New York City

"All you've got to do is decide to go
and the hardest part is over.

So go!"

TONY WHEELER, COFOUNDER – LONELY PLANET

P9-DDF-762

THIS EDITION WRITTEN AND RESEARCHED BY
Brandon Presser, Cristian Bonetto, Carolina A Miranda

Contents

Left: Times Square
(p176)

Above: Yankee Stadium
(p257)

Right: Greenwich Village
(p135)

Welcome to New York City

'As for New York City, it is a place apart. There is not its match in any other country in the world.' Pearl S Buck

Let Me Entertain You

From the chorus lines of Broadway down to the grungy cabarets of the Village, it's practically impossible to swing a dance belt without hitting a comedy club, jazz lounge or offbeat theater. And beyond the scope of live acts lurks an electric world of art and artifact housed in world-class museums of encyclopedic proportions and up-and-coming galleries showcasing relevant creators. So set your expectations as high as the skyscrapers and you'll quickly uncover myriad brilliant moments of sensory overload far beyond the twinkling lights of NYC's poster child, Times Square.

Take a Bite of the Big Apple

The Big Apple is, more than anything else, a wildly diverse urban ecosystem, and there's no better way to access the city's cornucopia of cultures than through the dinner plate. NYC's eating scene is a parade of superlatives culminating in a constellation of Michelin stars. From the Caribbean kitchens in Harlem to modern iterations of new American comfort cuisine downtown, New York offers endless opportunities to stamp your palate's passport.

Time & Trends

With topics that trend faster than a Twitter feed, New York City always seems to have its finger on the pulse, making it one of the most progressive and innovative pinpoints on the globe. In this land of perpendicular gridiron you can get anything at anytime, from the latest couture from the Parisian runways to the most ergonomic lounge chairs from the design ateliers of Tokyo. Sand passes through the hourglass much faster here – change is constantly afoot, as locals hunt down the latest and greatest with alacrity only to shift gears the following week in search of the next big hit. They don't call it a 'New York Minute' for nothin'!

Lady Liberty

One hundred years ago the torch-wielding icon, clad in copper greens, welcomed the 'tired, poor, and huddled masses' – she was quite the sight for sore eyes after a long journey from the other end of the globe. Today, Lady Liberty stands guard over a modern set of human pursuits. New York has become so much more than a gateway to opportunity – it's a city of triumph, a capital of exploration and experimentation; it's a place where one is truly free to be themselves. So come as you are, shed your apprehensions, let it all hang out and join the fray.

CHRISTOPHER GROENHOUT / LONELY PLANET IMAGES ©

Why I Love New York City

By Brandon Presser, Author

I used to have a theory about New York City: you could easily tell the difference between a tourist and local because tourists always look up. And I can safely say – after a decade of experiences both as a tourist and a local – that my half-baked hypothesis was indeed terribly wrong. For you see, 'the City' simply never ceases to amaze, and after all this time I still find myself staring skyward with awe.

My favorite spot? Standing on south side of 14th St looking uptown along Irving Pl – the Chrysler Building, with its gilded crown, waves hello from a distance every time I pass by.

For more about our authors, see p456.

Brooklyn Bridge (p71)

New York City's
Top 16

JEAN-PIERRE LESCOURRET / LONELY PLANET IMAGES ©

Central Park *(p229)*

1 London has Hyde Park. Paris has the Bois de Boulogne. And New York City has Central Park. One of the world's most renowned green spaces, it checks in with 843 acres of rolling meadows, boulder-studded outcrops, elm-lined walkways, manicured European-style gardens, a lake and a reservoir – not to mention an outdoor theater, a memorial to John Lennon, an idyllic waterside eatery (the Loeb Boathouse) and one very famous statue of Alice in Wonderland. The big challenge? Figuring out where to begin.

◉ *Upper West Side &*
Central Park

Skyscrapers *(p183)*

2 Ah, the skyscraper – mankind's phallic homage to human progress. New York City has plenty of 'em in every shape and size, from the imposingly elegant Chrysler Building (p183) to the iconic Empire State Building (p185) and dainty facade of the Flatiron Building (p163). And while staring into the city's infinite abyss of twinkling lights from atop a skyscraper ranks high on everyone's to-do list, we often prefer those quintessential New York moments down on the street when the crown of a soaring spire winks hello amid honking taxis in the early evening. EMPIRE STATE BUILDING

◉ *Midtown*

HUW JONES / LONELY PLANET IMAGES ©

Broadway Shows
(p200)

3 Only London's West End can rival Midtown's Theater District; a sea of premieres, revivals, smash hits and flops. Stretching from 40th St to 54th St, between Sixth and Eighth Aves, this is NYC's 'Dream Factory' – a place where romance, betrayal, murder and triumph come with dazzling costumes and stirring scores. Yet, the district is more than just the wicked vaudevillians of *Chicago,* or the in-tune wildlife of *The Lion King,* with enough off-Broadway and off-off-Broadway drama – both new and classic – to please the highest of theater brows.

⊙ *Midtown*

Classic New York Eats *(p34)*

4 If you want a real bite of the Apple, chow down a fat, juicy New York City classic. Start off with a 'bagel and a schmear' – a boiled-and-baked bagel pimped with cream cheese. Order an all-beef hot dog with the works, and bust your jaw with pastrami on rye and a side of pickles. But you're not done yet! Leave room for a slice of thin, cheesy New York–style pizza (tackled folded in half), and a slab of extra-creamy graham-cracker-crust cheesecake.
PASTRAMI SANDWICH

✕ *Eating*

Statue of Liberty & Ellis Island *(p58)*

5 Since its unveiling in 1886, Lady Liberty has welcomed millions of immigrants, sailing into New York Harbor in the hope of a better life. It now welcomes millions of tourists, many of whom head up to her crown for one of New York City's finest skyline and water views. Close by lies Ellis Island, the American gateway for more than 12 million new arrivals between 1892 and 1954. These days it's home to one of the city's most moving museums, paying tribute to these immigrants and their indelible courage.

⊙ *Lower Manhattan & the Financial District*

Museum Mile *(p217)*

6 A massive encyclopaedic museum that is one of the largest in the world? Check. An inverted ziggurat designed by Frank Lloyd Wright? Check. A landmark 1914 mansion stuffed with priceless Austrian and German expressionist paintings? Check, check and check. On Manhattan's Fifth Ave, some of the planet's most prestigious arts institutions – including the Metropolitan Museum of Art (p212), the Guggenheim Museum (p215) and the Neue Galerie (p218) – offer an overload for the eyeballs on a convenient 25-block stretch from 80th to 105th Sts.

GUGGENHEIM MUSEUM

◉ *Upper East Side*

Shopping *(p46)*

7 With enough opportunities for retail therapy to cure Woody Allen of his many neuroses, New York is a beacon of the material world where hundreds of creators – both local and international – descend upon the city with alacrity to display their wares. You'll find dozens of ways to empty your coffers, but at the end of the day shopping in New York isn't about collecting a closet full of items: it's about accessing the city's myriad subcultures through their art and artifacts.

BLOOMINGDALE'S (P206), MIDTOWN EAST

🔒 *Shopping*

Brooklyn Bridge & Beyond (p71)

8 There are three icons that make New York, New York: the skyscraper-packed skyline, the luminous presence of the Statue of Liberty, and the pointed arches of the Brooklyn Bridge. Completed in 1873, this Gothic Revival master-piece – crafted entirely from granite – has inspired poetry (Jack Kerouac's 'Brooklyn Bridge Blues'), music (Frank Sinatra's 'Brooklyn Bridge') and plenty of art (Walker Evans' photography). It is also the most scenic way to get from southern Manhattan to Brooklyn Heights.

◉ *Lower Manhattan & the Financial District*

Yankee Stadium
(p257)

9 Though not a thing of beauty (it looks like it was designed by Mussolini), this rebuilt South Bronx arena is home to one of the most storied outfits in American baseball: the Yankees. This was once the home of history-making players like the 'Sultan of Swat' Babe Ruth and 'Joltin' Joe' DiMaggio. These days, it gets packed with baseball fanatics who pour in to root, root, root for the home team, while inhaling pulled-pork sandwiches and cold beer. In other words: an all-American good time.

◉ *Harlem & Upper Manhattan*

MoMA *(p180)*

10 Quite possibly the greatest hoarder of modern masterpieces on earth, the Museum of Modern Art (MoMA) is a cultural promised land. It's here that you'll see Van Gogh's *The Starry Night,* Cézanne's *The Bather,* Picasso's *Le Demoiselles d'Avignon,* Pollock's *One: Number 31, 1950,* and Warhol's *Campbell's Soup Cans.* Just make sure you leave time for Chagall, Dix, Rothko, de Kooning and Haring, a free film screening, a glass of vino in the Sculpture Garden, a little designer retail therapy, and a fine-dining feed at its lauded in-house restaurant, the Modern.

◉ *Midtown*

The High Line
(p130)

11 A resounding triumph of urban renewal, the High Line is a great example of New York's continued effort to transform vestiges of its industrial past into comfortable, eye-pleasing spaces for city-center living. Once an unsightly elevated train track that snaked between butcheries and low-end domestic dwellings, today the High Line is an unfurled emerald necklace of park space that encourages calm and crowds alike. Unsurprisingly, it has acted as a veritable real estate magnet, luring world-class architects to the neighborhood to create residential eye candy.

◉ *Greenwich Village, Chelsea & the Meatpacking District*

MICHELLE BENNETT / LONELY PLANET IMAGES ©

GRAHAM CROUCH / LONELY PLANET IMAGES ©

Williamsburg *(p268)*

12 Here you'll find retro cocktail lounges peddling a Depression-era vibe, artsy eateries dishing out everything from humble pizza slices to Michelin-star gastronomy, and enough music halls and rowdy beer gardens to keep the most dedicated night owls up for weeks. Prefer the daylight hours? Williamsburg is stocked with an array of home design shops, plus fashion outposts of all stripes, from vintage thrift emporiums to design-y boutiques. It's not for nothing that this Brooklyn neighborhood – just one subway stop from downtown Manhattan – is the city's trendiest hangout.

◉ Brooklyn

STEFANO AMANTINI / SIME / 4CORNERS ©

DAN HERRICK / LONELY PLANET IMAGES ©

IZZET KERIBAR / LONELY PLANET IMAGES ©

Jazz in the West Village *(p151)*

13 The Village Vanguard and Blue Note may not ring a bell to most, but jazz aficionados raise an eyebrow in interest when these names are uttered amid music-savvy circles. Although the plumes of smoke have cleared from the West Village's coterie of clubs, the venues are still alive and riffin' to a mixed bag of local and international talent. This isn't just another soulful pocket in an anonymous, tower-clad city; this is the heart – the tree of Eden – of one of the most artistic and expression-filled genres of music.

⊙ *Greenwich Village, Chelsea & the Meatpacking District*

Times Square *(p176)*

14 Times Sq is more than just where Broadway and Seventh Ave meet. It's America in 'concentrate' – an intense, blinding, electrifying rush of Hollywood billboards, glittering cola signs, and buffed topless cowboys. True to the American dream, this 'Crossroads of the World' has invented and reinvented itself, from 1920s music-hall mecca to 1970s porn peddler to glossy, nonsmoking 21st-century role model. You might love it, you might loathe it, but do not miss it, especially when the sun goes down and its jumbotron screens turn night back into day.

⊙ *Midtown*

Staying Up Late in the City That Never Sleeps *(p38)*

15 Trendy all-night lounges tucked behind the walls of a Chinese restaurant, taco shops that clandestinely host late-night tranny cabarets, stadium-size discotheques that clang to the thump of DJ beats, and after-after-after-parties on the roof as the sun rises; an alternate universe lurks between the cracks of everyday life, and it welcomes savvy visitors just as much as locals in the know. If New York doesn't turn into a pumpkin come midnight, why should you?

BROOKLYN BOWL (P288), WILLIAMSBURG

🍷 *Drinking & Nightlife*

TREVOR COLLENS / ALAMY ©

FRANCES M. ROBERTS / ALAMY ©

Trailblazer Eating in Queens *(p303)*

16 Serious gastronomes go to Queens. New York City's most multicultural borough is also its tastiest – a sprawling, 'just-like-mom's' feast spanning all palates and kitchens of the world. From homemade bocconcini and momos (Nepalese dumplings), to Ecuadorian fish stew, Mexican hot chocolate, and green bean sheet jelly from northeast China, this is where your wildest culinary fantasies do come true. Go it alone or dive in with a foodie tour – either way, prepare for a thrill your taste buds won't forget.

👁 *Queens*

What's New

Seeing More Green

Brooklyn Bridge Park – the biggest new park to be built in Brooklyn since Prospect Park in the 19th century – has staggering views of Manhattan, the Brooklyn Bridge and a restored early 20th-century carousel. (p264)

Michelin Fare for a Song

Chef John Fraser has attracted a strong foodie following and a Michelin star status for Dovetail, an unpretentious Upper West Side eatery, which focuses on only the freshest produce. It's also a deal: on Mondays the restaurant offers a three-course vegetarian menu for only $46. (p236)

Eataly

Eataly is officially the largest Italian grocer and market space in the entire world, commanding over 50,000 sq ft in the heart of the city's Flatiron District. It is, without a doubt, a major game changer in New York's gourmet market scene. Don't miss the beer garden on the roof. (p172)

High Line 2.0

NYC's golden child of urban renewal recently made its first of two planned expansions, effectively doubling the size of this thin haven of green. Up next? Redevelopment of the veritable urban dead zone orbiting the Javits Center. (p130)

Cutting-Edge Design, Enter Stage Right

The top-notch Signature Theatre – a well-known company that champions contemporary American plays – has moved into its impressive new Frank Gehry–designed premises, the Signature Center on 42nd St. The center includes a bookshop, cafe and various performance spaces. (p200)

Downtown Yarmukle Chic

Check out Kutsher's Tribeca, a hot new contemporary-Jewish restaurant/bar in Tribeca, opened by Zach Kutscher – a fourth-generation member of Kutsher's Country Club (a legendary 'Borscht Belt' resort in the Catskills). (p73)

(S)wine & Cheese

Grilled-cheese sandwiches stuffed with kimchi and pork belly. Yum. Earl's Beer & Cheese is high-end eating for the budget gastronome, with craft beers to boot. (p220)

Old New York with a Twist of Lime

The guys behind cocktail bar Ward III in Tribeca have restored the Edison Hotel's old piano bar in Midtown and opened it as the Rum House. There's a pianist each night, and well-mixed drinks; a 'refreshed' slice of old New York. (p75)

Northern Star

Aloft Harlem is a new boutique hotel in the north that offers chic, reasonably priced sleeping quarters, a stone's throw from many of Manhattan's major attractions. (p345)

Chinese Cottage

These days fusion cuisine may seem a bit old hat, but the city's latest East-meets-West marriage on a plate – RedFarm – plays with a delightful assortment of international flavors, with scrumptious results. (p139)

For more recommendations and reviews, see **lonelyplanet.com/ usa/new-york-city**

Need to Know

Currency
US dollar (US$)

Language
English

Visas
The US Visa Waiver program (p397) allows nationals of 27 countries to enter the US without a visa.

Money
ATMs widely available; credit cards accepted at most hotels, stores and restaurants. Farmers markets, food trucks and some smaller eateries are cash-only.

Cell Phones
Most US cell phones, apart from the iPhone, operate on CDMA, not the European standard GSM; check compatibility with your phone service provider.

Time
Eastern Standard Time (GMT/UTC minus five hours)

Tourist Information
There are official NYC Visitor Information Centers (212-484-1222; www.nycgo.com; 53rd St at Seventh Ave, Midtown) throughout the city. The main office is in Midtown.

Your Daily Budget

Budget less than $100
➡ Dorm bed at Chelsea Hostel ($35–$80)
➡ Food truck burrito ($7)
➡ Walking the High Line (free)
➡ Staten Island Ferry (free)
➡ Drinks at an East Village dive bar ($4)
➡ NY Philharmonic rehearsal performance, Lincoln Center ($18)

Midrange $100–$300
➡ Swankified digs at Aloft Harlem ($150–$420)
➡ Brunch at Cookshop ($40)
➡ Dinner at Red Farm ($60)
➡ Innovative cocktails at an in-the-know lounge ($14)
➡ Discount TKTs tickets to a Broadway show ($80)
➡ Brooklyn Academy of Music orchestra seats (from $80)

Top end $300 plus
➡ Luxury stay at the Surrey ($350–$800)
➡ Tasting menu with wine pairings at Le Bernadin ($300)
➡ Snack at the Loeb Boathouse in Central Park ($18)
➡ Metropolitan Opera orchestra seats ($95–$320)

Advance Planning

Two months before Book hotel reservations as soon as possible – prices increase the closer you get to your arrival date. Snag tickets to your favorite Broadway blockbuster, too.

Three weeks before If you haven't done so already, score a table at your favorite high-end restaurant.

One week before Surf the interwebs for the newest and coolest in the city. Join email news blasts as well.

Useful Websites

➡ **Lonely Planet** (www.lonelyplanet.com/usa/new-york-city) Destination information, hotel bookings, traveler forum and more.

➡ **NYC: The Official Guide** (www.nycgo.com) New York City's official tourism portal.

➡ **Visit Brooklyn** (www.visitbrooklyn.org) NYC & Co's Brooklyn-specific website.

➡ **New York Magazine** (www.nymag.com) Comprehensive, current listings for bars, restaurants, entertainment and shopping.

➡ **New York Times** (www.nytimes.com) Local news coverage and theater listings.

➡ **Village Voice** (www.villagevoice.com) Solid resource for the various goings-on about town.

WHEN TO GO

Summers can be scorching hot; winters cold and not without blizzards. Spring or autumn are the best times to explore.

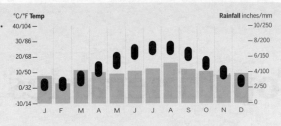

°C/°F Temp
40/104 —
30/86 —
20/68 —
10/50 —
0/32 —
-10/14 —

J F M A M J J A S O N D

Rainfall inches/mm
— 10/250
— 8/200
— 6/150
— 4/100
— 2/50
— 0

Arriving in New York

John F Kennedy International Airport (JFK) The AirTrain ($5) links to the Metropolitan Transport Authory's (MTA) subway ($2.50), which makes the one-hour journey into Manhattan; shared vans from Grand Central or Port Authority are $15 to $20; taxis cost a flat rate of $45 excluding tolls and tip.

LaGuardia Airport (LGA) The closest airport to Manhattan – take the M60 bus from 125th St ($2.50) directly to the airport (30 minutes). Vans and coach buses to Midtown cost $12 to $20. Taxis range from $25 to $45 (excluding tolls and tip) depending on traffic.

Newark Liberty International Airport (EWR) From Pennsylvania Station, the AirTrain ($12.50) links passengers to the airport with one transfer; shared shuttles from Midtown cost $15 to $20. Taxis range from $60 to $80 (excluding tolls and tip). Allow 45 minutes to one hour of travel time.

For much more on **arrival**, see p386.

Getting Around

Check out the Metropolitan Transportation Authority (www.mta.info) website for public transportation information (buses and subway), including a handy travel planner and regular notifications of delays and alternate travel routes during frequent maintenance.

➡ **Subway** Inexpensive, somewhat efficient and open around the clock, though can be confusing to the uninitiated. Single ride is $2.50 with a MetroCard. A 7-Day Unlimited Pass costs $29.

➡ **Buses** Convenient during off hours – especially when transferring between the city's east and west sides. Same price as the subway.

➡ **Taxi** Meters start at $2.50 and increase roughly $4 for every 20 blocks. See www.nyc.gov/taxi for more information.

➡ **Interborough ferries** Hop-on-hop-off service and free rides in harbor to Staten Island. Check out New York Waterway (www.nywaterway.com) and New York Water Taxi (www.nywatertaxi.com).

For much more on **getting around**, see p388.

Sleeping

In general, accommodation prices in New York City do not abide by any high season or low season rules; wavering rates usually reflect availability. With over 50 million tourists visiting in 2011, you can expect that hotel rooms fill up quick – especially in summer. In addition to the following websites, don't forget about global sites like Hotels.com, Hotwire.com and Orbitz.com.

Useful Websites

➡ **newyorkhotels.com** (www.newyorkhotels.com) The self-proclaimed official website for hotels in NYC.

➡ **airbnb** (www.airbnb.com) Choose furnished apartment or rooms in a New Yorker's house rather than pricey hotel digs.

➡ **Jetsetter** (www.jetsetter.com) Great selection of international sales on luxury hotels; excellent NYC selection.

For much more on **sleeping**, see p326.

Top Itineraries

Day One

Upper West Side & Central Park (p227)

☀️ Spend the morning exploring the wonders of **Central Park**, taking in the fortresslike wall of skyscrapers that surrounds the green. Start at **Columbus Circle**, then head in the northeast direction passing the **Central Park Zoo**, the **Bethesda Fountain**, the **Conservatory Water** and **Strawberry Fields** on the west side. If you have the kids in tow, check out the dinosaur skeletons at the **American Museum of Natural History** then hit up the **Loeb Boathouse** for a paddle around the lake.

🍴 **Lunch** Pick up supplies at Zabar's (p235) for a picnic in Central Park.

Midtown (p174)

☀️ After a morning exploring the green, it's time to uncover some of the city's architectural wonders, like **Grand Central Terminal**, the **Chrysler Building**, the **New York Public Library** and **Rockefeller Center**. Round off the afternoon with a visit to the city's museum darling: **MoMA**.

🍴 **Dinner** For Broadway-goers, do an early dinner at Marseille (p197).

Midtown (p174)

🌙 Spend the evening under the starry lights of **Broadway**, checking out a blockbuster show or something distinctly ahead of the curve at **Playwrights Horizon** or **Signature Theatre**. Soak up the atmosphere of **Times Square** from the **TKTS Booth**, swig cocktails at **Rum House** then climb to the top of the **Empire State Building** to wish the city 'goodnight'.

Day Two

Upper East Side (p210)

☀️ Start at the **Frick Collection**, one of the city's more underrated art spaces. The building itself is a true NYC treasure as it's one of the few remaining Fifth Ave mansions that hasn't been transformed into an apartment block. Say hello to the Vermeers and the Bellini, then stroll down **Madison Ave** for some shopping at **Crawford Doyle Booksellers**, **Encore** and **Michael's** for designer duds on consignment.

🍴 **Lunch** Join the ladies who lunch at Via Quadronno (p221).

SoHo & Chinatown (p80)

☀️ Head down to **SoHo** for an afternoon of shopping amid crowds of tourists seeking the best brands in the world. Wander over to **Chinatown**, which feels worlds away from the mainstream but is only a few blocks over. Stroll by the neighborhood's **Buddhist temples**, stopping for snacks like lacquered pork and almond ice cream.

🍴 **Dinner** Savor soup dumplings at Joe's Shanghai (p93), a Chinatown staple.

Upper West Side & Central Park (p227)

🌙 If you have concert tickets, then skip dinner downtown and hit up **Barcibo Enoteca** for a preshow glass of expertly curated Italian wine – go for some grub if you're seeing a full-length show. Then it's off to the **Lincoln Center** for opera at the **Metropolitan Opera House** or a symphony in **Avery Fisher Hall**. If you didn't do an early meal then hit up **Dovetail** – the neighborhood's new foodie hotspot – for a delectable dinner.

Day Three

Lower Manhattan & the Financial District (p56)

 Catch the **Staten Island Ferry** in the early morning and watch the sun come up over **Lower Manhattan's** skyscrapers. Then visit the **WTC Tribute Visitors Center** and **9/11 Memorial** before honoring some of New York's greatest luminaries buried in the cemetery at **Trinity Church**. Keep things light with a round of shopping at **Century 21**, then wave hello to the *Charging Bull* artwork at **Bowling Green**.

 Lunch Gorge on juicy burgers at Shake Shack (p74).

Brooklyn (p262)

Hit up the **Brooklyn Museum of Art** in South Brooklyn for a surplus of ancient Egyptian artifacts and American paintings. Stroll through **Prospect Park**, making sure to hit the vintage carousel in the **Children's Corner**.

Dinner Head to Dressler (p283) for a Michelin-star treat.

Brooklyn (p262)

Head to **Williamsburg**, on the other side of the borough, and join the veritable pub crawl – for snooty old-timey cocktails shaken by bewhiskered gents in suspenders (no joke), start with **Maison Premiere**. Go for vintage – though more trashy '70s than high-end '30s – at the **Commodore**. Swing by the **Brooklyn Bowl** afterwards for a side of bowling and some groovy musical acts.

Day Four

East Village & Lower East Side (p100)

 Wander through the **Lower East Side**, passing revelers returning home from a full night of partying. Start off with a visit to the **Lower East Side Tenement Museum** to gain insight into the city's fascinating immigration history, then wander down the East Village's **St Mark's Place** before stopping by the **New Museum of Contemporary Art**.

Lunch Cafe Orlin (p111) promises delicious Middle Eastern brunch fare.

Harlem & Upper Manhattan (p246)

Head up to **Harlem** and visit the **Studio Museum** to check out one of the most important African American art museums in the country. Move west to see the historic facade of the **Apollo Theater**, then do like the locals do and shop at **Atmos** for sneakers or **Swing** for more offbeat treats.

Dinner Try Red Rooster (p258) for wine-soaked, high-end comfort food.

Greenwich Village, Chelsea & the Meatpacking District (p128)

Continue your pilgrimage through all things soulful and head down to the **West Village** to sample some of the world's best jazz beats at **Blue Note** or **Village Vanguard**. Slip behind the inconspicuous brown door to swig bathtub gin cocktails amid Prohibition era–style surrounds at **Little Branch**, then make sure your name is on the guest list at **Le Bain**.

If You Like...

Museums

MoMA NYC's darling museum has brilliantly curated spaces boasting the best of the world's modern art. (p180)

Metropolitan Museum of Art The most incredible encyclopedic museum in the Americas comes stocked with its own Egyptian temple and the country's most famous canvas of George Washington. (p212)

Guggenheim Museum The exhibits can be uneven, but the architecture is the real star in this Frank Lloyd Wright–designed building. (p215)

Frick Collection A Gilded Age mansion has Vermeers, El Grecos and Goyas and a stunning courtyard fountain. (p217)

Cloisters Museum & Gardens Medieval treasures including a beguiling 16th-century tapestry that depicts a unicorn hunt. (p256)

Brooklyn Museum of Art Ancient Egyptian treasures, a stellar collection of American painting and a cutting-edge feminist arts center. (p265)

Lower East Side Tenement Museum Fantastic insight into life as an immigrant during the 19th and early 20th centuries. (p102)

Places of Worship

St Patrick's Cathedral A glorious neo-Gothic masterpiece – it's the largest cathedral in America. (p191)

Trinity Church This gorgeous Anglican church was tallest building in NYC in the mid-1800s. (p64)

KRZYSZTOF DYDYNSKI / LONELY PLANET IMAGES ©

St Patrick's Cathedral (p191), Midtown

Cathedral Church of St John the Divine The largest place of worship in the US was begun in 1892 – and still isn't completely finished. (p248)

Temple Emanu-el A Romanesque structure with gilded ceilings serves as one of New York's most beautiful synagogues. (p218)

Plymouth Church This Brooklyn Heights place of worship was a center of abolitionist activity in the 19th century. (p271)

Eldridge Street Synagogue Glittering after a multimillion-dollar restoration, the hallowed hall is now a museum space. (p107)

Staying Up All Night

Gray's Papaya You can't say you've done New York until you've eaten a recession special (two hot dogs and a papaya drink). (p236)

Der Schwarze Köelner A Fort Greene beer hall is the place for a late-night brew on weekends. (p285)

Chinatown A secreted scatter of late-night lounges tucked behind the unassuming facades of hole-in-the-wall chow spots. (p93)

Iggy's Get your karaoke on at this popular Upper East Side space. (p224)

Metropolitan Artsy gays congregate at this mixed space in Williamsburg. (p287)

Skyline Views

Brooklyn Bridge Park Brooklyn's newest park has wide open views of downtown Manhattan and the Brooklyn and Manhattan Bridges. (p264)

Top of the Strand Go one better than staring at Midtown's mix of scrapers and swig a drink while you're part of the view. (p198)

Top of the (other) Strand Check out the downtown views from the sleek bathrooms tucked high up between the Boom Boom Room and Le Bain. (p147)

Brooklyn Heights Promenade Staggering view of Manhattan 24 hours a day. (p270)

Roosevelt Island The island off the island of Manhattan has excellent views of Midtown and will soon be home to a new memorial designed by Louis Kahn. (p217)

Roof Garden Café & Martini Bar From late April through October, the rooftop garden at the Metropolitan Museum of Art offers incredible views of Central Park and the Midtown skyline. (p224)

Bargemusic Classical music with views of the Brooklyn Bridge and Manhattan – just beautiful. (p289)

Green Spaces

Central Park The city's most famous park has more than 800 acres of rolling meadows and boulder-topped hillocks. (p229)

Brooklyn Bridge Park A brand new park lines the waterfront along Dumbo, all the way to Carroll Gardens. (p264)

The High Line A thin stripe of green that unfurls up the western slice of downtown. (p130)

Woodlawn Cemetery Herman Melville and Duke Ellington's resting place is a stunner. (p257)

Riverside Park A 100-block park runs alongside the Hudson on Manhattan's west side – the ideal spot for a bike ride. (p235)

For more top New York City spots, see
➤ Eating (p34)
➤ Drinking & Nightlife (p38)
➤ Gay & Lesbian (p41)
➤ Entertainment (p43)
➤ Shopping (p46)
➤ Sports & Activities (p49)

PLAN YOUR TRIP IF YOU LIKE...

Historic Sights

Ellis Island The gateway to freedom and opportunity for so many of America's immigrants. (p60)

Frick Collection A rare mansion from the Gilded Age survives to this day as a museum on the Upper East Side. (p217)

Gracie Mansion A graceful Federal-style structure now serves as the Mayor's home (when that Mayor isn't Michael Bloomberg). (p220)

Jane's Carousel A 1922 carousel in Brooklyn Bridge Park is in the National Register of Historic Places. (p264)

Morris-Jumel Mansion Museum A Georgian-Federal structure is the oldest house in Manhattan. (p258)

Venturing off the Beaten Path

Flushing Go on a foodie safari deep in the heart of Queens and find Chinese restaurants serving dumplings. (p304)

New York Botanical Garden A sprawling garden is home to 50 acres of forest and a Victorian-style conservatory. (p257)

Inwood Hill Park It's part of Manhattan, but it doesn't

feel like it – this park remains wonderfully wild. (p257)

Queens Museum of Art Excellent exhibits without the fanfare and crowds of some of Manhattan's other museum spaces. (p301)

Dyckman Farmhouse Museum Manhattan's last surviving Dutch farmhouse. (p257)

Gowanus An old industrial canal is popular with urban decay types (and the Environmental Protection Agency). (p273)

Old School New York

Coney Island An amusement center that dates back to the early days of the 20th century; don't forget the hot dogs at Nathan's Famous. (p266)

Junior's Excellent cheesecake. Old school Brooklyn attitude. Bring it on. (p279)

Katz's Delicatessen Smoked meat that will please even the biggest kvetchers. (p114)

Bill's Gay Nineties Show tunes and singing patrons – many as old as the bar. (p198)

Zabar's An emporium for all types of Upper West Side food-a-holics since the 1930s. (p235)

William Greenberg Desserts The world's most perfect black and white cookie can be found on the Upper East Side. (p221)

Ultimate Indulgences

Retail therapy at Barneys The fashionista's aspirational closet comes with a hefty price tag – still, it's fun for window shopping. (p206)

Surrey A luxury hotel features brand-name art, a luxurious on-site spa and room service courtesy of Café Boulud. (p342)

Dough Best. Doughnuts. Ever. That is all. (p280)

Boom Boom Room Uber-selective nightclub high in the sky with enough room to twirl your trophy wife. (p147)

Rum House Slurp down a glass of rare Black Tot rum. (p199)

Exhale From four-handed massage to beginner yoga classes to acupuncture, you'll find it all at this Zen Upper East Side spa. (p226)

Free Things

Staten Island Ferry Hop on the free ferry to Staten Island for postcard-perfect views of Manhattan's southern edge. (p78)

Chelsea Galleries Over 300 galleries are open to the public along Manhattan's West 20s. (p134)

Brooklyn Brewery Tours Four-dollar draughts are easy on the wallet; free afternoon tours on weekends are even better. (p269)

Kayaking with Red Hook Boaters Paddle along the East River on gratis outings – arrange a few times a week during summer. (p295)

New Museum of Contemporary Art on Thursday nights Ethereal tooth-white boxes house a serious stash of contemporary art that's free for visitors on Thursday evenings. (p103)

Hidden Hangouts

Bathtub Gin Slide behind a false wall at the back of a modest coffee shop for Prohibition-chic styling and retro cocktails. (p149)

Mulberry Project An unassuming set of stairs leads to the swank cocktail laboratory of the international owners and their coterie of server-friends. (p93)

Smith & Mills Push the unmarked door to find a kooky industrial interior (think 1900s factory) and smooth libations. (p75)

Freemans Walk down a tiny alley to find quaint cabinlike surrounds and legions of faithful brunchers. (p114)

124 Old Rabbit Club Ring the buzzer when you spot the unassuming '124,' then down a tasty stout at the dimly lit bar. (p148)

Month by Month

January

The odd blizzard and below-freezing temperatures makes the New Year in New York a good time to snuggle up at your boutique digs or dine fireside at the next up-and-comer.

🍴 NYC Restaurant Week

You're not allowed to lose that extra holiday weight just yet! Usher in the new year with slash-cut meal deals at some of the city's finest eating establishments during New York's Winter Restaurant Week (www.nycgo.com/restaurantweek).

February

Cupid wields his quiver and everyone still shivers as crisp temperatures continue to hover above freezing. Someone get those fashion week models some coats!

✨ Mercedes-Benz Fashion Week

The infamous Bryant Park fashion shows (http://newyork.mbfashionweek.com) are sadly not open to the public. But whether or not you're invited or not, being in the city this week – when the couture world descends upon Manhattan to swoon over new looks – could provide a vicarious thrill, especially if you can find the after-parties.

✨ Lunar New Year

One of the biggest Lunar (Chinese) New Year (www.explorechinatown.com) celebrations in the country, this display of fireworks and dancing dragons draws mobs of thrillseekers into the streets of Chinatown. The date of Chinese New Year fluctuates from year to year, sometimes falling in late January but often in early February.

March

Months of dripping icicles and steamy winter breath come to a quiet close as spring pokes its nose out from behind the rain-bearing clouds.

✨ St Patrick's Day Parade

A massive audience, rowdy and wobbly from cups of green beer, lines Fifth Ave on March 17 for this popular parade (www.nycstpatricksparade.org) of bagpipe blowers, sparkly floats and Irish-lovin' politicians. The parade is the city's oldest and largest.

April

Spring is in full bloom: optimistic alfresco joints have a sprinkling of street-side chairs as the city squares overflow with skyscraping greens.

☆ Tribeca Film Festival

Created after the tragic events of 9/11, Robert De Niro's downtown film festival (www.tribecafilm.com) has quickly become a star in the indie movie circuit.

Gaggles of celebs come to walk the red carpets each spring.

fic or on waterfront paths through each of the city's five boroughs.

May

April showers bring May flowers in the form of brilliant bursts of cherry blossom and thick summer leaves adorning the hillocks of Central Park. The weather is warm without the steaming humidity of summer.

☆ Cherry Blossom Festival

Known in Japanese as Sakura Matsuri (www.bbg. org), this annual tradition, held the first weekend in May, celebrates the pink, puffy flowering of the Kwanzan cherry trees along the Brooklyn Botanic Garden's famous esplanade. It's complete with entertainment, refreshments and awe-inspiring beauty.

☆ Fleet Week

For one week at the end of the month, Manhattan resembles a 1940s movie set as fresh-faced, uniformed sailors go 'on the town' to look for adventures. The ships they leave behind, docked in the Hudson River, invite the curious to hop aboard for tours.

🏃 Five Boro Bike Tour

May is Bike Month, featuring two-wheelin' tours, parties and other events for pedal-pushing New Yorkers. TD Bank Five Boro Bike Tour (www. bikenewyork.org), the main event, sees thousands of cyclists hit the pavement for a 42-mile ride, much of it on roads closed to traf-

June

Summer's definitely here and locals crawl out of their office cubicles to relax in the city's green spaces. Parades roll down the busiest streets and portable movie screens are strung up in several parks.

☆ Puerto Rican Day Parade

The second weekend in June attracts thousands of flag-waving revelers for the annual Puerto Rican Day Parade (www.nationalpuer toricandayparade.org). Now in its fifth decade, it runs up Fifth Ave from 44th to 86th Sts.

☆ SummerStage

With over 100 performances spread across the five boroughs, SummerStage (p238) is NYC's biggest free performing arts festival. There's also a Summer-Stage Kids program, just in case you've got the little ones in tow. The festival runs until September.

☆ Gay Pride Parade

June is Gay Pride Month, and it culminates in a major march down Fifth Ave on the last Sunday of the month. It's a five-hour spectacle (www.nycpride.com) of dancers, drag queens, gay police officers, leathermen, lesbian soccer-moms and representatives of just about every other queer scene under the rainbow.

☆ HBO Bryant Park Summer Film Festival

From June to August, there are weekly outdoor screenings of some of the most beloved films during the Summer Film Festival (www.bryantpark.org).

☆ Mermaid Parade

Celebrating sand, sea and the beginning of summer is this quirky parade (www. coneyisland.com). It's a flash of glitter and glamour, as elaborately costumed folks walk along the Coney Island boardwalk. Held on the last Saturday of the month.

July

Visitors without room reservations must say a special prayer to the hotel gods – lodgings are crammed in the height of summer as tourists pour in and locals file out to their summer homes.

☆ Independence Day

America's Independence Day is celebrated on 4th July with fireworks and fanfare that can be seen from most NYC apartments with river views. Roosevelt Island also hosts a fireworks-viewing festival at its Southpoint Park.

☆ Shakespeare in the Park

The much-loved Shakespeare in the Park (www. shakespeareinthepark.org) pays tribute to the Bard, with free performances in Central Park. The catch? You'll have to wait hours in line to score tickets, or win them in the online lottery.

(above) Independence Day fireworks, East River

(below) Gay Pride Parade

BILL WASSMAN / LONELY PLANET IMAGES ©

ANGUS OBORN / LONELY PLANET IMAGES ©

August

Thick waves of summer heat slide between skyscrapers as everyone heads to the seashore nearby or gulps cool blasts of air-conditioning when stuck in the city. Myriad outdoor events and attractions add life to the languid urban heat.

☆ Fringe Festival

This annual mid-August theater festival (www.fringenyc.org) presents two weeks of performances from companies all over the world. It's the best way to catch the edgiest, wackiest and most creative up-and-comers around.

September

Labor Day officially marks the end of the Hampton's share-house season as the buzzing heat of summer fades to more tolerable levels. Locals return to their hectic work schedules and sidewalk brunches on weekends.

☆ BAM! Next Wave Festival

Celebrated for 30 years in 2012, the Brooklyn Academy of Music's Next Wave Festival (www.bam.org) showcases the newest iterations of avant-garde performance, music and dance.

☆ Electric Zoo

Celebrated over Labor Day Weekend, Electric Zoo (www.madeevent.com/electriczoo) is New York's electronic music festival held in sprawling Randall's Island Park. Past headliners have included Moby, David Guetta, Martin Solveig and The Chemical Brothers.

October

Brilliant bursts of orange, red and yellow fill the trees in Central Park as temperatures cool and alfresco cafes finally shutter their windows. It's one of the most comfortable and scenic months to visit NYC.

Open House New York

The country's largest architecture and design event, Open House New York (www.ohny.org), is held at the start of the month. It features special, architect-led tours, as well as lectures, design workshops and studio visits all over the city.

Comic-Con

Enthusiasts from near and far gather at this annual beacon of nerd-dom (www.newyorkcomiccon.com) to dress up as their favorite characters and cavort with like-minded anime aficionados. It's like a Trekkie convention only 20 times better... or worse...depending on who you ask.

Noah's Ark

In honor of the Feast Day of St Francis, which falls early in the month, pet owners flock to the grand Cathedral Church of St John the Divine for the annual Blessing of the Animals (www.stjohndivine.org) with their creatures – poodles, lizards, parrots, donkeys, you name it – in tow.

Halloween

What once started as simple door-to-door knocking, Halloween in the Village has transformed into an all-out parade (www.halloween-nyc.com) with costume-clad locals and interested onlookers gathering in equal numbers.

November

As the leaves tumble down to the street, light apparel is swapped for the latest iterations of stylish fall fashion. A headliner marathon is tucked into the final days of prehibernation weather.

Macy's Thanksgiving Day Parade

Massive helium-filled balloons soar overhead, high school marching bands rattle their snares and millions of onlookers bundle up with scarves and coats to celebrate Thanksgiving with Macy's world-famous 2.5-mile-long parade.

New York Comedy Festival

Funny-makers take the city by storm during the New York Comedy Festival (www.nycomedyfestival.com) with stand-up sessions, improv nights and big-ticket shows hosted by the likes of Rosie O'Donell and Ricky Gervais.

NYC Marathon

This annual 26-mile run (www.nycmarathon.org), held in the first week of November, draws thousands of athletes from around the world, and excited spectators line the streets to cheer the runners on.

Oh Christmas Tree

The flick of a switch ignites the massive Christmas tree in Rockefeller Center, officially ushering in the holiday season. Bedecked with over 25,000 lights, it is NYC's unofficial Yuletide headquarters and a must-see for anyone visiting the city during December.

December

Winter's definitely here, but there's plenty of holiday cheer to warm the spirit. Fairy lights adorn most buildings as everyone gears up to outdo one another with ostentatious interpretations of Christmas decor.

New Year's Eve

The ultimate place to ring in the New Year on planet earth, Times Square (p176) swarms with millions of gatherers who come to stand squashed together like boxed sardines, swig booze, freeze in subarctic temperatures, witness the annual dropping of the ball made entirely of Waterford Crystal and chant the '10...9...8...' in perfect unison.

With Kids

The city that never sleeps is surprisingly child-friendly. In recent years, imaginative new playgrounds have been built and kid-friendly staples – like the Central Park Zoo and the New York Aquarium – have been given makeovers.

DAVI HERRICK / LONELY PLANET IMAGES ©

View from the Top of the Rock lookout (p179)

Best Hotels for Kids

Hotel Beacon
The big rooms at Hotel Beacon (p343) accommodate cribs and extra beds and the in-room kitchenettes are ideal for whipping up light snacks. Located in the Upper West Side, the proximity to Central Park can't be beaten.

Hotel Gansevoort
The trendy Meatpacking District isn't known as a kid haven, but Hotel Gansevoort (p333) makes little scenesters feel like a million bucks with a welcome kit and a Wii on request.

Bubba & Bean Lodges
The charming Upper East Side guesthouse Bubba & Bean Lodges (p342) has a suite with kitchen that sleeps up to six. Perfect for a family caravan.

Top Attractions

Statue of Liberty
The boat ride to Lady Liberty offers the opportunity to chug around New York Harbor and get to know an icon that most kids only know from textbooks.

On Top of the World
A glass-roofed elevator leads to the Top of the Rock, a lookout that offers glittering views of New York.

Coasters on the Beach
Hot dogs. Vintage coasters. An open stretch of beach. Coney Island is just what the doctor ordered if the family is in need of some fun in the sun.

Urban Jungle
The city has a number of zoos. The best, by far, is the Bronx Zoo, which is known for its well-designed habitats. (The Congo Gorilla Forest is a stunner). Otherwise, if you're pressed for time, the Central Park Zoo will keep the tots entertained with polar bears and penguins.

NOT FOR PARENTS

For an insight into New York aimed directly at kids, pick up a copy of Lonely Planet's *Not for Parents: New York*. Perfect for children aged eight and up, it opens up a world of intriguing stories and fascinating facts about New York people, places, history and culture.

Best Museums

The big museums – the Metropolitan Museum of Art, the Museum of Modern Art and the Guggenheim Museum – all have kids' programs. But many smaller institutions offer some very unique experiences:

Toddler Time

For tots aged one to five, hit the Children's Museum of the Arts (p86) in West SoHo and the Brooklyn Children's Museum (p276) in Crown Heights. Both have story times, art classes and painting sessions.

Five & Over

Bigger kids can clamber on vintage subway cars at the New York Transit Museum (p270), slide down a pole at the New York City Fire Museum (p86) and impose law and order in a miniature cruiser at the New York City Police Museum (p70). Book 'em.

Best Parks

Central Park

More than 800 acres of green space, a lake that can be navigated by rowboat, 21 different playgrounds and a statue of Alice in Wonderland. There's a reason all the locals bring their kids to Central Park.

Prospect Park

Brooklyn's 585-acre Prospect Park has an entire Children's Corner (p275), including paddleboat rides and hands-on playthings.

Riverside Park

Riverside Park (p235) on the Upper West Side has a bicycle trail with views of the Hudson River. Take a break at the River Run Playground (at W 83rd St), with fountains for cooling off in summer.

Best Playgrounds

Creative Play

At the South Street Seaport (p70), the new Imagination Playground takes the concept of the playground and puts it entirely in kids' hands. Here kids play with oversized foam building blocks to construct their own play spaces.

On the Hudson

Kids under six will enjoy the Hudson River Park Playground (p70) in the West Village, which is well stocked with climbing equipment, slides and sandboxes. Parents will enjoy the sparkling Hudson River views.

Carousels

Midtown

Steps from Times Square and the New York Public Library, find Le Carrousel in Bryant Park (p191), which revolves to the tune of French cabaret music.

Central Park

At the level of 64th St in the heart of Central Park is a 1908 carousel with colorful painted horses.

Prospect Park

Prospect Park's Children's Corner (p275) contains a lovely 1912 ride that features a menagerie of 53 animals to sit on.

Jane's Carousel

Parents will love Jane's Carousel (p264) as much as kids. Located in the brand new Brooklyn Bridge Park, the 1920s ride offers spectacular Manhattan views and is housed in a structure by a Pritzker Prize–winning architect.

ALICE IN WONDERLAND, JOSE DE CREEFT. DENNIS JOHNSON / LONELY PLANET IMAGES ©

Alice in Wonderland statue, Central Park (p229)

Fun for Kids & Parents

Play Cafe

Tribeca's Moomah (p74) is part cafe, part play area – so parents can have a glass of wine while the kids make masterpieces at the 'Art Table.' Craft kits are available for sale.

Best Bets for a Rainy Day

Craft Hour

At the Upper East Side Craft Studio (Map p440), families can drop in to create ceramic masterpieces on the spot. Ages three and up.

Bounce Around

Little Athletes Exploration Center (Map p430) at the Chelsea Piers is a colorful indoor playground that lets six-month to four-year-old kids let off some steam.

Animal World

At Art Farm in the City (Map p440), on the Upper East Side, there are art supplies and craft sessions – not to mention bunnies and turtles. Ages six months to eight years.

Keep It Cheap

Ferry Tale

The Staten Island Ferry (p78) is free and offers spectacular views of New York Harbor and the Statue of Liberty.

Train Time

The subway can be a great adventure. The F train in Brooklyn comes out on an elevated track that has the highest stop in the city (Smith–9th Sts). The end of the line is even better: Coney Island.

Bird Brains

Pop into Belvedere Castle (p244) in Central Park for a free children's birding kit, an excellent way to get kids interested in nature.

Kid-Friendly Theater

The Manhattan Children's Theater (52 White St btwn Broadway & Church St) in Tribeca has productions geared at kids five and up, while Broadway can be a good bet for older children with shows such as *The Lion King* and *Spider-Man*.

NEED TO KNOW

➡ **Car seats** It's legal for children under the age of 7 to ride on an adult's lap in a taxi, but you can also install your own car seat.

➡ **Strollers** Strollers are not allowed on public buses unless they are folded.

➡ **Babysitters** Baby Sitters' Guild (☎212-682-0227; www.babysitters guild.com) can arrange for childcare at your hotel.

➡ **Online resource** Time Out New York Kids (www.timeoutnewyorkkids. com) has helpful tips.

Like a Local

Although it may seem easy to blend into a city that welcomes a diverse population of new citizens almost every day, New York can be unforgiving to the uninitiated. So, we've prepared a few pointers that will have you cleverly camouflaged among the legions of locals.

Commuter, 86th St & Central Park West subway station

BRENT WINEBRENNER / LONELY PLANET IMAGES ©

When in New York

Dos & Don'ts

➡ Hail a cab only if the roof light is on. Look carefully, though: if the middle light is on, the cab is available; if only the side lights are on, the cab is off-duty.

➡ You needn't obey 'walk' signs – simply cross the street when there isn't oncoming traffic.

➡ When negotiating pedestrian traffic on the sidewalk think of yourself as a vehicle – don't stop short, follow the speed of the crowd around you and pull off to the side if you need to take out your map or umbrella. Most New Yorkers are respectful of personal space, but they will bump into you – and not apologize – if you get in the way.

➡ When boarding the subway, wait until the passengers disembark, then be aggressive enough when you hop on so that the doors don't close in front of you.

➡ In New York you wait 'on line' instead of 'in line'.

➡ Oh, and it's How-sten Street, not Hew-sten.

Tipping Tips

In New York City, as in most places in the USA, tipping isn't merely an act of kindness – it's a requirement. At restaurants it's common practice to leave between 15% and 20% of the total bill (most people err on the side of 20%). The same goes for taxi drivers. Hotel housekeepers receive tips of between $1 and $5 per day, while a $1 tip for a porter is appreciated.

A Little Birdie Told Me

In New York City – more than most cities in the world – the internet is your friend. As much as locals covet their 'secret spots,' they love to brag about their cool new finds on blogs, Facebook and Twitter. Check out the following list of our favorite members of New York's Twitterati, who are always tweeting about the city's latest musts:

Michael Bloomberg (@mikebloomberg) NYC's mayor.

Soraya Darabi (@sorayadarabi) Media strategist and founder of www.foodspotting.com

Hyperallergic (@Hyperallergic) Tweets from NYC's favorite art blogazine.

Brian Braiker (@slarkpope) Brooklyn dweller and news editor for the *Guardian*.

Colson Whitehead (@colsonwhitehead) Manhattan native, novelist, erstwhile *Village Voice* critic and winner of the McArthur Fellowship.

Paul Goldberger (@paulgoldberger) Pulitzer Prize winner, architecture critic for the *New Yorker* and author of its Sky Line column.

Tom Colicchio (@tomcolicchio) Celebrity chef and owner of the popular Craft franchise.

Sam Sifton (@samsifton) National editor at the *New York Times*.

Everything NYC (@EverythingNYC) Hunting down the best things to see, do and eat in the Big Apple.

Eating & Drinking

Out on the Town

New Yorkers love to embrace the city's 'never sleep' motto by challenging the old-school notion that going out is a weekend sport. Here in NYC, locals joke that Fridays and Saturdays are for bridge and tunnel folk (people who need to take bridges and tunnels to reach the city) – a big night out on the town can occur any day of the week.

Booking a Table

If you can be flexible with your eating time, then chances are in your favor of scoring a seat at a Michelin-star affair one or two days before you plan on dining. Just be prepared to sit down for a 10:30pm booking. Another good approach to nabbing that impossible reservation is to swing by a restaurant in person before you plan to dine – a smile and some manners might get your name on the list, especially at restaurants that don't take reservations.

The Beauty of Lunch

If you're dying to try one of the city's headliner restaurants but don't want to break the bank (or can't get a reservation during your visit) then it's worth checking off your culinary bucket list during the daylight hours when prix fixe prices are slashed and seating is more likely to be available. Your celebrity chef may not be in the back searing your foie gras, but you'll get to soak in the atmosphere and taste-test the signature dishes nonetheless.

The Culture of Brunch

Long lines, curt hostesses, a mimosa, two cups of coffee, an egg-based main, a bread-y side and hungover friends – these are the ingredients that make up NYC's most coveted combination of chatting and chewing. Brunch in New York is deeply woven into the city's social fabric, much like teatime for British royals. Although the word 'brunch' is in itself a merging of 'breakfast' and 'lunch,' this special repast – reserved solely for weekends (particularly Sunday) – isn't quite one or the other. It's a special meal that can occur from 11am to around 4pm on weekends, when friends can catch up to rehash the week's events and weekend's shenanigans over dishes constructed of breakfast materials and an indiscriminant mix of cocktails of coffee.

Union Square Greenmarket (p172)

Eating

*From inspired iterations of world cuisine, to quintessentially local nibbles,
New York City's dining scene is infinite, all-consuming and a proud
testament to the kaleidoscope of citizens that call the city home. So go ahead,
take a bite out of the Big Apple – we promise you won't be sorry.*

Fine Dining

Dining trends in New York City come and
go, but there's one thing that will forever
remain certain: fine dining never goes out
of style. Sure, the culture of haute eats has
changed over the years, but locals and visitors alike will never tire of dressing up to
chow down. These days the scene very much
revolves around fresh, locally sourced, Modern American cuisine and high-end comfort
food (hello, gourmet burgers!)

Booking ahead is absolutely essential at
any popular venue where reservations are
taken. Sometimes you'll need to call the
restaurant long before you've even departed
on your vacation. If tables are booked up,
ask about bar service, or whether or not you
can sneak a seat at the very end of the night
(around 11pm). Lunch is another option –
many of the city's dinner darlings have mid-
day prix fixe service. Tables are less coveted
then, and oftentimes the price tag can be a
bit more wallet-friendly.

Food Trucks & Carts

The hot tin carts along the sides of busy intersections have long been a New York City staple as they dish out steaming halal snacks or plump bagels to overworked business folk or on-the-go tourists. But these days, there's a new crew in town that has classed up the meals-on-wheels culture with high-end treats and unique fusion fare. The trucks ply various routes, stopping in designated parking zones throughout the city – namely around Union Sq, Midtown and the Financial District – so if you're looking for a particular grub wagon, it's best to follow them on Twitter. A few of our favorites:

Big Gay Ice Cream Truck (www.twitter.com/biggayicecream)

Korilla BBQ (www.twitter.com/korillabbq)

Calexico Cart (www.twitter.com/calexiconyc)

Kelvin Natural Slush (www.twitter.com/kelvinslush)

Wafels & Dinges (www.twitter.com/waffletruck)

Tours & Courses

There's no better way to engage with the city's infinite dining scene than to link up with a savvy local for a food tour or cooking class. Check out the following winners:

Urban Oyster (www.urbanoyster.com) High-quality, themed foodie tours mostly in Lower Manhattan and Brooklyn.

Scott's Pizza Tours (www.scottspizzatours.com) Offbeat and always fun, Scott promises to unveil all of the secrets of the city's pizza pie scene.

Joshua M Bernstein (www.joshuambernstein.com) Joshua is a respected food blogger and journalist who leads tours with a special focus on craft beer and home brew.

I Want More Food (www.iwantmorefood.com) Food blogger specializing in Queens food-truck crawls.

Pizza A Casa (www.pizzaacasa.com) Much-loved pie school on the Lower East Side specializing in rolling and decorating dough.

To Market, to Market

Don't let the concrete streets and buildings fool you – New York City has a thriving greens scene that comes in many shapes and sizes. At the top of your list should be the New Amsterdam Market (p73) – a

PLAN YOUR TRIP EATING

NEED TO KNOW

Price Guide

For this guide, the following price symbols apply for a main dish, exclusive of tax and tip:

$	under $12
$$	$12–$25
$$$	more than $25

Opening Hours

Generally speaking, meal times often bleed together as New Yorkers march to the beat of their own drum: breakfast is served from 6am to noon, lunch goes from 11am to around 3pm, and dinner stretches between 5pm and 11pm. The popular Sunday brunch (often served on Saturdays, too) lasts from 11am to 4pm.

Useful Websites

➡ **Yelp** (www.yelp.com) Comprehensive user-generated content.

➡ **Open Table** (www.opentable.com) Reservation service for a wide spread of restaurants around town.

➡ **Tasting Table** (www.tastingtable.com) Sign up for handy news blasts about the latest and greatest.

Tipping

Waiters in the US are paid less than minimum wage, thus making tips essential. New Yorkers tip between 15% to 20% of the final price of the meal. You needn't tip for takeaway, though it's polite to drop a dollar in a tip jar at the register.

Reservations

Popular restaurants abide by one of two rules: either they take reservations and you need to plan in advance (even weeks or months early for the real treasures) or they only seat patrons on a first-come basis, in which case you should eat early or late to avoid the impossibly long lines.

seasonal Sunday food market outside the old Fulton St Fish Market near the South Street Seaport. It's here that you'll find the best artisanal meats, cheeses, pasta and bread from the Northeast. Also worth a look is the Union Square Greenmarket (p172), open Monday, Wednesday, Friday and Saturday throughout the year (with

Eating by Neighborhood

Harlem & Upper Manhattan
Comfort cuisine meets
Caribbean and
Latin American (p258)

**Upper West Side &
Central Park**
A few top eats tucked
between apartment
blocks (p235)

Central
Park

Upper East Side
Ladies who lunch meet
cafe culture (p220)

Midtown
Fine dining, cocktail-literate
bistros and old-school delis (p194)

Queens
A multicultural borough that
cures all cravings (p303)

**Greenwich Village, Chelsea &
the Meatpacking District**
See-and-be-seen brunch spots, wine bars
and New American darlings (p139)

**Union Square, Flatiron
District & Gramercy**
Everything from after-work tapas
to park-side burgers (p164)

MANHATTAN

**East Village &
Lower East Side**
Unpretentious spectrum of eats,
from Asia to the Middle East (p111)

SoHo & Chinatown
Bargain basement fare beside
high-end markets (p89)

**Lower Manhattan &
the Financial District**
Celebrity-chef hotspots and
a locavore market (p71)

Brooklyn
Neighborhood pizzerias,
Michelin-star dining and
retro–New American fare (p278)

reduced hours in the colder months).
Brought to the public by **Grow NYC** (www.
grownyc.org/ourmarkets), it could be considered the flagship venue of its market
movement – check out the website for more
locations throughout the city.

Also quite popular are high-end market-
cum-grocers like Eataly (p172) and Dean &
Deluca (p92).

Celebrity Chefs

The era of reality TV shows continues the
trend of celebrity chefdom in NYC; a city
where restaurateurs are just as famous as
their fare (if not more). It's not just buzz,
though – these taste masters really know
their trade. Big-ticket names abound:
Mario Batali (www.mariobatali.com) has
painted the town red with his spaghetti
sauces. Babbo (p142) and Otto Enoteca Pizzeria (p143) are old stand-bys and Eataly
(p172), his latest oeuvre, is a monstrous

marketplace dedicated to the Italian table.
David Chang's Momofuku (p237) empire
continues to expand with heart-stoppingly
delicious pork buns. And up-and-comers
like Hooni Kim (owner of Danji (p196) are
making a name for themselves as they rack
up Michelin stars with alacrity.

Food Reviews & Blogs

New Yorkers are famous for offering their
opinion, so why not capitalize on their
taste-bud experiences and click through
scores of websites catering to the discerning diner. Some of our favorite blog-style
rags:

Eater (http://ny.eater.com)

New York Magazine (www.nymag.com)

Serious Eats (http://newyork.seriouseats.com)

Grub street (http://newyork.grubstreet.com)

Lonely Planet's Top Choices

Le Bernardin (p196) Triple Michelin-star earner and New York's holy grail of fine dining.

Locanda Verde (p73) Insanely flavorful Italian grub from one of New York's most beloved chefs.

RedFarm (p139) Savvy Sino-fusion dishes boast bold flavors but it doesn't take itself too seriously.

Dovetail (p236) Simplicity is key at this Upper West Side stunner – vegetarians unite on Mondays for a divine tasting menu.

Danji (p196) Masterfully prepared and wildly inventive 'Korean tapas' crafted by a young-gun pro.

Best by Budget

$

Le Grainne (p146)

Nathan's Famous (p207)

Golden Shopping Mall (p304)

Earl's Beer & Cheese (p220)

Burger Joint (p196)

Cocoron (p114)

$$

Amy Ruth's Restaurant (p258)

Vinegar Hill House (p279)

Fatty Crab (p235)

Totto Ramen (p196)

Westville (p140)

$$$

Dressler (p283)

Café Boulud (p220)

Dutch (p89)

Best by Cuisine

Asian

Momofuku (p237)

Joe's Shanghai (p93)

Fu Run (p304)

Cocoron (p114)

Ippudo NY (p111)

Italian

Roberta's (p283)

L'Artusi (p140)

Luzzo's (p112)

Vesta Trattoria & Wine Bar (p303)

Maialino (p167)

Vegetarian

Candle Cafe (p221)

Champs (p284)

Hangawi (p194)

Souen (p143)

Angelica Kitchen (p113)

Best Brunch

Cookshop (p146)

Peaches (p280)

Cafe Orlin (p111)

Café Luxembourg (p236)

Marseille (p197)

Balthazar (p89)

Best for Old-School NYC

Junior's (p279)

Katz's Delicatessen (p114)

Zabar's (p235)

William Greenberg Desserts (p221)

Sarge's Deli (p195)

Best for Coffee

Abraço (p111)

Via Quadronno (p221)

Blue Bottle Coffee (p285)

Stumptown Coffee (p198)

Irving Farm (p168)

Kaffe 1668 (p75)

Best Celebrity-Chef Restaurants

Red Rooster (p258)

Dutch (p89)

Les Halles (p73)

Birreria (p166)

Best Bakeries

Dough (p280)

Birdbath (p112)

ChiKaLicious (p112)

Absolute Bagels (p236)

Make My Cake (p258)

City Bakery (p166)

Best Upscale Market Groceries

Eataly (p172)

Fairway (p237)

Zabar's (p235)

Grand Central Market (p188)

New Amsterdam Market (p73)

Best for Foodie Gifts

William Greenberg Desserts (p221)

Murray's Cheese (p155)

Pasanella & Son (p78)

MARTIN THOMAS PHOTOGRAPHY / ALAMY ©

McSorley's Old Ale House (p115), East Village

Drinking & Nightlife

Considering that 'Manhattan' is thought to be a derivation of the Munsee word manahactanienk ('place of general inebriation'), it shouldn't be surprising that New York truly lives up to its nickname: 'the city that never sleeps.' In fact, some 20 years after the city was founded, Peter Stuyvesant lashed out stating that a quarter of New Amsterdam's buildings were taverns. Sometimes it feels like things have barely changed.

Bars & Lounges

Here in the land where the term 'cocktail' was born, mixed drinks are still stirred with the utmost seriousness. And these days, researched cocktails are very much in – especially with a Prohibition or swinging '20s theme.

Once upon a time Brooklyn was a major beer exporter (p366), and although that's no longer the case, there's been a recent rise in craft brews. In fact, sampling designer beers has become such a popular evening pastime that it's starting to rival wine-bar soirees.

Clubbing

New Yorkers are always looking for the next big thing, and thus the city's club scene changes faster than a New York minute. Promoters drag revelers around the city for weekly events held at all of the finest addresses, and when there's nothing on, it's time to hit the dance floor stalwarts.

When clubbing it never hurts to plan ahead; having your name on a guest list can relieve unnecessary frustration and disappointment. If you're an uninitiated partier, then your best bet is to dress the part. If you're fed the 'private party' line, try to bluff – chances are high that you've been bounced. Also, don't forget a wad of cash as many nightspots (even the swankiest ones) often refuse credit cards, and in-house ATMs scam a fortune in fees.

Drinking & Nightlife by Neighborhood

➡ **Lower Manhattan & the Financial District** Manhattan's southern tip has its fair share of thirst-quenching drinking gems, from specialist beer and brandy bars, to an opium den turned cocktail peddler.

➡ **East Village & Lower East Side** The East Village is the proud home of the original flavor of dive bar; join the bands of youthful partygoers in the Lower East Side's mix of nightclubs.

➡ **Greenwich Village, Chelsea & the Meatpacking District** The jet set crowd flocks to the Meatpacking District, with wine bars, backdoor lounges and gay hangouts radiating out into the West Village and Chelsea.

➡ **Midtown** Whether you're after skyscraper views, historic cocktail salons, or a time-warped dive bar with Hollywood credentials, you're bound to find your perfect drinking hole in Midtown's canyons.

➡ **Brooklyn** Brooklyn offers everything on the nightlife spectrum with Williamsburg as its drinking capital; there are Depression-era theme bars and rowdy beer halls galore.

NEED TO KNOW

Websites

➡ **New York Magazine** (www.nymag.com/nightlife) Brilliantly curated nightlife options by the people who know best.

➡ **My Open Bar** (http://nyc.myopenbar.com) Offers a daily rundown of the spots in the city to score free booze.

➡ **Urbandaddy** (www.urbandaddy.com) Up-to-the-minute info and a handy 'hot right now' list.

➡ **Clubfone** (www.clubfone.com) Party in the palm of your hand. There's an app for that, and they made it.

Opening Hours

Opening times vary, though it's safe to say that most place get rollin' around 5pm – but some start as early as 8am. Most bars stay open until the legal closing time of 4am, though a few stop at 2am.

How Much

Happy Hour beers start at around $2; expect to pay about $6 for a regular draft, and from $8 for imported bottles. Glasses of wine start at around $7. Specialty cocktails run from $12 to well over $20.

Lonely Planet's Top Choices

Boom Boom Room (p147) Make it through the door here and you'll be clinking champagne with Vogue photographers and descendants of European royalty.

Bohemian Hall & Beer Garden (p308) Czech brews served with thick accents at NYC's favorite beer garden – a must during the warmer months.

Little Branch (p147) Speakeasy-chic is all the craze, but no one does it as well as this West Village hideout tucked behind an unassuming door.

Commodore (p286) Free arcade games and '70s-style beverages will draw you in, and the delicious pub grub will have you staying til closing.

Campbell Apartment (p188) In a hidden corner of Grand Central Terminal, this delightful throwback to the roaring '20s was once the office of a railroad magnate, and no expense has been spared in its inspired reproduction.

Best for Cocktails

RedFarm (p139)

Maison Premiere (p287)

Lantern's Keep (p198)

Lot 2 (p281)

Mulberry Project (p93)

Weather Up (p75)

Best for Wine Selection

Vin Sur Vingt (p147)

Terroir (p198)

Barcibo Enoteca (p238)

Immigrant (p118)

Best for Beer

Vol de Nuit (p147)

Spuyten Duyvil (p287)

McSorley's Old Ale House (p115)

Bier International (p259)

Keg No 229 (p76)

Birreria (p166)

Best for Spirits

Pravda (p93)

Brandy Library (p75)

Vandaag (p118)

Mayahuel (p118)

Best Bar Bites

Terroir (p198)

Commodore (p286)

Tertulia (p140)

Weather Up (p75)

Best Dance Clubs & House DJs

Le Bain (p147)

Sullivan Room (p148)

Brooklyn Bowl (p288)

Bell House (p288)

Best Happy Hours

Clem's (p287)

Ten Degrees Bar (p118)

John Dory Oyster Bar (p195)

Subway Inn (p198)

Alligator Lounge (p287)

Best for Date Night

Metropolitan Museum Roof Garden Café & Martini Bar (p224)

Vin Sur Vingt (p147)

Brandy Library (p75)

☆ Gay & Lesbian

The future has arrived in NYC: men seek out other men using apps with geolocators, drag queens are so 'out' that they're practically 'in,' bouncers thumb through guest lists on their iPads, and gay marriage is – at long last – legal. It's time to hop in your time machine and join the fray.

Weekdays are the New Weekend

Here in the Big Apple, any night of the week is fair game to paint the town rouge – especially for the gay community, who attack the weekday social scene with gusto. Wednesdays and Thursdays roar with a steady stream of parties, and locals love raging on Sundays (especially in summer). While there's undoubtedly much fun to be had on Friday and Saturday nights, weekend parties tend to be more 'bridge and tunnel.' Manhattanites use these days to catch up with friends and check out new restaurants.

Promoters

To dial into the party hotline, follow the various goings-on of your favorite promoter.

Josh Wood (www.joshwoodproductions.com)

Susanne Bartsch (www.susannebartsch.com)

Brian Rafforty and Shawn Paul Mazur (www. raffertymazurevents.com)

Sean B and Will Automagic (www.spankartmag.com)

Erich Conrad (Twitter @ZIGZAGLeBain)

Mo Money, no Matter

Although New York City has a smattering of neighborhoods that are infamous for their gay hangouts, the city's lesbian, gay, bisexual and transgender scene is hardly segregated, let alone ghettoized. With one of the largest disposable incomes of any demographic, the gays seem to run the city, from the fashion runways and major music labels to Wall St downtown. The new marriage laws of 2011 are a further acknowledgement that here in New York it's totally 'in' to be 'out.'

Gay & Lesbian by Neighborhood

➜ **East Village & Lower East Side** Slightly grittier, grungier versions of the West Side haunts.

➜ **Greenwich Village, Chelsea & the Meatpacking District** The original flavor of gay New York still shines as a rainbow beacon.

➜ **Union Square, Flatiron District & Gramercy** Hosts a spillover of gay venues from the East Village, West Village and Chelsea.

➜ **Midtown** Midtown West's Hell's Kitchen neighborhood is the 'new Chelsea,' with a booty of gay-friendly shops, bars, nosh spots and clubs.

➜ **Brooklyn** Multineighborhood borough with gays of every ilk, and diverse watering holes peppered throughout.

TAPPING INTO THE GAY SCENE

Benjamin Solomon, editor-in-chief of *Next Magazine*, gives us his top tips:

➜ There are few places all New York gays congregate, so figure out which scene you are a part of (Brooklyn hipster? Fashionista?) to find exactly the crowd you're after.

➜ Some of the best stuff happens at private parties, so make some friends then follow them.

➜ Unlike the '80s, backroom sex and bath houses are almost a nonexistent scene; most cruising happens on the dance floor.

➜ If it's hip and cool, odds are there will be plenty of gays in sight, so don't limit yourself to gay-specific places.

NEED TO KNOW

Websites

➜ **Next Magazine** (www.nextmagazine.com) Online version of the ubiquitous print guide to all things gay in NYC.

➜ **Gayletter** (www.gayletter.com) An e-newsletter about what to do in NYC.

➜ **La Daily Musto** (http://blogs.village voice.com/dailymusto) Michael Musto's queer-themed blog/column for the Village Voice.

Resources & Support

For almost 30 years, the **LGBT Community Center** (208 West 13th St btwn 7th & 8th Aves,West Village; www.gaycenter.org) has been the nexus of the Village's queer community. It allows endless groups to meet here and provides a ton of regional publications about gay events and nightlife, and hosts frequent special events – dance parties, art exhibits, Broadway-caliber performances and political panels.

Lonely Planet's Top Choices

Gay Pride Parade (p26) Rainbow-clad pomp and circumstance celebrating Marlo Thomas' credo after years of struggle.

LGBT Community Center Offers everything from a meeting space to performances and literature.

Industry (p200) Lounge chairs, dance beats and cute boys – the perfect gay ol' time.

Marie's Crisis (p147) The ultimate cramped piano bar where no one's afraid to be themselves.

Best for Weeknights

Splash Bar (p169)

Eastern Bloc (p118)

Therapy (p205)

Boxers NYC (p169)

Best Dance Floors

Splash Bar (p169)

Bar-Tini Ultra Lounge (p200)

Monster (p148)

Best for Women

Ginger's (p286)

Cubbyhole (p149)

Henrietta Hudson (p149)

Stonewall Inn (p149)

Best for Classic NYC Gay

Julius Bar (p148)

Stonewall Inn (p149)

Marie's Crisis (p147)

Rawhide (p150)

Cock (p119)

Best Places to Stay

Bubba & Bean Lodges (p342)

Chelsea Pines Inn (p333)

East Village B&B (p332)

Dream (p340)

Ink48 (p341)

Hotel Williamsburg (p347)

Eugene O'Neill Theater, featuring the Book of Mormon (p201)

RICHARD LEVINE / ALAMY ©

☆ Entertainment

Hollywood may hold court when it comes to the motion picture, but it's NYC that reigns supreme over the pantheon of other arts. Actors, musicians, dancers and artists flock to the bright lights of the Big Apple like moths to a flame. It's like the old saying goes: if you can make it here, you can make it anywhere.

Comedy

A good laugh is easy to find in the Big Apple, where comedians sharpen their stand-up and improv chops practicing new material or hoping to get scouted by a producer or agent. The best spots for some chuckles are downtown, particularly around Chelsea and Greenwich Village. Several festivals, like Comic-Con, draw big names throughout the year. You can also snag seats to tapings of America's popular late night variety shows.

Dance

Dance fans are spoiled for choice in this town, which is home to both the New York City Ballet (p239) and the American Ballet Theatre (p239). There are also modern dance companies galore that often take to the stage downtown and at the Brooklyn Academy of Music (p289). Note that there are two major dance seasons: first in spring from March to May, then in late fall from October to December.

NEED TO KNOW

Calendar & Reviews

➡ **Playbill** (www.playbill.com) Offers theater news, listings and tickets.

➡ **Talkin' Broadway** (www.talkingbroadway.com) Dishy reviews as well as a board for posting extra tickets.

➡ Print publications include *Time Out, New York Magazine, New York Times* and *Village Voice.*

Websites & Tickets

To purchase tickets for shows, head directly to the venue's box office or use ticket-service agencies.

➡ **Broadway Line** (www.livebroadway.com) Provides descriptions and good prices for Broadway shows.

➡ **SmartTix** (www.smarttix) A great resource for anything but Broadway.

➡ **Telecharge** (www.telecharge.com) Sells tickets for Broadway and off-Broadway shows.

➡ **Theatermania** (www.theatermania.com) For any form of theater; provides listings, reviews and ticketing.

Film & TV

Film-going is a serious venture here, as evidenced by the preponderance of movie houses that show indie, classic, avant-garde, foreign and otherwise non-standard fare. Frequent film festivals, like the Tribeca Film Festival, with different themes provide additional texture to the movie-going scene.

One of the least-known gems for films is Museum of Modern Art, which has a rich collection of movies spanning all genres and corners of the world. The Film Society at Lincoln Center (p239) stages an incredible array of documentary and art house films. Also worth checking is BAM Rose Cinemas (p289), which does similar fare as well as revivals.

Live Music

NYC is the country's capital of live music, and just about every taste can be catered for here. For current listings check out *New York Magazine* (p396) and the *Village Voice* (p396).

Opera & Classical Music

When thinking about opera, minds tend to go directly to the lavish images of Metropolitan Opera (p239) productions. However, many other forms live within the city limits. After the Amato Opera Theater closed, two spin-off companies formed: **Bleecker Street Opera** (Map p418; www.bleeckerstreetopera.org; 45 Bleecker St; [S] B/D/F/V to Broadway-Lafayette St; 6 to Bleecker St) and Amore Opera (p121) – joining Brooklyn's American Opera Projects (p289) in promising quality operas for just a fraction of what you'd pay uptown.

The choices for orchestras, chamber music and opera are abundant, with the more cutting-edge options often stealing center stage. Don't miss Lincoln Center (p233), the Brooklyn Academy of Music (p289) and Carnegie Hall (p204).

Theater

The most celebrated theater scene is, of course, that of Broadway, nicknamed the Great White Way in 1902 for its bright billboard lights. There's something truly magical about sitting in one of the ornate Broadway theaters and letting the show take you to another world. The term 'off-Broadway' is not a geographical one, it simply refers to theaters that are smaller in size (200 to 500 seats) and have less of a production budget than the Broadway big hitters.

Entertainment by Neighborhood

➡ **East Village & Lower East Side** Experimental performance spaces, poetry slams and stand-up comics.

➡ **Greenwich Village, Chelsea & the Meatpacking District** Unofficial headquarters of the world's jazz club scene, plus dance troupes galore in Chelsea.

➡ **Midtown** Razzle-dazzle extravaganzas, fresh American theater, world-class jazz sessions, stand-up comedy blue bloods.

➡ **Upper West Side & Central Park** The Lincoln Center supplies an endless amount of high culture, while the Beacon Theatre and Cleopatra's Needle provide more intimate settings for live music.

➡ **Brooklyn** There's a little bit of everything, from the classical offerings at BAM to the indie rock bands in Williamsburg.

Lonely Planet's Top Choices

Book of Mormon (p201) Uproariously brilliant Broadway musical appreciated citywide for its wit, charm and pitch-perfect performances.

Shakespeare in the Park (p26) Annual homage to the Bard in the form of wildly popular (and free!) performances in Central Park.

Jazz at Lincoln Center (p200) Glittering evening views of Central Park and world-class musical acts – what more could you ask for?

Carnegie Hall (p204) Legendary concert hall, blessed with perfect acoustics; hosts everything from opera to jazz.

Performance Space 122 (p120) Dedicated experimental performance space for up-and-coming artists.

Best Free Entertainment

SummerStage (p26)

HBO Bryant Park Summer Film Festival (p26)

World Financial Center (p77)

Ace Hotel live bands and DJs (p337)

Best for Laughs

Upright Citizen's Brigade Theatre (p151)

Comedy Cellar (p151)

Sweet (p120)

Caroline's on Broadway (p204)

Comic Strip Live (p225)

Best for Dance

City Center (p204)

Brooklyn Academy of Music (p289)

Lincoln Center (p233)

Kitchen (p152)

Best for Film

Angelika (p152)

Museum of Modern Art

92YTribeca (p77)

Anthology Film Archives (p121)

BAM Rose Cinema (p289)

Film Society of Lincoln Center (p239)

Best Broadway Shows

Book of Mormon (p201)

Chicago (p201)

Wicked (p201)

Best for Theater (Non-Broadway)

Playwrights Horizons (p204)

Signature Theatre (p200)

Flea Theater (p77)

Lincoln Center (p233)

Brooklyn Academy of Music (p289)

Best Pre-Broadway Show Hangouts

Rum House (p199)

Marseille (p197)

Jimmy's Corner (p200)

Best for Live Music

Jazz at Lincoln Center (p200)

Village Vanguard (p151)

Birdland (p204)

Music Hall of Williamsburg (p288)

Beacon Theatre (p242)

Blue Note (p151)

Best for Classical Music & Opera

Metropolitan Opera House (p239)

American Opera Projects (p289)

Brooklyn Academy of Music (p289)

Carnegie Hall (p204)

PETER HORREE / ALAMY ©

Barneys (p206), Midtown East

Shopping

You can blame the likes of Holly Golightly and Carrie Bradshaw for making it darned impossible not to associate New York City with diamonds for breakfast or designer labels for dinner – and the locals are all too happy to oblige. NYC may not be the world's fashion or technology capital, but private capital reigns supreme; so there's no better place on the planet to shop to your heart's content.

An Homage to Luxury

Shopping in NYC isn't, of course, just about purchasing items – it's also very much about experiencing the city in all of its incarnations. At the top of the pyramid are those bastions of aspirational trends. The high-end boutiques of big designer names dot the city, and they come together in heady conglomerations known worldwide as department stores. But New York brews a special blend – don't miss Barneys (p206), Bergdorf Goodman (p206), Macy's (p207) and Bloomingdale's (p206).

Sample Sales

While clothing sales happen year-round – usually when seasons change and old stock must be moved out – sample sales are held frequently, mostly in the huge warehouses in the Fashion District of Midtown or in SoHo. While the original sample sale was a way for designers to get rid of one-of-a-kind prototypes that weren't quite up to snuff, most sample sales these days are for high-end labels to get rid of overstock at wonderfully deep discounts. The semi-annual Barneys warehouse sale, held at Chelsea Barneys Co-op (p157), is one such frenzied event, bringing pushy crowds that resemble bread lines in their zeal for finding half-price Christian Louboutins or Diane Von Furstenburg dresses.

Flea Markets & Vintage Adventures

As much as New Yorkers gravitate towards all that's shiny and new, it can be infinitely fun to rifle through closets of unwanted wares and threads. The most popular flea market is the Brooklyn Flea, housed in all sorts of spaces throughout the year. The East Village is the city's de facto neighborhood for secondhand gyms – the uniform of the unwavering legion of hipsters.

Shopping by Neighborhood

➡ **Lower Manhattan** While not a shopping hotspot per se, Lower Manhattan serves up a trickle of gems, from vintage film posters and hard-to-find vino, to hipster-chic threads and outrageous retro fabrics.

➡ **SoHo & Chinatown** West Broadway is a veritable outdoor mall of encyclopedic proportions. It's like the UN of retail – if you can't find what you're looking for then it hasn't been invented yet. Try Mott St for something a bit more subdued.

➡ **East Village & Lower East Side** Hipster treasure trove of vintage wares and design goods. Go wild on E 9th St, St Marks Place and Orchard St.

NEED TO KNOW

Websites

➡ **Racked** (www.ny.racked.com) Informative shopping blog with its finger on the pulse.

➡ **NearSay** (www.newyork.nearsay.com/nyc/shopping) Personalized news bites about the latest in the consumer world.

➡ **New York Magazine** (www.nymag.com/shopping) Trustworthy opinions on the Big Apple's best places to swipe your plastic.

➡ **Daily Candy** (www.dailycandy.com) Curated selection of the best NYC has to offer.

Opening Hours

In general, most business are open from 10am to around 7pm on weekdays and 11am to around 8pm Saturdays. Sundays can be variable – some stores stay closed while others keep weekday hours. Stores tend to stay open later in the neighborhoods downtown. Small boutiques often have variable hours – many only open at noon.

Sales Tax

In New York City you'll have to tack on an 8.875% retail sales tax to every purchase.

➡ **Midtown** Epic department stores, global chains, historic music stores and the odd in-the-know treasure window shoppers unite!

➡ **Upper East Side** The country's most expensive boutiques along Madison Ave, but plenty of price-conscious consignment shops can be scouted as well.

➡ **Brooklyn** A healthy mix of independent boutiques, big-box shops and thrift stores. Go wild at the home design shops in Williamsburg. Try Bedford Ave and Boerum Hill's Smith St.

Lonely Planet's Top Choices

Barneys (p206) Serious fashionistas shop at Barneys, well-known for its spot-on collections of in-the-know labels.

Brooklyn Flea (p293) Brooklyn's collection of flea markets offer plenty of vintage furnishings, retro clothing and bric-a-brac, not to mention an array of loster rolls, tamales, chocolate and so much more.

ABC Carpet & Home (p172) Set up over six floors like a museum, ABC is filled with all sorts of furnishings, small and large, including easy-to pack knick-knacks, designer jewelry, global gifts and more bulky antique furnishings and carpets.

Barneys Co-Op (p157) Barneys' little brother, the Co-Op, has several locations scattered around Manhattan, offering discount deals on designer threads.

Best NYC Fashion Boutiques & Designers

Marc Jacobs (p154)

Patricia Field (p123)

John Varvatos (p95)

Castor & Pollux (p154)

John Bartlett (p156)

Best Department Stores

Bergdorf Goodman (p206)

Bloomingdales (p206)

Macy's (p207)

Jeffery New York (p155)

Best for Unique Souvenirs & Gifts

MoMA Design & Book Store (p206)

Philip Williams Posters (p77)

Black Gold (p292)

Amé Amé (East Village)

Citystore (p78)

Best for Women

Spiritual America (p125)

Michael's (p225)

Encore (p225)

Eva Gentry (p292)

Beacon's Closet (p292)

Best for Men

John Bartlett (p156)

Nepenthes New York (p207)

Nostylgia (p260)

Smith + Butler (p292)

C'H'C'M (p123)

Best for Reading Material

MoMA Design & Book Store (p206)

Strand Book Store (p154)

McNally Jackson (p94)

Book Thug Nation (p292)

Crawford Doyle Booksellers (p225)

Best for Foodies

William Greenberg Desserts (p221)

Murray's Cheese (p155)

Wine from Pasanella & Son (p78)

Books from Bonnie Slotnick Cookbook Store (p154)

Best for Children

FAO Schwartz (p206)

Yoyamart (p154)

Books of Wonder (p172)

Forbidden Planet (p156)

Sports & Activities

Although hailing cabs in New York City can feel like a blood sport, and waiting on subway platforms in summer heat is steamier than a sauna, New Yorkers still love to stay active in their spare time. And considering how limited the green spaces are in New York, it's surprising for some visitors just how active the locals can be.

Spectator Sports

BASEBALL

New York is one of the last remaining corners of the USA where baseball reigns supreme over football and basketball. With tickets starting at around $10, it's a steal to see and it's well worth visiting the city's two newly opened stadiums. The two Major League Baseball teams play 162 games during the regular season from April to October, when the playoffs begin.

New York Yankees (www.yankees.com) The Bronx Bombers are the USA's greatest dynasty, with over two dozen World Series championship titles since 1900.

New York Mets (www.mets.com) In the National League since 1962, the Mets remain New York's 'new' baseball team.

HOCKEY

The NHL (National Hockey League) has three franchises in the greater New York area; each team plays three or four games weekly during the season from September to April.

New York Rangers (www.nyrangers.com) Manhattan's favorite hockey squad.

New York Islanders (www.newyorkislanders.com) New York City hasn't given much Islander love since the unremarkable consecutive four-year Stanley Cup streak in the '80s.

New Jersey Devils (http://devils.nhl.com) The Devils may not be New Yorkers, but they've seen more wins than their neighbors.

BASKETBALL

Two NBA (National Basketball Association) teams, the Knicks and the Nets, call the New York metropolitan area home. The season lasts from October to May or June.

New York Knicks (p209) Occasional scandal aside, NYC loves its blue-and-orange basketball team.

New Jersey Nets (p295) Soon to be the Brooklyn Nets.

FOOTBALL

Football season runs from August to January or February. Most of New York tunes into its NFL (National Football League) teams – the Giants and Jets – both of whom play at the new Meadowlands Stadium at the Meadowlands Sports Complex in New Jersey (from Manhattan take NJ Transit via Seacaucus Junction, $7.75 return). The NFL season has 16 regular-season games (held on Sunday or Monday night), then up to three playoffs before the Super Bowl.

New York Giants (www.giants.com) One of the NFL's oldest teams.

New York Jets (www.newyorkjets.com) Games are always packed and new fans easily get swept away by the contagious 'J-E-T-S!' chants.

Outdoor Sports

RUNNING & JOGGING

Central Park's loop roads are best during traffic-free hours, though you'll be in the company of many cyclists and in-line skaters. The 1.6-mile path surrounding the Jacqueline Kennedy Onassis Reservoir (where Jackie O used to run) is for runners and walkers only; access it between 86th and 96th Sts. Running along the Hudson River is a popular path, best from 23rd St to Battery Park in Lower Manhattan. The Upper East Side has a path that runs along FDR Dr

NEED TO KNOW

Websites

➡ **NYC Parks** (www.nycgovparks.org) For details on park services, including free pools and basketball court opening times. Has detailed biking maps of the five boroughs.

➡ **New York Road Runners Club** (www.nyrrc.org) Organizes weekend runs citywide.

➡ **MeetUp** (www.meetup.com) Sign up and get access to thousands of city-wide activity groups – many dedicated to active pursuits.

➡ **Bloomspot** (www.bloomspot.com) Groupon-esque sales blast website with tons of pampering perks.

Buying Tickets

With so many teams and overlapping seasons, a game is rarely a day away. Some teams' hotlines or box offices sell tickets directly (available under 'tickets' on the relevant websites), but most go via **Ticketmaster** (www.ticketmaster. com). The other major buy/sell outlet is **StubHub** (www.stubhub.com).

and the East River (from 63rd St to 115th St). Brooklyn's Prospect Park has plenty of paths.

The New York Road Runners Club (p226) organizes weekend runs citywide, including the New York City Marathon.

BICYCLING

NYC has taken enormous strides in making the city more bike-friendly, adding well over 200 miles of bike lanes in the last five years. That said, we recommend that the uninitiated stick to the less hectic trails in the parks and along the waterways, like Central Park, Prospect Park, the **Manhattan Waterfront Greenway** (www.nyc.gov/html/dcp/html/mwg/mwghome.shtml) and the **Brooklyn Waterfront Greenway** (www.brooklyngreenway.org).

Check out the individual Explore chapters for details about bike rentals.

STREET SPORTS

With all that concrete around, New York has embraced a number of sports played directly on the streets themselves.

Those with hoop dreams will find pick-up basketball games all over the city, the most famous courts being the West 4th Street Basketball Courts (p158), known as 'the Cage.' Or try Holcombe Rucker Park (p256) up in Harlem – that's where many NBA big shots cut their teeth. You'll also find pick-up games in Tompkins Square Park (p106) and Riverside Park (p235).

Lesser-known handball and stickball are also quite popular in NYC – you'll find one-wall courts in outdoor parks all over the city. For stickball, link up with the Bronx-based **Emperors Stickball League** (www.stickball.com) to check out its Sunday games during the warmer months.

Indoor Activities

You can't do a child's pose without bumping into one of the many yoga or Pilates studios that dot the city. Yelp (www.yelp.com) is a great tool for selecting a spot in the neighborhood that suits your needs.

If you're looking to score some gym action and your hotel doesn't have adequate facilities, then you can try your luck at scoring a complimentary one-, three- or seven-day pass from one of the franchised studios – like **NYSC** (www.mysportsclubs.com) or **Equinox (www.equinox.com)** – around town. They tend to dole out free passes like after-dinner mints.

Sports & Activities by Neighborhood

➡ **Lower Manhattan & the Financial District** Boat rides galore offer brilliant skyline views from the harbor.

➡ **Greenwich Village, Chelsea & tge Meatpacking District** Pilates studios and hot yoga palaces are tucked betwixt crumbling brownstone walls.

➡ **Upper West Side & Central Park** Cycling, running, boating and baseball – all in the leafy surrounds of NYC's backyard, Central Park.

➡ **Brooklyn** Prospect Park holds its own as Brooklyn's answer to Central Park. Stay alert as you dodge the Park Slope stroller brigade!

➡ **Queens** Active or passive, Queens has you covered, from stadium baseball games and a world-famous Grand Slam, to urban kayaking and a giant Korean bathhouse.

Lonely Planet's Top Choices

Central Park (p229) The giant emerald jewel in New York's concrete crown, Central Park is the city's playground, complete with rolling hills for walking, green spaces for kicking a ball, and a beautiful lake that's perfect for boating.

New York Yankees (p257) Even if you're not a baseball enthusiast it's well worth trekking out to Queens to experience the rabid fandom.

Chelsea Piers Complex (p158) Every activity imaginable – from kickboxing to ice hockey – under one gigantic roof, just a stone's throw from the High Line.

New York Spa Castle (p308) Bathing behemoth with wallet-friendly prices. Inspired by ancient Korean traditions of wellness. You'll want to stay for days.

Best Urban Green Spaces

Inwood Hill Park (p257)

Governors Island (p65)

Bryant Park (p191)

Prospect Park (p274)

Madison Square Park (p164)

Brooklyn Bridge Park (p264)

Riverside Park (p235)

Best Indoor Activities

Gotham Girls Roller Derby (p294)

Brooklyn Boulders (p295)

New York Knicks (p209)

Soul Cycle (p173)

Best Out-of-the-Box Activities

Coney Island jet-ski tours (p267)

Hudson River kayak tours (p159)

Best Bowling

Brooklyn Bowl (p294)

300 New York (Map p430)

Lucky Strike (p209)

Bowlmor Lanes (p159)

Best Spas

Russian & Turkish Baths (p127)

Great Jones Spa (p99)

Caudalie Vinothérapie Spa (p208)

Best Retreats from the City

Rockaway Beach (p301)

Coney Island (p266)

Fire Island (p314)

Dia Beacon (p320)

Best Places to Go Jogging

Carl Schurz Park (Map p440)

Riverside Park (p235)

Battery Park (p70)

Brooklyn Bridge (p71)

BRENT WINEBRENNER / LONELY PLANET IMAGES ©

Explore
New York City

NEW YORK'S TOP SIGHTS

Neighborhoods at a Glance

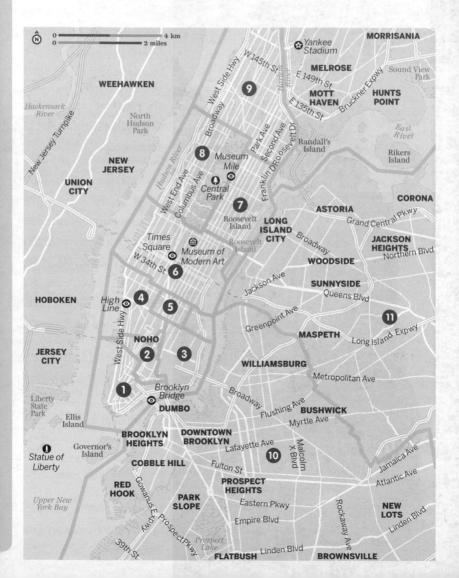

❶ Lower Manhattan & the Financial District (p56)

Home to icons like Wall Street, the 9/11 Memorial and the Statue of Liberty, the southern end of Manhattan pulses with businesslike energy during the day before settling into quiet nights. Tribeca, however, continues to hum well after dark with its cache of restaurants and lounges.

❷ SoHo & Chinatown (p80)

Sacred temples, hawkers peddling bric-a-brac and steam-filled soup dumpling parlors line hurried streets of Chinatown, with SoHo, next door, providing the counterpoint with streamlined thoroughfares and storefronts representing all of the biggest-name brands in the world. Tucked somewhere in between is Little Italy (emphasis on the 'little').

❸ East Village & Lower East Side (p100)

Old meets new on every block of this downtown duo – two of the city's hottest 'hoods for nightlife and cheap eats that lure students, bankers and scruffier types alike.

❹ Greenwich Village, Chelsea & the Meatpacking District (p128)

Quaint, twisting streets and well-preserved townhouses offer endless options for intimate dining and drinking in the West Village. The Meatpacking District next door has trendy nightlife options galore; further up is Chelsea, the unofficial headquarters of NYC's gay scene.

❺ Union Square, Flatiron District & Gramercy (p160)

This aptly named neighborhood is the tie that binds the colorful menagerie of surrounding areas. It's short on sights but big on buzz-worthy restaurants – and chances are high that you'll pass through on any New York visit.

❻ Midtown (p174)

This is the home of the NYC found on postcards: Times Sq, Broadway theaters, canyons of skyscrapers, and bustling crowds that rarely thin. Due to its position at the geographical center of the city's oft-visited sights, Midtown is a haven for tourists.

❼ Upper East Side (p210)

High-end boutiques line Madison Ave and sophisticated mansions run parallel along Fifth Ave, which culminates in an architectural flourish called Museum Mile – one of the most cultured strips in the city.

❽ Upper West Side & Central Park (p227)

New York's antidote to the endless stretches of concrete, Central Park is a verdant escape from honking horns and sunless sidewalks. Lining the park with inspired residential towers, the Upper West Side is home to Lincoln Center.

❾ Harlem & Upper Manhattan (p246)

Harlem and Hamilton Heights – a bastion of African American culture – offers good eats and jazz beats. Head up to Inwood for leafy park space, or try Morningside Heights to soak up some student life.

❿ Brooklyn (p262)

Brooklyn's sprawling checkerboard of distinct neighborhoods is over three times the size of Manhattan, not to mention more diverse and far-reaching. For skyline views and a pinch of history, try brownstone-studded Brooklyn Heights; or try Williamsburg for vintage wares and late-night bar crawls.

⓫ Queens (p296)

A patchwork of diverse communities, Queens is trailblazer territory for return visitors and locals alike. Gorge at the ethnic delis of Astoria, ogle contemporary art in Long Island City and ride the surf in Rockaway Beach.

Lower Manhattan & the Financial District

WALL STREET | FINANCIAL DISTRICT | NEW YORK HARBOR | BATTERY PARK CITY | SOUTH STREET SEAPORT | CITY HALL | CIVIC CENTER | TRIBECA

Neighborhood Top Five

1 Walking or biking across the glorious **Brooklyn Bridge** (p71). From the Gothic piers to the city view, this is one river crossing you won't forget.

2 Reflecting on loss and hope at the reborn **World Trade Center site** (p62).

3 Taking in skyscraper and Lady Liberty views from the free-and-fantastic **Staten Island Ferry** (p78).

4 Conjuring up the ghosts of the past at evocative **Ellis Island** (p60).

5 Hunting down a bargain at cheap 'n' chic **Century 21** (p77).

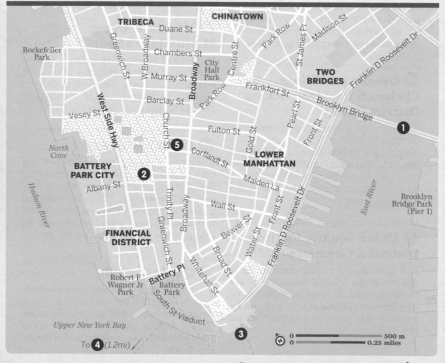

For more detail of this area, see Map p416 ➡

Explore Lower Manhattan & the Financial District

A little planning will save you a lot of time in Lower Manhattan. Book tickets online to the unmissable Ellis Island and Statue of Liberty, or catch the first ferry and avoid weekends, especially in summer. You'll need a good four hours to explore the two sights properly, and bring a picnic lunch – the food on-site is awful. You'll also need to book online to visit the 9/11 Memorial at the World Trade Center site. To experience the Financial District's power-broking intensity, head in during business hours, but, to calmly contemplate the area's Federal homes, Greek Revival temples and early modern skyscrapers, go after hours. To avoid the hordes at shopping mecca Century 21, raid the racks by 8am on weekdays. A good time for foodies is Sunday afternoon, with fantastic local produce at the seasonal New Amsterdam Market and free wine tastings at Pasanella & Son. If the weather is on your side, stock the hamper here and walk across the Brooklyn Bridge for a panoramic picnic. For an evening buzz, head to Tribeca's booty of fashionable bars and restaurants, the latter best booked ahead.

Local Life

➡ **Markets** Graze and shop with locavores at the gut-rumbling New Amsterdam Market (p73).

➡ **Coffee** Ditch the chains for in-the-know Kaffe 1668 (p75) and La Colombe (p75).

➡ **Wine** Swill free vino on Sunday afternoons at Pasanella & Son (p78).

➡ **Culture** Catch encore-inducing drama at the Flea Theater (p77).

Getting There & Away

➡ **Subway** The Financial District is well serviced by subway lines, connecting the area to the rest of Manhattan, Brooklyn, Queens and the Bronx. Fulton St is the main interchange station, servicing the A/C, J/M/Z, 2/3 and 4/5 lines. Line 1 terminates at South Ferry, from where the Staten Island Ferry departs.

➡ **Bus** From the Staten Island Ferry terminal, useful routes include the 15 (to East Village, Midtown East and Upper East Side) and the 20 (to Tribeca, West Village, Chelsea and Midtown West).

➡ **Boat** The Staten Island Ferry Terminal is at the southern end of Whitehall St. Ferries to Governors Island leave from the adjacent Battery Maritime Building. Services to Liberty and Ellis Islands depart from nearby Battery Park.

Lonely Planet's Top Tip

If you're after cut-price tickets to Broadway shows, ditch the main TKTS Booth in Times Sq for the TKTS branch at South Street Seaport (p392). Queues usually move a little faster and you can also purchase tickets for next-day matinees (something you can't do at the Times Sq outlet). Smartphone users can download the free TKTS app, which offers real-time listings of what's on sale.

✖ Best Places to Eat

➡ Locanda Verde (p73)
➡ Les Halles (p73)
➡ Kutsher's Tribeca (p73)
➡ New Amsterdam Market (p73)
➡ Shake Shack (p74)

For reviews, see p71 ➡

🍸 Best Places to Drink

➡ Macao (p75)
➡ Brandy Library (p75)
➡ Ward III (p75)
➡ Weather Up (p75)

For reviews, see 75 ➡

◉ Best Places to Relive the Past

➡ Ellis Island (p60)
➡ Historic Richmond Town (p67)
➡ Fraunces Tavern Museum (p63)
➡ South Street Seaport Museum (p70)
➡ Federal Hall (p64)

For reviews, see p63 ➡

TOP SIGHTS
STATUE OF LIBERTY

ANGUS OBORN / LONELY PLANET IMAGES ©

Lady Liberty has been gazing sternly across the waters to 'unenlightened Europe' since 1886. Dubbed the 'Mother of Exiles,' the statue serves as an admonishment to the rigid social structures of the old world. 'Give me your tired, your poor, Your huddled masses yearning to breathe free, The wretched refuse of your teeming shore. Send these, the homeless, tempest-tost to me, I lift my lamp beside the golden door!' she declares in Emma Lazarus' famous 1883 poem 'The New Colossus.' Ironically, these famous words were added to the statue's base only in 1903, more than 15 years after the poet's death.

DID YOU KNOW?

➡ The Statue of Liberty weighs 225 tonnes and stretches 93m from ground to torch-tip.

PRACTICALITIES

➡ ☑877-523-9849
➡ www.nps.gov/stli
➡ Liberty Island
➡ ⊘9:30am-5pm

Creating the Lady

One of America's most powerful symbols of kinship and freedom, 'Liberty Enlightening the World' was a joint effort between America and France to commemorate the centennial of the Declaration of Independence. It was created by commissioned sculptor Frédéric-Auguste Bartholdi. The artist spent most of 20 years turning his dream – to create the hollow monument and mount it in the New York Harbor – into reality. Along the way it was hindered by serious financial problems, but was helped in part by the fund-raising efforts of newspaper publisher Joseph Pulitzer. Lending a further hand was poet Emma Lazarus, whose aforementioned ode to Lady Liberty was part of a fund-raising campaign for the statue's pedestal, designed by American architect Richard Morris Hunt. Bartholdi's work on the statue was also delayed by structural challenges – a problem resolved by the metal framework mastery of railway engineer Gustave Eiffel (of, yes, the famous tower). The work of art was finally completed in France in 1884 (a bit off schedule for that centennial). It was shipped to NYC as 350 pieces packed into 214 crates, reassembled over a span of four months and placed on a US-made granite pedestal. Its spectacular October 1886 dedication included New York's first ticker-tape parade, and a flotilla of almost 300 vessels.

Put under the administration of the National Park Service in 1933, a restoration of the Lady's oxidized copper began in 1984, the same year the monument made it onto the UN's list of World Heritage Sites.

Liberty Today

Following the statue's 125th anniversary celebrations on 28 October 2011, the crown, museum and pedestal were closed for a major renovation. Due for completion in late 2012, the improvements will include access to the observation deck for mobility impaired visitors. In the meantime, visitors can still walk around the statue, take an audio tour, and pick up souvenirs in the gift shop. The cafeteria also remains open, though we strongly suggest you miss the sub-par offerings. Bring your own nibbles and (if the weather is behaving), enjoy it by the water, the Manhattan skyline before you.

Once the renovations are complete, folks who reserve in advance (more on that in a minute) will once again be able to climb the (steep) 354 steps to Lady Liberty's crown, where the city and harbor are even more impressive. As for the bad news: crown access is extremely limited, and the only way in is to reserve your spot in advance – and the further in advance you can do it, the better, as up to a full one-year lead time is allowed. Also know that each customer may only reserve a maximum of four crown tickets.

NEED TO KNOW

Although the ferry ride from Battery Park in Lower Manhattan lasts only 15 minutes, a trip to both the Statue of Liberty and Ellis Island is an all-day affair, and only those setting out on the ferry by 1pm will be allowed to visit both sites. Security screening at the ferry terminal can take up to 90 minutes. Reservations to visit the grounds and pedestal (the latter closed until late 2012) are strongly recommended, as they give you a specific visit time and a guarantee you'll get in. Your other option is to buy a Flex Ticket, which lets you enter any time within a three-day period.

The book of law in her left hand is inscribed with July IV MDCCLXXVI (4 July 1776), the date of American Independence. The seven rays on her crown represent the seven seas and continents, while the 25 windows adorning it symbolize gem stones. At her feet, chains and a broken shackle accentuate her status as free from oppression and servitude. As for the torch, it's a 1986 replacement of the original, the latter now housed at the on-site museum.

TOP SIGHTS
STATUE OF LIBERTY

TOP SIGHTS
ELLIS ISLAND

Ellis Island is America's most famous and historically important gateway – the very spot where old-world despair met new-world promise. Between 1892 and 1954, over 12 million immigrants passed through this processing station, their dreams in tow. Among them were Hungarian Erik Weisz (Harry Houdini), Rodolfo Guglielmi (Rudolph Valentino) and British Archibald Alexander Leach (Cary Grant). An estimated 40% of Americans today have at least one ancestor who was processed here, confirming the major role this tiny harbor island has played in the making of modern America.

After a $160 million restoration, the center was reopened to the public in 1990. Now anybody who rides the ferry to the island can experience a cleaned-up, modern version of the historic new-arrival experience at the impressive **Immigration Museum**, whose interactive exhibits pay homage to the hope, jubilation and sometimes bitter disappointment of the millions who came here in search of a new beginning.

Immigration Museum Exhibits

The three-level Immigration Museum is a poignant tribute to the immigrant experience. To get the most out of your visit, opt for the 50-minute self-guided audio tour ($8, available from the museum lobby). Featuring narratives from a number of sources, including historians, architects and the immigrants themselves, the tour brings to life the museum's hefty collection of personal objects, official documents, photographs and film footage. It's an evocative experience to relive personal memories – both good and bad – in the very halls and corridors in which they occurred.

The collection itself is divided into a number of permanent and temporary exhibitions. If you're very short on time, skip the 'Journeys: The Peopling of America 1550–1890' exhibit on the 1st floor and focus on the exhibitions on the second floor. It's here you'll find two of the most fascinating exhibitions. The first, 'Through America's Gate,' examines the step-by-step process faced by the newly arrived, including the chalk-marking of those suspected of illness, a wince-inducing eye examination, and 29 questions in the beautiful, vaulted Registry Room. The second must-see exhibition, 'Peak Immigration Years,' explores the motives behind the immigrants' journeys and the challenges they faced once they were free to begin their new American lives. For a history of the rise, fall and resurrection of the building itself, make time for the 'Restoring a Landmark' exhibition on the 3rd floor; its tableaux of trashed desks, chairs and other abandoned possessions are strangely haunting. Best of all, the audio tour offers optional, in-depth coverage for those wanting to delve deeper into the collections and the island's history. If you don't feel like opting for the audio tour, you can always pick up one of the phones in each display area and listen to the recorded, yet affecting memories of real Ellis Island immigrants, taped in the 1980s. Another option is the free, 45-minute guided tour with a park ranger (also available in American Sign Language).

DON'T MISS...

- ➡ Immigration Museum exhibits
- ➡ Main Building architecture
- ➡ American Immigrant Wall of Honor & Fort Gibson ruins

PRACTICALITIES

- ➡ Map p416
- ➡ ☎212-363-3200, Statue Cruises 877-523-9849
- ➡ www.statuecruises.com
- ➡ ferry departs Battery Park
- ➡ admission free, ferry (incl Statue of Liberty) adult/child $13/5
- ➡ 🕒ferries every 15-30min 9am-2pm
- ➡ [S]1 to South Ferry; 4/5 to Bowling Green

Main Building Architecture

With their Main Building, architects Edward Lippincott Tilton and William A Boring created a suitably impressive and imposing 'prologue' to America. The designing duo won the contract after the original wooden building burnt down in 1897. Having attended the Ecole des Beaux Arts in Paris, it's not surprising that they opted for a beaux arts aesthetic for the project. The building evokes a grand train station, with majestic triple-arched entrances, decorative Flemish bond brickwork, and granite quoins (cornerstones) and belvederes. Inside, it's the 2nd-floor, 338ft-long Registry Room (also known as the Great Hall) that takes the breath away. It was under its beautiful vaulted ceiling that the newly arrived lined up to have their documents checked, and that the polygamists, paupers, criminals and anarchists were turned back. The original plaster ceiling was severely damaged by an explosion of munition barges at nearby Black Tom Wharf. It was a blessing in disguise, the rebuilt version adorned with striking, herringbone-patterned tiles by Rafael Guastavino. The Catalan-born engineer is also behind the beautiful tiled ceiling at the Grand Central Oyster Bar & Restaurant (p188) at Grand Central Terminal.

American Immigrant Wall of Honor & Fort Gibson Ruins

Accessible from the 1st-floor 'Journeys: The Peopling of America' exhibit is the outdoor American Immigrant Wall of Honor, inscribed with the names of over 700,000 immigrants. Believed to be the world's longest wall of names, it's a fund-raising project, allowing any American to have an immigrant relative's name recorded for the cost of a donation. Construction of the wall in the 1990s uncovered the remains of the island's original structure, Fort Gibson – you can see the ruins at the southwestern corner of the memorial. Built in 1808, the fortification was part of a harbor defense system against the British that also included Castle Clinton in Battery Park and Castle Williams on Governors Island. During this time, Ellis Island measured a modest 3.3 acres of sand and slush. Between 1892 and 1934, the island expanded dramatically thanks to landfill brought in from the ballast of ships and construction of the city's subway system.

AN IRISH DEBUT

Ellis Island's very first immigrant arrival was 15-year-old Anna 'Annie' Moore. After a 12-day journey from County Cork, Ireland, on the steamship *Nevada*, the steerage passenger stepped onto the island on 1 January 1892, accompanied by her brothers Phillip and Anthony. The three siblings had headed to America to join their parents, who had migrated to New York City four years earlier. After tying the knot with German immigrant Joseph Augustus Schayer, the Irish-American gave birth to at least 11 children, only five of which survived. Annie died on 6 December 1924 and was laid to rest at Calvary Cemetery, Queens.

At the turn of the 20th century, the now-defunct hospital on Ellis Island was one of the world's largest. Consisting of 22 buildings and dubbed the 'Hospital of all Nations,' it was America's front line in the fight against 'imported' diseases. The institution's fascinating history is vividly relayed in writer/producer Lorie Conway's documentary and book *Forgotten Ellis Island*. For more on the project, visit www.forgottenellis island.com.

TOP SIGHTS
WORLD TRADE CENTER SITE

Plagued by design controversies, budget blowouts and construction delays, the first part of the World Trade Center (WTC) redevelopment – the National September 11 Memorial, or known more simply as the 9/11 Memorial – opened to the public on September 12, 2011. The wait was worth it. Titled *Reflecting Absence*, its two massive reflecting pools are as much a symbol of hope and renewal as they are a tribute to the thousands who lost their lives to terrorism.

Until surrounding construction projects at the World Trade Center are complete, you will need to reserve a visitor pass for a specific date and time. Visitor passes are free and available through the Memorial's online reservation system. Alternatively, paid admission to the WTC Tribute Visitor Center includes admission to the Memorial.

DON'T MISS...

- Reflecting Pools
- Memorial Museum

PRACTICALITIES

- Map p416
- www.911memorial.org
- cnr Greenwich & Albany Sts
- 9/11 Memorial free
- [S]A/C/E to Chambers St; R to Rector St; 2/3 to Park Pl

Reflecting Pools

Surrounded by a plaza planted with 400 swamp white oak trees, the 9/11 Memorial's reflecting pools occupy the very footprints of the ill-fated twin towers. From their rim, a steady cascade of water pours 30ft down towards a central void. The flow of the water is richly symbolic, beginning as hundreds of smaller streams, merging into a massive torrent of collective confusion, and ending with a slow journey towards an abyss. Bronze panels frame the pools, inscribed with the names of those who died in the terrorist attacks of September 11, 2001, and in the World Trade Center car bombing on February 26, 1993. Designed by Michael Arad and Peter Walker, the pools are both striking and deeply poignant.

Memorial Museum

When it opens, the National September 11 Memorial Museum will document the terrorist attacks of September 11, 2001 and February 26, 1993 in state-of-the-art subterranean galleries. With an exterior that evokes a toppled tower, the museum's interior will feature a soaring pair of giant tridents: the final beams removed from the catastrophic ruins. A ramp will lead down to the main exhibition space, which will include a history of the original WTC complex, tributes to the victims, and artifacts, including remnants from the 'Survivors' Stairs', used by hundreds to flee the WTC site. Until the museum's opening, visitors can reflect at the temporary **WTC Tribute Visitor Center** (Map p416; www.tributewtc.org; 120 Liberty St; admission $15; 🕘 10am-6pm Mon-Sat, to 5pm Sun; [S]E to World Trade Center; R/W to Cortland St), which features a gallery of moving images and artifacts, and join 75-minute tours of the WTC site's perimeter. Admission to the center also includes access to the neighboring 9/11 Memorial. Nearby is the temporary **9/11 Memorial Preview Site** (Map p416; www.911memorial.org; 20 Vesey St; admission free; 🕘9am-7pm Mon-Fri, 8am-7pm Sat & Sun), with models, renderings, artifacts and films related to the site and redevelopment.

One World Trade Center

At the northwest corner of the WTC site is architect David M Childs' *One World Trade Center* (1 WTC) – a redesign of Daniel Libeskind's original 2002 concept. Upon completion in late 2012, the tapered skyscraper will be America's tallest, with 105 stories and a total height of 1776ft, a symbolic reference to the year of American independence. An observation deck 1362ft above the ground is also planned. The cabled-stayed antenna was codesigned by sculptor Kenneth Snelson.

SIGHTS

Wall Street & the Financial District

WORLD TRADE CENTER SITE MONUMENT

See p62.

FRAUNCES TAVERN MUSEUM MUSEUM

Map p416 (www.frauncestavernmuseum.org; 54 Pearl St btwn Broad St & Coenties Slip; adult/child $7/free; ⏲noon-5pm; [S]J/M/Z to Broad St; 4/5 to Bowling Green) Combining five early-18th-century structures, this unique museum/restaurant combo is an homage to the nation-shaping events of 1783, when the British relinquished control of New York at the end of the Revolutionary War and General George Washington gave a farewell speech to the officers of the Continental Army in the 2nd-floor dining room on December 4.

The site was originally built as a tony residence for merchant Stephen Delancey's family; barkeeper Samuel Fraunces purchased it in 1762, turning it into a tavern in honor of the American victory in the Revolutionary War. After the war, when New York was the nation's first capital, the space was used by the Departments of War, Treasury and Foreign Affairs. The tavern was closed and fell into disuse in the 19th century – and soon after was damaged during several massive fires that destroyed most colonial buildings and Dutch-built structures in the area. In 1904, the Sons of the Revolution, a historical society, bought the building and returned it to an approximation of its colonial-era look – an act believed to be the first major attempt at historical preservation in the USA. Today, the museum hosts historical walking tours, lectures, Revolutionary War paintings, and some surprising Washington relics, including false teeth and a lock of hair.

[FREE] **NATIONAL MUSEUM OF THE AMERICAN INDIAN** MUSEUM

Map p416 (www.nmai.si.edu; 1 Bowling Green; ⏲10am-5pm Fri-Wed, to 8pm Thu; [S]4/5 to Bowling Green) An affiliate of the Smithsonian Institution, this elegant museum of Native American culture is set in Cass Gilbert's spectacular 1907 Custom House, one of NYC's finest beaux arts buildings. Beyond a vast elliptical rotunda, sleek galleries play host to changing exhibitions documenting Native American culture, life and beliefs. The museum's permanent collection includes stunning decorative arts, textiles and ceremonial objects.

It's an ironically grand space for the country's leading museum on Native American art, established by oil heir George Gustav Heye in 1916. The four giant female sculptures outside the building are the work of Daniel Chester French, who would go on to sculpt the seated Abraham Lincoln at Washington DC's Lincoln Memorial. Representing (from left to right) Asia, North America, Europe and Africa, the figures offer a revealing look at America's world view at the beginning of the 20th century; Asia 'bound' by its religions, America 'youthful and virile,' Europe 'wise yet decaying' and Africa 'asleep and barbaric.' Exhibitions

BLAST FROM THE PAST

If you wander past the former headquarters of JP Morgan Bank on the southeast corner of Wall and Broad Sts, take a minute to examine its limestone facade on the Wall St side. The pockmarks you see are the remnants of the so-called Morgan Bank bombing – America's deadliest terrorist attack until the Oklahoma City bombing of 1995.

The fateful day was Thursday, September 16, 1920, when at exactly 12.01pm, 500 pounds of lead sash weights and 100 pounds of dynamite exploded from a horse-drawn carriage. Thirty-eight people were killed and around 400 injured. Among the latter was John F Kennedy's father, Joseph P Kennedy.

The bomb's detonation outside America's most influential financial institution at the time led many to blame anticapitalist groups, from Italian anarchists to stock-standard Bolsheviks. Yet the crime has yet to solved, with the decision to reopen both the bank and New York Stock Exchange the following day leading to a swift clean-up of both debris and vital clues. Almost 100 years on, the shrapnel marks remain, purposely left by banker Jack Morgan as an act of remembrance and defiance.

aside, the museum also hosts a range of cultural programs, including dance and music performances, readings for children, craft demonstrations, films and workshops. The museum shop is well-stocked with Native American jewelry, books, CDs and crafts.

[FREE] **FEDERAL HALL** MUSEUM

Map p416 (www.nps.gov/feha; 26 Wall St, entrance on Pine St; ⏲9am-5pm Mon-Fri; [S]J/M/Z to Broad St; 2/3, 4/5 to Wall St) A Greek Revival masterpiece, Federal Hall houses a museum dedicated to postcolonial New York. Exhibition themes include George Washington's inauguration, Alexander Hamilton's relationship with the city, and the struggles of John Peter Zenger – jailed, tried and acquitted of libel here for exposing government corruption in his newspaper. There's also a visitor information hall which covers downtown cultural happenings.

The building itself, distinguished by a huge statue of George Washington, stands on the site of New York's original City Hall, where the first US Congress convened and Washington took the oath of office as the first US president on April 30, 1789. After that structure's demolition in the early 19th century, the current building rose in its place between 1834 and 1842, serving as the US Customs House until 1862.

BOWLING GREEN PARK

Map p416 (cnr Broadway & State St; 📶; [S]4/5 to Bowling Green) New York's oldest – and possibly tiniest – public park is purportedly the spot where Dutch settler Peter Minuit paid Native Americans the equivalent of $24 to purchase Manhattan Island. At its northern edge stands Arturo Di Modica's 7000lb bronze *Charging Bull,* placed here permanently after it mysteriously appeared in front of the New York Stock Exchange in 1989, two years after a market crash.

The tree-fringed triangle was leased by the people of New York from the English crown beginning in 1733, for the token amount of one peppercorn each. But an angry mob, inspired by George Washington's nearby reading of the Declaration of Independence, descended upon the site in 1776 and tore down a large statue of King George III; a fountain now stands in its place.

TRINITY CHURCH CHURCH

Map p416 (www.trinitywallstreet.org; Broadway at Wall St; ⏲7am-6pm Mon-Fri, 8am-4pm Sat, 7am-4pm Sun; [S]R to Rector St; 2/3, 4/5 to Wall St) New York City's tallest building upon completion in 1846, Trinity Church features a 280ft-high bell tower, an arresting stained glass window over the altar, and a small museum of historical church artifacts. Famous residents of its serene cemetery include Founding Father Alexander Hamilton, while its excellent music series includes Concerts at One (1pm Thursdays) and magnificent choir concerts, including an annual December rendition of Handel's *Messiah.*

The original Anglican parish church was founded by King William III in 1697 and once presided over several constituent chapels, including St Paul's Chapel at the corner of Fulton St and Broadway. Its huge landholdings in Lower Manhattan made it the country's wealthiest and most influential church throughout the 18th century. Burnt down in 1776, its second incarnation was demolished in 1839. The third and current church, designed by English architect Richard Upjohn, helped launch the picturesque neo-Gothic movement in America.

MUSEUM OF AMERICAN FINANCE MUSEUM

Map p416 (www.moaf.org; 48 Wall St btwn Pearl & William Sts; adult/child $8/free; ⏲10am-4pm Tue-Sat; [S]2/3, 4/5 to Wall St) Money makes this museum go round, its exhibits focusing on historic moments in American financial history. Permanent collections include rare, 18th-century documents, stock and bond certificates from the Gilded Age, the oldest known photograph of Wall St and a stock ticker from c 1875. The museum also runs themed walking tours of the area, advertised on the museum's website.

Once the headquarters for the Bank of New York, the building itself is a lavish spectacle, with 30ft ceilings, high arched windows, a majestic staircase to the mezzanine, glass chandeliers, and murals depicting historic scenes of banking and commerce.

ST PAUL'S CHAPEL CHURCH

Map p416 (www.trinitywallstreet.org; Broadway at Fulton St; ⏲10am-6pm Mon-Fri, to 4pm Sat, 7am-4pm Sun; [S]A/C, J/Z, 2/3, 4/5 to Fulton St) Despite George Washington worshipping here after his inauguration in 1789, this classic revival brownstone chapel found new fame in the aftermath of September 11. With the World Trade Center destruction occurring just a block away, the mighty structure became a spiritual support and volunteer center, movingly documented in its exhibition 'Unwavering Spirit: Hope & Healing at Ground Zero.'

Through photographs, personal objects and messages of support, the exhibition honors both the victims and the volunteers who worked round the clock, serving meals, setting up beds, doling out massages and counseling rescue workers. The chapel, built in 1766 and considered the oldest building in New York still in continuous use, also hosts workshops, special events and a popular classical-music series.

NEW YORK STOCK EXCHANGE
NOTABLE BUILDING

Map p416 (www.nyse.com; 11 Wall St; ⏲closed to the public; [S]J/M/Z to Broad St; 2/3, 4/5 to Wall St) Home to the world's best-known stock exchange (the NYSE), Wall Street is an iconic symbol of US capitalism. About one billion shares, valued at around $73 billion, change hands daily behind the portentous Romanesque facade, a sight no longer accessible to the public due to security concerns. Feel free to gawk outside the building, protected by barricades and the hawk-eyed NYPD (New York Police Department). The online shop has souvenirs like a hooded NYSE sweatshirt, as if you'd actually been inside.

Frantic buying and selling by those familiar red-faced traders screaming 'Sell! Sell!' goes on at the **New York Mercantile Exchange** (Map p416; ☎212-299-2499; www.nymex.com; 1 North End Ave; [S]2/3 to Park Place, E to World Trade Center), near Vesey St. This exchange deals in gold, gas and oil commodities, but no longer with tourists; like the NYSE, it's closed to visitors.

[FREE] FEDERAL RESERVE BANK OF NEW YORK
NOTABLE BUILDING

Map p416 (☎212-720-6130; www.newyorkfed.org; 33 Liberty St at Nassau St, entry via 44 Maiden Lane; reservation required; ⏲tours 11.15am, noon, 1:15pm, 2:30pm, 3:15pm & 4pm Mon-Fri; [S]A/C, J/Z, 2/3, 4/5 to Fulton St) The best reason to visit the Federal Reserve Bank is the chance to ogle at its high-security vault – more

WORTH A DETOUR

GOVERNORS ISLAND

Off-limits to the public for 200 years, former military outpost **Governors Island** (www.nps.gov/gois; admission free; ⏲10am-5pm Fri, to 7pm Sat & Sun, May 31-Oct 12; ferries leave from Battery Maritime Bldg, Slip 7, hourly 10am-3pm Fri & every 30min 10am-5pm Sat & Sun May-Oct; [S]4/5 to Bowling Green, 1 to South Ferry) is now one of New York's most popular seasonal playgrounds. Each summer, free ferries make the seven-minute trip from Lower Manhattan to the 172-acre oasis. Among the island's draws is Picnic Point, an 8-acre patch of green with picnic tables and hammocks; Figment (www.figmentproject.org), a one-weekend-only interactive art festival in June; and **Water Taxi Beach**, a spit of sand that hosts events from dance parties to live concerts. Then there's the smooth, 2.2-mile bicycle path around the perimeter of the entire island, which you can pedal with rental bikes from **Bike & Roll** for $15 per two hours (free on Fridays). Commencing in 2012, a major redevelopment of the island will see the addition of a striking new park across its southern half, commercial developments at its eastern and western ends, and a wide new promenade around its perimeter.

Besides serving as a successful military fort in the Revolutionary War, the Union Army's central recruiting station during the Civil War, and the take-off point for Wilbur Wright's famous 1909 flight around the Statue of Liberty, Governors Island is where the 1988 Reagan-Gorbachev summit signaled the beginning of the end of the Cold War. You can visit the spot where that famous summit took place at **Admiral's House**, a grand-colonnaded, 1843 military residence that's part of the elegant ghost-town area of Nolan Park. Other historic spots include **Fort Jay**, fortified in 1776 for what became a failed attempt to prevent the Brits from invading Manhattan; **Colonel's Row**, a collection of lovely, 19th-century brick officers' quarters; and the creepy **Castle Williams**, a 19th-century fort that was eventually used as a military penitentiary. The best way to explore it all is with the **National Park Service** (www.www.nps.gov/gois/index.htm), whose rangers conduct 90-minute guided tours of the historic district, usually on Wednesdays and Thursdays.

than 10,000 tons of gold reserves reside here, 80ft below ground. You'll only see a small part of that fortune, but signing on to a free tour (the only way down; book around six weeks ahead) is worth the effort.

While you don't need to join a guided tour to browse the bank's museum, which includes an interesting exhibition on the history of money, you will still need to book a time online. Bring your passport or other official ID.

New York Harbor

STATUE OF LIBERTY MONUMENT

See p58.

ELLIS ISLAND LANDMARK

See p60.

Battery Park City

MUSEUM OF JEWISH HERITAGE MUSEUM

Map p416 (www.mjhnyc.org; 36 Battery Pl; adult/child $12/free, 4pm-8pm Wed free; ⏲10am-5:45pm Sun-Tue & Thu, to 8pm Wed, to 5pm Fri; [S]4/5 to Bowling Green) This waterfront memorial museum explores all aspects of modern Jewish identity, with often poignant personal artifacts, photographs and documentary films. Its outdoor Garden of Stones – created by artist Andy Goldsworthy (and his first permanent exhibition in NYC) – in which 18 boulders form a narrow pathway for contemplating the fragility of life, is dedicated to those who lost loved ones in the Holocaust.

The building itself features a six-sided shape and three tiers to symbolize the Star of David and the six million Jews who perished in WWII. Exhibitions aside, the museum also hosts films, music concerts, ongoing lecture series and special holiday performances. Frequent, free workshops for families with children are also on offer, while the on-site, kosher Heritage Café serves light food during museum hours.

SKYSCRAPER MUSEUM MUSEUM

Map p416 (www.skyscraper.org; 39 Battery Pl; admission $5; ⏲noon-6pm Wed-Sun; [S]4/5 to Bowling Green) Fans of phallic architecture will love this compact, high-gloss gallery, examining skyscrapers as objects of design, engineering and urban renewal. Temporary exhibitions dominate the space, with one recent offering showcasing the world's next generation of 'Supertalls.' The permanent collection includes information on the design and construction of the Empire State Building, as well as of the World Trade Center.

The museum is also home to the cutting-edge technology known as VIVA – the Visual Index to the Virtual Archive. This visual-based interface uses a 3-D computer model of Manhattan as a clickable map, allowing users to see the city's past and present, and to explore the museum's collections through an online database (accessed via the museum's website).

CASTLE CLINTON HISTORIC SITE

Map p416 (www.nps.gov/cacl; Battery Park; ⏲8:30am-5pm; 📶; [S]1 to South Ferry; 4/5 to Bowling Green) Built as a fort to defend the New York Harbor during the war of 1812, this national monument has played numerous roles, including opera house, entertainment complex and aquarium. It's now a visitors center, with historical displays, as well as a massive performance space, where outdoor concerts are held on the open-air stage for summer shows under the stars.

The circular structure got its current moniker in 1817 to honor then mayor DeWitt Clinton. Later, and before Ellis Island opened to immigrants, Castle Garden (as it was then known) served as the major processing center for new immigrant arrivals, welcoming more than eight million people between 1855 and 1890. Rangers lead historic tours of the site daily at 10am, noon and 2pm, subject to staff availability.

IRISH HUNGER MEMORIAL MEMORIAL

Map p416 (290 Vesey St at North End Ave; admission free; [S]2/3 to Park Place) Artist Brian Tolle's compact labyrinth of low limestone walls and patches of grass pays tribute to the Great Irish Famine and Migration (1845–52), which prompted hundreds of thousands of immigrants to leave Ireland for better opportunities in the New World. Representing abandoned cottages, stone walls and potato fields, the work was created with stones from each of Ireland's 32 counties.

Tolle's proposal was the winning entry in a design competition organized by the Battery Park City Authority in 2000. Ironically, the sculpture is an even more fitting metaphor than Tolle probably meant it to be: it's turned out to be a delicate piece, having required extensive repairs due to New York's harsh winters.

WORTH A DETOUR

STATEN ISLAND

Most visitors to Staten Island exit the ferry – which docks in downtown St George, on the northern tip of the 58-sq-mile island – then reboard right away. Indeed, if not for its namesake ferry – or Robert Redford and Jane Fonda's wild night out with Armenians in *Barefoot in the Park* – New York's 'forgotten borough' might be a complete unknown. Despite its unfashionable reputation for suburbanism and conservatism, Staten Island is not without its drawcards, and a day out here promises a surprisingly different take on New York City life.

From the ferry terminal, turn left onto Richmond Tce (which becomes Bay St) and walk 0.3m south to the **Staten Island Chamber of Commerce** (718-727-1900; www.sichamber.com; 130 Bay St; 9am-5pm Mon-Fri) for tourist information. For organic coffee, books, political talks or, later on, live music, walk a further 0.2m south on Bay St to **Everything Goes Book Café & Neighborhood Stage** (www.etgstores.com/bookcafe; 208 Bay St; 10:30am-6:30pm Tue-Thu, 10:30am-10pm Fri & Sat, noon-5pm Sun), a Berkeley-style arts community. Close by you'll find its other sibling, **Everything Goes Furniture & Gallery** (17 Brook St; 10:30am-6:30pm Tue-Sat), which peddles eclectic antiques, collectibles and art.

An easy 0.3m northwest of the ferry terminal, the **Staten Island Museum** (718-727-1135; www.statenislandmuseum.org; 75 Stuyvesant Pl at Wall St; adult/child $2/1; noon-5pm Sun-Fri, 10am-5pm Sat) has a permanent display about the boat you just rode in on.

Staten Island's buses – which accept the MTA MetroCard and leave from outside the ferry terminal – are your best bet for reaching the island's more distant attractions. Top of the list is **Snug Harbor Cultural Center & Botanical Garden** (718-448-2500; www.snug-harbor.org; 1000 Richmond Tce; museum & gardens adult/child $6/3, gardens only $5/free, museum only $3/free; 10am-4pm Tue-Sun; S40 to Snug Harbor), a beautiful complex of themed gardens, historic buildings, art spaces and museums 2 miles west of the ferry terminal. Highlights include an ancient-style Chinese Scholar's Garden, a Tuscan Garden modeled on the Villa Gamberaia in Florence, and the Newhouse Center for Contemporary Art, which showcases changing exhibitions of modern art. From Henderson St on the southern edge of the Snug Harbor complex, the Staten Island Mall–bound S44 bus leads to **Denino's Pizzeria & Tavern** (www.deninos.com; 524 Port Richmond Ave; pizzas $11.50-20; S44). This Formica-laden family spot keeps it real with cushiony dough and extra cheese. The pizzas are insanely good and revered by gastronomes across the city.

In the very center of Staten Island, **Historic Richmond Town** (www.historicrichmondtown.org; 441 Clarke Ave; adult/child $5/3.50; 1pm-5pm Wed-Sun Sep-Jun, 10am-5pm Wed-Sat, 1pm-5pm Sun Jul & Aug; S74 to Richmond Rd & St Patrick's Pl) consists of 27 historic buildings (some dating back to a 1690s Dutch community) standing in a 100-acre preservation project maintained by the Staten Island Historical Society. The town includes the island's former county seat. Its most famous building, the two story, redwood Voorlezer's House, is the USA's oldest schoolhouse, dating back to c 1695. Guides lead tours (included with admission) at 2pm and 3:30pm; in July and August folks in period garb roam the grounds. From the ferry, catch bus S74; journey time is 40 minutes.

Another cultural highlight is **Alice Austen House** (www.aliceausten.org; 2 Hylan Blvd; admission $2; noon-5pm Thu-Sun; 551 to Hylan Blvd), the harbor-side home of the early-20th-century photographer. The museum offers glimpses into her world, including her life on Staten Island, as well as exhibiting many of her works. It's located just north of the Verrazano-Narrows Bridge, or about a 15-minute ride south from the ferry terminal on bus S51.

1. National September 11 Memorial (p62)
Contemplate the events of September 11 at the massive reflecting pools.

2. New York Stock Exchange (p65)
The famed stock exchange on Wall St is an iconic symbol of US capitalism.

3. Trinity Church (p64)
This cathedral was the city's tallest building when completed in 1846, and features a 280ft-high bell tower.

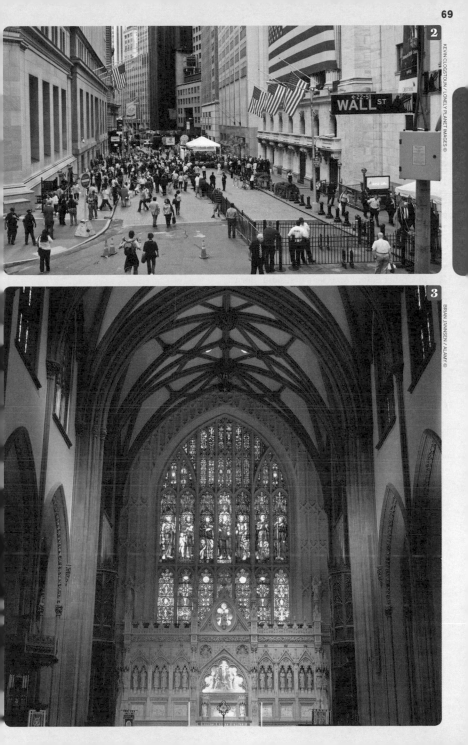

KEVIN CLOGSTOUN / LONELY PLANET IMAGES ©

BRIAN JANNSEN / ALAMY ©

HUDSON RIVER PARK OUTDOORS

Map p416 (www.hudsonriverpark.org; Manhattan's west side from Battery Park to 59th St) Stretching from Battery Park to Hell's Kitchen, the 5-mile, 550-acre Hudson River Park runs along the lower western side of Manhattan. Diversions include a bike/run/skate path snaking along its entire length, community gardens, playgrounds, and renovated piers reinvented as riverfront esplanades, miniature golf courses, and alfresco summertime movie theaters and concert venues. Visit website for a detailed map.

SHRINE TO ST ELIZABETH ANN SETON CHURCH

Map p416 (www.setonshrine.com; Our Lady of the Rosary Church, 7 State St; admission free; 🕒7am-5pm Mon-Fri, 8am-5pm Sat, 10am-5pm Sun; [S]R to Whitehall St; 1 to South Ferry) In 1801, this red-brick, Federal-style building was home to Mother Seton, America's first saint. Born in NYC, Elizabeth Ann married and had five children. When widowed, she became a nun and founded the Sisters of Charity. Inside you'll find a tiny church and shrine, popular with devotees and those craving a little respite from Manhattan's less-than-holy tendencies.

South Street Seaport

SOUTH STREET SEAPORT MUSEUM MUSEUM

Map p416 (☎212-748-8600; www.seany.org; 12 Fulton St; adult/child $5/free; 🕒10am-6pm Wed-Sun; [S]2/3, 4/5, A/C, J/M/Z to Fulton St) Recently renovated, this museum offers a glimpse of the seaport's history and a survey of the world's great ocean liners, with permanent exhibits and various other sites dotted around the 11-block area. Spanning three floors, the museum's new galleries include a battalion of model ships, antique shipping tools, and left-of-center shows covering anything from New York fashion to contemporary photography. The museum's booty also extends to a group of tall-masted sailing ships just south of Pier 17, including the *Ambrose* and *Pioneer*. Off-limits for restoration during research, access to their windswept decks and intimate interiors are normally included in the admission to the museum. It was hoped that from spring 2012, the gorgeous, iron-hulled *Pioneer*, built in 1885 to carry mined sand, is expected to once again offer two-hour sailing journeys through the warmer months; contact the museum for updates.

NEW YORK CITY POLICE MUSEUM MUSEUM

Map p416 (www.nycpolicemuseum.org; 100 Old Slip; adult/child $8/5; 🕒10am-5pm Mon-Sat, noon-5pm Sun; [S]1 to South Ferry; 2/3 to Wall St) Get the brief on 'New York's Finest' with cool old police vehicles, as well as the mug shots and weapons of notorious New York criminals like Willie Sutton and Al Capone. There's a collection of NYPD uniforms throughout the decades, insight into anti-terrorism tactics, and a 'Hall of Heroes' memorial to officers killed in the line of duty since 1845. The museum itself is housed in a neo-Renaissance palazzo on a landfilled inlet.

City Hall & Civic Center

WOOLWORTH BUILDING NOTABLE BUILDING

Map p416 (233 Broadway at Park Pl; [S]J/M/Z to Chambers St; 4/5/6 to Brooklyn Bridge-City Hall) The world's tallest building upon completion in 1913, Cass Gilbert's 60-story Woolworth Building is a neo-Gothic marvel, elegantly clad in masonry and terra-cotta. Surpassed in height by the Chrysler Building in 1930, the 792ft-tall tower is off-limits to visitors these days (try to sneak a peak at the beautifully preserved lobby). Alternatively, admire the facade from City Hall Park across the street.

At its dedication, the building was described as a 'cathedral of commerce' – though meant as an insult, FW Woolworth, head of the five-and-dime chain store empire headquartered there, took the comment as a compliment and began throwing the term around himself. Subversion at its effortless best.

AFRICAN BURIAL GROUND MEMORIAL

Map p416 (www.africanburialground.gov; 290 Broadway btwn Duane & Elk Sts; admission free; 🕒memorial 9am-5pm daily, visitors center 9am-5pm Mon-Fri; [S]4/5 to Wall St) In 1991, construction workers here uncovered over 400 stacked wooden caskets, just 16ft to 28ft below street level. The boxes contained the remains of enslaved Africans (nearby Trinity Church graveyard had banned the burial of Africans at the time). Today, a memorial and visitors center honors an estimated 15,000 Africans buried here during the 17th and 18th centuries.

BROOKLYN BRIDGE

A New York icon, the **Brooklyn Bridge** (Map p416) was the world's first steel suspension bridge. When it opened in 1883, the 1596ft span between its two support towers was the longest in history. Although its construction was fraught with disaster, the bridge became a magnificent example of urban design, inspiring poets, writers and painters. Today, the Brooklyn Bridge continues to dazzle – many regard it as the most beautiful bridge in the world.

Prussian-born engineer John Roebling designed the bridge, which spans the East River from Manhattan to Brooklyn; he died of tetanus poisoning before construction of the bridge even began. His son, Washington Roebling, supervised construction, which lasted 14 years and managed to survive budget overruns and the deaths of 20 workers. The younger Roebling himself suffered from the bends while helping to excavate the riverbed for the bridge's western tower and remained bedridden for much of the project; his wife Emily oversaw construction in his stead. There was one final tragedy to come in June 1883, when the bridge opened to pedestrian traffic. Someone in the crowd shouted, perhaps as a joke, that the bridge was collapsing into the river, setting off a mad rush in which 12 people were trampled to death.

The bridge entered its second century as strong and beautiful as ever following an extensive renovation in the early 1980s. The pedestrian walkway that begins just east of City Hall affords a wonderful view of Lower Manhattan; observation points under the support towers offer brass 'panorama' histories of the waterfront. Just take care to stay on the side of the walkway marked for folks on foot – one half is designated for cyclists, who use it en masse for both commuting and pleasure rides, and frustrated pedalers have been known to get nasty with oblivious tourists who wander, camera pressed to an eye, into the bike lane. Barring any such run-ins, you should reach Brooklyn after about a 20-minute walk. Bear left to Empire-Fulton Ferry State Park or Cadman Plaza West, which runs alongside Middagh St in the heart of Brooklyn Heights, taking you to Brooklyn's downtown area; don't miss the ornate Brooklyn Borough Hall and the Brooklyn Heights Promenade.

The site is permanently protected as a National Historic Landmark, and today it's part of the National Parks Service. The visitors center requires airportlike security screenings, so leave your nail files in the hotel.

⊙ Tribeca

HARRISON STREET HOUSES

NOTABLE BUILDING

Map p416 (Harrison St; [S]1 to Franklin St) Built between 1804 and 1828, the eight townhouses on the block of Harrison St immediately west of Greenwich St constitute the largest collection of Federal architecture left in NYC. Yet only the buildings at 31 and 33 Harrison St remain where they were originally constructed. The other six once stood two blocks away, on a stretch of Washington St that no longer exists.

In the early 1970s, that site was home to the Washington Market, a wholesale fruit and vegetable shopping complex. But development of the waterfront – which resulted in the construction of the Borough of Manhattan Community College and the Soviet-style concrete apartment complex that now looms over the townhouses – meant the market had to move uptown and the historic row of houses had to be relocated.

🍴 EATING

Frenzied lunch rushes for financial types fuel two extremes in Lower Manhattan: fast-food storefronts, and masculine dining rooms catering to steak-chomping bigwigs. Both genres offer plenty of satisfying experiences, whether it's *faux filet Bercy* at Les Halles or frozen custard at Shake Shack. Move just a bit north into Tribeca and the vibe is hipper and more fashion-forward, with buzzing hotspots like modern-Jewish Kutsher's Tribeca and revamped-Italian Locanda Verde.

START **LA COLOMBE**
END **FEDERAL HALL**
DISTANCE **2.5 MILES**
TIME **2½ TO 3 HOURS**

Neighborhood Walk
Lower Manhattan Landmarks

➤ Start with coffee at ❶ **La Colombe**.
In the 19th century, the site was a stop on the antislavery 'underground railway,' a secret network of routes and safe houses allowing African Americans to reach free states and Canada. A plaque on the Lispenard St side of the building commemorates the fact. Further west, the intersection of Varick and N Moore Sts is where you'll find ❷ **8 Hook & Ladder**, better known as ghost-control headquarters in '80s film *Ghostbusters*. Continue south on Varick St, turn left into Leonard St and stop at the intersection with Church St. On the southeast corner stands the ❸ **Textile Building**, built in 1901. Its architect, Henry J Hardenbergh, would go on to design Midtown's monumental Plaza Hotel. Head further south on Church St, turning left into Park Pl and right into Broadway. Before you is the neo-Gothic ❹ **Woolworth Building**, the world's tallest skyscraper upon completion in 1913. Security is tight, but you can usually poke your head in to inspect the opulent lobby and blue-and-gold-tiled ceiling. Heading south on Broadway, cross Vesey St and you'll see ❺ **St Paul's Chapel** on your right – it's the only pre–Revolutionary War church left intact in the city. Continue south on Broadway, turning right into Liberty St, home to the moving ❻ **WTC Tribute Visitor Center**. Admission includes access to the neighboring ❼ **World Trade Center Site** and its 9/11 Memorial – two giant reflecting pools. Soaring above them is the new, 1776ft One World Trade Center, America's tallest skyscraper. Further south on Broadway, ❽ **Trinity Church** was the city's tallest building upon completion in 1846 and its peaceful cemetery is the final resting place of steamboat inventor Robert Fulton. Pay your respects and head east onto Wall St, home of the ❾ **New York Stock Exchange** and the ❿ **Federal Hall**. You can visit the latter, in which John Peter Zenger was acquitted of seditious libel in 1735 – the first step, historians say, in establishing a democracy committed to a free press.

TOP
CHOICE **LOCANDA VERDE**   ITALIAN $$$

Map p416 (212-925-3797; www.locandaverde
nyc.com; 377 Greenwich St at Noore St; pasta $17-
19, mains $15-31 ; A/C/E to Canal St; 1 to Frank-
lin St) Step through the red velvet curtains
and into a sexy, buzzing scene of loosened
Brown Brothers' shirts, black dresses and
slick barmen behind a long, crowded bar.
Part of the Greenwich Hotel (p329), this
sprawling, brasserie-style hot spot is the
domain of celebrity chef Andrew Carmel-
lini, whose contemporary Italian grub is
seasonal, integrous and insanely flavorful.

Highlights to look out for include the
warm mushroom salad with poached eggs
and prosciutto, as well as the linguini with
rock shrimp, toasted garlic and Calabrian
chili. The desserts are especially impres-
sive, such as lemon tart with buttermilk
gelato and limoncello granita. Bookings
recommended.

KUTSHER'S TRIBECA   JEWISH $$$

Map p416 (212-431-0606; www.kutsherstribe
ca.com; 186 Franklin St btwn Greenwich & Hudson
Sts; mains $19-29; ⊘dinner; A/C/E to Canal
St; 1 to Franklin St) Thank Yahweh for new-
kid-on-the-block Kutsher's, where Jewish
comfort food gets a refreshing makeover.
Forget the starch and stodge: here you'll be
grazing on crispy artichokes with lemon,
garlic and Parmesan; borscht salad with
marinated goat cheese; or latkes with local
apple compote.

Classic flavors are not so much subverted
as enhanced thanks to top ingredients and
chef Mark Spangenthal's skilled hands,
while the menu itself is a democratic mix
of drink-friendly snacks, sharing plates and
more substantial mains. With names like
Bug Juice and Alan's 'Cherry Lime Ricky,'
the cocktails will have you pining for
long-gone summers...no coincidence given
that owner Zach Kutsher hails from the
legendary Kutsher's resort in the Catskill
Mountains.

NEW AMSTERDAM MARKET   MARKET $

Map p416 (www.newamsterdammarket.org; South
St btwn Peck Slip & Beekman Sts; ⊘11am-4pm
Sun late Apr–mid-Dec; A/C, J/Z, 1/2, 4/5 to Fulton St) Sophisticated locavore or basic glut-
ton, do not miss this Sunday food market
outside the old Fulton Fish Market. Usually
held from late April to mid-December, its
40-odd stalls showcase some of the region's
top food and drink producers. Pick up eve-

rything from organic Finnish Ruis bread
to handmade sausages and pasta. The
porchetta sandwiches ($6) have converted
vegetarians.

LES HALLES   FRENCH $$

Map p416 (212-285-8585; www.leshalles.net;
15 John St btwn Broadway & Nassau St; mains
$14.50-28.50; ☎; A/C, J/M/Z, 2/3, 4/5 to Ful-
ton St) Vegetarians need not apply at this
packed and serious brasserie, owned by
celebrity chef Anthony Bourdain. Among
the elegant light-fixture balls, dark wood
paneling and stiff white tablecloths you'll
find a buttoned-up, meat-lovin' crowd
who've come for rich and decadent favorites
like *cote de boeuf* and steak au poivre.

Standards like French onion soup, *moules
frites,* and salade Niçoise are equally sublime, while the lists of wine, single-malt
scotches and other liquors are impressive.
From the crème brûlée to the tarte tatin,
sweet tooths won't be disappointed.

THALASSA   GREEK $$$

Map p416 (212-941-7661; www.thalassanyc.
com; 179 Franklin St btwn Hudson & Greenwich
Sts; lunch prix fixe $24, dinner mains $28-46;
⊘lunch & dinner; 1 to Franklin St) Owned by
a family of passionate food importers, this
upmarket, mosaic-laced spot injects some
much needed attitude into Greek nosh
(there's even a cheese cave in the basement).
Ditch sad souvlakis for refreshing dishes
like baby arugula with graviera cheese,
beets, walnuts and honey oregano dressing,
or super-succulent calamari stuffed with
Dodonis fetta, tomato and pine nuts.

The vibe is stylish yet convivial, and the
wine list offers the city's best choice of Hel-
lenic drops.

TINY'S & THE BAR UPSTAIRS   AMERICAN

Map p416 (212-374-1135; 135 W Broadway btwn
Duane & Thomas Sts; mains $18 29; A/C, 1/2/3
to Chambers St) Snug and adorable (book
ahead!), Tiny's comes with a crackling
fire in the back room and an intimate bar
upstairs – try the signature Hot Buttered
Wassail (chamomile, apple cider, allspice,
cinnamon and whipped cream). Heading
the kitchen is chef John Martinez (formerly
of Michelin-starred Jean Georges), whose
seasonal, well-balanced dishes are served
on vintage porcelain. Expect soulful options like meatballs and garlic toast, beet
and crispy goat cheese salad, or a beautifully cooked pan-roasted hake.

LOCAL KNOWLEDGE

EDIBLE NEW YORK

Andrew Carmellini – chef, food writer and co-owner of Locanda Verde (p73) and the Dutch (p89) – talks food and hometown favorites.

Getting the Lowdown

Your best online tool for finding restaurants of all kinds is www.nymag.com, but if you're a little more intrepid, tap into the citizen-eaters on www.chow.com. Also, if the guy standing next to you at the coffee shop places a super-particular espresso order, chances are he knows where to get an amazing bowl of pappardelle, too.

The Inspiration Behind Locanda Verde & the Dutch

Locanda Verde was a response to how I wanted to eat every day: simply and relaxed. The food is 'urban Italian.' The menu at the Dutch is roots-inspired American. Downtown New York is such a diverse place, so we try and always reflect that in the cooking.

Old-School Favorites

Peter Pan Bakery (Map p446; 727 Manhattan Ave, Brooklyn) has great doughnuts (get the cruller), but it's the feeling of being back in 1965 that makes it really special. Everything from the staff's pink dresses to the swiveling stools is awesome. **Tortilleria Mexicana Los Hermanos** (☎718-456-3422; 271 Starr St at Wyckoff Ave; ⏰11am-9pm Mon-Sat; [S]L to Jefferson St), also at 271 Starr St, Brooklyn, does fantastic Mexican – I like the *carne asada.* The factory out back is incredible, all the workers laboring over big machines, cranking out tortillas all day. Gahm Mi Oak (p197) in Midtown is somewhere I'd always go for oxtail soup after a late shift cooking.

A Perfect New York Day

It starts with a cappuccino at Abraco (p111), or if I'm at Locanda Verde, one of Karen De Masco's pastries. My wife and I enjoy staying current with the art world, so we might check out the current set-up at Madison Square Park or a big ticket exhibition at the Museum of Modern Art or the Metropolitan Museum of Art. The day ends with friends and dinner at Tertulia (p140) or Hearth (p112).

SHAKE SHACK BURGERS $

Map p416 (www.shakeshack.com; 215 Murray St btwn West St & North End Ave; burgers $3.50-9; [S]A/C, 1/2/3 to Chambers St) Danny Meyer's cult burger chain is now undermining waistlines in Lower Manhattan. This is fast food at its finest: cotton-soft burgers made with prime, freshly ground mince; Chicago-style hot dogs in poppy-seed potato buns; and seriously good cheesy fries. Leave room for the legendary frozen custard and drink local with a Brooklyn Brewery Shackmeister ale.

BARBARINI ITALIAN $$

Map p416 (www.barbarinimercato.com; 225 Front St btwn Peck Slip & Beekman St; pasta $15, mains $16-20; [S]A/C, J/Z, 2/3, 4/5 to Fulton St) Deli? Cafe? Restaurant? Barbarini is all three, sleekly packaged in a combo of concrete floors, charcoal hues and brickwork. Stock the larder with artisanal pasta, salumi, cheeses and mini pistachio cannoli...but not before nabbing a table in the light-filled back room for better-than-mamma offerings like buckwheat pasta with wild boar. In a hurry? Opt for the *buonissimi* panini.

MOOMAH CAFE $

Map p416 (www.moomah.com; 161 Hudson St btwn Laight & Hubert Sts; meals $7-13; ⏰7:30am-6pm Mon-Thu, to 7pm Fri, 8am-7pm Sun, art space 9am-5pm Mon-Thu, to 6pm Fri & Sat ; 📶👪; [S]A/C/E, 1/2 to Canal St) Bond with your little munchkins at this trendy cafe/creative space hybrid, where you can buy art projects off the shelf and undertake them on-site. Whether you're making jewelry or a superhero costume, you'll be sensibly fueled by wholesome edibles like soups, wraps and salads. There are dairy- and gluten-free options for sensitive bellies and Counter Culture Coffee for caffeine snobs.

NELSON BLUE PUB $$

Map p416 (☎212-346-9090; www.nelsonblue.com; 233-235 Front St at Peck Slip; mains $15-26; [S]A/C, J/Z, 2/3, 4/5 to Fulton St) Good for a drink as well as a lamb curry pie, Nelson Blue is the only Kiwi pub in town. The wine list is heavy on New Zealand drops, a perfect match for standouts like zucchini and corn fritters, and green-lipped mussels in a curry and coconut broth. In true antipodean style, the vibe is friendly, laid-back and attitude-free.

🍷 DRINKING & NIGHTLIFE

Tie-loosening financial types don't always bolt for the 'burbs when 5pm hits. You'll find a smattering of wine bars and pubs around South St Seaport, Wall St and Stone St if you need a spirited recharge. To the north, trendy Tribeca keeps its cool with its coffee-cognoscenti cafes, plush lounges, and speakeasy-chic cocktail bars. Best of all – the drinks here tend to be stirred with a bit more precision than over on the East Side.

KAFFE 1668 CAFE

Map p416 (www.kaffe1668.com; 275 Greenwich St btwn Warren & Murray Sts; ⏲6:30am-10pm Mon-Fri, 7:30am-10pm Sat & Sun; 📶; [S]A/C, 1/2/3 to Chambers St) One for the coffee aficionado, with clover machines, coffee urns and dual synessos pumping out superlative single-origin magic. Seating includes a large communal table, speckled with a mix of office workers, designer Tribeca parents and laptop-hugging creatives. The vibe is chilled, the cafe latte seriously smooth, and the triple ristretto a hair-raising thrill.

MACAO COCKTAIL BAR

(☎212-431-8750; www.macaonyc.com; 311 Church St btwn Lispenard & Walker Sts; [S]A/C/E, N/Q/R, 4/6 to Canal St) Skip the lines for Macao restaurant and duck into the dark, red-walled opium den turned lounge downstairs. A fusion of Portuguese and Asian grub and liquor, Macao remains a top spot for late-night drinking and snacking, especially if you've a soft spot for creative, sizzle-on-the-tongue cocktails.

BRANDY LIBRARY BAR

Map p416 (www.brandylibrary.com; 25 N Moore St at Varick St; ⏲5pm-1am Sun-Wed, 4pm-2am Thu, 4pm-4am Fri & Sat; [S]1 to Franklin St) When sipping means serious business, settle into this uber-luxe library, with soothing reading lamps and club chairs facing backlit, floor-to-ceiling, bottle-filled shelves. Go for top-shelf cognac, malt scotch or 90-year-old brandies (prices range from $9 to $340). Libation-friendly nibbles includes the sublime house specialty Gougeres (Gruyere cheese puffs). Call ahead about tastings and other events.

SMITH & MILLS COCKTAIL BAR

Map p416 (www.smithandmills.com; 71 N Moore St btwn Hudson & Greenwich Sts; [S]1 to Franklin St) This petite drinking hole marks all the cool boxes: unmarked exterior, kooky industrial interior (think early 20th century factory) and smooth libations – the 'Carriage House' is a nod to the space's previous incarnation. Space is limited so head in early if you fancy kicking back on a plush banquette. A seasonal menu spans light snacks to more substantial options.

WARD III COCKTAIL BAR

Map p416 (www.ward3tribeca.com; 111 Reade St btwn Church St & W Broadway; [S]A/C/E, 1/2/3 to Chambers St) Ward III channels old-school jauntiness with its elegant cocktails, vintage vibe (tin ceilings, dark wood and old Singer sewing tables behind the bar), and gentlemanly house rules (No 2: 'Don't be creepy'). Reminisce over a Moroccan martini, or line the stomach first with top-notch bar grub, available every day til close at 4am.

WEATHER UP COCKTAIL BAR

Map p416 (www.weatherupnyc.com; 159 Duane St btwn Hudson St & W Broadway; [S]1/2/3 to Chambers St) Softly lit subway tiles, eye-candy bar staff and smooth, seductive libations underlie Weather Up's magic. Sweet talk the staff over a None But the Brave (cognac, homemade ginger syrup, fresh lime, Pimeto Dram Allspice and soda). Failing that, comfort yourself with some seriously fine bar grub, including spectacular green chile-spiked oysters.

LA COLOMBE CAFE

Map p416 (www.lacolombe.com; 319 Church St at Lispenard St; ⏲7:30am-6:30pm Mon-Fri, 8:30am-6:30pm Sat & Sun; [S]A/C/E, N/Q/R, 4/6

LOCAL KNOWLEDGE

DRINKING IN THE CITY

Sean Muldoon, Connoisseurs Club co-founder and cocktail consultant at Blue Bar at India House (p76), lets us in on his favorite Manhattan drinking holes.

Downtown Favorites

My favorite bar in town is Mayahuel (p118) in the East Village. From the cocktails and bartenders to the food and music, it's exactly what a tequila cocktail bar should be. They use a lot of Mezcal, a smoky, tequilalike spirit. For New York's best Negroni, reserve a spot at **PDT** (Map p422; ☑212-614-0386; www.pdtnyc.com; 113 St Marks Pl btwn First Ave & Ave A; ⓢL to 1st Ave), also in the East Village. You could try making the same drink using the same ingredients, but it would never turn out as good.

Employees Only (p147) in the West Village offers a different take on the speakeasy bar, with interesting art deco touches. The place was once only open to people in the hospitality industry, hence the name. While I don't necessarily love their drinks – I usually opt for a beer – the bartenders, music and vibe are absolutely brilliant.

Further south in Tribeca, don't miss the decor at Macao (p75) and the effortless cool of Weather Up (p75).

Midtown Classics

In Midtown, head to PJ Clarke's (p198) during the week to meet famous bartender Doug Quinn. He might not make the best drinks in town, but you can walk in here eight months later and he'll still remember your name, your life story and what you drank. The guy makes an absolute mint in tips. Close by is Bill's Gay Nineties (p198). It's genuine Prohibition bar, not a trendy reconstruction, with a nightly pianist and an electric crowd singing and dancing along. You're pretty much guaranteed one memorable night.

---

to Canal St) Coffee and a few baked treats is all you'll get at this roaster but, man, are they good. The espresso is dark and intense, brewed by hipster baristas and swilled by an endless stream of eye-candy creatives and clued-in Continentals. Don't leave without a bottle of 'Pure Black Coffee,' steeped in oxygen-free stainless steel wine tanks for 16 hours.

KEG NO 229   BEER HALL

Map p416 (www.kegno229.com; 229 Front St btwn Beekman St & Peck Slip; ⓢA/C, J/Z, 1/2, 4/5 to Fulton St) If you know that a Flying Dog Raging Bitch is a craft beer – not a nickname for your ex – this curated beer bar is for you. From Mother's Milk Stout to Whale's Tail Pale Ale, its booty of drafts, bottles and cans are a who's who of boutique American brews.

On hand to soak it all up is a solid selection of comfort grub, including fried pickles and mini cheeseburgers. Sibling bar Bin 220 across the street offers a similar set-up for vino-philes.

BLUE BAR AT INDIA HOUSE   COCKTAIL BAR

Map p416 (www.indiahouseclub.org; 1 Hanover Sq at Stone St; ⊙4pm-11pm Mon-Fri; ⓢR to Whitehall St; 1 to South Ferry) Head up the stairs to the lobby, turn left and slip into this bluewalled, wooden-floored beauty. A private members' bar during the day, it's a handsome, grown-up hideaway for all after 4pm. There's no shortage of Wall St old-timers, known by name and drink by the barmen. Reminisce about the crash of '87 over a smooth whiskey or a remastered 19th-century cocktail.

ANOTHER ROOM   BAR

Map p416 (www.anotheroomtribeca.com; 249 W Broadway btwn Beach & White Sts; ⓢ1/2 to Franklin St) Charcoal walls, candlelight and velvet banquettes: Another Room is a perfect spot to slip into darkness with a luscious glass of red. It's all beer and wine (no mixed drinks) with chalkboard scrawl announcing the daily catch, from boutique Italian drops to seasonal domestic brews. Expect a 30- and 40-something Tribecan crowd, clinking glasses over indie-folk tunes.

ENTERTAINMENT

FLEA THEATER THEATER

Map p416 (www.theflea.org; 41 White St btwn Church St & Broadway; [S]1 to Franklin St, A/C/E, N/Q/R, J/M/Z, 6 to Canal St) The Flea is one of New York's top off-off-Broadway companies, performing innovative, timely new works in its two intimate performance spaces. Luminaries including Sigourney Weaver and John Lithgow have trodden the boards here, and the year-round program also includes cutting-edge music and dance performances.

92YTRIBECA CINEMA

Map p416 (☎212-601-1000; www.92y.org; 200 Hudson St at Vestry St; [S]A/C/E, N/Q/R, J/M/Z, 6 to Canal St) Festival-circuit indies, underground classics, camp tear-jerkers – the film screenings at this Tribeca cultural center are as eclectic as they are brilliant. One night you're wincing at *The House by the Cemetery*, the next you're psychoanalyzing Woody Allen in *Broadway Danny Rose*. Regular themed events include 'sing-a-long' screenings (go on, you're dying to sing *Wind Beneath My Wings* in public, admit it!).

92Y Tribeca also hosts regular music, theater and comedy performances, as well as public lectures and themed city tours. Check the website for what's on.

TRIBECA CINEMAS CINEMA

Map p416 (www.tribecacinemas.com; 54 Varick St at Laight St; [S]A/C/E, N/Q/R, J/M/Z, 6 to Canal St) This is the physical home of the Tribeca Film Festival (p25), founded in 2003 by Robert De Niro and Jane Rosenthal. Throughout the year, the space hosts a range of screenings and educational panels, including festivals dedicated to video art, experimental films or kids' movies. Check the website for upcoming events and screening schedules.

WORLD FINANCIAL CENTER CONCERT VENUE

Map p416 (www.artsworldfinancialcenter.com; 200 Liberty St; [S]E to World Trade Center; R to Cortlandt St) Although the World Financial Center is best known as an office and retail complex, its palm-fringed Winter Garden hosts free concerts, theater and dance performances, as well as art exhibits, throughout the year. Head to the website to see what's on.

SHOPPING

While the Financial District is not a shopping destination per se, it is where you'll find two of the city's best-loved stores: cut-price fashion mecca Century 21, and electronics giant J&R Music & Computer World. You'll find chains galore at both South Street Seaport and the World Financial Center, while further north in Tribeca, hit the lower end of Hudson St and surrounding streets for high-end interior design, antiques and a handful of trendy boutiques.

[TOP CHOICE] **PHILIP WILLIAMS POSTERS** VINTAGE

Map p416 (www.postermuseum.com; 122 Chambers St btwn Church St & W Broadway; 🕒11am-7pm Tue-Sat; [S]A/C, 1/2/3 to Chambers St) You'll find over half a million posters in this cavernous treasure trove, from oversized French advertisements for perfume and cognac to Soviet film posters and retro-fab promos for TWA (we even found an Italian-language film poster for Billy Wilder's *Some Like It Hot*). Prices range from $15 to a few thousand bucks, and most of the stock is original.

STEVEN ALAN FASHION

Map p416 (www.stevenalan.com; 103 Franklin St btwn Church St & W Broadway; [S]A/C/E to Canal St; 1 to Franklin St) Head to this unisex boutique for cognoscenti labels like Sweden's Our Legacy, Canada's Dace and New York's very own Steven Alan. The look is chic, silhouetted and fun, with whimsical frocks, vintage-inspired shirts, woolen ties and detailed denim in the mix. Accessories include hard-to-find colognes, bags, jewelry and a lust-inducing selection of shoes from the likes of Saville Row.

CENTURY 21 FASHION

Map p416 (www.c21stores.com; 22 Cortlandt St at Church St; 🕒7:45am-9pm Mon-Wed, to 9:30pm Thu & Fri, 10am-9pm Sat, 11am-8pm Sun; [S]A/C, J/Z, 2/3, 4/5 to Fulton St) If you're a fashionista with more style than cents, this cut-price department store is your promised land. Raid the racks for designer duds at up to 70% off. Not everything is a knockout or a bargain, but persistence pays off. It gets crowded and competitive, so if you see something you like, get hold of it fast.

PASANELLA & SON WINE

Map p416 (www.pasanellaandson.com; 115 South St btwn Peck Slip & Beekman St; ⏰10am-9pm Mon-Sat, noon-7pm Sun; [S]A/C, J/Z, 2/3, 4/5 to Fulton St) Oenophiles will adore this savvy wine peddler, with its 400-plus drops both inspired and affordable. Long sheets of butcher's paper run down the wall, offering handwritten wine suggestions based on your menu. There's an impressive choice of American whiskeys, free wine tastings of the week's new arrivals on Sundays, and themed wine and cheese tastings throughout the year (check the website).

JEM FABRIC WAREHOUSE HANDICRAFTS

Map p416 (www.houseofjem.blogspot.com; 355 Broadway btwn Franklin & Leonard Sts; [S]N/R, 4/6 to Canal St) Looking for triple-layered satin topped with tulle and metallic spray paint? Chances are you'll find it here. Aside from stocking rare retro fabrics, JEM functions as a creative hub, with short- and longer-term workshops in anything from fabric dyeing to fashion illustration. There's even a drop-in sewing workshop on Thursdays between 5:30pm and 7pm. Check the website for upcoming events.

URBAN ARCHAEOLOGY HOMEWARES

Map p416 (www.urbanarchaeology.com; 143 Franklin St btwn Hudson & Varick Sts; ⏰8am-6pm Mon-Fri; [S]1 to Franklin St) A pioneer in recycled design, owner Gil Shapiro continues his tradition of remixing, reconstructing and reclaiming old parts from abandoned buildings and construction sites. What he salvages and restores (or repurposes) is now sought after in the hippest Manhattan apartments; even Robert De Niro headed here when furnishing his Greenwich Hotel. Check out the Tribeca showroom/studio for Shapiro's latest creations.

J&R MUSIC & COMPUTER WORLD MUSIC

Map p416 (www.jr.com; 15-23 Park Row; [S]A/C, J/M/Z, 2/3, 4/5 to Fulton St-Broadway-Nassau St) Located on what was once known as Newspaper Row – the center of NYC's newspaper publishing biz from the 1840s to the 1920s – this trio of electronics stores sells everything that's related to computers, phones, stereos, iPods, iPads, recording equipment and other electronic gadgetry. It's also packed with CDs, DVDs and video games.

CITYSTORE BOOKS

Map p416 (www.nyc.gov/citystore; 1 Centre St, North Plaza, Municipal Bldg; ⏰10am-6pm Mon-Fri; [S]J/M/Z to Chambers St; 4/5/6 to Brooklyn Bridge-City Hall) This small, little-known city-run shop stocks all manner of New York memorabilia, including authentic taxi medallions, manhole coasters, silk ties and baby clothes bearing the official 'City of New York' seal, Brooklyn Bridge posters, NYPD baseball caps, and actual streets signs ('No Parking,' 'Don't Feed the Pigeons'). There's also a great collection of city-themed books.

NEW YORK YANKEES CLUBHOUSE SPORTS

Map p416 (8 Fulton St btwn Front & Water Sts; ⏰10am-9pm Mon-Sat, 11am-8pm Sun; [S]A/C, J/Z, 2/3, 4/5 to Fulton St) It's on Schermerhorn Row, a block of old warehouses bordered by Fulton, Front and South Sts, that you'll find this commercial shrine to America's mightiest baseball dynasty. Salute the ballpark legends with logo-pimped jerseys, tees, caps…even dog bowls. Hardcore fans will appreciate the booty of signed bats, balls and posters. You can even purchase fee-free game tickets.

SPORTS & ACTIVITIES

[TOP CHOICE] **STATEN ISLAND FERRY** OUTDOORS

Map p416 (www.siferry.com; Whitehall Terminal at Whitehall & South Sts; fare free; ⏰24hr; [S]1 to South Ferry) Staten Islanders know these hulking, dirty-orange ferryboats as commuter vehicles, while Manhattanites like to think of them as their secret, romantic vessels for a spring-day escape. Yet many a tourist is clued into the charms of the Staten Island Ferry, whose 5.2-mile journey between Lower Manhattan and the Staten Island neighborhood of St George is one of NYC's finest free adventures.

In service since 1905, the ferry service carries more than 19 million passengers each year across the Hudson River. Whether you choose to simply ride it to Staten Island and back in one run – enjoying cinematic views of the city skyline, the Verrazano-Narrows Bridge (which connects Staten Island to Brooklyn) and the Statue of Liberty – or stay and explore New York's least-known borough before catching a later ferry, you're guaranteed a memorable experience. For maximum impact, catch the ferry an hour before sunset – this way your return trip view will be of a glittering, twilight Manhattan skyline.

DIALOG IN THE DARK WALKING TOUR

Map p416 (www.dialognyc.com; 11 Fulton St, South Street Seaport; adult/child weekdays $22.50/19.50, weekends $23.50/20.50; 🕒10am-7pm Sun-Thu, to 9pm Fri & Sat ; [S]A/C, J/M/Z, 2/3, 4/5 to Fulton St) If you've ever wondered what life is like for the blind, this incredible exhibition will answer your question. With a blind or visually impaired guide, you and your fellow visitors are led on a virtual tour of New York and its 'sights' – in complete darkness.

It's a powerful experience, bringing the city and its landmarks to life through sound, smell and temperature. It's also an opportunity to learn just how incredibly skilled people with a visual impairment are at navigating their way around. Prepare to have your perceptions rewritten.

BIKE & ROLL BICYCLE RENTAL

Map p416 (www.bikeandroll.com; Pier A, 18 Battery Place; rentals per day $49, tours adult/child $50/35; 🕒9am-7pm Mar-May, 8am-8pm Jun-Aug, 9am-5pm Sep-Nov; [S]4/5 to Bowling Green; 1 to South Ferry) Located in Battery Park, this place rents out bikes, as well as leading bike tours along the Hudson River to Central Park and across the Brooklyn Bridge from April to October.

BATTERY PARK CITY PARKS CONSERVANCY WALKING TOUR

(☎212-267-9700; www.bpcparks.org) Offers a range of free or low-fee walking tours, group swims, children's programs and classes. Check the website for upcoming events.

REAL PILATES HEALTH & FITNESS

Map p416 (☎212-625-0777; www.realpilatesnyc.com; 177 Duane St btwn Greenwich & Hudson Sts; private/group class $87.50/30; 🕒7am-9pm Mon-Thu, to 8pm Fri, 9am-3pm Sat & Sun; [S]A/C, 1/2/3 to Chambers St) Pilates guru (and author) Alycea Ungaro's studio hosts Pilates courses of all levels. There's a Pilates Sculpt class, as well as prenatal sessions. Check the website for specific class times and days.

SoHo & Chinatown

SOHO | NOHO | NOLITA | CHINATOWN | LITTLE ITALY

Neighborhood Top Five

1 Strutting your stuff down the concrete catwalks of **SoHo** (p94) – shopping bags in hand – then ducking down a side street to hunt for one-of-a-kind wares.

2 Slurping soup dumplings and browsing designer wares of ambiguous authenticity amid the sizzling lights of **Chinatown** (p84).

3 Stepping into the veritable time machine that is the **Merchant's House Museum** (p83) to explore what life was like in New York during the 1800s.

4 Wagging your pressed index finger and thumb in delight while devouring steaming slices of pizza in **Little Italy** (p82).

5 Escaping the urban frenzy for a meditative moment at the **Mahayana Buddhist Temple** (p88) – the largest in Chinatown.

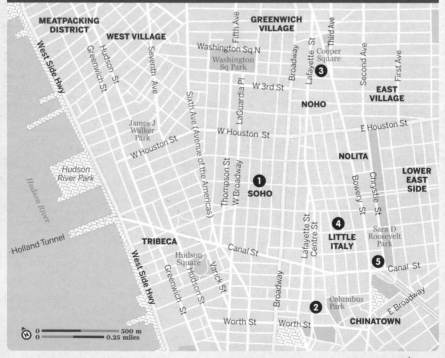

For more detail of this area, see Map p418 and p421 ➡

Explore SoHo & Chinatown

Like a colorful quilt of subneighborhoods sewn together in mismatched patches, the areas orbiting SoHo (or SOuth of HOuston) feel like urban crumbs mopped up from other countries and sprinkled throughout lower Manhattan. Down in SoHo, the boxy blocks of Midtown are swapped for a decidedly human scale, making a casual stroll feel as if you're walking through an elegant village (with the exception of Broadway, the main drag).

And while the sidewalks unfurl in a regal manner, there's a palpable anything-goes spirit that wafts up like stall smoke in Chinatown, where frenzied crowds and hawkers mingle under the winking lights of aging billboards (think Vegas in the '80s). The best way to weave your way around is on foot – you'll get nowhere fast on wheels. And don't bother planning your route of attack. It's all about absorbing the atmosphere and letting your senses guide you: follow your nose down an alleyway for freshly baked pork buns, let the prayer gong guide you to a Buddhist temple, or look down colorful Canal St.

Local Life

➡ **Family style** Chinatown has the best dining deals around, and locals love to head downtown to satisfy their hankering for hole-in-the-wall fare. Experience the area's bustling dining dens with a handful friends and eat 'family style' (order a ton of dishes and sample spoonsful of each). You'll be sure the waiter left a zero off the bill.

➡ **Side streets** The multilaned thoroughfares of SoHo are reserved for the legions of tourists – you'll find New Yorkers scouring the one-of-a-kind boutiques on the side streets for unique buys and slashed prices.

Getting There & Away

➡ **Subway** The subway lines dump off along various points of Canal St (J, M, Z, N, Q, R, W and 6). Once you arrive it's best to explore on foot. The neighborhood's downtown location makes it easy to access from Midtown and Brooklyn.

➡ **Bus & Taxi** Avoid taking cabs or buses – especially in Chinatown, as the traffic is full-on. For SoHo, have your taxi let you off along Broadway if you aren't fussed about your final destination. Don't take cabs south of Canal St if you're simply planning to wander around Chinatown.

Lonely Planet's Top Tip

Serious shopaholics should consult the city's in-the-know retail blogs before hitting the streets of SoHo – there's always some sort of 'sample sale' or marked-down offer going on.

✖ Best Places to Eat

➡ Dutch (p89)
➡ Balthazar (p89)
➡ Joe's Shanghai (p93)
➡ Café Gitane (p89)

For reviews, see p89 ➡

🍷 Best Places to Drink

➡ Pravda (p93)
➡ Jimmy (p94)
➡ Apotheke (p94)
➡ Randolph (p94)

For reviews, see p93 ➡

🔒 Best Places to Shop

➡ Housing Works Book Store (p94)
➡ Kiosk (p94)
➡ McNally Jackson (p94)
➡ Purl Soho (p95)
➡ Jack Spade (p95)

For reviews, see p94 ➡

SOHO & CHINATOWN

TOP SIGHTS
LITTLE ITALY

Unlike Chinatown, which feels as though it's bursting at the seams, Little Italy has been steadily shrinking over the last 50 years. The once strong Italian neighborhood (film director Martin Scorsese grew up on Elizabeth St) saw an exodus in the mid-20th century when many of its residents moved to more suburban neighborhoods in Brooklyn and beyond. Still, loyal Italian Americans flock here to gather around red-and-white-checked tablecloths for heaping pasta and pizza portions. If you're in town in late September, be sure to check out the raucous San Gennaro Festival, which honors the patron saint of Naples.

DON'T MISS...

➡ San Gennaro Festival in September
➡ Pizza by the slice
➡ St Patrick's Church
➡ Italian American Museum

PRACTICALITIES

➡ Map p421
➡ www.littleitalynyc.com
➡ Ⓢ F/V, N/R, 6; 🚌 M103

Mulberry Street

New York's tribute to the Boot-land is mostly concentrated on Mulberry St (p88) between Broome and Canal Sts. Here you'll find scores of restaurants with their signature checkerboard tablecloths spooning out bowlsful of homemade pasta and spinning hot tin trays of Neapolitan slices. It's got a pick-a-table-and-enjoy kinda vibe, so put down the guidebook and enjoy the *dolce vita*.

Italian American Museum

The small **Italian American Museum** (Map p421; www.italianamericanmuseum.org; 155 Mulberry St; admission free; ⊘11am-6pm Wed, Thu, Sat & Sun, to 8pm Fri) sits where one of the most important buildings in Little Italy once stood: the Banca Stabile, which was once the unofficial headquarters of the community, helping immigrants sort their monetary needs and providing a lifeline back to the homeland. Today, the former bank makes up much of the main exhibition space, which tells the New York Italian community's unique story of struggle.

St Patrick's Old Cathedral

Though **St Patrick's Cathedral** (Map p418; www.oldsaintpatricks.com; 263 Mulberry St; ⊘8am-5pm Mon-Fri) is now famously located on Fifth Ave in Midtown, its first congregation was housed here, on the northern edge of Little Italy, in this 1809–15 Gothic Revival church designed by Joseph-François Mangin. Back in its heyday, the church was the seat of religious life for the Archdiocese of New York, as well as an important community center for new immigrants, mainly from Ireland. Today it holds regular liturgies in English, Spanish and Chinese. Its ancient cemetery out the back is a beautiful respite in the midst of city chaos.

TOP SIGHTS
MERCHANT'S HOUSE MUSEUM

Walking through the doors of this perfectly preserved mansion is like stepping into a time machine that has transported you 150 years into the past. Everything in the house – from the polished floors to the crown moulding – is as it was during the bygone era; the facade is intact as well. The gorgeous red-brick house was once the home of merchant magnate Seabury Tredwell and his family. It remains to this day the most authentic Federal house (of which there are about 300) in New York City.

A Shrine to Decorative Arts

An antique dealer's dream, the Tredwell manse is as much about the city's mercantile past as it is a showcase of some of the finest domestic furnishings of the 19th century. Everything in the house is a testament to what money could buy, from the elaborate plaster ceiling medallions to the parlor chairs attributed to Duncan Phyfe (noted furniture designer with a collection of work in the White House) – even the elaborate system of multilevel call bells for the servants still functions today.

The Tredwell Family

Seabury Tredwell, a wealthy marine hardware merchant and a descendant of the *Mayflower* pilgrims, and his wife Eliza purchased what is now the Merchant's House Museum for $18,000 in 1821 when they sought to move further north up the island to escape the downtown congestion. They had eight children, of whom only three married – an anomaly for the time and for a family of such financial stature. Gertrude, the youngest member of the family, lived in the house for all 93 years of her life, and clung to the property even after the neighborhood around her largely fell into disrepair. She lived in the house alone – a spinster – for 24 years until her passing. A cousin saved the manse from foreclosure, turning the trove of period artifacts into a museum in 1936.

Unseen Residents

Perhaps just as well known as the contents and history of this brilliantly curated home are the museum's clan of unseen residents. It is popularly believed that many of the Tredwell ancestors haunt the old mansion, making cameo appearances late in evenings and sometimes at public events. In fact, at a Valentine's Day concert a few years back several attendees witnessed the shadow of a woman walk up to the performers and take a seat in the parlor chairs – it was commonly believed to be the ghost of Gertrude Tredwell, the last resident of the brownstone. Each year, during the last couple of weeks of October, the museum offers special ghost tours after dark.

DON'T MISS...

- ➡ Ghost Tours in late October
- ➡ Newly refurbished maid's quarters on the 4th floor
- ➡ Chairs attributed to Duncan Phyfe
- ➡ Piano in front parlor
- ➡ Plaster ceiling medallions
- ➡ Original (and still working) servant call bells

PRACTICALITIES

- ➡ Map p418
- ➡ ☎212-777-1089
- ➡ www.merchantshouse.org
- ➡ 29 E 4th St btwn Lafayette St & Bowery
- ➡ admission $10
- ➡ 🕒noon-5pm Thu-Mon
- ➡ [S]6 to Bleecker St

TOP SIGHTS
CHINATOWN

Endless exotic moments await in New York City's most colorfully cramped community, where a walk through the neighborhood is never the same no matter how many times you pass through. Catch the whiff of fresh fish and ripe persimmons, hear the clacking of mah-jongg tiles on makeshift tables, witness dangling duck roasts swinging in store windows and shop for anything imaginable, from rice-paper lanterns and 'faux-lex' watches to tire irons and a pound of pressed nutmeg. America's largest congregation of Chinese immigrants is your oyster – dipped in soy sauce, of course.

Canal Street

Walking down Canal St is like a game of Frogger played on the streets of Shanghai. This is Chinatown's main artery, where you'll dodge oncoming human traffic as you scurry into back alleys to scout treasures from the Far East. You'll pass stinky seafood stalls hawking slippery fish; mysterious herb shops displaying a witch's cauldron's worth of roots and potions; storefront bakeries with steamed-up windows and the tastiest 50-cent pork buns you've ever had; restaurants with whole, roasted ducks and pigs hanging by their skinny necks in the windows; produce markets piled high with fresh lychees, bok choy and Asian pears; and street vendors selling every iteration of knock-off, from Gucci sunglasses to faux Prada bags.

ANGUS OBORN / LONELY PLANET IMAGES ©

DON'T MISS...

➡ NYC & Company Explore Chinatown information kiosk (Baxter St between Canal and Walker Sts)

➡ A family-style meal at a bustling, back-alley dive

➡ Museum of Chinese in America

➡ Mahayana Buddhist Temple

PRACTICALITIES

➡ Map p421

➡ www.explorechina town.com

➡ south of Canal St & east of Broadway

➡ ⬜M1, M6, M9, M15, M22, M103, B39, B51, Ⓢ6, J/M/Z, N/Q/R/W to Canal St Station; B/D to Grand St Station; F to East Broadway Station

Buddhist Temples

Chinatown is home to Buddhist temples large and small, public and obscure. They are easily stumbled upon during a full-on stroll of the neighborhood, and at least two such temples are considered landmarks. The **Eastern States Buddhist Temple** (Map p421; 64 Mott St btwn Bayard & Canal Sts; ⊘9am-6pm; J/M/Z, 6 to Canal St) is filled with hundreds of Buddhas, while the **Mahayana Buddhist Temple** (Map p421; 133 Canal St) holds one golden, 16ft-high Buddha, sitting on a lotus and edged with offerings of fresh oranges, apples and flowers. Mahayana is the largest Buddhist temple in Chinatown, and its facade, right near the frenzied vehicle entrance to the Manhattan Bridge, features two giant golden lions for protection; its interior is simple, with a wooden floor, red chairs and red paper lanterns – but all these are trumped by the magnificent Buddha, thought to be the largest in the city.

Food Glorious Food

The most rewarding experience for Chinatown neophytes is to access this wild and wonderful world through their taste buds. More than any other area of Manhattan, Chinatown's menus sport wonderfully low prices, uninflated by ambience or reputation. But more than cheap eats, the neighborhood is rife with family recipes passed between generations and continents. Food displays and preparation remain unchanged and untempered by American norms; it's not unusual to walk by storefronts sporting a tangled array of lacquered animals – chickens, rabbit and duck, in particular – ready to be chopped up and served at a family banquet. Steaming street stalls clang down the sidewalk serving pork buns and other finger-friendly food. Don't forget to wander down the back alleys for a colorful assortment of spices and herbs to dress up your recipes back at home.

Museum of Chinese in America

Housed in a 12,350-sq-ft space designed by architect Maya Lin (who created the famed Vietnam Memorial in Washington DC), the Museum of Chinese in America is a multifaceted space with exhibit galleries, a bookstore and a visitors lounge, which, all together, serve as a national center of information about Chinese-American life. Browse through interactive multimedia exhibits, maps, timelines, photos, letters, films and artifacts. Its anchor exhibit, 'With a Single Step: Stories in the Making of America,' is an interactive display touching on subjects such as immigration, politics and history.

HISTORY

The history of Chinese immigrants in New York City is a long and tumultuous one. The first Chinese people to arrive in America came to work under difficult conditions on the Central Pacific Railroad; others were lured to the west coast in search of gold. When prospects dried up, many moved east to NYC to work in factory assembly lines and in the laundry houses of New Jersey.

A rising racist sentiment gave way to the Chinese Exclusion Act (1882–1943), which made naturalization an impossibility, and largely squashed the opportunity for mainland Chinese to find work in the US. When the ban was lifted, the Chinese were given a limited immigration quota that eventually expanded and grew. Today it's estimated that over 150,000 citizens fill the bursting, tenementlike structures orbiting Mott St.

SIGHTS

SoHo, NoHo & Nolita

SoHo (SOuth of HOuston), NoHo (NOrth of HOuston) and Nolita (NOrth of LIttle ITAly) represent three of the coolest city neighborhoods, known for their tangled thickets of hipness in the form of boutiques, bars and eateries. Real estate is through the roof in all three spots, and nights out (or days shopping) can prove to be expensive propositions. But in the end you'll be won over by the unique blend of industrial starkness and cobblestone coziness that lends these areas their character.

MERCHANT'S HOUSE MUSEUM — MUSEUM

See p83.

MUSEUM OF COMIC & CARTOON ART — MUSEUM

Map p418 (www.moccany.org; 594 Broadway; admission $5; ⏲noon-5pm Fri-Mon, by appt Tue-Thu; 👪; [S]R/W to Prince St) Cartoon aficionados can't get enough of this museum and its wealth of graphic novels, comic lore and long-lost posters. Special exhibits include both well-known cartoonists and up-and-coming artists, with frequent opening parties and various festivals. Check the website for online exhibits and upcoming lecture series.

NEW YORK CITY FIRE MUSEUM — MUSEUM

Map p418 (www.nycfiremuseum.org; 278 Spring St btwn Varick & Hudson Sts; suggested donation adult/child $5/1; ⏲10am-5pm Tue-Sat, to 4pm Sun; 👪; [S]C/E to Spring St) Occupying a grand 1904 firehouse, this museum houses a collection of gold, horse-drawn firefighting carriages and modern-day red firetrucks. Exhibits show the development of the NYC firefighting system, which began with the 'bucket brigades.' The New York Fire Department (FDNY) lost half of its members in the collapse of the World Trade Center, and memorials and exhibits have become a permanent part of the collection. An excellent gift shop sells books about firefighting history and official FDNY clothing and patches.

[FREE] NEW YORK EARTH ROOM — ART

Map p418 (www.earthroom.org; 141 Wooster St; ⏲noon-6pm Wed-Sun, closed 3pm-3:30pm; [S]N/R/W to Prince St) Since 1980 the oddity of the New York Earth Room, the work of artist Walter De Maria, has been wooing the curious with something not easily found in the city: dirt (250 cu yd, or 280,000lb, of it, to be exact). Walking into the small space is a heady experience, as the scent will make you feel like you've entered a wet forest; the sight of such beautiful, pure earth in the midst of this crazy city is surprisingly moving.

[FREE] AMERICAN NUMISMATIC SOCIETY — MUSEUM

Map p418 (www.numismatics.org; 1 Hudson Sq at Varick & Watts Sts; ⏲9am-5pm Mon-Fri; [S]1 to Houston St) The holdings here of more than 800,000 coins, medals and notes are rivaled by only one similar collection in Europe. The items are from all over the map and throughout history, including Greek, Roman, East Asian, medieval and Islamic items. Frequent small special exhibitions and lectures focus on the history of currency, while the Society's main exhibition space is at the nearby Federal Reserve Bank. It's best to call ahead before setting out to visit the headquarters here.

[FREE] DRAWING CENTER — GALLERY

Map p418 (www.drawingcenter.org; 35 Wooster St; ⏲noon-6pm Wed & Fri-Sun, to 8pm Thu; [S]A/C/E, 1 to Canal St) Here since 1977, this is the only nonprofit institute in the country to focus solely on drawings, using work by masters as well as unknowns to show various styles. Historical exhibitions have included work by Michelangelo, James Ensor and Marcel Duchamp, while contemporary shows have focused on Richard Serra, Ellsworth Kelly and Richard Tuttle; exhibits can range from the whimsical to the politically controversial. Artist lectures and performance-art programs are hot tickets here – as is the new Big Draw event, which invites folks of all ages to bring a sketchpad to any of several artist-led, hands-on happenings at locations around the city.

CHILDREN'S MUSEUM OF THE ARTS — MUSEUM

Map p418 (www.cmany.org; 182 Lafayette St btwn Broome & Grand Sts; admission $10, suggested donation 4pm-6pm Thu; ⏲noon-5pm Wed & Fri-Sun, to 6pm Thu; [S]N/R to Prince St; 6 to Spring St) A place for kids to unleash their inner artist, this small but worthy stop is home to a permanent collection of paintings, draw

Neighborhood Walk
Inside the Acronyms

➡️ Pop out of the B, D, F, V train and get an immediate sense of old-meets-new with NoHo's beaux arts ❶ **Cable Building**, built by famed architects McKim, Mead and White in 1894. Originally used as the power plant for the Broadway Cable Car (the nation's first), it features an oval window and caryatids on its Broadway facade. Today it houses the Angelika Film Center.

Head east across Houston St and make a right on Lafayette St, Turn left on Prince St and you'll be approaching ❷ **St Patrick's Old Cathedral**, dating from 1809 – the original location for the famous Fifth Ave cathedral's congregation. Don't miss the ancient, peaceful cemetery. Loop right along scenic Elizabeth St, then make another right on Spring St to enjoy the local neighborhood flavor until you hit Broadway; just half a block north is the ❸ **Singer Building**, one of the post–Civil War buildings that gave this area its 'Cast-Iron District' nickname. This one used to be the main warehouse for the famous sewing-machine company of the same name.

Head south down Broadway and you'll come to a rather generic Staples store with a surprising history: it's located in the ❹ **Haughwout Building**, the first structure to use the exotic steam elevator developed by Elisha Otis. Known as the 'Parthenon of Cast-Iron Architecture,' the Haughwout (pronounced how-out) is considered a rare structure for its two-sided design. Don't miss the iron clock that sits on the Broadway facade.

Cross Broadway at Broome St, walking west, and continue on to Wooster St. Turn right and head up to the ❺ **New York Earth Room**, where artist Walter De Maria's gallery filled with cool, moist soil will either thrill you or leave you scratching your head (maybe a bit of both).

ings and photographs by local school kids, with adorable exhibit titles like 'Beyond the Refrigerator Door.' For more hands-on activities, check out the museum's vast offering of public programs for kids of all ages, including guided workshops on art forms ranging from sculpture to collaborative mural painting, as well as movie nights and other special treats.

⊙ Chinatown & Little Italy

Although Chinatown and Little Italy are immigrant communities with yin and yang relationships, they have several points in common: both neighborhoods make for brilliant DIY adventures. Put down the guidebook and get lost in the tangle of cluttered streets and sidewalks.

CANAL STREET STREET
See p84.

ITALIAN AMERICAN MUSEUM MUSEUM
See p82.

ST PATRICK'S OLD CATHEDRAL CHURCH
See p82.

MAHAYANA TEMPLE TEMPLE
See p85.

MUSEUM OF CHINESE IN AMERICA MUSEUM
See p85.

CHURCH OF THE TRANSFIGURATION CHURCH
Map p421 (www.transfigurationnyc.org; 29 Mott St; admission $4; 🕐noon-6pm Tue-Sun; [S]J/M/Z, N/Q/R/W, 6 to Canal St) It's been serving New York's immigrant communities since 1801, and the Church of the Transfiguration doesn't stop adapting. First it was the Irish, then Italians and now Chinese. The same priest delivers sermons in Cantonese, English and sometimes Latin. This small landmark is not far from Pell St and Doyers St, two winding paths worth exploring.

COLUMBUS PARK OUTDOORS
Map p421 (Mulberry & Bayard Sts; [S]J/M/Z, 6 to Canal St) This is where outdoor mah-jongg and domino games take place at bridge tables while tai chi practitioners move through lyrical, slow-motion poses under shady trees. Judo-sparring folks and relaxing families are also common sights in this active communal space originally created in the 1890s and popular with local residents. Visitors are welcome, though (or at least ignored).

An interesting note is that the Five Points neighborhood, home to the city's first tenement slums and the inspiration for Martin Scorsese's *Gangs of New York*, was once located at the foot of where Columbus Park is now. The 'five points' were the five streets that used to converge here; now you'll find the intersection of only Mosco, Worth and Baxter Sts. (Another Columbus Park perk is its public bathroom, making it the perfect place for a pit stop.)

WING FAT SHOPPING MALL NOTABLE BUILDING
(8-9 Bowery btwn Pell & Doyers Sts; [S]J/M/Z, N/Q/R/W, 6 to Canal St) One of the most unique malls you'll ever see, Wing Fat lies underground and has businesses offering reflexology, collectible stamps and feng shui services. The most fascinating aspect is its history, as the tunnel is said to have served as a stop on the Underground Railroad as well as an escape route in the early 1900s for members of rival Tong gangs, who fought up on the street and then disappeared below before police could even begin to search.

MULBERRY STREET STREET
Map p421 ([S]6 to Spring St) Although it feels more like a theme park than an authentic Italian strip, Mulberry St is still the heart of Little Italy. It's the home of landmarks such as **Umberto's Clam House** (Map p421; www.umbertosclamhouse.com; 132 Mulberry St; [S]6 to Spring St), where mobster Joey Gallo was shot to death in the '70s, as well as the old-time **Mulberry Street Bar** (Map p421; 176½ Mulberry St btwn Broome & Grand Sts; [S]B/D to Grand St), one of the favorite haunts of the late Frank Sinatra. Just a half-block off of Mulberry is the legendary **Ferrara Cafe & Bakery** (Map p421; 195 Grand St; [S]B/D to Grand St), brimming with classic Italian pastries and old-school ambience. You'll see lots of red, white and green Italian flags sold in souvenir shops, and you'll also enjoy the lovely aroma of fresh-baked pastries and pizzas wafting out of doorways. Take a gander at what was once the **Ravenite Social Club** (Map p418; 247 Mulberry St; [S]6 to Spring St) to see how things have really changed around here, as these days it's host to a rotating roster of legit businesses, including

clothing and gift shops. It was once an organized-crime hangout (originally known as the Alto Knights Social Club), where big hitters such as Lucky Luciano and John Gotti (as well as the FBI, who kept raiding the place) logged time. For more about Mulberry St, see p82.

🍴 EATING

In the land of acronyms there are only three letters you need to know: Y.U.M. Though the area may not have a plethora of headliners like the East and West Villages just beyond, there are certainly a fair share of spots at which to sample some of the city's finest restaurants. You 99%ers should make a beeline for Chinatown, where heaping portions are served up for pennies.

🍴 SoHo, NoHo & Nolita

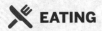

[TOP CHOICE] DUTCH AMERICAN **$$$**

Map p418 (☎212-677-6200; www.thedutchnyc.com; 131 Sullivan St btwn Prince & Houston Sts; mains $16-48; ⏰11:30am-3pm Mon-Fri, 5:30pm-midnight Mon-Thu & Sun, 5:30pm-1am Fri & Sat, 10am-3pm Sat & Sun; [S]A/C/E to Spring St; N/R to Prince St; 1/2 to Houston St) The foodie folks from Locanda Verde have done it again at the Dutch, with simple pleasures on the cobalt blue chalkboard and a shortlist of supper regulars that draw their inspiration from the new American table. Oysters on ice and freshly baked homemade pies are the notable bookends of the dining experience – in the middle is unfussy cuisine, fresh from the farm, served with the perfect amount of ceremony. Ever the award-winner, the Dutch promises a memorable night, if you manage to snag a table…

[TOP CHOICE] BALTHAZAR FRENCH **$$$**

Map p418 (www.balthazarny.com; 80 Spring St btwn Broadway & Crosby St; mains $11-34; ⏰breakfast, lunch & dinner daily, brunch Sat & Sun; [S]6 to Spring St) Retaining its long-held status as a superstar among the city's glut of French bistros, this bustling (OK, *loud*) spot still pulls in the discriminating mobs. That's all thanks to three winning details: the location, which makes it a convenient shopping-spree rest area; the uplifting ambience, shaped by big, mounted mirrors, cozy high-backed booths, airy high ceilings and wide windows; and, of course, the stellar something-for-everyone menu, which features an outstanding raw bar, steak frites, salade Niçoise, roasted beet salad and prawn risotto with sage and butternut squash. The kitchen stays open till 2am Thursday to Saturday, and weekend brunch here is a very crowded (and delicious) production.

CAFÉ GITANE MOROCCAN **$$**

Map p418 (www.cafegitanenyc.com; 242 Mott St; mains $12-18; ⏰9am-midnight Sun-Thu, to 12:30am Fri & Sat; [S]N/R/W to Prince St) Clear the Gauloise smoke from your eyes and blink twice if you think you're in Paris – Gitane has that louche vibe. Label-conscious shoppers love this authentic bistro, with its dark, aromatic coffee and dishes such as yellowfin tuna seviche, spicy meatballs in tomato-turmeric sauce with a boiled egg, Greek salad on focaccia and heart-of-palm salad, with plenty of lusty wines.

LA ESQUINA MEXICAN **$$**

Map p418 (www.esquinanyc.com; 114 Kenmare St; mains $9-20; ⏰24hr; [S]6 to Spring St) This mega-popular and quirky little spot is housed in a former greasy spoon that sits within the neat little triangle formed by Cleveland Pl and Lafayette St. It's a stand-while-you-eat taco window, a casual Mexican cafe and, downstairs, a cozy, overly hip cave of a dining room that requires reservations. Standouts include chorizo tacos, rubbed pork tacos and mango and jicama salads, among other authentic and delicious options (most of which are also available upstairs at the anyone-welcome area).

BALABOOSTA MODERN AMERICAN **$$**

Map p418 (www.balaboostanyc.com; 214 Mulberry St btwn Spring & Prince Sts; mains $20-29, small plates $5-10; ⏰noon-3pm Tue-Fri, 5:30pm-11pm Mon-Thu, 5:30pm-10pm Fri & Sat, 11am-4pm Sat & Sun, 5:30pm-10pm Sun; [S]J to Bowery; N/R to Prince St; 4/6 to Spring St) 'The Perfect Housewife,' as the Yiddish name suggests, truly does feel like a cram-packed evening at your Bubbie's…if your Bubbie were an amazing cook with an uncanny flair for whipping up delightfully inventive appetizers (crispy cauliflower!) and scrumptious mains (flavor-intensive lamb chops!). Seating is tight, but neighbors become fast friends when united by the collective chorus of 'yums'.

1. SoHo (p86)
A stroll around SoHo's elegant back streets is to see this neighborhood from a decidedly local viewpoint.

2. Opening Ceremony (p99)
Rub shoulders with fashion insiders at this off-the-beaten-path boutique that is known for its indie labels.

3. Little Italy (p82)
Loyal Italian Americans flock to this small enclave for helpings of pizza and pasta.

DAN HERRICK / LONELY PLANET IMAGES ©

DBIMAGES / ALAMY ©

BLUE RIBBON BRASSERIE
AMERICAN $$

Map p418 (www.blueribbonrestaurants.com; 97 Sullivan St near Spring St; mains $15-27; ⊙dinner; ⚇⚇; ⓈC/E to Spring St) Going strong since 1992, this comfort-food mecca is still a standout, especially for late-night dining, and the founding Bromberg Brothers have multiple offshoots: **Blue Ribbon Sushi** (Map p418; 119 Sullivan St), just a few doors away, **Blue Ribbon Bakery** (Map p426; 35 Downing St) and **Blue Ribbon Downing Street Bar** (Map p426; 34 Downing St). Blue Ribbon Brasserie's best-known dishes are the succulent, cheesy appetizers and sides; fresh, tangy salads; and delectable seafood, such as sweet and spicy catfish and red trout.

MERCER KITCHEN
AMERICAN $$

Map p418 (⚇212-966-5454; 99 Prince St at Mercer St; mains $12-28; ⊙breakfast, lunch & dinner; ⓈR/W to Prince St) Just peering into this soothing gem of a hideaway tells you something special is going on. It's part of chef-god Jean-Georges Vongerichten's top-echelon empire, and perches below street level in the endlessly fashionable Mercer Hotel. Basics, like baked salmon with fresh-corn pudding, sea scallops and pea-green ravioli, and a dessert of apricot tart with salted-caramel ice cream, excel thanks to the freshest, most seasonal ingredients. The same can be said for the customers, who work hard to look so divine.

TORRISI ITALIAN SPECIALTIES
ITALIAN $$$

Map p418 (www.piginahat.com; 250 Mulberry St btwn Spring & Prince Sts; prix fixe menu $65; ⓈN/R to Prince St; B/D/F, M to Broadway-Lafayette St; 4/6 to Spring St) Torrisi's tasting menu reads like an ode to Italy, with changes each week reflecting the whim of the owners (who also run popular Parm nearby) and the seasonal rotation of fresh ingredients. Expect market produce and less-common items (like rabbit and goat) spun into homemade platters that are both succulent and inspiring.

IL BUCO
ITALIAN $$$

Map p418 (www.ilbuco.com; 47 Bond St btwn Bowery & Lafayette St; mains $21-32; ⊙lunch & dinner Tue-Sun; ⓈB/D/F/V to Broadway-Lafayette St; 6 to Bleecker St) This magical nook is a real charmer – it boasts hanging copper pots, kerosene lamps and antique furniture, plus a stunning menu and wine list. Sink your teeth into seasonal and ever-changing highlights like white polenta with braised broc-

coli rabe and anchovies, homemade pappardelle with a mélange of mushrooms, and a succulent Dijon-crusted lamb chop.

DEAN & DELUCA
DELI $$

Map p418 (www.deananddeluca.com; 560 Broadway at Prince St; ⓈR/W to Prince St) New York City loves its luxury grocers and Dean & DeLuca is one of the biggest names around town; this reputation is well earned, as it boasts a seemingly infinite assortment of edibles from around the globe. Curious palates should make a beeline for the bakery.

RUBIROSA
PIZZERIA $$

Map p418 (www.rubirosanyc.com; 235 Mulberry St btwn Spring & Prince Sts; mains $12-25; ⊙11:30am-11pm Mon-Wed & Sun, 11:30am-midnight Thu-Sat; ⓈN/R to Prince St; B/D/F, M to Broadway-Lafayette St; 4/6 to Spring St) Rubirosa's infallible family recipe for the perfect, whisper-thin pie crust lures a steady stream of patrons from every corner of the city. Shovel slices from the bar stools or grab a table amid cozy surrounds and make room for savory apps and antipasti.

PEASANT
ITALIAN $$$

Map p418 (www.peasantnyc.com; 194 Elizabeth St btwn Spring & Prince Sts; mains $22-39; ⊙dinner; Ⓢ6 to Spring St) This homey house of gourmet comfort grub has a vibe of old-fashioned simplicity and quality. It has a warm dining area of bare oak tables around a brick hearth and an open kitchen, which lovingly turns out hearty, pan-Italian, mostly meat-based fare. Peasant has made it onto various best-restaurant lists in town, and always seems to be filled with a crowd of sophisticates who want in on solid stunners like gnocchi with wild mushrooms, grilled hen or octopus and thin-crusted pizzas – not to mention the winning bread and fresh ricotta that start off every meal.

SPRING STREET NATURAL
CAFE $$

Map p418 (www.springstreetnatural.com; 62 Spring St btwn Crosby & Lafayette Sts; mains $12-23; ⊙breakfast, lunch & dinner; ⚇; Ⓢ6 to Spring St) This cafe offers a selection of salads and entrées – from sashimi to risotto – that spans the continents. Many are aimed at the vegetarian set. A favorite of editors from nearby Scholastic, it's a good place to talk book biz over microbrews.

wobble atop the unceremonious scatter of slap-shut tables and chairs.

🍴 Chinatown & Little Italy

JOE'S SHANGHAI CHINESE $

Map p421 (www.joeshanghairestaurants.com; 9 Pell St btwn Bowery & Doyers St; mains $5-16; ⏰11am-11pm Mon-Sun; [S]J/Z, N/Q, 4/6 to Canal St; B/D to Grand St) Gather a gaggle of friends and descend upon Joe's en masse to spin the plastic lazy Susans and savor some of the best dumplings in town. A Flushing transplant, this Chinatown staple also tempts the budget-friendly palate with crispy beef, sticky pork buns and finger-licking shrimp platters.

MULBERRY PROJECT MODERN AMERICAN $$

Map p421 (www.mulberryproject.com; 149 Mulberry St btwn Hester & Grand Sts; mains $14-25; [S]J/Z, N/Q, 4/6 to Canal St; B/D to Grand St) An unmarked set of stairs – like those of a secreted Prohibition-era speakeasy – leads down to the doorway of the Mulberry Project, a veritable cocktail laboratory and the playground of the international owners and their coterie of server-friends. Lip-smacking beverages – the product of wisdom and whimsy in equal measure – are best enjoyed with the tasty assortment of small plates.

Come in summer when the courtyard out back fills with wafting DJed beats, curious graffiti art and a casual scatter of tables.

NICE GREEN BO CHINESE $

Map p421 (New Green Bow; ☎212-625-2359; 66 Bayard St btwn Elizabeth & Mott Sts; mains $4-10; [S]J/Z, N/Q, 4/6 to Canal St; B/D to Grand St) Not a shred of effort – not even a new sign (you'll see!) – has been made to spruce up Nice Green Bo, and that's the way we like it. It's all about the food here: gorgeous soup dumplings served in steaming drums, heaping portions of noodles, and savory pancakes.

PHO VIET HUONG VIETNAMESE, CHINESE $

Map p421 (www.phoviethuong.com; 73 Mulberry St btwn Bayard & Walker Sts; mains $6-14; ⏰11am-10:30pm; [S]J/Z, N/Q/R, 4/6 to Canal St) Shockingly inexpensive dishes is reason enough to visit; the delicious assortment of Vietnamese and Chinese selections will have you coming back for seconds. Slurp-worthy bowls of *pho* and dripping *bánh mì* (Vietnamese roast-pork sandwiches served on fat baguettes with piles of sliced cucumber, pickled carrots, hot sauce and cilantro)

BÁNH MÌ SAIGON BAKERY VIETNAMESE $

Map p421 (☎212-406-2292; 138 Mott St at Grand St; mains $4-6; ⏰10am-7pm Tue-Sun; [S]J/M/Z, N/Q/R/W, 6 to Canal St) This frequently mobbed, no-frills storefront doles out some of the best *bánh mì* in town. And none will cost you more than $5.

ORIGINAL CHINATOWN ICE CREAM FACTORY ICE CREAM $

Map p421 (www.chinatownicecreamfactory.com; 65 Bayard St; per scoop $4; ⏰11am-10pm; 👪; [S]J/M, N/Q/R/W, 6 to Canal St) Totally overshadowing the nearby Häagen-Dazs is this busy ice-cream shop, where you can savor scoops of green tea, ginger, passion fruit and lychee sorbet among dozens of flavors. The Factory also sells ridiculously cute, trademark yellow T-shirts with an ice cream-slurping happy dragon on them.

GREAT NEW YORK NOODLE TOWN CHINESE $

Map p421 (www.greatnynoodletown.com; 28 Bowery St at Bayard St; mains $4-13; ⏰9am-4am; [S]J/M/Z, N/Q/R/W, 6 to Canal St) The name of this Chinatown stalwart says it all: the specialties here are endless incarnations of the long and slippery strands, offered up through an easy-to-decipher picture menu. Among the long list of options are noodle soup with roast pork or duck, rice congee with frog or sliced fish, beef *chow fun*, spicy Singapore *mai fun*, wide Cantonese noodles with shrimp and egg or Hong Kong–style *lo main* with ginger and onions. What the no-frills spot lacks in ambience it makes up for in characters – especially once 2am or 3am rolls around.

🍷 DRINKING & NIGHTLIFE

PRAVDA COCKTAIL BAR

Map p418 (☎212-226-4944; 281 Lafayette St btwn Prince & Houston Sts; [S]B/D/F/V to Broadway-Lafayette St) This subterranean bar and brasserie lays on the Soviet-era nostalgia with heavy brushstrokes, from the Cyrillic lettering on the walls to the extensive vodka menu, including the caviar martini (vodka with dill, cucumber and a spoonful of you-know-what). Red leather banquettes and inviting armchairs provide a fine spot to enjoy blinis, handsomely made cocktails and a bit of eavesdropping on neighboring apparatchiks from the fashion or banking industry.

JIMMY BAR

Map p418 (www.jimmysoho.com; James Hotel, 15 Thompson St; [S]A/C/E, 1/2 to Canal St; A/C/E to Spring St) Lofted atop the James New York hotel in SoHo, Jimmy is a sky-high hangout with sweeping views of the city below. The summer months teem with tipsy patrons who spill out onto the open deck; in cooler weather drinks are slung indoors from the centrally anchored bar guarded by floor-to-ceiling windows.

APOTHEKE BAR BAR

Map p421 (www.apothekenyc.com; 9 Doyers St; 🕘6pm-2am Mon-Sat, 8pm-2am Sun; [S]J/M/Z to Canal St) It takes a little effort to track down this former opium-den-turned-apothecary bar located on Doyers St (known as the Bloody Triangle back when this was gang territory). Look for a Golden Flower sign. The sleek red interior, with marble bar and apothecary-type mortars, pestles and cylinders, gives the Apotheke Bar a cool vibe, enhanced when the owner passes around his homemade absinthe. The cocktails are intense and flavorful: try the Five Points (hibiscus, Italian bitters, grape juice and sugar-cane-infused rum) or the Saffron Sazerac (with saffron-infused bourbon).

RANDOLPH COCKTAIL BAR

Map p418 (www.randolphnyc.com; 349 Broome St btwn the Bowery & Elizabeth St; [S]J to Bowery) Brewing coffee by day, and swirling cocktails after dark (you can't go wrong with a 'Brambie'), Randolph has a Europe-meets-NYC vibe with a tin ceiling, knickknacks stacked on wobbly shelves and an extended happy hour that slashes prices around the clock.

MILADY'S BAR

Map p418 (☎212-226-9340; 160 Prince St btwn W Broadway & Thompson St; [S]A/C/E to Spring St; N/R to Prince St; 1/2 to Houston St) The last of the dive bars in SoHo where you can still score a brewski for under $5, MiLady's has all the ambience of the old neighborhood before high-end shops and sleek eats took over. The salads here are fresh, and you can't go wrong with the chicken wings and mac 'n' cheese – just avoid everything else.

SHOPPING

SoHo

Your swiping hand is going to get a lot of exercise during a visit to SoHo; there are many ways to swoosh your plastic, with hundreds of stores – big and small scattered along its streets. Broadway is one of the main corridors, and is lined with less-expensive chain stores. Hidden west along the tree-lined streets are pricier boutiques selling clothing, shoes, accessories and housewares. During the warmer months you'll also find street vendors hawking jewelry, art, T-shirts, hats and other crafts. Over on Lafayette, shops cater to the DJ and skate crowds with indie labels and vintage shops thrown into the mix.

If indie is your thing, continue east to Nolita, home of tiny jewel-box boutiques selling unique apparel, footwear, accessories and kitschy stuff at slightly lower prices than SoHo stores. Mott St is best for browsing, followed by Mulberry and Elizabeth.

HOUSING WORKS BOOK STORE BOOKS

Map p418 (www.housingworks.org/usedbookcafe; 126 Crosby St; 🕘10am-9pm Mon-Fri, noon-9pm Sat; [S]B/D/F/V to Broadway-Lafayette St) Relaxed, earthy and featuring a great selection of fabulous books you can buy for a good cause (proceeds go to the city's HIV-positive and AIDS homeless communities), this spacious cafe is a great place to while away a few quiet afternoon hours.

KIOSK HANDICRAFTS

Map p418 (www.kioskkiosk.com; 2nd fl, 95 Spring St btwn Mercer St & Broadway; 🕘noon-7pm Mon-Sat; [S]N/R to Prince St; B/D/F to Broadway-Lafayette St) 'Things from places' – the motto is as simple as that. Kiosk's owners scour the planet for the most interesting and unusual items, which they bring back to SoHo and proudly vend with museum-worthy acumen. Shopping adventures have brought back designer booty from the likes of Japan, Iceland, Sweden and Hong Kong.

MCNALLY JACKSON BOOKS, MAGAZINES

Map p418 (www.mcnallyjackson.com; 52 Prince St btwn Lafayette & Mulberry Sts; 🕘10am-10pm Mon-Sat, to 9pm Sun; [S]R/W to Prince St) This inviting indie bookshop stocks an excellent selection of magazines and books covering contemporary fiction, food writing, architecture and design, art and history. The cozy cafe is a fine spot to settle in with some reading material or to catch one of the frequent readings and book signings held here.

JACK SPADE
CLOTHING, ACCESSORIES

Map p418 (56 Greene St btwn Broome & Spring St; §N/R to Prince St; N/R to Canal St; 4/6 to Spring St) Menswear in rustic plaids along with a spectacular array of woven and leather satchels make this a must for the urban gentleman. Perfectly folded sweaters sit alongside a carefully curated selection of found objects, dog-eared paperbacks and vintage knickknacks undoubtedly found at the bottom of a cereal box in the '70s.

PURL SOHO
HANDICRAFTS

Map p418 (www.purlsoho.com/purl; 459 Broome St btwn Greene & Mercer Sts; §N/R to Canal St; N/R to Prince St; 4/6 to Spring St) The brainchild of a former *Martha Stewart Living* editor, Purl is a colorful library of fabric and yarn that feels like an in-person Etsy boutique, with inspiration for DIY crafts galore and a scatter of finished products that make unique stocking stuffers.

PEARL RIVER MART
BRIC-A-BRAC

Map p418 (www.pearlriver.com; 477 Broadway; ☉10am-7pm; §J/M/Z, N/Q/R/W, 6 to Canal St) An Asian emporium that stocks all sorts of knickknacks, Pearl River Mart's swanky storefront showcases bright kimonos, bejeweled slippers, Japanese teapots, paper lanterns, jars of mysterious spices, herbs, teas (and a Zen-like tea room) and more.

PRADA
FASHION, ACCESSORIES

Map p418 (☎212-334-8888; 575 Broadway; ☉11am-7pm Mon-Sat, noon-6pm Sun; §N/R/W to Prince St) Don't come just for the shoes: check out the space. Dutch architect Rem Koolhaas has transformed the old Guggenheim into a fantasy land full of elegant hardwood floors and small dressing spaces. Don't be afraid to try something on – those translucent changing-room doors do fog up when you step inside.

FLYING A
CLOTHING, ACCESSORIES

Map p418 (☎212-965-9090; 169 Spring St; ☉11am-7pm Mon-Thu, 11am-8pm Fri & Sat, noon-7pm Sun; §C/E to Spring St) Sporting a logo that bears a passing resemblance to those flying wings of Aerosmith, this Danish-owned store offers a little something for both rock-and-rollers and SoHo fashion mavens. You'll find vintage pieces (weathered cowboy boots, candy-colored '70s dresses, whisper-thin button-downs) as well as new apparel – jeans, graphic T-shirts and slim-fitting dresses. Books, watches, stylish air-tote bags, sunglasses and other accessories provide additional fun browsing.

JOHN VARVATOS
CLOTHING, SHOES

Map p418 (☎212-965-0700; 122 Spring St; ☉11am-7pm Mon-Sat, noon-6pm Sun; §R/W to Prince St) One of the city's most coveted menswear designers, John Varvatos creates a classic, timeless look – with a rock-and-roll soul – with his stylish and handsome-fitting sports coats, jeans, footwear and accessories. Head downstairs for JV's younger, edgier persona.

MOMA STORE
HOMEWARES, GIFTS

Map p418 (☎646-613-1367; 81 Spring St; ☉10am-8pm Mon-Sat, 11am-7pm Sun; §N/Q/R/W to Prince St) This sleek and stylish space carries a huge collection of handsomely designed objects for the home, office and wardrobe. You'll find modernist alarm clocks, wildly shaped vases, designer kitchenware and surreal lamps, plus brainy games, hand puppets, fanciful scarves, coffee-table books and lots of other great gift ideas.

JOE'S JEANS
CLOTHING

Map p418 (www.joesjeans.com; 77 Mercer St btwn Spring & Broome Sts; ☉11am-7pm Mon-Sat, noon-6pm Sun; §N/R to Prince St; N/R to Canal St; 4/6 to Spring St) The newest link in the elite Joe's Jeans chain firmly plants the name brand's flag in the heart of shop-happy SoHo. Clean lines and sparsely stacked racks of carefully curated denim give Joe's an effortlessly trendy vibe.

BOND 09
BEAUTY

Map p418 (www.bondno9.com; 9 Bond St; ☉11am-7pm Mon-Sat; §6 to Bleecker St) 'Making scents of New York' is the motto of this thoroughly unique perfume boutique, where the gimmick is everything NYC. Each bottle of home-brewed potion (prices begin at about $100) not only comes labeled with a trademark round label inspired by an old New York subway token, it gets filled with one of 20 fragrances that are named after and inspired by local nabes. Fragrances include Riverside Drive, Madison Soirée, Central Park, Nuits de Noho and Chinatown, none of which smells like wet pavement, exhaust fumes or simmering hot dogs. It also has a selection of body lotions, T-shirts and scented candles. Visit the website for Bond No 9's three other Manhattan locations.

UNIS CLOTHING

Map p418 (www.unisnewyork.com; 226 Elizabeth St; ⏲noon-7pm; [S]N/R/W to Prince St) Unis remains a Nolita favorite for its classic, rugged fashions for men – with clothing so comfortable you'll want to wear it right out of the store. You'll find slim, nicely cut pants, soft button-downs and well-made jackets, plus peacoats and lambswool scarves, come winter. Head here also for leather satchels, belts and journal covers.

YOUNG DESIGNERS MARKET ACCESSORIES, CLOTHING

Map p418 (☎212-580-8995; 268 Mulberry St; ⏲11am-7pm Sat & Sun; [S]B/D/F/V to Broadway-Lafayette St) This large colorful market takes over the gym of Old St Patrick's on weekends. As per the name, young and indie designers rule the roost, selling handmade jewelry, unique and witty T-shirts and one-of-a-kind stationery, plus dresses, hoodies and lots of other affordable items you won't find elsewhere.

DDC LAB CLOTHING

Map p418 (☎212-226-8980; 7 Mercer St; ⏲11am-7pm Mon-Sat, noon-6pm Sun; [S]N/Q/R/W, 6 to Canal St) A cool boutique for the latest flourishes of urban style, DDC Lab sells a range of nicely designed slim-fitting wares including sleek limited-edition sneakers, superbly comfortable T-shirts, leather jackets and peacoats as well as rubbery Nooka belts and other accessories. DDC Lab also sports a store in the **Meatpacking District** (Map p426; ☎212-414-5801; 427 W 14th St).

ELEVEN VINTAGE CLOTHING

Map p418 (☎212-334-5334; 15 Prince St; ⏲noon-8pm Mon-Sat, to 7pm Sun; [S]N/R/W to Prince St) Irish-owned Eleven may be small, but it contains a well-curated selection of vintage duds, particularly for men. Oversized leather mailbags, army knapsacks, jeans, leather jackets and softened leather cowboy boots – along with dresses and skirts for the gals – are among the regular finds at this inviting shop.

UNIQLO CLOTHING

Map p418 (☎917-237-8811; 546 Broadway; ⏲10am-9pm Mon-Sat, 11am-8pm Sun; [S]N/R/W to Prince St) The enormous three-story emporium owes its popularity to attractive apparel at discount prices. You'll find Japanese denim, Mongolian cashmere, graphic T-shirts, smart-looking skirts and endless racks of colorful ready-to-wear – with most things at the sub-$100 mark.

UNITED NUDE SHOES

Map p418 (www.unitednude.com; 268 Elizabeth St near Houston St; ⏲11am-7pm Mon-Sat, noon-8pm Sun; [S]N/R/W to Prince St) The flagship store is stocked with improbably beautiful and eye-catching footwear – flamboyant, classical, business-oriented or sporty. Whether you want strappy sandals, toweringly high stilettos or a solid pair of wedge-heeled pumps, you'll score here. The store has three basic groupings – Classics, Ultra Collection and Mono Series – and within those categories is a variety of shoe types.

OTHER MUSIC MUSIC

Map p418 (OM; www.othermusic.com; 15 E 4th St; ⏲noon-9pm Mon-Fri, to 8pm Sat, to 7pm Sun; [S]6 to Bleecker St) This indie-run CD store has created a loyal fan base with its informed selection of, well, other types of music: offbeat lounge, psychedelic, electronica, indie rock etc, available new and used. Friendly staffers like what they do, and may be able to help translate your inner musical whims and dreams to actual CD reality. OM also stocks a small but excellent selection of new and used vinyl.

ICE CREAM & THE BILLIONAIRE BOYS CLUB CLOTHING, SHOES

Map p418 (☎212-777-2225; 456 W Broadway; ⏲noon-7pm; [S]N/R/W to Prince St) Created by pop icon Pharell Williams and Japanese design guru Nigo, this slim little two-floor boutique stocks colorful, one-of-a-kind sneakers and imaginative T-shirts and outerwear. Head up the dark star-lit staircase at the back to check out the BBC part of the brand (more edgy sneakers and T-shirts) while talking a walk in outer space, courtesy of a moon print covering the floor.

MOSS HOMEWARES

Map p418 (☎212-204-7100; 146 Greene St; ⏲11am-7pm Mon-Sat, noon-6pm Sun; [S]N/R/W to Prince St) Converted from a gallery space, the two showrooms at Moss prop slick, modern and fun industrial designs behind glass, but they're definitely for sale. It's easy to find something that you'll just have to own – Boym's moving 'Buildings of Disaster' souvenirs, say, or a Van der Walls barrel-shaped world clock – and that you probably won't find at other places.

ATRIUM   FASHION, SHOES
Map p418 (☏212-473-3980; 644 Broadway at Bleecker St; ◷10am-9pm Mon-Sat, 11am-8pm Sun; ⓢB/D/F/V to Broadway-Lafayette St) Atrium has an excellent selection of funky designer-wear – including shoes and accessories – for both men and women, ranging from Diesel, G-Star and Miss Sixty to other popular labels. Best, though, is the grand range of high-end denim, from folks including Joe's, Seven, Blue Cult and True Religion.

ETIQUETA NEGRA   CLOTHING, SHOES
Map p418 (☏212-219-4015; 273 Lafayette St; ◷11am-7pm Mon-Sat, noon-7pm Sun; ⓢN/R/W to Prince St) The handsomely decorated two-floor boutique of the Argentine Etiqueta Negra exudes a timeless sense of style with its wood floors, black-and-white photos and fetching props such as the open-topped racecar parked near the cash register. Its designers aim to evoke much the same aesthetic in the men's wool suits, button-downs, soft polo jerseys and elegant leather boots. The women's collection is smaller, limited mostly to knits, denim and swimwear.

ODIN   CLOTHING, ACCESSORIES
Map p418 (☏212-966-0026; 199 Lafayette St; ◷11am-8pm Mon-Sat, noon-7pm Sun; ⓢ6 to Spring St) Named after the mighty Norse god, Odin offers a bit of magic for men seeking a new look. The large boutique carries stylish downtown labels like Phillip Lim, Band of Outsiders and Edward, and is a great place to browse for up-and-coming designers. Other eye candy at the minimalist store includes Comme des Garçons wallets, sleek sunglasses, Sharps grooming products and Taschen coffee-table books. Other branches are in the **East Village** (Map p422; ☏212-475-0666; www.odinnewyork.com; 328 E 11th St, East Village; ◷noon-9pm Mon-Sat, to 8pm Sun; ⓢL to First Ave; L, N/Q/R/W, 4/5/6 to 14th St-Union Sq) and the **West Village** (Map p426; ☏212-420-8446; 750 Greenwich St; ◷11am-8pm Mon-Sat, noon-7pm Sun; ⓢ1 to Christopher St-Sheridan Sq).

SCREAMING MIMI'S   VINTAGE CLOTHING
Map p418 (☏212-677-6464; 382 Lafayette St; ◷noon-8pm Mon-Sat, 1-7pm Sun; ⓢ6 to Bleecker St) A warm and colorful storefront that just begs to be entered; you'll find accessories and jewelry up front, and an excellent selection of clothing – organized, ingeniously, by decade, from the '50s to the '90s. It's all in great condition, from the prim, beaded wool cardigans to the suede minidresses and white leather go-go boots.

DAILY 235   TOYS
Map p418 (☏212-334-9728; 235 Elizabeth St; ◷noon-8pm Mon-Sat, to 7pm Sun; ⓢB/D/F/V to Broadway-Lafayette St) A fun little escape from the high-end boutiques of Nolita, Daily 235 lures in passersby with its quaint window displays of wind-up robots, cuddly creatures and old-fashioned toys. Inside, you'll find more curiosities, including unusual stationery, flip-books, glowing dog lamps, squishy frogs, lunch boxes, edible cigarettes (and other unusual candy – such as 'Frenching' gum) and more unique gifts.

RESURRECTION   VINTAGE CLOTHING
Map p418 (www.resurrectionvintage.com; 217 Mott St; ◷11am-7pm Mon-Sat, noon-7pm Sun; ⓢ6 to Spring St) A boudoir to the eye, Resurrection is a sleek and pricey red-walled boutique that gives new life to cutting-edge designs from past decades. Striking, mint-condition pieces cover the eras of mod, glam-rock and new-wave design, and well-known designers like Marc Jacobs have visited the shop for inspiration. Top picks include Gucci handbags, Halston dresses and Courrèges jackets.

SHAKESPEARE & CO   BOOKS
Map p418 (www.shakeandco.com; 716 Broadway; ◷10am-11pm Mon-Fri, noon-9pm Sat & Sun; ⓢN/R/W to 8th St; 6 to Astor Pl) This popular New York bookstore is one of the city's great indie options – with other locations, including the **Upper East Side** (Map p440; 939 Lexington Ave at 69th St; ◷9am-8pm Mon-Fri, 10am-7pm Sat, 11am-6pm Sun; ⓢ6 to 68th St). You'll find a wide array of contemporary fiction and nonfiction, art books and tomes about NYC, plus a small but unique collection of periodicals.

EVOLUTION   GIFTS
Map p418 (☏212-343-1114; 120 Spring St btwn Mercer & Greene Sts; ◷11am-7pm; ⓢR/W to Prince St) A great cabinet of curiosities, this

old-fashioned storefront sells natural-history collectibles of the sort usually seen in museums. This is the place to buy – or just gawk at – framed beetles and butterflies, bugs frozen in amber-resin cubes, stuffed parrots, zebra hides and shark teeth, as well as stony wonders, including meteorites, fragments from Mars and 100-million-year-old fossils.

ADIDAS ORIGINALS SHOES, CLOTHING

Map p418 (☎212-673-0398; 136 Wooster St; 🕙11am-7pm Mon-Sat, noon-6pm Sun; [S]R/W to Prince St) This ultrahip Adidas shop stocks a tempting selection of its iconic triple-striped sneakers plus sporty jackets, T-shirts and retro-looking gear. It's a tech- and music-savvy place, with DJs sometimes working the decks, and lawn chairs out front on hot summer days. You can also order custom-made sneakers. For the big-box retail experience, head to the 29,500-sq-ft **Adidas** (Map p418; ☎212-529-0081; 610 Broadway at Houston St; 🕙10am-8pm Mon-Sat, 11am-7pm Sun; [S]A/C/E to Spring St; N/R to Prince St; B/D/F to Broadway-Lafayette St) sneaker emporium a few blocks back.

ERICA TANOV CLOTHING, SHOES

Map p418 (☎212-334-8020; 204 Elizabeth St btwn Prince & Spring Sts; 🕙11am-7pm Mon-Sat, noon-6pm Sun; [S]6 to Spring St) This handsome, high-ceilinged boutique features Tanov's delicate feminine designs, such as hand-printed cotton tops, flirty dresses and delicate lingerie. In addition to Tanov's women's wear, you'll also find artistically crafted jewelry by other designers, handbags and kids' wear.

AMERICAN APPAREL CLOTHING

Map p418 (☎212-226-4880; www.americanapparel.net; 121 Spring St btwn Broadway & Mercer St; 🕙10am-8pm Mon-Thu, to 9pm Fri & Sat, 11am-8pm Sun; [S]R/W to Prince Street) Pick up American classics made with a conscience: no sweatshop labor goes into the making of these clothes. Everything is done with above-board in-house production. Sweats, hoodies, underwear and other apparel is available in a range of colors.

TOPSHOP FASHION

Map p418 (☎212-966-9555; www.topshopnyc.com; 478 Broadway at Broome St; 🕙10am-9pm Mon-Sat, 11am-8pm Sun; [S]6 to Spring St) The genius of Topshop is that the clothes always find that sweet spot between trendy and wearable. Everything's up-to-the-minute but still flattering and practical for the average person. Three floors for women, one for men, and all at fairly reasonable prices. Sales can get hectic: be prepared to dig for bargains.

Chinatown

Chinatown is a great place for wandering, particularly if you're in the market for some aromatic herbs, exotic Eastern fruits (like lychees and durians in season), fresh noodles or delicious bakery goodies. Canal St is the major thoroughfare, with lots of touristy merchandise and knock-off designer gear spilling onto the sidewalks. The backstreets are the real joy, however, with bubble-tea cafes, perfumeries, video arcades, plant shops and fishmongers all hawking their wares.

BUILT BY WENDY CLOTHING

Map p421 (☎212-925-6538; 7 Centre Market Pl; 🕙noon-7pm Mon-Sat, to 6pm Sun; [S]6 to Spring St) Hidden out of reach from the SoHo masses, Built by Wendy is a cozy boutique where sweaters, dresses and men's and women's denim sport a classic, flattering cut with interesting details. You can also pick up owner-designer Wendy Mullin's clever sewing book called *Sew U* or one of her ultrasuede guitar straps. A second branch is in **Williamsburg** (Map p446; ☎718-384-2882; 46 N 6th St; [S]L to Bedford Ave).

AJI ICHIBAN FOOD & DRINK

Map p421 (☎212-233-7650; 37 Mott St btwn Bayard & Mosco Sts; 🕙10am-8:30pm; [S]J/M/Z, N/Q/R/W, 6 to Canal St) This Hong Kong–based chain, the name of which means 'awesome' in Japanese, is a ubiquitous sight in Chinatown, as this is just one of five locations here. And though it is a candy shop, get ready for something a bit more exciting than malted balls and peppermint sticks. Here's where you'll find sesame-flavored marshmallows, Thai durian milk candy, preserved plums, mandarin peel, blackcurrant gummies and dried guava, as well as savory snacks like crispy spicy cod fish, crab chips, wasabi peas and dried anchovies with peanuts.

KAM MAN HOMEWARES

Map p421 (☎212-571-0330; 200 Canal St btwn Mulberry & Motts Sts; 🕙9am-9pm; [S]J/M/Z, N/Q/R/W, 6 to Canal St) Head past hanging ducks to the basement of this classic Canal St food store for cheap Chinese and Japanese tea sets, plus kitchen products such as chopsticks, stir-frying utensils and rice cookers.

OPENING CEREMONY FASHION

Map p418 (☎212-219-2688; 35 Howard St btwn Broadway & Lafayette St; 🕒11am-8pm Mon-Sat, noon-7pm Sun; [S]N/Q/R/W, 6 to Canal St) Just off the beaten SoHo path, Opening Ceremony is a favorite among fashion insiders for its unique collection of indie labels. Owners Carol Lim and Humberto Leon showcase a changing roster of labels from across the globe – though the look is always avant-garde, even if the prices are decidedly uptown.

DE VERA ANTIQUES

Map p418 (☎212-625-0838; 1 Crosby St btwn Grand & Howard Sts; 🕒11am-7pm Tue-Sat; [S]N/Q/R/W, 6 to Canal St) Federico de Vera travels the globe in search of rare and exquisite jewelry, carvings, lacquerware and other *objets d'art* for this jewel-box of a store. Illuminated glass cases display works like 200-year-old Buddhas, Venetian glassware and gilded inlaid boxes from the Meiji period, while tapestries and carvings along the walls complete the museumlike experience.

BABELAND EROTICA

Map p418 (☎212-966-2120; www.babeland.com; 43 Mercer St btwn Grand & Broome Sts; 🕒11am-10pm Mon-Sat, to 7pm Sun; [S]A/C/E to Canal St) This women-owned sex shop is the queen bee of sex toys, aflutter with open and supportive staffers who will gladly talk you through the chore of picking out the very best silicone dildo or butt plug, matching it with an appropriate leather harness and inspiring you to toss in a quality vibrator while you're at it. But it's also much more: it's a purveyor of sex-related books, magazines, adult DVDs, flavored lube and Babeland tees, and an educator, with a constant roster of how-to lectures, for all genders, from the knowledgeable staff. The original, but smaller, shop is on the **Lower East Side** (Map p424; ☎212-375-1701; 94 Rivington St; 🕒noon-10pm Sun-Wed, to 11pm Thu-Sat; [S]F, J/M/Z to Delancey St-Essex St).

DAFFY'S FASHION, ACCESSORIES

Map p418 (www.daffys.com; 462 Broadway at Grand St; 🕒10am-8pm Mon-Sat, noon-7pm Sun; [S]A/C/E to Canal St) Two floors of designer duds and accessories for men, women and children (as well as a random handful of homewares), with prices that can be blissfully low. And the tags – like those at most discount shops – show you the item's suggested retail price on top of Daffy's price, which, at an average of 50% off, just gives you more incentive to buy.

SCOOP FASHION

Map p418 (☎212-925-3539; 473 Broadway btwn Broome & Grand Sts; 🕒11am-8pm Mon-Sat, to 7pm Sun; [S]N/Q/R/W to Canal St) Scoop is a great one-stop destination for unearthing top contemporary fashion by Theory, Stella McCartney, Marc Jacobs, James Perse and many others. While there's nothing particularly edgy about the selections, there's a lot on offer (over 100 designers covering men's, women's and children's), and you can often score deals at season-end sales. Scoop has several stores in the city.

SPORTS & ACTIVITIES

GREAT JONES SPA DAY SPA

Map p418 (☎212-505-3185; www.greatjonesspa.com; 29 Great Jones St; 🕒4-10pm Mon, 9am-10pm Tue-Sun; [S]B/D/F/V to Broadway-Lafayette St; 6 to Bleecker St) Don't skimp on the services at this newish downtown spa designed with feng shui principles in mind, complete with three-story indoor waterfall. If you spend over $100 (not hard: hour-long massages or facials start at $130), you get free time in the water lounge's hot tub, rock sauna, chakra-light steam room and cold pool.

BUNYA CITISPA DAY SPA

Map p418 (☎212-388-1288; www.bunyacitispa.com; 474 W Broadway btwn Prince & W Housten Sts; 🕒10am-9pm Mon-Sat, to 7pm Sun; [S]N/R/W to Prince St; C/E to Spring St) This chic, Asian-style spa has taken over SoHo's spa front. Ex-models and shopping-bag toters subject aches and pains to the poking palms and thumbs of the popular 'Oriental herbal compress' massages (one houe, $120).

SCOTT'S PIZZA TOURS CULINARY TOUR

(www.scottspizzatours.com; tours from $35) Scott, pizza nerd extraordinaire, turns pizza delivery on its head by 'delivering the people to pizza' instead. Tours take in different swathes of the city, but always with the same goal in mind: scouting out the best slices in town.

East Village & Lower East Side

Neighborhood Top Five

1 Admiring the facade then wandering in to appreciate mind-bending iterations of art at the **New Museum of Contemporary Art** (p103).

2 Witnessing the shockingly cramped conditions of early immigrants at the brilliantly curated **Lower East Side Tenement Museum** (p102).

3 Passing knickknack shops and sake bars on **St Marks Place** (p105), then heading to the neighboring streets for a quieter round of nibbling and boutique-ing.

4 Pub-crawling through the East Village, stopping at **Terroir** (p115) and **McSorley's Old Ale House** (p115) along the way.

5 Sampling some of the finest flavors from around the world at restaurants scattered across the neighborhoods, starting with **Cafe Orlin** (p111).

For more detail of this area, see Maps p422 and p424 ➡

Explore the East Village & Lower East Side

If you've been dreaming of those quintessential New York City moments – graffiti on crimson brick, skyscrapers rising overhead, punks and grannies walking side by side, and cute cafes with rickety tables spilling out onto the sidewalks – then the East Village is your Holy Grail. Stick to the area around Tompkins Square Park, and the lettered avenues (known as Alphabet City) to its east, for interesting little nooks in which to imbibe and ingest – as well as a collection of great little community gardens (p107) that provide leafy respites and sometimes even live performances. The streets below 14th St and east of First Ave are packed with cool boutiques and excellent snack-food spots, offering styles and flavors from around the world. It's a mixed bag, indeed, and perhaps one of the most emblematic of today's city.

South of Houston on the Lower East Side, it's worth swinging by the Lower East Side Visitors Center (54 Orchard St) to orient yourself before willfully getting lost in the tangle of eclectic streets.

Local Life

➡ **One block over** Everyone knows that St Marks Place is the big cheese – chockablock with history and boutiques that overflow into the streets. And, as such, you'll find swarms of people shopping and carousing, so hop a block over in either direction for some great retail and restaurant finds with half the crowds.

➡ **Taste the rainbow** The East Village and the Lower East Side (LES) are like no other place in the city when it comes to sampling the finest spread of ethnic cuisine. Many of the area's restaurants don't take reservations, so have a wander and grab an open table to eat-pray-love your way through Italy, India, Indonesia or anywhere in between.

Getting There & Away

➡ **Subway** Trains don't go far enough east to carry you to most East Village locations, but it's a quick walk (and even quicker cab or bus ride) from the 6 at Astor Pl, the F, V at Lower East Side-2nd Ave or the L at First or Third Aves. The subway's F line (Lower East Side-2nd Ave or Delancey St stops) will let you off in the thick of the Lower East Side.

➡ **Bus** If you're traveling from the west side, it's better to take the M14 rather than the subway (L), as the bus will take you further into the East Village, making a southern turn along Aves A, B or C (depending on how the bus is marked).

Lonely Planet's Top Tip

A lot of the restaurants in this neck of the woods don't take reservations, so stop by the restaurant of your choosing in the early afternoon (2pm should do the trick) and place your name on the roster for the evening meal – chances are high that they'll take your name and you'll get seated right away when you return for dinner later on.

✖ Best Places to Eat

➡ Cafe Orlin (p111)
➡ Cocoron (p114)
➡ Westville East (p111)
➡ Katz's Delicatessen (p114)

For reviews, see p111 ➡

◉ Best Places to Drink

➡ Terroir (p115)
➡ Death + Co (p115)
➡ Angel's Share (p118)
➡ McSorley's Old Ale House (p115)
➡ Eastern Bloc (p118)

For reviews, see p115 ➡

🛍 Best Places to Shop

➡ Trash & Vaudeville (p122)
➡ Edith Machinist (p125)
➡ Amé Amé (p122)

For reviews, see p122 ➡

TOP SIGHTS
LOWER EAST SIDE TENEMENT MUSEUM

There's no museum in New York that humanizes the city's colorful past quite like the Lower East Side Tenement Museum, which puts the neighborhood's heartbreaking but inspiring heritage on full display in several re-creations of turn-of-the-20th-century tenements, including the late-19th-century home and garment shop of the Levine family from Poland, and two immigrant dwellings from the Great Depressions of 1873 and 1929. Always evolving and expanding, the museum has a variety of tours and talks beyond the museum's walls as well – a must for any curious visitor interested in old New York.

DON'T MISS...

- Themed walk around the neighborhood, either architecture, culture or food
- An American Story film screened in the visitors center
- Tenement Talks
- The bookshop
- The outhouse

PRACTICALITIES

- Map p424
- ☎212-431-0233
- www.tenement.org
- 108 Orchard St btwn Broome & Delancey Sts
- admission $22
- 🕑10am-6pm
- [S]B/D to Grand St; J/M/Z to Essex St; F to Delancey St

103 Orchard St

At the end of 2011, the museum unveiled its sparkling new visitor center and interpretive space housed at 103 Orchard St. The recent expansion has allowed for the addition of gallery space, an enlarged museum shop, a screening room that plays an original film and plenty of seminar space. The building itself was, naturally, a tenement too – ask the staff about the interesting families of Jewish and Italian descent that once dwelled here, or check out www.tenement.org/103-Orchard.html for black-and-white portraits of the former residents.

An American Life

The main portion of your visit is the tenement tour, during which you'll have the opportunity to interact with a guide, but don't forget to check out the one-of-a-kind film in the visitor center that details the difficult life endured by the people who once lived in the surrounding buildings. You'll become very aware of the squalid conditions most tenants faced: no electricity, no running water, and a wretched, communal outhouse.

Tenement Talks

Beyond the tours and displays, it is well worth stopping by the museum in the evenings when – at least twice a week – the staff hosts 'Tenement Talks.' This is a lecture and discussion series where a colorful cast of characters from historians through to anthropologists are invited to lead small seminars on a variety of wide-reaching topics about the city and its people. Not just about tenements, the soirees can be of interest even if the contents of the museum's permanent collection aren't.

Shop Life

The Tenement Museum's new permanent exhibit, which opened in the fall of 2012, is entitled 'Shop Life,' and is meant the shed some light on merchant life along Orchard St from 1863 all the way up to the 1970s.

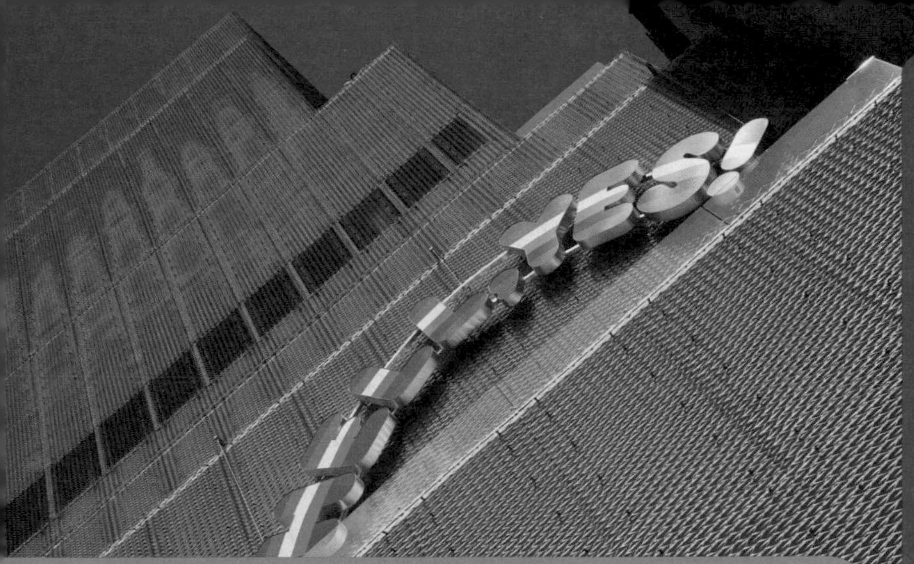

AA WORLD TRAVEL LIBRARY / ALAMY ©

TOP SIGHTS
NEW MUSEUM OF CONTEMPORARY ART

Like any modern-day museum worth its salt, its structure has to be as much of a statement as the artwork inside. The New Museum of Contemporary Art's Lower East Side avatar accomplishes just that and more with its inspired design by noted Japanese architecture firm SANAA. The Lower East Side has seen its fair share of physical changes over the last decade as the sweeping hand of gentrification has cleaned up slummy nooks and replaced them with glittering residential blocks. The New Museum manages to punctuate the neighborhood with something truly unique, and its cache of artistic work will dazzle and confuse just as much as its facade.

A Museum with a Mission

Founded in 1977 by Marcia Tucker and moved to five different locations over the years, the museum's mission statement is simple: 'New art, new ideas.' The institution has given gallery space to artists Keith Haring, Jeff Koons, Joan Jonas, Mary Kelly and Andres Serrano – all at the beginning of their careers – and continues to show contemporary heavy hitters. The city's sole museum dedicated to contemporary art has brought a steady menu of edgy works in new forms, such as seemingly random, discarded materials fused together and displayed in the middle of a vast room.

The museum also houses a small and healthy cafe, and has the added treat of a city-viewing platform, which provides a unique perspective on the constantly changing architectural landscape.

DON'T MISS...

- The facade from across the street
- Free Thursday evenings
- Birdbath cafe, created by City Bakery
- The New Museum Store

PRACTICALITIES

- Map p424
- ☎212-219-1222
- www.newmuseum.org
- 235 Bowery btwn Prince & Rivington Sts
- adult/child $14/free, 7pm-9pm Thu free
- 🕐11am-6pm Wed & Fri-Sun, to 9pm Thu
- [S]N/R to Prince St; F to 2nd Ave; J/Z to Bowery; 6 to Spring St

NEW MUSEUM SHOP

If you aren't so keen on the current exhibits, it's still worth stopping by the museum's store to peruse some of the greatest coffee table books – sometimes the take-homes include savvy collaborations with showcased artists. The shop has the same hours of operation as the museum.

Stop by on Thursday evenings between 7pm and 9pm to check out the latest rotating exhibits for free – saving yourself the $14 admission fee. We recommend lining up around 6.45pm.

In Orbit

It's now been several years since the New Museum has taken hold, inspiring nearby structures to adopt similarly ethereal designs. Perhaps most interestingly the museum has become somewhat of a magnetic force, keeping a clutch of small workshops and creative spaces in its orbit.

Though Chelsea may be the big shot when it comes to the New York gallery scene, the Lower East Side has its very own collection of about a dozen quality showplaces. Check out **Participant Inc** (Map p424; www.participantinc.org; 253 E Houston St btwn Norfolk & Suffolk Sts; S F to Lower East Side-2nd Ave), which showcases emerging talent and hosts varied performances. It was one of the places hailed as a LES gallery pioneer when it opened several years back. The **Sperone Westwater** (Map p424; www.speronewestwater.com; 257 Bowery; S F to Lower East Side-2nd Ave) gallery represents heavy hitters like William Wegman and Richard Long, and its new home was designed by the famed Norman Foster, who's already made a splash in NYC with his Hearst Building and Avery Fisher Hall designs.

Other popular, contemporary spaces include **Gallery Onetwentyeight** (Map p424; www.onetwentyeight.com; 128 Rivington St; ⊘ call for appt; S F to Lower East Side-2nd Ave), **Reena Spaulings Fine Art** (Map p424; www.reenaspaulings.com; 165 E Broadway), **Lehmann Maupin** (Map p424; ☎ 212-254-0054; www.lehmannmaupin.com; 201 Chrystie St; S F to Delancey-Essex Sts) and Angel Orensanz Foundation (p109).

SANAA's Vision

While exhibits rotate through the museum, regularly changing the character of the space within, the shell – an inspired architectural gesture – remains a constant, acting as a unique structural element in the diverse cityscape, while simultaneously fading into the background and allowing the exhibits to shine.

The building's structure is the brainchild of the hot Japanese firm SANAA – a partnership between two great minds, Sejima Kazuyo and Nishizawa Ryue. In 2010 SANAA won the much-coveted Pritzker Prize for its contributions to the world of design (think the Oscars of architecture). Its trademark vanishing facades are known worldwide for abiding by a strict adherence to a form-follows-function design aesthetic, sometimes taking the land plot's footprint into the overall shape of the structure. The box-atop-box scheme provides a striking counterpoint to the clusters of crimson brick and iron fire escapes outside, while alluding to the geometric exhibition chasms within.

WENDY CONNETT / ALAMY ©

TOP SIGHTS
ST MARKS PLACE

One of the most magical things about New York is that every street tells a story, from the action unfurling before your eyes to the dense history hidden behind colorful facades. St Marks Place is one of the best strips of pavement in the city for storytelling, as almost every building on these hallowed blocks is rife with tales from a time when the East Village embodied a far more lawless spirit.

Technically, St Marks Place is 8th St between Third Ave and Ave A; it earned its saintly moniker from the like-named church nearby on 10th St.

Astor Place

St Marks Place begins on the east side of Astor Place – a crowded crisscrossing of streets anchored by a curious square sculpture that's affectionately (and appropriately) known by locals as *The Cube*. A favorite meeting spot for neighborhood dwellers, this work of art – actually named *Alamo* – weighs over 1800 pounds and is made entirely of Cor-Tensteel.

Originally Astor Place was the home of the Astor Opera House (now gone), which attracted the city's wealthy elite for regular performances in the mid-1800s. The square was also the site of the notorious Astor Place riots, in which the city's protesting Irish population caused such a stir about their homeland potato famine that the police fired shots into the masses, injuring hundreds and killing at least 18 people.

Today, the square is largely known as the home of the *Village Voice* and the Cooper Union design institute. For more about the west side of Astor Place, see p135.

DON'T MISS...

➡ The *Physical Graffiti* buildings made famous by Led Zeppelin (numbers 96 and 98)

➡ Brunch at one of the tasty cafes

➡ Tompkins Square Park at the end of the street

➡ Sake bombs at one of the basement Japanese bars

➡ Shopping for knickknacks and odd souvenirs

PRACTICALITIES

➡ St Marks Pl, Ave A to Third Ave

➡ S N/R/W to 8th St-NYU; 6 to Astor Pl

EATING ON ST MARKS

In addition to all of its quirky and historical landmarks, St Marks has some wonderful places to stop for a bite. Weekend brunches in the East Village are a great bet, as the local restaurants are typically less expensive (and less scene-y) than the hotspots in neighboring 'hoods. Try Cafe Orlin (p111) and Yaffa (p113) – both fuse American favorites with an assortment of Middle Eastern plates.

The East Village was once the home base for emerging punk rock acts – many would frequent the clothing shops along St Marks to assemble their trademark looks. Although most joints have gone the way of the dodo in favor of more tourist-friendly wares, there are still a few spots that remain, like Trash & Vaudeville (p122).

Third Ave to Ave A

Easily one of NYC's most famous streets, St Marks Place is also one of the city's smallest, occupying only three blocks between Astor Pl and Tompkins Square Park. The road, however, is jam-packed with historical tidbits that would delight any trivia buff. Some of the most important addresses include numbers 2, 4, 96 and 98, and 122 St Marks Place. Number 2 St Marks Place is known as the **St Mark's Ale House**, but for a time it was the famous Five-Spot, where jazz fiend Thelonious Monk got his start in the 1950s. A cast of colorful characters have left their mark at 4 St Marks Place: Alexander Hamilton's son built the structure, James Fenimore Cooper lived here in the 1830s and Yoko Ono's Fluxus artists descended upon the building in the 1960s. The buildings at 96 and 98 St Marks Place are immortalized on the cover of Led Zeppelin's *Physical Graffiti* album. Though it closed in the 1990s, number 122 St Marks Place was the location of a popular cafe called Sin-é, where Jeff Buckley and David Gray often performed.

Tompkins Square Park

St Marks Place terminates at a welcome clearing of green deep in the heart of the East Village. The 10.5-acre Tompkins Square Park honors Daniel Tompkins, who served as governor of New York from 1807 to 1817 (and as the nation's vice president after that, under James Monroe). It's like a friendly town square for locals, who gather for chess at concrete tables, picnics on the lawn on warm days and spontaneous guitar or drum jams on various grassy knolls. It's also the site of basketball courts, a fun-to-watch dog run (a fenced-in area where humans can unleash their canines), frequent summer concerts and an always-lively kids' playground.

The park, which recently underwent a facelift, wasn't always a place for such clean fun, however. In the '80s, it was a dirty, needle-strewn homeless encampment, unusable for folks wanting a place to stroll or picnic. A contentious turning point came when police razed the band shell and evicted more than 100 squatters living in a tent city in the park in 1988 (and again in 1991). That first eviction turned violent; the Tompkins Square Riot, as it came to be known, ushered in the first wave of yuppies in the dog run, fashionistas lolling in the grass and undercover narcotics agents trying to pass as druggie punk kids. There's not much drama here these days, unless you count the annual Howl! Festival of East Village Arts, which brings Allen Ginsberg-inspired theater, music, film, dance and spoken-word events to the park each September.

TOP SIGHTS
ST MARKS PLACE

SIGHTS

East Village

ST MARKS PLACE STREET
See p105.

TOMPKINS SQUARE PARK OUTDOORS
See p106.

ST MARK'S IN THE BOWERY CHURCH
Map p422 (www.stmarksbowery.org; 131 E 10th St at Second Ave; ⏲10am-6pm Mon-Fri; [S]L to Third Ave; 6 to Astor Pl) Though it's most popular with East Village locals for its cultural offerings – such as poetry readings hosted by the Poetry Project or cutting-edge dance performances from Danspace and the Ontological Hysteric Theater – this is also a historic site. This Episcopal church stands on the site of the farm, or bouwerie, owned by Dutch Governor Peter Stuyvesant, whose crypt lies under the grounds.

The 1799 church, damaged by fire in 1978, has been restored, and you can enjoy an interior view of its abstract stained-glass windows during opening hours.

UKRAINIAN MUSEUM MUSEUM
Map p422 (www.ukrainianmuseum.org; 222 E 6th St btwn Second & Third Aves; adult/child $8/free; ⏲11:30am-5pm Wed-Sun; [S]F/V to Lower East Side-2nd Ave; L to 1st Ave) Ukrainians have a long history and still a strong presence here, hence the existence of several (though rapidly disappearing) *pierogi* (dumplings) joints – including the famous **Odessa** (Map p422; ☎212-253-1482; 119 Ave A btwn 7th St & St Marks Pl) and Veselka (p113) – and this interesting museum. Its collection of folk art includes richly woven textiles, ceramics, metalwork and traditional Ukrainian Easter eggs, as well as research tools for visitors to trace their own Ukrainian roots.

Diverse courses in craftwork, from embroidery to bead stringing, are also offered, as are rotating folk-art exhibits and educational lectures. This sleek and expansive museum is only a few years old.

Lower East Side

LOWER EAST SIDE TENEMENT MUSEUM MUSEUM
See p102.

NEW MUSEUM OF CONTEMPORARY ART GALLERY
See p103.

ELDRIDGE STREET SYNAGOGUE JEWISH
Map p424 (www.eldridgestreet.org; 12 Eldridge St btwn Canal & Division Sts; donations suggested;

COMMUNITY GARDENS

After a stretch of arboreal abstinence in New York City, the community gardens of Alphabet City are breathtaking. A network of gardens was carved out of abandoned lots to provide low-income neighborhoods with a communal backyard. Trees and flowers were planted, sandboxes built, found-art sculptures erected and domino games played – all within green spaces wedged between buildings or even claiming entire blocks. And while some were destroyed – in the face of much protest – to make way for the projects of developers, plenty of green spots have held their ground. You can visit most on weekends, when the gardens tend to be open to the public; many gardeners are activists within the community and are a good source of information about local politics.

Le Petit Versailles (Map p422; www.alliedproductions.org; 346 E Houston St at Ave C) is a unique marriage of a verdant oasis and an electrifying arts organization, offering a range of quirky performances and screenings to the public. The **6th & B Garden** (Map p422; www.6bgarden.org; E 6th St & Ave B; ⏲1pm-6pm Sat & Sun; 6 to Astor Pl) is a well-organized space that hosts free music events, workshops and yoga sessions; check the website for details. Three dramatic weeping willows, an odd sight in the city, grace the twin plots of 9th St Garden and **La Plaza Cultural** (Map p422; www.laplazacultural.org; E 9th St at Ave C). Also check out the **All People's Garden** (Map p422; E 3rd St btwn Aves B & C) and **Brisas del Caribe** (Map p422; 237 E 3rd St), easily located thanks to its surrounding white-picket fence.

E 10th St

Third Ave

Tompkins
Square Park

7
END

Astor Pl
E 8th St

St Marks Pl

4

6

EAST VILLAGE

Astor Pl

3

Fourth Ave

Cooper
Square

5

E 6th St

Lafayette St

Second Ave

First Ave

Ave A

**ALPHABET
CITY**

E 4th St

NOHO

Bowery St

E 2nd St

**LOWER
EAST SIDE**

Bond St

2
START **1**

Bleecker St
Bleecker St

EAST VILLAGE & LOWER EAST SIDE NEIGHBORHOOD WALK

Neighborhood Walk
East Village Nostalgia

From the Bleecker St subway station, head east along the leafy like-named street for a few blocks until you reach the former **1** **CBGB** (315 Bowery), a famous music venue that opened in 1973 and launched punk rock via the Ramones. Today, it's a John Varvatos boutique selling rock-inspired leather jackets – the old walls of fading posters and wild graffiti remain untouched. The corner just north of here marks the block-long **2** **Joey Ramone Place**, named after the Ramones' singer who succumbed to cancer in 2001.

Head north on Bowery to Astor Pl. Turn right and head east through the square to come to **3** **Cooper Union**, where in 1860 presidential hopeful Abraham Lincoln rocked a skeptical New York crowd with a rousing antislavery speech that ensured his candidacy.

Continue east on St Marks Pl, a block full of tattoo parlors and cheap eateries that haven't changed much at all since the 1980s. Poke your head into **4** **Trash &**

Vaudeville, a landmark goth-and-punk shop.

Head south down Second Ave to the site of the long-defunct **5** **Fillmore East** (105 Second Ave), a 2000-seat live-music venue run by promoter Bill Graham from 1968 to 1971. In the '80s the space was transformed into the Saint – the legendary, 5000-sq-ft dance club that kicked off a joyous, drug-laden, gay disco culture.

Cross Second Ave at 6th St and head down the block-long strip of Indian restaurants and curry shops. At First Ave, turn left, rejoin St Marks Pl and turn right. The row of tenements is the site of Led Zeppelin's **6** **Physical Graffiti cover** (96-98 St Marks Pl), where Mick and Keith sat in 1981 in the Stones' hilarious video for 'Waiting on a Friend.' End your stroll at the infamous **7** **Tompkins Square Park**, where drag queens started the Wigstock summer festival at the bandshell where Jimi Hendrix played in the 1960s.

⊙10am-5pm Sun-Thu; S F to East Broadway) This landmarked house of worship, built in 1887, was once the center of Jewish life, before falling into squalor in the 1920s. Left to rot, it's only recently been reclaimed, and now shines with original splendor. Its on-site museum gives **tours** ($10; ⊙10am to 5pm) every half-hour, with the last one departing at 4pm.

ESSEX STREET MARKET   MARKET

Map p424 (www.essexstreetmarket.com; 120 Essex St btwn Delancey & Rivington Sts; ⊙8am-7pm Mon-Sat; S F to Delancey St, J/M/Z to Essex St) This 60-year-old historic shopping destination is the local place for produce, seafood, butcher-cut meats, cheeses, Latino grocery items, and even a barber's shop and small art gallery. Though the legendary local stall of Schapiro's kosher wine disappeared with the 2007 death of the company founder, now newer spots, like Formaggio Essex, with a grand display of artisanal cheeses, or Roni-Sue's Chocolates, are attracting a new-generation clientele who want to shop in an old-school environment.

ORCHARD STREET
BARGAIN DISTRICT   NEIGHBORHOOD

Map p424 (Orchard; Ludlow & Essex Sts btwn Houston & Delancey Sts; ⊙Sun-Fri; S F, J/M/Z to Delancey-Essex Sts) Back in the day, this large intersection was a free-for-all, as Eastern European and Jewish merchants sold anything that could command a buck from their pushcarts. The 300-plus shops you see now aren't as picturesque, but it's a good place to pick up some cheap shirts, tees and jeans. If you like to haggle, take a shot at bargaining over the price.

KEHILA KEDOSHA JANINA
SYNAGOGUE & MUSEUM   JEWISH

Map p424 (www.kkjsm.org; 280 Broome St at Allen St; ⊙11am-4pm Sun, worship service 9am Sat; S F, J/M/Z to Delancey-Essex Sts) This small synagogue is home to an obscure branch of Judaism, the Romaniotes, whose ancestors were slaves sent to Rome by ship but rerouted to Greece by a storm. This is their only synagogue in the Western Hemisphere, and includes a small museum bearing artifacts like handpainted birth certificates, an art gallery, a Holocaust memorial for Greek Jews and costumes from Janina, the Romaniote capital of Greece. An upcoming renovation has plans for a Greek cafe, too.

EAST RIVER PARK   PARK

Map p422 (FDR & E Houston; S F to Delancey-Essex Sts) In addition to the great ballparks, running and biking paths, 5000-seat amphitheater for concerts and expansive patches of green, this park has got cool, natural breezes and stunning views of the Williamsburg, Manhattan and Brooklyn

EAST VILLAGE & LOWER EAST SIDE SIGHTS

ART INVASION

Creativity is no stranger to the Lower East Side (LES). Long before uptown galleries started arriving, the LES was home to artists, musicians, writers and painters who often shared space and resources in order to do their work. Many of those collectives are still around today, and are open to the public for browsing.

ABC No Rio (Map p424; ☑212-254-3697; www.abcnorio.org; 156 Rivington St; admission varies; ⊙hrs vary; S F, J/M/Z to Delancey-Essex Sts) Founded in 1980, this internationally known art and activism center features weekly hard-core/punk and experimental music shows, as well as regular fine-arts exhibits, poetry readings and more.

Angel Orensanz Foundation (Map p424; ☑212-529-7194; www.orensanz.org; 172 Norfolk St; admission varies; S F to Delancey-Essex Sts) Inside one of the oldest synagogues in the city, this artist-run foundation hosts art and photography exhibits and various live-music events.

Artists Alliance (Map p424; ☑212-420-9202; www.aai-nyc.org; 107 Suffolk St; admission varies; ⊙hrs vary; S F, J/M/Z to Delancey-Essex Sts) A nonprofit artists' collective with more than 40 members, Artists Alliance has a rotating list of exhibits and contributors on its website.

Clemente Soto Velez (p122) Inside the Artists Alliance building, this collective focuses on the work of Puerto Rican poet Velez, but also brings in theater, music, art and film from artists across the world.

START **NEW MUSEUM OF CONTEMPORARY ART**

END **KEHILA KEDOSHA JANINA SYNAGOGUE**

DISTANCE **2 MILES**

TIME **2 HOURS**

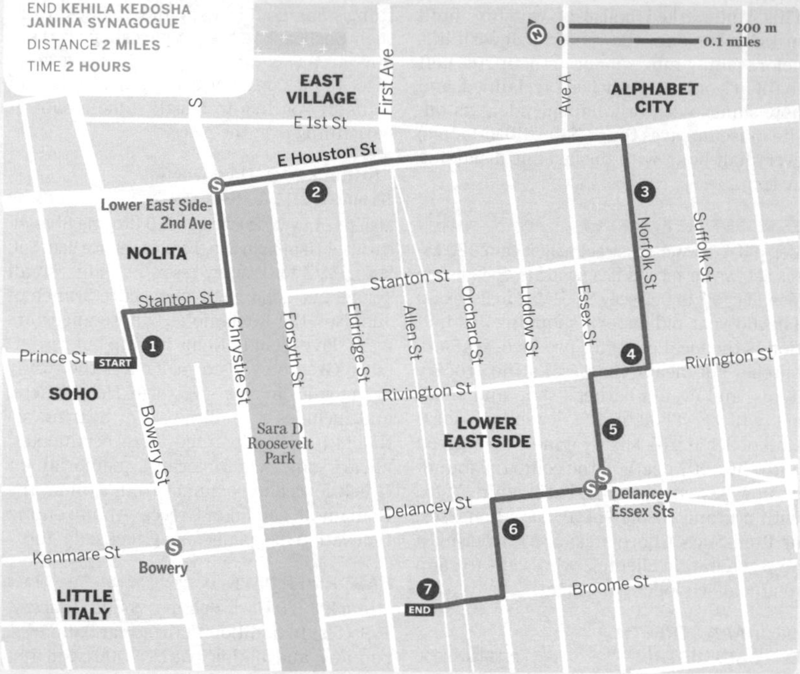

Neighborhood Walk

Art & Religion on the Lower East Side

Kick off by seeing one of its most buzzed-about attractions: the 1 **New Museum of Contemporary Art**, a stunning work of architecture that towers above the gritty Bowery.

Follow Chrystie St north to Houston St, then make a right. Just past Forsyth St, on your right, you'll see the 2 **Landmark Sunshine Cinema**, which was shuttered for 70 years before being reopened in its current form as an indie-movie cinema. In its heyday it was a Yiddish theater and a boxing venue, and was originally built as a Dutch church in the 1840s.

Continue walking east along Houston St for several blocks until you reach Norfolk St. Turn right and halfway down the block on your left will be the 3 **Angel Orensanz Foundation**, a neo-Gothic building designed as a synagogue in 1849. Spanish sculptor Angel Orensanz purchased the fading gem in 1986 to use it as his studio; it's now an arts foundation that hosts performances, exhibits and other cultural happenings.

Continue along Norfolk St, and at the corner of Rivington St you'll get to the always thought-provoking 4 **Gallery Onetwentyeight**, where installations can range from the playful to the political.

Turn right on Rivington St and left onto Essex; on your left is the 5 **Essex Street Market**, a great place to browse and indulge in gourmet treats from fresh fruit and cheese to prepared bistro fare.

Continue heading down Essex, turn right onto Delancey St and then left onto Orchard St. Here you'll find the visitors center for the 6 **Lower East Side Tenement Museum**, where a guided tour of the collection of former tenements will show you how life was for Jewish and Italian immigrants living in poverty.

From Orchard St, turn right on Broome St to reach the 7 **Kehila Kedosha Janina Synagogue & Museum**, home to the Romaniotes, an obscure branch of Greek Judaism.

Bridges. A drawn-out renovation brought great nighttime lighting and surprisingly clean bathrooms to the mix.

Although flanked by a looming housing project and the clogged FDR Dr on one side and the less-than-pure East River on the other, it's a cool spot for a picnic or a morning run.

SARA D ROOSEVELT PARK
PARK

Map p424 (Houston St at Chrystie St; S F to Delancey-Essex Sts) Spiffed up just in time for the arrival of its tony new luxury-condo neighbors, this remade little park is a place that most New Yorkers will remember as more of a junkie's spot for scoring than an actual plot of green space. But it's joined the ranks of other rejuvenated 'needle parks' – such as Bryant Park and Tompkins Square Park –and is now a three-block respite from urban chaos.

Grab an ethnic picnic-to-go at any of the nearby food spots and settle into a shady corner; if you've got kids with you, there's a nice little playground that's perfect for letting off steam.

ST AUGUSTINE'S
EPISCOPAL CHURCH
CHURCH

Map p424 (✆212-673-5300; 290 Henry St btwn Jackson & Montgomery Sts; S F to East Broadway) St Augustine's Episcopal Church is an 1828 landmark housing the largest African American congregation on the LES. Peek inside to see the restored 'slave galleries,' created to separate worshippers by race in the church's early days.

EATING

Here lies the epitome of what's beautiful in New York's dining scene: mind-blowing variety which can cover the full spectrum of continents and budgets – in just a single city block. You'll find every type of taste-bud tantalizer under the sun from Ukrainian *pierogi* (dumpling) palaces and dozens of sushi joints to pizza parlors and falafel huts galore. There's tons of Indian fare too, especially on the carnival-esque strip of E 6th St between First and Second Aves, otherwise known as Curry Row, where cheap, decent restaurants from the subcontinent are a dime a dozen.

🍴 East Village

CAFE ORLIN
MIDDLE EASTERN $

Map p422 (www.cafeorlin.com; 41 St Marks Pl btwn First & Second Aves; mains $7-14; ⊗breakfast, lunch & dinner; S L to 3rd Ave; N/R to 8th St-NYU; 4/6 to Astor Pl) Toeing the line between Middle Eastern and homegrown American fare, Cafe Orlin is the star of the brunching and lunching scene along St Marks Pl. The perfect omelets, with fresh fixings folded deep within, lure a colorful assortment of characters from angsty hipster types guzzling red wine while toying with their iPads to hung-over Saturday Night Live cast members recovering from last night's show.

Find the subtle 'cafe' sign scribbled in cursive and step inside to discover an unholy assemblage of black wooden furniture spread among three rooms.

ABRAÇO
CAFE $

Map p422 (www.abraconyc.com; 86 E 7th St btwn First & Second Aves; snacks $2-7; ⊗Tue-Sat 8am-6pm, Sun 9am-6pm; S F to 2nd Ave; L to 1st Ave; 4/6 to Astor Pl) With hardly room to move – let alone sit – Abraço is an East Village refuge where good coffee and good taste combine to form one of the finest cafes in the entire city. Slurp your perfectly crafted espresso while inhaling a slice of delicious olive cake. If you're stopping by with a friend you'll each need to order a slice – fights are known to break out over the last bite.

IPPUDO NY
RAMEN $

Map p422 (www.ippudo.com/ny; 65 4th Ave btwn 9th & 10th Sts; ramen $10-13; ⊗11am-3:30pm Mon-Sat, 5-11:30pm Mon-Thu, 5pm-12:30am Fri & Sat, 11am-10:30pm Sun; S N/R 8th St-NYU; 4/5/6 to 14th St-Union Sq; 4/6 to Astor Pl) In Tokyo, Ippudo is the veritable equivalent of America's Olive Garden, with hundreds of franchised outposts tucked into every urban fold. In New York, the good folks from Ippudo have kicked things up a notch – they've taken their mouthwatering ramen recipe (truly, it's delish) and spiced it up with sleek surrounds (hello shiny black surfaces and streamers of cherry red) and blasts of rock and roll on the overhead speakers.

WESTVILLE EAST
NEW AMERICAN $$

Map p422 (www.westvillenyc.com; 173 Ave A; mains $12-20; ⊗11:30am-11pm Mon-Fri, 10am-11pm Sat & Sun; S L to 1st Ave; 4/6 to Astor Pl) Market-fresh veggies and delicious mains is the name of the game at Westville, and it doesn't hurt that the cottage-chic surrounds are undeniably charming. The chicken reuben is the ultimate hangover cure-all, though most people opt to take four vegetable side dishes and turn them into a gorge-ous meal (the brussels sprouts are heavenly).

There are three locations in the city – the other two are in Chelsea and the West Village. This one is our favorite.

LUZZO'S
PIZZERIA $$

Map p422 (☏212-473-7447; 211-213 First Ave btwn 12th & 13th Sts; pizzas $14-17; ⏱5-11pm Mon, noon-11pm Tue-Sun; ⬛L to 1st Ave) Fan-favorite Luzzo's occupies a thin sliver of real estate in the East Village, which becomes stuffed to the gills each evening as discerning diners feast on thin-crust pies, kissed with ripe tomatoes and cooked in an illusive coal-fired stove.

CARACAS AREPA BAR
SOUTH AMERICAN $

Map p422 (www.caracasarepabar.com; 93 ½ E 7th St btwn First Ave & Ave A; dishes $6-16; ⏱noon-11pm; ✎; ⬛6 to Astor Pl) Cram into this tiny joint and order a crispy, hot *arepa* (corn tortilla stuffed with veggies and meat) such as the Pepi Queen (chicken and avocado) or La Pelua (beef and cheddar). You can choose from 17 types of *arepa* (plus empanadas and daily specials like oxtail soup), served in baskets with a side of *nata* (sour cream) and fried plantains.

CHIKALICIOUS
DESSERTS $

Map p422 (www.chikalicious.com; 203 E 10th St btwn First & Second Aves; desserts $3-12; ⏱3-10:30pm Thu-Sun; ⬛L to 1st Ave; 4/6 to Astor Pl) An ice cream served atop an éclair instead of a cone? We're in! ChiKaLicious is an East Village favorite taking traditional sweet-tooth standards and transforming them into inspired calorie concoctions. Transcontinental desserts – like green-tea ice cream – are a big hit, too. Due to popular demand, ChiKaLicious recently opened a 'dessert club' (more seating space) across the street.

HEARTH
ITALIAN $$$

Map p422 (www.restauranthearth.com; 403 E 12th St at First Ave; mains $20-40; ⏱6-10pm Sun-Thu, to 11pm Fri & Sat; ⬛L to 1st Ave; L, N/Q/R/W, 4/5/6 to 14th St-Union Sq) A staple for finicky, deep-pocketed diners, Hearth boasts a warm, brick-walled interior. The seasonal

menu includes specials such as roasted sturgeon with lentils and bacon, zucchini ravioli and rabbit pappardelle with fava beans.

REDHEAD
SOUTHERN COOKING $$

Map p422 (www.theredheadnyc.com; 349 E 13th St btwn First & Second Aves; mains $13-25; ⏱4pm-2am Mon-Sun; ⬛L to 1st Ave or 3rd Ave; 6 to Astor Pl) Cozy corners of exposed bricks and warm smiles from the staff mirror the home-style comfort food, which has a distinctly Southern bent. There are stacks of fried chicken and rounds of pucker-inducing cocktails on everyone else's table, and you should follow suit. Ask about the 'hoho' for dessert – you won't be sorry.

MINCA
RAMEN $

Map p422 (www.newyorkramen.com; 536 E 5th St btwn Aves A & B; ramen $10-13; ⏱noon-11:30pm Mon-Sun; ⬛F to 2nd Ave; J/M/Z to Essex St; F to Delancey St) The epitome of an East Village hole-in-the-wall, Minca focuses all of its attention on the food: cauldron-esque bowls of steaming ramen served with a recommended side order of fried gyoza. When you're nearing the end, the waitress will bring you a mug of complimentary tea. Yum.

MOTORINO
PIZZERIA $$

Map p422 (www.motorinopizza.com; 349 E 12th St btwn First & Second Aves; pizza $9-17; ⏱11am-midnight Sun-Thu, to 1am Fri & Sat; ✎; ⬛L to First Ave; 4/5/6 to 14th St-Union Sq) Crusts are both chewy and pillowy at this intimate East Village restaurant.

BIRDBATH
BAKERY $

Map p422 (www.thecitybakery.com/birdbath; 223 1st Ave btwn 13th & 14th Sts; desserts $3-9; ⏱8am-10pm Mon-Sat, 9am-10pm Sun; ⬛L to 1st Ave or 3rd Ave; 4/6 to Astor Pl) The brainchild of the savvy City Bakery clan, Birdbath touts itself as an ecofriendly bakery, though the audible 'yums' from customers is enough to lure in the discerning sweet tooth. Warning: you're about to try the best cookies in downtown Manhattan.

PRUNE
AMERICAN $$$

Map p422 (www.prunerestaurant.com; 54 E 1st St btwn First & Second Aves; mains $12-34; ⏱lunch & dinner daily, brunch Sat & Sun; ⬛F/V to Lower East Side-2nd Ave) Expect lines around the block on the weekend, when the hungover show up to cure their ills with Prune's brunches and excellent Bloody Marys (in nine varieties). The small room is always busy as diners pour in for roast suckling pig, rich sweetbreads and sausage-studded concoctions.

RAI RAI KEN — RAMEN $

Map p422 (☎212-477-7030; 214 E 10th St btwn First & Second Aves; ramen $9-13; 🕐noon-midnight Mon-Thu, to 2am Fri & Sat; [S]L to 1st Ave; 4/6 to Astor Pl) Rai Rai Ken's storefront may only be the size of its door, but it's pretty hard to miss since there's usually a small congregation of hungry locals lurking out front. Inside, low-slung wooden stools are arranged around the noodle bar, where the cooks are busily churning out piping-hot portions of tasty pork-infused broth. Lines generally move quite fast, as patrons are subtly encouraged to slurp and dash.

KANOYAMA — SUSHI $

Map p422 (www.kanoyama.com; 175 Second Ave near E 11th St; rolls from $4.50; 🕐dinner; 🍷; [S]L to 3rd Ave; L, N/Q/R/W, 4/5/6 to 14th St-Union Sq) Providing no-fuss, no-muss sushi with fresh daily specials in the heart of the East Village, Kanoyama is a local favorite that has so far been overlooked by the city's big-name food critics (that might explain its unpretentious air). You can order sushi à la carte or in rolls, or choose from the many tempura plates.

VESELKA — UKRAINIAN $

Map p422 (www.veselka.com; 144 Second Ave at 9th St; mains $6-14; 🕐24hr; [S]L to 3rd Ave; 6 to Astor Pl) A bustling tribute to the area's Ukrainian past, Veselka dishes out borscht and stuffed cabbage amid the usual suspects of greasy comfort food. The cluttered spread of tables is available to loungers and carbo-loaders all night long, though it's a favorite any time of day.

YAFFA — AMERICAN $

Map p422 (www.yaffacafe.com; 97 St Marks Pl btwn First Ave & Ave A; mains from $9; 🕐breakfast, lunch & dinner; [S]L to 1st Ave; F to 2nd Ave; 4/6 to Astor Pl) Yaffa seems to embody a similar spirit to some of the other eating spots peppered along St Marks Pl – the vibe is on the funky side and the menu walks the line between American comfort food and Middle Eastern flavors. What sets Yaffa apart is the quiet courtyard in the back that provides the perfect amount of respite from traffic on the main drag.

PORCHETTA — ITALIAN $

Map p422 (☎212-777-2151; 110 E 7th St; dishes from $9; 🕐11:30am-1am Sun-Thu, to 3am Fri & Sat; [S]6 to Astor Pl) This white-tiled storefront is short on seating (with just six stools) but long on taste, as renowned chef Sara Jenkins is the talent behind this pork-lovers' takeout haven. The porchetta in question – tender boneless roasted pork that's been wrapped in a pork belly and seasoned with fennel pollen, rosemary, sage, thyme and garlic – is available in sandwich or platter-with-sides versions. For herbivore tag-alongs, there's a mozzarella sandwich on the small menu, too.

MUD — CAFE $$

Map p422 (www.themudtruck.com; 307 E 9th St btwn Second & First Aves; [S]L to 3rd Ave or 1st Ave; 4/6 to Astor Pl) Offering trustworthy beans and a foolproof brunch, this 9th St nook is a favorite among East Villagers looking for a quick caffeine fix or a friendly place to loiter with a book. Keep an eye out for the MUD trucks that roam the streets of the city, dispensing caffeine jolts to weary pedestrians.

BANJARA — INDIAN $$

Map p422 (☎212-477-5956; 97 First Ave at 6th St; mains $12-18; 🕐lunch & dinner; [S]L to 1st Ave) On 6th St between First and Second Aves you'll find a row of Indian restaurants. A little more upscale than some of the other options, Banjara has delicious, well-prepared Indian food without all the headache-inducing Christmas lights that festoon many of the other restaurants on the block.

M2M — GROCERY $

Map p422 (☎212-353-2698; 55 Third Ave btwn 10th & 11th Sts; [S]L to 3rd Ave; N/R to 8th St-NYU; 4/6 to Astor Pl) Open 'morning to midnight,' as the acronym suggests, this Asian grocer is the perfect place to assemble a picnic of Japanese and Korean eats if an outdoor adventure is on the cards. The fresh-cut sushi and spicy kim chi platters can't be beaten, especially for the price.

ANGELICA KITCHEN — VEGAN, CAFE $$

Map p422 (www.angelicakitchen.com; 300 E 12th St btwn First & Second Aves; dishes $14-20; 🕐lunch & dinner; [S]L to 1st Ave) This enduring herbivore classic has a calming vibe – candles, tables both intimate and communal, and a mellow, longtime staff – and enough creative options to make your head spin.

Some dishes get too-cute names (Sacre-Coeur Basmatica in Paris, Thai Mee Up), but all do wonders with tofu, seitan, spices and soy products, and sometimes an array of raw ingredients.

Standards like the Pantry Plate – which lets you choose from a list of a dozen or so veggie concoctions and special salads – or the Dragon Bowl, a Buddha's delight with seasonal greens, tubers, tofu, seaweed and brown rice piled high, will leave you feeling both virtuous and full. Creative puddings and cakes only sweeten the deal.

🍴 Lower East Side

COCORON SOBA $

Map p424 (☎212-925-5220; www.cocoron-soba.com; 61 Delancey St btwn Eldridge & Allen Sts; dishes $9-13; ⏲noon-3pm Tue-Sun, 6-11pm Tue-Sat, 6-10:30pm Sun; [S]F to Delancey St; B/D to Grand St; J to Bowery) Oh Cocoron, if soba weren't so messy, we'd fill our pockets with your brilliant recipes. A short menu of delicious hot and cold noodle dishes (go for the cold) reads like a haiku dedicated to savory, vegetable-driven fare. Minimalist surrounds and clean wooden tables help offset the cramped quarters, though the tight seating means that you'll have a front-row seat to watch the pan-wielding geniuses.

FREEMANS AMERICAN $$$

Map p424 (☎212-420-0012; www.freemansrestaurant.com; end of Freeman Alley; mains $24-30; ⏲5-11:30pm; [S]F to 2nd Ave) Tucked down a back alley befitting the metropolitan likes of Paris or London, Freeman's is staunchly reserved for hipster brunchophiles who let their chunky jewelry clang on the wooden tables as they lean forward to sip overflowing martinis. Potted plants and taxidermic antlers lend an endearing hunting-cabin vibe – a charming escape from the bustle (when there isn't a crowd inside).

KATZ'S DELICATESSEN DELI $$

Map p424 (☎212-254-2246; www.katzsdelicatessen.com; 205 E Houston St at Ludlow St; pastrami on rye $15, knockwurst $6; ⏲breakfast, lunch & dinner; [S]F/V to Lower East Side-2nd Ave) Though visitors won't find many remnants of the classic, old-world-Jewish Lower East Side dining scene, there are a few stellar holdouts, among them the famous Katz's Delicatessen, where Meg Ryan faked her famous orgasm in the 1989 Hollywood flick *When Harry Met Sally*. If you love classic deli grub like pastrami and salami on rye, it just might have the same effect on you.

KUMA INN PAN-ASIAN $

Map p424 (☎212-353-8866; 113 Ludlow St btwn Delancey & Rivington Sts; small dishes $7-11; ⏲dinner Tue-Sun; [S]F, J/M/Z to Delancey-Essex Sts) Reservations are a must at this popular spot in a secretive 2nd-floor location (look for a small red door next to a Chinese deli with 113 painted on the concrete side). The Filipino- and Thai-inspired tapas runs the gamut, from vegetarian summer rolls (with chayote) and edamame (soybean) drizzled with basil-lime oil to an oyster omelet and grilled salmon with mung beans and pickled onions. Pair anything with some chilled sake or mango nectar.

MEATBALL SHOP ITALIAN $

Map p424 (☎212-982-8895; www.themeatballshop.com; 84 Stanton St btwn Allen & Orchard Sts; dishes from $9; ⏲noon-2am Mon-Wed & Sun, to 4am Thu-Sat; [S]F to 2nd Ave; F to Delancey St; J/M/Z to Essex St) Masterfully executed meatball sandwiches have suddenly spiked in popularity, and the Meatball Shop is riding the wave of success with moist incarnations of the traditional hero. Come early to ensure you'll get a seat – there's always a line when we swing by. There's also a branch in Williamsburg (p283).

IL LABRATORIO DEL GELATO ICE CREAM $

Map p424 (☎212-343-9922; www.laboratoriodelgelato.com; 188 Ludlow St btwn Houston & Stanton Sts; ice cream from $4; ⏲7:30am-10pm Mon-Thu, to midnight Fri, 10am-midnight Sat, 10am-10pm Sun; 📶; [S]F to 2nd Ave; F to Delancey St; J/M/Z to Essex St) A fortuitous marriage between cryogenics and farm-fresh bounty, Il Labratorio del Gelato puts the *dolce* in the *dolce vita* with over 200 varieties of rotating gelato flavors (of which only 20 are on daily display). All are created in-house using market-bought ingredients and tried-and-true recipes.

'INOTECA ITALIAN $$

Map p424 (☎212-614-0473; 98 Rivington St at Ludlow St; dishes $7-17; ⏲lunch & dinner daily, brunch Sat & Sun; [S]F/V to Lower East Side-2nd Ave) It's worth joining the crowd waiting at the cramped bar of this airy, dark-wood-paneled corner haven to choose from *tramezzini* (small sandwiches on white or whole-wheat bread), panini (pressed sandwiches) and bruschetta options, all delicious and moderately priced. The truffled egg toast, a square of bread hollowed out in its center and filled with egg, truffles and fontina cheese, is a signature favorite.

You can't go wrong, whether you choose the beet-orange-mint salad, vegetable lasagna built with layers of eggplant rather than pasta, or a plate of garlicky mussels. There's also a list of 200 wines, 25 of them available by the glass.

PROSPERITY DUMPLING   CHINESE $

Map p424 (212-343-0683; 46 Eldridge St btwn Hester & Canal Sts; dumplings $1-5; 7:30am-10pm Mon-Sun; B/D to Grand St; F to East Broadway; J to Bowery) The Lower East Side's reigning ambassador of cheap eats churns out plump pockets stuffed with a tangy mishmash of chives and pork. Toss a sesame pancake into the mix and you'll still be getting back a chunk of change when you hang the cashier a fiver.

VANESSA'S DUMPLING HOUSE   CHINESE $

Map p424 (212-625-8008; 118 Eldridge St btwn Grand & Broome Sts; dumplings $1-5; B/D to Grand St; J to Bowery; F to Delancey St) If it weren't for Vanessa, the entire campus of New York University would starve. Dumplings – served steamed, fried or in soup (our favorite) – are whipped together in iron skillets at light speed and tossed into hungry mouths at unbeatable prices. There's also a branch at 14th St and Third Ave.

CLINTON STREET
BAKING COMPANY   AMERICAN $$

Map p424 (www.clintonstreetbaking.com; 4 Clinton St btwn Stanton & Houston Sts; mains $8.50-17; 8am-4pm Mon-Fri, 6-11pm Mon-Sat, 9am-4pm Sat, 9am-6pm Sun; J/M/Z to Essex St; F to Delancey St; F to 2nd Ave) Mom-and-pop shop extraordinaire, Clinton Street Baking Company gets the blue ribbon in so many categories – best pancakes (blueberry! Swoon!), best muffins, best po'boys (southern-style sandwiches), best biscuits etc – that you're pretty much guaranteed a stellar meal no matter which time of day (or night) you stop by. Half-priced vino sweetens the already sweet pot on Mondays and Tuesdays, officially keeping the doors spinning every night of the week.

🍷 DRINKING &
🍸 NIGHTLIFE

🍸 East Village

In the East Village, as a general rule, the further east you go the looser things gets. Like the myriad eating options in the area, nightlife is served up across quite the gamut: you'll find dirty dive bars stuffed to the gills with NYU students, and secreted swanky lounges tucked behind the Japanese restaurant right next door. Things are positively packed come the weekend.

TERROIR   WINE BAR

Map p422 (www.wineisterroir.com; 413 E 12th St btwn First Ave & Ave A; L to 1st Ave; L to 3rd Ave; 4/6 to Astor Pl) Removing the pretension from the wine bar experience, Terroir serves vino at smooth communal tables made from large scraps of wood. A delightful assortment of bar bites (including superlative paninis) makes a strong case for teetotalers with boozy friends.

There are two other locations – one in Tribeca, and a newer shaking things up in Murray Hill.

MCSORLEY'S OLD ALE HOUSE   BAR

Map p422 (212-474-9148; 15 E 7th St btwn Second & Third Aves; 6 to Astor Pl) Around since 1854, McSorley's feels far removed from the East Village veneer of cool: you're more likely to drink with firemen, Wall St refugees and a few tourists. But (didn't you know?) that's become cool again. It's hard to beat the cobwebs and sawdust floors and flip waiters who slap down two mugs of the house's ale for every one ordered.

DEATH + CO   LOUNGE

Map p422 (www.deathandcompany.com; 433 E 6th St btwn First Ave & Ave A; 6pm-1am Mon-Thu & Sun, to 2am Fri & Sat; F to 2nd Ave; L to 1st Ave; 4/6 Astor Pl) 'Death & Co' is scrawled in ornate cursive on the ground at Death's door, so to speak – the only hint that you're in the right place to try some of the most perfectly concocted cocktails in town.

Relax amid dim lighting and thick wooden slatting and let the bartenders – with their PhDs in mixology – work their magic as they shake, rattle and roll your blended poison of choice.

EAST VILLAGE & LOWER EAST SIDE DRINKING & NIGHTLIFE

WENDY CONNETT / ALAMY ©

1. Tompkins Square Park (p106)
This 10.5-acre space of urban greenery is like a friendly town square for East Village locals.

2. Lower East Side (p107)
Willfully get lost in the tangle of eclectic streets, including Clinton St, where you'll find this mural.

3. St Mark's Bookshop (p123)
Browse the shelves of this indie bookshop tucked around the corner from St Marks Pl.

MICHELLE BENNETT / LONELY PLANET IMAGES ©

ANGEL'S SHARE BAR

Map p422 (☎212-777-5415; 2nd fl, 8 Stuyvesant St near Third Ave & 9th St; ⏲5pm-midnight; [S]6 to Astor Pl) Show up early and snag a seat at this hidden gem, behind a Japanese restaurant on the same floor. It's quiet and elegant with creative cocktails, but you can't stay if you don't have a table, and they tend to go fast.

EASTERN BLOC GAY

Map p422 (www.easternblocnyc.com; 505 E 6th St btwn Aves A & B; ⏲7pm-4am; [S]F/V to Lower East Side-2nd Ave) Though the theme may be 'Iron Curtain,' the drapery is most definitely velvet and taffeta at this East Village gay bar. Hang your jacket at the 'Goat Czech' and spring forth into the cramped and crowded sea of boys – some flirting with the topless barkeeps, others pretending not to stare at the retro '70s porn on the TVs.

HEATHERS BAR

Map p422 (☎212-254-0979; 506 E 13th St btwn Aves A & B; [S]L to 1st Ave) Heathers is a tiny and stylish unsigned drinking den with frosted windows, a painted tin ceiling and whitewashed brick walls. A mishmash of regulars lingers over eye-catching artworks (courtesy of the artist owner and her friends), two-for-one drink specials and gluten-free beer options. The DJ tucked in the corner spins eclectic sounds: sometimes indie rock, other times bubble-gum pop.

TEN DEGREES BAR WINE BAR

Map p422 (www.10degreesbar.com; 121 St Marks Pl btwn First Ave & Ave A; ⏲noon-4am Mon-Sun; [S]L to 1st Ave or 3rd Ave; F to 2nd Ave) The decor doesn't suggest anything particularly special about this St Marks stalwart, but one glance at the drinks list and you'll quickly appreciate one of the best happy hour deals around town: half-priced bottles of wine. And there's no gimmick about it; a fantastic selection from across the globe (grab the Malbec) comes heavily discounted when you show up early – go for the couches up front or grab a tiny table in the back nook.

IMMIGRANT WINE BAR

Map p422 (www.theimmigrantnyc.com; 341 E 9th St btwn First & Second Aves; ⏲5pm-1am Mon-Wed & Sun, to 2am Thu, 5pm-3am Fri & Sat; [S]L to 1st Ave or 3rd Ave; 4/6 to Astor Pl) Wholly unpretentious, this East Village wine bar – housed in a former tenement (hence the name) – could easily become your *Cheers* if you decide to stick around town. The owners are on the floor doing the dirty work, mingling with faithful regulars while dishing out tangy olives and topping up glasses with imported snifters.

CIENFUEGOS BAR

Map p422 (www.cienfuegosny.com; 95 Ave A btwn 6th & 7th Sts ; [S]F to 2nd Ave; L to 1st Ave; 4/6 to Astor Pl) If Fidel Castro had a stretched Cadillac, its interior would look something like the inside of New York's foremost rum-punch joint. A sampler of tasty Cuban dishes makes the perfect midnight snack. If you like this place, then make a pit stop at the connected **Amor y Amargo** (Map p422; www.amoryamargo.com; 443 E 6th St btwn Ave A & First Ave; ⏲5-11pm Mon-Wed & Sun, to midnight Thu, to 1am Fri & Sat; [S]F to 2nd Ave; L to 1st Ave; 4/6 to Astor Pl) – Cienfuegos' bitters-centric brother.

JIMMY'S NO 43 BAR

Map p422 (www.jimmysno43.com; 43 E 7th St btwn Third & Second Aves; ⏲noon-2am Mon-Thu & Sun, to 4am Fri & Sat; [S]N/R to 8th St-NYU; F to 2nd Ave; 4/6 to Astor Pl) It doesn't look like much from outside – the generic awning and plastic weather shield do it no favors – but when you enter the basement beer hall the story quickly changes. Barrels and stag antlers line the walls up to the ceiling as locals chug their drinks. Select from over 50 imported favorites, to go with a round of delectable bar nibbles (betcha didn't think a hot plate could cook pork belly so darn well!).

MAYAHUEL COCKTAIL BAR

Map p422 (☎212-253-5888; 304 E 6th St at Second Ave; [S]L to 1st Ave or 3rd Ave; 6 to Astor Pl) About as far from your typical Spring Break tequila bar as you can get – it's more like the cellar of a monastery. Devotees of the fermented agave can seriously indulge themselves experimenting with dozens of varieties (all cocktails $13); in between drinks, snack on tamales and tortillas.

VANDAAG COCKTAIL BAR

Map p422 (www.vandaagnyc.com; 103 Second Ave btwn 6th & 7th Sts; ⏲9am-10pm Mon, to 2am Tue-Sat, 11am-10pm Sun; [S]N/R to 8th St-NYU; F to 2nd Ave; 4/6 to Astor Pl) A relative newcomer to the East Village, Vandaag specializes in Dutch food (there's a window in the window, if you're as confused as we are), though we much prefer coming here simply for a smooth gin- or genever-based cocktail while enjoying the Scandi-sleek decor.

COCK GAY

Map p422 ([☎]212-777-6254; 29 Second Ave at 2nd St; [S]F/V to Lower East Side-2nd Ave) A dark, dank spot that's proud of its sleazy-chic reputation, this is the place to join lanky hipster boys and rage until you're kicked out at 4am. Varying theme nights present popular parties with live performers, DJs, drag-queen hostesses, nearly naked go-go boys and porn videos on constant loops. It's wild and friendly.

CHERRY TAVERN BAR

Map p422 ([☎]212-777-1448; 441 E 6th St at Ave A; [S]L to 1st Ave) Not for the 40-year-old virgin – hard-drinking 20- and 30-somethings get their flirt on at this small, dimly lit dive. Arrive before 9pm and you have a shot at the bar or a seat at one of the few tables. Otherwise, clunk your quarters down for a game of pool or sidle up to the jukebox filled with indie/alt songs.

♟ Lower East Side

The Lower East Side (LES) still clings to its status as the coolest 'hood in Manhattan. While some bars are favored by the 'bridge and tunnel' gang (not to mention tourists, ahem), the locals still adore newfound clubs that stage Manhattan's next indie-rock kings. There's something for everyone here, with booze and beer usually a lot cheaper than in most of the island's other areas – just walk up and down the tiny blocks and peek in.

MILK & HONEY BAR

Map p424 (www.mlkhny.com; 134 Eldridge btwn Delancey & Broome Sts; [S]B/D to Grand St) You can't beat the '40s-era low-key ambience of the most infamous bar on the Lower East Side – the cocktails are superb (and priced accordingly at $15 each), and the staff are even friendly – it's just that you have to know people to get in. No number listed, no sign outside but a graffitied door. Go if you can, but we can't shake the feeling that the exclusivity is pretty lame.

WHISKEY WARD BAR

Map p424 (www.thewhiskeyward.com; 121 Essex St btwn Delancey & Rivington Sts; [⏱]5pm-4am; [S]F, J/M/Z to Delancey-Essex Sts) Once upon a time, city officials divided Manhattan into wards, and the Lower East Side was the 'Whiskey Ward,' courtesy of its many drinking establishments. Modern owners of the Whiskey Ward apparently appreciate history as much as they adore single malts, rye whiskey, blended Scotch, Irish whiskey and bourbon. Patrons enjoy the single-mindedness of this brick-walled bar.

NURSE BETTIE COCKTAIL BAR

Map p424 (www.nursebettieles.com; 106 Norfolk St btwn Delancey & Rivington Sts; [⏱]6pm-2am Sun-Tue, to 4am Wed-Sat; [S]F, J/M/Z to Delancey-Essex Sts) Something a bit new is going on with this pint-sized charmer: plenty of roaming space between slick '00s-modern lounges and '50s-style ice-cream-shop stools and painted pin-ups on the brick walls. Cocktails get freaky: fruity vodka and brandies, plus bubble-gum martinis. You can bring food in, and many won-over locals do.

BARRIO CHINO COCKTAIL BAR

Map p424 ([☎]212-228-6710; 253 Broome St btwn Ludlow & Orchard Sts; [S]F, J/M/Z to Delancey-Essex Sts) An eatery that spills easily into a party scene, with an airy Havana-meets-Beijing vibe and a focus on fine sipping tequilas (the menu offers 50, some breaking $25 per shot). Or stick with fresh blood-orange or black-plum margaritas, guacamole and chicken tacos.

WELCOME TO THE JOHNSONS BAR

Map p424 ([☎]212-420-9911; 123 Rivington St btwn Essex & Norfolk Sts; [S]F, J/M/Z to Delancey-Essex Sts) Set up like a '70s game room – a bit sleazier than the one on *That '70s Show* – the Johnsons' irony still hasn't worn off for the devoted 20-something crowd. It could have something to do with the $2 Buds till 9pm, the pool table, the blasting garage-rock jukebox or the plastic-covered sofas.

BARRAMUNDI LOUNGE

Map p424 ([☎]212-529-6999; 67 Clinton St btwn Stanton & Rivington Sts; [S]F, J/M/Z to Delancey-Essex Sts) This Australian-owned arty place fills an old tenement building with convivial booths, reasonably priced drinks (including Aussie imports) and some cool tree-trunk tables. Happy hour runs 6pm to 9pm.

BACK ROOM BAR

Map p424 ([☎]212-228-5098; 102 Norfolk St btwn Delancey & Rivington Sts; [S]F, J/M/Z to Delancey-

Essex Sts) Yet another speakeasy-style bar in the LES, the Back Room is entered through a cavernlike alley off Norfolk. The drinks are pricey and served in teacups, and we'd write the whole thing off if it weren't for its undeniable allure. Handsome copper ceilings, art nouveau flourishes, vintage wallpaper, a mirrored bar and an oversized fireplace – all pure eye candy for the not-terribly-sophisticated 20-something crowd.

EDEN @ R BAR LESBIAN

Map p424 (www.myspace.com/edenevents; R Bar, 218 Bowery btwn Rivington & Prince Sts; [S]F/V to Lower East Side-2nd Ave) This weekly lesbian lounge soiree, held on Wednesdays from 8pm to 3am, is known for drawing sexy, sophisticated ladies with its charming hostess, Maggie C, and music from the oddly named DJ sHErOCK.

☆ ENTERTAINMENT

☆ East Village

PERFORMANCE SPACE 122 THEATER

Map p422 (PS 122; ☎212-477-5288; www.ps122.org; 150 First Ave at 9th St; [S]R/W to 8th St-NYU; 6 to Astor Pl) This former schoolhouse has been committed to fostering new artists and their far-out ideas since its inception in 1979. Its two stages have hosted such now-known performers as Meredith Monk, Eric Bogosian and the late Spalding Gray, and it's also home to dance shows, film screenings and various festivals for up-and-coming talents.

SWEET COMEDY

Map p422 (Comedy at Ella's; ☎212-777-2230; sethzog@aol.com; 9 Ave A near Houston St; admission $5; ⏲show starts 9pm Tue; [S]F to 2nd Ave or Delancey St; J/M/Z to Essex St) There are tons of small comedy houses scattered around the city, but we're pretty sure you haven't heard of this one – a local gig hosted every Tuesday by Seth Herzog and his gang of friends (including his mother, who loves to get up in front of the small crowd and discuss her weekly list of grievances).

Seth brings in his industry friends – everyone from unknown up-and-comers to SNL mainstays – to test out their new material. Laughs aplenty.

STONE LIVE MUSIC

Map p422 (www.thestonenyc.com; Ave C at 2nd St; [S]F/V to Lower East Side-2nd Ave) Created by renowned downtown jazz cat John Zorn, the Stone is about the music and nothing but the music, in all its experimental and avant-garde forms. Shows take place nightly (except Mondays) in the unsigned space, with a repertoire of psychedelically tinged Dixieland, alternative folk, electro-acoustic provocation and other instrumentalists working in a sometimes aurally challenging landscape.

The $10 cover goes entirely to the musicians, and there's no bar or frills of any kind; just folding chairs on a concrete floor.

BANJO JIM'S LIVE MUSIC

Map p422 (☎212-777-0869; 700 E 9th St at Ave C; [S]L to 1st Ave; 6 to Astor Pl) The latest addition to the nonrock scene on Ave C, Banjo Jim's – a tiny dive with a good jukebox and friendly atmosphere – hosts a nightly crew of banjo pickers and lap-steel players. Most nights have standard lineups of a few acts, with no cover but a pass-the-hat policy.

SIDEWALK CAFÉ COUNTRY, FOLK

Map p422 (www.sidewalkmusic.net; 94 Ave A at 6th St; [S]F/V to Lower East Side-2nd Ave; 6 to Astor Pl) Anti-folk forever! Never mind the Sidewalk's burger-bar appearance outside; inside is the home of New York's 'anti-folk' scene, where the Moldy Peaches carved out their legacy before Juno got knocked up. The open-mic 'anti-hootenanny' is Monday night.

LA MAMA ETC THEATER

Map p422 (☎212-475-7710; www.lamama.org; 74A E 4th St; Annex Theater $20, 1st fl Theater $15, the Club $15; ⏲hrs vary; [S]F/V to Lower East Side-2nd Ave) A long-standing home for on-stage experimentation (the ETC stands for Experimental Theater Club), La MaMa is now a three-theater complex with a cafe, an art gallery and a separate studio building that features cutting-edge dramas, sketch comedy and readings of all kinds.

NEW YORK THEATER WORKSHOP THEATER

Map p422 (www.nytw.org; 79 E 4th St btwn Second & Third Aves; [S]F/V to Lower East Side-2nd Ave) Recently celebrating its 25th year, this innovative production house is a treasure to those seeking cutting-edge, contemporary plays with purpose. It was the originator of two big Broadway hits, *Rent* and *Urine-*

town, and offers a constant supply of high-quality drama.

It has staged works from Rebecca Gilman *(The Heart Is a Lonely Hunter),* Geoffrey Cowan and Leroy Aarons *(Top Secret)* – and even Samuel Beckett, whose quartet of one-act plays was adapted here by director JoAnne Akalaitis and composer Phillip Glass in *Beckett Shorts,* starring Mikhail Baryshnikov.

ANTHOLOGY FILM ARCHIVES CINEMA

Map p422 (www.anthologyfilmarchives.org; 32 Second Ave at 2nd St; [S]F/V to Lower East Side-2nd Ave) This theater, opened in 1970 by film buff Jonas Mekas and a supportive crew, is dedicated to the idea of film as an art form. It screens indie works by new filmmakers and also revives classics and obscure oldies that are usually screened in programs organized around a specific theme or director, from Luis Buñuel to Ken Brown's psychedelia.

AMORE OPERA OPERA

Map p422 (www.amoreopera.org; Connelly Theater, 220 E 4th St btwn Aves A & B; [S]F/V to Lower East Side-2nd Ave) This new company, formed by several members of the recently defunct Amato Opera, presents good-value ($35) works. Its inaugural season offerings included *La Bohème, The Merry Widow, The Mikado* and *Hansel and Gretel,* performed at this East Village theater.

BOWERY POETRY CLUB LITERARY

Map p422 (☎212-614-0505; www.bowerypoetry.com; 308 Bowery btwn Bleecker & Houston Sts; [S]6 to Bleecker St) Just across from the old CBGB site on the East Village/NoHo border, this funky cafe and performance space has eccentric readings of all genres, from plays to fiction, plus frequent themed poetry slams and literary-focused parties that celebrate new books and their authors.

SING SING KARAOKE KARAOKE

Map p422 (www.karaokesingsing.com; 9 St Marks Pl; [S]N/R to 8th St-NYU; L to 3rd Ave; 4/6 to Astor Pl) A chuckle-worthy reference to the nearby state prison, Sing Sing is exactly as it sounds – swing by to belt your heart out. Go for a classic ballad, or try for a top 40 hit – no matter what you choose, you're likely to be joined by a chorus of tipsy backup singers.

☆ Lower East Side

BOWERY BALLROOM LIVE MUSIC

Map p424 (www.boweryballroom.com; 6 Delancey St at Bowery St; ⏲performance times vary; [S]J/M/Z to Bowery St) This terrific, medium-sized venue has the perfect sound and feel for more blown-up indie-rock acts (The Shins, Stephen Malkmus, Patti Smith).

DELANCEY LIVE MUSIC

Map p424 (www.thedelancey.com; 168 Delancey St at Clinton St; [S]F, J/M/Z to Delancey-Essex Sts) Surprisingly stylish for the Lower East Side, the Delancey hosts some popular indie bands like Clap Your Hands Say Yeah for doting indie-rock crowds. Also a good early-evening spot at which to drink, particularly from the airy 2nd-floor patio deck.

SAPPHIRE CLUB

Map p424 (www.sapphirenyc.com; 249 Eldridge St at E Houston St; admission $5; ⏲7pm-4am; [S]F/V to Lower East Side-2nd Ave) Fun without attitude! This tiny, hoppin' venue has survived the crowds of the mid-'90s Ludlow St boom with its hip factor intact, and its $5 cover keeps snootiness to a minimum. The tightly packed dance floor gets lit with a mix of R&B, rap, disco and funk.

PIANOS LIVE MUSIC

Map p424 (www.pianosnyc.com; 158 Ludlow St at Stanton St; cover charge $8-17; ⏲noon-4am; [S]F/V to Lower East Side-2nd Ave) Nobody's bothered to change the sign at the door, a leftover from the location's previous incarnation as a piano shop. Now it's a musical mix of genres and styles, leaning more toward pop, punk and new wave, but throwing in some hip-hop and indie bands for good measure. Sometimes you get a double feature – one act upstairs and another below.

ROCKWOOD MUSIC HALL LIVE MUSIC

Map p424 (www.rockwoodmusichall.com; 196 Allen St btwn Houston & Stanton Sts; [S]F/V to Lower East Side-2nd Ave) Opened by indie rocker Ken Rockwood, this breadbox-sized, two-room concert space features a rapid-fire flow of bands and singer/songwriters across the stage. With no cover, and a max of one hour per band (die-hards can see five or more a night), what's to lose? Music kicks off at 3pm on weekends, 6pm on weeknights.

DIXON PLACE
THEATER

Map p424 (www.dixonplace.org; 161A Chrystie St btwn Rivington & Delancey Sts; Ⓢ B/D to Grand St; F/V to Lower East Side-2nd Ave) An intimate showcase for experimental theater that began as a reading space in 1985, Dixon Place recently moved from its longtime home – a cramped, apartmentlike space with mismatched chairs and couches – to a sleek, brand-new space. It's fronted by a lovely bar and lounge area for post-show discussions that has performers and audience members breathing a sigh of relief.

Luckily, the move hasn't at all altered the constant flow of exciting shows: brand-new dramas, comedy and readings, often with a queer bent. Its summer HOT! series is a great time to catch the newest works.

LANDMARK SUNSHINE CINEMA
CINEMA

Map p424 (www.landmarktheatres.com; 143 E Houston St at Forsyth St; Ⓢ F/V to Lower East Side-2nd Ave) A renovated Yiddish theater, the wonderful Landmark shows foreign and first-run mainstream art films on massive screens. It also has much-coveted stadium-style seating, so it doesn't matter what giant sits in front of you after the lights go out.

CLEMENTE SOTO VELEZ
PERFORMING ARTS

Map p424 (www.csvcenter.com; 107 Suffolk St; admission varies; ⊘ hrs vary; Ⓢ F, J/M/Z to Delancey-Essex Sts) Inside the AAI building, this collective focuses on the work of Puerto Rican poet Velez, but also brings in theater, music, art and film from artists across the world.

🔒 SHOPPING

🔒 East Village

In the East Village – once known as the archetype of underground downtown style – you'll find urban and outsider fashion, but new local designers, sleeker shops and chain stores have also moved into the area, taking away from neighborhood's former edginess. More than a whiff of those rockin' '80s days remains at punk-rock T-shirt shops, tattoo parlors and dusty stores selling furniture and vintage clothing, and the record stores are the real deal, with New York's best selection of vinyl. You'll have

to pound the pavement to see it all; the old-school stuff is on St Marks Pl between Third and First Aves, and much of the new stuff is along parallel strips, from 13th St to Houston St, and as far east as Ave C. On weekends, vendors line St Marks Pl and Ave A, and a greenmarket hits Tompkins Square Park. The blocks of E 2nd through E 7th Sts, between Second Ave and Ave B especially, are good for finding vintage wear, curiosity shops and record stores.

TRASH & VAUDEVILLE
CLOTHING

Map p422 (4 St Marks Pl; Ⓢ 6 to Astor Pl) The capital of punk-rocker-dom, Trash & Vaudeville is the veritable costume closet for singing celebs like Debbie Harry, who found their groove in the East Village when it played host to a much grittier scene. On any day of the week you'll find everyone from drag queens to themed partygoers scouting out the most ridiculous shoes, shirts and hair dye.

TOY TOKYO
TOYS

Map p422 (☎ 212-673-5424; 121 Second Ave btwn St Marks Pl & 7th St; ⊘ 1-9pm; Ⓢ 6 to Astor Pl) For a nostalgic journey into the past, head to this 2nd-floor toy emporium. The narrow warren of rooms hides all sorts of icons from previous decades. You'll find Superman watches, scowling Godzillas, shiny Transformers, painted toy soldiers and action figures from all genres. As per the name, Japanese toys are particularly well represented – an essential destination for all Japanophiles.

VILLAGE STYLE
VINTAGE CLOTHING

Map p422 (☎ 212-260-6390; 111 E 7th St btwn First & Second Aves; ⊘ 1-9pm Mon-Thu, noon-10pm Fri & Sat, noon-8pm Sun; Ⓢ 6 to Astor Pl) On a quiet stretch of the East Village, Vintage Style is a fine little place to stumble upon, with an impressive selection of leather jackets, furs and cowboy boots, as well as handbags, old-school T-shirts, sweaters, hats and '80s dresses. Prices are generally decent and the unpretentious setting encourages digging.

AMÉ AMÉ
FASHION

Map p422 (www.amerain.com; 318 E 9th St btwn First & Second Aves; ⊘ 1-7pm Tue-Sun; Ⓢ L to 3rd Ave or 1st Ave; 4/6 to Astor Pl) Rain gear and candy? Teresa (p126), the kindly owner, will explain what Amé Amé means if you're perplexed by this unusual juxtaposition. She'll also tell you that there's no such thing as bad weather – only bad fashion. This teeny hipster haven will set you straight when it comes to drizzle-friendly fashion, and the imported candy is discounted on rainy days. Score!

C'H'C'M CLOTHING

Map p422 (Clinton Hill Classic Menswear; www.chcmshop.com; 2 Bond St btwn the Bowery & Second Ave; [S]B/D/F, M to Broadway-Lafayette St; N/R to 8th St-NYU; 4/6 to Bleecker St) The acronym-y shortening of Clinton Hill Classic Menswear shows not a pinch of pretension when displaying carefully selected threads for the fashion-forward man. The store's decor has unadulterated design decoys, letting shopping focus solely on the beautifully crafted wares.

TOKIO 7 CONSIGNMENT STORE

Map p422 (☎212-353-8443; 64 E 7th St near First Ave; 🕒noon-8:30pm Mon-Sat, to 8pm Sun; [S]6 to Astor Pl) This revered, hip consignment shop, down a few steps on a shady stretch of E 7th St, has good-condition designer labels for men and women at some fairly hefty prices. Best of all is the selection of men's suits – there's nearly always something tip-top in the $100 to $150 range that's worth trying on.

ESKANDAR FASHION, ACCESSORIES

Map p422 (☎212-533-4200; 33 E 10th St btwn Broadway & Fourth Ave; [S]6 to Astor Pl) Located on one of the prettiest blocks in the Village, Eskandar offers women's fashions and chunky jewelry that would appeal to any Vassar professor of performance studies – mature and refined.

SUSTAINABLE NYC CLOTHING

Map p422 (☎212-254-5400; 139 Ave A btwn St Marks Pl & 9th St; 🕒8am-9pm Mon-Fri, 9am-9pm Sat & Sun; [S]6 to Astor Pl) Across from Tompkins Square Park, this ecofriendly shop offers all sorts of home and office gear for living green. Organic T-shirts, shoes made out of recycled auto tires, compost bins, biodegradable beauty products, recycled stationery, and books on going green are all on hand. The store itself sets a fine example: the interior is built from 300-year-old reclaimed lumber and fixtures are recycled (and for sale).

A small cafe on-site sells snacks and fair-trade coffee.

ST MARK'S BOOKSHOP BOOKS

Map p422 (www.stmarksbookshop.com; 31 Third Ave btwn St Marks Pl & 9th St; 🕒10am-midnight Mon-Sat, 11am-midnight Sun; [S]6 to Astor Pl) Actually located around the corner from St Marks Pl (it moved long ago), this indie bookshop specializes in political literature, poetry, new nonfiction and novels and academic journals. There's also a superior collection of cookbooks, travel guides and magazines, both glossy and otherwise. Staffers are a bit on the unsociable side, but hey, they're bookish and they really know their stuff.

JOHN DERIAN HOMEWARES

Map p422 (☎212-677-3917; 6 E 2nd St btwn the Bowery & Second Ave; 🕒noon-7pm Tue-Sun; [S]F/V to Lower East Side-2nd Ave) John Derian is famed for its decoupage – pieces from original botanical and animal prints stamped under glass. The result is a beautiful collection of one-of-a-kind plates, paperweights, coasters, lamps, bowls and vases. The atmospheric store hides many other curiosities: T-shirts with roguish 19th-century graphics, handmade terra-cotta pottery, linoleum cut prints and papier-mâché figurines. For eclectic bed linens and such, visit nearby **John Derian's Dry Goods** (Map p422; ☎212-677-8408; 10 E 2nd St; 🕒noon-7pm Tue-Sun; [S]F/V to Lower East Side-2nd Ave).

PATRICIA FIELD FASHION

Map p422 (☎212-966-4066; 302 Bowery at 1st St; 🕒11am-8pm Mon-Thu, to 9pm Fri & Sat, to 7pm Sun; [S]F/V to Lower East Side-2nd Ave) The move from its SoHo digs to the new Bowery location brings much-needed space (4000 sq ft to be exact) to this fun, whimsical design shop. The fashion-forward stylist for *Sex and the City,* Patricia Field isn't afraid of flash, with feather boas, pink jackets, disco dresses, graphic and color-block T-shirts and leopard-print heels, plus colored frizzy wigs, silver spandex and some wacky gift ideas for good measure.

OBSCURA ANTIQUES ANTIQUES

Map p422 (☎212-505-9251; 280 E 10th St btwn First Ave & Ave A; 🕒2-8:30pm; [S]L to 1st Ave) This small cabinet of curiosities pleases both lovers of the macabre and inveterate antique hunters. Here you'll find taxidermy specimens (like a bear's head), butterfly displays in glass boxes, photos of dead people, a mounted deer-hoof, disturbing little (dental?) instruments, old poison bottles, glass eyes, frock coats, Victorian corsets, miscellaneous

EAST VILLAGE VINYL

The East Village has a rich history of producing some of the finest musicians – from indie and jazz to mainstream – so it's no surprise that the area has some of the best spots in the city to score some analog tunes.

A-1 Records (Map p422; ☎212-473-2870; 439 E 6th St btwn First Ave & Ave A; 🕐1-9pm; [S]F/V to Lower East Side-2nd Ave) A huge selection.

Gimme Gimme Records (Map p422; ☎212-475-2955; 325 E 5th St btwn Second & First Aves; 🕐1-10pm Fri & Sat, to 7pm Sun; [S]F/V to Lower East Side-2nd Ave) A great place to browse (with good variety and fair prices), but open three days only.

Good Records (Map p422; ☎212-529-2081; 218 E 5th St btwn Third & Second Aves; 🕐noon-8pm Mon-Sat, 1-8pm Sun; [S]6 to Astor Pl) The selection is overwhelming, but it is well chosen, allowing for some great finds.

Tropicalia in Furs (Map p422; ☎212-982-3251; 304 E 5th St btwn First & Second Aves; 🕐1-8pm Tue-Sun; [S]F/V to Lower East Side-2nd Ave) Specializing in '60s-era Brazilian tropicalia, with offerings of rock, soul and blues.

Turntable Lab (Map p422; ☎212-677-0675; 120 E 7th St btwn First Ave & Ave A; 🕐1-9pm Mon-Fri, noon-8pm Sat, noon-6pm Sun; [S]F/V to Lower East Side-2nd Ave) Electronic music and DJ mixes.

beakers and other items not currently available at the local department store.

KIEHL'S
BEAUTY

Map p422 (☎212-677-3171, 800-543-4571; 109 Third Ave btwn 13th & 14th Sts; 🕐10am-8pm Mon-Sat, 11am-6pm Sun; [S]L to 3rd Ave) Making and selling skincare products since it opened in NYC as an apothecary in 1851, this Kiehl's flagship store has doubled its shop size and expanded into an international chain, but its personal touch remains – as do the coveted, generous sample sizes.

Pick up some of the legendary moisturizers, masks and emollients, including Creme with Silk Groom for the hair, Creme de Corps for the body or Abyssine Serum for the face. Kiehl's has another NYC branch on the **Upper West Side** (Map p442; ☎212-799-3438; 154 Columbus Ave; 🕐10am-8pm Mon-Sat, 11am-7pm Sun; [S]1 to 66th St-Lincoln Center).

DE LA VEGA
STREET ART

Map p422 (☎212-876-8649; 102 St Marks Pl btwn First Ave & Ave A; 🕐1pm-8pm Mon, Tue & Thu-Sat, 1-6pm Sun; [S]6 to Astor Pl) The 30-something artist De La Vega is sometimes described as a blend of Keith Haring and Francisco de Goya. If you don't have time to hunt for his street murals in Spanish Harlem, head to his small gallery space in the East Village.

Small canvases, T-shirts and other curios feature De La Vega's iconic motifs like two fish gazing at one another from opposite fish bowls.

JOHN VARVATOS
CLOTHING, SHOES

Map p422 (☎212-358-0315; 315 Bowery btwn 1st & 2nd Sts; 🕐noon-9pm Mon-Sat, to 7pm Sun; [S]F/V to Lower East Side-2nd Ave; 6 to Bleecker St) Set in the hallowed halls of former punk club CBGB, the John Varvatos Bowery store is either a grievous insult to rock history or a creative reconfiguration of the past – depending on which side of the gentrification aisle you happen to stand on. The store goes to great lengths to tie fashion with rock and roll, with records, '70s audio equipment and even electric guitars for sale alongside JV's denim, leather boots, belts and graphic tees. It also has a small stage (not original) and old show posters that pay homage to the space's colorful past.

FOOTLIGHT RECORDS
MUSIC

Map p422 (☎212-533-1572; 113 E 12th St btwn Third & Fourth Aves; 🕐11am-7pm Mon-Fri, 10am-6pm Sat, noon-5pm Sun; [S]R/W to 8th St-NYU; 6 to Astor Pl) Home to a well-chosen collection of out-of-print Broadway and foreign-movie soundtracks, Footlight is a must-visit for vinyl hounds, show-tune lovers and anyone searching for a particular version of a hard-to-find cabaret song.

Lower East Side

The downtown fashion crowd looking for that edgy, experimental, or 'old-school hip-hop' look head to the shops in the Lower

East Side. Sprinkled among the area's many bars and restaurants are dozens of stores selling vintage apparel, vegan shoes (yes, you read that right), old-fashioned candy, sex toys, left-wing books and more. You'll find the most shops on Orchard and Ludlow Sts, between Houston and Delancey Sts, but it's worth wandering to other strips, too.

EDITH MACHINIST VINTAGE CLOTHING

Map p424 (☎212-979-9992; 104 Rivington St at Essex St; 🕒1-8pm; [S]F, J/M/Z to Delancey-Essex Sts) To properly strut about the Lower East Side, you've got to dress the part. Edith Machinist can help you get that rumpled but stylish look in a hurry – a bit of vintage glam via 1930s silk dresses and ballet-style flats, with military jackets and weather-beaten leather satchels for the gents.

DRESSING ROOM CLOTHING

Map p424 (www.thedressingroomnyc.com; 75A Orchard St btwn Broome & Grand Sts; 🕒1pm-midnight Sun, Tue & Wed, 1pm-2am Thu-Sat; [S]F, J/M/Z to Delancey-Essex Sts) The Dressing Room is a creative hybrid that's equal parts indie fashion boutique and low-key neighborhood bar. On the 1st floor, you'll find a rotating mix of local and emerging designers with pieces ranging from clever graphic T-shirts to flouncy black dresses and wildly patterned knits, while downstairs is a small selection of vintage clothes.

Adjoining the space is a casual bar with a regular lineup of DJs, film screenings and shopping parties. The drink-shop combo can be quite handy for some couples who can't quite resolve their disparate interests in looking at clothes versus swilling some martinis.

SPIRITUAL AMERICA CLOTHING

(☎212-960-8564; 5 Rivington St btwn the Bowery & Chrystie St; [S]F to Lower East Side 2nd Ave) It's everything you're looking for in a one-of-a-kind clothing boutique: carefully selected items gathered by a discerning eye and prices that feel refreshingly reasonable when compared to the neighboring bank-breakers.

TG170 CLOTHING

Map p424 (☎212-995-8660; 170 Ludlow St btwn Stanton & Housten Sts; 🕒noon-8pm; [S]F, J/M/Z to Delancey-Essex Sts) One of the first boutiques to blaze the trail into the Lower East Side way back in 1992, TG170 is still a major destination for downtown style-seekers. Inside the graffiti-covered storefront, you'll find both young and established designers pushing a fashion-forward look. Vivienne Westwood dresses, Lauren Moffatt jackets and vinyl Freitag bags look all the better beneath the wild ice-planet-style chandeliers.

REED SPACE FASHION, ACCESSORIES

Map p424 (www.thereedspace.com; 151 Orchard St btwn Stanton & Rivington Sts; 🕒1-7pm Mon-Fri, noon-7pm Sat & Sun; [S]F to Delancey-Essex Sts) Sneakers, accessories, youthful tees, pants and jackets for both sexes line the bright and varied shelves at Reed Space. Designer Jeff Ng has found a blueprint for the urban casual lifestyle.

LAS VENUS ANTIQUES

Map p424 (☎212-982-0608; 163 Ludlow St btwn Stanton & Housten Sts; 🕒11am-8pm Mon-Fri, noon-8pm Sat & Sun; [S]F, J/M/Z to Delancey-Essex Sts) Down a couple of steps from the street, this colorful shop packs in cool Danish-modern furniture (from the 1950s, '60s and '70s) and other vintage furnishings. Much of it edges toward the pricey, but some deals await the prodder (as well as old *Playboys*, if that's your thing). Las Venus has another inviting store nearby – **LV2** (Map p424; ☎212-358-8000; 113 Stanton St;

UP-AND-COMING WOMEN'S CLOTHING BOUTIQUES

In NYC's ever-ephemeral shopping scene, boutiques – like style trends – come and go on a whim. The following three shops offer up some of the hippest threads around. Hit them up in one go – they're all around the corner from one another.

Reformation (www.thereformation.com; 156 Ludlow St btwn Rivington & Stanton Sts; 🕒noon-8pm Mon-Sat, to 7pm Sun; [S]F to Delancey St or 2nd Ave; J/M/Z to Essex St)

Dolce Vita (www.shopdolcevita.com; 136 Orchard St btwn Delancey & Rivington Sts; [S]F to Delancey St or 2nd Ave; J/M/Z to Essex St)

Yumi Kim (www.yumikimshop.com; 105 Stanton St btwn Ludlow & Essex Sts; 🕒noon-7pm Mon-Sun; [S]F to Delancey St or 2nd Ave; J/M/Z to Essex St)

S F, J/M/Z to Delancey-Essex Sts) – and also stocks chrome furnishings on the 2nd floor of ABC Carpet & Home.

MOO SHOES
SHOES

Map p424 (www.mooshoes.com; 78 Orchard St btwn Broome & Grand Sts; ⊙11:30am-7:30pm Mon-Sat, noon-6pm Sun; S F, J/M/Z to Delancey-Essex Sts) Socially and environmentally responsible fashion usually tends to entail certain sacrifices in the good-looks department. Bucking the trend is Moo Shoes, a vegan boutique where style is no small consideration in the design of inexpensive microfiber (faux leather) shoes, bags and motorcycle jackets. Look for smart-looking Novacas, Crystalyn Kae purses, Queenbee Creations messenger bags and sleek Matt & Nat wallets.

For more ecofriendly designs, head across the street to the cute boutique **Kaight** (Map p424; www.kaightnyc.com; 83 Orchard St; ⊙11:30am-7:30pm; S F, J/M/Z to Delancey-Essex Sts).

ALIFE RIVINGTON CLUB
FASHION, ACCESSORIES

Map p424 (ARC; www.rivingtonclub.com; 158 Rivington St near Clinton St; ⊙11am-7pm Mon-Sat, noon-6pm Sun; S J/M/Z to Delancey-Essex Sts) Concealed behind an unmarked entrance (ring the buzzer), ARC feels more like the VIP lounge of a nightclub than a shoe store. You'll find royal-hued carpeting, a long leather couch and a handsome display case of rare, limited-edition sneakers.

Stocks of those coveted Nikes and Adidases change often and sell out fast, so don't dawdle if you see something you like. For more upscale streetwear, check out Alife's spinoff, **ARC Sports** (Map p424; ☎212-253-0363; 157 Rivington St; S F, J/M/Z to Delancey-Essex Sts) across the road.

ESSEX STREET MARKET
MARKET

Map p424 (www.essexstreetmarket.com; 120 Essex St btwn Delancey & Rivington Sts; ⊙8am-7pm Mon-Sat; S F/V to Delancey St; J/M/Z to Delancey-Essex Sts) This 60-year-old historic shopping

---

LOCAL KNOWLEDGE

RAIN CHECKLIST
....

Teresa Soroka, rainy day guru and owner of Amé Amé (p122), gives us her insider tips for making the most of those inevitable days of drizzle.

Circle Line
Take the **Circle Line** (☎212-563-3200; www.circleline42.com; Pier 83, W 42nd St; tickets $16-34) ferry around Manhattan while absorbing the changing scenery and the grand stature of New York's skyscrapers – it's especially magical in the rain.

Lower East Side Tenement Museum
While everybody's at the Met or MoMA, check out the history of American immigrants at this wonderfully interactive museum (p102).

Upright Citizens Brigade Theatre
There's nothing like a good laugh at one of the city's best improvisational theaters (p151) when you feel like the weather is raining on your parade.

Grand Central Terminal
New Yorkers hustle and bustle differently when it's raining, and you can feel it when you're at Grand Central (p187). Don't miss the historic, celestial ceiling, and if you meet the dress code, have a chic cocktail at the Campbell Apartment.

American Museum of Natural History
No matter your age, it's hard not to let your imagination wander at the dinosaur displays at the American Museum of Natural History (p234). Take a rainy day nap under the big blue whale.

Cloisters Museum & Gardens
A nice drizzle is the perfect background to take in the Medieval architecture at the Cloisters Museum & Gardens (p256) while having a mini escape within Manhattan. Stroll through Fort Tryon Park and then immerse yourself in the castles and arches of mystery and wonder.

destination is the local place for produce, seafood, butcher-cut meats, cheeses, Latino grocery items, and even a barber. It's a fun place to explore, with snack stands and an attached restaurant when you really want to get down to business.

BLUESTOCKINGS BOOKS

Map p424 (www.bluestockings.com; 172 Allen St btwn Stanton & Rivington Sts; ⏰11am-11pm; [S]F/V to Lower East Side-2nd Ave) This independent bookstore, first opened with a lesbian bent, has now expanded to radicalism of all kinds. It's still women-owned, though, and its shelves have a strong selection of dyke and feminist lit and crit – along with tomes on gender studies, global capitalism, democracy studies, black liberation and police and prison systems.

It's also the site of a vegan, organic, fair-trade cafe, as well as myriad readings and speaking events, including women's poetry readings, workshops on radical protests and even a monthly Dyke Knitting Circle.

SPORTS & ACTIVITIES

RUSSIAN & TURKISH BATHS BATHHOUSE

Map p422 (☎212-674-9250; www.russianturkishbaths.com; 268 E 10th St btwn First Ave & Ave A; per visit $30; ⏰noon-10pm Mon,Tue, Thu & Fri, 10am-10pm Wed, 9am-10pm Sat, 8am-10pm Sun; [S]L to 1st Ave; 6 to Astor Pl) Since 1892, this has been the spa for anyone who wants to get naked (or stay in their swimsuit) and romp in steam baths, an ice-cold plunge pool, a sauna and on the sundeck. The baths are open to both men and women most hours (wearing shorts is required at these times). Check the website for more detailed opening hours.

PIZZA A CASA COOKING COURSE

Map p424 (☎212-209-3370; www.pizzaacasa.com; 371 Grand St btwn Essex & Norfolk Sts; class $150) Housed in a kitchen that doubles as a laboratory and classroom, Pizza A Casa walks 12 pie-ophiles through the process of making their own slices, from designing the dough from scratch to adding a selection of gourmet ingredients. Sessions last around two hours, and at the end you'll have four handmade pies to devour with friends.

Greenwich Village, Chelsea & the Meatpacking District

Neighborhood Top Five

1 Packing a picnic lunch from Chelsea Market and having a uniquely pastoral moment on the **High Line's** (p130) thin strand of green as it soars above the grid-iron.

2 Checking out the city's brightest art stars at the

gaggles of galleries in **Chelsea** (p134).

3 Walking through **Washington Square Park** (p133), pausing under the signature arch then loitering at the fountain to eavesdrop on gossiping NYU kids.

4 Putting on the ritz in the **Meatpacking District** (p135) then breezing by guest lists for cocktails in exclusive lounges.

5 Sipping lattes alfresco on cobblestone corners and searching for out-of-print paperbacks in the **West Village** (p146).

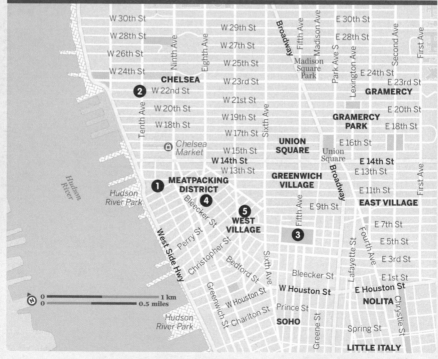

For more detail of this area, see Maps p426 and p430 ➡

Explore Greenwich Village, Chelsea & the Meatpacking District

There's a very good reason why this area is known as the Village: it kinda looks like one! Quaint, quiet lanes carve their way between brown-brick townhouses offering endless strolling fodder for locals appreciating good weather, or tourists coming to see what all the fuss is about. The Village is cute indeed, and the best way to uncover its treasures is to simply have a wander, and when your feet grow tired of negotiating the cobbled streets, plunk yourself down at a cafe with a soup-bowl-sized cappuccino.

Stroll through the Meatpacking District – once filled with slaughterhouses and now brimming with sleek boutiques and roaring nightclubs – to reach Chelsea just a smidge to the north. Chelsea bridges the gap between the West Village and Midtown, importing bits and bobs from both. It's the de facto neighborhood for the city's sociable gay community, and its broad avenues are lined with breezy cafes, themed bars and sweaty clubs. The neighborhood's massive gallery scene can be found in the West 20s, with starkly contrasting mega-mart retailers orbiting Sixth Ave.

Local Life

→ **Eighth Ave brunch** If you're a dude looking to meet (or at least look at) other dudes, but the cruise-y bar scene isn't your style, then opt for the weekend brunch scene along Eighth Ave. You'll spot piles of friendly Chelsea boys drinking off their hangovers in tight jeans and even tighter T-shirts.

→ **West Village cafes** The West Village is one of the most desirable residential neighborhoods in the city, so do as the locals do and make the most of this quaint district stacked to the brim with cute cafes. Grab a book and a latte and hunker down for a blissful afternoon of people-watching.

Getting There & Away

→ **Subway** Sixth Ave, Seventh Ave and Eighth Ave are graced with convenient subway stations, but public transportation slims further west. Take the A, C, E or 1, 2, 3 to reach this colorful clump of neighborhoods – disembark at 14th St (along either service) if you're looking for a good place to make tracks.

→ **Bus** Try M14 or the M8 if you're traveling across town and want to access the westernmost areas of Chelsea and the West Village by public transportation. It's a shame, however, to use the bus or a taxi to get around the West Village – the charming cobblestone streets are perfect for a stroll.

Lonely Planet's Top Tip

It's perfectly acceptable to arm yourself with a map (or rely on your smartphone) to get around the West Village's charming-but-challenging side streets. Even some locals have a tricky time finding their way! Just remember that 4th St makes a diagonal turn north – breaking away from usual east-west street grid – and you'll quickly become a Village pro.

✗ Best Places to Eat

→ RedFarm (p139)
→ Chelsea Market (p132)
→ Cookshop (p146)
→ Tartine (p139)

For reviews, see p139 ➡

♀ Best Places to Drink

→ Little Branch (p147)
→ Marie's Crisis (p147)
→ Boom Boom Room (p147)
→ Vin Sur Vingt (p147)
→ Art Bar (p147)

For reviews, see p146 ➡

Best Bookshops

→ Printed Matter (p157)
→ Strand Book Store (p154)
→ Three Lives & Company (p154)
→ Posman Books (p157)
→ Bonnie Slotnick Cookbooks (p154)

For reviews, see p154 ➡

HUW JONES / LONELY PLANET IMAGES ©

TOP SIGHTS
THE HIGH LINE

In the early 1900s, the western area around the Meatpacking District and Chelsea was the largest industrial section of Manhattan, and a set of elevated tracks were created to move freight off the cluttered streets below. As NYC evolved, the rails eventually became obsolete, and in 1999 a plan was made to convert the scarring strands of metal into a public green space. On June 9, 2009, part one of the city's most beloved urban renewal project opened with much ado, and it's been one of New York's star attractions ever since.

Industrial Past

It's hard to believe that the High Line – a shining example of brilliant urban renewal – was once a dingy rail line that anchored a rather unsavory district of thugs, trannies and slaughterhouses. The tracks that would one day become the High Line were commissioned in the 1930s when the municipal government decided to raise the street-level tracks after years of accidents that gave Tenth Ave the nickname 'Death Avenue.' The project drained over $150 million in funds (equivalent to around $2 billion by today's dime) and took roughly five years to complete. After two decades of effective use, a rise in truck transportation and traffic led to the eventual decrease in usage, and finally, in the 1980s, the rails became obsolete. Petitions were signed by local residents to remove the eyesores, but in 1999 a committee called the Friends of the High Line – founded by Joshua David and Robert Hammond – was formed to save

DON'T MISS...

- ➡ Cut-out box at 17th St
- ➡ Cut-out box at 30th St
- ➡ Views down to the High Line from the Standard Hotel
- ➡ Public art scattered about

PRACTICALITIES

- ➡ Map p426
- ➡ ☎212-500-6035
- ➡ www.thehighline.org
- ➡ Gansevoort St
- ➡ 🕒7am-7pm
- ➡ [S]L or A/C/E to 14th St-8th Ave; C/E to 23rd St-8th Ave, 🚌M11 to Washington Street; M11, M14 to 9th Avenue; M23, M34 to 10th Avenue

the rusting iron and transform the tracks into a unique elevated green space.

A Green Future

On a warm spring day in 2009, the High Line – full of blooming flowers and Kelly-green trees – opened to the public, the first of three planned phases that will one day link the Meatpacking District and Midtown. Section 1 starts at Gansevoort St and runs parallel to Tenth St up to West 20th St. Full of sitting space in various forms – from giant chaise lounges to bleacherlike benching – the first part quickly became the setting for various public works and activities, many geared towards the neighborhood's growing population of families. Section 2 opened in June of 2011, adding another 10 blocks of green-ified tracks, and the final section will meander across the partially privately owned West Side Rail Yards up to 34th St in a U-like fashion. Negotiations for renovation are still under way and an official opening date has – at the time of writing – yet to be slated.

More than Just a Public Space

The High Line's civic influence extends far beyond being the trendsetter in the island's re-green-ification. As the West Village and Chelsea continue to embrace their new-found residential nature, the High Line is making a dedicated move towards becoming more than just a public place but an inspired meeting point for families and friends. As you walk along the High Line you'll find dedicated staffers wearing shirts with the signature double-H logo who can point you in the right direction or offer you additional information about the converted rails. There are also myriad staffers behind the scenes organizing public art exhibitions and activity sessions for family and friends. Group tours for children can be organized on a variety of topics from the plantlife of the high-rise park to the area's history.

PUBLIC ART DISPLAYS

In addition to being a haven of hovering green, the High Line is also an informal art space featuring a variety of installations, both site-specific and standalone. For detailed information about the public art on display at the time of your visit, check out www. thehighline.org/about/ public-art.

Like the smattering of ever-evolving art, the High Line also invites various gastronomic establishments from around the city to set up vending carts and stalls so that strollers can enjoy to-go items on the green. Expect a showing of the finest coffee and ice cream establishments during the warmer months.

GREENWICH VILLAGE, CHELSEA & THE MEATPACKING DISTRICT THE HIGH LINE

TOP SIGHTS
CHELSEA MARKET

ALEX SEGRE / ALAMY ©

In a shining example of redevelopment and preservation, the Chelsea Market has taken a former factory of cookie giant Nabisco (creator of the Oreo) and turned it into an 800ft-long shopping concourse that caters to foodies. And that's only the lower part of a larger, million-sq-ft space that occupies a full city block – upstairs you'll find the current home of several TV channels, including the Food Network, Oxygen Network and NY1, the local news channel.

National Biscuit Company

Continuing the building's significance as a major land-mark, the renamed Chelsea Market opened in the '90s as a base camp for gourmet outlets and apparel boutiques.

A New Generation of Sweets

Taking the place of the old factory ovens that churned out massive numbers of biscuits are the boutique bakeries that fill the renovated hallways of this foodie haven. **Eleni's** (212-255-6804; Chelsea Market) is of special note – Eleni Gianopulos was one of the first tenants here, and her expertly designed cookies are a big hit for one-time biters as well as repeat visitors.

Also worth a stop is **Sarabeth's** (www.sarabeths.com; Chelsea Market), where tasty incarnations of flour and dough are whipped into perfect desserts. Sweet-tooths will fawn over **l'Arte Del Gelato** (www.lartedelgelato.com; Chelsea Market). Gelato flavors are made fresh every day and come in over 20 varieties – it's the perfect snack to take up to the High Line.

Although geared more towards the savory, **Amy's Bread** (Map p430; www.amysbread.com; Chelsea Market) has fine loaves that make a brilliant tribute to the hundreds of ovens that once inhabited the buildings.

DON'T MISS...

➡ Amy's Bread
➡ Dickson Meats
➡ Posman Books
➡ The High Line out back

PRACTICALITIES

➡ Map p430
➡ www.chelsea market.com
➡ 75 Ninth Ave at 15th St
➡ ⏰7am-9pm Mon-Sat, 10am-8pm Sun
➡ Ⓢ A/C/E to 14th St; L to 8th Ave

TOP SIGHTS
WASHINGTON SQUARE PARK

What was once a potter's field and a square for public executions is now the unofficial town square of the Village, and plays host to lounging NYU students, fire-eating street performers, curious canines and their owners, and legions of speed-chess pros. Encased in perfectly manicured brownstones and gorgeous twists of modern architecture (all owned by NYU), Washington Square Park is one of the most beautiful garden spaces in the city – especially as you are welcomed by the iconic Stanford White Arch on the north side of the green.

History

Although quite ravishing today, Washington Square Park has had a long and sordid history before finally blossoming into the paradigm of public space we see today (thanks largely to a $16 million renovation that began in 2007).

When the Dutch settled Manhattan to run the Dutch East India Company, they gave what is now the park to their freed black slaves. The land was squarely between the Dutch and Native settlements, so, in a way, the area acted as a buffer between enemies. Though somewhat marshy, it was arable land and farming took place for around 60 years.

At the turn of the 19th century, the municipality of New York purchased the land for use as a burial ground straddling the city's limit. At first the cemetery was mainly for indigent workers, but the space quickly reached capacity during an outbreak of yellow fever. Over 20,000 bodies remain buried under the park today.

By 1830 the grounds were used for military parades, and then quickly transformed into a park for the wealthy elite who were constructing lavish townhouses along the surrounding streets.

Stanford White Arch

The iconic Stanford White Arch, colloquially known as the Washington Square Arch, dominates the park with its 72ft of beaming white Dover marble. Originally designed in wood to celebrate the centennial of George Washington's inauguration in 1889, the arch proved so popular that it was replaced with stone six years later and adorned with statues of the general in war and peace. In 1916 artist Marcel Duchamp famously climbed to the top of the arch by its internal stairway and declared the park the 'Free and Independent Republic of Washington Square.'

In Recent Years

Once it was clear that the park was here to stay, the public green became a haven for beatniks and political outcry, especially when urban planners sought to change the shape and usage of the space. Locals vehemently protested, and the square's shape has remained largely unchanged since the 1800s.

The political tradition continues even today, when Barack Obama led a rally here in 2007 to drum up support for his presidential bid. Turnout was, unsurprisingly, overwhelming.

DON'T MISS...

- ➡ Stanford White Arch
- ➡ Central fountain
- ➡ Greek Revival houses surrounding the park

PRACTICALITIES

- ➡ Map p426
- ➡ www.washingtonsquareparkcouncil.org
- ➡ Fifth Ave at Washington Sq N
- ➡ [S]A/C/E, B/D/F/V to W 4th St-Washington Sq; N/R/W to 8th St-NYU

TOP SIGHTS
CHELSEA GALLERIES

Chelsea is home to the highest concentration of art galleries in the entire city – and the cluster continues to grow with each passing season. Most lie in the 20s, on the blocks between Tenth and Eleventh Aves. With hundreds of galleries peppering the area's westernmost avenues and streets it can be downright difficult to figure out which showcase to visit when; fortunately, a casual wander can reveal interesting installations that capture the imagination. But for a complete guide and map, pick up Artinfo's *Gallery Guide,* available for free at most galleries, or visit www.westchelseaarts.com. Wine-and-cheese openings for their new shows are typically held on Thursday evenings, while most art houses tend to shutter their doors on Sundays and Mondays.

DON'T MISS...

- Thursday openings

PRACTICALITIES

- [S]C/E to 23rd St

Galleries at a Glance

The showcases that generate the most buzz are the so-called 'blue-chip' galleries – and there are many. In addition to some of the favorites below, it's well worth checking out the **Andrea Rosen Gallery** (Map p430; www.andrearosengallery.com; 525 W 24th St; admission free; 🕒10am-6pm Tue-Sat; [S]C/E, 1 to 23rd St), with gems by Katy Moran, Rita Ackerman and Felix Gonzalez-Torres; the **Mary Boone Gallery** (Map p430; www.maryboonegallery.com; 541 W 24th St; [S]C/E, 1 to 23rd St), whose owner found fame in the '80s with her eye for Jean-Michel Basquiat and Julian Schnabel in SoHo; and the **Matthew Marks Gallery** (Map p430; www.matthewmarks.com; 523 W 24th), a Chelsea pioneer known for exhibiting big names, from Jasper Johns to Ellsworth Kelly.

Alexander & Bonin

Since moving to Chelsea in 1997, the three-story **Alexander & Bonin gallery** (Map p430; www.alexanderandbonin.com; 132 Tenth Ave near 18th St; 🕒11am-6pm Tue-Sat; [S]C/E to 23rd St) has made excellent use of its airy space with a stellar roster of artists, including several prestigious Turner Prize winners. Carolyn Alexander and Ted Bonin, the directors, can sometimes be seen at their 2nd-story desks. Recent shows include Willie Cole and Willie Doherty.

Barbara Gladstone

The curator of this eponymous **gallery** (Map p430; www.gladstonegallery.com; 515 W 24th St btwn Tenth & Eleventh Aves; 🕒10am-6pm Tue-Sat, closed weekends Jul & Aug; [S]C/E, 1 to 23rd St) has learned a thing or two after 27 years in the Manhattan art world. Ms Gladstone consistently puts together the most talked-about and well-critiqued displays, and artists such as Shirin Neshat, Magnus von Plessen and Anish Kapoor are frequently shown.

Cheim & Read

Sculptures of every shape, size and material abound at **Cheim & Read** (Map p430; www.cheimread.com; 547 W 25th St btwn Tenth & Eleventh Aves; 🕒10am-6pm Tue-Sat; [S]C/E to 23rd St), and monthly changes keep the exhibits fresh. If the timing is right, you might catch William Eggleston's bouncy color photographs hanging on the wall.

Greene Naftali

Sharp, edgy and youth-oriented **Greene Naftali** (Map p430; www.greenenaftaligallery.com; 526 W 26th St; admission free; 🕒10am-6pm Tue-Sat; [S]C/E to 23rd St) has an ever-rotating display of art in all kinds of media: film/video, installation, painting, drawing and performance art.

SIGHTS

Greenwich Village & the Meatpacking District

THE HIGH LINE — OUTDOORS

See p130.

WASHINGTON SQUARE PARK — SQUARE

See p133.

NEW YORK UNIVERSITY — UNIVERSITY

Map p426 (NYU; www.nyu.edu; information center 50 W 4th St; [S]A/C/E, B/D/F/V to W 4th St-Washington Sq; R/W to 8th St-NYU) In 1831 Albert Gallatin, formerly Secretary of the Treasury under President Thomas Jefferson, founded an intimate center of higher learning open to all students, regardless of race or class background. He'd scarcely recognize the place today, as it's swelled to a student population of more than 54,000, with more than 16,000 employees, and schools and colleges at six Manhattan locations.

It just keeps growing, too – to the dismay of landmark activists and business owners, who have seen buildings rapidly bought out by the academic giant (or destroyed such as with the historic Provincetown Playhouse) and replaced with dormitories or administrative offices. Still, some of its crevices are charming, such as the leafy courtyard at its School of Law, or impressively modern, like the Skirball Center for the Performing Arts, where top-notch dance, theater, music, spoken-word and other performers wow audiences at the 850-seat theater. NYU's academic offerings are highly regarded and wide-ranging, especially its film, theater, writing, medical and law programs. For a unique experience that will put you on the fast track to meeting locals, sign up for a weekend or one-day class – from American history to photography – offered by the School of Professional Studies and Continuing Education, and open to all.

ASTOR PLACE — SQUARE

Map p422 (8th St btwn Third & Fourth Aves; [S]R/W to 8th St-NYU; 6 to Astor Pl) This square is named after the Astor family, who built an early New York fortune on beaver pelts (check out the tiles in the wall of the Astor Place subway platform) and lived on Colonnade Row, just south of the square. Four of the original nine marble-faced, Greek Revival residences on Lafayette St still exist. The large, brownstone Cooper Union, the public college founded in 1859 by millionaire Peter Cooper, dominates the square – now more than ever – as the school now has its first new academic building in over 50 years, a striking, twisting, nine-story sculpture of glazed glass wrapped in perforated stainless steel (and LEED-certified, too) by architect Thom Mayne of Morphosis.

GRACE CHURCH — CHURCH

Map p426 (www.gracechurchnyc.org; 802 Broadway at 10th St; ⏲10am-5pm, services daily; [S]R/W to 8th St-NYU; 6 to Astor Pl) This Gothic Revival Episcopal church, designed in 1843 by James Renwick Jr, was made of marble quarried by prisoners at 'Sing Sing,' the state penitentiary in the town of Ossining, 30 miles up the Hudson River (which, legend has it, is the origin of the expression 'being sent upriver'). After years of neglect, Grace Church is being spiffed up in a major way; now it's a National Landmark, whose elaborate carvings, towering spire and verdant, groomed yard are sure to stop you in your tracks as you make your way down this otherwise ordinary stretch of the Village. The stained-glass windows inside are stunning, and the soaring interior makes a perfect setting for the frequent organ and choir concerts.

FORBES COLLECTION — MUSEUM

Map p426 (www.forbesgalleries.com; 62 Fifth Ave at 12th St; admission free; ⏲10am-4pm Tue-Sat; [S]L, N/Q/R/W, 4/5/6 to 14th St-Union Sq) These galleries, located in the lobby of the headquarters of *Forbes* magazine, house rotating exhibits and curios from the personal collection of the late publishing magnate Malcolm Forbes. The eclectic mix of objects on display includes Fabergé eggs, toy boats, early versions of Monopoly and over 10,000 toy soldiers.

ABINGDON SQUARE — SQUARE

Map p426 (Hudson St at 12th St) This historic dot on the landscape (just a quarter-acre) is a lovely little patch of green, home to grassy knolls, beds of perennial flowers and winding bluestone paths, as well as a popular Saturday greenmarket. It's a great place to enjoy a lunchtime picnic or rest after an afternoon of wandering the winding West Village streets. After getting horizontal, look up at the southern end of the park and you'll see the *Abingdon Doughboy,* a bronze statue dedicated to servicemen from the

GREENWICH VILLAGE, CHELSEA & THE MEATPACKING DISTRICT NEIGHBORHOOD WALK

Neighborhood Walk

It Takes a Village...

Of all the neighborhoods in New York City, Greenwich Village is the most pedestrian-friendly, with its cobbled corners that stray from the signature gridiron that unfurls across the rest of the island. Start your walkabout at the **1 Cherry Lane Theatre**. Established in 1924, the small theater is the city's longest continuously running off-Broadway establishment, and was the center of creative activity during the 1940s. Make a left on Bedford and you'll find **2 90 Bedford** on the right-hand side at the corner of Grove St. You might recognize the apartment block as the fictitious home of the cast of *Friends* (sadly, Central Perk was just a figment of the writers' imaginations). For another iconic TV landmark, wander up Bleecker St and make a right on Perry St, stopping at **3 66 Perry St**, which was used as the facade and stoop of the city's 'It Girl', Carrie Bradshaw, in *Sex and the City*. Make a right on W 4th St until you reach **4 Christopher Park**, where two white, life-sized statues of same-sex

couples stand guard. On the north side of the greenspace is the legendary Stonewall Inn, where a clutch of fed-up drag queens rioted for their civil rights in 1969, signaling the start of what would become the gay revolution.

Follow Christopher St to Sixth Ave to find the **5 Jefferson Market Library** straddling a triangular plot of land. The 'Ruskinian gothic' spire was once a fire lookout tower; today the structure houses a branch of the public library; in the 1870s it was used as a courthouse. Stroll down Sixth Ave taking in the flurry of passersby, then make a left on Minetta Lane to swing by **6 Café Wha?**, the notorious institution where many young musicians and comedians – like Bob Dylan and Richard Pryor – got their start. End your wandering further along MacDougal St in **7 Washington Square Park**, the Village's unofficial town square, which plays host to loitering NYU students, buskers and a regular crowd of protestors chanting about various global and municipal injustices.

neighborhood who gave their lives in WWI (when soldiers were commonly known as 'doughboys').

PIER 45 OUTDOORS

Map p426 (Christopher St at Hudson River; [S]1 to Christopher St-Sheridan Sq) Still known to many as the Christopher Street Pier, this is an 850ft-long finger of concrete, spiffily renovated with a grass lawn, flowerbeds, a comfort station, an outdoor cafe, tented shade shelters and a stop for the New York Water Taxi as part of the ongoing Hudson River Park project. And it's a magnet for downtowners of all stripes, from local families with toddlers in daylight to mobs of young gay kids who flock here at night from all over the city (and beyond) because of the pier's long-established history as a gay cruising hangout. That's been the source of ongoing conflict in the neighborhood, where moneyed West Village residents say that the clutches of youths who stream there along Christopher St are disorderly and disrespectful late into the night. The kids say they've got nowhere else to go, and deserve a claim to the pier just like anyone else. It's unclear how it'll all work out, but one thing's for sure: the spot offers sweeping views of the Hudson and cool, relieving breezes in the thick of summer.

WHITE COLUMNS GALLERY

Map p426 (www.whitecolumns.org; 320 W 13th St; admission free; ⏲noon-6pm Tue-Sat; [S]A/C/E, L to 8th Ave-14th St) Geographically, White Columns is part of the Meatpacking District, but aesthetically speaking, it's in Chelsea. The sedate, four-room space has ample installations and exhibits, many of which are by fairly well-known names like Andrew Serrano, Alice Aycock, Lorna Simpson and a White Columns founder, Gordon Matta-Clark. One of its most successful recent installations came from South London's Studio Voltaire, which presented different works all related to the public persona of singer Michael Jackson.

⊙ Chelsea

CHELSEA GALLERIES GALLERY

See p134.

CHELSEA MARKET MARKET

See p132.

CHELSEA HOTEL HISTORIC BUILDING

Map p430 (☎212-243-3700; 222 W 23rd St btwn Seventh & Eighth Aves; [S]1, C/E to 23rd St) It's probably not any great shakes as far as hotels go – and besides, it mainly houses long-term residents – but as a place of mythical proportions, the Chelsea Hotel is top of the line. The red-brick hotel, featuring ornate iron balconies and no fewer than seven plaques declaring its literary landmark status, has played a major role in pop-culture history. It's where the likes of Mark Twain, Thomas Wolfe, Dylan Thomas and Arthur Miller hung out; Jack Kerouac allegedly crafted *On the Road* during one marathon session here, and it's where Arthur C Clarke wrote *2001: A Space Odyssey*. Dylan Thomas died of alcohol poisoning while staying here in 1953, and Nancy Spungeon died here after being stabbed by her Sex Pistols boyfriend Sid Vicious in 1978. Among the many celebs who have logged time living at the Chelsea are Joni Mitchell, Arthur Miller, Stanley Kubrick, Dennis Hopper, Edith Piaf, Bob Dylan and Leonard Cohen, whose song 'Chelsea Hotel' recalls a romp with Janis Joplin (who spent time here, too). The art-filled lobby is worth a look-see, and its basement-level Star Lounge is a sexy, low-lit spot for a martini.

GENERAL THEOLOGICAL SEMINARY CHURCH

Map p430 (www.gts.edu; 175 Ninth Ave btwn 20th & 21st Sts; ⏲noon-3pm Mon-Fri, 11am-3pm Sat; [S]C/E to 23rd St) Founded in 1817, this is the oldest seminary of the Episcopal Church in America – as well as home to the Desmond Tutu Center, which hosts various peace and reconciliation conferences. The school, which sits in the midst of the beautiful Chelsea historic district, has been working hard lately to make sure it can preserve its best asset – the gardenlike campus snuggled in the middle of its full block of buildings – even as Chelsea development sprouts up all around it. This peaceful haven is the perfect spot for finding respite, either before or after your neighborhood gallery crawl.

RUBIN MUSEUM OF ART MUSEUM

Map p430 (www.rmanyc.org; 150 W 17th St at Seventh Ave; adult/child $10/free, 7-10pm Fri free; ⏲11am-5pm Mon & Thu, to 7pm Wed, to 10pm Fri, to 6pm Sat & Sun; [S]1 to 18th St) This is the first museum in the Western world to dedicate itself to the art of the Himalayas and surrounding regions. Its impressive collections

START **529 W 20TH ST**
END **27TH ST**
DISTANCE **1.5 MILES**
TIME **2 HOURS**

Neighborhood Walk
Chelsea's Art Tour

➤ Follow this zigzagging route and you'll hit up some of the finest galleries in Chelsea's famed district. Start on 20th St at the High Line and enter the eight-floor building at ❶ **529 W 20th St**, where you'll find ACA Galleries, Admit One Gallery, the Bill Maynes Gallery and many others.

Stroll north along Tenth Ave, taking a left on 22nd St; at the junction of Eleventh Ave check out the ❷ **Chelsea Art Museum**, a unique collection of 'Informal Art' near the Hudson River. Head north on Eleventh Ave and turn right on 24th St, where you'll find a trio of excellent showcases: the famous ❸ **Mary Boone Gallery**, ❹ **Luhring Augustine**, which often shows large-format photography, and ❺ **Metro Pictures**, best known for representing photographer Cindy Sherman.

Go north once more on Tenth Ave and turn left on 27th St for a stop at ❻ **Aperture Gallery**, the exhibit space of the photography-focused Aperture Foundation, which mounts shows from pros and newcomers alike. Continue along ❼ **27th St** to find an excellent gallery group where, in 2006, a collection of showcases – including Derek Eller Gallery, Foxy Production, Wallspace, John Connelly Presents and a couple of others that have since relocated or closed – moved from other Chelsea spots into the old loading-dock bays of what used to be the Tunnel nightclub.

include embroidered textiles from China, metal sculptures from Tibet, Pakistani stone sculptures and intricate Bhutanese paintings, as well as ritual objects and dance masks from various Tibetan regions, spanning from the 2nd to the 19th centuries. Rotating exhibitions have included the educational 'The Red Book of CJ Jung' and 'Victorious Ones,' which comprises sculptures and paintings of Jinas, the founding teachers of Jainism. A small cafe serves traditional Himalayan foods, and the K2 Lounge offers performances and cocktails, and is the perfect nightcap after visiting the galleries on free Friday evenings.

CHELSEA ART MUSEUM GALLERY

Map p430 (☎212-255-0719; www.chelseaart museum.org; 556 W 22nd St; adult/child $8/free; 🕒noon-6pm Tue, Wed, Fri & Sat, to 8pm Thu; [S]C/E to 23rd St) Occupying a three-story red-brick building dating from 1850, this popular museum stands on land once owned by writer Clement Clarke Moore (author of the famous poem 'A Visit from St Nicholas'). Its focus is on postwar abstract expressionism, especially by national and international artists, and its permanent collection includes works by Antonio Corpora, Laszlo Lakner, Jean Arp and Ellen Levy. The museum is also the headquarters of the Miotte Foundation, dedicated to archiving the works of Jean Miotte, a SoHo-based artist who has played a large role in creating the genre known as 'Informel' (Informal Art).

🍴 EATING

While the West Village is known for its classy, cozy and intimate spots, the adjacent Meatpacking District's dining scene is a bit more ostentatious, complete with nightclublike queues behind velvet ropes, bold decor and swarms of trend-obsessed patrons.

Chelsea, further beyond, strikes a balance between the two with a brash assortment of très gay eateries along the uber-popular Eighth Ave (a must for see-and-be-seen brunch), and more cafes lining Ninth Ave further west. In the warmer months expect windows and doors to fling open and plenty of alfresco seating to spill out onto the streets, be they the concrete of Chelsea or the cobblestone of the Village.

🍴 Greenwich Village & the Meatpacking District

[TOP CHOICE] **REDFARM** ASIAN FUSION $$

Map p426 (☎212-792-9700; www.redfarmnyc.com; 529 Hudson St btwn 10th & Charles Sts; mains $14-39; 🕒5pm-12:30am Mon-Thu, to midnight Fri, 11am-2:30pm & 5pm-midnight Sat, 11am-2:30pm & 5-11pm Sun; [S]1/2 to Christopher St-Sheridan Sq; A/C/E, B/D/F, M to W 4th St; 1/2/3 to 14th St) Savvy Sino fusion is this cottage-style restaurant's signature on its flavorful dishes. A recent chart-topper on the best lists of foodies, RedFarm earns our devotion for preparing mouthwatering mains (rib steak!) without a hint of pretension. Besides the heavily touted mixed-bag recipes, RedFarm also sports some of the best drinks in town – the Suntory Old-Fashioned is one of the finest scotch cocktails out there.

TARTINE FRENCH $$

Map p426 (☎212-229-2611; www.tartinecafenyc.com; 253 W 11th St btwn 4th St & Waverly Pl; mains $10-24; 🕒9am-10:30pm Mon-Sat, to 10pm Sun; [S]1/2/3 to 14th St; 1/2 to Christopher St-Sheridan Sq; L to 8th Ave) Tartine is the corner bistro of your French-ified dreams: wobbly stacks of chairs and tables, pink steaks and escargot, found treasures nailed to wooden walls, and a good-cop-bad-cop duo of waitresses who bounce dishes around the teeny-tiny room. It's BYOB, and staff will gladly uncork your bottle for some covert street-side sips while you wait for your table.

TOMOE SUSHI $$

Map p426 (☎212-777-9346; www.tomoesushi.com; 172 Thompson St btwn Houston & Bleecker Sts; sushi roll from $4.50, combo platter $19.95; 🕒1-3pm Tue-Sat, 5-11pm Mon-Sat, 5-10pm Sun; [S]A/C/E to Spring St; N/R to Prince St; B/D/F, M to Broadway-Lafayette St) Slap-dash scrawls and scribbles on the wall about credit-card restrictions and house specials are oddly juxtaposed with elegant California rolls (the size of hockey pucks!) and impossibly tender strips of sashimi resting on wasabi-tinged clouds of rice.

Known with half-mocking affection as 'Garbage Sushi' due to the large dumpster outside that partially hides the facade, Tomoe has somehow missed the critics' reviews, making it everyone's favorite sushi spot for people in the know.

SPOTTED PIG PUB $$

Map p426 (☎212-620-0393; www.thespottedpig.com; 314 W 11th St at Greenwich St; mains $14-30; ⏲lunch & dinner; 🍷 👪; [S]A/C/E to 14th St; L to 8th Ave) This Michelin-starred gastro-pub is a favorite of Villagers, serving a hearty, upscale blend of mains from Italy and the UK. Two floors are bedecked in old-timey souvenirs that serve to make the experience both casual and refined. It doesn't take reservations, so there is often a wait for a table. Brunch and lunch are less packed, so you can usually get a seat straight away.

MINETTA TAVERN BISTRO $$

Map p426 (☎212-475-3850; www.minettatavernny.com; 113 MacDougal St; mains $17-34; ⏲dinner daily, brunch Sat & Sun; [S]A/C/E, B/D/F/V to W 4th St) Book in advance, or come early to snag a table on a weeknight, because Minetta Tavern is pretty much always packed to the rafters. The snug red-leather banquettes, dark-paneled walls with black-and-white photos, classic checkered floors, tin ceilings and flaring yellow bistro lamps will lure you in. The flavor-filled bistro fare – pan-seared marrow bones, roasted chicken, crisp fries and big burgers, and mustn't-miss French dip sandwiches – will have you wishing you lived upstairs.

CAFÉ CLUNY CAFE $$

Map p426 (☎212-255-6900; www.cafecluny.com; 284 W 12th St; mains $10-32; [S]L to 8th Ave; A/C/E, 1/2/3 to 14th St) As the name might suggest, Café Cluny brings the whimsy of Paris to the West Village, with woven bistro-style bar chairs, light wooden upholstery, and a selection of joie-de-vivre-inducing platters like *steak frites* (fries), mixed green salads and roasted chicken.

WESTVILLE MODERN AMERICAN $$

Map p426 (☎212-741-7971; www.westvillenyc.com; 210 W 10th St btwn 4th & Bleecker Sts; mains $12-20; ⏲11:30am-11pm Mon-Fri, 10am-11pm Sat & Sun; [S]1/2 to Christopher St-Sheridan Sq; A/C/E, B/D/F, M to W 4th St; 1/2/3 to 14th St) A triumvirate of market-fresh tributes to New American cuisine, Westville has a location in the West Village, Chelsea, and – our favorite – the East Village (p111).

BLUE HILL AMERICAN $$$

Map p426 (☎212-539-1776; 75 Washington Pl btwn Sixth Ave & Washington Sq W; mains $32-36; ⏲dinner; [S]A/C/E, B/D/F/V to W 4th St-Washington Sq) A place for Slow Food junkies with deep pockets, Blue Hill was an early crusader in the local-is-better movement. Gifted chef Dan Barber, who hails from a farm family in the Berkshires, Massachusetts, uses harvests from that land, as well as from farms in upstate New York, to create his widely praised fare. Expect barely seasoned, perfectly ripe vegetables, which serve to highlight centerpieces of cod in almond broth, Berkshire pork stewed with four types of beans, and grass-fed lamb with white beans and new potatoes. The space itself, slightly below street level and housed in a landmark former speakeasy on a quaint Village block, is sophisticated and serene.

L'ARTUSI ITALIAN $$

Map p426 (☎212-255-5757; www.lartusi.com; 228 W 10th St; mains $16-30; ⏲5:30-11pm Mon-Thu, to midnight Fri & Sat; [S]A/C/E, B/D/F, M to W 4th St; 1/2 to Houston St) A storm of steel pots and pans hangs above the kitchen, while patrons dine amid unfussy flourishes of black and white in the two tiny floors of dining space. A curated collection of small Italian mains are bookended by tempting nibbles from the raw bar and cheese counter. Founded by Batali protégés, l'Artusi has a sister restaurant – **Dell'Anima** (38 Eighth Ave) – that's also well worth a looksee.

ALTA TAPAS $$

Map p426 (☎212-505-7777; 54 W 10th St btwn Fifth & Sixth Aves; small plates $5-18.50; ⏲dinner; [S]A/C/E, B/D/F/V to W 4th St-Washington Sq) This gorgeous townhouse highlights the neighborhood's quaintness, with plenty of exposed brick, wood beams, flickering candles, massive mirrors and romantic fireplace glows. A small-plates menu of encyclopedic proportions cures indecision with the likes of succulent lamb meatballs (butternut-squash foam! Yum!), white-truffle and porcini deviled eggs, warm artichoke salad, fried goat cheese, and blue-crab risotto. The wine list is outstanding, too.

TERTULIA TAPAS $$$

Map p426 (☎646-559-9909; www.tertulianyc.com; 359 Sixth Ave; small plates $5-19; [S]A/C/E, B/D/F, M to W 4th St; 1/2 to Christopher St-Sheridan Sq or Houston St) A favorite of Gwyneth Paltrow (without the pretension of her GOOP-y blog), Tertulia offers perfected Spanish tapas in cozy surrounds with plenty of blonde-wood bar seating and exposed brick. Waiters tend to patrons with the utmost care, offering thoughtful suggestions from both the small-plates menu and the wine list. Tiny portions and pricier vino means the bill can add up rather quickly – you've been warned.

TAÏM ISRAELI $

Map p426 (☎212-691-1287; 222 Waverly Pl btwn Perry & W 11th Sts; mains $5-9.50; 🕒lunch & dinner; [S]1/2/3 to 14th St) Not all Middle Eastern fare is alike, and this tiny falafel joint proves it with its smoothies, salads and sass – and its falafel, which ranges from the traditional type to those spiced up with roasted red pepper or hot harissa. Whichever fried balls you choose, you'll get them stuffed into pita with creamy tahini sauce and a generous dose of Israeli salad, or you can try them all in a platter that gets you three tasty dips.

Refreshing salads include carrots spiced with garlic and cumin, and smoothies are blended with exotics that range from dates to tamarind. This place is beloved by Israeli regulars, who pop into the tiny storefront to chat in Hebrew with the friendly owners.

JOE THE ART OF COFFEE CAFE $

Map p426 (www.joetheartofcoffee.com; 141 Waverly Pl; [S]A/C/E, B/D/F/V to W 4th St-Washington Sq) Superb coffee is served at this always-bustling joint sitting squarely on bucolic Waverly Place in the heart of the Village. Some say this is the best cup of joe in town; others just come to sip their latte while doodling on their iPad in quaint surrounds.

BUVETTE FRENCH $$

Map p426 (☎212-255-3590; www.ilovebuvette.com; 42 Grove St btwn Bedford & Bleecker Sts; mains $10-15; [S]1/2 to Christopher St-Sheridan Sq; A/C/E, B/D/F, M to W 4th St; 1/2 to Houston St) The delicate tin tiling on the ceiling is reflected in the swooshing marble countertop at the bar, the perfect place for an early evening glass of wine. For the full dinner experience at this self-proclaimed *gastrotèque,* grab a seat at one of the tables – it's decidedly romantic, with Dutch porcelain hanging from the wooden accents on the walls.

BARBUTO MODERN AMERICAN $$

Map p426 (☎212-924-9700; www.barbutonyc.com; 775 Washington St btwn 12th & Jane Sts; mains $18-25; [S]L to 8th Ave; A/C/E to 14th St; 1/2 to Christopher St-Sheridan Sq) Occupying a cavernous garage space with sweeping see-through doors that roll up and into the ceiling during the warmer months, Barbuto slaps together a delightful assortment of Modern American faves like roast chicken and moist risotto. A cluster of photography studios is upstairs, so you might spot some models and artsy types filing by.

CRISPO ITALIAN $$

Map p426 (☎212-229-1818; www.crisporestaurant.com; 240 W 14th St; mains $18-28; 🕒dinner; [S]A/C/E, 1/2/3 to 14th St; L to 8th Ave) Funky '80s-style art adorns the walls of this no-fuss Italian restaurant with a sprawling patio out back. Kick off a round of eats with the heart prosciutto platter, then dip into the homemade pastas before making a move on the excellent carnivore entrées, such as duck with figs and skirt steak.

GOTHAM BAR & GRILL AMERICAN $$

Map p426 (☎212-620-4020; www.gothambarandgrill.com; 12 E 12th St btwn Fifth Ave & University Pl; prix fixe lunch $25, mains $19-26; 🕒noon-2:15pm Mon-Fri, 5:30-10pm Mon-Thu, to 11pm Fri, 5-11pm Sat, 5-10pm Sun; [S]L, N/Q/R, 4/5/6 to Union Sq-14th St) Classically American like a crisp, just-pressed tuxedo, Gotham offers the finest fine-dining experience, with an assortment of perfect dishes and top-shelf cocktails. Expertly trained waiters bounce carefully prepared gourmet treats (the oysters and foie gras are particularly divine) around a white-clothed room accented with fresh flowers.

JOE'S PIZZA PIZZA $

Map p426 (☎212-366-1182; www.joespizzanyc.com; 7 Carmine St btwn Sixth Ave & Bleecker St; slices from $2.75; 🕒10am-4:30am; [S]A/C/E, B/D/F, M to W 4th St; 1/2 to Christopher St-Sheridan Sq or to Houston St) Joe's is the Meryl Streep of pizza parlors, collecting dozens of awards and accolades over the last three decades while safely cementing its reputation as one of the top spots for a slice in NYC. No-frills pies are served up indiscriminately to students, tourists and celebrities alike (everyone's stopped by for a bite, from Kirsten Dunst to Bill Murray).

BILL'S BAR & BURGER BURGERS $

Map p426 (☎212-414-3003; www.billsbarandburger.com; 22 Ninth Ave near 13th St; mains $5-10.50; 🕒lunch & dinner; [S]A/C/E, L to 8th Ave-14th St) There are ways to navigate around the meat-centric menu at Bill's – a veggie burger, fresh salads, crispy fries – but it's mainly a carnivore's kinda place. Classic burgers, bacon-and-cheddar burgers, mushroom-and-swiss burgers and even a short-rib-style burger are what keep the place hopping. There are also 'disco fries' (smothered in gravy and melted cheese), sweet-potato fries, all types of hot dogs (chili dogs, sauerkraut dogs etc), blackened catfish sammies and chicken wings, not to mention apple-crumb pie for dessert.

KIN SHOP
THAI **$$**

Map p426 (212-675-4295; www.kinshopnyc.com; 469 Sixth Ave; mains $9-28; 11:30am-3pm daily, 5:30-11pm Mon-Thu, 5:30-11:30pm Fri & Sat, 5-10pm Sun; S L to 6th Ave; 1/2/3, F, M to 14th St) The second avatar of *Top Chef* winner Harold Dieterle (the first being Perilla – also a great find – nearby) is this Thai-inspired joint that finds its place somewhere between neighborhood haunt and forward-thinking fusion kitchen. Curry pastes are crushed in-house – a testament to the from-scratch methods used to craft every item on the colorful menu.

EMPELLON
MEXICAN **$$**

Map p426 (212-367-0999; www.empellon.com; 230 W 4th St btwn Seventh Ave & 10th St; mains $8-19; 5-11pm Mon-Wed, 5pm-midnight Thu-Sat; S 1/2 to Christopher St-Sheridan Sq; A/C/E, B/D/F, M to W 4th St; 1/2/3 to 14th St) Chef Alex Stupak has transformed the all-important avocado into the most inventive and flavorsome guacamole in town. He's also dropped the 'Tex' from Tex-Mex, creating imaginative south-of-the-corner fare that is wholly elegant and beautifully presented. The white-brick walls further accentuate the mural of luscious red petals behind the bar.

GROUNDED ORGANIC COFFEE & TEA HOUSE
CAFE **$**

Map p426 (212-647-0943; 28 Jane St; mains $7-9; 7am-8pm; S A/C/E, L to 14th St) We won't blame you for flashing back to your '90s grunge look when you step into this coffeehouse, which seems as if it has been encased in amber since *Reality Bites*. As well as brag-worthy coffee blends and teas, Grounded also serves up guilt-free lunch entrées using healthy staples like quinoa.

BABBO
ITALIAN **$$$**

Map p426 (212-777-0303; www.babbonyc.com; 110 Waverly Pl; mains $19-29; dinner; S A/C/E, B/D/F/V to W 4th St; 1 to Christopher St-Sheridan Sq) Celebrity chef Mario Batali has multiple restaurants in Manhattan, but everyone has a sneaking suspicion that this two-level split townhouse is his favorite. Whether you order mint love letters, lamb's brain *francobolli* (small, stuffed ravioli) or pig's foot *milanese* (Milan-style), you'll find Batali at the top of his innovative, eclectic game. Reservations are in order.

GROM
ICE CREAM **$**

Map p426 (212-206-1738; www.grom.it/eng; 233 Bleecker St; gelato from $5.25; 11am-11pm Mon-Thu & Sun, to midnight Fri & Sat; S A/C/E, B/D/F, M to W 4th St; 1/2 to Houston St or Christopher St-Sheridan Sq) With an unwavering dedication to creating gelato the old fashion way, Grom leads the Italian dessert movement with a delectable assortment of homegrown flavors using products directly imported from Boot-land.

FATTY CRAB
PAN-ASIAN **$$**

Map p426 (212-352-3590; www.fattycrab.com; 643 Hudson St btwn Gansevoort & Horatio Sts; mains $16-28; noon-midnight Mon-Wed, to 2am Thu & Fri, 11am-2am Sat, 11am-midnight Sun; S L to 8th Ave; A/C/E, 1/2/3 to 14th St) The Fatty folks have done it again with their small Malaysian-inspired joint in the thick of things on the west side. It's super hip and always teeming with locals who swing by in droves to devour fish curries and pork belly accompanied by a signature selection of cocktails.

PERILLA
MODERN AMERICAN **$$**

Map p426 (212-929-6868; 9 Jones St; mains $22-27; 5:30am-11pm Mon-Thu, to 11:30pm Fri & Sat, 11am-10pm Sun; S A/C/E, B/D to W 4 St; 1/2 to Christopher St-Sheridan Sq) Belonging to one of the winners of popular reality-TV show *Top Chef*, Perilla is an extremely creative yet well-grounded American bistro. The spicy duck meatballs and roasted main sardines are good ways to start off a meal.

SPICE MARKET
SOUTHEAST ASIAN **$$**

Map p426 (212-675-2322; www.jean-georges.com; 403 W 13th St at Ninth Ave; lunch prix fixe $24, mains $8-36; lunch & dinner; S A/C/E to 14th St; L to 8th Ave) Yet another innovation from Jean-Georges Vongerichten, Spice Market lives in a dark, clublike realm where every fantasy of a faraway souk comes to life through thick waves of gossamer drapery, glinting meditative Buddhas, and pots that steam and bubble as the waiter rushes them by. Fusion fare is distinctively Asian in taste, but many of the dishes have lost their initial luster now that the shiny veneer of newness has worn away.

SNACK TAVERNA
GREEK $$

Map p426 (212-929-3499; 63 Bedford St; mains $15-25; noon-11pm Mon-Sat, to 10pm Sun; A/C/E, B/D to W 4 St; 1/2 to Christopher St-Sheridan Sq) So much more than your usual Greek restaurant, Snack Taverna eschews gyros for a seasonal selection of scrumptious small plates to accompany the flavorsome selection of market mains. The regional wines are worth a miss, but the Med beers are surprisingly refreshing.

OTTO ENOTECA PIZZERIA
PIZZERIA $$

Map p426 (212-995-9559; 1 Fifth Ave near 8th St; mains $8-15; lunch & dinner; A/C/E, B/D/F/V to W 4th St-Washington Sq) An intimate trattoria in the heart of the Village, this is (a refreshingly affordable) part of Mario Batali's empire, a pizza palace where thin pizzas are cooked on flat iron griddles till they crackle perfectly. They come topped with items far beyond your standard pizza joint – fennel, goat cheese, fresh chilies, capers, fresh mozzarella – and sauce that has the perfect balance of smoky and sweet.

Pasta dishes (for just nine bucks!) veer toward the exotic, like penne with hazelnuts and butternut squash, spaghetti with zucchini, chilies and mint, and rigatoni with sausage and black Tuscan kale. And don't even think of leaving without trying the house-made gelato.

BONSIGNOUR
SANDWICHES $

Map p426 (212-229-9700; 35 Jane St at Eighth Ave; mains $7-12; breakfast, lunch & dinner; L to 8th Ave; A/C/E, 1/2/3 to 14th St) Nestled on a quiet Village street, this sandwich shop offers dozens of delicious choices as well as salads, frittatas and a wonderful beef chili. Get a sandwich or a chicken curry salad to go and wander down the street to Abingdon Sq for alfresco dining.

SOUEN
ASIAN FUSION $$

Map p426 (www.souen.net; 28 E 13th St btwn 5th Ave & University Pl; mains $9-25.50; 10am-11pm Mon-Sat, to 10pm Sun; 4/5/6, L, N/Q/R to Union Sq-14th St) A paradigm of pure food, Souen delivers a traditional Japanese macrobiotic diet to eager diners who come to clear their minds and cleanse. Pure grains are reputed to have curative properties – just make sure to chew a lot (as the waitstaff will often remind you)!

LOCAL KNOWLEDGE

PARK IN THE SKY

Robert Hammond, cofounder and executive director of Friends of the High Line, talks about what, in his opinion, makes the 'park in the sky' and its surrounding neighborhood so special.

Highline Hightlights

To me, the West Village is a reminder of New York's industrial past and residential future. What I love most about the High Line are its hidden moments, like at the Tenth Ave cut-out near 17th St, most people sit on the bleachers, but if you turn the other way you can see the Statue of Liberty far away in the harbor. Architecture buffs will love looking down 18th St, and up on 30th is my favorite moment – a steel cut-out where you can see the cars underneath.

Stop-Offs

For lunch near the High Line, I recommend **Hector's Café & Diner** (Map p426; 44 Little W 12th St; mains $8-12.95; 2am-10pm Mon-Sat). It's cheap, untouristy and not at all a see-and-be-seen spot – the cookies are great. If you're in the area, you have to visit the galleries in Chelsea – there are over 300, and check out Printed Matter (p157), with its artist-made books. Check out the Hôtel Americano (p333) in northern Chelsea – it's very up-and-coming. For an evening out on the town, head to the Boom Boom Room (p147) at the top of the Strand – go early and book ahead.

Family-Friendly Activities

The High Line is also great for children, with scheduled kids' programming on Saturdays and Wednesdays.

GREENWICH VILLAGE, CHELSEA & THE MEATPACKING DISTRICT EATING

1. Washington Square Park (p133)
Pausing under the signature arch while strolling through this energetic public space is a must.

2. Spotted Pig (p140)
Italian meets British at this buzzing Michelin-starred gastro-pub.

3. Duplex (p152)
Not for the bashful, this legendary haunt is famous for cabaret, karaoke and dance.

DAN HERRICK / LONELY PLANET IMAGES ©

ROGER GAESS / LONELY PLANET IMAGES ©

🍴 Chelsea

CHELSEA MARKET MARKET

See p132.

COOKSHOP MODERN AMERICAN $$

Map p430 (www.cookshopny.com; 156 Tenth Ave btwn 19th & 20th Sts; mains $14-33; 🕘lunch & dinner; [S]L to 8th Ave; A/C/E to 14th St or 23rd St) A brilliant brunching pit stop before (or after) tackling the verdant High Line across the street, Cookshop is a lively place that knows its niche and does it oh so well. Excellent service, eye-opening cocktails (good morning Bloody Maria!), a perfectly baked breadbasket and a selection of inventive egg mains make this a favorite in Chelsea on a Sunday afternoon. Dinner is a sure-fire win as well.

LE GRAINNE FRENCH $$

Map p430 (www.legrainnecafe.com; 183 Ninth Ave btwn 21st & 22nd Sts; mains $9.50-27; 🕘8am-midnight; [S]A/C/E, 1/2 to 23rd St; A/C/E to 14th St) Tap the top of your French onion soup as you dream of that Pollyanna ingénue Amélie cracking open her crème brulée; Le Grainne transports the senses from the busy blocks of Chelsea to the backstreets of Paris. The tin-topped eatery really excels at lunchtime, when baguette sandwiches and savory crepes are scarfed down amid cramped quarters; come for dinner to breath in the wafting garlic as heartier pastas are tossed in the kitchen.

BILLY'S BAKERY BAKERY $

Map p430 (www.billysbakerynyc.com; 184 Ninth Ave btwn 21st & 22nd Sts; cupcakes $3; 🕘8:30am-11pm Mon-Thu, 8:30am-midnight Fri & Sat, 9am-10pm Sun; [S]A/C/E, 1/2 to 23rd St; A/C/E to 14th St) New York's *Sex and the City*–fueled cupcake craze has come and gone, but Billy's is still cranking out its four-bite bits of heaven. Red velvet and banana cream top the recipe list, and a clutch of retro-style pastries are created by the I-don't-care-what-I'm-wearing hipsters in the back. Why buy one when six fit oh so perfectly into their cute little boxes.

CO PIZZERIA $$

Map p430 (☎212-243-1105; 230 Ninth Ave at 24th St; pizza $9-18; 🕘dinner Mon, lunch & dinner Tue-Sun; [S]C/E to 23rd St) Masterfully prepared pizza is served in bright, wooden surrounds that feel like a Scandinavian cafeteria. Expect a faithful reproduction of the trademark Neapolitan thin crust pies topped with an assortment of fresh-from-the-farm items like fennel and buffalo mozzarella. Salads of artichoke, beet or radicchio – as well as global wines and a sprinkling of sweets – round out the offerings.

TÍA POL TAPAS $$

Map p430 (www.tiapol.com; 205 Tenth Ave btwn 22nd & 23rd Sts; small plates $2-16; 🕘dinner Tue-Sun; [S]C/E to 23rd St) Wielding Spanish tapas amid closet-sized surrounds, Tía Pol is the real deal, as the hordes of locals swarming the entrance can attest. The red-wine options will have your tongue doing backflips, as will the array of small plates: Spanish tortillas, lemony salad topped with tuna, lima-bean-puree bruschetta and sautéed cockles with razor clams.

It's the perfect post-gallery-opening pit stop. Come on the early side to take your best stab at grabbing one of the handful of tables in the back.

BLOSSOM VEGAN $$

Map p430 (☎212-627-1144; 187 Ninth Ave btwn 21st & 22nd Sts; mains $12-22; 🕘lunch & dinner; [S]C/E to 23rd St) This Chelsea veg oasis – with a sinful new wine and chocolate bar attached – is a peaceful, romantic dining room that offers imaginative tofu, seitan and vegetable creations, some raw, all kosher. The stellar Autumn Sweet Potato Rolls have raw strips of the orange root wrapped around tangy strips of coconut, carrots and peppers, and will leave your taste buds reeling.

Seitan scaloppini has a perfect blend of richness and a light lemony zing, while the hickory-roasted tempeh gets tempered with creamy horseradish crème fraîche. Desserts are so rich, you'll swear they're filled with butter and cream. A second Upper West Side location is **Cafe Blossom** (Map p442; ☎212-875-2600; 466 Columbus Ave btwn 82nd & 83rd Sts; [S]1 to 79th St).

🍷 DRINKING & NIGHTLIFE

The key word in the West Village is 'west' – the further towards the Hudson you go, the more likely you are to sidestep the frat party scene found

around the NYU campus – generally the going gets good around the crooked lanes west of Sixth Ave.

Just to the north, the Meatpacking District is strictly contemporary in vibe, with sprawling, modern spaces boasting long cocktail lists, velvet-roped entrances and dins that'll rattle your brain. Jetsetters and your entourage: this is your kingdom.

Chelsea is still very much the territory for gay men, but there's a handful of options for all tastes, from speakeasy-chic digs to well-worn dive bars.

🍷 Greenwich Village & the Meatpacking District

LITTLE BRANCH — COCKTAIL BAR

Map p426 (☎212-929-4360; 22 Seventh Ave S at Leroy St; [S]1 to Houston St) If it weren't for the casual bouncer dressed in slacks and suspenders, you'd never guess that a charming bar lurked behind the boring brown door positioned at the odd triangular intersection. When you get the go-ahead to enter, you'll find a basement bar that feels like a wonder kickback to Prohibition times. Squeaky tunes waft overhead as locals clink glasses and sip inventive, old-timey cocktails.

MARIE'S CRISIS — BAR

Map p426 (☎212-243-9323; 59 Grove St btwn Seventh Ave S & Bleecker St; 🕙4pm-4am; [S]1 to Christopher St-Sheridan Sq) Aging Broadway queens, wide-eyed out-of-town gay boys, giggly tourist girls and various other fans of musical theater assemble around the piano here and take turns belting out campy numbers, often joined by the entire crowd. It's old-school fun, no matter how jaded you were when you went in.

ART BAR — BAR

Map p426 (☎212-727-0244; 52 Eighth Ave near Horatio St; 🕙4pm-4am, happy hour 4-7pm; [S]L to 8th Ave-14th St; A/C/E to 14th St) A decidedly bohemian crowd favors Art Bar, which doesn't look like much up front (oval booths crowded too close to the wooden bar), but has a bit more going on in the back. Grab your beer or one of the house specials (usually martinis) and head for the couches, placed under a huge *Last Supper* mural featuring Jimmy Dean and Marilyn Monroe, among others.

VIN SUR VINGT — WINE BAR

Map p426 (www.vinsur20nyc.com; 201 W 11th St btwn Seventh Ave & Waverly Pl; 🕙5pm-2am Mon-Fri, 11am-2am Sat, 11am-midnight Sun; [S]1/2/3 to 14th St; 1/2 to Christopher St-Sheridan Sq; L to 8th Ave) A cozy spot just off Seventh Ave's bustle, Vin Sur Vingt is a thin wine bar with a strip of bar seating and a quaint row of two-seat tables, perfect for a first date. Warning: if you come for a pre-dinner drink, you'll inevitably be charmed into staying through dinner as you munch on the excellent selection of bar bites. Reasonably priced vino keeps the locals coming back for seconds.

VOL DE NUIT — PUB

Map p426 (☎212-982-3388; 148 W 4th St; [S]A/C/E, B/D/F/V to W 4th St-Washington Sq) Even all the NYU students can't ruin this: a cozy Belgian beer bar, with a few dozen zonkers like Lindemans Framboise (strawberry beer!) and *frites* to share at the front patio seats, the lounge, the communal wood tables or under the dangling red lights at the bar.

BOOM BOOM ROOM — LOUNGE

Map p426 (☎212-645-4646; 848 Washington St btwn 13th & Little W 12th Sts; 🕙10pm-4am Wed & Thu, 11pm-4am Fri & Sat; [S]L to 8th Ave; 1/2/3, A/C/E to 14th St) Smooth beige surrounds, softer music and plenty of room to swig your top-shelf tipple, the Boom Boom Room is strictly VIP and the favored hangout for the vogue elite (and *Vogue* elite) – expect models, their photographer and the occasional celeb sighting. Come early and book ahead – that's the only way to gain access if you're not a cornerstone of New York's social scene.

EMPLOYEES ONLY — BAR

Map p426 (☎212-242-3021; 510 Hudson St near Christopher St; 🕙6pm-4am; [S]1 to Christopher St-Sheridan Sq) Duck behind the neon 'Psychic' sign to find this hidden hangout. The bar gets busier as the night wears on. Bartenders are ace mixologists, fizzing up crazy, addictive libations like the 'Ginger Smash' and the 'Mata Hari.' Great for late-night drinking, and eating, courtesy of the on-site restaurant that serves past midnight.

LE BAIN — CLUB

Map p426 (☎212-645-4646; 848 Washington St btwn 13th & Little W 12th Sts; 🕙10pm-4am Wed & Thu, 11pm-4am Fri & Sat; [S]L to 8th Ave; 1/2/3, A/C/E to 14th St) The sweeping rooftop venue at the tragically hip Standard Hotel, Le Bain sees a garish parade of party promoters who do their thang on any day of the week. Have you seen those Stefon sketches on *Saturday Night Live*? If not, brace yourself for plumes of smoke on the turf-laced balconies, make-out sessions in the jet-black bathrooms, a giant Jacuzzi built right into the dance floor, and an ambassador from every walk of life in New York getting wasted on pricy snifters. Best. Night. Ever.

SULLIVAN ROOM BAR

Map p426 (www.sullivanroom.com; 218 Sullivan St btwn Bleecker & 3rd Sts; 🕘9pm-5am Wed-Sat; [S]A/C/E, B/D/F/V to W 4th St) You'll have to look hard to find the entrance to this below-ground hangout, which attracts its share of the beautiful people with DJ-hosted dance parties, a foreign beer collection and generous mixed cocktails. Best after 1am.

KETTLE OF FISH BAR

Map p426 (www.kettleoffishnyc.com; 59 Christopher St at Seventh Ave; 🕘3pm-4am Mon-Fri, 2pm-4am Sat & Sun; [S]1 to Christopher St-Sheridan Sq) Step into this dimly lit spot, full of couches and plump chairs, and prepare to stay for a while because the crowd is simply beguiling. It's a dive bar, a sports bar and a gay bar in one, and everyone mixes happily. There are stacks of board games like Monopoly and checkers, which patrons are encouraged to play, as well as darts. And if you get hungry, the barkeeps will offer menus from nearby restaurants that deliver here. The owner is a Packers' fan, so expect raucous activity on game days.

124 OLD RABBIT CLUB BAR

Map p426 (☎212-254-0575; 124 MacDougal St; [S]A/C/E, B/D/F, M to W 4th St; 1/2 to Christopher St-Sheridan Sq or Houston St) You'll wanna pat yourself on the back when you a) find the darn place, and b) gain access to this speakeasy-style joint (hint: look for the '124' and ring the buzzer). Once you're here, grab a seat at the dimly lit bar and reward yourself with a quenching stout or one of the dozens of imported brews.

BRASS MONKEY BAR

Map p426 (www.brassmonkeybar.com; 55 Little W 12th St at Washington St; 🕘11:30am-4am; [S]A/C/E to 14th St; L to 8th Ave) While most Meatpacking District bars tend toward the chic, the Monkey is more for beer lovers than those worrying about what shoes to wear. The multifloor Monkey is at-ease and down-to-earth, with squeaking wood floors and a nice long list of beers and scotch. The roof deck is a fine destination in warm weather.

675 BAR LOUNGE

Map p426 (www.675bar.com; 675 Hudson St btwn 13th & 14th Sts; 🕘6pm-2am Mon-Sat; [S]L to 8th Ave; 1/2/3, A/C/E to 14th St) Tucked under Bill's Bar & Burger in the Meatpacking District is this unpretentious hangout, which feels like a cross between a '70s rec room and your uncle's retro library. Come for the low-priced wines and draughts and stay for the rousing match of Mancala.

JULIUS BAR GAY

Map p426 (☎212-243-1928; 159 W 10th St at Waverly Pl; [S]A/C/E, B/D/F, M to W 4th St; 1/2/3 to 14th St; 1/2 to Christopher St-Sheridan Sq) One of the infamous originals – in fact, it's the oldest operating gay bar in NYC – Julius is a dive bar through and through. The only hint of its homo roots is the clientele, a mixed bag of faithful locals and the occasional newbie. It's refreshingly unpretentious, and just steps away from the better known Stonewall and Duplex.

MONSTER BAR

Map p426 (☎212-924-3558; 80 Grove St at Sheridan Sq; [S]1 to Christopher St-Sheridan Sq) It's old-school gay-man heaven in here, with a small dance floor as well as a piano bar and cabaret space. Spirited theme nights range from Latino parties to drag-queen-hosted soirees.

G2 BAR

Map p426 (www.gaslightnyc.com; 39 Ninth Ave at 14th St; no cover charge; 🕘8pm-4am Mon-Sat; [S]A/C/E, L to 8th Ave-14th St) For adult coolness in the hipster-mad Meatpacking District, do your drinking at G2. It's funky, with its crazy potted plants, bookshelves, marble-topped tables and distressed velvet couches. A DJ spins house, electronica and hip-hop most nights.

STANDARD BAR

Map p426 (☎212-645-4646, 877-550-4646; www.standardhotels.com; 848 Washington St; [S]A/C/E to 14th St; L to 8th Ave) Rising on concrete stilts over the new High Line, the Standard is one of the celebrated destinations of the moment, with two choice drinking spots and a grill (plus hotel rooms where some high-paying guests allegedly exposed themselves to High Line saunterers...but we digress). There's an outdoor beer garden with a classic German menu and frothy drafts, plus the Living Room bar, a swankier indoor affair (p147) with marvelous views over the Hudson and a trendy Euro-loving crowd.

HENRIETTA HUDSON LESBIAN
Map p426 (www.henriettahudson.com; 438 Hudson St; S1 to Houston St) All sorts of cute young dykes, many from neighboring New Jersey and Long Island, storm this sleek lounge, where varying theme nights bring in spirited DJs, who stick to particular genres (hip-hop, house, rock). The owner, Brooklyn native Lisa Canistraci, is a favorite promoter in the world of lesbian nightlife, and she is often on hand to mix it up with her fans.

CORNER BISTRO BAR
Map p426 (www.cornerbistrony.com; 331 W 4th St btwn Jane & 12th Sts; 11:30am-4am Mon-Sat, noon-4am Sun; SL to 8th Ave; 1/2/3, A/C/E to 14th St) An old-school dive bar with cheap beers on tap – it all sounds pretty standard until you take a mouthwatering bite out of Corner Bistro's bar burger. Nothing beats this juicy meat sandwich with a side scatter of fries.

STONEWALL INN BAR
Map p426 (212-463-0950; 53 Christopher St; S1 to Christopher St-Sheridan Sq) Site of the Stonewall riots in 1969, this historic bar was losing its fan base to trendier spots until new owners came along several years back, gave it a facelift and opened it to a new and welcoming crowd. Since then, it's been pulling in varied crowds nightly for parties catering to everyone under the gay rainbow.

ONE IF BY LAND, TWO IF BY SEA BAR
Map p426 (212-255-8649; 17 Barrow St; dinner; S1 at Christopher St-Sheridan Sq; A/C/E, B/D/F/V to W 4th St-Washington Sq) Famous for its beef Wellington and graceful, aged location in Aaron Burr's old carriage house, this is quite possibly New York's favorite date restaurant. But it's even better as a quiet watering hole, perfect for a cocktail-hour or late-night libation for those who need a break from the harried streets.

KISS & FLY CLUB
Map p426 (www.kissandflyclub.com; 409 W 13th St near Ninth Ave; cover charge $10-25; 11pm-4am Wed-Sat; SA/C/E, L to 8th Ave-14th St) A heavily European crowd moves and grooves to French electronica and pop into the wee hours at Kiss & Fly, a unique club designed to look a bit like a Roman bathhouse. The circular room flows around a central bar, and arches pull the eye upward to elaborately decorated walls and ceilings.

CUBBYHOLE BAR
Map p426 (212-243-9041; 281 W 12th St; SA/C/E to 14th St; L to 8th Ave) A tiny hideaway festooned with brightly patterned bar stools and strings of colorful lights, this no-attitude neighborhood watering hole has that truly rare mix of lesbians and gay men who are out to make friends rather than hit the road with the first trick they find. It's got a great jukebox, friendly bartenders and plenty of regulars.

BAR NEXT DOOR BAR
Map p426 (212-529-5945; 129 MacDougal St btwn W 3rd & W 4th Sts; 6pm-2am Sun-Thu, to 3am Fri & Sat; SA/C/E, B/D/F/V to W 4th St) One of the loveliest hangouts in the neighborhood, the basement of this restored townhouse is all low ceilings, exposed brick and romantic lighting. You'll find mellow, live jazz nightly, as well as the tasty Italian menu of the restaurant next door, La Lanterna di Vittorio.

WHITE HORSE TAVERN BAR
Map p426 (212-243-9260; 567 Hudson St at 11th St; S1 to Christopher St-Sheridan Sq) It's a bit on the tourist trail, but that doesn't dampen the century-old, pubby dark-wood, tin-ceiling atmosphere of this bar, where Dylan Thomas had his last drink (too many beers led to his 1953 death), a tipsy Jack Kerouac got kicked out, and we had a friendly NBA debate with the *South Park* guys one night. Sit at the long oak bar inside or on sidewalk tables.

Chelsea

BATHTUB GIN BAR
Map p430 (www.bathtubginnyc.com; 132 Ninth Ave btwn 18th & 19th Sts; 6pm-1:30am Sun-Tue, 6pm-3:30am Wed-Sat; SA/C/E to 14th St; L to 8th Ave; A/C/E to 23rd St) Amid New York City's serious obsession with speakeasy-styled

hangouts, Bathtub Gin manages to poke its head above the crowd with its super-secret front door, which doubles as a wall for an unassuming cafe. Inside, chill seating, soft background beats and kindly staff make it a great place to sling back bespoke cocktails with friends.

G LOUNGE BAR

Map p430 (www.glounge.com; 223 W 19th St btwn Seventh & Eighth Aves; no cover charge; ⏰4pm-4am; [S]1 to 18th St) Glossy and unpretentious, this gay bar is as straight-friendly as they come, and it's really all about the music. DJs rotate daily, but Tuesday is always BoyBox night. Check out the website to find out who's spinning while you're in town. For heavy drinking and dancing with no cover, you can't beat G – although you may have to wait in line to get in. Dress at G Lounge is refreshingly casual. Cash only.

CHELSEA BREWING COMPANY PUB

Map p430 (☎212-336-6440; West Side Hwy at W 23rd St, Chelsea Piers, Pier 59; ⏰noon-midnight; [S]C/E to 23rd St) Enjoy a quality microbrew, waterside, in the expansive outdoor area of this way-west beer haven. It's a perfect place to re-enter the world after a day of swimming, golfing or rock climbing as a guest at the Chelsea Piers Complex.

BARRACUDA GAY

Map p430 (☎212-645-8613; 275 W 22nd St at Seventh Ave; [S]C/E to 23rd St) This longtime favorite holds its own even as newer, slicker places come and go. That's because it's got a simple, winning formula: affordable cocktails, a cozy rec-room vibe and free entertainment from some of the city's top drag queens.

1OAK CLUB

Map p430 (☎212-242-1111; 453 W 17th St; cover charge $10-25; ⏰10pm-4am Tue-Sat; [S]A/C/E, L to 8th Ave-14th St) Part Nordic hunting lodge and part Moroccan hookah lounge, this celebrity favorite has a DJ spinning house and techno tunes, a roaring corner fireplace and bottle service at tables, and it stays packed into the wee hours.

PETER MCMANUS TAVERN BAR

Map p430 (☎212-929-9691; 152 Seventh Ave at 19th St; ⏰10am-4pm Mon-Sat, noon-4pm Sun; [S]A/C/E to 14th St) Pouring drafts since the 1930s, this family-run dive is something of a museum to the world of the McManuses: photos of yesteryear, an old telephone booth and Tiffany glass. There's also greasy bar food to eat at the cute green booths. Hurrah for the McManus!

BAR VELOCE BAR

Map p430 (☎212-629-5300; 176 Seventh Ave near 20th St; ⏰5pm-3am; [S]C/E to 23rd St) Sip your wine, eat a few panini, watch the well-dressed world walk by, or strike up a conversation with an interesting stranger (or two). What could be better than that? Small and friendly Bar Veloce caters to a sophisticated crowd that likes wine and a few laughs at the end of a hard day.

EAGLE NYC CLUB

Map p430 (www.eaglenyc.com; 555 W 28th St btwn Tenth & Eleventh Aves; cover charge $10; ⏰10pm-4am Mon-Sat; [S]C/E to 23rd St) A bi-level club full of hot men in leather, the Eagle is the choice for out-and-proud fetishists. Its two levels plus roof deck leave plenty of room for dancing and drinking, which are done with abandon. Thursdays are 'code' nights, meaning everyone must meet the dress code (wear leather, or nothing at all). Located in a renovated 19th-century stable, the inside joke is that 'the studs keep coming.'

RAWHIDE GAY

Map p430 (☎212-242-9332; 212 Eighth Ave btwn 20th & 21st Sts; [S]A/C/E, 1/2 to 23rd St; 1/2 to 18th St) Brand your behind with a rainbow flag and jump into Rawhide, one of the last reminders of Chelsea's grittier days. Bartenders serve a mixed bag of queens, though it traditionally attracts a leather crowd.

FRYING PAN BAR

Map p430 (☎212-989-6363; Pier 66 at W 26th St; [S]C/E to 23rd St) Salvaged from the bottom of the sea (or at least the Chesapeake Bay), the lightship *Frying Pan* and the two-tiered dockside bar where it's parked are fine go-to spots for a sundowner. On warm days, the rustic open-air space brings in the crowds, who come to laze on deck chairs, eat burgers off the sizzling grill, drink ice-cold bottles of Corona ($7) and admire the fine views across the water to, uh, New Jersey.

HIRO CLUB

Map p430 (www.themaritimehotel.com; 371 W 16th St; ⏰Thu-Sun; [S]A/C/E to 14th St; L to 8th Ave) In the Maritime Hotel, this chic Japanese space looks a little like the place where Uma kicked a lot of ass at the end of *Kill Bill: Vol 1*. It's Japanese chic, with bamboo wall dividers and low-slung banquettes, and is most popular on Thursday and Sunday nights when a gay crowd hits the dance floor.

PINK ELEPHANT CLUB

Map p430 (www.pinkelephantclub.com; 527 W 27th St; cover $25; ⌚Thu-Sun; [S]1 to 28th St) The name is coy, but the place is all class – so much so that it can be tough getting in the door. DJ-blasted deep house resonates throughout the tight, low-ceilinged dance floor, so don't expect to hear your taxi driver's chatter at 4am.

HOME CLUB

Map p430 (☎212-273-3700; 532 W 27th St near Tenth Ave; cover charge $20; ⌚10pm-4am Tue-Sun; [S]C/E to 23rd St; 1 to 28th St) Most homes aren't multilevel, cavernous spaces with dark leather couches lining the walls and eerily lit passageways taking you from nook to nook, but maybe that's a growing trend. Either way, there's lots to make you feel comfortable at Home – ample seating and space, and deep electronic, funk and pop coming from the live DJ. Sometimes the doors between Home and the neighboring club Guesthouse are opened and you can pass from one to the other.

☆ ENTERTAINMENT

UPRIGHT CITIZENS BRIGADE THEATRE COMEDY

Map p430 (www.ucbtheatre.com; 307 W 26th St btwn Eighth & Ninth Aves; [S]C/E to 23rd St) Pros of comedy sketches and outrageous improvisations reign at this popular 74-seat venue, which gets drop-ins from casting directors. Getting in is cheap ($5 to $8), and so is the beer (from $2 a can). You may recognize pranksters on stage from late-night comedy shows. It's free Wednesdays after 11pm, when newbies take the reins. Check the website for popular classes on sketch and improv, now spilling over to an annex location on W 30th St.

COMEDY CELLAR COMEDY

Map p426 (www.comedycellar.com; 117 MacDougal St btwn W 3rd & Bleecker Sts; cover charge $20; ⌚shows start approx 9pm Sun-Fri, 7pm & 9:30pm Sat; [S]A/C/E, B/D/F/V to W 4th St-Washington Sq) This long-established basement club in Greenwich Village features mainstream material and a good list of regulars (eg *Saturday Night Live's* Darrell Hammond, Wanda Sykes), plus an occasional high-profile drop-in like Dave Chappelle.

SLEEP NO MORE THEATER

Map p430 (www.sleepnomorenyc.com; McKittrick Hotel, 530 W 27th St; ⌚7pm-midnight Mon-Sat) After a smashing success in London, British theatre company Punchdrunk has reimagined their evocative performance installation in a series of Chelsea warehouses that have been redesigned to look like an abandoned hotel. It's a choose-your-own adventure kind of experience where audience members are free to wander the grounds and interact with the actors who perform a variety of scenes that range from the bizarre to the risqué.

VILLAGE VANGUARD LIVE MUSIC

Map p426 (www.villagevanguard.com; 178 Seventh Ave at 11th St; [S]1/2/3 to 14th St) Possibly the city's most prestigious jazz club, the Vanguard has hosted literally every major star of the past 50 years. It started as a home to spoken-word performances and occasionally returns to its roots, but most of the time it's just smooth, sweet jazz all night long. Mind your step on the steep stairs, and close your eyes to the signs of wear and tear – acoustically, you're in one of the greatest venues in the world.

BLUE NOTE LIVE MUSIC

Map p426 (www.bluenote.net; 131 W 3rd St btwn Sixth Ave & MacDougal St; [S]A/C/E, B/D/F/V to W 4th St-Washington Sq) This is by far the most famous (and expensive) of the city's jazz clubs. Most shows are $20 at the bar, $35 at a table, but can rise for the biggest jazz stars, and a few outside the normal jazz act (um, Doobie Brothers' Michael McDonald, anyone?). Go on an off night, and be quiet – all attention is on the stage!

CHERRY LANE THEATER PERFORMING ARTS

Map p426 (www.cherrylanetheater.com; 38 Commerce St; ⌚hrs vary; [S]1 to Christopher St-Sheridan Sq) A theater with a distinctive charm, Cherry Lane has a long and distinguished history. It was started by poet Edna St Vincent Millay and has given a voice to numerous playwrights and actors over the years. It remains true to its mission of creating 'live' theater that's accessible to the public. Readings, plays and spoken-word performances rotate frequently.

IFC CENTER
CINEMA

Map p426 (www.ifccenter.com; 323 Sixth Ave at 3rd St; SA/C/E, B/D/F/V to W 4th St-Washington Sq) This arthouse cinema in NYU-land has a great cafe and a solidly curated lineup of new indies, cult classics and foreign films. Catch shorts, documentaries, '80s revivals, director-focused series, weekend classics and frequent special series, such as midnight screenings of holiday classics at Christmas.

KITCHEN
DANCE

Map p430 (www.thekitchen.org; 512 W 19th St btwn Tenth & Eleventh Aves; SA/C/E to 14th St; L to 8th Ave) A loftlike experimental space in west Chelsea that also produces edgy theater, readings and music performances, Kitchen is where you'll find new, progressive pieces and works-in-progress from local movers and shakers.

ANGELIKA FILM CENTER
CINEMA

Map p426 (www.angelikafilmcenter.com; 18 W Houston St at Mercer St; tickets $10-14; ; SB/D/F/V to Broadway-Lafayette St) The Angelika Film Center specializes in foreign and independent films and has some quirky charms (such as the rumble of the subway, long lines and occasionally bad sound). But the on-site, roomy cafe is a great place to meet before or after a film and the beauty of its Stanford White–designed, beaux arts building is undeniable.

ATLANTIC THEATER COMPANY
THEATER

Map p430 (www.atlantictheater.org; 336 W 20th St btwn Eighth & Ninth Aves; ⊙10am-6pm Mon-Fri, 8-10pm Tue-Sat, 2-4pm Sat, 3-5pm & 7-9pm Sun; SA/C/E to 23rd St or 14th St; 1/2 to 18th St) Founded by David Mamet and William H Macy in 1985, the Atlantic Theater is a pivotal anchor for the off-Broadway community, hosting many Tony Award and Drama Desk winners over the last 25-plus years.

13TH ST REPERTORY COMPANY
THEATER

Map p426 (www.13thstreetrep.org; 50 W 13th St btwn Fifth & Sixth Aves; SL to 6th Ave; F, M, 1/2/3 to 14th St) Celebrating 40 years in 2012, this rep theater offers tons of weekly offerings, including productions workshops, children's theater and the New Works Reading Series. The company is also home to the longest running off-off-Broadway show, Line.

BARROW STREET THEATER
THEATER

Map p426 (www.barrowstreettheatre.com; 27 Barrow St, btwn Seventh Ave & W 4th St; S1/2 to Christopher St-Sheridan Sq; A/C/E, B/D/F, M to W 4th St; 1/2 to Houston St) A fantastic off-Broadway space in the heart of the West Village showcasing a variety of local and international theater.

ACTOR'S PLAYHOUSE
THEATER

Map p426 (www.nyactorsplayhouse.com; 100 Seventh Ave, btwn Grove & Barrow Sts; S1/2 to Christopher St-Sheridan Sq; A/C/E, B/D/F, M to W 4th St; 1/2 to Houston St) A West Village mainstay that dabbles in all sorts of theater in its tiny 150-seat space. Cheap tickets and carefully selected and produced shows make this an easy crowd-pleaser for those looking for some off-off-Broadway fun.

IRISH REPERTORY THEATER
THEATER

Map p430 (www.irishrep.org; 132 W 22nd St btwn Sixth & Seventh Aves; ⊙10am-6pm Mon & Tue, to 8pm Wed-Fri, 11am-8pm Sat; S1/2, F, M to 23rd St; 1/2 to 18th St) This repertory troupe, with a space in a renovated Chelsea warehouse, showcases the finest contributions to the theater world from the Irish and Irish American community.

SMALLS JAZZ CLUB
LIVE MUSIC

Map p426 (www.smallsjazzclub.com; 183 W 10th St at Seventh Ave; S1 to Christopher St-Sheridan Sq) Living up to its name, this cramped but appealing basement jazz den offers a grab-bag collection of jazz acts who take the stage nightly. Cover for the evening is $20 (including a free drink Sunday through Thursday), with a come-and-go policy if you need to duck out for a slice.

55 BAR
LIVE MUSIC

Map p426 (www.55bar.com; 55 Christopher St at Seventh Ave; cover charge $3-15, 2-drink minimum; ⊙1pm-4am; S1 to Christopher St-Sheridan Sq) Dating back to the Prohibition era, this friendly basement dive is great for low-key shows without high covers or dressing up. There are regular performances twice nightly by quality artists-in-residence, some blues bands and Miles Davis' super '80s guitarist Mike Stern.

DUPLEX
CABARET, KARAOKE

Map p426 (www.theduplex.com; 61 Christopher St; cover charge $10-20; ⊙4pm-4am; S1 to Christopher St-Sheridan Sq) Cabaret, karaoke and campy dance moves are par for the course at the legendary Duplex. Pictures of Joan Rivers line the walls, and the performers like to mimic her sassy form of self-deprecation, while getting in a few jokes about audience members as well. It's a fun and unpretentious place, and certainly not for the bashful.

LE POISSON ROUGE LIVE MUSIC

Map p426 (www.lepoissonrouge.com; 158 Bleecker St; [S]A/C/E, B/D/F/V to W 4th St-Washington Sq) This newish high-concept art space (complete with dangling fish aquarium) hosts a highly eclectic lineup, with the likes of Deerhunter, Marc Ribot, Lou Reed and Laurie Anderson performing in past years. Aside from the main (high-tech) concert space, there's also an art gallery and a bar-cafe open during the day.

CORNELIA ST CAFÉ LITERARY

Map p426 (www.corneliastreetcafe.com; 29 Cornelia St btwn Bleecker & W 4th Sts; [S]A/C/E, B/D/F/V to W 4th St-Washington Sq) This intimate cafe is known for its various lit series, including monthly storytelling gatherings, open-mic poetry nights, and readings dedicated to Italian Americans, Greeks, Caribbean Americans, NYC-area grads, members of the Writers Room (a local writers' collective), scribes of prose and emerging poets. There are also music performances and art exhibits, plus a nice cafe menu.

NEW SCHOOL UNIVERSITY EVENTS

Map p426 (www.newschool.edu; 66 Fifth Ave at 12th St; [S]F/V to 14th St) This forward-thinking university – which includes the Parsons School of Design and various arts, music and urban studies divisions – hosts a series of public discourses for anyone interested in attending; if you can't be there in person, the school's website has webcasts available for downloading. Discussions have revolved around topics such as strengthening the middle class, recovering from the mortgage crisis in NYC neighborhoods, how to organize protests, global warming, and the history of the AIDS pandemic.

DANCE THEATER WORKSHOP DANCE

Map p430 (www.dancetheaterworkshop.org; 219 W 19th St btwn Seventh & Eighth Aves; [S]1 to 18th St) You'll find a program of more than 110 experimental, contemporary works annually at this sleek dance center, led by artistic director Carla Peterson. Residency showcases, First Light Commissions and various international productions bring fresh works to the stage, with shows that often include pre- or post-show discussions with choreographers or dancers.

GOTHAM COMEDY CLUB COMEDY

Map p430 (www.gothamcomedyclub.com; 208 W 23rd St btwn Seventh & Eighth Aves; [S]F/V, R/W to 23rd St) Fancying itself as a NYC comedy hall of fame, and backing it up with regular big names and Gotham All-Stars shows, this expanded club provides space for comedians who've cut their teeth on HBO, Letterman and Leno.

JOYCE THEATER PERFORMING ARTS

Map p430 (www.joyce.org; 175 Eighth Ave; ⏲hrs vary; [S]C/E to 23rd St; A/C/E to 8th Ave-14th St; 1 to 18th St) A favorite among dance junkies because of its excellent sight lines and offbeat offerings, this is an intimate venue, seating 470 in a renovated cinema. Its focus is on traditional modern companies such as Pilobolus and Parsons Dance, which make annual apperances. Its other, more intimate, branch, **Joyce Soho** (Map p418; www.joyce.org; 155 Mercer St at Prince St, SoHo; [S]R/W to Prince St), occupies a former firehouse in SoHo and has dance studios and a performance space that seats just 74.

CLEARVIEW'S CHELSEA CINEMA

Map p430 (☎212-777-3456; 260 W 23rd St btwn Seventh & Eighth Aves; [S]C/E to 23rd St) In addition to showing first run films, this multiscreen complex hosts weekend midnight showings of the *Rocky Horror Picture Show*. It also hosts a great Thursday-night series, Chelsea Classics, which features local drag star Hedda Lettuce presenting old-school camp fare from Joan Crawford, Bette Davis, Barbra Streisand and the like.

SHOPPING

Greenwich Village & the Meatpacking District

The picturesque, tranquil streets of the West Village are home to some lovely boutiques, with a few antique dealers, bookstores, record stores, and quirky gift and curio shops adding a bit of eclecticism to an otherwise fashion-focused 'hood. High-end shoppers stick to top-label stores along Bleecker St between Bank and W 10th. There's much more color along Christopher St, with its stores selling leather play gear and rainbow-colored T-shirts.

The Meatpacking District is all about that sleek, high-ceilinged industrial-chic vibe, with ultramodern designers reigning at expansive boutiques that are among the most fashionable haunts in town (some stores indeed look like sets for futuristic and beautifully stylized Kubrick films).

YOYAMART — CHILDREN

Map p426 (www.yoyashop.com; 15 Gansevoort St; 🕐11am-7pm Mon-Sat, noon-6pm Sun; [S]A/C/E to 14th St; L to 8th Ave) Ostensibly geared toward the younger set, Yoyamart is a fun place to browse for adults – even if you're not packing a child. Sure, you'll find adorable apparel for babies and toddlers, but there are also cuddly robots, Gloomy Bear gloves, plush ninjas, build-your-own-ukulele kits, CD mixes and anime-style amusements. For more kiddy clothes and accessories, visit the nearby **Yoya** (Map p426; ☎646-336-6844; 636 Hudson St; 🕐11am-7pm Mon-Sat, noon-5pm Sun; [S]A/C/E to 14th St; L to 8th Ave).

STRAND BOOK STORE — BOOKS

Map p426 (www.strandbooks.com; 828 Broadway at 12th St; 🕐9:30am-10:30pm Mon-Sat, 11am-10:30pm Sun; [S]L, N/Q/R/W, 4/5/6 to 14th St-Union Sq) Book fiends (or even those who have casually skimmed one or two) shouldn't miss New York's most loved and famous bookstore. In operation since 1927, the Strand sells new, used and rare titles, spreading an incredible 18 miles of books (over 2.5 million of them) among three labyrinthine floors. Check out the staggering number of reviewers' copies in the basement, or sell off your own tomes before you get back on the plane, as the Strand buys or trades books at a side counter on weekdays.

MARC BY MARC JACOBS — FASHION

Map p426 (www.marcjacobs.com; 403-405 Bleecker St; 🕐noon-8pm Mon-Sat, to 7pm Sun; [S]A/C/E to 14th St; L to 8th Ave) With five small shops sprinkled around the West Village, Marc Jacobs has established a real presence in this well-heeled neighborhood. Large front windows allow easy peeking – assuming there's not a sale, during which you'll only see hordes of fawning shoppers. Here's the layout: on Bleecker St, you'll find the women's line at Nos 403 to 405, women's accessories (fun wallets, rubber boots and T-shirts) at No 385 and the children's line (Little Marc) at No 382. Men should head one block over, where they'll find the men's collection at 301 W 4th St and men's accessories at 298 W 4th. For men's and women's apparel from the Marc Jacobs Collection (the priciest stuff of all), head to the SoHo **Marc Jacobs** (Map p418; ☎212-343-1490; 163 Mercer St; 🕐11am-7pm Mon-Sat, noon-6pm Sun; [S]B/D/F/V to Broadway-Lafayette St; R/W to Prince St).

MCNULTY'S TEA & COFFEE CO, INC — FOOD & DRINK

Map p426 (☎212-242-5351; 109 Christopher St; 🕐10am-9pm Mon-Sat, 1-7pm Sun; [S]1 to Christopher St-Sheridan Sq) Just down from a few sex shops, sweet McNulty's, with worn wooden floorboards and fragrant sacks of coffee beans and large glass jars of tea, flaunts a different era of Greenwich Village. It's been selling gourmet teas and coffees here since 1895.

BONNIE SLOTNICK COOKBOOKS — BOOKS

Map p426 (www.bonnieslotnickcookbooks.com; 163 W 10th St btwn Waverly Pl & Seventh Ave; [S]1/2 to Christopher St-Sheridan Sq; A/C/E, B/D/F, M to W 4th St; 1/2/3 to 14th St) Bonnie, the kindly owner, dotes on her customers, who are searching for the perfect cooking tome. Stocked to the ceiling with shelf after shelf of the best recipes on earth, the shop – bedecked like grandma's pantry – is bound to reveal some truly unique finds, like themed references (Jewish, gay, soup-specific etc) to antique wares.

CASTOR & POLLUX — CLOTHING

Map p426 (www.castorandpolluxstore.com; 238 W 10th St; [S]1/2 to Christopher St-Sheridan Sq; A/C/E, B/D/F, M to W 4th St; 1/2 to Houston St) Kerrilynn uses the dual nature of Castor and Pollux to design and refine her collection of gorgeous threads. Carefully edited fashions feel wearable yet undeniably chic.

THREE LIVES & COMPANY — BOOKS

Map p426 (www.threelives.com; 154 W 10th St, btwn Seventh Ave & Waverly Pl; [S]1/2 to Christopher St-Sheridan Sq; A/C/E, B/D/F, M to W 4th St; 1/2/3 to 14th St) Your neighborhood bookstore extraordinaire, Three Lives & Company is a wondrous spot that's tended by a coterie of exceptionally well-read individuals, which makes a trip to the store not just a pleasure, but an adventure in the magical world of words.

THE BATHROOM BEAUTY, HOMEWARES

Map p426 (http//:store.inthebathroom.com; 94 Charles St btwn W 4th & Bleecker Sts; 🕐noon-8pm Mon-Fri, 11am-8pm Sat, noon-7pm Sun; [S]1/2 to Christopher St-Sheridan Sq; A/C/E, B/D/F, M to W 4th St; 1/2/3 to 14th St) Although most New York shops tend to be kitchen obsessed, Colin Heywood's boutique knows that the most important room in the house (or – in NYC – the apartment) is the bathroom. Styled like an old-school apothecary, this West Village wonder offers browsers a charming collection of handmade brands from home goods to luxury soaps.

JEFFREY NEW YORK FASHION

Map p426 (www.jeffreynewyork.com; 449 W 14th St; 🕐10am-8pm Mon-Sat, 12:30-6pm Sun; [S]A/C/E to 14th St; L to 8th Ave) One of the pioneers in the Meatpacking District's makeover, Jeffrey sells several high-end designer clothing lines – Versace, Pucci, Prada, Michael Kors and company – as well as accessories, shoes and a small selection of cosmetics. DJs spinning pop and indie add to the very hip vibe.

MURRAY'S CHEESE FOOD & DRINK

Map p426 (www.murrayscheese.com; 254 Bleecker St btwn Sixth & Seventh Aves; 🕐8am-8pm Mon-Sat, 10am-7pm Sun; [S]1 to Christopher St-Sheridan Sq) Founded in 1914, this is probably New York's best cheese shop. Owner Rob Kaufelt is known for his talent of sniffing out devastatingly delicious varieties from around the world. You'll find (and be able to taste) all manner of *fromages* (cheeses), be it stinky, sweet or nutty, from European nations and from small farms in Vermont and upstate New York. There are also prosciutto and smoked meats, freshly baked breads, olives, antipasto, chocolate and all manner of goodies for a gourmet picnic – plus a counter for freshly made sandwiches and melts. Murray's also has a branch in the food market at Grand Central Terminal. You'll find other delectable *fromages* at the restaurant/cheese counter of **Artisanal** (Map p434; www.artisanalbistro.com; 2 Park Ave S at 32nd St; 🕐noon-11pm Mon-Thu, to midnight Fri & Sat, to 10pm Sun; ✎; [S]6 to 33rd St), which you enter on 32nd St.

BUCKLER FASHION, ACCESSORIES

Map p426 (www.bucklershowroom.com; 13 Gansevoort St; 🕐11am-7pm Mon-Sat, noon-6pm Sun; [S]A/C/E, L, 1/2/3 to 8th Ave-14th St) Producing cult menswear that blends 'roguish American icons with British edge,' Buckler is famous for its selection of brash and boyish denim designs. If you like the way Lenny Kravitz and Iggy Pop dress, you've found the perfect store.

CO BIGELOW CHEMISTS HEALTH, BEAUTY

Map p426 (☎212-473-7324; 414 Sixth Ave btwn 8th & 9th Sts; 🕐7:30am-9pm Mon-Fri, 8:30am-7pm Sat, 8:30am-5:30pm Sun; [S]1 to Christopher St-Sheridan Sq; A/C/E, B/D/F/V to W 4th St-Washington Sq) The 'oldest apothecary in America' is now a slightly upscale fantasyland for the beauty-product obsessed (though there's still an actual pharmacy for prescriptions and standard drugstore items for sale on the premises, too). In addition to its own CO Bigelow label products, including lip balms, hand and foot salves, shaving creams and rosewater, you can browse through lotions, shampoos, cosmetics and fragrances from makers including ADP, Dr Hauschka, Weleda, Fekkai and many more.

GREENWICH LETTERPRESS STATIONERY

Map p426 (www.greenwichletterpress.com; 39 Christopher St btwn Seventh Ave & Waverly Pl; 🕐1-6pm Mon, 11am-7pm Tue-Fri, noon-6pm Sat & Sun; [S]1/2 to Christopher St-Sheridan Sq; A/C/E, B/D/F, M to W 4th St; 1/2/3 to 14th St) Founded by two sisters, this cute card shop specializes in wedding announcements and other specially made letterpress endeavors, so skip the stock postcards of the Empire State Building and send your loved ones a bespoke greeting card from this stalwart stationer.

DESTINATION ACCESSORIES, CLOTHING

Map p426 (www.destinationny.net; 32-36 Little W 12th St at Washington St; 🕐11am-8:30pm Tue-Sun; [S]A/C/E to 14th St; L to 8th Ave) The eclectic merchandise provides the spots of color in this vast, all-white space. You'll find hard-to-get jewelry from designers such as Serge Thoraval and Ema Takahashi. Then there are the elegant fashion pieces by Lia Lintern and Mercy, wonderfully beaded totes by Jamin Puech and whimsical, hand-stitched bags and sneakers by Nelma.

EARNEST SEWN CLOTHING

Map p426 (www.earnestsewn.com; 821 Washington St; 🕐11am-7pm Sun-Fri, to 8pm Sat; [S]A/C/E to 14th St; L to 8th Ave) Wood plank floors and a shiny open-top Jeep set the scene for the high-quality apparel on display. Earnest Sewn denim has become famous for its craftsmanship, and customers sign on to long waiting lists to order customized and tailored jeans. The atmospheric store is a fun place to browse, and you'll find an odd mix of delicate jewelry, outerwear and pocketknives among the antique (still working) machinery. You can also check out its **Lower East Side store** (Map p424; ☎212-979-5120; 90 Orchard St; 🕐noon-8pm Mon-Sat, to 7pm Sun; [S]F, J/M/Z to Essex St-Delancey St), which has a smaller selection of apparel (mostly denim).

ADAM FASHION, ACCESSORIES

Map p426 (www.shopadam.com; 678 Hudson St btwn W 13th & W 14th Sts; 🕐11am-7pm Mon-Wed & Fri, to 8pm Thu, 10am-7pm Sat, noon-6pm Sun; [S]A/C/E to 8th Ave-14th St) Oscar de la Renta protégé Adam Lippes' Meatpacking store is full of the smart, modern clothes that have made him a rising star. There's something for men and women (on the left and right sides of the store, respectively) amid the casually hung chic separates, polos, T-shirts and sweaters. Emphasis is on unusual and sensuous materials, like buttery suede and plump quilting.

FLIGHT 001 TRAVEL GEAR

Map p426 (www.flight001.com; 96 Greenwich Ave; 🕐11am-8pm Mon-Sat, noon-6pm Sun; [S]A/C/E to 14th St; L to 8th Ave) Travel is fun, sure – but getting travel gear is even more fun. Check out Flight 001's range of luggage and smaller bags by brands ranging from Bree to Rimowa, kitschy 'shemergency' kits (breath freshener, lip balm, stain remover, etc), pin-up-girl flasks, brightly colored passport holders and leather luggage tags, travel guidebooks (Lonely Planet included, of course), toiletry cases and a range of mini toothpastes, eye masks, pillboxes and the like.

FORBIDDEN PLANET COMICS, GAMES

Map p426 (☎212-473-1576; 840 Broadway; 🕐10am-10pm Mon-Sat, 11am-8pm Sun; [S]L, N/Q/R/W, 4/5/6 to 14th St-Union Sq) Indulge your inner sci-fi nerd. Find heaps of comics, books, manga, video games and figurines (ranging from *Star Trek* to *Where the Wild Things Are*). Fellow Magic and Yu-Gi-Oh! card-game lovers play upstairs in the public sitting area.

MXYPLYZYK GIFTS

Map p426 (www.mxyplyzyk.com; 125 Greenwich Ave at W 13th St; 🕐11am-7pm Mon-Sat, noon-5pm Sun; [S]A/C/E to 14th St; L to 8th Ave) There's nothing usual about this totally fun home shop – including its odd name (pronounced mix-ee-*pliz*-ik). Here you'll find life-sized owl lamps, LED mini-chandeliers, candy-striped sock monkeys, oversized animal books, fruit baskets made from chopsticks, cardboard animal heads, colorful nesting bowls for the kitchen, alphabet soaps and other intriguing objects.

PLEASURE CHEST EROTICA

Map p426 (www.thepleasurechest.com; 156 Seventh Ave btwn Charles & Perry Sts; 🕐10am-midnight; [S]1 to Christopher St-Sheridan Sq) No trip to the Village is complete without a stop at the Pleasure Chest, a gay-friendly, clean, upbeat and inclusive sex shop with zero sleaze factor. Its wildly colorful window displays of creams, oils, funny (and risqué) cards and toys lure a wide variety of shoppers.

SUSAN PARRISH ANTIQUES ANTIQUES

Map p426 (☎212-645-5020; 390 Bleecker St; 🕐noon-7pm Mon-Sat, or by appt; [S]1 to Christopher St) American furniture, textiles, folk art and paintings are offered at this well-respected West Village antiques store. There are early-20th-century Amish quilts and furnishings, as well as 19th-century items in good condition. Navajo and hooked rugs come in dozens of floral and geometric designs.

AEDES DE VENUSTAS BEAUTY

Map p426 (www.aedes.com; 9 Christopher St; 🕐noon-8pm Mon-Sat, 1-7pm Sun; [S]A/C/E, B/D/F/V to W 4th St; 1 to Christopher St-Sheridan Sq) Plush and inviting, Aedes de Venustas ('Temple of Beauty' in Latin) provides more than 40 brands of luxury European perfumes, including Hierbas de Ibiza, Mark Birley for Men, Costes, Odin and Shalini. It also has skincare products created by folks such as Found and Jurlique, and everyone's favorite scented candles from Diptyque.

JOHN BARTLETT CLOTHING

Map p426 (☎212-633-6867; 143 Seventh Ave at Charles St; [S]B, Q to 7th Ave; 2/3, 4 to Grand Army Plaza) Rugby players and Ivy Leaguers will go gaga for the selection of extra-masculine clothing that comes with a wink at this underrated designer's Village shop. There's women's wear, too.

STELLA MCCARTNEY FASHION

Map p426 (www.stellamccartney.com; 429 W 14th St; 🕐11am-8pm Tue-Sat, noon-6pm Sun; [S]A/C/E, L to 8th Ave-14th St) More showroom than full-fledged store, McCartney's Meatpacking outpost has a minimal selection on hand, but, oh, what a selection it is. Drapey, gauzy, muted in color yet high on femininity, the delicate, ethereal clothes shine in this pared-down setting. Of course, McCartney's clothes are animal-product free, in keeping with her vegan philosophy.

ALEXANDER MCQUEEN FASHION, ACCESSORIES

Map p426 (www.alexandermcqueen.com; 417 W 14th St; 🕒11am-7pm Mon-Sat, noon-6pm Sun; [S]A/C/E, L, 1/2/3 to 8th Ave-14th St) The brand's rambunctious outfits are shown to perfection in this massive Meatpacking District store, and the edgy creations seem made to be worn in this fashion-forward district.

🛍 Chelsea

Better known for its dining and nightlife scenes, Chelsea has a decent selection of antiques, discount fashion, chain stores and kitsch, along with a hidden bookstore and well-edited thrift shop. The neighborhood standout is the beloved Chelsea Market, a huge concourse packed with shops selling fresh baked goods, wines, veggies, imported cheeses and other temptations.

202 CLOTHING, HOMEWARES

Map p430 (☎646-638-0115; 75 Ninth Ave at 16th St; 🕒11:30am-10pm Mon-Fri, 10am-10pm Sat, 10am-6pm Sun; [S]A/C/E to 14th St; L to 8th Ave) On the edge of Chelsea Market, this spacious wood-floored boutique and restaurant sates many appetites with its elegant glasswares and homewares, beautifully designed men's and women's clothing, trim leather armchairs – and of course those delectable fluffy pancakes served at brunch. The 202 store is the brainchild of designer Nicole Farhi, who has a similar store in London's Notting Hill.

BARNEYS CO-OP FASHION, ACCESSORIES

Map p430 (☎212-593-7800; 236 W 18th St; 🕒11am-8pm Mon-Fri, to 7pm Sat, noon-6pm Sun; [S]1 to 18th St) The edgier, younger, less expensive version of Barneys has good deals. At this expansive, loftlike space, with a spare, very selective inventory of clothing for men and women, plus shoes and cosmetics, the biannual warehouse sale (February and August) packs the place, with both endless merchandise and mobs of customers.

HOUSING WORKS THRIFT SHOP FASHION, BRIC-A-BRAC

Map p430 (☎212-366-0820; 143 W 17th St; 🕒10am-6pm Mon-Sat, noon-5pm Sun; [S]1 to 18th St) This shop, with its swank window displays, looks more boutique than thrift, but its selections of clothes, accessories, furniture and books are great value. All proceeds benefit the charity serving the city's HIV-positive and AIDS homeless communities. There are 10 other branches around town.

POSMAN BOOKS BOOKS

Map p430 (www.posmanbooks.com; 75 Ninth Ave btwn Fifth Ave & 15th St; [S]A/C/E to 14th St; L to 8th Ave; 1/2 to 18th St) Family-run Posman is a shining star in a night darkened by big-box booksellers. But as the seas once again ebb in favor of the next iteration in book sales (oh, hi Amazon!), this sleekly designed reading hub has evolved into an inviting social space that hosts talks and activities for the little ones. Definitely worth stopping by for a snoop.

PRINTED MATTER BOOKS

Map p430 (☎212-925-0325; 195 Tenth Ave btwn 21st & 22nd Sts; 🕒11am-6pm Tue & Wed, to 7pm Thu-Sat; [S]C/E to 23rd St) Printed Matter is a wondrous little two-room shop dedicated to limited-edition artist monographs and strange little zines. Here you will find nothing carried by mainstream bookstores; instead, trim little shelves hide call-to-arms manifestos, critical essays about comic books, flip books that reveal Jesus' face through barcodes and how-to guides written by prisoners.

BALENCIAGA FASHION, ACCESSORIES

Map p430 (☎212-206-0872; 522 W 22nd St at Eleventh Ave; 🕒10am-7pm Mon-Sat, noon-5pm Sun; [S]C/E to 23rd St) Come and gaze at this cool, gray, Zen-like space. It's the gallery district's showcase, appropriately enough, for the artistic, post-apocalypse, avant-garde styles of this French fashion house. Expect strange lines, goth patterns and pants for very skinny (and deep-pocketed) gals.

192 BOOKS BOOKS

Map p430 (www.192books.com; 192 Tenth Ave btwn 21st & 22nd Sts; 🕒11am-7pm Tue-Sat, noon-6pm Sun & Mon; [S]C/E to 23rd St) Located right in the gallery district is this small indie bookstore, with sections on literature, history, travel, art and criticism. A special treat is its offerings of rotating art exhibits, during which the owners organize special displays of books that relate thematically to the featured show or artist. Weekly book readings feature acclaimed (often NY-based) authors.

UNIVERSAL GEAR CLOTHING

Map p430 (www.universalgear.com; 140 Eighth Ave btwn 16th & 17th Sts; [S]A/C/E to 14th St; L to 8th Ave) A more accurate name might be 'Chelsea Gear,' as the place is bursting with all that's de rigueur for handsome Chelsea boys and wannabes. Here's where you'll find cute-boy staples like G-Star and Diesel denim, pouch-heightening underwear by 2(x)ist and C-IN2, plus swimwear, jackets, shoes and accessories from Ben Sherman bags to D&G watches.

ANTIQUES GARAGE FLEA MARKET ANTIQUES

Map p430 (☎212-243-5343; 112 W 25th St at Sixth Ave; 🕒9am-5pm Sat & Sun; [S]1 to 23rd St) This weekend flea market is set in a two-level parking garage, with more than 100 vendors spreading their wares. Antique-lovers shouldn't miss a browse here, as they'll find clothing, shoes, records, books, globes, furniture, rugs, lamps, glassware, paintings, artwork and many other relics from the past. Weekend antique hunters should also visit the affiliated Hell's Kitchen Flea Market.

NASTY PIG CLOTHING

Map p430 (☎212-691-6067; 265 W 19th St btwn Seventh & Eighth Aves; [S]A/C/E to 14th St; 1/2 to 18th St or 23rd St) T-shirts, socks and underwear bearing the store's namesake, along with a bit of rubber and leather fetish wear, makes this an ideal stop for Chelsea boys and their admirers.

BEHAVIOUR CLOTHING, ACCESSORIES

Map p430 (☎212-352-8380; 231 W 19th St btwn Seventh & Eighth Aves; [S]A/C/E to 8th Ave-14th St; 1/2 to 18th St or 23rd St) A terribly well-curated men's shop for the stylish dandy. From sunglasses to T-shirts, they are all excellent. Usually a dash of seersucker in the spring.

ABRACADABRA ACCESSORIES

off Map p430 (☎212-627-5194; 19 W 21st St btwn Fifth & Sixth Aves; [S]N/R, 4/6 to 23rd St) It's not just a Steve Miller Band song, it's also an emporium of horror, costumes and magic. Those who like this sort of thing will be hard-pressed to leave without racking up some credit-card bills.

SPORTS & ACTIVITIES

CHELSEA PIERS COMPLEX SPORTS

Map p430 (www.chelseapiers.com; Hudson River at end of W 23rd St; [S]C/E to 23rd St) This massive waterfront sports center caters to the athlete in everyone. You can set out to hit a bucket of golf balls at the four-level driving range, ice skate on the complex's indoor rink or rent in-line skates to cruise along the new bike path on the Hudson River Park – all the way down to Battery Park. The complex has a jazzy bowling alley, Hoop City for basketball, a sailing school for kids, batting cages, a huge gym facility with an indoor pool (day passes for nonmembers are $50), indoor rock-climbing walls – the works. There's even waterfront dining and drinking at the Chelsea Brewing Company, which serves great pub fare and delicious home brews for you to carb-load on after your workout. Though the complex is somewhat cut off by the busy West Side Hwy (Twelfth Ave), the wide array of attractions here brings in the crowds; the M23 crosstown bus, which goes right to the main entrance, saves you the long, four-avenue trek from the subway.

WEST 4TH STREET BASKETBALL COURTS BASKETBALL

Map p426 (Sixth Ave btwn 3rd & 4th Sts; 🕒hrs vary; [S]A/C/E, B/D/F/V to W 4th St-Washington Sq) Also known as 'the Cage,' this small basketball court that stands enclosed within chain-link fencing is home to some of the best streetball in the country. Though it's more touristy than its counterpart, Rucker Park in Harlem, that's also part of its charm, as the games held here in the center of the Village draw massive, excitable crowds who often stand 10-deep to hoot and holler for the skilled, competitive guys who play here. Prime time is summer, when the W 4th St Summer Pro-Classic League, with daily high-energy games, hits the scene. While the height of this court's popularity was back in 2001 – the year Nike capitalized on the raw energy of the place by shooting a commercial here – b'ball-lovin' throngs still storm the place on weekends.

BOWLMOR LANES BOWLING

Map p426 (www.bowlmor.com; 110 University Pl; individual games from $10, shoe rental $6; ⏰4pm-1am Mon-Thu, 11am-3:30am Fri & Sat, 11am-midnight Sun; [S]L, N/Q/R/W, 4/5/6 to 14th St-Union Sq) Among retro-crazed New Yorkers, a night of bowling qualifies as quite a hoot. Maybe it's the shoes, or all the pitchers of beer. Open since 1938, Bowlmor has Manhattan's go-to lanes for stars, bar mitzvah parties and beer-slugging NYU students. After 9pm Monday, it goes DJ-blasting glow-in-the-dark, with unlimited bowling for $24 including shoe rental (age 21 and up).

NEW YORK TRAPEZE SCHOOL SPECTATOR SPORTS

Map p426 (http://newyork.trapezeschool.com; Pier 40 at West Side Hwy; classes $47-65, 5-week course $270; [S]1 to Houston St) Fulfill your circus dreams, like Carrie did on *Sex and the City,* flying trapeze to trapeze in this open-air tent by the river. It's open from May to September, on top of Pier 40. The school also has an **indoor facility** (Map p438; 518 W 30th St btwn Tenth & Eleventh Aves; [S]A/C/E to 34th St-Penn Station) open year round. Call or check the website for daily class times. There's a one-time $22 registration fee.

OM YOGA CENTER YOGA

Map p426 (www.omyoga.com; 6th fl, 826 Broadway; classes $18; [S]L, N/Q/R/W, 4/5/6 to 14th St-Union Sq) This inviting space – with redwood floors, high ceilings and showers – has popular *vinyasa* classes run by former dancer (and choreographer of videos such as 'Girls Just Want to Have Fun') Cyndi Lee, a practitioner of hatha yoga and Tibetan Buddhism. Classes are run for all levels; an hour-long 'yoga express' is $12.

DOWNTOWN BOATHOUSE KAYAKING

Map p426 (www.downtownboathouse.org; Pier 40, near Houston St; tours free; ⏰9am-6pm Sat & Sun mid-May–mid-Oct, some weekday evenings mid-Jun–mid-Sep; [S]1 to Houston St) New York's most active public boathouse offers free walk-up 20-minute kayaking (including equipment) in the protected embayment in the Hudson River on weekends and some weekday evenings. Longer rides (eg to Governors Island) usually go from the Midtown location at **Clinton Cove** (Map p438; Pier 96, W 56th St; ⏰9am-6pm Sat & Sun, 5-7pm Mon-Fri mid-Jun–Aug; [S]A/C, B/D, 1 to 59th St-Columbus Circle); there's another boathouse at **Riverside Park** (Map p442; W 72nd St; ⏰10am-5pm Sat & Sun; [S]1/2/3 to 72nd St) on the Upper West Side.

TONY DAPOLITO RECREATION CENTER SWIMMING

Map p426 (☎212-242-5228; 3 Clarkson St; ⏰7am-10pm Mon-Fri, 9am-4:30pm Sat & Sun; [S]1 to Houston St) This West Village center (formerly the Carmine) has one of the city's best public pools, but it's only available by annual membership ($75 not including the indoor pool, which is $50). It has an indoor and outdoor swimming pool – the latter was used for the pool scene in *Raging Bull.*

Union Square, Flatiron District & Gramercy

Neighborhood Top Five

1 Perusing floor after floor of wildly priced home goods amid the glorious warehouse-chic surrounds of **ABC Carpet & Home** (p172).

2 Wandering between stalls stuffed with leafy farm produce at the **Union Square Greenmarket** (p172), which transforms into a delightful Christmas market in winter.

3 Slurping handcrafted brews at Eataly's secreted Beer Garden, **Birreria** (p166), lofted high up among the Flatiron District's clock towers.

4 Walking square around **Gramercy Park** (p165), enjoying one of the city's most intimate urban moments.

5 Snacking on **Shake Shack** (p166) burgers amid audacious art installations in Madison Square Park.

For more detail of this area, see Map p432 ➡

Explore Union Square, Flatiron District & Gramercy

Although Union Sq earned its moniker from rather practical and prosaic roots, the name today has become so much more than the junction of two roads. In many ways the neighborhood is the union of many disparate parts of the city, acting as the veritable urban glue linking unlikely cousins. Some may criticize the area for not having a distinct personality of its own, but upon closer inspection, Union Sq and the Flatiron District seem to borrow rather cautiously and selectively from their neighbors.

There's not a lot of ground to cover, so the best plan of attack is to use the two major public spaces – Union Sq and Madison Square Park – as your anchors. From Union Sq you'll feel the Village vibe spilling over with the likes of quirky cafes, funky storefronts and dreadlocked buskers in the square. Up towards 23rd St you'll find the namesake Flatiron Building looming over the commercial quarter, replete with crowded lunch spots and after-work watering holes. East of both public spaces is Gramercy, which feels predominantly residential save for a generous peppering of restaurants throughout.

Local Life

➡ **Meals on wheels** The Union Sq and Flatiron areas have designated parking spaces for some of the best food trucks and carts in town. Head to the southwest corner of 14th St and Third Ave to check out trucks hawking their edible wares. The halal food cart at 28th St and Madison Ave has garnered quite a cult following – some say it's the best one in town.

➡ **Gourmet groceries** Eataly (p172) is making a name for itself as the place to go for Italophile food buffs, but locals do much more of their everyday shopping at Whole Foods (p173) and Trader Joe's (p172).

Getting There & Away

➡ **Subway** A slew of subway lines converge below Union Sq, shuttling passengers up Manhattan's East Side on the 4, 5 and 6 lines straight across to Williamsburg on the L or up and over to Queens on the N, Q and R lines. The L also travels across to the West Side, although when there's no traffic it costs about the same to take a cab (if you're two or more people). Take the Q for an express link up to Times Sq.

➡ **Bus** Easy to remember, the M14 and the M23 provide cross-town service along 14th St and 23rd St respectively. Go for the bus over the subway if you're traveling between two eastern points in Manhattan – it's not worth traveling over to Union Sq to walk back to First Ave.

Lonely Planet's Top Tip

Human traffic can be overwhelming in Union Sq, especially along 14th St. If you're in a rush, or trying to hoof it on foot, then switch over to 13th St and you'll cover a lot more ground in much less time.

✖ Best Places to Eat

➡ Birreria (p166)
➡ ABC Kitchen (p166)
➡ Casa Mono (p166)
➡ Ess-a-Bagel (p166)

For reviews, see p164 ➡

🍷 Best Places to Drink

➡ Raines Law Room (p168)
➡ Beauty Bar (p169)
➡ Gramercy Tavern (p167)
➡ Boxers NYC (p169)
➡ Crocodile Lounge (p169)

For reviews, see p168 ➡

⊙ Best Places to Take Photos

➡ Trader Joe's (p172), looking up Irving Pl toward the Chrysler Building
➡ Birreria (p166), from the roof deck
➡ The south side of Madison Square Park (p164) for a full-frontal of the Flatiron Building
➡ From the stone steps on the southern end of Union Sq (p162), capturing the chanting protestors or scurrying buskers

For reviews, see p164 ➡

UNION SQUARE, FLATIRON DISTRICT & GRAMERCY

TOP SIGHTS
UNION SQUARE

Union Sq is like the Noah's Ark of New York, rescuing at least two of every kind from the curling seas of concrete. In fact, one would be hard-pressed to find a more eclectic cross-section of locals gathered in one public place. Here, amid the tapestry of stone steps and fenced-in foliage it's not uncommon to find denizens of every ilk: suited businessfolk gulping fresh air during their lunch breaks, dreadlocked loiterers tapping beats on their tabla, skateboarding punks flipping tricks on the southeastern stairs, rowdy college kids guzzling student-priced eats, and throngs of protesting masses chanting fervently for various causes.

Riches & Rags

Opened in 1831, Union Sq quickly became the central gathering place for those who lived in the mansions nearby. Concert halls and artist societies further enhanced the cultured atmosphere, and high-end shopping quickly proliferated along Broadway, which was dubbed 'Ladies' Mile.'

When the Civil War broke out, the vast public space (large by New York standards, of course) was center stage for protesters of all sorts – from union workers to political activists. By the height of WWI, the area had fallen largely into disuse, allowing politically and socially driven organizations like the American Civil Liberties Union, the Communist and Socialist Parties and the Ladies' Garment Workers Union to move in. The square is still the site for political and social protests today.

The Factory

After over a century of the continuous push-and-pull between dapper-dom and political protest, a third – artistic, if not thoroughly hippie-ish – ingredient was tossed into the mix when Andy Warhol moved his Factory to Union Sq West. The building is now a Puma sportswear store – a telling sign of the times.

Metronome

A walk around Union Sq will reveal almost a dozen notable pieces of art – there's Rob Pruitt's 10ft homage to Andy Warhol (erected on the exact spot where he was shot by Valerie Solanas), and the imposing equestrian statue of George Washington (one of the first public pieces of art in New York City). But on the south side of the square sits a massive art installation that either earns confused stares or simply gets overlooked by passersby. A symbolic representation of the passage of time, *Metronome* has two parts – a digital clock with a puzzling display of numbers, and a wandlike apparatus with smoke puffing out of concentric rings. We'll let you ponder the latter while we give you the skinny on what exactly the winking orange digits denote: the 14 numbers must be split into two groups of seven – the seven from the left tell the current time (hour, minute, second, 10th-of-a-second) and the seven from the right are meant to be read in reverse order; they represent the remaining amount of time in the day.

DON'T MISS...

- Union Square Greenmarket
- Andy Warhol statue
- Gandhi statue
- *Metronome* art installation
- Protests, sit-ins and buskers

PRACTICALITIES

- Map p432
- www.unionsquarenyc.org
- 17th St btwn Broadway & Park Ave S
- [S]L, N/Q/R/W, 4/5/6 to 14th St-Union Sq

RACHEL LEWIS / LONELY PLANET IMAGES ©

TOP SIGHTS
FLATIRON BUILDING

Built in 1902, the 20-story Flatiron Building, designed by Daniel Burnham, has a uniquely narrow triangular footprint that resembles the prow of a massive ship. It also has a traditional beaux arts limestone facade, built over a steel frame, that gets more complex and beautiful the longer you stare at it. Best viewed from the traffic island north of 23rd St between Broadway and Fifth Ave, this unique structure dominated the plaza back in the skyscraper era of the early 1900s. In fact, until 1909 it was the world's tallest building.

The construction of the Flatiron Building (originally known as the Fuller Building) coincided with the proliferation of mass-produced picture postcards – the partnership was kismet. Even before its completion, there were images of the soon-to-be tallest tower circulating the globe, creating much wonder and excitement.

Publisher Frank Munsey was one of the building's first tenants. From his 18th-floor offices, he published *Munsey's Magazine,* which featured short-story writer William Sydney Porter, whose pen name was 'O Henry.' His musings (in popular stories such as 'The Gift of the Magi'), the paintings of John Sloan and photographs of Alfred Stieglitz best immortalized the Flatiron back in the day – along with a famous comment by actress Katherine Hepburn, who said that she'd like to be admired as much as the grand old building.

Like many of New York City's monumental homages to civic progress, the Flatiron Building is still fully functional and houses private businesses. The famed structure is therefore best appreciated from the exterior. Plans are underway to transform the building into a five-star hotel, but progress is on permanent hold until the final tenants willingly vacate the premises.

DON'T MISS...

- The view of the facade from Madison Square Park
- An up-close-and-personal look to appreciate the fine exterior detail

PRACTICALITIES

- Map p432
- Broadway cnr Fifth Ave & 23rd St
- [S]N/R, 6 to 23rd St

SIGHTS

UNION SQUARE
SQUARE

See p162.

FLATIRON BUILDING
LANDMARK

See p163.

MADISON SQUARE PARK
PARK

Map p432 (www.nycgovparks.org; 23rd to 26th Sts btwn Broadway & Madison Ave; ⏲6am-1am; [S]N/R, 6 to 23rd St) This park defined the northern reaches of Manhattan until the island's population exploded after the Civil War. It has enjoyed a rejuvenation in the past few years thanks to a renovation and re-dedication project, and now locals unleash their dogs here in the popular dog-run area, as workers enjoy lunches – which can be bought from the hip, on-site Shake Shack (p166) – while perched on the shaded benches or sprawled on the wide lawn. These are perfect spots from which to gaze up at the landmarks that surround the park, including the Flatiron Building (p163) to the southwest, the art deco **Metropolitan Life Insurance Tower** to the southeast and the **New York Life Insurance Building**, topped with a gilded spire, to the northeast.

The space also sports 19th-century statues of folks including Senator Roscoe Conkling (who froze to death in a brutal 1888 blizzard) and Civil War admiral David Farragut. Between 1876 and 1882 the torch-bearing arm of the Statue of Liberty was on display here, and in 1879 the first Madison Square Garden arena was constructed at Madison Ave and 26th St. In warm months, various park programs feature readings and music performances, many for kids, while eclectic sculptures are shown year-round. And, at the southeast corner of the park, you'll find one of the city's few self-cleaning, coin-operated toilets.

TIBET HOUSE
CULTURAL CENTER

Map p432 (www.tibethouse.org; 22 W 15th St btwn Fifth & Sixth Aves; suggested donation $5; ⏲noon-5pm Mon-Fri; [S]F to 14th St, L to 6th Ave) With the Dalai Lama as the patron of its board, this nonprofit cultural space is dedicated to presenting Tibet's ancient traditions through art exhibits, a research library and various publications, while programs on offer include educational workshops, open meditations, retreat weekends and docent-led tours to Tibet, Nepal and Bhutan. Exhibits here tend to attract a diverse and passionate crowd, and have recently ranged from 'Modern Buddhist Visions by Pema Namdol Thaye,' with traditional Tibetan *tangka* painting and sculpture, to 'Masterpieces of Contemporary Buddhist and Hindu Tantric Art,' featuring works from a special collection. Open on Saturdays by appointment.

[FREE] THEODORE ROOSEVELT'S BIRTHPLACE
HISTORIC SITE

Map p432 (www.nps.gov/thrb; 28 E 20th St btwn Park Ave S & Broadway; adult/child $3/free; ⏲9am-5pm Tue-Sat; [S]N/R/W, 6 to 23rd St) This National Historic Site is a bit of a cheat, since the physical house where the 26th president was actually born was demolished in his own lifetime. But this building is a worthy reconstruction by his relatives, who joined it with another family residence next door. If you're interested in Roosevelt's extraordinary life, which has been somewhat overshadowed by the enduring legacy of his younger cousin Franklin D, visit here – especially if you don't have the time to see his spectacular summer home in Long Island's Oyster Bay. Included in the admission price are half-hour house tours, offered on the hour from 10am to 4pm.

NATIONAL ARTS CLUB
CULTURAL CENTER

Map p432 (www.nationalartsclub.org; 15 Gramercy Park S; [S]6 to 23rd St) This club, founded in 1898 to promote public interest in the arts, boasts a beautiful, vaulted, stained-glass ceiling above the wooden bar in its picture-lined front parlor. Calvert Vaux, who was one of the creators of Central Park, designed the building, originally the private residence of Samuel J Tilden, governor of New York and failed presidential candidate in 1876. The club holds art exhibitions, ranging from sculpture to photography, that are sometimes open to the public from 1pm to 5pm (check the website for schedules). Other events include sketch classes, jazz lunches and French lessons.

🍴 EATING

A veritable goldmine of eateries, this multinamed area stretches from E 14th St to about the mid-30s. One precious perk is the Union Square Greenmarket – a sprawling sensory delight held Monday, Wednesday, Friday

START **MADISON SQUARE PARK**
END **DSW**
DISTANCE **2 MILES**
TIME **2 HOURS**

Neighborhood Walk
Be There, Be Square

Start off in the peaceful green space of
❶ Madison Square Park, dotted with
historic statues and contemporary sculptures. If you'd like to eat before the walk, hit
up **❷ Shake Shack** for a gourmet burger
and fries. Before exiting the park, stand at
its southwest corner and take in the lovely
❸ Flatiron Building, Chicago architect
Daniel Burnham's clever response to the
awkward space where Fifth Ave and Broadway meet. Its beaux arts style and triangular plan are mesmerizing from across the
street; cross the street to stand up close
and admire the city's oddest skyscraper
from a whole new angle.

Follow Broadway south to 21st St and
take a left. Past Park Ave S you'll find yourself alongside **❹ Gramercy Park**, created
by Samuel Ruggles in 1831 after he drained
the swamp in this area and laid out streets
in an English style. You can't enter the
park, as it's private, but go ahead and peer
through the gate.

Head back west along 20th St, stopping
at the reconstructed version of
❺ Theodore Roosevelt's Birthplace,
which is run by the National Parks Service
and offers hourly tours.

Once back on Broadway continue south
and you'll soon find yourself at the northwest corner of **❻ Union Square**. Check
out the produce, cheese, baked goods and
flowers of the Greenmarket farmers market
or amuse yourself by watching the skate-
boarders, visiting the Gandhi statue near
the southwest corner, or grabbing some
food at one of the surrounding eateries for a
picnic in the park.

Standing like a beacon of retail on Union
Sq South (14th St) is **❼ DSW**, a massive
warehouse dedicated to heavily discounted
designer shoes and accessories. Shop
if you wish, but the real attraction is the
store's massive, north-facing window, which
lets you look down over the park and across
to the top of the Empire State Building from
a 4th-floor perch.

UNION SQUARE, FLATIRON DISTRICT & GRAMERCY NEIGHBORHOOD WALK

and Saturday – where discerning chefs, both pro and amateur, scour the wares of upstate farmers and get inspiration for their next meals. But beyond this patch of green is a large range of offerings – both pricey destination dining events and low-key neighborhood gems. Madison Square Park is host to the popular alfresco Shake Shack, with foodie-focused burgers and the like. And Lexington Ave in the high 20s is known as Curry Hill, thanks to its preponderance of spots serving South Indian fare. But the rest of the region covers all the global bases.

[TOP CHOICE] **BIRRERIA** AMERICAN **$$**

Map p432 (www.eatalyny.com; 200 Fifth Ave at 23rd St; mains $15-24; ⌚11:30am-midnight Sun-Wed, to 1am Thu-Sat ; [S]F, N/R, 6 to 23rd St) The crown jewel of Italian gourmet market Eataly is its rooftop beer garden tucked betwixt the Flatiron's corporate towers. A beer menu of encyclopedic proportions offers drinkers some of the best brews on the planet (watch out, though – some bottles cost more than a main!). The signature pork shoulder is your frosty one's soul mate; big bellies should tack on a heaping side of farm-fresh mushrooms.

Oh, and if you can find the hidden access elevator without asking an Eataly employee then congrats – you have better hunting skills than a foxhound.

ABC KITCHEN MODERN AMERICAN **$$**

Map p432 (www.abckitchennyc.com; 35 E 18th St btwn Broadway & Park Ave; small plates $9-15; ⌚ 5:30-10pm Sun-Thu, to 11:30pm Fri & Sat, last reservations half-hour prior; [S]L, N/Q/R, 4/5/6 to Union Sq) A culinary avatar of the wildly wonderful home goods department store, ABC Kitchen's trim, cottagelike surrounds is neatly tucked behind the ballroom chandeliers and drapery out front. Plates are as eclectic as the fairy tale decor – though you'll never go wrong with an organic app and one of the scrumptious whole-wheat pizzas.

CASA MONO TAPAS **$$**

Map p432 (www.casamononyc.com; 52 Irving Pl btwn 17th & 18th Sts; small plates $9-20; ⌚noon-midnight; [S]4/5/6, N/R/Q, L to Union Sq) Another winner from Mario Batali and chef Andy Nusser, Casa Mono has a great, long bar where you can sit and watch your *pez espada a la plancha* and *gambas al ajillo* take a grilling. Or grab one of the wooded tables and nosh on tapas with *jerez* (sherry) from the bottles lining the walls. For a cheese dessert, hop next door to Bar Jamon, also owned by Batali; you may have to squeeze in – the place is communal and fun.

ESS-A-BAGEL DELI **$**

Map p432 (www.ess-a-bagel.com; 359 First Ave at 21st St; bagels from $1; ⌚6am-9pm Mon-Fri, to 5pm Sat & Sun; [S]L, N/Q/R, 4/5/6 to Union Sq) It's simply impossible to resist the billowy tufts of sesame-scented smoke that waft out onto First Ave. Inside, crowds of lip-smacked locals yell at the bagel mongers for their classic New York snack topped with generous gobs of cream cheese. And those gaudy, jewel-dripping chandeliers jammed into the Styrofoam ceiling? You stay classy, Ess-a-Bagel.

CITY BAKERY BAKERY **$**

Map p432 (www.thecitybakery.com; 3 W 18th St btwn Fifth & Sixth Aves; hot chocolate $3, cafeteria lunch per pound $14; [S]L, N/Q/R, 4/5/6 to 14th St-Union Sq) A happy marriage between gourmet entrées and cafeteria service, City Bakery is best known for its scrumptious drip coffee (look at how they pour the milk in first – yum!) and world-famous homemade hot chocolate crowned by a plump marshmallow in the shape of a fairy's pillow.

SHAKE SHACK BURGERS **$**

Map p432 (www.shakeshack.com; cnr 23rd St & Madison Ave; hamburgers from $3.50; ⌚lunch & dinner; [S]R/W to 23rd St) Part of chef Danny Meyer's gourmet burger chainlet, Shake Shack whips up hyper-fresh burgers, crinkle-cut fries and a rotating lineup of frozen custards. Veg-heads can dip into the crisp Portobello burger. Lines are long, but worth it.

BAOHAUS TAIWANESE **$**

Map p432 (www.baohausnyc.com; 238 E 14th St near Second Ave; bao from $3; ⌚11am-midnight Sun-Thu, 11.30am-4am Fri & Sat; [S]L, N/Q/R, 4/5/6 to Union Sq) Blink and you'll miss this hole-in-the-wall and bastion of food-related pun-dom. Three-bite *bao* (Taiwanese pocket sandwiches) are whipped up in seconds by the sociable staffers. Go for the signature Chairman Bao (har har) – a thick slice of pork belly hugged by a cloudlike bun.

BITE SANDWICHES $

Map p432 (www.bitenyc.com; 211 E 14th St btwn Second & Third Aves; sandwiches $7.50; ⏲8am-noon Mon-Sat, 11am-9pm Sun; [S]L, N/Q/R, 4/5/6 to Union Sq) A sweet play on words ('bite' or 'bayit' means 'house' in Hebrew), this tribute to the hummus homeland is a no-frills snacking spot that whips up light, Med-inspired fare amid wood-paneled surrounds. Go for one of the pressed paninis – the eggplant pesto is a veggie's dream – and wash it down with a muddy, home-brewed coffee.

ELEVEN MADISON PARK FRENCH $$$

Map p432 (www.elevenmadisonpark.com; 11 Madison Ave btwn 24th & 25th Sts; four-course dinner $125; ⏲lunch & dinner; [S]N/R, 6 to 23rd St) An art deco wonder often overlooked in this star-studded town, Eleven Madison Park is welcoming enough to bring children into fine dining, and delicious enough to please even the most discerning diner. Dishes include Muscovy duck with honey sauce, wild salmon with horseradish crust and fennel risotto, halibut *mi-cuit* (half-cooked) with carrots, and seasonal surprises.

NUELA PERUVIAN $$$

Map p432 (www.nuelany.com; 43 W 24th St btwn Broadway & Sixth Ave; ceviches $10-18, mains $25-35; ⏲5:30-9pm Sun & Mon, to 10pm Tue-Thu, to 11pm Fri & Sat; [S]F, N/R, 6 to 23rd St) Though the smooth lipstick reds and reflective black decor are somewhat reminiscent of a Shanghai bordello, Nuela's over-sleek surrounds can be easily forgiven with generous portions of fresh-from-the-sea ceviches, brilliantly battered potato wedges, and frothy, meringue-topped pisco sours.

DOS TOROS TAQUERIA MEXICAN $

Map p432 (www.dostoros.com; 137 Fourth Ave btwn 13th & 14th Sts; burritos from $7; ⏲11:30am-10:30pm Mon, to 11pm Tue-Fri, noon-11pm Sat, noon-10:30pm Sun; [S]L, N/Q/R, 4/5/6 to Union Sq) Skip the national chain gang (ahem…Chipotle) in favor of this citywide favorite that promises high-quality meats tucked safely in a sea of thick guacamole and refried beans. Lines can be long (so you know it's good) but efficient staffers whip up your Tex-Mex treat in minutes.

GRAMERCY TAVERN AMERICAN $$$

Map p432 (www.gramercytavern.com; 42 E 20th St btwn Broadway & Park Ave S; tasting menu lunch/dinner $58/116; ⏲lunch & dinner; [S]6 to 23rd St) Though superstar chef Tom Colicchio (who put this legendary spot on the foodie map) recently passed the torch, Michael Anthony was the capable guy who grabbed it. And so the country-chic restaurant, aglow with copper sconces, bright murals and dramatic floral arrangements, is still in the spotlight – perhaps now more than ever. That's thanks to the lighter fish-and-vegetable menu that has replaced what was meat-heavy and hearty. Smoked lobster, Spanish mackerel, blackfish and tuna-and-beet tartare are packed with punches, as are the heavenly desserts and excellent wine options.

MAIALINO ITALIAN $$

Map p432 (www.maialinonyc.com; 2 Lexington Ave at 21st St; mains $15-36; ⏲breakfast, lunch & dinner; [S]4/5, N/R to 23rd St) Danny Meyer's done it again – take your taste buds on a Roman holiday and sample exquisite iterations of Italian peasant fare created from the greenmarket produce from down the street in Union Sq. You can come for a fresh cup of breakfast brew, but the lunchtime prix fixe (at a reasonable $35) should not be passed up.

BOQUERIA FLATIRON TAPAS $$

Map p432 (www.boquerianyc.com/flatiron.html; 53 W 19th St btwn Fifth & Sixth Aves; tapas $5-19; ⏲noon-midnight; [S]N/R/W to 23rd St) A holy union between Spanish-style tapas and market-fresh fare, Boqueria has wooed the after-work crowd with a brilliant assortment of smooth wines that wash down small plates showcasing the spectrum of recipes one can whip up using aged cheese, from-the-farm ham and organic vegetables.

CRAFT AMERICAN $$$

Map p432 (www.craftrestaurantsinc.com/craft-new-york; 43 E 19th btwn Park Ave S & Broadway; mains $18-50; ⏲dinner; [S]L, N/Q/R/W, 4/5/6 to 14th St-Union Sq) When super chef Tom Colicchio opened this fine-food palace in a sweeping architectural space several years ago, the concept was completely new: create your own meal with à la carte items, and enjoy the feeling that not a plate on your table was cookie cutter. Copycats sprang up around town, but this spot still reigns – and still feels fresh – as ingredients change seasonally, and are always finely prepared. Menu items can be found under their appropriate subject headings – fish, 'farm egg,' meat, vegetables, salad – and it's up to you to make the matches (or ask for some expert direction). You might wind up with a plate of Spanish mackerel with fennel, mizuna with truffle vinaigrette and some roasted Jerusalem artichoke. Or perhaps some roasted pheasant with prunes, braised escarole, and beets and tarragon will float your boat. If you can't decide, you can always go for the tasting menu: a seven-course feast paired with wines. You can't lose either way.

PURE FOOD & WINE VEGAN **$$**

Map p432 (www.oneluckyduck.com/purefoodandwine; 54 Irving Pl btwn 17th & 18th Sts; mains $19-26; ⏰dinner; 🌿; [S]L, N/Q/R/W, 4/5/6 to 14th St-Union Sq) The 'chef' (there's no oven in the kitchen) at this gem achieves the impossible: churning out not just edible but also extremely delicious and artistic concoctions, made completely from raw organics that are put through blenders, dehydrators and the capable hands of Pure's staff. Results are creative, fresh and alarmingly delicious, and include the wonderful tomato-zucchini lasagna (sans cheese and pasta), Thai coconut 'noodles' with red curry, and the white-corn tamales with raw cacao *mole* (sauce) and salsa verde. The dining room is sleek and festive, but in warmer months don't miss a chance to settle into a table in the shady oasis of a backyard.

71 IRVING PLACE CAFE **$**

Map p432 (Irving Farm Coffee Company; www.irvingfarm.com; 71 Irving Pl btwn 18th & 19th Sts; mains $6-10; ⏰7am-10pm Mon-Fri, 8am-10pm Sat & Sun; [S]4/5/6, N/Q/R to 14th St-Union Sq, 4/6 to 23rd St) No one takes their coffee more seriously than Irving Farm – a quaint cafe just steps away from the peaceful Gramercy Park. Hand-picked beans are lovingly roasted on a farm in the Hudson Valley (about 90 miles from NYC), and imbibers can tell – this is one of the smoothest cups of joe you'll find in Manhattan.

CURRY HILL

It's not exactly politically correct, but a small four-block section north of Union Sq and Gramercy, traditionally known as Murray Hill, is sometimes also referred to as Curry Hill – a nod to the numerous Indian restaurants, shops and delis that proliferate here. Starting around E 28th St and flowing north on Lexington Ave to about E 33rd St, you'll find some of the finest Indian eateries in town – and most at bargain prices. The all-time local fave? **Curry in a Hurry** (Map p434; www.curryhurry.net; 119 Lexington Ave at E 28th St; ⏰lunch & dinner; [S]6 to 28th St). It's not fancy, but even Bono of U2 fame has been spotted having a nosh here.

ARTICHOKE BASILLE'S PIZZA PIZZERIA **$**

Map p432 (www.artichokepizza.com; 328 E 14th St btwn First & Second Aves; slices from $4.50; ⏰lunch & dinner; [S]L, N/Q/R/W, 4/5/6 to 14th St-Union Sq) Some say this pizzeria is in the East Village, others say Union Sq but, hey, wherever Artichoke Basille's is, count yourself lucky to be there. Run by two Italian guys from Staten Island, the pizza here is authentic, tangy and piled high with all sorts of toppings. The signature pie is a rich, cheesy treat with artichokes and spinach; the plain Sicilian is thinner, with emphasis solely on the crisp crust and savory sauce. Hours are from around noon to about midnight, but sometimes it doesn't open until 3pm. Lines usually form fast.

MAX BRENNER DESSERTS **$**

Map p432 (Chocolate by the Bald Man; www.maxbrenner.com; 841 Broadway btwn 13th & 14th Sts; desserts from $7; ⏰9am-midnight Mon-Thu, to 2am Fri & Sat, to 11pm Sun; [S]L, N/Q/R/W, 4/5/6 to 14th St-Union Sq) Sweet-toothed Aussie Max Brenner has brought his chocolate empire to Union Sq, and his wildly popular cafe-cum-chocolate-bar, looking from the outside like a gingerbread house, is all the rage. Besides the sweets he's got a full menu (great breakfast) and also does low-cal variations mixed by hand on the spot. Divine!

🍷 DRINKING & NIGHTLIFE

As the village morphs into Midtown you'll find a great diversity of drinking spots from stylish hotel lounges to fancy eatery bars and a few down-and-dirty basics thrown in for good measure. If you need a regular-guy Irish pub, look on Third Ave north of 14th St.

RAINES LAW ROOM COCKTAIL BAR

Map p432 (www.raineslawroom.com; 48 W 17th St btwn Fifth & Sixth Aves; [S]F/M to 14th St, L to 6th Ave, 1/2 to 18th St) A sea of velvet drapes and overstuffed leather lounge chairs, tin-tiled ceilings, the perfect amount of exposed brick, and expertly crafted cocktails using perfectly aged spirits – these guys are about as serious as a mortgage payment when it comes to amplified atmosphere. Walk through the unassuming entrance and let Raines Law Room transport you to a far more sumptuous era.

BEAUTY BAR — THEME BAR

Map p432 (www.thebeautybar.com/new_york; 231 E 14th St btwn Second & Third Aves; ⏰5pm-4am Mon-Fri, 7pm-4am Sat & Sun; [S]L to 3rd Ave) A kitschy favorite since the mid-'90s, this homage to old-fashioned beauty parlors pulls in a cool local crowd with its gritty soundtrack, nostalgic vibe and around US$10 manicures (with a free Blue Rinse margarita thrown in) from Wednesday to Sunday.

ROLF'S BAR & RESTAURANT — THEME BAR

Map p432 (www.rolfsnyc.com; 281 Third Ave btwn 21st & 22nd Sts; ⏰noon-4am; [S]N/R, 4/6 to 23rd St; 4/6 to 28th St) During the six weeks before Christmas, Rolf's transforms itself from a standard-fare German bar into a whimsical tribute to the yuletide season that falls somewhere between Santa's workshop and an Addams Family holiday party, with bulbous ornaments and hundreds of dolls that stare at you blankly while you swig your pint.

CROCODILE LOUNGE — LOUNGE

Map p432 (☎212-477-7747; 325 E 14th St btwn First & Second Aves; [S]L to 1st Ave) Williamsburg comes to Manhattan! The Brooklyn success story Alligator Lounge – a 20-something hideout with free pizza – has set up a 14th St outpost hauling in East Villagers seeking free dinner, some Skee-Ball and a few unusual microbrews on tap.

BOXERS NYC — GAY

Map p432 (www.boxersnyc.com; 37 W 20th St, btwn Fifth & Sixth Aves; [S]F, N/R, 6 to 23rd St) Dave & Busters meets David Bowie at this self-proclaimed gay sports bar in the heart of the Flatiron District. There's football on the TV, buffalo wings at the bar, and topless waitstaff keeping the pool cues polished. Monday's drag theme keeps everyone keenly aware that Boxers has a different definition of 'bromance'.

NOWHERE — GAY

Map p432 (☎212-477-4744; 322 E 14th St; [S]L, N/Q/R, 4/5/6 to Union Sq) Dark, dank and rife with flannel-clad fellas in super-skinny jeans: everything your local gay dive bar should be. The booze is priced for the '99%' and there's a pizza joint nearby, which keeps crowds hanging out 'til the wee hours of the morn.

SPLASH BAR — CLUB

Map p432 (www.splashbar.com; 50 W 17th St btwn Fifth & Sixth Aves; ⏰5pm-4am Wed-Sat; [S]L to 6th Ave, F/V to 14th St) As megaclubs come and go, this staple (found near Chelsea's eastern border with the Flatiron District) has become hotter than ever. It's a multilevel club that balances both a lounge and dance-club vibe, thanks to a mix of hang-out spaces, an unrivaled lineup of DJs, great special events, and some of the most smokin' bartenders around.

OLD TOWN BAR & RESTAURANT — BAR

Map p432 (www.oldtownbar.com; 45 E 18th St btwn Broadway & Park Ave S; [S]L, N/Q/R/W, 4/5/6 to 14th St-Union Sq) It still looks like 1892 in here, with the original tile floors and tin ceilings – the Old Town is an 'old world' drinking-man's classic (and woman's: Madonna lit up at the bar here, when lighting up was still legal, in her 'Bad Girl' video). There are cocktails around, but most come for an afternoon beer and burger (around $10), both very good.

PETE'S TAVERN — BAR

Map p432 (www.petestavern.com; 129 E 18th St at Irving Pl; ⏰noon-2am; [S]L, N/Q/R/W, 4/5/6 to 14th St-Union Sq) This dark and atmospheric watering hole has all the earmarks of a New York classic – pressed tin, carved wood and an air of literary history. You can get a respectable burger here, and choose from more than 15 draft beers. The pub draws in everyone from post-theater couples and Irish expats to no-nonsense NYU students.

☆ ENTERTAINMENT

FUERZA BRUTA — PERFORMING ARTS

Map p432 (Daryl Roth Theatre, 101 E 15th St at Union Sq; tickets $79-89, rush tickets $27; ⏰shows 8pm Wed-Fri, 7pm & 10pm Sat, 7pm Sun) Defying the laws of gravity and the theater-going experience in general, Fuerza Bruta is sensory overload on steroids as a visceral world of sound and fury is unleashed upon unwitting audience members. You've gotta see it to believe it.

1. ABC Carpet & Home (p172)
Six wonderful museum-like floors of furnishings, knickknacks, jewelry, gifts and more.

2. Gramercy Park (p165)
You can't enter, but you can peer into one of the city's most intimate urban spaces of greenery.

3. George Washington statue (p162)
The equestrian statue was one of New York's first public pieces of art.

AA WORLD TRAVEL LIBRARY / ALAMY ©

RICHARD CUMMINS / LONELY PLANET IMAGES ©

UNION SQUARE THEATER THEATER

Map p432 (www.nytheater.com; 100 E 17th St at Union Sq; [S]L, N/Q/R/W, 4/5/6 to 14th St-Union Sq) The coolest thing about this theater is that it's built in what used to be Tammany Hall, seat of the most corrupt Democratic political machine that's ever ruled the city. Now the theater outrages the public in other ways, by hosting searing works like *The Laramie Project*, and the side-splittingly funny (and un-PC) puppet show *Stuffed and Unstrung* (not for children). Campy musicals also pop up sometimes.

SHOPPING

There's plenty of shopping to be had in this big block of neighborhoods. First and foremost is Union Sq, home to a delightful greenmarket, which hits the park several times a week all year round. Meanwhile, huge chain stores flank the park to the north and south, offering books, discount fashion and music. Fourteenth St, more to the west than to the east, is a shopping adventure all of its own, with store upon store hawking discount electronics, cheap linens and a great range of shoes and hit-and-miss clothing, from bargain indies as well as chains like Urban Outfitters and Diesel. You'll find more upmarket chain stores heading up Fifth Ave, with Paul Smith, BCBG, Anthropologie, Zara and Intermix among the standouts.

ABC CARPET & HOME HOMEWARES

Map p432 (www.abccarpetandhome.com; 888 Broadway at 19th St; 🕒10am-7pm Mon-Wed & Fri, to 8pm Thu, 11am-7pm Sat, noon-6pm Sun; [S]L, N/Q/R/W, 4/5/6 to 14th St-Union Sq) Home designers and decorators stroll here to brainstorm ideas. Set up like a museum on six floors, ABC is filled with all sorts of furnishings, small and large, including easy-to-pack knickknacks, designer jewelry, global gifts and more bulky antique furnishings and carpets. Come Christmas season the shop is a joy to behold: the decorators here go all out with lights and other wondrous touches.

UNION SQUARE GREENMARKET MARKET

Map p432 (17th St btwn Broadway & Park Ave S; 🕒10am-6pm Mon, Wed, Fri & Sat) The Union Square Greenmarket is arguably the most famous greenmarket in NYC. It attracts many of the city's top chefs to its stalls – to finger aromatic greens, fresh yellow corn and deep-orange squashes.

EATALY FOOD & DRINK

Map p432 (www.eatalyny.com; 200 Fifth Ave at 23rd St; [S]F, N/R, 6 to 23rd St) A 50,000-sq-ft tribute to the *dolce vita*, Mario Batali's food-filled wonderland is a New York-ified version of those dreamy Tuscan markets you find in Diane Lane films. Decked stem to the stern with gourmet edibles, Eataly is a must for a picnic lunch – though make sure to leave room for some pork shoulder at the rooftop beer garden, Birreria (p166).

IDLEWILD BOOKS BOOKS

Map p432 (www.idlewildbooks.com; 12 W 19th St btwn Fifth & Sixth Aves; 🕒11:30am-8pm Mon-Fri, noon-7pm Sat & Sun; [S]L, N/Q/R/W, 4/5/6 to 14th St-Union Sq) One of the best new indie bookshops to open in recent years, Idlewild is a great shopping destination when planning or even daydreaming about travel. Books are divided by region, and cover guidebooks as well as fiction, travelogues, history, cookbooks and other stimulating fare for delving into a country. The big windows overlooking the street, high ceilings and world globe display (all for sale) add to the charm. Check 'Events' on the website for Idlewild's lineup of readings and book-launch parties; sometimes with drinks, music and dance.

BOOKS OF WONDER BOOKS

Map p432 (www.booksofwonder.com; 18 W 18th St btwn Fifth & Sixth Aves; 🕒10am-7pm Mon-Sat, 11am-6pm Sun; 👪; [S]F/V, L to 6th Ave-14th St) Chelsea folks adore this small, fun-loving bookstore devoted to children's and young-adult titles. It's a great place to take the kids on a rainy day, especially when a children's author is giving a reading, or a storyteller is on hand.

TRADER JOE'S FOOD & DRINK

Map p432 (☎212-529-4612; 142 E 14th St at Irving Pl; 🕒9am-10pm; [S]L, N/Q/R/W, 4/5/6 to 14th St-Union Sq) Most people love Trader Joe's, it seems. It's a slightly smaller version of Whole Foods, with fair-trade coffee, organic produce, beef and poultry, and an odd smattering of exotic goods not normally stocked in stores. In fact, so many people love the E 14th St Trader Joe's that shopping there takes enormous patience; the store is small and awkwardly laid out, and crowds form quickly.

WHOLE FOODS FOOD & DRINK

Map p432 (☎212-673-5388; 4 Union Sq S; 🕗8am-11pm; [S]L, N/Q/R/W, 4/5/6 to 14th St-Union Sq) One of several locations of the healthy food chain that is sweeping the city, this is an excellent place to shop for a picnic. Find endless rows of gorgeous produce, both organic and non-organic, plus a butcher, a bakery, a health and beauty section, and aisles packed with natural packaged goods.

SPORTS & ACTIVITIES

SOUL CYCLE CYCLING

Map p432 (http://east.soul-cycle.com; 12 E 18th St btwn Fifth & Sixth Aves; classes $35; 🕗classes 6-9:30am; [S]L, N/Q/R, 4/5/6 to Union Sq) 'Boutique fitness' is all the buzz in NYC, and the reigning queen is Soul Cycle, whose wellness recipe (one part spinning class, one part dance party, one part therapy session) makes exercise an easy pill to swallow. There are no membership fees, so locals and tourists alike are welcome. You may even spot a celeb – Jake Gyllenhaal is known to take a class here and there.

JIVAMUKTI YOGA

Map p432 (www.jivamuktiyoga.com; 841 Broadway; classes $20; 🕗classes 8am-8pm Mon-Thu, 8am-6:45pm Fri, 9:15am-5pm Sat & Sun; [S]L, N/Q/R/W, 4/5/6 to 14th St-Union Sq) *The* yoga spot in Manhattan, Jivamukti – in a 12,000-sq-ft locale on Union Sq – is a posh place for *vinyasa* and hatha classes (chanting alert). You can study Sanskrit if you're ready to get serious; Uma's little bro Dechen Thurman teaches classes, too.

Midtown

MIDTOWN EAST | FIFTH AVENUE | MIDTOWN WEST | TIMES SQUARE

Neighborhood Top Five

1 Playing spot the landmark at **Top of the Rock** (p179), the Rockefeller Center's jaw-dropping observation deck. Sure, the Empire State Building might be more famous, but it's from here that you'll be able to see it. Charge your camera.

2 Hanging out with Picasso, Warhol and Rothko at the **Museum of Modern Art** (p180).

3 Indulging in a little retail rampage on and around Fifth and Madison Aves (p206).

4 Dirty martinis, skyline views and hot, hot sax at **Jazz at Lincoln Center** (p200).

5 Adding a little sparkle to life with a **Broadway** (p200) show.

For more detail of this area, see Maps p434 and p438 ➡

Explore Midtown

Midtown is big, bold and best seen on foot, so slice it up and enjoy it bit by bit. The top end of Fifth Ave (around the 50s) makes for a fabled introduction. It's here that you'll find glam icons, not to mention the incredible Museum of Modern Art (MoMA). You could easily spend an entire day at MoMA, ogling masterpieces, eating, drinking and catching a film. Unlike most major museums, it's open on Monday. From here, it's only a few blocks south to the Rockefeller Center and its sky-high Top of the Rock observation decks. A day in Midtown East could easily incorporate rare manuscripts at the Pierpont Morgan Library, beaux arts architecture at Grand Central Terminal, the art deco lobby of the Chrysler Building and a tour of the United Nations.

Across in Midtown West, design and fashion buffs shouldn't miss the Museum of Arts & Design and the Museum at FIT. Between the two is bright, blinding Times Square, most spectacular at night. It's here you'll find a TKTS Booth selling cut-price Broadway tickets. The real gems of Times Square, however, are on its periphery, such as sheet-music specialist Colony, cocktail den the Rum House and dive bar Jimmy's Corner.

Local Life

➜ **Dive bars** Stiff drinks, loosened ties and the whiff of nostalgia await at no-bull bars like Subway Inn, Jimmy's Corner (p200) and PJ Clarke's (p198).

➜ **Theater** Look beyond the glitz of Broadway for fresh, innovative drama at Playwrights Horizons (p204).

➜ **Food** For a slice of old New York, join the locals at time-warped Sarge's Deli (p195) or El Margon (p197).

Getting There & Away

➜ **Subway** Times Sq–42nd St, Grand Central–42nd St and 34th St–Herald Sq are Midtown's main interchange stations. A/C/E and 1/2/3 lines run north to south through Midtown West. The 4/5/6 lines run north to south through Midtown East. The central B/D/F/M lines run up Sixth Ave, while N/Q/R lines follow Broadway.

➜ **Bus** Useful for the western and eastern extremes of Midtown. Routes include the 11 (northbound on Tenth Ave and southbound on Ninth Ave), the M101, M102 and M103 (northbound along Third Ave and southbound along Lexington Ave) and the M15 (northbound on First Ave and southbound on Second Ave).

➜ **Train** Long-distance Amtrak and Long Island Rail Road trains terminate at Penn Station. Jersey's PATH trains stop at 33rd St, while Metro–North commuter trains terminate at Grand Central Terminal.

Lonely Planet's Top Tip

Savoring Midtown's A-list restaurants without mortgaging the house is possible if you go for the prix fixe lunch menu where available. Participants include triple–Michelin starred Le Bernardin (p196) and the one-starred A Voce (p197). The former offers dishes usually featured in its evening menu. How far in advance you should book depends on the restaurant. While you can usually secure a lunch table at A Voce with a few days notice, it can sometimes be a one-month wait at Le Bernardin. Both offer online reservations.

✖ Best Places to Eat

➜ Le Bernardin (p196)
➜ Danji (p196)
➜ A Voce (p197)
➜ Burger Joint (p196)

For reviews, see p194 ➜

☐ Best Places to Drink

➜ Campbell Apartment (p188)
➜ Rum House (p199)
➜ Bill's Gay Nineties (p198)
➜ Terroir (p198)

For reviews, see p197 ➜

◉ Best Places for a Skyline View

➜ Top of the Rock (p179)
➜ Empire State Building (p185)
➜ Top of the Strand (p198)
➜ Robert (p199)

CHRISTOPHER GROENHOUT / LONELY PLANET IMAGES ©

TOP SIGHTS
TIMES SQUARE

'I had traveled eight thousand miles around the American continent and I was back on Times Square; and right in the middle of a rush-hour, too, seeing with my innocent road-eyes the absolute madness and fantastic hoorair of New York with its millions and millions hustling forever for a buck among themselves, the mad dream...' Jack Kerouac, *On the Road.*

Love it or hate it, the intersection of Broadway and Seventh Ave (better known as Times Square) is New York City's hyperactive heart. It's a restless, hypnotic torrent of glittering lights, bombastic billboards and raw, urban energy. Times Square is not hip, fashionable or in-the-know, and it couldn't care less. It's too busy pumping out iconic, mass-marketed NYC: yellow cabs, golden arches, soaring skyscrapers and razzle-dazzle Broadway marquees. This is the New York of collective fantasies – the place where Al Jolson 'makes it' in the 1927 film *The Jazz Singer,* where photojournalist Alfred Eisenstaedt famously captured a sailor and nurse lip-locked on V-J Day in 1945, and where Alicia Keys and Jay-Z waxed lyrically about this 'concrete jungle where dreams are made.'

For several decades, the dream here was a sordid, wet one. The economic crash of the early 1970s led to a mass exodus of corporations from Times Square. Billboard niches went dark, stores shut and once grand hotels were converted into SROs (single-room occupancy) dives. What was once an area bathed in light and showbiz glitz became a dirty den of drug dealers and crime. While the adjoining Theater District survived, its respectable playhouses shared the streets with porn cinemas, strip clubs and adult bookstores. That all changed with tough-talking Mayor

DON'T MISS...

- Getting your face on the Forever 21 jumbo screen
- A drink at R Lounge, the Renaissance Hotel
- Taking in Times Sq from the TKTS Booth steps
- Discount tickets to a Broadway show
- The Centennial Dropping Ball, Times Square Visitor Center

PRACTICALITIES

- Map p438
- www.timessquare.com
- Broadway at Seventh Ave
- [S] N/Q/R, S, 1/2/3, 7 to Times Sq-42nd St

Rudolph Giuliani, who, in the 1990s, forced out the skin flicks, boosted police numbers and lured a wave of 'respectable' retail chains, restaurants and attractions. By the new millennium, Times Square had gone from 'X-rated' to 'G-rated,' drawing almost 40 million annual visitors and raking in more than $1.8 billion annually from its 17,000 hotel rooms.

For a panoramic overview over the square, order a drink at the Renaissance Hotel's **R Lounge**, which offers floor-to-ceiling glass windows of the neon-lit spectacle below. It might not be the best-priced sip in town, but with a view like this, who's counting?

A Subway, a Newspaper & a Very Famous Dropping Ball

At the turn of last century, Times Square was known as Longacre Square, an unremarkable intersection far from the city's commercial epicenter of Lower Manhattan. This would change with a deal made between friends: subway pioneer August Belmont and *New York Times* publisher Adolph Ochs. Heading construction of the city's first subway line (from Lower Manhattan to the Upper West Side and Harlem), Belmont astutely realized that a Midtown business hub along 42nd St would maximize profit and patronage on the route. On his mission to draw business into the area, Belmont approached Ochs, who had recently turned around the fortunes of the *New York Times*. Belmont argued that moving the newspaper's operations to the intersection of Broadway and 42nd St would be a win-win for Ochs, for not only would an in-house subway station mean faster distribution of the newspaper around town, the influx of commuters to the square would also mean more sales right outside its headquarters. Belmont even convinced New York Mayor George B McClellan Jr to rename the square in honor of the broadsheet.

It was an offer to good to resist and in the winter of 1904–05, both subway station and the *Times'* new headquarters at One Times Sq made their debut. In honor of the move, the *Times* hosted a New Year's Eve party in 1904, setting off fireworks from its skyscraper rooftop. By 1907, however, the square had become so built-up that fireworks were deemed a safety hazard, forcing the newspaper to come up with alternative crowd-puller. It came in the form of a 700-pound, wood-and-iron ball, lowered from the roof of One Times Sq to herald the arrival of 1908.

While the *Times* may have left the building (its current home is a Renzo Piano–designed skyscraper at 620 Eighth Ave), up to one million people still gather in Times Square every New Year's Eve to watch an illuminated Waterford Crystal ball de-

BRILL BUILDING

At the northwest corner of Broadway and 49th St, the Brill Building (Map p438; Broadway at 49th St) might look unassuming, but this 1930s veteran is widely considered the most important generator of popular songs in the western world. By 1962, over 160 music businesses were based here, from songwriters, managers and publishers, to record companies and promoters. It was a one-stop shop for artists, who could craft a song, hire musicians, cut a demo and (hopefully) convince a producer without ever leaving the building. Among the legends who did were Carol King, Bob Dylan, Joni Mitchell and Paul Simon. A few legacies from that gilded era live on, from on-site sheet-music megastore Colony (p208) to music outfitter Rudy's Music (p208) on nearby W 48th St, a street once dubbed Music Row.

If you simply must have your 15 seconds of fame, look for the giant digital monitor above the Forever 21 store at 1540 Broadway. The screen features a strutting fashion model who, every now and then, takes a Polaroid of the crowd, shakes it out and zooms in on it. Ready for your close-up?

scend at midnight. It's a mere 90-second spectacle that is arguably one of NYC's greatest anticlimaxes. Thankfully, you don't have to endure the crowds and winter cold to experience this short-lived thrill: the **Times Square Visitor Center** (www.timessquarenyc.org; 1560 Broadway btwn 46th & 47th Sts; ⏰8am-8pm; [S]N/Q/R, S, 1/2/3, 7 to Times Sq-42nd St) offers a simulated NYE light show every 20 minutes year-round, as well as a close-up look at the Centennial Dropping Ball used in 2007 – an 11,875-pound geodesic globe created using Waterford crystal and over 32,000 LEDs.

On Broadway

By the 1920s, Belmont's dream for Times Square had kicked into overdrive. Not only was it the heart of a growing commercial district, but it had overtaken Union Sq as New York's theater hub. The neighborhood's first playhouse was the long-gone Empire, opened in 1893 and located on Broadway between 40th and 41 Sts. Two years later, cigar manufacturer and part-time comedy scribe Oscar Hammerstein opened the Olympia, also on Broadway, before opening the Republic (now children's theater **New Victory**) in 1900. This lead to a string of new venues, among them the still-beating **New Amsterdam Theatre** and **Lyceum Theatre**.

The Broadway of the 1920s was well-known for its lighthearted musicals, commonly fusing vaudeville and music hall traditions, and producing classic tunes like George Gershwin's *Rhapsody in Blue* and Cole Porter's *Let's Misbehave*. At the same time, Midtown's theater district was evolving as a platform for new American dramatists. One of the greatest was Eugene O'Neill. Born in Times Square at the long-gone Barrett Hotel (1500 Broadway) in 1888, the playwright debuted many of his works here, including Pulitzer Prize–winners *Beyond the Horizon* and *Anna Christie*. O'Neill's success on Broadway paved the way for other American greats like Tennessee Williams, Arthur Miller and Edward Albee – a surge of serious talent that led to the establishment of the annual Tony Awards in 1947, Broadway's answer to Hollywood's Oscars.

These days, New York's Theater District covers an area stretching roughly from 40th St to 54th St between Sixth and Eighth Aves, with dozens of Broadway and off-Broadway theaters spanning blockbuster musicals to new and classic drama. Unless there's a specific show you're after, the best – and cheapest – way to score tickets in the area is at the **TKTS Booth** (www.tdf.org/tkts; Broadway at W 47th St; ⏰3-8pm Wed-Sun, 2-8pm Tue, also 10am-2pm Tue-Sat, 11am-3pm Sun during matinee performances; [S]N/Q/R, S, 1/2/3, 7 to Times Sq-42nd St), where you can line up and get same-day, half-price tickets for top Broadway and off-Broadway shows. Smart phone users can download the free TKTS app, which offers rundowns of both Broadway and off-Broadway shows, as well as real-time updates of what's available on that day. Always have a back-up choice in case your first preference sells out, and never buy tickets from scalpers on the street.

The TKTS Booth is an attraction in its own right, its illuminated roof of 27 ruby-red steps rising a panoramic 16ft 1in above the 47th St sidewalk. Needless to say, the view across Times Square from the top is a crowd pleaser, so good luck finding a spot to park your booty.

TOP SIGHTS
ROCKEFELLER CENTER

This 22-acre 'city within a city' debuted at the height of the Great Depression. Taking nine years to build, it was America's first multiuse retail, entertainment and office space – a modernist sprawl of 19 buildings (14 of which are the original art deco structures), outdoor plazas and big-name tenants. Developer John D Rockefeller Jr may have sweated over the cost (a mere $100 million), but it was all worth it, with the Center declared a National Landmark in 1987.

Top of the Rock

There are views, and then there is *the* view from the **Top of the Rock** (www.topoftherocknyc.com; 30 Rockefeller Plaza at 49th St, entrance on W 50th St btwn Fifth & Sixth Aves; adult/child $25/16, sunrise & sunset $38/20; 🕑8am-midnight, last elevator at 11pm). Crowning the GE Building, 70 stories above Midtown, its jaw-dropping vista includes one icon that you won't see from atop the Empire State Building – *the* Empire State Building. The Chrysler Building, however, is partially obscured. Heading up to watch the sun set over the city is worth the price hike.

DON'T MISS...

- Top of the Rock
- Public artworks
- NBC Studio Tour
- Rockefeller Plaza

PRACTICALITIES

- Map p434
- www.rockefellercenter.com
- Fifth to Sixth Aves & 48th to 51st Sts
- 🕑24hr, times vary for individual businesses
- [S]B/D/F/M to 47th-50th Sts-Rockefeller Center

Public Artworks

Rockefeller Center is graced with the creations of 30 great artists, commissioned around the punchy theme 'Man at the Crossroads Looks Uncertainly But Hopefully at the Future.' Paul Manship contributed *Prometheus,* overlooking the sunken plaza, and *Atlas,* in front of the International Building (630 Fifth Ave). Isamu Noguchi's *News* sits above the entrance to the Associated Press Building (50 Rockefeller Plaza), while José Maria Sert's oil *American Progress* awaits in the lobby of the GE Building. The latter work replaced Mexican artist Diego Rivera's original painting, rejected by the Rockefellers for containing 'communist imagery.'

NBC Studio Tour

TV comedy *30 Rock* gets its name from the GE Building, and the tower is the real-life home of NBC TV. **NBC Studio Tours** (☎212-664-6298; www.nbcstudiotour.com; 30 Rockefeller Plaza at 49th St; tours adult/child $24/20, children under 6yr not admitted; 🕑tours every 15 mins 8:30am-5:30pm Mon-Thu, to 6:30pm Fri & Sat, to 4.30pm Sun) leave from inside the NBC Experience Store every 15 minutes and include a sneak peak of the legendary *Saturday Night Live* set. Tours last 70 minutes and there's a strict 'no bathrooms' policy, so empty your bladder beforehand! Advanced phone bookings are strongly recommended. Across 49th St, opposite the plaza, is the glass-enclosed studio of the NBC Today show, which broadcasts live from 7am to 10am daily.

Rockefeller Plaza

Come the festive season, Rockefeller Plaza is where you'll find New York's most famous Christmas tree. Ceremoniously lit just after Thanksgiving, it's a tradition that dates back to the 1930s, when construction workers set up a small tree on the site. In its shadow, Rink at Rockefeller Center is the city's most famous ice-skating rink. Incomparably magical, it's also undeniably small and crowded. Opt for the first skating period (at 8.30am) to avoid a long wait. Come summer, the rink becomes a cafe.

HUW JONES / LONELY PLANET IMAGES ©

TOP SIGHTS
MUSEUM OF MODERN ART

Superstar of the modern art scene, MoMA's booty makes many other collections look, well, endearing. You'll find more A-listers here than at an Oscars after party: Van Gogh, Matisse, Picasso, Warhol, Lichtenstein, Rothko, Pollock, Bourgeois. Since its founding in 1929, the museum has amassed over 150,000 artworks, documenting the emerging creative ideas and movements of the late 19th century through to those that dominate today. For art buffs, it's Valhalla. For the uninitiated, it's a thrilling crash course in all that is beautiful and addictive about art.

Collection Highlights

It's easy to get lost in MoMA's vast collection, so to maximize your time here, create a plan of attack. MoMA's permanent collection spans four levels, with prints, illustrated books and the unmissable Contemporary Galleries on level two; architecture, design, drawings and photography on level three; and painting and sculpture on levels four and five. Many of the big hitters are on these last two levels, so tackle the museum from the top down before the fatigue sets in. Must-sees include Van Gogh's *The Starry Night,* Cézanne's *The Bather,* Picasso's *Les Demoiselles d'Avignon,* and Henri Rousseau's *The Sleeping Gypsy,* not to mention iconic American works like Warhol's *Campbell's Soup Cans* and *Gold Marilyn Monroe,* Lichtenstein's equally poptastic *Girl With Ball,* and Hopper's haunting *House by the Railroad.*

DON'T MISS...

- ➡ Collection highlights
- ➡ Abby Aldrich Rockefeller Sculpture Garden
- ➡ Museum eateries
- ➡ Film screenings

PRACTICALITIES

- ➡ MoMA
- ➡ Map p438
- ➡ www.moma.org
- ➡ 11 W 53rd St btwn Fifth & Sixth Aves, Midtown West
- ➡ adult/child $25/free, 4-8pm Fri free
- ➡ 🕒10:30am-5:30pm Sat-Mon, Wed & Thu, to 8pm Fri, to 8:30pm the first Thu of every month
- ➡ [S]E/M to Fifth Ave-53rd St

Abby Aldrich Rockefeller Sculpture Garden

With architect Yoshio Taniguchi's acclaimed reconstruction of the museum in 2004 came the restoration of the Sculpture Garden to the original, larger vision of Philip Johnson's 1953 design. Johnson described the space as a 'sort of outdoor room,' and on warm, sunny days, it's hard not to think of it as a soothing alfresco lounge. One resident who can't seem to get enough of it is Aristide Maillol's *The River*, a larger-than-life female sculpture that featured in Johnson's original garden. She's in fine company, too, with fellow works from greats including Auguste Rodin, Alexander Calder and Henry Moore. Sitting above the garden's eastern end is possibly MoMA's least noticed work, *Water Tower*, a resin installation by British artist Rachel Whiteread.

A Fabulous Feed

MoMA's eateries have a stellar reputation. For communal tables and a super-casual vibe. Nosh on Italian-inspired panini, pasta dishes, salads, salumi and cheeses at **Cafe 2** (Map p434; www.momacafes.com; ⊙11am-5pm Sat-Mon, Wed & Thu, to 7.30pm Fri). For table service, à la carte options and Danish design, opt for **Terrace Five** (Map p438; www.momacafes.com; ⊙11am-5pm Sat-Mon, Wed & Thu, to 7.30pm Fri), which features an outdoor terrace overlooking the Sculpture Garden. If you're after a luxe feed, however, book a table at fine-dining **Modern** (Map p438; www.themodernnyc.com; 9 W 53rd St btwn Fifth & Sixth Aves; 3-/4-course lunch $55/70, 4-course dinner $98; ⊙restaurant lunch Mon-Fri, dinner Mon-Sat, Bar Room 11.30am-10.30pm Mon-Thu, to 11pm Fri & Sat, to 9.30pm Sun). The Michelin-starred menu offers decadent, French-American creations like 'pralines' of foie gras terrine with mango puree and balsamic vinegar. Fans of *Sex and the City* will be keen to know that it was here that scribe-about-town Carrie announced her impending marriage to 'Mr Big.' (If you're on a *real* writer's wage, you can always opt for simpler, cheaper Alascan-inspired grub in the adjacent Bar Room.) The Modern has its own entrance on W 53rd St.

Film Screenings

Not only a palace of visual art, MoMA screens an incredibly well-rounded selection of celluloid gems from its collection of over 22,000 films, including the works of the Maysles Brothers and every Pixar animation film ever produced. Expect anything from Academy Award–nominated documentary shorts and Hollywood classics to experimental works and international retrospectives. Best of all, your museum ticket will get you in for free.

GALLERY CONVERSATIONS

To delve a little deeper into MoMA's collection, join one of the museum's daily 'Gallery Conversations,' which sees lecturers, graduate students and the odd curator offer expert insight into specific works and exhibitions on view. The talks take place each day at 11:30am and 1:30pm (except on Tuesdays, when the museum is closed). To check upcoming topics, click the 'Learn' link on the MoMA website.

One of the greatest strengths of MoMA's collections is abstract expressionism, a radical movement that emerged in New York in the 1940s and boomed a decade later. Defined by its penchant for irreverent individualism and monumentally scaled works, this so-called 'New York School' helped turn the metropolis into the epicenter of Western contemporary art. Among the stars are Rothko's *Magenta, Black, Green on Orange*, Pollock's *One (Number 31, 1950)* and de Kooning's *Painting*.

TOP SIGHTS
RADIO CITY MUSIC HALL

Ladies and gentleman, boys and girls, welcome to the one and only Radio City Music Hall. A spectacular art deco diva, this 5901-seat movie palace was the brainchild of vaudeville producer Samuel Lionel 'Roxy' Rothafel. Never one for understatement, Roxy launched his venue on 23 December 1932 with an over-the-top extravaganza that included a *Symphony of the Curtains* (starring, you guessed it, the curtains), and the high-kick campness of precision dance troupe the Roxyettes (mercifully renamed the Rockettes).

By the 1940s, Radio City had become the greatest single attraction in New York, its red carpet well-worn with a string of movie premieres. Alas, the good times didn't last, dwindling popularity and soaring rents forcing the theater's closure in 1978. However, the venue escaped demolition with a last-minute reprieve, and its interior and was declared a landmark worthy of a $5 million restoration.

For a real treat, join a one-hour guided tour of the sumptuous interiors, designed by Donald Deskey. But first, eye-up the building's 50th St facade, where Hildreth Meière's whimsical brass rondels represent (from left to right) dance, drama and song. Celebrated artists also lavished the interiors. Among them was Lithuanian-born William Zorach, whose nude sculpture *Spirit of the Dance* sparked enough controversy to have the work temporarily removed. Less scandalous gems include Stuart Davies' abstract wall mural *Men Without Women* in the Smoking Room, and Witold Gordon's classically inspired *History of Cosmetics* in the Women's Downstairs Lounge. The adjoining restroom (open to all) sports the world's first modern hand dryers.

While the original, wood-paneled elevators are sublime, the pièce de résistance is the main auditorium, its radiating arches evoking a setting sun. Here you'll see Radio City Music Hall's legendary pipe organ (the biggest built for a movie palace) and the landmark-listed Great Stage, famed for its still-sophisticated hydraulics. Much smaller but *tres* exclusive is the VIP Roxy Suite, lavished with rich cherrywood walls, 20ft-high domed ceilings and an acoustically clever dining area.

As far as catching a show here goes, be warned: the vibe doesn't quite match the theater's splendor now that it's managed by the folks from Madison Square Garden. Latecomers are allowed, disrupting performances, and glow-in-the-dark cocktails often create an ugly sea of purple drinks more akin to a stadium rock concert than a sophisticated show in an elegant theater. Still, there are often some fabulous talents in the lineup, with past performers including Rufus Wainwright, Aretha Franklin and Dolly Parton. And while the word 'Rockettes' provokes eye rolling from most self-consciously cynical New Yorkers, fans of glitz and kitsch might just get a thrill from the troupe's annual Christmas Spectacular (your secret is safe with us – promise!).

You can buy tour tickets online or at the candy store beside the Sixth Ave entrance.

DON'T MISS...

- Artworks
- Main auditorium
- Roxy Suite
- Vintage hand dryers

PRACTICALITIES

- Map p438
- www.radiocity.com
- 1260 Sixth Ave at 51st St
- tours adult/child $22.50/16
- ⏲tours 11am-3pm
- [S]B/D/F/M to 47th-50th Sts-Rockefeller Center

DAVID R. FRAZIER PHOTOLIBRARY, INC./ALAMY ©

TOP SIGHTS
CHRYSLER BUILDING

The 77-floor Chrysler Building makes most other skyscrapers look like uptight geeks. Designed by Willian Van Alen in 1930, it's a dramatic fusion of art deco and Gothic aesthetics, adorned with stern steel eagles and topped by a spire that screams *Bride of Frankenstein*. The building was constructed as the headquarters for Walter P Chrysler and his automobile empire. Unable to compete on the production line with bigger rivals Ford and General Motors, Chrysler decided to trump them on the skyline. More than 80 years on, Chrysler's ambitious $15 million statement remains one of New York's most poignant symbols.

The Lobby

Although the Chrysler Building has no restaurant or observation deck, its deco-licious lobby is an evocative consolation prize. Bathed in an amber glow, its Jazz Age vintage is echoed in its architecture – dark, exotic African wood and marble, contrasted against the brash, man-made steel of industrial America. The elaborately veneered elevators are especially beautiful, their Egyptian lotus motifs made of inlaid Japanese ash, Oriental walnut and Cuban plum-pudding wood. When the doors open, you almost expect Bette Davis to strut on out. Above you is painter Edward Trumbull's ceiling mural *Transport and Human Endeavor*. Purportedly the world's largest mural at 97ft by 100ft, its depiction of buildings, airplanes and industrious workers on Chrysler assembly lines show the golden promise of industry and modernity.

The Spire

Composed of seven radiating steel arches, the Chrysler Building's 185ft spire was as much a feat of vengeance as it was of modern engineering. Secretly constructed in the stairwell,

DON'T MISS...

- The lobby
- The spire
- The gargoyles
- The view from Third Ave–44th St & the Empire State Building
- Chanin Building

PRACTICALITIES

- Map p434
- Lexington Ave at 42nd St, Midtown East
- ⏰lobby 8am-6pm Mon-Fri
- [S]S, 4/5/6, 7 to Grand Central-42nd St

CLOUD CLUB

Nestled at the top of the Chrysler Building between 1930 and 1979 was the famed Cloud Club. Its regulars included tycoon John D Rockefeller, publishing magnate Condé Montrose and boxing legend Gene Tunney. Comprising floors 66 to 68, the art deco–meets-Hunting Lodge hangout featured a lounge, dining rooms (including a private room for Walter Chrysler), as well as kitchens, a barber shop and a locker room with sneak cabinets for hiding booze during Prohibition. Chrysler merrily boasted about having the highest toilet in town.

The Chrysler Building's lobby and crown feature in *Cremaster 3* **(2002), an avant-garde film by award-winning visual artist and filmmaker Matthew Barney. The third installment of an epic five-part film project, it delivers a surreal take on the skyscraper's construction, fusing Irish mythology with genre elements from both zombie and gangster films. To read more about the project, check out www.cremaster.net.**

the 200ft creation (dubbed 'the vertex') was raised through a false roof and anchored into place in an impressive 1½ hours. The novel reveal shocked and outraged architect H Craig Severance, who had hoped that his Manhattan Company skyscraper on Wall Street would become the world's tallest building. Van Alen' fait accompli was especially humiliating given that Severance had personally fallen out with architect William Van Alen, a former colleague. Karmic retribution may have been served with the 1931 debut of the even-taller Empire State Building, but Van Alen's crowning glory endures as a showstopping symbol of 20th-century daring.

The Gargoyles

If the spire is the building's diva, the gargoyles are its supporting cast. Pairs of gleaming steel American eagles look ready to leap from the corners of the 61st floor, giving the building a brooding, Gothic edge. Further down on the 31st floor, giant winged hubcaps echo the Chrysler radiator caps of the late 1920s. For a dramatic view of the gargoyles from street level, head to the corner of Lexington Ave and 44th St and look up.

Two Impressive Views

For a great view of the Chrysler Building, head to the corner of Third Ave and 44th St from where you can appreciate the building's slimline profile, gargoyles and spire in one hit. If you have binoculars, bring them for a close-up view of the facade's detailing, which includes basket-weave motifs and a band of abstract automobiles. Alternatively, head to the top of the Chrysler Building's taller rival, the Empire State Building, where pay-per-view telescopes will get you up close and personal with that gleaming steel spire.

Chanin Building: a Neighboring Gem

Across the street from the Chrysler Building, on the southwest corner of Lexington Ave and 42nd St, stands another art deco gem: the **Chanin Building** (Map p434; 122 E 42nd St at Lexington Ave, Midtown East; [S]S, 4/5/6, 7 to Grand Central-42nd St). Completed in 1929, the 56-storey brick and terra-cotta tower is the work of unlicensed architect Irwin S Chanin, who teamed up with the legally recognized firm Sloan & Robertson to achieve his dream. Yet, the star attractions here are the work of René Chambellan and Jacques Delamarre, creators of the exquisite bands of relief at the building's base. While birds and fish create a sense of whimsy in the lower band, the upper band of terra-cotta steals the show with its rich botanical carvings.

TOP SIGHTS
CHRYSLER BUILDING

RICHARD I'ANSON / LONELY PLANET IMAGES ©

TOP SIGHTS
EMPIRE STATE BUILDING

The Chrysler Building may be prettier and the One World Trade Center may now be taller, but the Queen Bee of the New York skyline remains the Empire State Building. It's NYC's tallest film star, enjoying more than its fair share of close-ups in around 100 movies, from *King Kong* to *Independence Day*. No other building screams New York quite like it, and heading up to the top is as quintessential an experience as pastrami, rye and pickles at Katz's Delicatessen.

The statistics are astounding: 10 million bricks, 60,000 tons of steel, 6400 windows and 328,000 sq ft of marble. Built on the original site of the Waldorf-Astoria, construction took a record-setting 410 days, using seven million hours of labor and costing a mere $41 million. It might sound like a lot, but it fell well below its $50 million budget (just as well given it went up during the Great Depression). Coming in at 102 stories and 1472ft from top to bottom, the limestone phallus opened for business on May 1, 1931. Generations later, Deborah Kerr's words to Gary Grant in *An Affair to Remember* still ring true: 'It's the nearest thing to heaven we have in New York.'

DON'T MISS...

- Observation decks at sunset
- Live jazz Thursday to Saturday nights

PRACTICALITIES

- Map p434
- www.esbnyc.com
- 350 Fifth Ave at 34th St
- 86th-floor observation deck adult/child $20/15, incl 102nd-floor observation deck $37/31
- ⏲8am-2am, last elevators up 1.15am
- [S]B/D/F/M, N/Q/R to 34th St-Herald Sq

Observation Decks

Unless you're Ann Darrow (the unfortunate blonde caught in King Kong's grip), heading to the top of the Empire State Building should leave you beaming. There are two observation decks. The open-air 86th-floor deck offers an alfresco experience, with coin-operated telescopes for close-up glimpses of the metropolis in action. Further up, the enclosed 102nd-floor deck is New York's highest – at least until the observation deck at One World Trade Center opens in mid-2014. Needless to say, the views over the city's five boroughs (and five neighboring

LANGUAGE OF LIGHT

Since 1976, the building's top 30 floors have been floodlit in a spectrum of colors each night, reflecting seasonal and holiday hues. Famous combos include red, pink and white for Valentine's Day; green for St Patrick's Day; red and green for Christmas; and lavender for Gay Pride weekend in June. For a full rundown of the color schemes and meanings, check the website.

The Empire State Building was designed by the prolific architectural firm Shreve, Lamb and Harmon. According to legend, the skyscraper's conception began with a meeting between William Lamb and building co-financier John Jakob Raskob, during which Raskob propped up a No 2 pencil and asked, 'Bill, how high can you make it so that it won't fall down?'

states, weather permitting) are quite simply exquisite. The views from both decks are especially spectacular at sunset, when the city dons its nighttime cloak in dusk's afterglow. For a little of that *Arthur's Theme* magic, head to the 86th-floor between 10pm and 1am from Thursday to Saturday, when the twinkling sea of lights is accompanied by a soundtrack of live sax (yes, requests are taken). Alas, the passage to heaven will involve a trip through purgatory: the queues to the top are notorious. Getting here very early or very late will help you avoid delays – as will buying your tickets online, ahead of time, where an extra $2 purchase charge is well worth the hassle it will save you.

An Ambitious Antenna

A locked, unmarked door on the 102nd-floor observation deck leads to one of New York's most outrageous pie-in-the-sky projects to date: a narrow terrace intended to dock zeppelins. Spearheading the dream was Alfred E Smith, who went from failed presidential candidate in 1928 to head honcho of the Empire State Building project. When architect William Van Alen revealed the secret spire of his competing Chrysler Building, Smith went one better, declaring that the top of the Empire State Building would sport an even taller mooring mast for transatlantic airships. While the plan looked good on paper, there were just two (major) oversights: dirigibles require anchoring at both ends (not just at the nose as planned) and passengers (traveling in the zeppelin's gondola) cannot exit the craft through the giant helium-filled balloon. Regardless, it didn't stop them from trying. In September 1931, the *New York Evening Journal* threw sanity to the wind, managing to moor a zeppelin and deliver a pile of newspapers fresh out of Lower Manhattan. Years later, an aircraft met up with the building with less success: a B-25 bomber, which crashed into the 79th floor on a foggy day in 1945, killing 14 people.

TOP SIGHTS
EMPIRE STATE BUILDING

TOP SIGHTS
GRAND CENTRAL TERMINAL

Threatened by the debut of rival Penn Station (the majestic original, that is), shipping and railroad magnate Cornelius Vanderbilt set to work on transforming his 19th-century Grand Central Depot into a 20th-century showpiece. The fruit of his envy is Grand Central Terminal, New York's most breathtaking beaux arts building. More than just a station, Grand Central is an enchanted time machine. Its swirl of chandeliers, marble, and historic bars and restaurants is a porthole into an era where train travel and romance were not mutually exclusive.

For better or worse, there are no teary goodbyes for people traveling across the country from here today, as Grand Central's underground electric tracks serve only commuter trains en route to northern suburbs and Connecticut. Whether you're traveling somewhere or not, Grand Central is one stop you cannot afford to miss.

DON'T MISS...

- 42nd St facade
- Main Concourse
- Whispering Gallery and the Oyster Bar & Restaurant
- Campbell Apartment
- Grand Central Market

PRACTICALITIES

- Map p434
- www.grandcentralterminal.com
- 42nd St at Park Ave
- 🕘5:30-2am
- [S]S, 4/5/6, 7 to Grand Central-42nd St

42nd Street Facade

Clad in Connecticut Stony Creek granite at its base and Indiana limestone on top, Grand Central's showpiece facade is crowned by America's greatest monumental sculpture, *The Glory of Commerce*. Designed by the French sculptor Jules Félix Coutan, the piece was executed in Long Island City by respected local carvers Donnely and Ricci. Once completed, it was hoisted up, piece by piece, in 1914. The star of the sculptural group is a wing-capped Mercury, the Roman god of travel and commerce. To the left, Hercules is portrayed in an unusually placid stance, while looking down on the mayhem of 42nd St is Minerva, the ancient guardian of cities. The splendid clock beneath Mercury foot contains the largest example of Tiffany glass in the world.

Main Concourse

Grand Central's glorious trump card is more akin to a glorious ballroom than a transit thoroughfare. The marble floors are Tennessee pink, while the vintage ticket counters are Italian Bottocino marble. The vaulted ceiling is (quite literally) heavenly, its turquoise and gold-leaf mural depicting eight constellations...backwards. A mistake? Apparently not. Its French designer, painter Paul César Helleu, wished to depict the stars from God's point of view – from the out, looking in. The original, frescoed execution of Helleu's design was by New York–based artists J Monroe Hewlett and Charles Basing. Moisture damage saw it faithfully repainted (alas, not in fresco form) by Charles Gulbrandsen in 1944. By the 1990s, however, the mural was in ruins again – soiled by decades of cigarette smoke. Enter renovation architects Beyer Blinder Belle, who restored the work, but left a tiny patch of soot (in the northwest corner) as testament to what a fine job they did. A bridge links the southern end of the Main Courcourse to Vanderbilt Hall, once the station's waiting room. The massive, gold-plated chandeliers that are visible from the bridge were made in Williamsburg.

GUIDED TOURS

The Municipal Art Society (p394) walks you through Grand Central on Wednesdays at 12.30pm. Tours start at the Information Booth in the Main Concourse and a $10 donation is suggested. The Grand Central Partnership (www.grandcentralpartnership.com) leads free tours of the terminal and the surrounding neighborhood on Fridays at 12:30pm. Tours commence in the sculpture court at 120 Park Ave. Both tours run for 1½ hours.

Grand Central's Platform 61 was custom built for polio-afflicted President Franklin D Roosevelt. Determined to hide his affliction from public view, the platform features a custom-made elevator to fit the President's limousine. Upon arrival at the station, the car would be driven straight out of the carriage, along the platform and into the elevator. The area is off-limits to the public but you can still catch a glimpse of the President's armored carriage from the upper level (look right if you're heading away from the platform, left if heading towards it).

Whispering Gallery, Oyster Bar & Restaurant, and Campbell Apartment

The vaulted landing directly below the bridge linking the Main Concourse and Vanderbilt Hall harbors one of Grand Central's quirkier features, the so-called Whispering Gallery.

If you're in company, stand facing the walls diagonally opposite each other and whisper something. Operator! If your partner proposes (it happens a lot down here), chilled champagne is just through the door at the station's oldest nosh spot, **Grand Central Oyster Bar & Restaurant** (www.oysterbarny.com; Grand Central Terminal, 42nd St at Park Ave; mains $23.95-33.95; 🕘closed Sun). Hugely atmospheric (with a vaulted tiled ceiling by Catalan-born engineer Rafael Guastavino and retro attendants in the restrooms), stick to what it does exceptionally well: oysters (expect up to 30 varieties to slurp on).

An elevator beside the restaurant leads up to another historic gem: the sublime, deliciously snooty bar **Campbell Apartment** (Map p434; www.hospitalityholdings.com; 15 Vanderbilt Ave at 43rd St; 🕘noon-1am Mon-Thu, to 2am Fri, 2pm-2am Sat, 3pm-midnight Sun; [S]S, 4/5/6, 7 to Grand Central-42nd St). Once the home of a '20s railroad magnate, its Euro-chic detailing includes Florentine-style carpets, decorative ceiling beams and a soaring leaded glass window. You can also reach the bar from the stairs to the West Balcony.

Grand Central Market

More drooling awaits at the **Grand Central Market** (Lexington Ave at 42nd St; 🕘7am-9pm Mon-Fri, 10am-7pm Sat, 11am-6pm Sun), a 240ft corridor lined with fresh produce and artisan treats. Stock up on anything from crusty bread and fruit tarts to lobsters, chicken pot pies, Spanish quince paste, fruit and vegetables, and roasted coffee beans. There's even a Murray's Cheese stall, where you will find milky wonders including moreish smoked mozzarella and cave-aged Gruyère. Hovering above the Lexington St entrance is Donald Lipski's striking sculptural chandelier, *Sirshasana,* depicting the sprawling branches of an olive tree and adorned with 5000 crystal pendants.

SIGHTS

Midtown East

CHRYSLER BUILDING NOTABLE BUILDING

See p183.

GRAND CENTRAL TERMINAL NOTABLE BUILDING

See p187.

UNITED NATIONS NOTABLE BUILDING

Map p434 (www.un.org/tours; First Ave at 46th St; guided tour adult/child $16/11, children under 5yr not admitted; ⏲tours 9:45am-4:45pm Mon-Fri, 10am-4:15pm Sat & Sun, closed Sat & Sun Jan & Feb; 📶; [S]S, 4/5/6, 7 to Grand Central-42nd St) Welcome to the headquarters of the UN, a worldwide organization overseeing international law, international security and human rights. While the soaring, Le Corbusier-designed Secretariat building is off-limits, one-hour guided tours do take in the General Assembly, where the annual convocation of member nations takes place in fall, as well as exhibitions about the UN's work and artworks given by member states.

To the north of the complex, which technically stands on international territory, is a serene park featuring Henry Moore's *Reclining Figure* as well as several other peace-themed sculptures. The UN visitors' entrance is at 46th St.

PIERPONT MORGAN LIBRARY CULTURAL BUILDING

Map p434 (www.morganlibrary.org; 29 E 36th St at Madison Ave; adult/child $15/10; ⏲10:30am-5pm Tue-Thu, to 9pm Fri, 10am-6pm Sat, 11am-6pm Sun; [S]6 to 33rd St) Part of the 45-room mansion once owned by steel magnate JP Morgan, this sumptuous library features a phenomenal array of manuscripts, tapestries and books (with no fewer than three Gutenberg Bibles). There's a study filled with Italian Renaissance artwork, a marble rotunda and a program of top-notch rotating exhibitions.

Recent exhibition themes include Islamic manuscript painting, drawings from Revolutionary France and Charles Dickens.

JAPAN SOCIETY CULTURAL CENTER

Map p434 (www.japansociety.org; 333 E 47th St btwn First & Second Aves; adult/child $12/free, 6-9pm Fri free; ⏲11am-6pm Tue-Thu, to 9pm Fri, to 5pm Sat & Sun; [S]S, 4/5/6, 7 to Grand Central-42nd St) Fresh, rotating exhibitions of Japanese art, textiles and design are the main draw at this cultural center. Its theater hosts a range of films and dance, music and theatrical performances, while those who want to dig deeper can browse through the 14,000 volumes of the research library or attend one of its myriad lectures.

Founded in 1907 by a group of NYC businesspeople with a deep admiration for Japan, this nonprofit society has played a large role in strengthening American-Japanese relations. Its expansion into a full arts and cultural center was thanks, in no small part, to philanthropist John D Rockefeller III, an ardent fan of the country.

MUSEUM OF SEX MUSEUM

Map p434 (MoSex; www.museumofsex.com; 233 Fifth Ave at 27th St; adult/child $17.50/$15; ⏲11am-8pm Sun-Thu, to 9pm Fri & Sat; [S]N/R to 23rd St) From vintage vibrators to homosexual necrophilia in the mallard duck, 'MoSex' explores the world of sex in culture and nature. One long-running exhibition, 'Action: Sex and the Moving Image,' examines representations of sex in mainstream cinema and pornography, while the permanent collection showcases everything from vintage blow-up dolls and homemade copulation machines to anti-onanism devices.

Don't expect any sex parties or naked go-go dancers – although various folks do take the stage from time to time for presentations including erotica readings, one-person shows and sex-ed seminars. The museum shop sells a variety of sex-themed books and designer sex toys, while the in-house bar serves 'stimulating' drinks with names like New Orleans Brothel and Frida Calor.

Fifth Avenue

EMPIRE STATE BUILDING NOTABLE BUILDING

See p185.

ROCKEFELLER CENTER NOTABLE BUILDING

See p179.

TOP OF THE ROCK LOOKOUT

See p179.

NEW YORK PUBLIC LIBRARY CULTURAL BUILDING

Map p434 (Stephen A Schwarzman Building; www.nypl.org; Fifth Ave at 42nd St; ⏲10am-6pm Mon

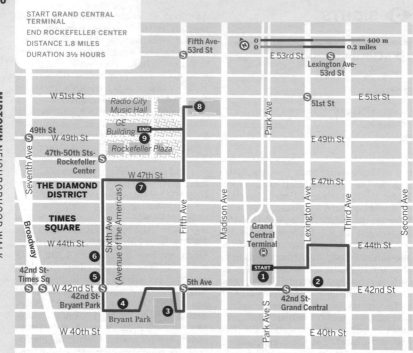

MIDTOWN NEIGHBORHOOD WALK

Neighborhood Walk
A Midtown Meander

Start your Midtown saunter at beaux arts marvel **❶ Grand Central Terminal**. Star gaze at the Main Concourse ceiling, share sweet nothings at the Whispering Gallery and pick up a gourmet treat at the Grand Central Market. Exit onto Lexington Ave and walk one block east along 44th St to Third Ave for a view of William Van Alen's 1930 masterpiece, the **❷ Chrysler Building**. Walk down Third Ave to 42nd St, turn right and slip into the Chrysler Building's sumptuous art deco lobby, lavished with exotic inlaid wood, marble and purportedly the world's largest ceiling mural.

At the corner of 42nd St and Fifth Ave stands the stately **❸ New York Public Library**, guarded by a pair of regal lions called Patience and Fortitude. Step inside to peek at its spectacular Rose Reading Room, then nibble on your market treat in neighboring **❹ Bryant Park**, home to cafes and a vintage carousel.

On the northwest corner of 42nd St and Sixth Ave soars the **❺ Bank of America Tower**, NYC's third-tallest building and one of its most ecofriendly. The next block north along Sixth Ave is home to the **❻ International Center of Photography**. Take in the current exhibitions before continuing north to 47th St. Between Sixth and Fifth Aves is the **❼ Diamond District**, home to more than 2600 independent businesses selling diamonds, gold, pearls and watches. Walk towards Fifth Ave, taking in its swirl of Jewish traders, persistent hawkers and ring-hunting couples.

Turn left into Fifth Ave and visit the Gothic Revival splendor of **❽ St Patrick's Cathedral**, its impressive rose window the work of American artist Charles Connick. Across the street is your last stop, **❾ Rockefeller Center**, a magnificent complex of art deco skyscrapers and sculptures.

& Thu-Sat, to 8pm Tue & Wed, 1-5pm Sun, guided tours 11am & 2pm Mon-Sat, 2pm Sun; ☎; [S]B/D/F/M to 42nd St-Bryant Park; 7 to Fifth Ave) Loyally guarded by 'Patience' and 'Fortitude' (the famous marble lions overlooking Fifth Ave), this beaux arts show-off is one of NYC's best free attractions. When dedicated in 1911, New York's flagship library ranked as the largest marble structure ever built in the US, and to this day, its Rose Main Reading Room will steal your breath with its lavish, coffered ceiling.

The library's Exhibition Hall contains precious manuscripts by just about every author of note in the English language including an original copy of the Declaration of Independence and a Gutenberg Bible. The Map Division is equally astounding, with a collection that holds some 431,000 maps, 16,000 atlases and books on cartography, dating from the 16th century to the present.

To properly explore this mini-universe of books, art, chandeliers and porticoes, join a free guided tour, which leaves from the information desk in Astor Hall.

BRYANT PARK PARK

Map p434 (www.bryantpark.org; 42nd St btwn Fifth & Sixth Aves; ⌚7am-midnight Mon-Sat, to 11pm Sun in May-Sep, to 10pm Sun-Thu, to midnight Fri & Sat Nov-Feb, to 7pm Mar, to 10pm Apr & Oct; ☎; [S]B/D/F/M to 42nd St-Bryant Park; 7 to Fifth Ave) European coffee kiosks, alfresco chess games, summer film screenings and winter ice-skating: it's hard to believe that this leafy oasis was dubbed 'Needle Park' in the '80s. Nestled behind the show-stopping New York Public Library building, it's a handy spot for a little time-out from the Midtown madness.

It's a shamelessly charming place, complete with a Brooklyn-constructed, French-inspired Le Carrousel offering rides for $2, and frequent special events, from readings to concerts. This is where the famed Fashion Week tent goes up every winter. It's also the site of the wonderful Bryant Park Summer Film Festival, which packs the lawn with post-work crowds lugging cheese-and-wine picnics. And it becomes a winter wonderland at Christmastime with holiday gift vendors lining the park's edge and a popular ice-skating rink sprouting in its middle. **Bryant Park Grill** (Map p434; www.arkrestaurants.com/bryant_park.html; 25 W 40th St btwn Fifth & Sixth Aves; [S]B/D/F/M to 42nd St-Bryant Park; 7 to Fifth Ave), a lovely restaurant and bar situated at the eastern end of the park, is the site of many a New York wedding come springtime. When it's not closed for a private event, the patio bar is a perfect spot for a twilight cocktail or three.

PALEY CENTER FOR MEDIA CULTURAL BUILDING

Map p434 (www.paleycenter.org; 25 W 52nd St btwn Fifth & Sixth Aves; adult/child $10/5; ⌚noon-6pm Wed & Fri-Sun, to 8pm Thu; [S]E/M to Fifth Ave-53rd St) Heaven for pop-culture fans, the Paley Center offers more than 150,000 TV and radio programs from around the world on its computer catalog. While reliving your favorite TV shows on one of the museum's consoles is sheer bliss on a rainy day, the radio-listening room is an unexpected pleasure – as are the excellent, regular screenings, festivals, speakers and performers.

ST PATRICK'S CATHEDRAL CHURCH

Map p434 (www.saintpatrickscathedral.org; Fifth Ave btwn 50th & 51st Sts; ⌚6:30am-8:45pm; [S]B/D/F/M to 47th-50th Sts-Rockefeller Center) America's largest Catholic cathedral is a vision in neo-Gothic. Built at a cost of nearly $2 million during the Civil War, the building did not originally include the two front spires; those were added in 1888. Highlights include the Louis Tiffany–designed altar and Charles Connick's stunning Rose Window, the latter gleaming above a 7000-pipe church organ.

The cathedral is the seat of the Archbishop of New York, the staunchly conservative Timothy Dolan, and the place that's been largely recognized as the center of Catholic life in the US – drawing a steady stream of both revelers and protesters alike. A basement crypt behind the altar contains the coffins of every New York cardinal and the remains of Pierre Touissant, a champion of the poor and the first black American up for sainthood (he emigrated from Haiti).

⊙ Midtown West & Times Square

MUSEUM OF MODERN ART GALLERY

See p180.

RADIO CITY MUSIC HALL NOTABLE BUILDING

See p182.

MIDTOWN SKYSCRAPERS: BEST OF THE REST

Midtown's skyline is more than just the Empire State and Chrysler Buildings, with enough modernist and postmodern beauties to satisfy the wildest of high-rise dreams. Celebrate all things phallic with five of Midtown's finest.

Seagram Building (1956–58; 514ft)

A textbook regular, the 38-floor **Seagram Building** (Map p434; 100 E 53rd St at Park Ave; S 6 to 51st St; E, M to Fifth Ave-53rd St) is one of the world's finest examples of the International Style. Its lead architect, Ludwig Mies van der Rohe, was recommended for the project by Arthur Drexler, then-curator of architecture at the Museum of Modern Art. With its low podium, colonnade-like pillars and bronze cladding, Mies cleverly references classical Greek influences.

Lever House (1950–52; 306ft)

Upon its debut, 21-storey **Lever House** (Map p434; 390 Park Ave btwn 53rd & 54th Sts; S E, M to Fifth Ave-53rd St) was at the height of the cutting-edge. The UN' Secretariat Building was the only other skyscraper to feature a glass skin, an innovation that would redefine urban architecture. The building's form was equally bold: two counter-posed rectangular shapes consisting of a slender tower atop a low-rise base. The open courtyard features marble benches by Japanese-American sculptor Isamu Noguchi, while the lobby exhibits contemporary art especially commissioned for the space.

Citigroup Center (1974–77; 915ft)

With its striking triangular roof and candy-like striped facade, Hugh Stubbins' 59-storey **Citigroup Center** signaled a shift from the flat-roof sobriety of the International Style. Even more dramatic is the building's base, which is cut away at the four corners, leaving the tower to perch dramatically on a cross-shaped footing. This unusual configuration allowed for the construction of St Peter's Lutheran Church on the site's northwest corner. This replaced the original neo-Gothic church demolished during the skyscraper's construction.

Hearst Tower (2003–06; 597ft)

Foster & Partners' **Hearst Tower** is hands down one of New York's most creative works of contemporary architecture. Its diagonal grid of trusses evokes a jagged glass-and-steel honeycomb, best appreciated up close and from an angle. The tower rises above the hollowed-out core of John Urban's 1928 cast-stone Hearst Magazine Building, itself originally envisioned as a skyscraper. The 46-floor structure is also one of the city's greenest creations: around 90% of its structural steel is from recycled sources. In the lobby you'll find *Riverlines*, a mural by Richard Long.

Bank of America Tower (2004–09; 1200ft)

While striking for its crystal shape and piercing, 255ft spire, the **Bank of America Tower** hit the headlines for its enviable green credentials. The stats are impressive: a clean-burning, on-site cogeneration plant providing around 65% of the tower's annual electricity requirements; CO_2-detecting air filters that channel filtered air where needed; and even destination-dispatch elevators designed to avoid empty car trips. Designed by Cook & Fox Architects, the 58-floor role model was awarded Best Tall Building in America by the Council on Tall Buildings & Urban Habitat awards in 2010.

MUSEUM OF ARTS & DESIGN MUSEUM
Map p438 (MAD; www.madmuseum.org; 2 Columbus Circle btwn Eighth Ave & Broadway; adult/child $15/free; ⊗11am-6pm Tue, Wed, Sat & Sun, to 9pm Thu & Fri; S A/C, B/D, 1 to 59th St-Columbus Circle) Museum of Arts & Design (MAD) offers four floors of superlative design and handicrafts, from blown glass and carved wood to elaborate metal jewelry. Its temporary exhibitions are nothing short of innovative, with past shows exploring anything from American modernism to art made from dust, ash, dirt and sand. Stock up on contemporary jewelry and design objects in

the gift shop or sip cocktails at the 9th-floor restaurant/bar.

Formerly housed around the corner on 53rd St, the museum made a big splash when it moved into this Columbus Circle building after much controversy from folks who wanted to landmark and protect the long-empty building, originally the Gallery of Modern Art in 1964, with a unique, all-white design by Edward Durell Stone. But the Museum of Arts & Design won out, drastically changing the shape of the place and moving in in late 2008.

INTERNATIONAL CENTER OF PHOTOGRAPHY — GALLERY

Map p438 (ICP; www.icp.org; 1133 Sixth Ave at 43rd St; admission $12, by donation Fri 5-8pm; ⌚10am-6pm Tue, Wed, Sat & Sun, to 8pm Thu & Fri; [S]B/D/F/M to 42nd St-Bryant Park) ICP is New York's paramount showcase for photography, with a strong emphasis on photojournalism and changing exhibitions focused on a wide range of creative themes. Past shows in its two-floor space have included work by Henri Cartier-Bresson, Man Ray and Robert Capa. The center is also a school, offering coursework (for credit) and a public lecture series.

DIAMOND DISTRICT — STREET

Map p438 (www.diamonddistrict.org; 47th St btwn Fifth & Sixth Aves; [S]B/D/F/M to 47th-50th Sts-Rockefeller Center) Like Diagon Alley in *Harry Potter,* the Diamond District is a world unto itself. A frenetic whirl of Hasidic Jewish traders, aggressive hawkers and lovestruck couples looking for the perfect rock, its 2600-plus businesses peddle all manner of diamonds, gold, pearls, gemstones and watches. In fact, the strip handles approximately 90% of the cut diamonds sold in the country. Marilyn, eat your heart out!

HERALD SQUARE — SQUARE

Map p438 (cnr Broadway, Sixth Ave & 34th St; [S]B/D/F/M, N/Q/R to 34th St-Herald Sq) This crowded convergence of Broadway, Sixth Ave and 34th St is best known as the home of the gigantic Macy's department store, where you can still ride some of the original wooden elevators. And, as part of the city's 'traffic-free Times Square' plan, you can also (try to) relax in a lawn chair outside the store, slap-bang in the middle of Broadway.

The square gets its name from a long-defunct newspaper, the New York Herald (1835–1924), and the small, leafy park here bustles during business hours thanks to a much-needed facelift. Skip the indoor malls south of Macy's on Sixth Ave, which are packed with dull, suburban chain stores – the exception being Daffy's, which offers great discounts on big labels.

GARMENT DISTRICT — NEIGHBORHOOD

Map p438 (Seventh Ave btwn 34th St & Times Sq; [S]N/Q/R, S, 1/2/3 & 7 to Times Sq-42nd St) Otherwise known as the Fashion District, this thread-obsessed area might look like an unremarkable-looking stretch of designers' offices and wholesale and retail shops, but it's where you'll find a huge selection of fabrics, sequins, lace and, chances are, those day-glo velvet buttons you've been missing since 1986.

Look down at the sidewalk when you hit Seventh and 39th St and you'll catch the Fashion Walk of Fame, honoring the likes of Betsey Johnson, Marc Jacobs, Geoffrey Beene, Halston and other fashion visionaries. It's on the same corner as Claes Oldenburg's sculpture of the world's largest button, held upright by a 31ft-tall steel needle.

INTREPID SEA, AIR & SPACE MUSEUM — MUSEUM

Map p438 (www.intrepidmuseum.org; Pier 86, Twelfth Ave at 46th St; adult/child $24/12; ⌚10am-6pm daily Apr-Oct, to 5pm Tue-Sun Nov-Mar; [S]A/C/E to 42nd St-Port Authority Bus Terminal, 🚌M42 bus westbound) The USS *Intrepid* survived both a WWII bomb and kamikaze attacks. Thankfully, this hulking aircraft carrier is now less stressed, playing host to a multimillion dollar interactive military museum that tells its tale through videos, historical artifacts and frozen-in-time living quarters. The flight deck features fighter planes and military helicopters, which might inspire you try the museum's high-tech flight simulators.

The rides include the G Force Encounter, which allows you to experience the virtual thrill of flying a supersonic jet plane, and the Transporter FX, a flight simulator that promises six full minutes of a 'complete sensory overload.' The museum is also home to the guided-missile submarine *Growler,* (not for the claustrophobic), a decommissioned Concorde, and from summer 2012 the former NASA space shuttle Orbiter Enterprise. Come May, the *Intrepid* is also the nexus for the Fleet Week celebrations, when

BENTON, POLLOCK & A SECRET MASTERPIECE

While New York bursts with superlative artworks, some are too easy to miss. An outstanding example is Thomas Hart Benton's *America Today*, an epic, multipanel mural in the lobby of the **AXA Equitable Building**.

Painted between 1930 and 1931, its intense color and rhythm are an energy-packed ode to American industry, progress and optimism during the Jazz Age. The panels capture a range of scenes, from the stoic toil of steel industry workers to the wild hedonism of dance-hall culture.

Many of the images were based on sketches drawn by Benton on trips across the country in the 1920s, and the work's distinctly American flavor is testament to Benton's legacy as a leading proponent of Regionalism, a realist art movement popular in the 1930s. The movement would become a precursor to the abstract expressionism of the 1940s and 50s, a radical style that would launch the career of greats like Jackson Pollock.

Like many of New York's abstract expressionists, Pollock was a student of Benton at the Art Students League on W 57th St. The young painter would spend many hours watching his mentor at work. In fact, Benton used Pollock as the model for the muscular worker at the right in the *Steel* panel.

Ironically, with the rising success of Benton's students and their abstract expressionist ways came a waning interest in Benton and his regionalist works. Though snubbed by an art world that had moved on, Benton continued to paint, though his epic murals gave way to more modestly scaled bucolic compositions – scenes he painted until his death, aged 86, in 1975.

thousands of the world's sailors descend on Manhattan for shore leave.

[FREE] **MUSEUM AT FIT** MUSEUM

Map p438 (www.fitnyc.edu/museum; Seventh Ave at 27th St; ⏲noon-8pm Tue-Fri, 10am-5pm Sat; [S]1 to 28th St) The Fashion Institute of Technology (FIT) lays claim to one of the world's richest collections of garments, textiles and accessories. At last count, there were around 50,000 items spanning the 18th century to the present day. The school's museum is the place to catch a glimpse, it's rotating exhibitions showcasing both permanent collection items and on-loan treasures.

KOREATOWN NEIGHBORHOOD

Map p438 (31st to 36th Sts & Broadway to Fifth Ave; [S]B/D/F/M, N/Q/R to 34th St-Herald Sq) For kimchi and karaoke, it's hard to beat Koreatown (Little Korea). Mainly concentrated on 32nd St, with some spillover into the surrounding streets both south and north of this strip, it's a Seoul-ful jumble of Korean-owned restaurants, shops, salons and spas.

Authentic BBQ is available around the clock at many of the all-night spots on 32nd St, some with microphone, video screen and *Manic Monday* at the ready.

🍴 EATING

Despite the ubiquitous chains and tourist-trap deprestaurants – mostly around Times Square and the Theater District – Midtown is no culinary slouch. You'll find 16 Michelin-starred restaurants here, some with million-dollar skyline views. Tuck into authentic *chingudi jhola* (spicy prawn curry) in the 'Curry Hill' district (Lexington Ave around 28th St), organic zen noodles in Koreatown, or homemade cheese blintzes at an all-night Jewish deli on Third Ave. The rising tide of hipster hotspots includes a speakeasy burger dive, while Ninth Ave in Hell's Kitchen continues its evolution as a see-and-be-seen, locally loved sip-and-sup strip.

🍴 Midtown East & Fifth Avenue

[TOP CHOICE] **HANGAWI** KOREAN $$

Map p434 (☎212-213-0077; www.hangawirestaurant.com; 12 E 32nd St btwn Fifth & Madison Aves; dinner mains $17-25; ⏲lunch Mon-Sat, dinner daily; [S]B/D/F/M, N/Q/R to 34th St-Herald Sq) Sublime, flesh-free Korean is the draw at high-achieving Hangawi. Leave your shoes at the entrance and slip into a soothing, Zen-like space of meditative music, soft low seating and clean, complexly flavored dishes. Show-stoppers include the leak pancakes and a seductively smooth tofu claypot in ginger sauce.

Organic and gluten-free options add to the holistic vibe, while the $20 prixe-fixe lunch is good value. Book ahead for dinner.

THE SMITH AMERICAN $$

Map p434 (www.thesmithnyc.com; 956 Second Ave at 51st St; mains $17-29; [S]6 to 51st St) Its name aglow in bold red neon, the Smith has sexed-up dining in the far eastern throws of Midtown with its industrial-chic interior, buzzing bar and well-exectued brasserie grub. With much of the food made from scratch on-site, the emphasis is on regional produce, retro American and Italian-inspired flavors and slick, personable service.

Graze on fresh oysters or bacon-wrapped apricots with spicy glaze, get nostalgic over chicken pot pie with cheddar chive biscuit, or tuck into fabulous handmade pasta creations like goat cheese ravioli with creamy spinach pesto. All the desserts are in the form of a sundae, including the candle-topped 'Birthday Cake' for those who just can't wait.

JOHN DORY OYSTER BAR SEAFOOD $$$

Map p434 (www.thejohndory.com; 1196 Broadway at 29th St; small plates $9.50-25 ; [S]N/R to 28th St) This loud, vibey seafood favorite sits just off the Ace Hotel (p337) lobby. Only hotel guests can book, so head in early for clever, tapas-style creations like sea urchin with pomegranate and black pepper, or chorizo stuffed squid with smoked tomato. Between 5pm and 7pm, $15 gets you six oysters or clams and a glass of sparkling vino or ale.

While you're bound to have better cocktails and desserts elsewhere, the raw bar here is worth any wait.

SOCIAL EATZ FUSION $

Map p434 (www.socialeatz.com; 232 E 53rd St btwn Second & Third Aves, Midtown East; burgers $8-11, salads $6-7; [S]E/M to Lexington Ave-53rd St) American comfort food gets an Asian twist at this hip, '70s-inspired diner. Celebrate inter-racial harmony with Korean beef tacos, St Louis pork ribs with gochujang-spiked BBQ sauce or Korean spiced slaw. Topping them all is the mighty Bibimbap Burger, voted America's best by prolific foodie website **Eater** (www.eater.com). Well-priced and super tasty, this spot is a justifiable hit.

EL PARADOR CAFE MEXICAN $$

Map p434 (☎212-679-6812; www.elparadorcafe.com; 325 E 34th St; dinner mains $18-29; ⏲closed Sun Aug; [S]6 to 33rd St) Back in the day, the far-flung location of this Mexican stalwart (serving here since 1970) was much appreciated by philandering husbands. The shady regulars may have gone, but the old-school charm remains, from the beveled candleholders and dapper Latino waiters to the satisfying south-of-the-border standbys.

House classics include the *mejillones al vino* (mussels in red wine, cilantro and garlic, served with green chili corn bread), the Baja California fish tacos, and the signature *Mole Poblano* (chicken stewed in a rich, chili and chocolate-spiked sauce). End the night with a shot or three of the homemade pineapple tequila.

SARGE'S DELI DELI $$

Map p434 (www.sargesdeli.com; 548 Third Ave btwn 36th & 37th Sts, Midtown East; mains $15-26; ⏲24hr; [S]6 to 33rd St) Sarge's is the underdog of historic Manhattan delis, leaving the tourists to its more famous rivals. It's like a scene from a '70s sitcom: brown vinyl booths filled with weathered cabbies, loud-mouthed businesspeople and neurotic couples. Eavesdrop 24/7 over a pastrami sandwich, blintzes and matza-ball chicken soup, but leave room for the pornographically good strawberry cheesecake – one slice is enough for two.

BHATTI INDIAN $$

Map p434 (www.bhattinyc.com; 100 Lexington Ave at 27th St ; dishes $7-21; [S]6 to 28th St) One of your best options in 'Curry Hill' (Murray Hill), well-priced Bhatti has no shortage of extended Indian families tucking into expat-approved north Indian dishes. Service may be patchy but the food more than compensates. Suncontinental 'kebabs' are the specaility, among them a succulent, intensely spiced lamb Gilauti kebab.

A must for herbivores is the creamy Bharwaan Mushroom (grilled mushrooms stuffed with spices and cheese and coated in yogurt).

BI LOKMA TURKISH $

Map p434 (www.bi-lokma.com; 212 E 45th St btwn Second & Third Aves, Midtown East; mains $8.50-10.50; ⏲lunch & dinner Mon-Sat; [S]S, 4/5/6, 7 to

Grand Central-42nd St) Behind a dainty wooden facade, eccentric Orhan Yegem keeps Midtowners nourished with honest, fresh Ottoman staples like stuffed cabbage, eggplant salad and creamy yogurt soup. Stake a table, then head to the counters to order. Top of the list is the Ali Nazik (eggplant puree topped with succulent lamb and tomato mince), the culinary equivalent of a hug from a Turkish grandmother.

SPARKS STEAKHOUSE **$$$**

Map p434 (www.sparkssteakhouse.com; 210 E 46th St btwn Second & Third Aves; ⏲lunch & dinner Mon-Fri, dinner Sat; [S]S, 4/5/6, 7 to Grand Central-42nd St) Get an honest-to-goodness New York steakhouse experience at this classic joint, a former mob hangout that's been around for nearly 50 years and still packs 'em in for a juicy carnivorous feed.

Rub elbows with red-meat lovers of all stripes and choose your cut: prime sirloin, filet mignon, steak *fromage* (topped with Roquefort) or medallions of beef topped with bordelaise sauce. Thick chops of veal and lamb and various seafood options are also on tap, as are heaping portions of character thanks to the skilled waiters.

99 CENT PIZZA PIZZERIA **$**

Map p434 (473 Lexington Ave; pizza slice $1; [S]S, 4/5/6, 7 to Grand Central-42nd St) Serving up quick and cheap pizza, the barebones 99 Cent Pizza does a brisk business – always a sign that you've found a good bargain. It's not gourmet and doesn't claim to be, but if you're craving a good slice with a nice balance of tangy tomato sauce and creamy cheese, this barebones joint won't disappoint.

🍴 Midtown West & Times Square

[TOP CHOICE] **LE BERNARDIN** SEAFOOD **$$$**

Map p438 (☎212-554-1515; www.le-bernardin.com; 155 W 51st St btwn Sixth & Seventh Aves; prix fixe lunch/dinner $75/125, tasting menus $145-190; ⏲lunch Mon-Fri, dinner Mon-Sat; [S]1 to 50th St; B/D/E to 7th Ave) The interiors may have been slightly sexed-up for a 'younger clientele' (the stunning storm-themed triptych is by Brooklyn artist Ran Ortner), but triple Michelin-starred Le Bernardin remains a luxe, fine-dining holy grail. At the helm is celebrity chef Eric Ripert, whose deceptively simple-looking seafood often borders on the transcendental.

The menu works simply: four lunch courses for $75 or four dinner courses for $125, with ample choices per course, and two tastings menus for those with more time and money. While it's hard to go wrong, especially outstanding dishes include a peekytoe crab cake served with tequila-spiked guacamole and petite-sized potato crisps, and Ripert's signature tuna and foie gras creation. Book at least three weeks ahead for dinner and one week ahead for lunch.

[TOP CHOICE] **DANJI** KOREAN **$$**

Map p438 (www.danjinyc.com; 346 W 52nd St; plates $7-20; ⏲lunch Mon-Fri, dinner Mon-Sat; [S]C/E to 50th St) Young-gun chef Hooni Kim has captured tastebuds with his Michelin-starred Korean 'tapas.' Served in a snug contemporary space, his drool-inducing creations are divided into 'traditional' and 'modern' options. Though the highlights are many, the celebrity dish is the sliders, a duo of *bulgogi* beef and spiced pork belly, each dressed with scallion vinaigrette and served on butter-grilled buns. Head in early or prepare to wait.

[TOP CHOICE] **BURGER JOINT** BURGERS **$**

Map p438 (www.parkermeridien.com/eat4.php; Le Parker Meridien, 119 W 56th St; burgers $7; [S]F to 57th St) With only a small neon burger as your clue, this speakeasy burger hut loiters behind the curtain in the lobby of the Le Parker Meridien hotel. Find it and you'll stumble onto a thumping scene of graffiti-strewn walls, retro booths and attitude-loaded staff slapping up beef-n-patty brilliance.

The menu is a no-fuss, no-bull affair: hamburger or cheeseburger, cooked to your liking and pimped with your choice of garnishes. Order a side of golden fries, a pitcher of beer and scan the walls for celebrity scribbles. It gets packed, so head in early, late or wait.

TOTTO RAMEN JAPANESE **$**

Map p438 (www.tottoramen.com; 366 W 52nd St; ramen $9.50-12.50; ⏲lunch Mon-Sat, dinner daily; [S]C/E to 50th St) Good things come to those who wait. Like tiny Totto. Write your name and number of guests on the clipboard by the door and wait for your (cash-only) ramen revelation. Skip the chicken and go for the pork, which sings in dishes like miso ramen (with fermented soybean paste, egg, scallion, bean sprouts, onion and home-made chili paste).

If you're lucky you'll get a seat at the counter, behind which the ramen masters tackle bubbling vats of fragrant broth and char the melt-in-your-mouth pork with a blowtorch. Specials are pinned on the wall corkboards: the *ika-yaki* (skewered and torched sea urchin) is unmissable. Avoid the place on weekends as waiting times are particularly excruciating.

A VOCE
ITALIAN $$$

Map p438 (📞212-823-2523; www.avocerest aurant.com; 10 Columbus Circle at 59th St; Mon-Fri prix fixe lunch $29, dinner mains $25-39; ⓢlunch & dinner daily, brunch Sat & Sun; ⓢA/C, B/D, 1 to 59th St-Columbus Circle) Inside the swanky Time Warner mall, light, airy and modern A Voce combines sweeping views of Central Park with high-end interpretations of Ital-ian classics – think caramelized onion-filled ravioli with foie gras, balsamico and bread-crumbs or grilled swordfish with chickpeas, broccoli and a sucker-punch *nduja* (spicy salami spread) vinaigrette. The well-versed wine list includes almost 20 drops by the glass. Book ahead.

MARSEILLE
FRENCH, MEDITERRANEAN $$

Map p438 (www.marseillenyc.com; 630 Ninth Ave at 44th St; mains $19-28.50; ⓢA/C/E to 42nd St-Port Authority Bus Terminal) A nostalgic fusion of theatrical lighting, sweeping curves and mirrored panels, this Hell's Kitchen gem looks somewhere between an old cinema lobby and an art deco brasserie. At once buzzing and romantic, it's a fabulous spot to kick back with a spiced pear martini and nibble on flavor-packed French-Med fare.

Not to be missed is the tuna tartar appe-tizer, served in three crispy wonton wrap-pers and topped with diced jalapeños, cu-cumbers and spicy mayo. Prepare to swoon.

BOCCA DI BACCO
ITALIAN $$

Map p438 (📞212-265-8828; www.boccadibacco nyc.com; 828 Ninth Ave btwn 54th & 55th Sts; mains $16-24; ⓢdinner daily; ⓢA/B, C/D, 1 to 59th St-Columbus Circle) With its art-slung walls and rustic interior, this electric res-taurant/wine bar combo is Hell's Kitchen's take on the classic Italian enoteca. Sit at the bar for vino and impromptu conversation or book a table for a more private tête-à-tête. Fueling the conversation is a repertoire of beautifully prepared Italian dishes, from soulful *zuppe* (soups) to sublime meats and seafood mains.

Seafood stars in several pasta options, including a sublime spaghetti bottarga (with Sardinian tuna caviar and rape broc-coli), while desserts include a decadent *sgroppino* (an 'adult smoothie' made with chamapagne, vodka, lemon, sorbet and mango cream).

GAHM MI OAK
KOREAN $$

Map p438 (43 W 32nd St btwn Broadway & Fifth Ave; dishes $10-22; ⓢ24hr; ⓢN/Q/R, B/D/F/M to 34th St-Herald Sq) If you're craving *yook hwe* (raw beef and Asian pear matchsticks) at 3am, this K-Town savior has you covered. The shtick here is authenticity, shining through in dishes like the house speciality *sul long tang* (a milky broth of ox bones, boiled for 12 hours and pimped with brisket and scallion). Korean wise man say *sul long tang* cure evil hangover.

EL MARGON
CUBAN $

Map p438 (136 W 46th St btwn Sixth & Seventh Aves; sandwiches from $4, mains $9; ⓢB/D/F/M to 47-50th Sts-Rockefeller Center) It's still 1973 at this ever-packed Cuban lunch counter, where orange Laminex and greasy good-ness never went out of style. Go for gold with their legendary cubano sandwich (a pressed panino jammed with rich roast pork, salami, cheese, pickles, mojo and mayo). It's obscenely good.

🍷 DRINKING & NIGHTLIFE

The massive belly of Manhattan covers about everyone – cheesy tourist, barely-legal suburbanite, martini princesses, you name it. The drinking holes east of Times Square may be a little more old-school than to the west, but they're among the most atmospheric in town, from baronial hideaways and historic pubs to a sing-song former speakeasy. Head to Midtown West and quench your thirst anywhere from lofty cocktail bars to sleazy dive joints and even a country-and-western gay bar. Those around Seventh Ave, Times Square and Hell's Kitchen are within easy striking distance

of Broadway theaters – an ideal spot for a little post-show commentary.

🍷 Midtown East & Fifth Avenue

[TOP CHOICE] **BILL'S GAY NINETIES** BAR

Map p434 (☎212-355-0243; www.billsnyc.com; 57 E 54th St; ⏲11am-2am Mon-Sat; [S]E/M to Fifth Ave-53rd St) Back in the day, Bill's was a real speakeasy bar, with boarded-up windows and three floors of spirit-fueled song, dance and hedonism. The boards have gone, but the bonhomie lives on with nightly piano sessions and a motley crew of Midtown baby boomers, Jersey girlfriends and the odd Jewish matriarch bonding over Do Re Mi. You *will* break into song.

PJ CLARKE'S BAR

Map p434 (www.pjclarkes.com; 915 Third Ave at 55th St; [S]E/M to Lexington Ave-53rd St) A bastion of old New York, this lovingly worn wooden saloon has been straddling the scene since 1884; Buddy Holly proposed to his fiancée here and Old Blue Eyes pretty much owned table 20. Choose a jukebox tune, order a round of crab cakes and settle in with a come-one-and-all crowd of collar-and-tie colleagues, college students and nostalgia-longing urbanites.

STUMPTOWN COFFEE CAFE

Map p434 (www.stumptowncoffee.com; 18 W 29th St btwn Broadway and Fifth Ave; ⏲6am-8pm Mon-Sun; [S]N/R to 28th St) Hipster baristas in fedora hats brewing killer coffee? No, you're not in Williamsburg, you're at the Manhattan outpost of Portland's most celebrated coffee roaster. The queue is a small price to pay for proper espresso in Midtown, so count your blessings. It's standing-room only, though weary punters might find a seat in the adjacent Ace Hotel (p337) lobby.

TERROIR WINE BAR

Map p434 (www.wineisterroir.com; 439 Third Ave; ⏲5pm-1am Mon-Thu, to 2am Fri & Sat, to 11pm Sun; [S]6 to 28th St) Restaurateur/sommelier Paul Grieco and chef Marco Canora have injected a little cred into Murray Hill's drinking scene with this, the third branch of their acclaimed wine bar. Low-slung bulbs, exposed brickwork and long communal tables ooze downtown cool, while the well-versed, well-priced wine list features a mind-boggling array of drops by the glass. The vino-friendly grub is inspired and delicious.

SUBWAY INN BAR

Map p434 (143 E 60th St btwn Lexington & Third Aves; [S]4/5/6 to 59th St, N/Q/R to Lexington Ave-59th St) Booze in this part of town for this cheap? Count us in. Occupying its own world across from Bloomingdale's, this old-geezer watering hole is a vintage cheap-booze spot that, despite the classic rock and worn red booths, harkens to long-past days when Marilyn Monroe would drop in.

CULTURE ESPRESSO CAFE

Map p434 (www.cultureespresso.com; 72 W 38th St; ⏲7am-7pm Mon-Fri, 9am-5pm Sat & Sun; [S]B/D/F/M to 42nd St-Bryant Park) The line says it all: Culture knows good coffee. The single-origin espresso here is nutty, complex and creamy, with other coffee-geek options including Chemex and cold brew varieties. The clued-in vibe extends to the edibles, with SCRATCHbread scones from Brooklyn (the citrus-rosemary–grey salt combo will improve the worst of days), super-gooey choc-chip cookies made on-site and fresh locavore sandwiches.

🍷 Midtown West & Times Square

TOP OF THE STRAND COCKTAIL BAR

Map p438 (www.topofthestrand.com; Strand Hotel, 33 W 37th St btwn Fifth & Sixth Aves; [S]B/D/F/M to 34th St) For that 'Oh my God, I'm in New York' feeling, head to the Strand (p340) hotel's rooftop bar, order a martini (extra dirty) and drop your jaw (discreetly). Sporting slinky cabanas and a sliding glass roof, its view of the Empire State Building is unforgettable.

Expect DJ-spun tunes Thursday to Sunday and a mixed crowd of post-work locals and international hotel guests.

LANTERN'S KEEP COCKTAIL BAR

Map p438 (☎212-453-4287; www.thelanternskeep.com; Iroquois Hotel, 49 W 44th St; ⏲5pm-midnight Tue-Sat; [S]B/D/F/M to 42nd St-Bryant Park) Can you keep a secret? If so, cross the lobby of the Iroquois Hotel (p340) and slip into this dark, intimate cocktail salon. Its speciality is pre-Prohibition libations, shaken and stirred by passionate, personable mixologists. If you're feeling spicy, request a Groom's Breakfast, a fiery melange of gin, hot sauce, Worcestershire sauce, muddled lime, cucumber, and salt and pepper. Reservations are recommended.

ROBERT
COCKTAIL BAR

Map p438 (www.robertnyc.com; Museum of Arts & Design, 2 Columbus Circle btwn Eighth Ave & Broadway; S A/C, B/D, 1 to 59th St-Columbus Circle) Perched on the 9th floor of the Museum of Arts & Design, '60s-inspired, pink-tastic Robert is technically a high-end, Modern-American restaurant. While the food is satisfactory, it's a little overpriced, so head in late afternoon or post-dinner, find a sofa and gaze out over Central Park with a MAD Manhattan (Bourbon, Blood Orange Vermouth and liquored cherries). Magic.

RUM HOUSE
COCKTAIL BAR

Map p438 (www.edisonrumhouse.com; 228 W 47th St btwn Broadway & Eighth Ave; ⊙11am-4am daily; S N/Q/R to 49th St) Not long ago, this was Hotel Edison's crusty old piano bar. Enter the capable team from Tribeca bar Ward III (p75), who ripped out the green carpet, polished up the coppertop bar and revived this slice of old New York. You'll still find a nightly pianist, but he's now accompanied by well-crafted drinks and an in-the-know medley of whiskies and rums.

MIDTOWN DRINKING & NIGHTLIFE

LOCAL KNOWLEDGE

SEEING STARS ON BROADWAY

Broadway's biggest name – Tony Award winner Nikki M James, star of The Book of Mormon (p201) – gives us her top picks for a perfect night out on the town.

Best Places to Go Pre-Show

The Book of Mormon has a 7pm curtain, which means I get to the theater around 6pm, and that makes for a rather awkward time to eat. I usually swing by **Thalia's Kitchen** (www.restaurantthalia.com) – the take-away offshoot of Thalia – for a delicious salads. Thalia Kitchen is where all the Broadway types go – from actors to crew members – before taking the stage. I also like to stop by **Juice Generation** (www.juicegeneration.com) for a 'Lemon Lozenge' – a fresh pressed smoothie with lemon, apple and ginger. It's the perfect drink to coat my throat before I go on stage.

A Perfect Night Out On Broadway

I definitely recommend eating dinner after the show and having a little snack beforehand. It's always a bummer when people fill up on giant bowls of pasta and then fall into a food coma while watching the show. And we see a lot more in the audience than people think. Afterwards It's fun to swing by Don't Tell Mama (p204) to check out some fun, offbeat cabaret – the gypsies, tramps and thieves of Midtown. Or, class things up at **Print** (653 11th Ave at 48th St; S C/E to 50th St) at the Ink48 (p341) hotel for sky-high views of the city and great drinks.

Best Place to Check Out the City's Latest Performances

There's a lot of badass theater downtown. I love the **Public Theater** (Map p418; ☏212-260-2400; www.publictheater.org; 425 Lafayette St btwn Astor Pl & 4th St; ⊙hours vary; S N/R to 8th St-NYU; 6 to Astor Pl) – they're always pushing boundaries. Sleep No More (p151) is this choose-your-adventure kind of experience; like a crazy cool '60s 'happening.' I go to BAM (p289), too – they import an amazing variety of theater from around the world from German contemporary to incredible classics like obscure Shakespeare.

Tips & Tricks for Scoring Tickets

If you're looking for cheap seats, then I recommend the lottery. Show up around two hours before the show and put your name in the lottery to score front-row seats. The Book of Mormon gives away around 20 tickets every night for $32. It's not easy to get tickets, but it can be a lot of fun hanging out with other fans.

As told to Brandon Presser

JIMMY'S CORNER DIVE BAR

Map p438 (140 W 44th St btwn Sixth & Seventh Aves; ⏰10am-4am; [S]N/Q/R, 1/2/3, 7 to 42nd St-Times Sq; B/D/F/M to 42nd St-Bryant Park) This skinny, welcoming, completely unpretentious dive off Times Square is run by an old boxing trainer – as if you wouldn't guess by all the framed photos of boxing greats (and lesser-known fighters, too).

The jukebox covers Stax to Miles Davis (plus Lionel Ritchie's most regretful moments), kept low enough for post-work gangs to chat away.

[TOP CHOICE] **INDUSTRY** GAY

Map p438 (www.industry-bar.com; 355 W 52nd St btwn Eighth & Ninth Aves; ⏰4pm-4am; [S]C/E, 1 to 50th St) What was once a parking garage is now the hottest gay bar in Hell's Kitchen – a slick 4000-sq-ft watering hole with handsome lounge areas, a pool table and a stage for top-notch drag divas. Head in between 4pm and 9pm for the two-for-one drinks special or squeeze in later to party with the eye-candy party hordes. Cash only.

FLAMING SADDLES GAY

Map p438 (www.flamingsaddles.com; 793 Ninth Ave btwn 52nd & 53rd Sts; [S]C/E to 50th St) Butter my butt and call me a biscuit, there's a country and western gay bar in Midtown! *Coyote Ugly* meets *Calamity Jane* at this new Hell's Kitchen hangout, complete with studly boot-scotin' barmen, aspiring urban cowboys and a rough-n-ready vibe. So slip on them Wranglers and hit the Saddle, partner. You're in for a wild and boozy ride.

RUDY'S DIVE BAR

Map p438 (www.rudysbarnyc.com; 627 Ninth Ave at 44th St; [S]A/C/E to 42nd St-Port Authority Bus Terminal) The big pantless pig in a red jacket out front marks Hell's Kitchen's best divey mingler, with cheap pitchers of Rudy's two beers, half-circle booths covered in red duct tape and free hot dogs. A mix of folks come to flirt or watch muted Knicks games as classic rock plays.

BAR-TINI ULTRA LOUNGE GAY

Map p438 (www.bar-tiniultralounge.com; 642 Tenth Ave btwn 45th & 46th Sts; [S]A/C/E to 42nd St-Port Authority Bus Terminal) Still going strong, this white-on-white lounge remains a gay staple in Hell's Kitchen. Its happy hour is a hit, as are its nightly special events, with open drag comps, karaoke nights, guest singers and a rotating lineup of favorite local DJs.

☆ ENTERTAINMENT

☆ Midtown East & Fifth Avenue

ST BARTHOLOMEW'S CHURCH CLASSICAL MUSIC

Map p434 (www.stbarts.org; 109 E 50th St btwn Park & Lexington Aves; [S]E/M to 5th Ave-53rd St; 6 to 51st St) Several free performance series have found an extraordinary home at this landmark Anglican church, where the fine acoustics add a special touch to choir, cello, piano, violin and ensemble performances.

NEW YORK PUBLIC LIBRARY LECTURES

Map p434 (www.nypl.org/events; 42nd St at Fifth Ave; [S]S, 4/5/6 to 42nd St-Grand Central; 7 to Fifth Ave; B/D/F/M to 42nd St-Bryant Park) The public library offers lectures and public seminars at its myriad branch locations, on topics from contemporary art to the writings of Jane Austen. You'll find some of the best at the main branch on 42nd St. You can search all happenings at the library's website.

☆ Midtown West & Times Square

[TOP CHOICE] **JAZZ AT LINCOLN CENTER** JAZZ

Map p438 (www.jazzatlincolncenter.org; Time Warner Center, Broadway at 60th St; [S]A/C, B/D, 1 to 59th St-Columbus Circle) Perched high atop the Time Warner Center, Jazz at Lincoln Center consists of three state-of-the-art venues: the mid-sized Rose Theater; the panoramic, glass-backed Allen Room; and the intimate, atmospheric Dizzy's Club Coca-Cola. It's the last one you're likely to visit given its regular, nightly shows. The talent is often exceptional, as are the dazzling Central Park views.

[TOP CHOICE] **SIGNATURE THEATRE** THEATER

Map p438 (☎tickets 212-244-7529; www.signaturetheatre.org; 480 W 42nd St btwn Ninth & Tenth Aves; [S]A/C/E to 42nd St-Port Authority Bus Terminal) Now in its new Frank Gehry-

TV TAPINGS

Wanna be part of a live studio audience for the taping of one of your favorite shows? NYC is the place to do it. Follow the instructions below to gain access to some of TV's big-ticket tapings.

Saturday Night Live

One of the most popular NYC-based shows and known for being difficult to get into. That said, you can try your luck by getting your name into the mix in the fall, when seats are assigned by lottery. Simply send an email to snltickets@nbcuni.com in August, or line up by 7am the day of the show on the 49th St side of Rockefeller Plaza (p179) for standby lottery tickets (16 years and older only).

Late Show with David Letterman

Another late-night show that draws the crowds. You can try to request tickets for a specific date through the online request form at www.cbs.com/lateshow, or submit a request in person by showing up at the theater (1697 Broadway between 53rd and 54th Sts) to speak to a representative. Hours for requests are 9:30am to 12:30pm Monday to Friday and 10am to 6pm Saturday and Sunday. Or else try for a standby ticket by calling 212-247-6497 at 11am on the day of the taping you would like to attend; taping begins at 5:30pm Monday to Thursday.

Daily Show with Jon Stewart

Get on the *Daily Show* on Comedy Central by reserving tickets at least three months ahead at www.thedailyshow.com/tickets. If the day of taping you want is filled, try emailing requesttickets@thedailyshow.com.

For more show ticket details, visit the websites of individual TV stations, or try www.tvtickets.com.

designed home – complete with three theaters, bookshop and cafe – Signature Theatre devotes entire seasons to the body of work of its playwrights in residence. To date, featured dramatists have included Tony Kushner, Edward Albee, Athol Fugard and Kenneth Lonergan.

[TOP CHOICE] BOOK OF MORMON — THEATER

Map p438 (Eugene O'Neill Theatre; www.bookofmormonbroadway.com; 230 W 49th St btwn Broadway & Eigth Ave; [S]N/Q/R to 49th St; 1, C/E to 50th St) Subversive, obscene and ridiculously hilarious, this cutting musical satire is the work of *South Park* creators Trey Parker and Matt Stone and *Avenue Q* composer Robert Lopez. Winner of nine Tony Awards, it tells the story of two naive Mormons on a mission to 'save' a Ugandan village.

Book six months ahead for standard-price tickets or prepare to pay a premium for tickets at shorter notice. If you're feeling particularly lucky, head to the theater 2½ hours before the show to enter the ticket lottery, which offers a limited number of tickets for $32.

CHICAGO — THEATER

Map p438 (Ambassador Theater; www.chicagothemusical.com; 219 W 49th St btwn Broadway & Eighth Ave; [S]N/Q/R to 49th St; 1, C/E to 50th St) This beloved Bob Fosse/Kander & Ebb classic – a musical about showgirl Velma Kelly, wannabe Roxie Hart, lawyer Billy Flynn and the fabulously sordid goings-on of the Chicago underworld – has made a great comeback. This version, revived by director Walter Bobbie, is seriously alive and kicking.

WICKED — THEATER

Map p438 (Gershwin Theatre; www.wickedthemusical.com; 221 W 51st St btwn Broadway & Eighth Ave; [S]B/D/F/M to 47th-50th Sts-Rockefeller Center) A whimsical, mythological and extravagantly produced prequel to *The Wizard of Oz*, this pop-rock musical – a stage version of Gregory Maguire's 1995 novel – gives the story's witches a turn to tell the tale. Its followers are an insanely cultish crew, attending frequent performances and launching all sorts of fan clubs, fansites and obsessive blogs to keep themselves occupied.

1

1. Grand Central Terminal (p187)

This is NYC's beaux arts masterpiece, from the pink marble floors and vaulted ceilings to the vintage ticket counters.

2. FAO Schwarz (p206)

This giant toy store has everything to enthrall visiting kids, including life-sized stuffed animals and air-hockey sets.

3. Radio City Music Hall (p182)

Join a tour to get the most out of this spectacular art deco movie theater. Don't miss the legendary pipe organ!

COREY WISE / LONELY PLANET IMAGES ©

COREY WISE / LONELY PLANET IMAGES ©

TOP CHOICE CARNEGIE HALL — LIVE MUSIC

Map p438 (☏212-247-7800; www.carnegiehall. org; W 57th St & Seventh Ave; ⓈN/Q/R to 57th St-Seventh Ave) This legendary music hall may not be the world's biggest, nor grandest, but it's definitely one of the most acoustically blessed venues around. Opera, jazz and folk greats feature in the Isaac Stern Auditorium, with edgier jazz, pop, classical and world music in the hugely popular Zankel Hall.

MAGNET THEATER — COMEDY

Map p438 (☏212-244-8824; www.magnettheater. com; 254 W 29th St btwn Seventh & Eighth Aves; ⏱6:30-11pm Tue & Wed, to midnight Thu & Fri, to 1am Sat, 6-11pm Sun; Ⓢ1/2 to 28th St; A/C/E to 23rd St; 1/2/3 to 34th St-Penn Station) A jam-packed schedule featuring tons of comedy in several incarnations (mostly improv) lures crowds of rowdy youngsters. Our favorite is the musical improv but you can't go wrong with the sketch-comedy workshops.

PLAYWRIGHTS HORIZONS — THEATER

Map p438 (☏tickets 212-279-4200; www.play wrightshorizons.org; 416 W 42nd St btwn Ninth & Tenth Aves, Midtown West; ⓈA/C/E to 42nd St-Port Authority Bus Terminal) An excellent place to catch what could be the next big thing, this veteran 'writers' theater' is dedicated to fostering contemporary American works. Notable past productions include *Saved*, a musical by Michael Friedman based on the quirky film, as well as *I Am My Own Wife* and *Grey Gardens*, both of which moved on to Broadway.

BIRDLAND — LIVE MUSIC

Map p438 (☏212-581-3080; www.birdlandjazz. com; 315 W 44th St btwn Eighth & Ninth Aves, Theater District; admission $10-50; ⏱club from 7pm, shows around 8:30pm & 11pm; ☎; ⓈA/C/E to 42nd St-Port Authority Bus Terminal) Off Times Square, it's got a slick look, not to mention the legend – its name dates from bebop legend Charlie Parker (aka 'Bird'), who headlined at the previous location on 52nd St, along with Miles, Monk and just about everyone else (you can see their photos on the walls). Covers run from $20 to $50 and the line-up is always stellar.

Regular highlights include razzle-dazzle cabaret of John Caruso's Cast Party on Mondays, the Louis Armstrong Centennial Band on Wednesdays, and the Chico O'Farrill Afro-Cuban Orchestra on Sundays.

CAROLINE'S ON BROADWAY — COMEDY

Map p438 (☏212-757-4100; www.carolines.com; 1626 Broadway at 50th St; ⓈN/Q/R to 49th St; 1 to 50th St) You may recognize this big, bright, mainstream classic from comedy specials filmed here on location. It's a top spot to catch US comedy big guns and sitcom stars, but for something a little more subversive, don't miss the late-late Friday night show The Degenerates.

SECOND STAGE THEATRE — THEATER

Map p438 (Tony Kiser Theatre; ☏212-246-4422; www.2st.com; 305 W 43rd St at Eighth Ave; ⓈA/C/E to 42nd St-Port Authority Bus Terminal) Second Stage is well known for debuting the work of talented emerging writers as well as that of the country's more established names. If you're after top-notch contemporary American theater, this is a good place to find it.

CITY CENTER — DANCE

Map p438 (☏212-581-1212; www.nycitycenter.org; 131 W 55th St btwn Sixth & Seventh Aves; ⓈN/Q/R to 57th St-7th Ave) This Moorish, red-domed wonder almost went the way of the wrecking ball in 1943, but it was saved by preservationists, only to face extinction again when its major ballet companies departed for Lincoln Center. Today, it hosts dance troupes including the Alvin Ailey and American Dance Theater, theater productions, and the New York Flamenco Festival in February or March.

OAK ROOM — CABARET

Map p438 (www.algonquinhotel.com; Algonquin Hotel, 59 W 44th St btwn Fifth & Sixth Aves; ⓈB/D/F/V to 42nd St-Bryant Park) Glam up, order a martini and get the Dorothy Parker vibe at this famous piano bar. Famed for launching the careers of Harry Connick Jr, Diana Krall and Michael Feinstein, its Sunday brunch often sees jazz veteran Barbara Carroll grace the piano.

DON'T TELL MAMA — CABARET

Map p438 (www.donttellmamanyc.com; 343 W 46th St; 2-drink minimum; ⏱4pm-1am; ⓈN/Q/R, S, 1/2/3, 7 to Times Sq-42nd St) Piano bar and cabaret venue extraordinaire, Don't Tell Mama is an unpretentious little spot that's been around for more than 25 years and has the talent to prove it. Its regular roster of performers aren't big names, but true lovers of cabaret who give each show their all and don't mind a little singing help from the audience sometimes.

If you want your cabaret a bit more sinister and sexy, head to the **Box** (www.theboxnyc.com) on the Lower East Side. It's risqué and ribald, but its (very) late-night shows might just tickle your fancy.

THERAPY GAY

Map p438 (www.therapy-nyc.com; 348 W 52nd St btwn Eighth & Ninth Aves; [S]C/E, 1 to 50th St) Industry may be the street's new hot shot, but this multilevel, contemporary space was the first gay man's lounge/club to draw throngs to Hell's Kitchen. It still draws the crowds with its nightly shows (from music to comedy) and decent fare Sunday to Friday (burgers, hummus, salads). Drink monikers team with the theme: Oral Fixation and Size Queen, to name a few.

AMC EMPIRE 25 CINEMA

Map p438 (www.amctheatres.com/empire; 234 W 42nd St at Eighth Ave; [S]N/Q/R, S, 1/2/3, 7 to 42nd St-Times Sq) It's pretty cool to gaze out of over illuminated 42nd St at this massive cinema complex, and even more thrilling to settle into the stadium-style seating. While it's not the best place to catch mainstream Hollywood flicks (crowds can be massive and rowdy), it's the perfect off-the-radar spot for indies, which screen frequently to well-behaved, manageable numbers.

MADISON SQUARE GARDEN LIVE MUSIC

Map p438 (www.thegarden.com; Seventh Ave btwn 31st & 33rd Sts; [S]1/2/3 to 34th St-Penn Station) NYC's major performance venue – part of the massive complex housing Penn Station and the WaMu Theater – hosts big-arena performers, from Kanye West to Madonna. It's also a sports arena, with New York Knicks, New York Liberty and New York Rangers games, as well as boxing matches and events like the Annual Westminster Kennel Club Dog Show.

🛍 SHOPPING

Midtown retail may lack the edge of downtown neighborhoods like the Lower East Side, but it's here that you'll find

LOCAL KNOWLEDGE

THE NEW YORK STAGE

Jason Zinoman, theater critic for the *New York Times*, shares his tips on New York's dynamic theater scene.

Don't Miss Musicals

The Book of Mormon (p201) is irreverent, obscene satire wrapped inside a truly old-fashioned Broadway musical entertainment. It's the rare show that will appeal to lovers of *South Park* and *The Music Man*. If you can't get a ticket, which is quite likely, you can't go wrong with the long-running Kander and Ebb classic Chicago (p201).

For Contemporary American Theater

Playwrights Horizons (p204), Signature Theatre (p200) and Second Stage Theatre (p204) are good places to see great new writing. But if you are in a more adventurous mood, check out PS 122 or the Brooklyn Academy of Music (p289). Troupes like the **Civilians** (www.thecivilians.org), specialized in tricky docu-dramas, and the giddy pop-culture obsessed **Vampire Cowboys** (www.vampirecowboys.com) are always worth seeing.

Talented Locals

There are far too many to mention, but Annie Baker and Young Jean Lee (YJL) are young, brilliant and prolific. Annie Baker is known for quiet, careful observed naturalism, while YJL is more experimental and provocative, playing more with form. This said, Kenneth Lonergan, Edward Albee and Tony Kushner are probably this city's greatest playwrights, with an honorable mention for Wallace Shawn.

Final Tip

Skip Broadway altogether and see a show downtown where ticket prices are often barely more than a movie and popcorn, and the shows are often inspired and far more accessible than you think.

fabled department stores like Fifth Ave's Bergdorf & Goodman and Madison Ave's Barneys. Rockstars pick up pedals on W 48th St, while gem hunters scour the wild-and-wacky Diamond District on W 47th St. If you're a self-made style maven, hit the Garment District, around Seventh Ave in the 30s, for massive shops peddling DIY fashion props. A handful of trend-sensitive boutiques dot Ninth Ave in hip Hell's Kitchen, while down in Herald Square you'll find love-it-or-loathe-it Macy's, the planet's largest store.

Midtown East & Fifth Avenue

BARNEYS DEPARTMENT STORE

Map p434 (www.barneys.com; 660 Madison Ave at 61st; [S]N/Q/R to Fifth Ave-59th St) Serious fashionistas shop at Barneys, well known for its spot-on collections of in-the-know labels like Holmes & Yang, Kitsuné, Miu Miu and Derek Lam. For less expensive deals (geared to a younger market), check out Barneys Co-op on the 7th and 8th floors, or on the Upper West Side, in Chelsea, SoHo or Brooklyn.

A sharp collection of bags, cosmetics, fragrances and homewares complete the picture. When you're done, head to Fred's on the 9th floor for a well-earned prosecco.

[TOP CHOICE] **MOMA DESIGN & BOOK STORE** BOOKS, GIFTS

Map p434 (www.momastore.org; 11 W 53rd St btwn Fifth & Sixth Aves; [S]E/M to Fifth Ave-53rd St) The flagship store at the Museum of Modern Art is a savvy spot to souvenir shop in one fell swoop. Aside from stocking must-have books (from art and architecture tomes to pop culture readers and kids' picture books), you'll find art prints and posters, edgy homewares, jewelry, bags and one-of-a-kind knick-knacks. For furniture, lighting and MUJI merchandise, head to the MoMA Design Store across the street.

BLOOMINGDALE'S DEPARTMENT STORE

Map p434 (www.bloomingdales.com; 1000 Third Ave at 59th St; ⏲10am-8:30pm Mon-Fri, to 7pm Sat, 11am-7pm Sun; 📶; [S]4/5/6 to 59th St, N/Q/R to Lexington Ave-59th St) Fresh from a major revamp, epic 'Bloomie's' is something like the Metropolitan Museum of Art to the shopping world: historic, sprawling, overwhelming and packed with bodies, but you'd be sorry to miss it. Raid the racks for clothes and shoes from a who's who of US and global designers, including an increasing number of 'new-blood' collections. Refuel pitstops include a branch of cupcake heaven Magnolia Bakery.

BERGDORF GOODMAN DEPARTMENT STORE

Map p434 (www.bergdorfgoodman.com; 754 Fifth Ave btwn 57th & 58th Sts; [S]N/Q/R to Fifth Ave-59th St; F to 57th St) Not merely loved for its Christmas windows (the city's best), BG gets the approval of the fashion cognoscenti for its exclusive labels and all-round fabulousness. Reinvent yourself with threads from the likes of John Varvatos, Marc Jacobs and Etro, then complete the picture with a lust-inducing booty of handbags, shoes, jewelery, cosmetics and homewares. The men's store is across the street.

SAKS FIFTH AVE DEPARTMENT STORE

Map p434 (www.saksfifthavenue.com; 611 Fifth Ave at 50th St; [S]B/D/F/M to 47th-50th Sts-Rockefeller Center; E/M to Fifth Ave-53rd St) Complete with beautiful vintage elevators, Saks' 10-floor flagship store fuses old-world glamor with solid service and must-have labels. Go luxe with the likes of Escada, Kiton and Brunello, or opt for younger, edgier, more less expensive labels like Scotch & Soda, Vince and Rag & Bone. There's a decent selection of cosmetics and homewares, and its January sale is legendary.

TIFFANY & CO JEWELRY, HOMEWARES

Map p434 (www.tiffany.com; 727 Fifth Ave; [S]F to 57th St) This fabled jeweler, with its trademark clock-hoisting Atlas over the door, has won countless hearts with its luxe diamond rings, watches, silver Elsa Peretti heart necklaces, crystal vases and glassware. Swoon, drool, but whatever you do, don't harass the elevator attendants with tired 'Where's the breakfast?' jokes.

FAO SCHWARZ CHILDREN

Map p434 (www.fao.com; 767 Fifth Ave; [S]4/5/6 to 59th St; N/Q/R to Fifth Ave-59th St) The toy store giant, where Tom Hanks played footsy piano in the movie *Big*, is number one on the NYC wish list of most visiting kids. Why not indulge them? The magical (over-the-top) wonderland, with dolls up for 'adoption,' life-size stuffed animals, gas-powered kiddie convertibles, air-hockey sets and much more, might even thrill you, too.

UNIQLO FASHION

Map p434 (www.uniqlo.com; 666 Fifth Ave at 53rd St; [S]E/M to Fifth Ave-53rd St) Uniqlo is Japan's answer to H&M and this is its showstopping 89,000-sq-ft flagship megastore. Grab a mesh bag at the entrance and let the elevators woosh you up to the 3rd floor to begin your retail odyssey. The forte here is affordable, fashionable, quality basics, from tees and undergarments, to Japanese denim, cashmere sweaters and high-tech parkas. Prepare to queue.

DYLAN'S CANDY BAR FOOD & DRINK

Map p434 (www.dylanscandybar.com; 1011 Third Ave at 60th St; ⏲10am-9pm Mon-Thu, to 10pm Fri & Sat, 11am-9pm Sun; [S]N/Q/R to Lexington Ave-59th St) Willy Wonka has nothing on this three-level feast of giant swirly lollipops, crunchy candy bars, glowing jars of jelly beans, softball-sized cupcakes and a luminescent staircase embedded with scrumptious, unattainable candy. Stay away on weekends to avoid being pummeled by small, sugar-crazed kids. There's a cafe for hot chocolate, espresso, ice cream and other pick-me-ups on the 2nd floor.

ARGOSY BOOKS

Map p434 (www.argosybooks.com; 116 E 59th St; ⏲10am-6pm Mon-Fri year-round, to 5pm Sat Sep–mid-May; [S]4/5/6 to 59th St; N/Q/R to Lexington Ave-59th St) Since 1925, this landmark used bookstore has stocked fine antiquarian items such as leatherbound books, old maps, art monographs and other classics picked up from high-class estate sales and closed antique shops. Interesting extras including autographed publicity stills from classic TV shows like *MASH*. Prices range from costly to clearance.

Midtown West & Times Square

NEPENTHES NEW YORK FASHION, ACCESSORIES

Map p438 (www.nepenthesny.com; 307 W 38th St btwn Eighth & Ninth Aves; ⏲noon-7pm Mon-Sat, to 5pm Sun; [S]A/C/E to 42nd St-Port Authority Bus Terminal) Occupying an old sewing shop in the Garment District, this cult Japanese collective stocks in-the-know labels like Engineered Garments and Needles, famed for their quirky detailing and artisanal production value (think tweed lace-up hem pants). While there's a small, well-curated selection of women's pieces, the focus is on menswear. Accessories include bags and satchels, hard-to-find fragrances and obscure magazines.

TAGG FASHION, ACCESSORIES

Map p438 (www.taggnyc.com; 720 Ninth Ave at 49th St; ⏲noon-9pm Mon-Thu, 11am-9pm Fri & Sat, noon-8pm Sun ; [S]C/E to 50th St) Everything a 'Hellsea' boy needs to turn heads, this compact boutique cranks up the pull-factor with preppy knits and shirts, pec-flaunting graphic tees, and sexy denim and briefs. Labels include J Brand, Diesel, Scotch & Soda, and Paul Frank Industries, while neighborhood essentials include sexy shades, gym bags and 'make a statement' headphones.

HOUSING WORKS VINTAGE

Map p438 (www.shop-housingworks.com; 730-732 Ninth Ave; [S]C/E to 50th St) As one shopper put it: 'They have some fabulous s$*t in here.' Welcome to the Hell's Kitchen branch of this much-loved thrift store, where Burberry shirts go for $25 and Joseph suede pants are yours for $40. While it's all about luck, the daily consignments mean a sterling find is never far off. Profits go to helping homeless people living with HIV/AIDS.

B&H PHOTO-VIDEO ELECTRONICS

Map p438 (www.bhphotovideo.com; 420 Ninth Ave btwn 33rd & 34th Sts; ⏲9am-7pm Mon-Thu, to 1pm Fri, 10am-6pm Sun, closed Sat; [S]A/C/E to 34th St-Penn Station) Visiting NYC's most popular camera shop is an experience in itself – it's massive and crowded, and bustling with black-clad (and tech-savvy) Hasidic Jewish salesmen. Your chosen item is dropped into a bucket, which then moves up and across the ceiling to the purchase area (which requires a second queue).

It's all very orderly and fascinating, and the selection of cameras, camcorders, computers and other electronics is outstanding.

MACY'S DEPARTMENT STORE

Map p438 (www.macys.com; 151 W 34th St at Broadway; [S]B/D/F/M, N/Q/R to 34th St-Herald Sq) The world's largest department store covers most bases, with clothing, furnishings, kitcheware, sheets, cafes, hair salons and even a branch of the Metrpolitan Museum of Art gift store. It's more 'mid-priced' than 'exclusive,' with mainstream labels and big-name cosmetics. Plus, riding the creaky wooden elevators between the eighth and ninth floors on the Broadway side is a must-do NYC experience.

COLONY MUSIC

Map p438 (www.colonymusic.com; 1619 Broadway; 🕒9am-1am Mon-Sat, 10am-midnight Sun; [S]N/Q/R to 49th St) Located in the Brill Building (onetime home of Tin Pan Alley song crafters), historic Colony once sold sheet music to the likes of Charlie Parker and Miles Davis. Its collection remains the city's largest. Extras include a 60,000-strong LP collection, karaoke CDs and an eclectic booty of memorabilia (Beatles gear, unused Frank and Sammy tickets, Jimmy Osmond dolls), all for sale.

DRAMA BOOK SHOP BOOKS

Map p438 (www.dramabookshop.com; 250 W 40th St btwn Seventh & Eighth Aves; 🕒11am-7pm Mon-Wed, Fri & Sat, to 8pm Thu; [S]A/C/E to 42nd St-Port Authority Bus Terminal) Broadway fans will find treasures in print at this expansive bookstore, which has taken its theatre (both plays and musicals) seriously since 1917. Staffers are good at recommending worthy selections, which span the classics to current hits. Check the website for regular events, which include talks with playwrights.

TIME WARNER CENTER MALL

Map p438 (www.shopsatcolumbuscircle.com; 10 Columbus Circle; [S]A/C, B/D, 1 to 59th St-Columbus Circle) A great add-on to an adventure in Central Park, the swank Time Warner Center has a fine booty of largely upscale vendors including Coach, Stuart Weitzman, Williams-Sonoma, True Religion, Hugo Boss, Godiva, Sephora, J Crew, Armani Exchange, and Tourneau. For delectable picnic fare, visit the enormous **Whole Foods** (www.wholefoodsmarket.com; 🕒8am-11pm; [S]A/C, B/D, 1 to 59th St-Columbus Circle) in the basement for ready-to-go salads, sandwiches, sushi and hot foods.

RUDY'S MUSIC MUSIC

Map p438 (www.rudysmusic.com; 169 W 48th St at Seventh Ave; 🕒closed Sun; [S]N/Q/R to 49th St) The stretch of 48th St just off Times Square was known as Music Row, and it's where rock royals like the Beatles, Jimi Hendrix and the Stones dropped in for acoustic essentials. Rudy's is one of the last vestiges of this venerable block, particularly for high-end acoustic and classical guitars.

Its newer **SoHo store** (Map p418; ☎212-625-2557; 461 Broome St) is even more impressive, with the world's best collection of D'Angelico guitars and the odd Swarovski Crystal-embedded number.

SPORTS & ACTIVITIES

RINK AT ROCKEFELLER CENTER SKATING

See p179.

NBC STUDIO TOURS CULTURAL TOUR

See p179.

CENTRAL PARK BIKE TOURS BICYCLE RENTAL

Map p438 (www.centralparkbiketours.com; 203 W 58th St at Seventh Ave; rentals per 2hr/day $20/40, tours from adult/child $49/40; 🕒9am-6pm daily; [S]A/C, B/D, 1 to 59th St-Columbus Circle) This place rents good quality bikes and leads various tours of the city, including a two-hour tour of the park, a three-hour tour of Midtown and Downtown, as well as themed movie-location and architecture tours. Rental prices include lock and helmet, and bikes can be delivered straight to your hotel. See the website for daily tour times.

CAUDALIE VINOTHÉRAPIE SPA DAY SPA

Map p434 (☎212-265-3182; www.caudalie-usa.com; 1 W 58th St; 🕒10am-8pm Mon & Tue, 9am-9pm Wed-Fri, 9am-7pm Sat, 10am-6pm Sun; [S]N/Q/R to Fifth Ave-59th St; F to 57th St) Wine therapy gets holistic at this luxe French spa, where treatments harness the antioxidant properties of grapes and vine leaves. Treatments include a Crushed Cabernet Scrub ($145) and a Wine Maker's Massage ($195). Our favorite is the Red Vine Bath ($75), yours to enjoy in a cherrywood barrel tub. You'll find the spa on the fourth floor of the Plaza Hotel (p338).

24 HOUR FITNESS GYM

Map p434 (www.24hourfitness.com; 153 E 53rd St btwn Lexington & Third Aves; day pass $25; 🕒gym 24hr, pool 5am-11pm; 📶; [S]E/M to Lexington Ave-53rd St) Work up a sweat at this smart, well-equipped chain, which includes top-of-the-range cardio equipment, weights, classes (including weights, boot camp and pilates), a sauna, steamroom and whirlpool. This branch also has a lap pool. Check the website for information on all three Manhattan branches.

LUCKY STRIKE BOWLING ALLEY
Map p438 (646-829-0170; www.bowllucky strike.com; 624 W 42nd St; individual games from $12, shoe rental $6; noon-2am Sun-Thu, to 4am Fri & Sat; A/C/E to 42nd St-Port Authority Bus Terminal) One of the world's few bowling alleys with a dress code, Lucky Strike has pricey drinks, plush lounge fittings and a fashion-conscious crowd – which makes the whole experience more akin to a nightclub than a bowling alley. Reservations are recommended.

NEW YORK KNICKS BASKETBALL
Map p438 (212-465-6073, tickets 866-858-0008; www.nyknicks.com; Madison Square Garden, Seventh Ave btwn 31st & 33rd Sts; tickets $13-330; A/C/E, 1/2/3 to 34th St-Penn Station) Occasional scandal aside, NYC loves its blue-and-orange basketball team. Indeed, the first song to popularize hip-hop gives it up for the beloved Knickerbockers (Sugar Hill Gang sings 'I have a color TV so I can watch the Knicks play basketball'). Yet, despite big crowds of Spike Lee and 18,999 others at the Garden, the Knicks haven't won a championship since 1973.

Upper East Side

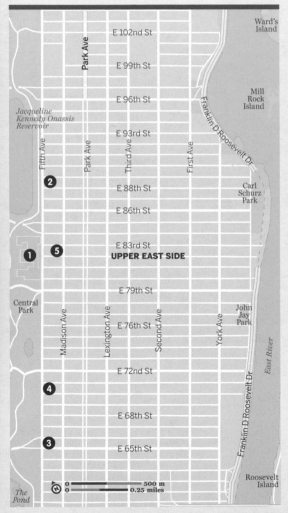

Neighborhood Top Five

1 Getting lost inside the priceless collections at the sprawling **Metropolitan Museum of Art** (p212), admiring Egyptian artifacts and contemporary rooftop installations. The new Art of the Arab Lands galleries and the revamped American Wing are both worth seeing.

2 Walking the spiraling ramps of Frank Lloyd Wright's architectural masterpiece, the **Guggenheim Museum** (p215).

3 Visiting **Temple Emanu-El** (p218), a dazzling Romanesque synagogue lined with splendid mosaics and stained glass.

4 Listening to Sunday classical music in a beaux arts mansion at **Frick Collection** (p224).

5 Sinking a tooth into one of the city's best black-and-white cookies at **William Greenberg Desserts** (p221).

For more detail of this area, see Map p440 ➡

Explore Upper East Side

There are infinite ways to tackle the neighborhood that contains some of the richest zip codes in the US. Begin with a walk south down Fifth Ave, starting at about 96th St. This will take you down storied Museum Mile (studded with vintage mansions and prestigious museums). At 72nd St, scoot east to Madison Ave and head south, where you can then enjoy the sight of some of the country's most extravagant flagship boutiques (Vera Wang, Prada and Lanvin, to name a few). The path is strewn with old-world cafes and opulent bars. Welcome to the rarefied air of uptown.

Local Life

➡ **Lunch with the upper crust** The Upper East Side is all about lunch – specifically ladies who lunch, a well-coiffed breed known for dispensing air kisses while armed with designer handbags the size of steam trunks. The best places to see 'em include Sant Ambroeus (p220) and Café Boulud (p220), on weekdays.

➡ **(Window) shop 'til you drop** Sure, the ritzy Madison Ave boutiques are jaw-dropping to look at, but aren't within reach of everyone's budgets. Local fashionistas hit the neighborhood for its high-end consignment shops and thrift stores – like Encore (p225), Michael's (p225) and Arthritis Foundation Thrift Shop (p225) – to hunt down good deals on mildly worn frocks tossed aside by New York society types.

➡ **Get jittery with it** The neighborhood seems to have the highest per capita ratio of coffee emporiums anywhere in the city. And when the locals aren't shopping or doing Pilates, they're sipping steamy skim-milk macchiatos at cafes like Via Quadronno (p221), Sant Ambroeus (p220) and Cafe 3 (p216) at the Guggenheim Museum.

Getting There & Away

➡ **Subway** The sole subway lines here are the 4, 5 and 6, which travel north and south on Lexington Ave. Note that these trains get packed to sardine levels at rush hour, which means that if you're just traveling one or two stops, you'll be better off walking. A new stretch of subway track underneath Second Ave is expected to be completed by late 2016.

➡ **Bus** The M1, M2, M3 and M4 buses make the scenic drive down Fifth Ave along the eastern edge of Central Park. The M15 can be handy for getting around the far east side, traveling up First Ave and down Second. Cross-town buses at 66th, 72nd, 79th, 86th and 96th Sts take you across the park and into the Upper West Side.

Lonely Planet's Top Tip

The Upper East Side is ground zero for all things luxurious, especially the area that covers the blocks from 60th to 86th Sts between Park and Fifth Aves. As a general rule, if you're looking for eating and drinking spots that are easier on the wallet, head east of Lexington Ave. First, Second and Third Aves are lined with less pricey neighborhood spots.

UPPER EAST SIDE

✖ Best Places to Eat

➡ Earl's Beer & Cheese (p220)

➡ Café Boulud (p220)

➡ Sandro's (p221)

➡ Café Sabarsky (p221)

For reviews, see p220 ➡

🍷 Best Places to Drink

➡ Metropolitan Museum Roof Garden Café & Martini Bar (p224)

➡ Heidelberg (p224)

➡ Bemelmans Bar (p224)

For reviews, see p224 ➡

🔒 Best Places to Shop

➡ Encore (p225)

➡ Crawford Doyle Booksellers (p225)

➡ Zitomer (p225)

➡ Arthritis Foundation Thrift Shop (p225)

For reviews, see p225 ➡

JEAN-PIERRE LESCOURRET / LONELY PLANET IMAGES ©

TOP SIGHTS
METROPOLITAN MUSEUM OF ART

This sprawling encyclopedic museum, founded in 1870, houses one of the biggest art collections in the world. Its permanent collection has more than two million individual objects, from Egyptian temples to American paintings. Known colloquially as 'the Met,' the museum attracts almost six million visitors a year to its 17 acres of galleries – making it the largest single-site attraction in New York City. (Yup, you read that right: 17 acres.) In other words, plan on spending some time here. It is B-I-G.

DON'T MISS...

- The Temple of Dendur
- European paintings
- Arab Lands galleries
- Roof Garden Café & Martini Bar

PRACTICALITIES

- Map p440
- ☎212-535-7710
- www.metmuseum.org
- 1000 Fifth Ave at 82nd St
- suggested donation adult/child $25/free
- 🕐9:30am-5:30pm Tue-Thu & Sun, to 9pm Fri & Sat
- [S]4/5/6 to 86th St

Egyptian Art

The museum has an unrivaled collection of ancient Egyptian art, some of which dates back to the Paleolithic era. Located to the north of the Great Hall, the 39 Egyptian galleries open dramatically with one of the Met's prized pieces: the Mastaba Tomb of Perneb (c 2300 BC), an Old Kingdom burial chamber crafted from limestone. From here, a web of rooms is cluttered with funerary stele, carved reliefs and fragments of pyramids. (Don't miss the irresistible quartzite sculpture of a lion cub in Gallery 103.) These eventually lead to the Temple of Dendur (Gallery 131), a sandstone temple to the goddess Isis that resides in a sunny atrium gallery with a reflecting pool – a must-see for the first-time visitor.

European Paintings

Want Renaissance? The Met's got it. On the museum's 2nd floor, the European Paintings' galleries display a stunning collection of masterworks. This includes more than 1700 canvases from the roughly 500-year-period starting in the 13th century, with works by every important painter from Duccio to Rembrandt. In fact, everything here is, literally, a masterpiece. On the north end, in Gallery 615, is Vermeer's tender 17th century painting *A Maid Asleep*. Gallery 608, to the west, contains a luminous 16th-century altar by Renaissance master Raphael. And in a room stuffed with works by Zurbarán and Murillo (Gallery 618), there is an array of paintings by Velázquez, the most extraordinary of which depicts the dashing Juan de Pareja. And that's just the beginning. You can't go wrong in these galleries.

Art of the Arab Lands

The newly renovated 2nd-floor space comes with a very unwieldy name. The 'New Galleries for the Art of the Arab Lands, Turkey, Iran, Central Asia, and Later South Asia' comprises 15 incredible rooms that showcase the museum's extensive collection of art from the Middle East and Central and South Asia. In addition to garments, secular decorative objects and manuscripts, you'll find treasures such as a 12th-century ceramic chess set from Iran (Gallery 453) that is downright modernist in its simplicity. There is also a superb array of Ottoman textiles (Gallery 459), a medieval-style Moroccan court (Gallery 456) and an 18th-century room from Damascus (Gallery 461).

American Wing

In the northwest corner, the recently revamped American galleries showcase a wide variety of decorative and fine art from throughout US history. These include everything from colonial portraiture to Hudson River School masterpieces to John Singer Sargent's unbearably sexy *Madame X* (Gallery 771) – not to mention Emanuel Leutze's massive canvas of *Washington Crossing the Delaware* (Gallery 760). The galleries are stacked around an interior sculpture court abutted by a pleasant cafe.

Greek & Roman Art

The 27 galleries devoted to classical antiquity are another Met doozy, some of which are dramatically illuminated by natural daylight. From the Great Hall, a passageway takes viewers through a barrel vaulted room flanked by the chiseled torsos of Greek figures. This spills right into one of the Met's loveliest spaces: the airy Roman sculpture court (Gallery 162), full of marble carvings of gods and historical figures. The statue of a bearded Hercules from AD 68–98 is particularly awe-inspiring.

UPPER EAST SIDE METROPOLITAN MUSEUM OF ART

THE MET FOR KIDS

The most popular galleries with children are generally the Egyptian galleries, the Africa and Oceania galleries and the collection of medieval arms and armor – all of which are on the 1st floor. The Met hosts plenty of kid-centric happenings (check the website) and distributes a special museum brochure and map made specifically for the tykes. Inquire at the information desk.

One of the best spots at the museum is the roof garden (open from April to October). It features rotating sculpture installations by contemporary and 20th-century artists, but its best asset is the views of the city and Central Park. It's also home to the Roof Garden Café & Martini Bar, the best place for a sip.

SEEING THE MUSEUM

A desk inside the Great Hall has audio tours in several languages ($7), while docents offer guided tours of specific galleries. These are free with admission. Check the website or information desk for details. If you can't stand crowds, avoid weekends.

METROPOLITAN MUSEUM OF ART

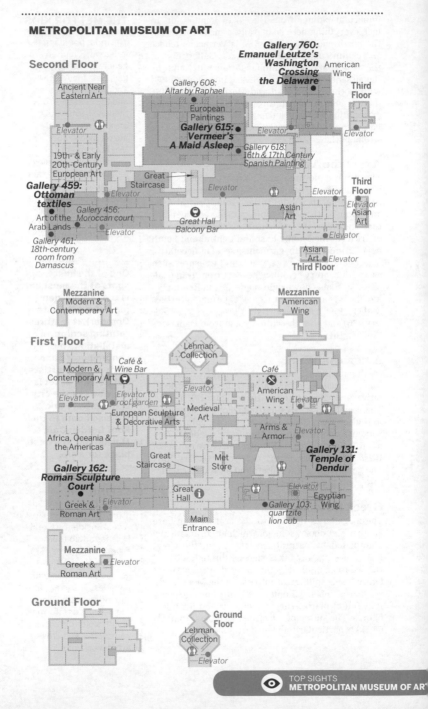

Second Floor

Ancient Near Eastern Art

Gallery 608: Altar by Raphael

Gallery 760: Emanuel Leutze's Washington Crossing the Delaware

American Wing

Third Floor

European Paintings

Gallery 615: Vermeer's A Maid Asleep

Elevator

Third Floor

Elevator

19th- & Early 20th-Century European Art

Gallery 618: 16th & 17th-Century Spanish Painting

Gallery 459: Ottoman textiles

Great Staircase

Elevator

Elevator

Third Floor

Elevator

Asian Art

Gallery 456: Moroccan court

Art of the Arab Lands

Elevator

Great Hall Balcony Bar

Asian Art

Gallery 461: 18th-century room from Damascus

Elevator

Asian Art *Elevator*

Third Floor

Mezzanine
Modern & Contemporary Art

Mezzanine
American Wing

First Floor

Lehman Collection

Café & Wine Bar

Café

Modern & Contemporary Art

Elevator to roof garden

Elevator

American Wing *Elevator*

Elevator

European Sculpture & Decorative Arts

Medieval Art

Africa, Oceania & the Americas

Arms & Armor

Elevator

Gallery 131: Temple of Dendur

Gallery 162: Roman Sculpture Court

Great Staircase

Met Store

Greek & Roman Art

Elevator

Great Hall

Egyptian Wing

Elevator

Main Entrance

Gallery 103: quartzite lion cub

Mezzanine
Greek & Roman Art

Elevator

Ground Floor

Ground Floor

Lehman Collection

Elevator

EXTERIOR OF THE SOLOMON R. GUGGENHEIM MUSEUM, NEW YORK. © THE SOLOMON R. GUGGENHEIM FOUNDATION, NEW YORK. USED WITH PERMISSION. DONALD C. & PRISCILLA ALEXANDER EASTMAN / LONELY PLANET IMAGES ©

TOP SIGHTS
GUGGENHEIM MUSEUM

A sculpture in its own right, architect Frank Lloyd Wright's building almost overshadows the collection of 20th century art that it houses. Completed in 1959, the inverted ziggurat structure was derided by some critics, but it was hailed by others who welcomed it as a beloved architectural icon. Since it first opened, this unusual structure has appeared on countless postcards, TV programs and films.

Abstract Roots

Like many museums, the Guggenhcim came out of the collection of a single individual: Solomon R Guggenheim, a New York mining magnate who began acquiring abstract art in his 60s at the behest of his art adviser, an eccentric German baroness named Hilla Rebay. His impressive collection included pieces by early Modernists like Vasily Kandinsky, Paul Klee and Marc Chagall.

In 1939, with Rebay serving as director, Guggenheim opened a temporary museum on 54th St titled Museum of Non-Objective Painting. (Incredibly, it had grey velour walls, piped-in classical music and burning incense.) Four years later, the pair commissioned Wright to construct a permanent home for the collection.

Years in the Making

Like any development in New York City, the project took forever to come to fruition. Construction was delayed for almost 13 years due to budget constraints, the outbreak of WWII and outraged neighbors who weren't all that excited to see an architectural spaceship land in their midst. Construction was completed in 1959, after both Wright and Guggenheim had passed away.

DON'T MISS...

➡ Permanent Collection Galleries

➡ Cafe 3

➡ Exterior views of the facade

PRACTICALITIES

➡ Map p440

➡ ☏212-423-3500

➡ www.guggenheim.org

➡ 1071 Fifth Ave at 89th St

➡ adult/child $18/free, by donation 5:45-7:45pm Sat

➡ ⊙10am-5:45pm Sun-Wed & Fri, to 7:45pm Sat

➡ Ⓢ4/5/6 to 86th St

A PINK GUGGENHEIM

Wright made hundreds of sketches and pondered the use of various materials for the construction of the museum. At one point, he considered using red marble for the exterior facade – a 1945 model sketch shows a pink building – but the color scheme was rejected.

While Wright was thrilled to create a museum, the idea of working in Manhattan didn't exactly captivate him. 'I can think of several more desirable places in the world to build his great museum,' wrote the famously acerbic architect in 1949, 'but we will have to try New York.'

SAVE TIME

The line to get in to the museum can be brutal. You'll save time if you purchase tickets online in advance.

Bring on the Critics

When the Guggenheim finally opened its doors in October 1959, the ticket price was 50¢ and the works on view included pieces by Kandinsky, Alexander Calder and abstract expressionists Franz Kline and Willem De Kooning.

The structure was savaged by the *New York Times,* which lambasted it as 'a war between architecture and painting in which both come out badly maimed.' But others quickly celebrated it as 'the most beautiful building in America.' Whether Wright intended to or not, he had given the city one of its most visible landmarks.

To the Present

Various changes have been made to the structure since the '50s. A renovation in the early 1990s by Gwathmey Siegel added an eight-story tower to the east, which provided an extra 50,000 sq ft of exhibition space. These galleries show the permanent collection and other exhibits, while the ramps are occupied by rotating exhibits.

The museum's holdings include works by Kandinsky, Picasso and Jackson Pollock. Over time, other key additions have been made, including paintings by Monet, Van Gogh and Degas, photographs by Robert Mapplethorpe, and key surrealist works donated by Guggenheim's niece Peggy.

Visiting the Museum

The museum's ascending ramp is occupied by rotating exhibitions of modern and contemporary art. Though Wright intended visitors to go to the top and wind their way down, the cramped, single elevator doesn't allow for this. Exhibitions, therefore, are installed from bottom to top.

There are two good on-site food options: **Wright** (Map p440; 212-427-5690; www.thewrightrestaurant.com; mains $21-27; 11:30am-3:30pm Fri-Wed; S4/5/6 to 86th St), at ground level, a space-age eatery serving steamy risotto and classic cocktails, and **Cafe 3** (Map p440; sandwiches $8; 10:30am-5pm Fri-Wed, to 7pm Sat; S4/5/6 to 86th St), on the 3rd floor, which offers sparkling views of Central Park and excellent coffee and light snacks.

SIGHTS

METROPOLITAN MUSEUM OF ART MUSEUM

See p212.

GUGGENHEIM MUSEUM MUSEUM

See p215.

WHITNEY MUSEUM OF AMERICAN ART MUSEUM

Map p440 (www.whitney.org; 945 Madison Ave at 75th St; adult/child $18/free; ⏲11am-6pm Wed, Thu, Sat & Sun, 1-9pm Fri; [S]6 to 77th St) The Whitney makes no secret of its mission to provoke, which starts with its imposing Brutalist building, a structure that houses works by 20th century masters Edward Hopper, Jasper Johns, Georgia O'Keeffe and Mark Rothko. In addition to rotating exhibits, there is a biennial on even years, an ambitious survey of contemporary art that rarely fails to generate controversy.

The museum was opened in 1931 by society doyenne Gertrude Vanderbilt Whitney, who was known for her lively Greenwich Village salons. During her lifetime, she collected more than 600 works of art, including canvases by painters such as Thomas Hart Benton and George Bellows. These works comprise the core of the museum's permanent collection, which is beautifully displayed on the 5th floor.

After inhabiting various locations downtown, the Whitney moved to its current Marcel Breuer–designed building in 1975. But, having outgrown these digs, it is set to move again. A new Renzo Piano–designed structure is currently under construction in the Meatpacking District and is scheduled to be completed in 2015.

For food, try the museum's new Danny Meyer comfort eatery in the basement, Untitled. In addition to a variety of snacks and sandwiches, it serves breakfast all day (pancakes $10).

FRICK COLLECTION GALLERY

Map p440 (www.frick.org; 1 E 70th St at Fifth Ave; admission $18, by donation 11am-1pm Sun, children under 10 not permitted; ⏲10am-6pm Tue-Sat, 11am-5pm Sun; [S]6 to 68th St-Hunter College) This spectacular art collection sits in a mansion built by prickly steel magnate Henry Clay Frick, one of the many such residences that made up Millionaires' Row. The museum has 12 splendid rooms that display masterpieces by Titian, Vermeer, Gilbert Stuart, El Greco and Goya. The Oval Room is graced by Jean-Antoine Houdon's stunning figure *Diana the Huntress*.

This museum is a treat for a number of reasons. One, it resides in a lovely, rambling beaux arts structure built from 1913 to 1914 by Carrère and Hastings. Two, it is

WORTH A DETOUR

ROOSEVELT: THE ISLAND OFF THE ISLAND OF MANHATTAN

Roosevelt Island, the tiny sliver of land that sits in the middle of the East River, has never had much to offer in the way of sights. For much of the 19th century, when it was known as Welfare Island, it was cluttered with hospitals, including a mental hospital and a crenelated small-pox ward. In the 1970s, a series of cookie-cutter apartment buildings were built along the island's only road. For years, the only thing Roosevelt Island really had going for it were the good views of Manhattan and the picturesque ruins of the old small-pox hospital (kept fenced off from those with SLR cameras).

But the island will be hitting the architectural map in the fall of 2012, when a five-acre memorial to President Franklin D Roosevelt opens on the southern tip. Designed by architect Louis Kahn in the 1960s, construction of the 4½-acre park stalled in the 1970s when Kahn died and New York City almost went into bankruptcy. Funding has been resuscitated and so has the park, which is being built with few changes to Kahn's original design. Once complete, it should be an interesting architectural time capsule – and the only structure by this monumental modernist in the city.

The best way to get to Roosevelt Island is to take the picturesque four-minute aerial tram trip across the East River. Trams leave from the **Roosevelt Island Tramway Station** (www.rioc.com/transportation.htm; 60th St at Second Ave; one-way fare $2.25; ⏲every 15min 6am-2am Sun-Thu, to 3am Fri & Sat). Otherwise, take the F train to the Roosevelt Island stop.

generally not crowded. And, three, it feels refreshingly intimate, with a trickling indoor courtyard fountain and gardens that can be explored on warmer days. A demure new Portico Gallery, opened in 2011, displays decorative works and sculpture.

A worthwhile audio tour (available in several languages) is included in the price of admission. Classical music fans will enjoy the frequent piano and violin concerts (p224) that take place on Sundays.

NEUE GALERIE — GALLERY

Map p440 (www.neuegalerie.org; 1048 Fifth Ave at 86th St; admission $20, children under 12 not admitted, 6-8pm 1st Fri of every month free; ⏲11am-6pm Thu-Mon, 6-8pm 1st Fri of every month; [S]4/5/6 to 86th St) This restored Carrère and Hastings mansion from 1914 is a resplendent showcase for German and Austrian art, featuring works by Paul Klee, Ernst Ludwig Kirchner and Egon Schiele. In pride of place on the 2nd floor is Gustav Klimt's golden 1907 portrait of Adele Bloch-Bauer – which was acquired for the museum by cosmetics magnate Ronald Lauder for a whopping $135 million.

This is a small but beautiful place with winding staircases and wrought-iron banisters. It also boasts the lovely, street-level eatery, Café Sabarsky. Avoid weekends if you don't want to deal with gallery-clogging crowds.

JEWISH MUSEUM — MUSEUM

Map p440 (www.jewishmuseum.org; 1109 Fifth Ave at 92nd St; adult/child $12/free, Sat free; ⏲11am-5:45pm Thu-Tue, to 4pm Fri; 👪; [S]6 to 96th St) This New York City gem is tucked into a French-Gothic mansion from 1908, which houses 30,000 items of Judaica, as well as sculpture, painting and decorative arts. It is well regarded for its thoughtful temporary exhibits, featuring retrospectives on influential figures such as Chaim Soutine and sprawling examinations of socially conscious photography in New York.

There are frequent lectures and events, as well as an array of activities for children. Every January, the museum collaborates with the Film Society of Lincoln Center to present the New York Jewish Film Festival.

NATIONAL ACADEMY MUSEUM — MUSEUM

Map p440 (www.nationalacademy.org; 1083 Fifth Ave at 89th St; adult/child $12/free; ⏲noon-5pm Wed & Thu, 11am-6pm Fri-Sun; [S]4/5/6 to 86th St) Co-founded by painter/inventor Samuel Morse in 1825, the National Academy Museum comprises an incredible permanent collection of paintings by figures such as Wil Barnet, Thomas Hart Benton and George Bellows. (This includes some highly compelling self-portraits.) It is housed in a beaux arts structure designed by Ogden Codman and featuring a marble foyer and spiral staircase.

TEMPLE EMANU-EL — SYNAGOGUE

Map p440 (www.emanuelnyc.org; 1 E 65th St at Fifth Ave; ⏲10am-5pm Mon-Thu; [S]6 to 68th St-Hunter College) Founded in 1845 as the first Reform synagogue in New York, this temple, completed in 1929, is now one of the largest Jewish houses of worship in the world. An imposing Romanesque structure, it is more than 175ft long and 100ft tall, with a brilliant, hand-painted ceiling that contains details in gold.

The structure also boasts 60 stained glass windows and a massive rose window whose dozen panels represent the 12 tribes of Israel. Other stained glass elements pay tribute to notable synagogues, including the Altneuschul in Prague (the oldest continually used Jewish house of worship in the world). The ark containing the Torah scrolls, on the eastern wall, is surrounded by a glittering glass-and-marble mosaic arch. The synagogue's 2500 seats all have an unobstructed view of this point.

The temple is home to the small **Herbert & Eileen Bernard Museum of Judaica**, with more than 650 pieces that date back to the 14th century. Worth a visit.

MUSEUM OF THE CITY OF NEW YORK — MUSEUM

Map p440 (www.mcny.org; 1220 Fifth Ave btwn 103rd & 104th Sts; suggested donation $20; ⏲10am-6pm; [S]6 to 103rd St) Situated in a colonial Georgian-style mansion, this local museum focuses solely on New York City's past, present and future. You'll find internet-based historical resources, lots of vintage photographs and a scale model of New Amsterdam shortly after the Dutch arrival. The 2nd-floor gallery includes entire rooms from demolished homes of New York grandees.

One of the museum's star attractions is the 12-room mansion dollhouse fabricated by Carrie Stettheimer over 25 years at the turn of the 20th century – replete with tiny artworks (including miniatures of pieces by Marcel Duchamp and Gaston Lachaise).

START BLOOMINGDALE'S
END THE MET
DISTANCE 1.5 MILES
DURATION 2 HOURS

Neighborhood Walk
Manhattan Movie Sites

➡ An exploration of Manhattan's most storied film sites takes you past film locations big and small.

Start outside ➊ **Bloomingdale's**, on Third Ave, where Darryl Hannah and Tom Hanks shattered televisions in *Splash* (1984) and Dustin Hoffman hailed a cab in *Tootsie* (1982).

West of here, 10 60th St is the site of the now defunct ➋ **Copacabana**, a nightclub (now a health food restaurant) that hosted Ray Liotta and Lorraine Bracco in *Goodfellas* (1990) and a coked-up lawyer played by Sean Penn in *Carlito's Way* (1993).

Continue west to ➌ **Central Park**, which has appeared in *The Royal Tenenbaums* (2001), *Ghostbusters* (1983), *The Muppets Take Manhattan* (1983), *Barefoot in the Park* (1967) and the cult classic *The Warriors* (1979).

From here, head east to Park Ave. At 620 Park Ave at 65th St, you'll find the building that served as ➍ **John Malkovich's apartment** in Charlie Kaufman's *Being John Malkovich* (1999). And to the north at 114 72nd St is the ➎ **high-rise** where Sylvia Miles lured Jon Voight in *Midnight Cowboy* (1969).

One block to the east and south is 171 E 71st St, a townhouse featured in one of the most famous movies to star New York: this was ➏ **Holly Golightly's apartment** in *Breakfast at Tiffany's* (1961).

Continuing east to Third Ave, you'll find ➐ **JG Melon** at the corner of 74th St, a good spot for beer and burger – plus the site of a meeting between Dustin Hoffman and Meryl Streep in *Kramer vs. Kramer* (1979).

Heading west to Madison Ave, the tony ➑ **Carlyle** hotel stands at 35 76th St where Woody Allen and Dianne Wiest had a date from hell in *Hannah and Her Sisters* (1986).

From the Carlyle, it's a short jaunt west to the ➒ **Metropolitan Museum of Art** at 82nd St and Fifth Ave, where Angie Dickinson had a fatal encounter in *Dressed to Kill* (1980) and Billy Crystal chatted up Meg Ryan in *When Harry Met Sally* (1989).

ASIA SOCIETY & MUSEUM
MUSEUM

Map p440 (www.asiasociety.org; 725 Park Ave at 70th St; admission $10, 6-9pm Fri mid-Sept–Jun free; ⊘museum 11am-6pm Tue-Sun, 6-9pm Fri mid-Sept–Jun; Ⓢ6 to 68th St-Hunter College) Founded in 1956 by John D Rockefeller, this cultural center is meant to strengthen Western understanding of Asia and the relationships between that region and the US. There are events and lectures, but the biggest draw is the museum, which shows rotating contemporary exhibits, as well as treasures – such as Jain sculptures and Nepalese Buddhist paintings.

GRACIE MANSION
HISTORIC BUILDING

Map p440 (⊘tour reservations 311 or 212-NEW-YORK, outside NYC 212-570-4773; www.nyc.gov/gracie; East End Ave at E 88th St; admission $7; ⊘tours 10am, 11am, 1pm & 2pm Wed; Ⓢ4/5/6 to 86th St) This Federal-style home served as the country residence of merchant Archibald Gracie in 1799. Since 1942, it has been where New York's mayors have lived – with the exception of megabillionaire Mayor Michael Bloomberg, who prefers his own plush, Upper East Side digs. The house has been added to and renovated over the years. Reservations required.

The home is bordered by the pleasant, riverside Carl Schurz Park.

COOPER-HEWITT NATIONAL DESIGN MUSEUM
MUSEUM

Map p440 (www.cooperhewitt.org; 2 E 91st St at Fifth Ave; adult/child $15/free; Ⓢ4/5/6 to 86th St) Part of the Smithsonian Institution in Washington, DC, this house of culture is the only museum in the country that's dedicated to both historic and contemporary design. The collection is housed in the 64-room mansion built by billionaire Andrew Carnegie in 1901. The museum closed in 2011 for a two-year renovation and expansion. Check the website for updates.

MUSEUM FOR AFRICAN ART
MUSEUM

off Map p440 (www.africanart.org; Fifth Ave at E 110th St; Ⓢ2/3, 6 to 110th St) First opened in an Upper East Side townhouse in 1984, this museum, dedicated to African artists, will tentatively open its doors in mid-2012, at which time it will become the first addition to Fifth Ave's Museum Mile since the Guggenheim in 1959. Opening dates have been pushed back several times, so check the website before heading out.

✖ EATING

⟨TOP CHOICE⟩ EARL'S BEER & CHEESE
AMERICAN $

Map p440 (www.earlsny.com; 1259 Park Ave btwn 97th & 98th Sts; grilled cheese $6-8, mains $8-17; ⊘4pm-midnight Tue-Fri, 11am-midnight Sat & Sun; Ⓢ6 to 96th St) Chef Corey Cova's comfort food outpost channels a hipster hunting vibe, complete with buck's head on the wall. Rest assured that these aren't warmed-over American classics. Basic grilled cheese is a paradigm shifter, served with pork belly, fried egg and kimchi. There is also mac 'n' cheese and waffles (with foie gras), none of it like anything you've ever eaten.

Earl's is tiny and fills up fast, so order at the bar and grab a seat at the communal picnic table. There is a good selection of craft beers.

CAFÉ BOULUD
FRENCH $$$

Map p440 (⊘212-772-2600; www.danielnyc.com/cafebouludny.html; 20 E 76th St at Madison Ave; mains $24-44; ⊘breakfast, lunch & dinner; ⊘; Ⓢ6 to 77th St) Now steered by Gavin Kaysen, this Michelin-starred bistro – part of Daniel Boulud's gastronomic empire – attracts a staid crowd with its globe-trotting French cuisine. Seasonal menus include classic dishes such as coq au vin, as well as more inventive fare (scallop crudo with white miso). Foodies on a budget will be interested in the two-course, $37 prix fixe lunch.

The adjacent 40-seat **Bar Pleiades** (open 'til midnight) serves seasonal cocktails, along with a full bar menu (think beef sliders and grilled baby octopus). Gents should consider wearing a jacket in the evenings. Reservations recommended.

SANT AMBROEUS
CAFE $$

Map p440 (⊘212-570-2211; www.santambroeus.com; 1000 Madison Ave btwn 77th & 78th St; tea sandwiches $8, pastries $10, mains $22-48; ⊘8am-11pm; ⊘; Ⓢ6 to 77th St) Behind a demure facade lies this dressy Milanese bistro and cafe that oozes old-world charm. Up front, a long granite counter dispenses inky espressos, pastries and tea sandwiches (think vegetable frittata and parma ham), while the elegant dining room in the back dishes up northern Italian specialties such as octopus salad and saffron risotto.

SANDRO'S ITALIAN **$$**

Map p440 (☎212-288-7374; www.sandrosnyc.com; 306 E 81st St near Second Ave; mains $20-35; 🕐4:30-11pm Mon-Sat, to 10pm Sun; [S]6 to 77th St) This neighborhood trattoria serves up fresh Roman dishes and homemade pastas by chef Sandro Fioriti. Specialties include crisp fried artichokes and sea urchin ravioli. From 4:30pm to 6:30pm on weekdays, all pasta dishes are priced according to the closing average of the Dow Jones Index. (If the Dow closes at 11,000, your pasta will be $11.)

Or as Sandro likes to say: 'When the Dow goes down, your value goes up!'

CAFÉ SABARSKY AUSTRIAN **$$**

Map p440 (☎212-288-0665; www.wallse.com; 1048 Fifth Ave at E 86th St; mains $12-20; 🕐breakfast, lunch & dinner; 🌿👪; [S]4/5/6 to 86th St) The lines get long at this popular cafe, which evokes opulent turn-of-the-20th-century Vienna. But the well-rendered Austrian specialties make the wait worth it. Expect crepes with smoked trout, goulash soup and creamed *spatzle* (a type of German noodle). And save room for dessert: there is a long list of specialty sweets, including a divine *sachertorte* (dark chocolate cake laced with apricot preserves).

LUKE'S SEAFOOD **$$**

Map p440 (www.lukeslobster.com; 242 E 81st St near Second Ave; lobster roll $15; 🕐11am-10pm Sun-Thu, to 11pm Fri & Sat; [S]6 to 77th St) This place delivers one hell of a succulent lobster roll: a buttered, toasted, split-top bun stuffed with chilled lobster salad that is dabbed with a swipe of mayonnaise and a sprinkle of lemon butter. It is simple and delicious.

WILLIAM GREENBERG DESSERTS BAKERY **$**

Map p440 (www.wmgreenbergdesserts.com; 1100 Madison Ave btwn 82nd & 83rd; baked goods from $1.50; 🕐8am-6:30pm Mon-Fri, to 6pm Sat, 10am-4pm Sun; 👪; [S]4/5/6 to 86th St) This pristine bakery serves up a delectable array of traditional Jewish treats including *hamantaschen* (a triangular, jam-filled cookie), cupcakes, brownies and what has to be New York City's finest black-and-white cookie, a soft vanilla disc dipped in white sugar and dark chocolate glazes. Takeout only.

VIA QUADRONNO CAFE **$$**

Map p440 (☎212-650-9880; www.viaquadronno.com; 25 E 73rd St btwn Madison & Fifth Aves; sandwiches $7-17, mains $20-26; 🕐8am-11pm Mon-Fri, 9am-11pm Sat, 10am-9pm Sun; 🌿; [S]6 to 77th St) A little slice of Italy that looks like it's been airlifted into New York, this cozy cafe-bistro has exquisite coffee (rich, not bitter), as well as a mind-boggling selection of sandwiches – one of which is stuffed with venison prosciutto and Camembert. There are soups, pastas and a very popular daily lasagna.

If you're pressed for time, belly up to the granite counter for a quick macchiato and a cookie snack.

CANDLE CAFE VEGETARIAN **$$**

Map p440 (☎212-472-0970; www.candlecafe.com; 1307 Third Ave btwn 74th & 75th Sts; mains $15-20; 🕐11:30am-10:30pm Mon-Sat, to 9:30pm Sun; 🌿; [S]6 to 77th St) The moneyed, yoga set piles into this attractive vegan cafe serving a long list of sandwiches, salads, comfort food and market-driven specials. The specialty here is the house-made seitan. (Try it crusted with porcini and served with mashed potatoes and gravy – the perfect cold-day dish.) There is a juice bar and a gluten-free menu.

For a more upscale take on the subject, check out its sister restaurant, **Candle 7** (Map p440; www.candle79.com; 154 E 79th St at Lexington Ave; mains $19-24; 🕐lunch & dinner; 🌿; 6 to 77th St), two blocks away.

JG MELON PUB **$**

Map p440 (☎212-744-0585; 1291 Third Ave at 74th St; burgers $10; 🕐11:30am-4am; [S]6 to 77th St) JG's is a loud, old-school, melon-themed pub that has been serving basic burgers on tea plates since 1972. It's a local favorite for both eating and drinking (the Bloody Marys are excellent) and it gets crowded in the after-work hours. If you're feeling claustrophobic, try lunchtime instead.

YURA ON MADISON DELI **$**

Map p440 (www.yuraonmadison.com; 1292 Madison Ave at 92nd St; sandwiches $6-9, box lunches $7-10; 🕐6:30am-7pm Mon-Fri, 7am-4pm Sat & Sun; 🌿👪; [S]6 to 96th St) This crisp, white emporium of yuppiedom sells fresh sandwiches, premade salads and excellent scones. Everything here is designed for quick eating or takeout. The ready-made box lunches are ideal for Central Park picnics.

DAN HERRICK / LONELY PLANET IMAGES ©

3

DAN HERRICK / LONELY PLANET IMAGES ©

1. Whitney Museum of American Art (p217)
The Whitney houses works by 20th-century masters and holds a biennial survey of contemporary art.

2. Neue Galerie (p218)
Works by German and Austrian artists are on show in a restored 1914 mansion.

3. Frick Collection (p217)
This beaux arts building is just as beautiful as the spectacular collection of art housed inside.

DRINKING & NIGHTLIFE

The choices here are extreme: luxury lounges or frat-house vomitoriums (the latter are along Second Ave in the high 70s into the 90s), with little to choose from in between.

METROPOLITAN MUSEUM ROOF GARDEN CAFÉ & MARTINI BAR — COCKTAIL BAR

Map p440 (www.metmuseum.org; 1000 Fifth Ave at 82nd St; ⏲10am-4:30pm Sun & Tue-Thu, to 8pm Fri & Sat, Martini Bar 5:30-8pm Fri & Sat May-Oct; [S]4/5/6 to 86th St) The sort of setting you can't get enough of (even if you are a jaded local). The roof garden's bar sits right above Central Park's tree canopy, allowing for splendid views of the park and the city skyline all around. Sunset is when you'll find fools in love – then again, it could all be those martinis.

BEMELMANS BAR — LOUNGE

Map p440 (www.thecarlyle.com/dining/bemelmans_bar; Carlyle Hotel, 35 E 76th St at Madison Ave; ⏲noon-2am Mon-Sat, to 12:30am Sun; [S]6 to 77th St) Sink into a chocolate leather banquette and take in the glorious 1940s elegance of this fabled bar – the sort of place where the waiters wear white jackets, a baby grand is always tinkling and the ceiling is 24-carat gold leaf. Show up before 9:30pm if you don't want to pay a cover (per person $15 to $30).

HEIDELBERG — BEER GARDEN

Map p440 (www.heidelbergrestaurant.com; 1648 Second Ave btwn 85th & 86th Sts; ⏲11:30am-10pm Sun-Thu, to 11pm Fri & Sat; [S]4/5/6 to 86th St) Beer, schnapps and schnitzel. This old-school German beer garden supplies the trifecta of Teutonic pleasure – as well as servers decked out in Bavarian costume. Feeling thirsty? You can order your Spaten in a 2L Stiefel (glass boot). Hokey-good fun. *Ein Prosit!*

LUKE'S BAR & GRILL — PUB

Map p440 (www.lukesbarandgrill.com; 1394 Third Ave btwn 79th & 80th St; ⏲11:30am-1am Mon-Fri, to 2am Sat; [S]6 to 77th St) This laid-back local hangout offers a respite from Red Bull and ridiculous drink prices, with an inexpensive selection of beers and solid pub grub. Cash only.

IGGY'S — KARAOKE

Map p440 (www.iggysnewyork.com; 1452 Second Ave; ⏲noon-4am; [S]6 to 77th St) How much you love this skinny Irish-lite pub with its 100ft long bar depends on how badly you need to misbehave in the Upper East Side. The karaoke mic certainly helps the raucous regulars, who bring on a bit of a frat-house atmosphere some nights.

ENTERTAINMENT

FEINSTEIN'S AT THE REGENCY — CABARET

Map p440 (☎212-339-4095; www.feinsteinsattheregency.com; 540 Park Ave at 61st St; tickets $40-280; [S]F to Lexington Ave-63rd St, N/Q/R to Lexington Ave-59th St) You'll be puttin' on the ritz at this old-school cabaret spot from crooner Michael Feinstein. The storied stage has hosted everyone from Rosemary Clooney to Vikki Carr to Tony Danza. (Yes, Tony Danza.) It's a small room, so buy tickets in advance for big-name Broadway acts.

CAFÉ CARLYLE — CLUB

Map p440 (☎212-744-1600; www.thecarlyle.com/dining/cafe_carlyle; 35 E 76th St at Madison Ave; cover $90-175; [S]6 to 77th St) This swanky spot at the Carlyle Hotel draws top-shelf talent, from Bettye Lavette to Woody Allen, who plays his clarinet here with the Eddy Davis New Orleans Jazz Band on Mondays at 8:45pm (September through May). Bring bucks: the cover doesn't include food or drinks.

FRICK COLLECTION — CLASSICAL MUSIC

Map p440 (☎212-288-0700; www.frick.org; 1 E 70th St at Fifth Ave; [S]6 to 68th St-Hunter College) This opulent mansion-museum also hosts Sunday concerts that bring world-renowned performers such as cellist Yehuda Hanani and violinist Thomas Zehetmair. This is a lovely, intimate space and a very special type of concert experience.

92ND STREET Y — PERFORMING ARTS

Map p440 (☎212-415-5500; www.92y.org; 1395 Lexington Ave at 92nd St; 👪; [S]6 to 96th St) In addition to its wide spectrum of wonderful readings, this nonprofit cultural center hosts an excellent lecture and conversation series. Past presenters have included playwright Edward Albee, cellist Yo-Yo Ma, crooner Lou Reed and novelist Gary Shteyngart.

COMIC STRIP LIVE
COMEDY

Map p440 (☎212-861-9386; www.comicstriplive. com; 1568 Second Ave btwn 81st & 82nd Sts; $22-28 plus 2-drink min; ⊘shows 8:30pm Sun-Thu; 8:30pm, 10:30pm & 12:30am Fri; 8pm, 10:30pm & 12:30am Sat; Ⓢ4/5/6 to 86th St) Adam Sandler, Jerry Seinfeld and Eddie Murphy have all performed at this club. Not recently, but you're sure to find somebody stealing their acts here most nights. Seriously folks, it'll get you out of your hotel room for a few laughs – at least until you get your bill. *Is this thing on?* Reservations required.

🛍 SHOPPING

The Upper East Side isn't for amateurs. Madison Ave (from 60th St to 72nd St) features one of the globe's glitziest stretches of retail: the flagship boutiques of some of the world's top designers, including Gucci, Prada and Cartier. The neighborhood is also a good spot to hunt down designer deals at consignment shops.

ENCORE
CONSIGNMENT STORE

Map p440 (www.encoreresale.com; 1132 Madison Ave btwn 84th & 85th Sts; ⊘10:30am-6:30pm Fri-Wed, to 7:30pm Thu, noon-6pm Sun; Ⓢ4/5/6 to 86th St) An exclusive consignment store has been emptying out Upper East Side closets since the 1950s. (Jacqueline Kennedy Onassis used to sell her clothes here.) Expect to find a gently worn array of name brands such as Louboutin, Fendi and Dior. Prices are high but infinitely better than retail.

ARTHRITIS FOUNDATION THRIFT SHOP
THRIFT STORE

Map p440 (1430 Third Ave at 81st St; ⊘9:30am-6pm Mon-Wed & Sat, to 8pm Thu; Ⓢ4/5/6 to 86th St) When local bargain hunters are looking for steals, this is where they head: a charity-driven Upper East Side thrift store where cheap designer frocks are known to materialize within stacks of everyday cast-offs. Closed on the weekends in July and August.

MICHAEL'S
CONSIGNMENT STORE

Map p440 (www.michaelsconsignment.com; 2nd fl, 1041 Madison Ave btwn 79th & 80th Sts; ⊘9:30am-6pm Mon-Wed, Fri & Sat, to 8pm Thu; Ⓢ6 to 77th St) In operation since the 1950s, this is a vaunted Upper East Side resale store that is strong on high-end labels, including Chanel, Gucci and Prada. Almost everything on display is less than two years old. It's pricey, but cheaper than shopping the flagship boutiques on Madison Ave.

CRAWFORD DOYLE BOOKSELLERS
BOOKS

Map p440 (1082 Madison Ave btwn 81st & 82nd Sts; ⊘10am-6pm Mon-Sat, noon-5pm Sun; Ⓢ6 to 77th St) This genteel Upper East Side bookshop invites browsing, with stacks devoted to art, literature and the history of New York – not to mention plenty of first editions. A wonderful place to while away a chilly afternoon.

BLUE TREE
CLOTHING, GIFTS

Map p440 (www.bluetreenyc.com; 1283 Madison Ave btwn 91st & 92nd Sts; ⊘10am-6pm Mon-Fri, 11am-6pm Sat & Sun; Ⓢ4/5/6 to 86th St) This charming (and pricey) little boutique sells a dainty array of women's clothing, Lucite objects, and quirky home design like pig butter dishes and metallic Harry Allen banana bowls.

ZITOMER
BEAUTY

Map p440 (www.zitomer.com; 969 Madison Ave btwn 75th & 76th Sts; ⊘9am-8pm Mon-Fri, to 7pm Sat, 10am-6pm Sun; Ⓢ6 to 77th St) This three-story retro pharmacy carries all things European, including products that aren't exactly (ahem) FDA approved. We're not talking illicit drugs, just high-powered sunscreens and skin-care creams that are usually only available across the pond. An excellent spot to cure what ails you, or simply window shop.

🏃 SPORTS & ACTIVITIES

ASPHALT GREEN
SWIMMING

Map p440 (☎212-369-8890; www.asphaltgreen. org; 555 E 90th St btwn York & East End Aves; gym & pool pass $35; ⊘5:30am-9:45pm Mon-Fri, 8am-7:45pm Sat & Sun; ♿; Ⓢ4/5/6 to 86th St) Not to be confused with the 1973 Charlton Heston sci-fi film *Soylent Green*, the Asphalt Green fitness center is set in a former municipal asphalt plant. There is an excellent 50m Olympic-size pool, as well as a smaller pool for classes. Some hours are for members only. There are programs for kids.

NEW YORK ROAD RUNNERS CLUB

RUNNING

Map p440 (☎212-860-4455; www.nyrrc.org; 9 E 89th St btwn Madison & Fifth Aves; ☉10am-8pm Mon-Fri, to 5pm Sat, to 3pm Sun; Ⓢ4/5/6 to 86th St) This long-time club, and organizer of the New York City Marathon, coordinates runs throughout the year, including a midnight fun run on New Year's Eve.

EXHALE

SPA

Map p440 (☎212-561-6400; www.exhalespa. com; 980 Madison Ave btwn 76th & 77th Sts; 1hr massage from $130) This Zen-like spa offers all the standard treatments, including massages, facials and scrubs. There is also yoga, acupuncture and cupping. Prepare to emerge relaxed.

Upper West Side & Central Park

UPPER WEST SIDE | CENTRAL PARK | LINCOLN CENTER

Neighborhood Top Five

1 Escaping the city's frantic urban madness to lounge on a great lawn, stroll amid statues honoring literary heroes or jog around a lovely reservoir in one of the world's most famous green zones: **Central Park** (p229).

2 Going to the **Metropolitan Opera House** (p239) to wallow in the operatic trials of Rigoletto, Carmen and Figaro.

3 Walking among the world's largest dinosaurs at the **American Museum of Natural History** (p234).

4 Taking a pilgrimage to Tibet without leaving New York City at the **Nicholas Roerich Museum** (p234).

5 Stocking up on gut-filling knishes and German marble cake at **Zabar's** (p235).

For more detail of this area, see Map p442 ➡

Lonely Planet's Top Tip

The best way to cover all 840 acres of Central Park is to rent a bicycle. Bike & Roll (p244) at Columbus Circle and the Loeb Boathouse (p244) inside the park both offer rentals. If starting at the Loeb Boathouse, pedal north along East Dr to see the Great Lawn, the reservoir, the Conservatory Garden and Harlem Meer. From the Great Hill, you can coast down West Dr, past the Delacorte Theater and end up at Strawberry Fields. (Weather permitting.)

✖ Best Places to Eat

➡ Fatty Crab (p235)

➡ Absolute Bagels (p236)

➡ Gray's Papaya (p236)

➡ Dovetail (p236)

For reviews, see p235 ➡

🍷 Best Places to Drink

➡ Ding Dong Lounge (p238)

➡ Dead Poet (p238)

➡ Barcibo Enoteca (p238)

➡ Malachy's (p238)

For reviews, see p238 ➡

☆ Best Places for Music

➡ Metropolitan Opera House (p239)

➡ SummerStage (p238)

➡ Cleopatra's Needle Club (p242)

➡ Beacon Theatre (p242)

For reviews, see p238 ➡

Explore Upper West Side & Central Park

Manhattan's midsection is a lot of ground to cover – and the best plan of attack will depend on your flavor. Traveling with tykes? Then wear them out with a visit to the Museum of Natural History, followed by a journey through the sprawling adventure wonderland that is Central Park. If the high arts are your pleasure, then make for Lincoln Center – where the Metropolitan Opera, the New York Philharmonic and the New York City Ballet all inject the city with vibrant doses of culture. And, if your idea of a good time is just ambling around, then take in the sights in and off Broadway in the 70s, an area cluttered with bustling shops and fine architecture.

Local Life

➡ **Go fishing** Wood-smoked lox. Briny pickled herring. Meaty sturgeon. It doesn't get more Upper West Side than examining the seafood treats at Zabar's (p235) and Barney Greengrass (p236).

➡ **Central chill** You can pick out the tourists in Central Park because they're rushing to see sights. Make like a local by picking out a patch of green with good views and letting the world come to you.

➡ **Catch a flick** Manhattan's diehard film buffs can be found taking in quality cinema courtesy of the Film Society of Lincoln Center (p239).

➡ **Late-night munchies** Nothing is more New York than soaking up the evening's liquor damage with a midnight hot dog from Gray's Papaya (p236).

Getting There & Away

➡ **Subway** On the Upper West Side, the 1, 2 and 3 subway lines are good for destinations along Broadway and points west, while the B and C trains are best for points of interest and access to Central Park. The park can be accessed from all sides, making every subway that travels north/south through Manhattan convenient. The A, C, B, D and 1 all stop at Columbus Circle at Central Park's southwestern edge, while the N, R or Q will leave you at the southeast corner. The 2 or 3 will deposit you at the northern gate in Harlem.

➡ **Bus** The M104 bus runs north to south along Broadway, and the M10 plies the scenic ride along the western edge of the park. Crosstown buses at 66th, 72nd, 79th, 86th and 96th Sts take you through the park to the Upper East Side. Note that these pick up and drop off passengers at the edge of the park – not inside.

RACHEL LEWIS / LONELY PLANET IMAGES ©

CENTRAL PARK

Comprising more than 800 acres of picturesque meadows, ponds and woods, it might be tempting to think that Central Park represents Manhattan in its raw state. It does not. Designed by Frederick Law Olmsted and Calvert Vaux, the park is the result of serious engineering: thousands of workers shifted 10 million cartloads of soil to transform swamp and rocky outcroppings into the 'people's park' of today.

Birth of the Park

In the 1850s, the area was occupied by pig farms, a garbage dump, a bone-boiling operation and an African American village. It took 20,000 laborers 20 years to transform this terrain into a park. Today, Central Park has more than 24,000 trees, 136 acres of woodland, 21 playgrounds and seven bodies of water. It attracts more than 38 million visitors a year.

Strawberry Fields

This tear-shaped **garden** (Map p442; at 72nd St on the west side; ♿; S A/C, B to 72nd St) serves as a memorial to former Beatle John Lennon. The garden is composed of a grove of stately elms and a tiled mosaic that reads, simply, 'Imagine.'

Bethesda Terrace & the Mall

The arched walkways of **Bethesda Terrace**, crowned by the magnificent **Bethesda Fountain** (Map p442; at the level of 72nd St), have long been a gathering area for New Yorkers of all flavors. To the south is the Mall (featured in countless movies), a promenade shrouded in

DON'T MISS...

➡ The Mall
➡ The Reservoir
➡ Conservatory Garden
➡ Central Park Zoo

PRACTICALITIES

➡ Map p442
➡ www.central parknyc.org
➡ 59th & 110th Sts btwn Central Park West & Fifth Ave
➡ ◷6am-1am
➡ ♿

THE LUNGS OF NEW YORK

The rectangular patch of green that occupies Manhattan's heart began life in the mid-19th century as a swampy piece of land that was carefully bulldozed into the idyllic naturescape you see today. Since officially becoming Central Park, it has brought New Yorkers of all stripes together in interesting and unexpected ways. The park has served as a place for the rich to show off their fancy carriages (1860s), for the poor to enjoy free Sunday concerts (1880s) and for activists to hold be-ins against the Vietnam War (1960s). Since then, legions of locals – not to mention travelers from all kinds of faraway places – have poured in to stroll, picnic, sunbathe, play ball and catch free concerts and performances of works by Shakespeare.

The park's varied terrain offers a wonderland of experiences. There are quiet, woodsy knolls in the north. To the south is the

Loeb Boathouse
Perched on the shores of the Lake, the historic Loeb Boathouse is one of the city's best settings for an idyllic meal. You can also rent rowboats and bicycles and ride on a Venetian gondola.

Duke Ellington Circle

Harlem Meer

The Blockhouse

North Woods

97th St Transverse

Fifth Ave

86th St Transverse

The Great Lawn

Central Park West

Conservatory Garden
The only formal garden in Central Park is perhaps the most tranquil. On the northern end, chrysanthemums bloom in late October. To the south, the park's largest crab apple tree grows by the Burnett Fountain.

STEVEN GREAVES / LPI ©

Jacqueline Kennedy Onassis Reservoir
This 106-acre body of water covers roughly an eighth of the park's territory. Its original purpose was to provide clean water for the city. Now it's a good spot to catch a glimpse of waterbirds.

ANGUS OSBORN / LPI ©

Belvedere Castle
A so-called 'Victorian folly,' this Gothic-Romanesque castle serves no other purpose than to be a very dramatic lookout point. It was built by Central Park co-designer Calvert Vaux in 1869.

reservoir, crowded with joggers. There are European gardens, a zoo and various bodies of water. For maximum flamboyance, hit the Sheep Meadow on a sunny day, when all of New York shows up to lounge.

Central Park is more than just a green space. It is New York City's backyard.

FACTS & FIGURES

» **Landscape architects** Frederick Law Olmsted and Calvert Vaux

» **Year that construction began** 1858

» **Acres** 843

» **On film** Hundreds of movies have been shot on location, from Depression-era blockbusters such as *Gold Diggers* (1933) to the monster-attack flick *Cloverfield*.

Conservatory Water
This pond is popular in the warmer months, when children sail their model boats across its surface. Conservatory Water was inspired by 19th-century Parisian model-boat ponds and figured prominently in EB White's classic book, *Stuart Little*.

Bethesda Fountain
This neoclassical fountain is one of New York's largest. It's capped by the *Angel of the Waters*, who is supported by four cherubim. The fountain was created by bohemian-feminist sculptor Emma Stebbins in 1868.

Metropolitan Museum of Art

Alice in Wonderland Statue

79th St Transverse

The Ramble

Delacorte Theater

The Lake

Fifth Ave

Central Park Zoo

65th St Transverse

Sheep Meadow

Strawberry Fields
A simple mosaic memorial pays tribute to musician John Lennon, who was killed across the street outside the Dakota Building. Funded by Yoko Ono, its name is inspired by the Beatles song 'Strawberry Fields Forever.'

The Mall / Literary Walk
A Parisian-style promenade – the only straight line in the park – is flanked by statues of literati on the southern end, including Robert Burns and Shakespeare. It is lined with rare North American elms.

Columbus Center

CONSERVATORY GARDEN

If you want a little peace and quiet (as in, no runners, cyclists or boom boxes), the six-acre Conservatory Garden serves as one of the park's official quiet zones. And it's beautiful, to boot: bursting with crabapple trees, meandering boxwood and, in the spring, lots of flowers. It's located at 105th St off of Fifth Ave. Otherwise, you can catch maximum calm (and maximum bird life) in all areas of the park just after dawn.

The North Woods, on the west side between 106th and 110th Sts, is home to the park's oldest structure, the Blockhouse, a military fortification from the War of 1812.

VISITING THE PARK

Free and custom walking tours are available via the Central Park Conservancy (www.centralparknyc.org/walkingtours), the nonprofit organization that supports park maintenance.

mature North American elms. The southern stretch, known as **Literary Walk** (Map p442), is flanked by statues of famous authors.

Central Park Zoo

Officially known as the Central Park Wildlife Center (no one calls it that), this small **zoo** (Map p442; ☎212-861-6030; www.centralparkzoo.com; 64th St at Fifth Ave; adult/child $12/7; ⌚10am-5pm Apr-Oct, to 4:30pm Nov-Mar; 👪; [S]N/Q/R to 5th Ave-59th St) is home to penguins, polar bears, snow leopards and red pandas. Feeding times in the sea lion and penguin tanks make for a rowdy spectacle. Check the website for times.

The attached **Tisch Children's Zoo** (Map p442; www.centralparkzoo.com; cnr 65th & Fifth Ave), a petting zoo, has alpacas and mini-Nubian goats and is perfect for small children.

Conservatory Water & Around

North of the zoo at the level of 74th St is the Conservatory Water, where model sailboats drift lazily and kids scramble about on a toadstool-studded statue of Alice in Wonderland. There are Saturday story hours at the Hans Christian Andersen statue to the west of the water (at 11am from June to September).

Great Lawn & the Ramble

The **Great Lawn** (Map p442; btwn 72nd & 86th Sts; [S]B, C to 86th St) is a massive emerald carpet at the center of the park – between 79th and 86th Sts – and is surrounded by ball fields and London plane trees. (This is where Simon & Garfunkel played their famous 1981 concert.) Immediately to the southeast is the **Delacorte Theater** (Map p442; enter at Central Park West at 81st St), home to an annual Shakespeare in the Park (p26), as well as Belvedere Castle (p244), a lookout.

Further south, between 72nd and 79th Sts, is the leafy **Ramble** (Map p442; mid-park from 73rd to 79th Sts), a popular birding destination (and legendary gay pick-up spot). On the southeastern end is the Loeb Boathouse (p244), home to a waterside restaurant that offers rowboat and bicycle rentals.

Jacqueline Kennedy Onassis Reservoir

The reservoir takes up almost the entire width of the park at the level of 90th street and serves as a gorgeous reflecting pool for the city skyline. It is surrounded by a 1.58-mile track that draws legions of joggers in the warmer months. Nearby, at Fifth Ave and 90th St, is a statue of New York City Marathon founder Fred Lebow, peering at his watch.

TOP SIGHTS
LINCOLN CENTER

This stark arrangement of gleaming modernist temples contains some of Manhattan's most important performance spaces: Avery Fisher Hall (home to the New York Philharmonic), David H Koch Theater (site of the New York City ballet), and the iconic Metropolitan Opera House, whose interior walls are dressed with brightly saturated murals by painter Marc Chagall. Various other venues are tucked in and around the 16-acre campus, including a theater, two film screening centers and the renowned Juilliard School.

A History of Building & Rebuilding

Built in the 1960s, this imposing campus replaced a group of tenements called San Juan Hill, a predominantly African American neighborhood where the exterior shots for the movie *West Side Story* were filmed. In addition to being a controversial urban planning move, Lincoln Center wasn't exactly well received at an architectural level – it was relentlessly criticized for its conservative design, fortress-like aspect and poor acoustics. For the center's 50th anniversary (2009–10), Diller Scofidio + Renfro and other architects gave the complex a much-needed and critically acclaimed freshening up.

Highlights

A survey of the three classic buildings surrounding Revson Fountain is a must. These include the Metropolitan Opera, Avery Fisher Hall and the David H Koch Theater, the latter designed by Philip Johnson. The fountain is spectacular in the evenings when it puts on Las Vegas–like light shows. These are all located on the main plaza at Columbus Ave, between 62nd and 65th Sts.

Of the refurbished structures, there are a number that are worth examining, including **Alice Tully Hall** (Map p442; cnr 65th St & Broadway), now displaying a very contemporary translucent, angled facade, and the **David Rubenstein Atrium** (Map p442; Broadway btwn 62nd & 63rd Sts), a public space offering a lounge area (free wi-fi), a cafe, an information desk and a ticket vendor plying day-of discount tickets to Lincoln Center performances. Free events are held here on Thursday evenings.

Performances & Screenings

On any given night, there are at least 10 performances happening throughout Lincoln Center – and even more in summer, when Lincoln Center Out of Doors (a series of dance and music concerts) and Midsummer Night Swing (ballroom dancing under the stars) lure those who love parks and culture. For details on seasons, tickets and programming – which runs the gamut from opera to dance to theater to ballet – turn to the Entertainment section (p238) of this chapter.

Tours

Daily tours of the complex explore the Metropolitan Opera House, Revson Fountain and Alice Tully Hall and are a great way to get acquainted with the complex.

DON'T MISS...

- Metropolitan Opera House
- Revson Fountain at night
- Alice Tully Hall

PRACTICALITIES

- Map p442
- ☎212-875-5456, tours 212-875-5350
- www.lincolncenter.org
- Columbus Ave btwn 62nd & 66th Sts
- public plazas free, tours adult/child $15/8
- 🕒performance hrs vary, tours 10:30am & 4:30pm
- 👪
- [S]1 to 66th St-Lincoln Center

SIGHTS

The stretch of Manhattan that lies to the west of Central Park was once a lively mix of African American, Latino and German Jewish immigrant communities. These days it's still holding on to its Jewish bonafides (this is where you'll find some of the best smoked fish in town), but in recent decades the neighborhood has also been a base for well-to-do artsy types, young professionals and the stroller set.

While real estate developers have seen fit to carpet long stretches of Broadway with charmless chain stores, the rest of the neighborhood is an architectural bonanza, featuring residential dwellings built in beaux arts, baroque, neo-Gothic and postwar styles. You'll find some of the poshest pads lining Central Park West, among them the Dakota (on the northwest corner of 72nd St), where John Lennon once lived.

Upper West Side

LINCOLN CENTER — CULTURAL CENTER

See p233.

AMERICAN MUSEUM OF NATURAL HISTORY — MUSEUM

Map p442 (www.amnh.org; Central Park West at 79th St; admission suggested donation adult/child $16/9, interactive exhibits $14-24; ⏲10am-5:45pm, Rose Center to 8:45pm Fri, Butterfly Conservancy Oct-May; 👪; [S]B, C to 81st St-Museum of Natural History; 1 to 79th St) Founded in 1869, this classic museum contains a veritable wonderland of more 30 million artifacts, including lots of menacing dinosaur skeletons, as well as the Rose Center for Earth & Space, with its cutting-edge planetarium. From October through May, the museum is home to the Butterfly Conservatory, a glasshouse featuring 500-plus butterflies from all over the world.

On the natural history side, the museum is perhaps best known for its Fossil Halls, containing nearly 600 specimens on view, including the skeletons of a massive mammoth and a fearsome Tyrannosaurus Rex.

There are also plentiful animal exhibits (the stuffed Alaskan brown bear is popular), galleries devoted to gems and an IMAX theater that plays films on natural phenomena. The Milstein Hall of Ocean Life contains dioramas devoted to ecologies, weather and conservation, as well as a beloved 94ft replica of a blue whale. At the 77th St Lobby Gallery visitors are greeted by a 63ft canoe carved by the Haida people of British Columbia in the middle of the 19th century.

For the space set, it's the Rose Center that is the star of the show. With its mesmerizing glass box facade, home to space-show theaters and the planetarium – it is indeed an otherworldly setting. Every half-hour between 10:30am and 4:30pm, you can drop yourself into a cushy seat to view *Journey to the Stars*, which charts the life and death of astral bodies using telescopic images and hallucinatory visualizations – the sort of thing that will have you exclaiming, 'Whoaaaaaa.'

Needless to say, the museum is a hit with kids, and as a result, it's swamped on weekends. Early on a weekday is the best time to go.

NICHOLAS ROERICH MUSEUM — MUSEUM

Map p442 (www.roerich.org; 319 W 107th St btwn Riverside Dr & Broadway; suggested donation $5; ⏲noon-5pm Tue-Fri, 2-5pm Sat & Sun; [S]1 to Cathedral Pkwy) This compelling little museum, housed in a three-story townhouse from 1898, is one of the city's best-kept secrets. It contains more than 200 paintings by the prolific Nicholas Konstantinovich Roerich (1874–1947), a Russian-born poet, philosopher and painter. His most remarkable works are his stunning depictions of the Himalayas, where he often traveled.

While the collection includes early modern figure paintings and religious scenes (the latter of which are quite forgettable), his mountainscapes are truly a wonder to behold: icy Tibetan peaks in shades of blue, white, green and purple channeling a Georgia O'Keeffe/Rockwell Kent vibe. This is a curious and intriguing place. Worth a visit.

NEW-YORK HISTORICAL SOCIETY — MUSEUM

Map p442 (www.nyhistory.org; 2 W 77th St at Central Park West; adult/child $15/5, by donation 6-8pm Fri, library free; ⏲10am-6pm Tue-Thu & Sat, to 8pm Fri, 11am-5pm Sun; [S]B, C to 81st St-Museum of Natural History) As the antiquated hyphenated name implies, the Historical Society is the city's oldest museum, founded in 1804 to preserve the city's historical and cultural artifacts. Its collection of more than 60,000 objects is quirky and fascinating and includes everything from George

Washington's inauguration chair to a 19th century Tiffany ice cream dish (gilded, of course).

Other treasures include a leg brace worn by President Franklin D Roosevelt, a 19th century mechanical bank in which a political figure slips coins into his pocket and photographer Jack Stewart's graffiti-covered door from the 1970s (featuring tags by known graffiti writers such as Tracy 168). In the lobby, be sure to look up: the ceiling mural from Keith Haring's 1986 'Pop Shop' hangs above the admissions desk.

ZABAR'S
MARKET

Map p442 (www.zabars.com; 2245 Broadway at 80th St; ⊙8am-7:30pm Mon-Fri, to 8pm Sat, 9am-6pm Sun; ⓢ1 to 79th St) A bastion of gourmet-Kosher foodie-ism, this sprawling local market has been a neighborhood fixture since the 1930s. And what a fixture it is: featuring a heavenly array of cheeses, meats, olives, caviar, smoked fish, pickles, dried fruits, nuts and baked goods, including pillowy fresh-out-of-the-oven knishes (Eastern European–style potato dumplings wrapped in dough). Street vendors sell knishes all over New York. Most are of the frozen-industrial variety and have all the flavor of freeze-dried hockey pucks. Zabar's is the place to try the real deal.

FREE AMERICAN FOLK ART MUSEUM
MUSEUM

Map p442 (www.folkartmuseum.org; 2 Lincoln Sq, Columbus Ave at 66th St; ⊙noon-7:30pm Tue-Sat, to 6pm Sun; ⓢ1 to 66th St-Lincoln Center) This tiny institution contains a couple of centuries' worth of folk and outsider art treasures, including pieces by Henry Darger (known for his girl-filled battlescapes) and Martín Ramírez (producer of hallucinatory *caballeros* on horseback). There is also an array of wood carvings, paintings, hand-tinted photographs and decorative objects. On Wednesdays there are guitar concerts, and there's free music on Fridays.

RIVERSIDE PARK
OUTDOORS

Map p442 (www.riversideparkfund.org; Riverside Dr btwn 68th & 155th Sts; ⊙6am-1am; ⓹; ⓢ1/2/3 to any stop btwn 66th & 157th Sts) A classic beauty designed by Central Park creators Frederick Law Olmsted and Calvert Vaux, this waterside spot, running north on the Upper West Side and banked by the Hudson River from 59th to 158th Sts, is lusciously leafy. Plenty of bike paths and playgrounds make it a family favorite.

From late March through October (weather permitting), a rowdy waterside restaurant, the **West 79th Street Boat Basin Café** (Map p442; www.boatbasincafe. com; W 79th St at Henry Hudson Parkway; ⊙lunch & dinner Apr-Oct, weather permitting; ⓢ1 to 79th St) serves a light menu at the level of 79th St.

CHILDREN'S MUSEUM OF MANHATTAN
MUSEUM

Map p442 (www.cmom.org; 212 W 83rd St btwn Amsterdam Ave & Broadway; admission $11; ⊙10am-5pm Tue-Sun; ⓹; ⓢB, C to 81st St-Museum of Natural History; 1 to 86th St) This small museum features interactive exhibits scaled down for the little people. This includes toddler discovery programs and exhibits that stimulate play, like operating a giant heart with a pedal or tumbling around a set with *Dora the Explorer* elements. It's not very exciting, but it can be a rainy-day saver if you're traveling with antsy toddlers.

⊙ Central Park

CENTRAL PARK
PARK

See p229.

✗ EATING

Though not known for its dining scene, this huge swath of neighborhood nonetheless manages to serve up everything from chewy bagels to fancy French cassoulets to the latest in New American cooking.

It is also ground zero for off-the-hook picnic fixings: head to Zabar's (p235) to pick up delicacies for an alfresco meal in Central Park.

✗ Upper West Side

FATTY CRAB
MALAYSIAN $

Map p442 (☎212-496-2722; www.fattycrab.com; 2170 Broadway btwn 76th & 77th Sts; Fatty Dog $12, mains $16-29; ⊙noon-11pm Mon-Wed, to midnight Thu-Sat, to 10pm Sun; ⓹; ⓢ1 to 79th St) This brick-lined, industrial chic spot steered by chef Zakary Pelaccio serves winning Malaysian-influenced specialties.

Start with sweet and sticky Julan Alor chicken wings, follow up with shrimp and pork wontons and then dig into the Dungeness crab with chili sauce. Don't forget to request extra napkins and an ice cold beer to wash it all down.

In the mood for a devastating snack? Try the 'Fatty Dog,' a plump sausage laced with chili sauce, fresh cilantro and pickled radish on a toasty bun.

CAFÉ LUXEMBOURG — FRENCH $$$

Map p442 (☎212-873-7411; www.cafeluxembourg.com; 200 W 70th St btwn Broadway & West End Ave; lunch mains $16-34, dinner mains $25-34; 🕒breakfast, lunch & dinner daily, brunch Sun; [S]1/2/3 to 72nd St) This quintessential French bistro is generally crowded with locals – and it's no mystery why: the setting is elegant, the staff is friendly, and there's an outstanding menu, to boot. The classics – salmon tartare, cassoulet and *steak frites* (fries) – are all deftly executed, and its proximity to Lincoln Center makes it a perfect pre-performance destination. There is a lighter lunch menu and there are eggy dishes at brunch.

ABSOLUTE BAGELS — BAKERY $

Map p442 (☎212-932-2052; 2788 Broadway btwn 107th & 108th Sts; bagel $1; 🕒6am-9pm Mon-Sat, to 8pm Sun; 🥕👪; [S]1 to Cathedral Parkway-110th St) This popular neighborhood bagel joint has 16 varieties of hot, chewy, hand-rolled bagels – and myriad cream cheeses to top them with (including the tofu variety).

GRAY'S PAPAYA — HOT DOGS $

Map p442 (☎212-799-0243; 2090 Broadway at 72nd St; hot dog $2; 🕒24hr; [S]A/C, B, 1/2/3 to 72nd St) It doesn't get more New York than bellying up to this classic stand-up joint in the wake of a beer bender. The lights are bright, the color palette is 1970s and the hot dogs are good. A sign on the wall says, 'Best damn frankfurter you ever ate.'

Granted, the papaya drink is more 'drink' than papaya, but you can't go wrong with Gray's famous 'Recession Special' – $4.95 for two grilled dogs and a beverage. Deal.

BARNEY GREENGRASS — DELI $$

Map p442 (☎212-724-4707; www.barneygreengrass.com; 541 Amsterdam Ave at 86th St; mains $9-18, bagel with cream cheese $5; 🕒8:30am-4pm Tue-Fri, to 5pm Sat & Sun; 👪; [S]1 to 86th St) The self-proclaimed 'King of Sturgeon' Barney Greengrass serves up the same heaping dishes of eggs and salty lox, luxuriant caviar, and melt-in-your mouth chocolate babkas that first made it famous when it opened a century ago. Pop in to fuel up in the morning or for a quick lunch; there are rickety tables set amid the crowded produce aisles.

In addition to an array of Jewish delicacies (seriously, try the smoked sturgeon), you can, of course, get a perfect New York bagel. On weekends, it has fresh garlic bialys (a type of chewy, baked roll).

[TOP CHOICE] DOVETAIL — MODERN AMERICAN $$$

Map p442 (☎212-362-3800; www.dovetailnyc.com; 103 W 77th St at Columbus Ave; tasting menu/Mon vegetarian menu $85/46, mains $34-55; 🕒5:30-10pm Mon-Sun, brunch 11:30am-2:30pm Sun; 🥕; [S]A/C, B to 81st St-Museum of Natural History; 1 to 79th St) Everything about this Michelin-starred restaurant is simple, from the decor (exposed brick, bare tables) to the uncomplicated seasonal menus focused on bracingly fresh produce and quality meats (think: pistachio crusted duck with sunchokes, dates and spinach). On Mondays, chef John Fraser has a three-course vegetarian tasting menu that is winning over carnivores with dishes like crisp cauliflower in jerk spice.

An encyclopedic wine list (from $31 per bottle) features top vintages from all over the world, including charming anecdotes about some of the vineyards. For foodies who are watching their dollars, the tasting menu is a bargain.

SHAKE SHACK — BURGERS $

Map p442 (☎646-747-8770; www.shakeshacknyc.com; 366 Columbus Ave, btwn 77th & 78th Sts; burgers $4-9, shakes $5-7; 🕒10:45am-11pm; 👪; [S]B, C, 1/2/3 to 72nd St) To the delight of moms, pops and kids all over the Upper West Side, organic eats guru Danny Meyer brought the Shake Shack to their 'hood. The burger stand has sundaes, shakes, thick fresh burgers and crispy curly fries, just like the original in Madison Square Park.

KEFI — GREEK $$

Map p442 (☎212-873-0200; www.kefirestaurant.com; 505 Columbus Ave btwn 84th & 85th Sts; lunch mains $9-18, dinner mains $11-18; 🕒noon-3pm Mon-Fri, dinner 5-10pm daily, brunch 11am-3pm Sat & Sun; 👪; [S]B, C to 86th St) This homey, whitewashed eatery run by chef Michael Psilakis channels a sleek taverna vibe while dispensing excellent rustic Greek dishes.

Expect favorites like spicy lamb sausage, sheep-milk dumplings and grilled octopus. The platter featuring four types of spreads is delicious, as is the flat pasta with braised rabbit. The wine list features a vast selection of Greek vintages (from $22 per bottle).

MOMOFUKU MILK BAR ASIAN $

Map p442 (www.momofuku.com; 561 Columbus Ave btwn 87th & 88th Sts; pork buns $8; 🕑8am-10pm; [S]A/C, B to 86th St) Two words: pork buns. And not just any pork buns, but David Chang's slow-braised-pork on a puffy-steamed-bun-concoction, which will make you wish that pork was a major food group. There are also plenty of diabetes-inducing baked goods, including chewy-delicious cornflake-marshmallow cookies that seem to be designed to rip out your fillings. Check the website for Chang's other NYC offerings.

PEACEFOOD CAFE VEGAN $$

Map p442 (☎212-362-2266; www.peacefoodcafe.com; 460 Amsterdam Ave at 82nd St; panini $13, mains $10-17; 🕑lunch & dinner; 🌶; [S]1 to 79th St) This bright and airy vegan haven run by Eric Yu dishes up a popular fried seitan panino (served on homemade focaccia and topped with cashew, arugula, tomatoes and pesto), as well as an excellent quinoa salad. There are daily raw specials, organic coffees and delectable bakery selections. Healthy and good.

SALUMERIA ROSI PARMACOTTO ITALIAN $$

Map p442 (☎212-877-4800; www.salumeriarosi.com; 284 Amsterdam Ave at 73rd St; mains $11-14; 🕑11am-11pm; [S]1/2/3 to 72nd St) This is an intimate little meat-loving nook where you can dip into tasting plates that feature cheeses, salumi, slow-roasted pork loin, sausages, cured hams and every other piece of the pig you care to imagine. There are other tasty Tuscan-inspired offerings, too, including homemade lasagna, savory leek tart, escarole-anchovy salad and hand-rolled sweet-potato gnocchi.

PJ CLARKE'S PUB $$

Map p442 (☎212-957-9700; www.pjclarkes.com; 44 W 63rd St at Broadway; burgers $10-14, mains $18-40; 🕑11:30am-1am; [S]1 to 66th St-Lincoln Center) Right across the street from Lincoln Center, this red-checker-tablecloth spot has a buttoned down crowd, friendly bartenders and solid eats. If you're in a rush, belly up to the bar for a Black Angus burger and a Brooklyn Lager. A raw bar offers fresh Long Island Little Neck and Cherry Stone clams, as well as jumbo shrimp cocktails.

HUMMUS PLACE MIDDLE EASTERN $

Map p442 (☎212-799-3335; www.hummusplace.com; 305 Amsterdam Ave btwn 74th & 75th Sts; hummus from $8, mains $8-11; 🕑lunch & dinner; 🌶; [S]1/2/3 to 72nd St) Hummus Place is nothing special in the way of ambience – about eight tables tucked just below street level, fronting a cramped, open kitchen – but it's got amazing hummus platters. They're served warm and with various toppings, from whole chickpeas to fava-bean stew with chopped egg. You'll also find tasty salads, couscous and stuffed grape leaves. A great value.

BIG NICK'S BURGERS $

Map p442 (www.bignicksnyc.com; 2175 Broadway btwn 76th & 77th Sts; burgers $7-13; 🕑24hr; [S]1 to 79th St) This grimy dive is an institution – not for its food, but for its overwhelming 27-page menu and cluttered walls. (There isn't a surface that doesn't have a framed something on it.) It serves everything from pizza to baked clams, but do yourself a favor and stick to the burgers, a good way of countering a night of boozing. It's better in summer when you can sit at one of the outdoor tables and avoid smelling like french fries.

FAIRWAY SELF-CATERING $

Map p442 (☎212-595-1888; www.fairwaymarket.com; 2127 Broadway at 75th St; 🕑6am-1am; [S]1/2/3 to 72nd St) Like a museum of good eats, this incredible grocery spills its lovely mounds of produce into its sidewalk bins, seducing you inside with international goodies, fine cooking oils, nuts, cheeses, prepared foods and, upstairs, an organic market and cafe.

🍴 Central Park

LOEB BOATHOUSE AMERICAN $$$

Map p442 (☎212-517-2233; www.thecentralparkboathouse.com; Central Park Lake, Central Park at 74th St; mains $22-44; 🕑lunch daily, brunch Sat & Sun year-round, dinner daily Apr-Nov; [S]A/C, B to 72nd St; 6 to 77th St) Perched on the northeastern tip of the Central Park Lake, the Loeb Boathouse, with its views of the Midtown skyline in the distance, provides one of New York's most idyllic spots for a meal. That said, what you're paying for is the setting. While the food is generally good (the crab cakes are the standout), we've often found the service to be indifferent.

If you want to experience the location without having to lay out the bucks, a better bet is to hit the adjacent Bar & Grill, which offers a limited bar menu (plates $16), where you can still get crabcakes and excellent views.

🍷 DRINKING & NIGHTLIFE

A noted family neighborhood, the Upper West Side isn't exactly the number one destination for hardcore drinkers. But it has its moments, with some good dives, pubs and wine bars.

MALACHY'S — PUB

Map p442 (www.malachys.com; 103 W 72nd St btwn Amsterdam & Columbus Aves; 🕒noon-4am; [S]B/C, 1/2/3 to 72nd St) Giving new meaning to the word 'dive,' this crusty local holdout has a long bar, a lineup of regulars and a bartender with a sense of humor. In other words: the perfect place for day-time drinking. There's also a cheap menu.

BARCIBO ENOTECA — WINE BAR

Map p442 (www.barciboenoteca.com; 2020 Broadway at 69th St; 🕒4:30pm-2am; [S]1/2/3 to 72nd St) Just north of Lincoln Center, this casual chic marble-table spot is ideal for sipping, with a long list of vintages from all over Italy, including 40 different varieties sold by the glass. There is a short menu of small plates and light meals. The staff is knowledgeable; ask for recommendations.

DEAD POET — BAR

Map p442 (www.thedeadpoet.com; 450 Amsterdam Ave btwn 81st & 82nd Sts; 🕒9am-4am Mon-Sat, noon-4am Sun; [S]1 to 79th St) This skinny, mahogany-paneled pub has been a neighborhood favorite for over a decade, with a mix of locals and students nursing pints of Guinness. There are cocktails named after dead poets, including a Jack Kerouac margarita ($12) and a Pablo Neruda spiced rum sangria ($9). Funny, because we always pegged Neruda as a pisco sour kind of guy.

DING DONG LOUNGE — BAR

Map p442 (www.dingdonglounge.com; 929 Columbus Ave btwn 105th & 106th Sts; [S]B, C, 1 to 103rd St) It's hard to be too bad-ass in the Upper West, but this former crack den turned punk bar makes a wholesome attempt by supplying graffiti-covered bathrooms to go with its exposed-brick walls. It also, interestingly, features an array of cuckoo clocks. It's popular with Columbia students and guests from nearby hostels for its beer-and-a-shot combo (only $6).

SIP — COCKTAIL BAR

Map p442 (www.sipbar.com; 998 Amsterdam Ave btwn 109th & 110th Sts; 🕒10:30am-4am; [S]1 to Cathedral Parkway-110 St) This quirky storefront decked out in bright tile and red leather serves as coffeehouse by day and friendly little cocktail lounge by night. The mixologists here produce various signature drinks including, appropriately enough, a cappuccino martini. There are tapas, too, including small plates of chorizo and cheeses.

☆ ENTERTAINMENT

☆ Lincoln Center

This vast cultural complex is ground zero for high art in Manhattan. In addition to the venues and companies listed below, the Vivian Beaumont Theater and the Mitzi

SUMMER HAPPENINGS IN CENTRAL PARK

During the warm months, the park is home to countless cultural events, many of which are free. The two most popular are: Shakespeare in the Park (p26), which is managed by the Public Theater, and SummerStage (p26), a series of free concerts.

Shakespeare tickets are given out at 1pm on the day of the performance, but if you want to lay your hands on a seat, get there by 8am and make sure you have something to sit on and your entire group with you. Tickets are free and one per person; no latecomers are allowed in line.

SummerStage concert venues are generally opened to the public 1½ hours prior to the start of the show. But if it's a popular act, start queuing up early or you're not getting in.

E Newhouse Theater showcase works of drama and musical theater. Both of these have programming information listed on Lincoln Center's main website at www.new.lincolncenter.org.

METROPOLITAN OPERA HOUSE OPERA

Map p442 (www.metopera.org; Lincoln Center, 64th St at Columbus Ave; S1 to 66th St-Lincoln Center) New York's premier opera company, the Metropolitan Opera is the place to see classics such as *Carmen*, *Madame Butterfly* and *Macbeth*, not to mention Wagner's *Ring Cycle*. The Opera also hosts premieres and revivals of more contemporary works, such as Peter Sellars' *Nixon in China*, which played here in 2011. The season runs from September to April.

Ticket prices start at $30 and can get close to $500. Note that the box seats can be a bargain, but unless you're in boxes right over the stage, the views are dreadful. Seeing the stage requires sitting with your head cocked over a handrail – a literal pain in the neck.

For last-minute ticket-buyers there are other deals. You can get bargain-priced standing-room tickets ($17 to $22) starting at 10am on the day of the performance. (You won't see much, but you'll hear everything.) Two hours before shows on Mondays through Thursdays, 200 rush tickets are put on sale for starving artist types – just $20 for an orchestra seat (excluding galas and opening nights)! Line up early.

And don't miss the gift shop, which is chock full of operatic bric-a-brac, including Met curtain cufflinks and Rhinemaidens soap. (Seriously.)

FILM SOCIETY OF LINCOLN CENTER CINEMA

Map p442 (☎212-875-5456; www.filmlinc.com; S1 to 66th St-Lincoln Center) The Film Society is one of New York's cinematic gems, providing an invaluable platform for a wide gamut of documentary, feature, independent, foreign and avant-garde art pictures. Films screen in one of two facilities at Lincoln Center: the new **Elinor Bunin Munroe Film Center** (Map p442; www.filmlinc.com; Lincoln Center, 144 W 65th St; S1 to 66 St-Lincoln Center), a more intimate, experimental venue, or the **Walter Reade Theater** (Map p442; www.filmlinc.com; Lincoln Center, 165 W 65th St; S1 to 66th St-Lincoln Center), with wonderfully-wide, screening room–style seats.

Every September, both venues host the New York Film Festival, featuring plenty of New York and world premieres. In the spring, you'll find the New Directors/New Films series on view. For the cinephiles, it's highly recommended.

NEW YORK PHILHARMONIC CLASSICAL MUSIC

Map p442 (www.nyphil.org; Avery Fisher Hall, Lincoln Center; ♿; S1 to 66 St-Lincoln Center) The oldest professional orchestra in the US (dating back to 1842) holds its season every year at Avery Fisher Hall. Directed by Alan Gilbert, the son of two Philharmonic musicians, the orchestra plays a mix of classics (Tchaikovsky, Mahler, Haydn) and some contemporary works, as well as concerts geared towards children.

Tickets run in the $33 to $83 range. If you're on a budget, check out its open rehearsals on Thursdays during the day (at the discretion of the conductor) for only $18. In addition, students with a valid school ID can pick up rush tickets for $12.50 up to 10 days before an event.

NEW YORK CITY BALLET DANCE

Map p442 (☎212-870-5656, student rush tickets 212-870-7766; www.nycballet.com; David H Koch Theater Lincoln Center, Columbus Ave at 62nd St; ♿; S1 to 66th St-Lincoln Center) This prestigious company was first directed by renowned Russian-born choreographer George Balanchine back in the 1940s. Today, the company has 90 dancers and is the largest ballet organization in the US, performing 23 weeks a year at Lincoln Center's David H Koch Theater. During the holidays the troop is best known for its annual production of *The Nutcracker*.

Depending on the ballet, ticket prices can range from $29 to $250. Student rush tickets (valid school ID required) are posted on Mondays and cost $15. Fourth-ring seats are often a deal, but the views can be lousy.

AMERICAN BALLET THEATRE DANCE

Map p442 (☎212-477-3030; www.abt.org; Lincoln Center, 64th St at Columbus Ave; S1 to 66th St-Lincoln Center) This seven-decade-old traveling company presents a classic selection of ballets at the Metropolitan Opera House every spring (generally in May). Tickets are by subscription only. The Orchestra, Parterre and Grand Tier sections offer the best views. Avoid the top tier or all you'll see is the dancers' heads. Box seats towards the rear have highly obscured views.

1. Upper West Side (p227)
Admire the grand residences along Central Park West, such as the Dakota Building, where John Lennon once lived.

2. Lincoln Center (p233)
The modernist Lincoln Center contains some of NYC's most renowned entertainment venues, such as the Metropolitan Opera House.

3. American Museum of Natural History (p234)
More than 30 million artifacts are housed in this classic, family-friendly museum.

RICHARD CUMMINS / LONELY PLANET IMAGES ©

RICHARD CUMMINS / LONELY PLANET IMAGES ©

☆ Upper West Side

Outside of Lincoln Center, there are numerous other venues in the Upper West Side that cater to the cultured set.

BEACON THEATRE
LIVE MUSIC

Map p442 (www.beacontheatre.com; 2124 Broadway btwn 74th & 75th Sts; Ⓢ1/2/3 to 72nd St) This historic theater from 1929 is a perfect in-between-size venue, with 2600 seats (not a terrible one in the house) and a constant flow of popular acts, from The Cure to Paul Simon to Adele. A $15 million restoration in 2009 has left the gilded interiors – a mix of Greek, Roman, Renaissance and Rococo design elements – totally sparkling.

CLEOPATRA'S NEEDLE
CLUB

Map p442 (www.cleopatrasneedleny.com; 2485 Broadway btwn 92nd & 93rd Sts; ⊘4pm-late; Ⓢ1/2/3 to 96th St) Named after an Egyptian obelisk that resides in Central Park, this venue is small and narrow like its namesake. There's no cover, but there's a $10 minimum spend. Come early and you can enjoy happy hour, when martinis are half-price. But be prepared to stay late: Cleopatra's is famous for all-night jam sessions that hit their peak around 4am.

SMOKE
JAZZ

Map p442 (www.smokejazz.com; 2751 Broadway btwn 105th & 106th Sts; ⊘5pm-4am; Ⓢ1 to 103rd St) This swank but laid-back lounge – with good stage views from plush sofas – brings

---

LOCAL KNOWLEDGE

NYC'S BEST SPOTS FOR LIVE MUSIC

A jazz and pop music critic who writes for *JazzTimes* and the *New York Times*, Nate Chinen covers the music scene in New York City and beyond. (He's @natechinen on Twitter.) He gives us a list of his favorite music venues.

The Village Vanguard

The Vanguard (p151) is run by Lorraine Gordon, an authentic New York character with a real take-no-nonsense attitude. It's the oldest jazz club in the city, and it's sort of bare bones but the acoustics are perfect and the vibe is terrific. This is my favorite room for music in the world.

The Jazz Standard

One of the city's other great jazz clubs is the **Jazz Standard** (Map p434; www.jazz standard.net; 116 E 27th St btwn Lexington & Park Aves; Ⓢ6 to 28th St). The service is impeccable. The food is great. There's no minimum and it's programmed by Seth Abramson, a guy who really knows his stuff.

Bowery Ballroom

For rock and pop, this is my favorite space. The Bowery Ballroom (p121) is a room with history (it was built in the 1920s), and it has really good sound and strong booking. This is where bigger acts will sometimes do their small shows.

Brooklyn Bowl

Brooklyn Bowl (p288) is kind of a weird venue because people are also bowling, but it's where you'll find plenty of groovier gigs, including jam bands. Questlove, the drummer for The Roots, DJs every Thursday night.

Joe's Pub

The room here feels cozy and elegant. **Joe's Pub** (Map p418; www.joespub.com; Public Theater, 425 Lafayette St btwn Astor Pl & 4th St; Ⓢ R/W to 8th St-NYU; 6 to Astor Pl) has a high concentration of tongue-in-cheek cabaret, and the sensibility is pretty young. (It's attached to the Public Theater, so there's a performance aspect to it a lot of the time.)

Beacon Theatre

The Beacon (p242) generally skews to classic rock. But it's a great concert hall, and the renovation was spectacular. It's like a mini–Radio City Music Hall: it doesn't swallow the artist.

out old-timers and local faves, like George Coleman and Wynton Marsalis. Most nights there's a $10 cover, plus a $20 to $30 food and drink minimum. Smoke is smoke-free but then again so is the rest of NYC.

MERKIN CONCERT HALL CLASSICAL MUSIC

Map p442 (www.kaufman-center.org/mch; 129 W 67th St btwn Amsterdam Ave & Broadway; admission varies; [S]1 to 66th St-Lincoln Center) Just north of Lincoln Center, this 450-seat hall, part of the Kaufman Center, is one of the city's more intimate venues for classical music, as well as jazz, world music and pop. The hall hosts Tuesday matinees (a deal at $17) that highlight emerging classical solo artists. Every January, it is home to the New York Guitar Festival.

SYMPHONY SPACE LIVE MUSIC

Map p442 (www.symphonyspace.org; 2537 Broadway btwn 94th & 95th Sts; 👪; [S]1/2/3 to 96th St) Home to National Public Radio's renowned literary readings, Symphony Space is a multidisciplinary gem supported by the local community. It often hosts three-day series that are dedicated to one musician, and has an affinity for world music, theater, film and dance.

NEW YORK CITY OPERA OPERA

(www.nycopera.com; various venues) The 'people's opera,' founded by Mayor Fiorella LaGuardia in 1944, is one of New York's more interesting companies, producing updated classics, neglected operas, and new and recent work. Unfortunately, it also has profound financial troubles, and in late 2011, was experiencing all kinds of labor problems. For now, the show is going on in venues around the city. But that may change. Check its website for the latest.

🛍 SHOPPING

The Upper West Side is chain store central, so local flavor can be hard to find. That said, there are some good shopping stops.

GREENFLEA MARKET

Map p442 (www.greenfleamarkets.com; Columbus Ave btwn 76th & 77th Sts; 🕒10am-5:30pm Sun; [S]B, C to 81st St-Museum of Natural History; 1 to 79th St) One of the oldest open-air shopping spots in the city, this friendly, well-stocked flea market is a perfect activity for a lazy Upper West Side Sunday morning. You'll find a little bit of everything here, including vintage and contemporary furnishings, antique maps, custom eyewear, hand-woven scarves and handmade jewelry. Check the website for weekly vendor details. The market is also open on occasional Saturdays in warm months.

WESTSIDER BOOKS BOOKS

Map p442 (www.westsiderbooks.com; 2246 Broadway btwn 80th & 81st Sts; 🕒10am-late; [S]1 to 79th St) This great little shop is packed to the gills with rare and used books, including a good selection of fiction and illustrated tomes. There are first editions and there's a smattering of vintage vinyl. There is a sister shop, Westsider Records, that dispenses vinyl, too.

WESTSIDER RECORDS MUSIC

Map p442 (☎212-874-1588; www.westsiderbooks.com; 233 W 72nd St btwn Broadway & West End Ave; 🕒11am-7pm Mon-Thu, 11am-9pm Fri-Sat, noon-6pm Sun; [S]1/2/3 to 72nd St) Featuring more than 30,000 LPs, this shop has got you covered when it comes to everything from funk to jazz to classical. A good place to lose all track of time.

CENTURY 21 DEPARTMENT STORE

Map p442 (www.c21stores.com; 1972 Broadway btwn 66th & 67th Sts; 🕒9am-10pm Mon-Sat, 11am-8pm Sun; [S]1 to 66th St-Lincoln Center) Exceedingly popular with fashionable locals and foreign travelers, the Century 21 chain is a bounty of season-old brand name and designer brands sold at steeply discounted prices. Featuring everything from Missoni to Marc Jacobs, prices may sometimes seem high, but compared to retail, they're a steal.

HARRY'S SHOES SHOES

Map p442 (www.harrys-shoes.com; 2299 Broadway at 83rd St; 🕒10am-6:45pm Tue, Wed, Fri & Sat, to 7:45pm Mon & Thu, 11am-6pm Sun; [S]1 to 86th St) Around since the 1930s, Harry's is a classic. It's staffed by gentlemen who measure your foot in an old-school metal contraption and then wait on you patiently, making sure the shoe fits. If your feet are killing you from all the walking, you'll find sturdy, comfortable brands (Merrel, Dansko, Birkenstock) as well as Earth, a vegan brand.

TIME FOR CHILDREN
TOYS

Map p442 (www.atimeforchildren.org; 506 Amsterdam Ave btwn 84th & 85th Sts; ⏰10am-7pm Mon-Sat, 11am-6pm Sun; 🚺; §1 to 86th St) This small store sells adorable clothes for babies and toddlers, colorful books and plush toys, block sets, handmade cards and other treasures for the under-10 gang. Bonus: feel good about your purchase. Time donates 100% of its profits to the Children's Aid Society of New York.

🏃 SPORTS & ACTIVITIES

LOEB BOATHOUSE
BOATING, BICYCLE RENTAL

Map p442 (www.thecentralparkboathouse.com; Central Park btwn 74th & 75th Sts; boating per hr $12, bike rentals per hr $9-15; ⏰10am-dusk Apr-Nov; 🚺; §B, C to 72nd St; 6 to 77th St) Central Park's boathouse has a fleet of 100 rowboats plus three kayaks available for rent from April to November. In the summer, there is also a Venetian-style gondola that seats up to six (per 30 minutes $30). Bicycles are also available from April to November. Rentals require an ID and credit card and are weather permitting. Helmets included.

BIKE & ROLL
BICYCLE RENTAL

Map p442 (www.bikeandroll.com/newyork; Columbus Circle at Central Park West; per hr/day from $12/39; ⏰9am-7pm Mar-May, 8am-8pm Jun-Aug, 9am-5pm Sep-Nov; 🚺; §A/C, B/D, 1/2 to 59th St-Columbus Circle) At the southwestern entrance to the park, a small, pop-up kiosk dispenses beach cruisers and 10-speeds for rides around Central Park. It also has child seats and tandem bikes.

CHAMPION BICYCLES INC
BICYCLE RENTAL

Map p442 (www.championbicycles.com; 896 Amsterdam Ave at 104th St; rentals per 24hr $40; ⏰10am-7pm Mon-Fri, to 6pm Sat & Sun; §1 to 103rd St) This places stocks a variety of bikes for rent and has free copies of the helpful **NYC Cycling Map** (www.nyc.gov/bikes), which details more than 50 miles of bike lanes around New York City.

TOGA BIKE SHOP
BICYCLE RENTAL

Map p442 (www.togabikes.com; 110 West End Ave btwn 64th & 65th Sts; rentals per 24hr $35-75; ⏰11am-7pm Mon-Fri, 10am-6pm Sat, 11am-6pm Sun; §1 to 66th St-Lincoln Center) This friendly

and long-standing bike shop is conveniently located between Central Park and the Hudson River bike path. Rentals are available in good weather (typically April through October). You'll need to leave a credit card deposit. Prices include a helmet.

FIVE BOROUGH BICYCLE CLUB
BICYCLE RENTAL

Map p442 (www.5bbc.org; 891 Amsterdam Ave at 104th St; §1 to 103rd St) For a $20 annual fee, you can participate in this local club's myriad day rides as well as long-haul rides. The club office is at Hostelling International New York (p344).

CHARLES A DANA DISCOVERY CENTER
FISHING

Map p442 (www.centralparknyc.org; Central Park at 110th St btwn Fifth & Lenox Aves; ⏰10am-3pm Tue-Sat, to 1pm Sun; 🚺; §2/3 to Central Park North) Get your bass on! You can borrow a rod and bait (corn kernels) for catch-and-release fishing at the Harlem Meer from April through October. Photo ID and a fishing license are required ($5 per day, www.dec.ny.gov) for persons 16 and older.

STARR SAPHIR BIRDING
BIRDWATCHING

Map p442 (☎212-304-3808, 917-306-3808; cnr 81st St & Central Park West; tours $8; ⏰tours Apr-Jun, Sept & Oct; 🚺; §A/C, B to 81st St-Museum of Natural History) Ornithologist Starr Saphir leads regular birding walks through Central Park during migration seasons – roughly April to June and September and October. Tours depart at 7:30am Monday and Wednesday from the corner of 81st St and Central Park West, or from 103rd St and Central Park West at 9am Tuesday and 7:30am Saturday.

You can show up without a reservation or call ahead to confirm your attendance by leaving Starr a message.

FREE BELVEDERE CASTLE
BIRDWATCHING

Map p442 (☎212-772-0210; Central Park at 79th St; admission free; ⏰10am-5pm Tue-Sun; 🚺; §B, C, 1/2/3 to 72nd St) For a DIY birding expedition with kids, pick up a 'Discovery Kit' at Belvedere Castle in Central Park. It comes with binoculars, a bird book, colored pencils and paper – a perfect way to get the kids excited about birds. Picture ID required.

WEST SIDE YMCA
SPORTS

Map p442 (☎212-912-2600; www.ymcanyc.org/west-side; 5 W 63rd St btwn Central Park West &

Columbus Ave; day pass $25; ⊘5am-10:45pm Mon-Fri, 8am-7:45pm Sat & Sun; ⬛; ⓢA/C, B/D, 1 to 59th St-Columbus Circle) Near Central Park, the West Side Y – one of 20 YMCAs in the city – boasts two swimming pools, an indoor running track, a basketball court, six racquetball/squash courts and a big weight room. Membership is $93 monthly (with a $125 initiation fee).

WOLLMAN SKATING RINK   SKATING

Map p442 (www.wollmanskatingrink.com; Central Park btwn 62nd & 63rd Sts; adult Mon-Thu $11, Fri-Sun $16, child $6, skate rentals $7, lock rental $5, spectator fee $5; ⊘mid-Oct–Apr; ⬛; ⓢF to 57 St; N/Q/R to 5th Ave-59th St) Larger than the Rockefeller Center skating rink, and allowing all-day skating, this rink is at the south-eastern edge of Central Park and offers nice views. It's open mid-October through April. Cash only.

CENTRAL PARK TENNIS CENTER   TENNIS

Map p442 (☏212-280-0205; www.centralpark. com; Central Park btwn 94th & 96th Sts, enter at 96th St & Central Park West; ⊘6:30am-dusk Apr-Oct or Nov; ⓢB, C to 96th St) This daylight-hours-only facility has 26 clay courts for public use and four hard courts for lessons. You can buy single-play tickets ($15) here. You can reserve a court if you pick up a $15 permit at the **Arsenal** (Map p442; www.nyc govparks.org; Central Park at Fifth Ave & E 64th St; ⊘9am-4pm Mon-Fri, to noon Apr-May; ⓢN/Q/R to 5th Ave-59th St). The least busy times are roughly noon to 4pm on weekdays.

Harlem & Upper Manhattan

MORNINGSIDE HEIGHTS | HARLEM | EAST HARLEM | HAMILTON HEIGHTS | SUGAR HILL | WASHINGTON HEIGHTS | INWOOD

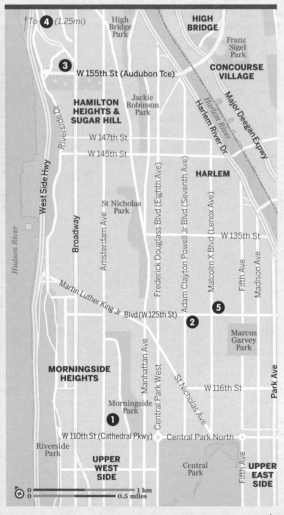

Neighborhood Top Five

1 Taking in the overwhelming scale of **Cathedral Church of St John the Divine** (p248), the largest place of worship in the US. This glorious Gothic-style treasure is a work in progress; the north tower has yet to be built.

2 Admiring the myriad contributions of African American artists at **Studio Museum in Harlem** (p250).

3 Spending quiet time with priceless works by Goya at the underrated **Hispanic Society of America Museum & Library** (p256).

4 Strolling through **Cloisters Museum & Gardens** (p256), among the remains of medieval monasteries.

5 Savoring Harlem's global soul at Marcus Samuelsson's fashionable bistro, **Red Rooster** (p258).

For more detail of this area, see Map p444 ➡

Explore Harlem & Upper Manhattan

The top half of Manhattan is a lot of territory to cover, with a number of historical sights – many on opposing sides of the island. So pick a neighborhood (or better yet, a couple of contiguous neighborhoods) and stick to them. If you like your cities to feel a little bit country, then start with Inwood – which has lovely parks, an extravagant museum and a super chilled-out vibe – and then work your way down the west side to the soaring Cathedral Church of St John the Divine. Prefer an urban vibe? Then it's all about Harlem and Hamilton Heights, a bastion of African American culture that offers good eating and shopping, and jazzy places to sip a drink.

Local Life

➡ **Get your chic on** When Harlem ladies and gents go out on the town, they are usually dressed to the nines. The commercial strip on 125th provides plenty of shopping opportunities. For glam frocks, hit Swing (p260); for killer kicks, head to Atmos (p260).

➡ **Tune in** For off-the-beaten-path musical events, nothing beats Morningside Heights. Riverside Church (p251), the Cathedral Church of St John the Divine (p248) and Columbia University (p251) all host regular concerts.

➡ **Take a hike** New Yorkers jogging, hiking and biking is what you'll find at Inwood Hill Park (p257) on any given sunny day. Join in!

Getting There & Away

➡ **Subway** Harlem's main drag – 125th St – is just one subway stop from the 59th St–Columbus Circle Station in Midtown on the A and D trains. Other areas of Harlem and northern Manhattan can be reached on the A/C, B/D, 1/2/3 and 4/5/6 trains.

➡ **Bus** Dozens of buses ply the north–south route between upper and lower Manhattan along all the major avenues. The M10 bus provides a scenic trip along the west side of Central Park into Harlem. The M100 and the M101 run east to west along 125th St.

➡ **Taxi** If yellow cabs are in short supply, look for livery cabs (big town cars bearing a company name and number); negotiate a price before you get in.

Lonely Planet's Top Tip

Manhattan's uptown communities tend to be locally minded, with bars, restaurants and shops catering to a neighborhood scene. These tend to be sleepiest on weekday mornings but come to life on evenings and weekends when locals are out and about.

To make the most of your visit, hit one of the museums or other historic sights in the afternoon, then stick around for dinner when these areas are at their liveliest.

✖ Best Places to Eat

➡ Charles' Pan-Fried Chicken (p259)
➡ Red Rooster (p258)
➡ Mamajuana (p259)
➡ Community Food & Juice (p258)

For reviews, see p258 ➡

◗ Best Places to Drink

➡ Bier International (p259)
➡ Yankee Stadium (p257)
➡ Lenox Lounge (p259)

For reviews, see p259 ➡

🔒 Best Places to Browse

➡ Atmos (p260)
➡ Nostylgia (p260)
➡ Jumel Terrace Books (p260)
➡ Malcolm Shabazz Harlem Market (p252)

For reviews, see p260 ➡

STEVEN GREAVES / LONELY PLANET IMAGES ©

TOP SIGHTS
CATHEDRAL CHURCH OF ST JOHN THE DIVINE

The largest place of worship in the United States has yet to be completed – and probably won't be any time soon. But this storied Episcopal cathedral nonetheless commands attention with its ornate Byzantine-style facade, booming vintage organ and extravagantly scaled nave – twice as wide as Westminster Abbey in London.

An Unfinished History

Founded in the 19th century by Bishop Horatio Potter, the first cornerstone for the Cathedral was laid on St John's Day in 1892. But the construction – as its incomplete state will attest – was hardly smooth. The engineers had to dig 70ft in order to find bedrock to which they could anchor the building. Architects died and were fired. And in 1911, the initial Romanesque design was exchanged for something bigger and more Gothic.

Construction has been halted on countless occasions (whenever funds run out). To this day, the north tower remains unbuilt, and a 'temporary' domed roof, constructed out of terra-cotta tile in 1909, still shelters the Crossing. In 2001, there was a raging fire to contend with, too. Much of the church has since been restored, but the north transept, which was severely damaged, has not been rebuilt.

If it is ever completed, the 601ft-long Cathedral will rank as the third-largest church in the world, after St Peter's Basilica in Rome and Basilica of Our Lady of Peace at Yamoussoukro in Côte d'Ivoire. Just don't count on this happening any time soon.

DON'T MISS...

- ➡ Portal sculptures
- ➡ Great Rose Window
- ➡ Great Organ
- ➡ Keith Haring Triptych

PRACTICALITIES

- ➡ Map p444
- ➡ ☎tours 212-932-7347
- ➡ www.stjohndivine.org
- ➡ 1047 Amsterdam Ave at W 112th St
- ➡ admission by donation, tours $6, vertical tours $15
- ➡ 🕒7am-6pm Mon-Sat, to 7pm Sun
- ➡ [S]B, C, 1 to 110th St-Cathedral Pkwy

The Portal Sculptures

Framing the western entrance are two rows of Gothic-inspired sculptures that were carved in the 1980s and '90s by British artist Simon Verity (b 1945). On the central pillar stands St John the Divine himself, author of the *Book of Revelation*. (Note the Four Horsemen of the Apocalypse under his feet.) Flanking him are various biblical figures, including Moses, John the Baptist and Noah.

Themes of devastation are rife, but most unnerving is the statue of Jeremiah (third on the right), which stands on a base that shows the New York City skyline – Twin Towers included – in the process of being destroyed.

The Nave

The nave is laid out west to east. Lining this monumental passageway are two magisterial sets of 17th-century tapestries. The Barberini Tapestries from Italy depict scenes from the life of Christ, while the Mortlake Tapestries, based on cartoons by Raphael, show the *Acts of the Apostles*.

Great Rose Window

Installed in 1932, the largest stained glass window in the country contains more than 10,000 individual pieces of glass. The design features a red-robed image of Christ at the center, from which trumpet-bearing angels radiate outward to the prophets.

Great Organ

One of the most powerful organs in the world, the Great Organ was originally installed in 1911 and then enlarged and rebuilt in 1952. It contains 8035 pipes arranged in 141 ranks. The 2001 fire damaged the instrument, but a careful five-year restoration brought it back. You can hear it roar during services and concerts.

Keith Haring Triptych

Behind the choir is the silver triptych 'Life of Christ,' carved by '80s pop artist Keith Haring (1958–90). It's one of the last works of art he produced prior to succumbing to an AIDS-related illness at the age of 31.

Gardens

The Cathedral is situated on a lovely 11-acre plot. On the south side of the building you'll find the whimsical Children's Sculpture Garden (check out the bizarre Peace Fountain, which shows the archangel Michael and Satan doing battle) and the Biblical Garden, containing plants mentioned in the Bible.

VISITING THE CATHEDRAL

Tours are offered at 11am and 1pm Saturdays and at 1pm Sundays. Vertical tours, which take you on a steep climb to the top of the Cathedral (bring your own flashlight), are at noon and 2pm Saturdays. Regular prayer services are held four times daily (see the website for the schedule). Two special services worth seeing are the annual Blessing of the Animals (p28), a pilgrimage for pet owners held on the first Sunday of October. If attending a regular service, remain seated and refrain from taking pictures.

The Cathedral has a storied institutional history. It was involved in civil rights issues back in the early 1950s and has regularly worked with members of the community on issues of inequity. It is also a long-running cultural outpost, hosting holiday concerts, lectures and exhibits. And it has been the site of memorial services for many famous New Yorkers, including choreographer George Balanchine, jazz trumpeter Louis Armstrong and artist Haring.

HARLEM & UPPER MANHATTAN CATHEDRAL CHURCH OF ST JOHN THE DIVINE

TOP SIGHTS
CATHEDRAL CHURCH OF ST JOHN THE DIVINE

TOP SIGHTS
STUDIO MUSEUM IN HARLEM

This small, cultural gem has been exhibiting the works of African American artists for more than four decades. While it contains a notable permanent collection, and its exhibition program is always challenging, the museum is not just another art display center. It is an important point of connection for Harlem cultural figures of all stripes, who arrive to check out a rotating selection of shows, attend film screenings or sign up for gallery talks.

DON'T MISS...

- African American Flag
- The well-stocked gift shop

PRACTICALITIES

- Map p444
- ☎212-864-4500
- www.studio museum.org
- 144 W 125th St at Adam Clayton Powell Jr Blvd
- suggested donation $7
- ⏲noon-9pm Thu & Fri, 10am-6pm Sat, noon-6pm Sun
- 👪
- [S]2/3 to 125th St

From Loft to Museum

Founded in 1968, the museum originally came to life in a small loft space off 125th St that was sandwiched between a couple of garment factories and a supermarket. But it quickly became known for its thoughtful, contemporary-minded exhibits and vibrant event programming, which included concerts, poetry readings and lectures. Roughly a dozen years after its establishment, it moved to its present location, a renovated bank building that offered more room for exhibits, archives and the growing permanent collection.

You'll also find the **Harlem Visitor Information Kiosk** (www.nycgo.com/harlem; 144 W 125th St at Adam Clayton Powell Jr Blvd; ⏲noon-6pm Mon-Fri, 10am-6pm Sat & Sun; [S]2/3 to 125th St) located here.

Collecting African American Artists

The permanent collection is small (roughly 1700 objects), but it is rich. The Studio Museum has been an important patron to African American artists, and the collection features work by more than 400 of them. This includes important pieces by painter Jacob Lawrence, photographer Gordon Parks and collagist Romare Bearden – all of whom are represented in major museum collections in the US.

In addition, its photography holdings include an extensive archive of work by James VanDerZee (1886–1983), an unparalleled chronicler of early-20th-century Harlem life. He shot portraits of prominent entertainers and black nationalists, and continued to take pictures well into his nineties. One well-known snap shows Jean-Michel Basquiat, the '80s graffiti artist and painter, sitting pensively with a Siamese cat on his lap.

African American Flag

Look up on your way in. One of the museum's most iconic works hangs right outside the front door: Hammons' 1990 piece *African-American Flag* replaces the traditional red, white and blue of the stars and stripes with the red, green and black of the pan-African flag. It is a sly comment on the African American presence in the US.

Artists in Residence

The museum's long-running artist-in-residence program has provided crucial support to a long list of well-known artists, including conceptualist David Hammons, figurative painter Mickalene Thomas and portraitist Kehinde Wiley. There are regular open studio sessions (check the website) and residents' works can often be found on display in the out-of-the-way basement gallery or in one of the small display areas upstairs.

 SIGHTS

⊙ Morningside Heights

Covering the area between 110th and 125th Sts on the far west side, this neighborhood serves as a bedroom community for Columbia University, which occupies the neighborhood's southern half.

CATHEDRAL CHURCH OF ST JOHN THE DIVINE
CHURCH

See p248.

FREE GENERAL ULYSSES S GRANT NATIONAL MEMORIAL
MEMORIAL

Map p444 (www.nps.gov/gegr; Riverside Dr at 122nd St; ⊙9am-5pm; S1 to 125th St) Popularly known as Grant's Tomb ('Who's buried in Grant's Tomb?' 'Who?' 'Grant, stupid!' goes a classic joke), this landmark holds the remains of Civil War hero and 18th president Ulysses S Grant and his wife, Julia. Completed in 1897 – 12 years after his death – the imposing granite structure cost $600,000 and is the largest mausoleum in the country.

Seventeen Gaudi-inspired mosaic benches, designed by Chilean artist Pedro Silva in the 1970s, surround the mausoleum. It's a downright hallucinatory installation – and a good spot to contemplate the musings of the late, great comedian George Carlin, who was known to light up here back in the day.

FREE RIVERSIDE CHURCH
CHURCH

Map p444 (www.theriversidechurchny.org; 490 Riverside Dr at 120th St; ⊙7am-10pm; ⊕; S1 to 116th St) Built by the Rockefeller family in 1930, this Gothic beauty overlooks the Hudson River, and in good weather you can climb to the 355ft observation deck for expansive river views. The church rings its 74 carillon bells with an extraordinary 20-ton bass bell (the world's largest) at noon and 3pm on Sundays.

Interdenominational services are held at 10:45am on Sundays, with free tours available to the public immediately after. The church also hosts high-quality events such as concerts and lectures, many with an activist, queer-friendly and antiwar bent.

FREE COLUMBIA UNIVERSITY
UNIVERSITY

Map p444 (www.columbia.edu; Broadway at 116th St; S1 to 116th St-Columbia University) Founded in 1754 as King's College downtown, the oldest university in New York is now one of the premiere research institutions in the world. It moved to its current location (the site of a former insane asylum) in 1897, where its gated campus now channels a staid, New England vibe and offers plenty in the way of cultural happenings.

The principal point of interest is the main courtyard (located on College Walk at the level of 116th St), which is surrounded by various Italian Renaissance–style structures. Here, you'll find the statue of the open-armed *Alma Mater* seated before the Low Memorial Library. On the south end of College Walk, on the corner of Amsterdam Ave, is Hamilton Hall, a key site during the infamous student uprising of 1968.

There are other newer buildings by architects of note. Your best bet for navigating the grounds is to download the self-guided audio tour by architectural historian Andrew Dolkart from the Columbia University (www.columbia.edu/content/self-guided-walking-tour.html) website.

FREE MORNINGSIDE PARK
OUTDOORS

Map p444 (www.morningsidepark.org; 110th to 123rd Sts btwn Manhattan Ave, Morningside Ave & Morningside Dr; ⊕; S B, C, 1 to 110th St-Cathedral Pkwy) This 13 block finger of green has playgrounds, shaded pathways, an arboretum and several sculpture memorials. (The Seligman Fountain, featuring a bear and a faun, is delightfully weird.) In the area behind the Cathedral Church of St John the Divine, you'll find a pond and waterfall. A farmers market is held here on Saturdays from June through December.

⊙ Harlem

This is the neighborhood where Cab Calloway crooned. Where Ralph Ellison penned his epic novel on truth and intolerance, *Invisible Man*. Where acclaimed artist Romare Bearden pieced together his first collages. It's a place that is soaked in history – and then some. And it remains one of the country's most fabled centers of black American life.

Like everywhere else in New York, however, it's changing. National chains now blanket 125th St, Harlem's historic main drag. Of-the-moment eateries, luxury condos and young professionals (of all creeds and races) have also moved in. But the neighborhood nonetheless retains its trademark charm:

sidewalk vendors still dispense Malcolm X T-shirts and end-of-the-world types preach politics and hellfire. In Harlem, there's a little something for everybody.

STUDIO MUSEUM IN HARLEM MUSEUM
See p250.

APOLLO THEATER HISTORIC BUILDING
Map p444 (☎212-531-5305, tours 212-531-5337; www.apollotheater.org; 253 W 125th St at Frederick Douglass Blvd; admission weeknights $16, weekends $18; [S]A/C, B/D to 125th St) The Apollo has been Harlem's leading space for concerts and political rallies since 1914 and, with its gleaming marquee, is one of the neighborhood's most visible icons. Virtually every major black artist in the 1930s and '40s performed here, including Duke Ellington and Billie Holiday. And to this day it hosts regular concerts by high-profile entertainers. Everyone from Tony Bennett to Usher has played here.

The theatre is most famous, however, for its long-running Amateur Night – 'where stars are born and legends are made' – which takes place every Wednesday night. The wild and ruthless crowd is as fun to watch as the performers.

Tours of the interior are only available for groups of 20 or more with advance reservation.

[FREE] **MALCOLM SHABAZZ HARLEM MARKET** MARKET
Map p444 (52 W 116th St btwn Malcolm X Blvd & Fifth Ave; ⏲10am-8pm; 👪; [S]2/3 to 116th St) This semi-enclosed market does a brisk trade in just about everything: leather goods, crafts, textiles, bootleg CDs, oils, drums, clothing, sculptures and a stupendous array of assorted African everything. It's also, coincidentally, an excellent spot to get your hair braided. The market is run by the Malcolm Shabazz Mosque, the former pulpit of slain Muslim orator Malcolm X.

CRACK IS WACK PLAYGROUND PARK
Map p444 (www.nycgovparks.org/parks/M208E; Harlem River Park, E 127th St & 2 Ave; ⏲dawn-dusk; [S]4/5/6 to 125th St) This small, out-of-the-way playground is named for the bright orange 'Crack is Wack' mural painted by pop graffiti artist Keith Haring on a handball court back in October 1986. It has since been restored, harkening back to a time when Haring's works covered walls all over New York.

[FREE] **SCHOMBURG CENTER FOR RESEARCH IN BLACK CULTURE** LIBRARY
Map p444 (☎212-491-2200; www.nypl.org/research/sc/sc.html; 515 Malcolm X Blvd; ⏲noon-8pm Tue-Thu, 10am-6pm Fri & Sat; [S]2/3 to 135th St) The nation's largest collection of documents, rare books and photographs relating to the African American experience resides at this scholarly center run by the New York Public Library. It is named after Arthur Schomburg, a black Puerto Rican activist who amassed a singular collection of manuscripts, slave narratives and other important artifacts. Regular concerts, lectures and exhibits are held on-site.

WEST HARLEM PIERS PARK
Map p444 (www.nycgovparks.org/parks/M376; 125th St at the Hudson River; 👪; [S]1 to 125th St) On the site of a former milk factory, this 2-acre waterfront oasis has parkland, fishing spots, bike lanes and running paths. It is part of a narrow chain of pier parks along the Hudson River that link down to Battery Park, making it possible to bike all the way downtown without ever having to dismount.

HARLEM STREET NAMES

Many of the major avenues in the area have been renamed in honor of prominent African Americans; however, many locals still call the streets by their original names. Hence, Malcolm X Blvd is still frequently referred to as Lenox Ave.

East Harlem

The working class district of East Harlem above 96th St and east of 5th Ave, known colloquially as Spanish Harlem or El Barrio, has been home to one of the city's biggest Puerto Rican communities since the 1950s. Today, it remains a vibrant Latino neighborhood, where a mix of Puerto Rican, Dominican, Mexican and South American immigrants all come together.

EL MUSEO DEL BARRIO MUSEUM
Map p444 (www.elmuseo.org; 1230 Fifth Ave btwn 104th & 105th Sts; suggested donation adult/child $9/free, 3rd Sat of month & 6-9pm Wed free;

FULL PEWS: GOSPEL CHURCH SERVICES IN HARLEM

What began as an occasional pilgrimage has turned into a tourist-industry spectacle: entire busloads of travelers now make their way to Harlem every Sunday to attend a gospel service. The volume of visitors is so high that some churches turn away people due to space constraints. In some cases, tourists have been known to outnumber congregants.

Naturally, this has led to friction. Many locals are upset by visitors who chat during sermons, leave in the middle of services or show up in skimpy attire. Plus, there's the uncomfortable sense that black spirituality is something to be consumed like a Broadway show.

The churches, to their credit, remain welcoming spaces. But if you do decide to attend, be respectful: dress modestly (Sunday best!), do not take pictures, and remain present for the duration of the service.

Sunday services generally start at 11am and can last for two or more hours. Below are just a few of the roughly five dozen participating churches.

Abyssinian Baptist Church (Map p444; www.abyssinian.org; 132 W 138th St btwn Adam Clayton Powell Jr & Malcolm X Blvds; ⓜ; Ⓢ2/3 to 135th St) This famed congregation, now more than a century old, is the number one spot for foreign travelers (hence the separate tourist seating section). It's so popular, in fact, that you may not get in.

Canaan Baptist Church (Map p444; www.cbccnyc.org; 132 W 116th St btwn Adam Clayton Powell Jr & Malcolm X Blvds; ⓜ; Ⓢ2/3 to 116th St) A neighborhood church, founded in 1932.

Convent Avenue Baptist Church (Map p444; www.conventchurch.org; 420 W 145th St btwn St Nicholas Pl & Convent Ave; ⓜ; ⓈA/C, B/D, 1 to 145th St) Traditional baptist services since the 1940s.

Greater Hood Memorial AME Zion Church (Map p444; www.greaterhood.org; 160 W 146th St btwn Adam Clayton Powell Jr & Malcolm X Blvds; ⓜ; Ⓢ3 to 145th) Also hosts hip-hop services on Thursdays at 7pm.

St Paul Baptist Church (Map p444; 249 W 132nd St btwn Frederick Douglass & Adam Clayton Powell Jr Blvds; ⓜ; ⓈB, C to 135th St) A neighborhood-focused church.

⏱11am-6pm Tue-Sat, 1-5pm Sun; Ⓢ6 to 103rd St) Facing Central Park at the top of Museum Mile, this beloved museum is one of New York's premiere Latino institutions. In addition to a thoughtful exhibition program, El Museo has a strong permanent collection that includes pre-Columbian artifacts, traditional folk works and a stellar array of postwar art made by a wide gamut of Latino and Latin American artists.

This includes pieces by well-known historical figures (including Chilean surrealist Roberto Matta) and established contemporary artists such as Felix Gonzalez-Torres, Pepón Osorio and Tony Capellán.

There is a good gift shop and a cafeteria that sells pan-Latin foods.

JUSTO BOTANICA　　　　　MARKET

Map p444 (134 E 104th St btwn Park & Lexington Aves; ⏱10:30am-7pm Mon-Wed, noon-7pm Thu-Sat, noon-6pm Sun; Ⓢ6 to 103rd St) This eight-decade-old emporium of spiritual ephemera is a wonder to behold: bursting with crucifixes, candles, incense and mystery herbs. Tell the staff what you're seeking (love, success, protection against the evil eye) and they'll recommend the right fix. Just don't pepper them with questions unless you plan on buying something.

⊙ Hamilton Heights & Sugar Hill

Basically the northwestern extension of Harlem, Hamilton Heights takes its name from the former estate of Alexander Hamilton, one of the drafters of the US Constitution, who had an estate in the area.

During the Harlem Renaissance, the northern edge of the neighborhood was dubbed 'Sugar Hill' since this is where the Harlem elite came to live the 'sweet life.' This area is tangentially linked to hip-hop history. It is from here that the Sugarhill Gang, the group behind 'Rapper's Delight,' the first hip-hop single to become a mainstream hit, takes its name.

1. Apollo Theater (p252)
Harlem's leading concert space has hosted virtually every major black artist of the 1930s and '40s.

2. Lenox Lounge (p259)
Grab a drink at this art deco spot, once the haunt of jazz legends Miles Davis and John Coltrane.

3. Malcolm Shabazz Harlem Market (p252)
Browse the myriad wares on sale or get your hair braided at this semi-enclosed market.

DESIGN PICS INC. - RM CONTENT / ALAMY ©

VESPASIAN / ALAMY ©

[FREE] **HAMILTON GRANGE** HISTORIC BUILDING

Map p444 (www.nps.gov/hagr; St Nicholas Park at 141st St; ⏲9am-5pm Wed-Sun; [S]A/C, B/D to 145th St) This Federal-style retreat belonged to US founding father Alexander Hamilton, who owned a country estate here in the early 1800s. The home was recently moved from Convent Ave to its present location (and is now bizarrely situated on the side of a hill). But it's beautifully refurbished – of interest to history and architecture buffs as well as really grange people.

STRIVERS' ROW NEIGHBORHOOD

Map p444 (138th & 139th Sts btwn Frederick Douglass & Adam Clayton Powell Jr Blvds; [S]B, C to 135th St) Also known as the St Nicholas Historic District, these streets was popular with Harlem's elite in the 1920s. Its graceful row houses and apartments, many of which date back to the 1890s, draw visitors from all over. Keep your eyes peeled for informative historical plaques and alleyway signs advising visitors to 'walk your horses.'

HAMILTON HEIGHTS HISTORIC DISTRICT NEIGHBORHOOD

Map p444 (Convent Ave & Hamilton Tce btwn 140th & 145th Sts; [S]A/C, B/D to 145th St) Two parallel streets in Hamilton Heights – Convent Ave and Hamilton Tce – contain a landmark stretch of historic limestone and brownstone townhouses from the period between 1866 and 1931.

HOLCOMBE RUCKER PARK PARK

Map p444 (www.nycgovparks.org/parks/M216; W 155th St at Frederick Douglass Blvd; [S]B/D to 155th St) For die-hard fans of basketball, the riverside courts at Rucker are a venerated spot, consistently delivering some of the most exciting street ball games in the city. Throughout its history, NBA stars like Wilt Chamberlain, Kareem Abdul-Jabbar and Kobe Bryant have all stopped in for hoops.

Washington Heights & Inwood

Located at Manhattan's narrow, northern tip (above 155th St), Washington Heights takes its name from the first president of the US, who set up a Continental Army fort here during the Revolutionary War. For much of the 20th century, it has been a bastion of Dominican life – though it has recently seen an influx of downtown hipsters in search of affordable rent.

Inwood, at Manhattan's northern tip (from about 175th St), is a chilled-out residential zone that retains an almost suburban vibe.

CLOISTERS MUSEUM & GARDENS MUSEUM

off Map p444 (www.metmuseum.org/cloisters; Fort Tryon Park; suggested donation adult/child $25/free; ⏲9:30am-4:45pm Tue-Sun Nov-Feb, to 5:15pm Mar-Oct; [S]A to 190th St) On a hilltop overlooking the Hudson River, the Cloisters is a mesmerizing mish-mash of various European monasteries. Built in the 1930s to house the Metropolitan Museum's medieval treasures, it also contains the beguiling 16th-century tapestry *The Hunt of the Unicorn*. Summer is the best time to visit, when the garden's flowers and herbs are in bloom.

The frescoes, tapestries and paintings are set in galleries that sit around an airy courtyard, connected by grand archways and topped with Moorish terra-cotta roofs. Among the many rare treasures you'll get to gaze at are a 9th-century gold plaque of St John the Evangelist and an English-made ivory sculpture of the Virgin and Child from 1290, not to mention the stunning 12th-century Saint-Guilhem Cloister, made of French limestone standing 30ft high.

An on-site cafe serves snacks.

[FREE] **HISPANIC SOCIETY OF AMERICA MUSEUM & LIBRARY** MUSEUM

Map p444 (www.hispanicsociety.org; Broadway at 155th St, Washington Heights; ⏲10am-4:30pm Tue-Sat, 1-4pm Sun; [S]1 to 157th St) This underrated museum is housed in the ornate beaux arts structure where naturalist John James Audubon once lived. Open since 1908, it contains the largest collection of 19th-century Spanish art and manuscripts outside of Spain – including a substantial selection of works by El Greco, Goya and Velázquez, as well as a library featuring 600,000 rare books and manuscripts. Greeting visitors at the entrance is Goya's alluring 1797 masterpiece *The Duchess of Alba,* while a majestic sculpture of El Cid by Anna Hyatt Huntington dominates the exterior courtyard.

At the time of research, the Society was considering a name change to honor its founder, Archer Milton Huntington.

DYCKMAN FARMHOUSE MUSEUM MUSEUM
off Map p444 (www.dyckmanfarmhouse.org; 4881 Broadway at 204th St; admission $1; ⊙11am-4pm Wed-Sat, noon-4pm Sun; ⑤A to Inwood-207th St)
Built in 1784 on a 28-acre farm, the Dyckman House is Manhattan's lone surviving Dutch farmhouse – and is better than ever following an extensive renovation. Excavations of the property have turned up valuable clues about colonial life, and the museum includes period rooms and furniture, decorative arts, a half-acre of gardens and an exhibition on the neighborhood's history. To get to the Dyckman House, take the subway to the Inwood–207th St station (not Dyckman St) and walk one block south.

INWOOD HILL PARK OUTDOORS
off Map p444 (Dyckman St at the Hudson River; ⑤A to Inwood-207th St) This gorgeous

---

WORTH A DETOUR

THE BRONX

The only borough on the US mainland, the 42-sq-mile Bronx lies just north of Manhattan between the Hudson, Harlem and East Rivers and Long Island Sound. It was named after Scandinavian sea captain Jonas Bronck, who settled here in 1639, in an area previously inhabited by the Lenape Nation. Today nearly 1.4 million residents call it home.

The house that Babe Ruth built, **Yankee Stadium** (⊿tickets 877-469-9849; www.yankees.com; E 161st St at River Ave; tours $20, tickets $5-375; ⑪; ⑤B/D, 4 to 161st St-Yankee Stadium), is known for its very expensive team, its very expensive stadium ($1.5 billion; opened in 2009), and its 27 World Series wins. The 52,000-seat stadium channels the intimacy of the '23 original, so if you're into baseball – or *béisbol* or *beysbol* or *baseboll* – consider this a must.

For the kids, there's the **Bronx Zoo** (www.bronxzoo.com; 2300 Southern Blvd; basic ticket adult/child $16/12, suggested donation Wed; ⊙10am-5pm Mon-Fri, to 5:30pm Sat & Sun Apr-Oct, to 4:30pm Nov-Mar; ⑪; ⑤2, 5 to West Farms Sq-E Tremont Ave). Opened in 1899, this beautifully designed 265-acre zoo is home to some 4000 animals and there are a number of leafy areas that recreate different habitats, including African plains and Asian rain forests.

Immediately to the north is the **New York Botanical Garden** (www.nybg.org; Bronx River Pkwy & Fordham Rd; adult/child $20/8, Wed & 10am-noon Sat free; ⊙10am-6pm Tue-Sun; ⑪; ⑭Metro North to Botanical Garden), spread across 50 acres of forest. It opened in 1891 and is home to the restored Enid A Haupt Conservatory, a grand, Victorian iron-and-glass edifice that is now a New York landmark.

Art and architecture aficionados will enjoy the **Bronx Museum** (www.bxma.org; 1040 Grand Concourse at 165th St; admission $5, free Fri; ⊙11am-6pm Thu, Sat & Sun, to 8pm Fri; ⑤B/D to 167th St) for its angled facade and its well-executed contemporary exhibits.

Further up the Concourse is the renovated **Poe's Cottage** (www.bronxhistorical society.org/poecottage; Grand Concourse at Kingsbridge Rd; admission $5; ⊙10am-4pm Sat, 1-5pm Sun; ⑤B/D to Kingsbridge Rd), where author Edgar Allan Poe (1809–49) lived for three years at the end of his life. This is where he penned his famous poems 'Annabel Lee' and 'The Bells.'

On the borough's northern edge is the incredibly scenic **Woodlawn Cemetery** (www.thewoodlawncemetery.org; Webster Ave at E 233rd St; ⊙8:30am-5pm; ⑤4 to Woodlawn), a 400-acre burial ground that dates back to the Civil War (1863) and contains more than 300,000 headstones. Buried here are Cuban singer Celia Cruz, jazz legends Miles Davis and Duke Ellington, and *Moby Dick* scribe Herman Melville, among many others.

For some of the best Italian food in the borough, head to Arthur Ave, the Bronx's answer to Little Italy. For stellar brick-oven pizzas and fresh pasta, try **Zero Otto Nove** (www.roberto089.com; 2357 Arthur Ave at 186th St; pizzas from $14; ⊙lunch Mon-Sat, dinner daily; ⑭Metro-North to Fordham), a tempting trattoria set inside a cavernous (and wondrously fake) Salerno-inspired piazza.

197-acre park contains the last natural forest and salt marsh in Manhattan. It's a cool escape in summer and a great place to explore anytime, as you'll find hilly paths for hiking and mellow, grassy patches and benches for quiet contemplation. It's so peaceful and un-urban here, in fact, that the treetops serve as frequent nesting sites for bald eagles.

You'll find helpful rangers and a slew of educational programs, many geared toward children, at the **Inwood Hill Nature Center**. Let your sporty side rip on basketball courts, horseback-riding trails, and soccer and football fields; you can also join locals who barbecue at designated grills on summer weekends. The views of New Jersey and the Bronx from high points in the forest are wonderful.

MORRIS-JUMEL MANSION MUSEUM HISTORIC BUILDING

Map p444 (www.morrisjumel.org; 65 Jumel Tce at 160th St, Washington Heights; adult/child $5/4, guided tours per person $6; ⌚10am-4pm Wed-Sun, other times by appt; [S]C to 163rd St-Amsterdam Ave) Built in 1765 as a country retreat for Roger and Mary Morris, this columned mansion is the oldest house in Manhattan. It is also famous for having served as George Washington's headquarters after it was seized by the Continental Army in 1776. The mansion's rooms contain many original furnishings, including a bed that reputedly belonged to Napoleon.

🍴 EATING

🍴 Morningside Heights

COMMUNITY FOOD & JUICE AMERICAN $$

Map p444 (www.communityrestaurant.com; 2893 Broadway btwn 112th & 113th Sts; sandwiches $10-14, dinner mains $14-29; ⌚breakfast, lunch & dinner Mon-Fri, brunch & dinner Sat & Sun; 🍸 👪; [S]1 to 110th St) This loud and lofty spot is a great place for brunch for frenzied families and hungover Columbia University students. Get here before 10:30am or be prepared to wait for your veggie scramble. Better yet, skip the weekend rush and bop in for a candlelit dinner. The warm lentil salad and grass-fed burger are tops.

TOM'S RESTAURANT DINER $

Map p444 (www.tomsrestaurant.net; 2880 Broadway cnr 112th St; burgers with fries from $7; [S]1 to 110th St) The exteriors of Tom's may look familiar if you're a fan of the TV series *Seinfeld*, but the interiors are all New York Greek diner. As in, *busy*. The menu consists of classic items like burgers and gyros, as well as gut-warming homemade soups (creamy broccoli is good). Breakfast is served all day and it's open 24 hours Thursday to Saturday.

🍴 Harlem

[TOP CHOICE] **RED ROOSTER** NEW AMERICAN $$

Map p444 (www.redroosterharlem.com; 310 Malcolm X Blvd btwn 125th & 126th Sts; dinner mains $16-35; ⌚lunch Mon-Fri, dinner daily, brunch Sat & Sun; [S]2/3 to 125th St) This hot spot is run by Ethiopian-Swedish chef Marcus Samuelsson, who laces upscale comfort food with a world of flavors. Grilled salmon is garnished with peanuts while dirty rice features aged basmati. Best of all are the Swedish meatballs, served with potatoes and lingonberries. There is a long menu of beers and a wine list strong on California and Mediterranean vintages.

Tip: the menu is largely the same and significantly cheaper at lunch and on Sundays when it hosts a popular gospel brunch.

MAKE MY CAKE BAKERY $

Map p444 (www.makemycake.com; 121 St Nicolas Ave at 116th St; cupcakes $4; ⌚8am-8pm Mon-Thu, 9am-9pm Fri & Sat, 9am-7pm Sun; [S]2/3 to 116th St) A solid choice for sweet treats is this cozy, wood-lined spot dispensing tasty red velvet and German chocolate cupcakes, as well as sweet-potato cheesecake and yummy pies.

AMY RUTH'S RESTAURANT SOUTHERN COOKING $$

Map p444 (www.amyruthsharlem.com; 113 W 116th St near Malcolm X Blvd; chicken & waffles $10, mains $12-20; ⌚11:30am-11pm Mon, 8:30am-11pm Tue-Thu, 8:30am-5:30pm Fri & Sat, 7:30am-11pm Sun; [S]B, C, 2/3 to 116th St) This perennially crowded restaurant is *the* place to go for classic soul food, serving up delicious fried catfish, mac 'n' cheese and fluffy biscuits. But it's the waffles (served at all hours) that are most famous – dished up 13 different ways, including with shrimp. Our favorite is the 'Al Sharpton,' waffles topped with succulent fried chicken.

🍴 East Harlem

EL AGUILA MEXICAN $

Map p444 (137 E 116th St cnr Lexington Ave; tacos $2, burritos $7; ⏲24hr; [S]6 to 116th St) This bright, tile-clad taqueria serves up solid chicken, tongue and *bistec* (grilled steak) tacos that won't break the bank. It also has tasty tamales, tostadas, tortas (sandwiches) and veggie burritos. And for breakfast, there is even *pan dulce* (a sweet Mexican bun).

🍴 Hamilton Heights

[TOP CHOICE] **CHARLES' PAN-FRIED CHICKEN** SOUTHERN COOKING $

Map p444 (2839-2841 Frederick Douglass Blvd btwn 151st & 152nd Sts; fried chicken with two sides $12; ⏲11am-11pm Sun-Thu, to 2am Fri & Sat; [S]B/D to 155th St) It's a hole-in-the-wall place, but the charismatic Charles Gabriel makes the best damn chicken we've ever tasted: crisp and beautifully seasoned, it's served with mountains of collard greens, mac 'n' cheese and corn bread. The setting is informal (meals are dished out in Styrofoam) and there are just four tables, but the food is wonderful and the portions are big enough for two.

🍴 Inwood

NEW LEAF CAFE MODERN AMERICAN $$$

(www.newleafrestaurant.com, 1 Margaret Corbin Dr; lunch mains $14-20, dinner mains $26-34; ⏲lunch & dinner; [S]A to 190th St) Nestled into Fort Tryon Park, a short jaunt from the Cloisters Museum & Gardens, this 1930s stone edifice has idyllic views and a lofty, wood-ceiling dining room that feels like a stylish country tavern. The seasonal menu is an international mix of pasta, seafood and salads. On nice days, the outdoor patio is a perfect spot for brunch.

MAMAJUANA LATINO $$$

(www.mamajuana-cafe.com; 247 Dyckman St at Seaman Ave; mains $15-30; ⏲dinner daily, brunch & dinner Sun; [S]A to Dyckman St) This Latin fusion eatery gets its moniker from the traditional Dominican brew of rum, wine and spices. Starters like the mixed empanadas and shrimp ceviche get the party started, while the hearty mains – think slow-roasted pork with pigeon-pea rice – keep it going into the night. There are a couple of types of paella, including one for vegetarians.

🍷 DRINKING & NIGHTLIFE

LENOX LOUNGE LOUNGE

Map p444 (www.lenoxlounge.com; 288 Malcolm X Blvd btwn W 124th & W 125th Sts, Harlem; ⏲noon-4am; [S]2/3 to 125th St) A classic art-deco spot in the heart of Harlem – once the haunt of big-time jazz cats Miles Davis and John Coltrane – is now a lovely place to imbibe. Don't miss the luxe Zebra Room in the back. The bar is home to semi-regular jazz and other musical performances.

PARIS BLUES BAR

Map p444 (2012 Adam Clayton Powell Jr Blvd cnr 121st St, Harlem; ⏲noon-2am Sun-Wed, noon-4am Thu-Sat; [S]A/C, B to 116th St; 2/3 to 125th St) This down-home dive is named after the 1961 Sidney Poitier and Paul Newman flick about two expats living and loving in Paris. It's a little worn in places and the booze selection is limited, but it makes up for it with plenty of charm, and with jazz performances on Wednesdays and Thursdays from about 8pm.

BIER INTERNATIONAL BEER GARDEN

Map p444 (www.bierinternational.com; 2099 Frederick Douglass Blvd at 113th St, Harlem; ⏲noon-1am Sun & Mon, to 2am Tue-Thu, to 4am Fri & Sat) A fun and friendly beer garden featuring more than a dozen drafts and a full menu of eats to choose from. The truffle fries with Parmesan ($7) make a great accompaniment to the Bier Stiefel ($15) – beer in a boot glass.

☆ ENTERTAINMENT

MAYSLES INSTITUTE CINEMA

Map p444 (www.mayslesinstitute.org; 343 Malcolm X Blvd btwn 127th & 128th Sts, Harlem; suggested donation $10; [S]2/3 to 125th St) This small not-for-profit cinema founded by director Albert Maysles (of *Grey Gardens* fame) shows documentary and other independent films. There are also live performances, lectures and presentations. Check the website for details of upcoming screenings and events.

SHOPPING

In Harlem, the Malcolm Shabazz Harlem Market (p252) and Justo Botanica (p253) are ideal for small gifts and good browsing. Otherwise, give the following spots an ogle.

ATMOS — SHOES

Map p444 (www.atmosnyc.com; 203 W 125th St at Adam Clayton Powell Jr Blvd, Harlem; ⏲11am-8pm Mon-Sat, noon-7pm Sun; [S]A/C, B/D, 2/3 to 125th St) This gleaming white temple draws sneaker fetishists both high and low. (Method Man from the Wu-Tang Clan has been spotted here.) A perfect place for high-end kicks, as well as limited edition releases and re-releases.

JAZZ AT HOME

The city's top jazz destinations all reside downtown – but that doesn't mean you can't hear good jazz uptown. In addition to bars and restaurants that regularly host performances, two incredible New Yorkers both open their homes once a week, every week, for unforgettable gigs:

Marjorie Eliot (Map p444; ☎212-781-6595; Apt 3F; 555 Edgecombe Ave at 16th St, Washington Heights; [S]A/C to 163rd St-Amsterdam Ave; 1 to 157th St) The renowned Eliot offers free jams in her home every Sunday at 4pm in honor of her two deceased sons. Warmly recommended.

Bill's Place (Map p444; www.billsaxton.com; 148 W 133rd St btwn Adam Clayton Powell Jr & Malcolm X Blvds, Harlem; [S]2/3 to 135th St) Bill Saxton, a noted sax man, gives concerts every Friday at 9pm and 11pm on the 1st floor of his narrow brownstone home. The cover is $20. Bring your own drinks.

JUMEL TERRACE BOOKS — BOOKS

Map p444 (☎212-928-9525; www.jumelterracebooks.com; 426 W 160th St, Washington Heights; ⏲11am-6pm Fri-Sun & by appointment; [S]C to 163rd St-Amsterdam Ave) Housed in a brownstone from 1891, this shop specializes in tomes on Africana, Harlem history and African American literature. You have to call to set up an appointment outside weekend hours, but if you're fascinated by rare books – and a rare opportunity to shop at a beautiful home – it's worth it.

NOSTYLGIA — FASHION

(www.nostylgia.com; 251 Dyckman St, Inwood; ⏲noon-9pm; [S]A to Dyckman St) This intimate neighborhood haberdashery just north of the Cloisters Museum dispenses handcrafted tees, sweaters for men, shirts and other locally designed articles of hipster clothing. There is also a tea bar (try the blood orange black tea) and a minuscule chess lounge to hang out in.

HUE-MAN BOOKSTORE — BOOKS

Map p444 (www.huemanbookstore.com; 2319 Frederick Douglass Blvd btwn 124th & 125th Sts, Harlem; ⏲10am-8pm Mon-Sat, 11am-7pm Sun; [S]A/C, B/D to 125th St) The largest independent African American bookstore in the country offers a good selection of works from black literary heavyweights and pop writers alike. A small cafe plies coffee, and there are regular book signings and poetry readings.

SWING — FASHION

Map p444 (www.swing-nyc.com; 1960 Adam Clayton Powell Jr Blvd at 118th St, Harlem; ⏲11am-6pm Thu-Mon; [S]A/C, B, 2/3 to 116th St) A chic little boutique that carries a stylish mix of fashion, jewelry and home design. Included in the mix are pieces by local and international designers as well as a line of 'I love Harlem' tees.

SPORTS & ACTIVITIES

TREAD — BICYCLE RENTAL

(www.treadbikeshop.com; 250 Dyckman St, Inwood; per hour $8, per day $30; ⏲10am-7pm Mon-Sat, to 6pm Sun; 👪; [S]A to Dyckman St) Located in Inwood Hill Park, right off the New York Greenway Bike Trail, is this family-friendly rentals shop – perfect for navigating the long and winding paths of upper Manhattan.

RIVERBANK STATE PARK SPORTS

Map p444 (http://nysparks.state.ny.us; 679 Riverside Dr at 145th St, Hamilton Heights; pool adult/child $2/1, fitness room $10, roller/ice skating $1.50/5, skate rental $6; ⏲park 6am-11pm; 👪; [S]1 to 145th St) This modern, 28-acre five-building facility, perched atop a waste refinery (not as crazy as it sounds), has an indoor Olympic-size pool, an outdoor lap pool, a fitness room, basketball and tennis courts, a running track around a soccer field, a kids' area and a roller-skating rink (with ice skating from November to March).

Brooklyn

BROOKLYN HEIGHTS | DUMBO | DOWNTOWN BROOKLYN | FORT GREENE | CLINTON HILL | BOERUM HILL | COBBLE HILL | CARROLL GARDENS | RED HOOK | GOWANUS | PARK SLOPE | PROSPECT PARK | PROSPECT HEIGHTS | BEDFORD-STUYVESANT | CROWN HEIGHTS | CONEY ISLAND | BRIGHTON BEACH | WILLIAMSBURG | BUSHWICK

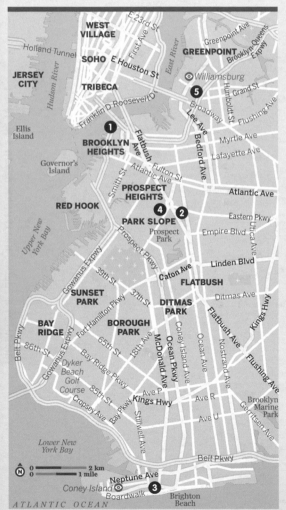

Neighborhood Top Five

1 Taking in the incredible views of Lower Manhattan from the new **Brooklyn Bridge Park** (p264) in Dumbo. Tucked between the Brooklyn and Manhattan Bridges, this East River green space has good spots for picnicking and a magnificent vintage carousel.

2 Seeing the impressive collections at the **Brooklyn Museum of Art** (p265), strong on Egyptian, American and feminist works.

3 Riding the rickety **Cyclone roller coaster** (p266) in Coney Island, one of America's oldest amusement parks.

4 Admiring the historic turn-of-the–20th-century architecture on **Montgomery Place** (p274) in Park Slope.

5 Poring through New York ephemera at the **City Reliquary** (p268).

For more detail of this area, see Maps p446 and p452 ➡

Explore Brooklyn

If Brooklyn were its own city, it'd be the fourth largest in the US – bigger than Houston, Philadelphia and Phoenix. It is home to more than 2.5 million people and is a rambling 71 sq miles (easily three times larger than Manhattan). It is split in two, with one set of subway lines servicing the north end of the borough, and another set traveling to points south. So if you think you can see it all in a day, as the locals say: 'Fuhgeddaboudit!'

For day-trip purposes, it is best to pick a neighborhood and stick to it. South Brooklyn, especially brownstone-studded Brooklyn Heights, offers lots of history and great Manhattan views. Fans of vintage amusement parks should head to Coney Island. For the night owls, the trendy enclave of Williamsburg lies just a single subway stop from Manhattan and is loaded with bars and restaurants.

If you are interested in other parts of town, ask around first. The borough may be all the rage, but it's not without its sketchy parts.

Local Life

➡ **Rock and roll** Hit the hot music spots in Williamsburg and Bushwick to hear the latest indie sounds. Bonus local points if you go on a weeknight.

➡ **Roller girls** Watch the Brooklyn Bombshells roller derby squad tear up the track in competition.

➡ **Park sloping** Join the stroller brigade for a lap or two around Prospect Park.

Getting There & Away

➡ **Subway** Sixteen subway lines travel between Manhattan and Brooklyn, with an additional line (the G) connecting the Park Slope area of Brooklyn to Williamsburg and Queens. For southern Brooklyn, you'll want the A/C line that stops in Brooklyn Heights, downtown and Bed-Stuy. Park Slope and Coney Island are serviced by the D/F and the N/Q. Brooklyn Heights, downtown and Prospect Heights can be accessed by the 2/3 and the 4/5. In north Brooklyn, Bushwick and Williamsburg are reached primarily on the L.

➡ **Bus** If you have a lot of time on your hands, the B62 bus travels within Brooklyn between downtown and Williamsburg. In downtown, find a stop at the intersection of Smith and Fulton Sts. In Williamsburg, look for stops along Driggs St.

Lonely Planet's Top Tip

If you want to get a sense of what old New York was like, be sure to wander around Brighton Beach. Under the elevated tracks on Brighton Beach Ave, the bustling Russian district known as 'Little Odessa' is packed with greengrocers and emporiums dispensing smoked fish and pierogis. On the street, you'll find a cross section of humanity – from grandmas to sulky teens – chattering in a million different languages as the trains rumble overhead. It's unmistakably New York.

✗ Best Places to Eat

➡ Roberta's (p283)
➡ Vinegar Hill House (p279)
➡ Lot 2 (p281)
➡ Varenichnaya (p283)
➡ Mile End (p280)

For reviews, see p278 ➡

🍷 Best Places to Drink

➡ Freddy's (p286)
➡ Commodore (p286)
➡ Ruby's (p267)
➡ Pine Box Rock Shop (p287)
➡ 61 Local (p285)

For reviews, see p285 ➡

◉ Best Places to Channel Your Inner Hipster

➡ Bell House (p288)
➡ Beacon's Closet (p294)
➡ Mermaid Parade (p267)

BROOKLYN

TOP SIGHTS
BROOKLYN BRIDGE PARK

This 85-acre park is one of Brooklyn's most talked-about new sights. Wrapping around a bend on the East River, it runs for 1.3 miles from Jay St in Dumbo to the west end of Atlantic Ave in Cobble Hill. It has revitalized a once-barren stretch of shoreline, turning a series of abandoned piers into public park land. Two of these are now open (Piers 1 and 6); others are scheduled to open in 2012 and 2013. Once completed, it will be the biggest new park in Brooklyn since Calvert Vaux and Frederick Olmsted designed the 585-acre Prospect Park in the 19th century.

Empire Fulton Ferry

Just east of the Brooklyn Bridge, in the northern section of Dumbo, a 9-acre state park has been transformed into a grassy lawn that faces the East River. It is bordered on one side by the **Empire Stores & Tobacco Warehouse** (Map p452), a series of hollow, Civil War–era structures. It is in this section that you'll find Jane's Carousel.

Jane's Carousel

Behold the star attraction: a vintage **carousel** (Map p452; www.janescarousel.com; Brooklyn Bridge Park, Empire Fulton Ferry, Dumbo; tickets $2; ⏰11am-7pm Wed-Mon, to 6pm Nov-Apr; 👪; [S]F to York St) built by the Philadelphia Toboggan Company back in 1922. It was purchased by Dumbo artist Jane Walentas in 1984, who spent the next two decades faithfully restoring the vintage paint scheme on the ornate, carved-wood elements.

The carousel has 48 horses in rows of three, two chariots and 1200 lights. It is the first carousel to be placed on the National Register of Historic Places. Housing this treasure is an acrylic glass pavilion designed by Pritzker Prize–winning architect Jean Nouvel. The combination of crisp contemporary architecture and vintage carousel is staggering. Do not miss.

Pier 1

A 9-acre pier just south of the Fulton Ferry Terminal is home to a brand new stretch of park featuring a playground, walkways and the Harbor and Bridge View lawns, both of which overlook the river. On the latter, you'll find artist Mark di Suvero's 30ft kinetic sculpture *Yoga* (1991). The seasonal Brooklyn Bridge Wine Bar (open May to October) can be found on the pier's north end.

Pier 6

The other major pier to be operational is this one, at the southern end of the park, off Atlantic Ave. There are walkways and seasonal concessions (May to October), including hot dogs and Italian ices. There is a pedestrian greenway that connects this area with Pier 1 to the north, though as long as the park is incomplete, this will remain a barren, lonely walk.

There are plans for a seasonal weekend ferry to ply the waters between this point and the South Street Seaport in lower Manhattan. Check the website for details.

DON'T MISS...

- ➡ Views of downtown Manhattan from Pier 1
- ➡ Jane's Carousel
- ➡ Empire Fulton Ferry at sunset

PRACTICALITIES

- ➡ Map p452
- ➡ ☎718-222-9939
- ➡ www.brooklynbridgeparknyc.org
- ➡ East River Waterfront btwn Atlantic Ave & Adams St
- ➡ ⏰6am-1am
- ➡ 👪
- ➡ [S]A/C to High St, 2/3 to Clark St, F to York St

TOP SIGHTS
BROOKLYN MUSEUM OF ART

This encyclopedic museum is housed in a five-story, 560,000-sq-ft beaux arts building designed by McKim, Mead & White. Construction on the building began in the early 1890s (when Brooklyn was still independent) with the intention of making it the largest single-site museum in the world. But the plan lost steam in 1898, when Brooklyn was incorporated into New York. Today, the building houses more than 1.5 million objects, including ancient artifacts, 19th-century period rooms, and sculptures and painting from across several centuries.

Egyptian Art

One of the highlights here is the excellent collection of Egyptian art, which spans a period of 5000 years. Housed in the 3rd-floor galleries, it includes bas-reliefs and Roman-era portraits, some of which are drawn from the museum's ongoing excavations in Egypt. A mummy chamber holds sarcophagi and ritual objects. But the most incredible piece is the so-called 'Bird Lady,' a delicate terra-cotta figurine with an abstracted face and claw-like hands, dating back to 3300–3650 BC. Look for her in a stand-alone vitrine.

All-American

An iconic portrait of George Washington by Gilbert Stuart. Childe Hassam's celebrated urban landscape, *Late Afternoon, New York, Winter*, from 1900. And dozens of paintings by late-19th-century portraitist John Singer Sargent. The Brooklyn is in possession of one of the great collections of American art. Do not miss a trip to the 5th floor to see it.

A Room of Their Own

This is the rare mainstream arts institution that devotes permanent space to showcasing women. The 8300-sq-ft Elizabeth Sackler Center for Feminist Art on the 4th floor exhibits an engaging mix of one-person and historical shows that examine topics like women in video or pop art. At the gallery's core, you'll find Judy Chicago's seminal 1979 installation, *The Dinner Party*.

What to Know

There are other worthwhile galleries devoted to African sculpture, Latin American textiles and contemporary art. If you want a peek behind the scenes, head to the Visible Storage and Study Center on the 5th floor to see glass cases stuffed with everything from vintage bicycles to a bulbous Gaston Lachaise sculpture.

The museum offers a great alternative to the packed-to-the-gills institutions in Manhattan. And the modern plaza out front is a good place to hang out when it's sunny.

Admission is free on the first Saturday of every month after 5pm.

DON'T MISS...

➡ Egyptian Collection
➡ Elizabeth Sackler Center for Feminist Art
➡ Visible Storage
➡ American Collection

PRACTICALITIES

➡ Map p450
➡ ☏718-638-5000
➡ www.brooklyn museum.org
➡ 200 Eastern Pkwy at Washington Ave
➡ suggested donation $12
➡ ⊙11am-6pm Wed & Fri-Sun, to 10pm Thu, to 11pm first Sat of the month
➡ ⊞
➡ ⓢ2/3 to Eastern Parkway-Brooklyn Museum

NATALIE GRONO / LONELY PLANET IMAGES ©

TOP SIGHTS
CONEY ISLAND

Named by the Dutch for the *konijn* (wild rabbits) that once ran loose on Brooklyn's extreme southern point, Coney Island achieved worldwide fame as a working-class resort area at the turn of the 20th century. Though it is no longer the booming, peninsula-wide attraction it was then, it has blossomed in recent years with new crowds, fresh rides and plentiful places to eat and drink.

Sodom by the Sea

The area traces its amusement park roots to the mid-1800s, when inhabitants of the increasingly industrialized city began to seek relief from their sweltering tenements in summer. By the late 19th century, the area was a rough-and-tumble party spot dubbed 'Sodom by the Sea.'

In the early 1900s, however, family amusements began to materialize. The most famous, Luna Park, opened in 1903 – a dream world with live camels and elephants, illuminated by more than a million bulbs. Today, it is still possible to ride the Wonder Wheel (opened in 1920) and the clackety Cyclone roller coaster (1927).

The area was a bit of a ghost town in the '80s, but it has experienced a resurgence in recent years, drawing New Yorkers who come to chow on hot dogs, catch a sideshow and dress up like punk mermaids at the annual Mermaid Parade.

DON'T MISS...

- Cyclone roller coaster
- Wonder Wheel
- Cold beer at Ruby's
- Nathan's Famous hot dogs

PRACTICALITIES

- Map p453
- www.coneyisland.com
- Surf Ave & the Boardwalk btwn 19th & 5th Sts
- 👪
- [S]D/F, N/Q to Coney Island-Stillwell Ave

Riding the Cyclone at Luna Park

Luna Park (Map p453; www.lunaparknyc.com; Surf Ave & 10th St; 🕐late Mar-Oct; 👪; [S]D/F, N/Q to Coney Island-Stillwell Ave) is one of Coney Island's most popular amusement parks and contains one of its most legendary rides: the Cyclone ($8), a wood roller coaster that reaches speeds of 60mph and makes near-vertical drops. It is now listed on the National Register of Historic Places.

Wheel of Wonder

The pink-and-mint-green **Deno's Wonder Wheel** (Map p453; ☎718-372-2592; www.wonderwheel.com; W 12th St btwn Surf Ave & the Boardwalk; ride $6; 🕒mid-Mar–Oct; 👪; [S]D/F, N/Q to Coney Island-Stillwell Ave) dates all the way back to 1920. It is the best place to survey Coney Island from up high.

Sideshows

A complex called **Coney Island USA** (Map p453; ☎718-372-5159; www.coneyisland.com; 1208 Surf Ave at 12th St; 🕒May-Sep; [S]D/F, N/Q to Coney Island-Stillwell Ave) is home to various activities. The best of the bunch is the **Sideshows by the Seashore** (adult/child $7.50/5), where you can see a face-tattooed fire-eater and a Mormon sword swallower. Upstairs, the small **Coney Island Museum** ($5) showcases local memorabilia. Most attractions operate in the afternoon from Wednesday to Sunday in summer. Check the website for details.

Coney by Jet Ski

Release your inner Kenny Powers by signing up for an excursion with **Jetty Jumpers** (Map p453; ☎917-734-9919; www.jettyjumpers.com; tours $275), which offers one-hour jet-ski tours of Coney Island (as well as epic, three-hour tours of the New York Harbor area). Reservations required.

Beer on the Boardwalk

The only dive bar on the Coney Island boardwalk is an institution: **Ruby's** (Map p453; www.rubysconeyisland.com; 1213 Boardwalk btwn Stillwell Ave & 12th St; 🕒11am-10pm Mon-Thu & Sun, to 1am Fri-Sat, Apr-Oct; [S]D, N/Q to Coney Island-Stillwell Ave), around since 1934, has been threatened with extinction by real estate developers. The bar, however, hangs on. So grab a stool, order a pint of Ruby's Ale ($7), and watch the waves and the salty locals roll in.

Let's Be Frank

The hot dog was invented in Coney Island in 1867, which means that eating a frankfurter is practically obligatory here. The top choice: **Nathan's Famous** (Map p453; 1310 Surf Ave cnr Stillwell Ave; hot dog $4; 🕒breakfast, lunch & dinner till late; [S]D/F to Coney Island-Stillwell Ave), which has been around since 1916. The annual 4th of July hot dog eating contest here is the stuff of legends.

ARCTIC DIP

It's never too cold for the Coney Island Polar Bear Club (www.polarbearclub.org) to take a dip in the Atlantic Ocean. Founded in 1903 by health crusader Bernarr Macfadden, the club organizes outdoor swims every Sunday from October through April. It is best known for its New Year's Day Swim, when hundreds of hungover New Yorkers plunge into Coney Island's frigid waters. Check the website for details of this and other swims.

HONOR THY MERMAID

The official start of the season is the wacky annual procession known as the Mermaid Parade (www.coneyisland.com/mermaid.shtml), which takes place the last Saturday in June. It is a sea of sequined, bejeweled, face-painted and topless revelers – not to mention drag queens in spangly aquatic getups. Things get rolling at 2pm, with the parade kicking off along the boardwalk between 10th and 15th Sts. It then moves chaotically along Surf Ave before winding up at the 'Mermaid Parade Ball' at the New York Aquarium.

Williamsburg is essentially a college town without a college – it's New York's of-the-moment Bohemian magnet, drawing slouchy, baby-faced artists, musicians, writers and graphic designers. Once a bastion of Latino working-class life, it's become a prominent dining and nightlife center – and, as a result, has attracted plenty of young urban professionals (and their attendant condo towers). It may not be full of major museums and picturesque architecture, but Williamsburg nonetheless offers plenty to do.

DON'T MISS...

➡ City Reliquary
➡ Brooklyn Brewery Tour
➡ Williamsburg Bridge
➡ All those bars!

PRACTICALITIES

➡ Map p446
➡ blocks between the BQE & the East River & Williamsburg Bridge & N 12th St
➡ S L to Bedford or Lorimer, J/M/Z to Marcy Ave

Bushwick to Williamsburg

The neighborhood now known as Williamsburg was once part of the greater community of Bushwick, a settlement founded by Dutch colonists in 1660. Williamsburg broke off into its own town in the 1820s, when the area began to industrialize. By the late 19th century, a steady stream of Jewish, German, Italian and Irish immigrants were arriving to fill factory jobs. By the 1920s, Puerto Rican immigrants began gaining a foothold.

The area attracted textile manufacturers and beer brewers. One of the biggest companies in the area was Domino Sugar, which kept a plant on the East River until 2004. The factory (built in the late 19th century) is now a landmark and a favorite graffiti spot.

Orientation

Most of the neighborhood is located along the East River waterfront, to the north of the Williamsburg Bridge. Bedford Ave serves as the main drag, with clusters of side-by-side cafes, boutiques and restaurants tucked into the area between N 10th St and Metropolitan Ave.

Wiliamsburg Bridge

Built in 1903 to link Williamsburg and the Lower East Side, this steel-frame suspension **bridge** (Map p446; www.nyc.gov/html/dot/html/bridges/willb.shtml; access at Havemayer St & 4th St Broadway & Roebling St; S J/M/Z to Marcy Ave) helped transform the area into a teeming industrial center. It is bigger than the more famous Brooklyn Bridge to the south. In fact, at the time of construction, it was the world's longest suspension bridge, with a span of 1600ft and a length of 7308ft.

Its uncrowded foot and bike paths offer excellent views of Manhattan and the East River. These are also the ideal spots from which to take in the graffiti that covers the nearby rooftops, the Domino Sugar plant and the bridge itself.

Bonus: unlike the more attractive Brooklyn Bridge, which is capped by less-than-interesting civic center zones, the Williamsburg connects two neighborhoods with plenty of bars and restaurants, offering the possibility of refreshments on both ends.

The City Reliquary

A tiny community museum housed in a former bodega, the curiously fascinating **City Reliquary** (Map p446; www.cityreliquary.org; 370 Metropolitan Ave near Havemeyer St; by donation; ⊘noon-6pm Sat & Sun, 7pm-10pm Thu; S L to Lorimer Ave) is filled with New York–related ephemera. Cases and shelves are stuffed full of old shop signs, Statue of Liberty postcards, vintage pencil sharpeners, subway tokens, seltzer bottles and paint chips off the L train.

There is also, according to the display text, a 'very old shovel.'

The exterior windows are reserved for odd collections of bric-a-brac owned by New York City residents, allowing for the odd sight of someone's ceramic frog collection to be viewed by passersby. In addition, the miniscule gift shop sells small tins of dirt from all five boroughs for $10. A quirky-excellent experience.

Brooklyn Brewery

Harkening back to a time when this area of New York was a beer brewing center, the **Brooklyn Brewery** (Map p446; ☎718-486-7422; www.brooklynbrewery. com; 79 N 11th St btwn Berry St & Wythe Ave; ⊘free tours on the hr 1-4pm Sat & Sun; Ⓢ L to Bedford Ave) not only brews and serves tasty local suds but offers tours of their facilities on weekends. For those who want to quaff while waiting for their 30-minute tour to begin, there is a selection of brews on tap (from $4).

Interesting fact: the brewery's cursive logo was designed by none other than Milton Glazer, of 'I heart New York' fame, who did the job in exchange for a share of the profits and free beer for life.

East River State Park

The seven-acre waterfront **East River State Park** (Map p446; www.nysparks.com/parks/155; Kent Ave btwn 8th and 9th Sts; ⊘9am-dusk; 🚻; Ⓢ L to Bedford Ave) is the latest hot spot for outdoor parties and free summer concerts in Williamsburg. Its grassy lawn is also home to a vast assortment of other events and activities. During the summer, the Brooklyn Flea (p293) can be found here, and there is ferry service to Manhattan and Governor's Island. No pets allowed.

UP TO DATE

Visit the Free Williamsburg (www.free williamsburg.com) and Wagmag (www.wag mag.org) websites to keep tabs on the latest music gigs, art openings and more.

For a time in the 1830s, Williamsburg was a fashionable resort area for wealthy New York magnates such as Commodore Vanderbilt and James Fisk. It began to grow more industrial in the late 1840s.

BEST TIME TO GO

Weekends is when Williamsburg is at its busiest and sidewalks overflow with street vendors, hipsters with sleeve tattoos, fashion-conscious couples and skate punks. It's prime people-watching time.

BROOKLYN WILLIAMSBURG

⊙ SIGHTS

⊙ Brooklyn Heights

New York's first suburb is also its first designated historic district, with 19th century brownstones (some of which date back to the 1820s) in the panoply of architectural styles: Victorian Gothic, Romanesque, neo-Greco, Italianate and Federal, to name but a few. This is a district of narrow streets and towering London plane trees – an ideal place to walk.

BROOKLYN HEIGHTS
PROMENADE   LOOKOUT
Map p452 (btwn Orange & Remsen Sts; ⊘24hr; ♦; ⓢ2/3 to Clark St) All of the neighborhood's east–west lanes (such as Clark and Pineapple Sts) lead to the neighborhood's number-one attraction: a narrow park with breathtaking views of Lower Manhattan and New York Harbor. Though it hangs over the busy Brooklyn–Queens Expressway (BQE), this little slice of urban perfection is a great spot for a sunset walk.

BROOKLYN HISTORICAL SOCIETY   MUSEUM
Map p452 (⌂718-222-4111; www.brooklynhistory.org; 128 Pierrepont St near Clinton St; adult/child $6/free; ⊘noon-5pm Wed-Sun; ⓢA/C, F to Jay St, M, R to Court St, 2/3, 4/5 to Borough Hall) Housed in an 1881 Queen Anne–style landmark building (a gem in itself, with striking terracotta details on the facade), this library and museum is devoted to all things Brooklyn. Its priceless collection contains a rare 1770 map of New York City and a signed copy of the Emancipation Proclamation (both too fragile, unfortunately, for permanent display).

Be sure to check out the vintage library, with its original black ash balcony from the 19th century. The society organizes regular exhibitions and neighborhood walks. Check the website for details.

⊙ Dumbo

Dumbo – short for Down Under the Manhattan Bridge Overpass – is a cobble-stone district lined with old 19th-century warehouses (now luxury condos) that offers incredible views of Manhattan from its waterfront areas. It's not the easiest neighborhood to navigate, so be prepared to do some walking around.

Visitors from Manhattan often combine Dumbo with a visit to Brooklyn Heights.

BROOKLYN BRIDGE PARK   PARK
See p264.

⊙ Downtown Brooklyn

Jammed into the area between Cadman Plaza West and Flatbush Ave, the modern downtown consists of the borough's civic center buildings (the courts and such), as well as functional office buildings. Here, the Fulton St Mall, a pedestrian strip, is chock-full of discount clothing and sneaker shops.

BROOKLYN TOURISM &
VISITORS CENTER   INFORMATION
(⌂718-802-3846; www.visitbrooklyn.org; 209 Joralemon St btwn Court St & Brooklyn Bridge Blvd; ⊘10am-6pm Mon-Fri; ⓢ2/3, 4/5 to Borough Hall) Housed in the Greek Revival Brooklyn Borough Hall (built 1845), the city's tourism office has maps and a list of recommended local tour operators. Here, you can also buy a Brooklyn Pass (adult/child $25/15) that will gain you admittance to various Brooklyn attractions.

NEW YORK TRANSIT MUSEUM   MUSEUM
Map p452 (⌂718-694-1600; www.mta.info/mta/museum; Schermerhorn St at Boerum Pl; adult/child $7/5; ⊘10am-4pm Tue-Fri, 11am-5pm Sat & Sun; ♦; ⓢ2/3, 4/5 to Borough Hall, R to Court St) Occupying an old subway station built in 1936 (and out of service since 1946), this kid-friendly museum takes on 100-plus years of getting around town. The best part is the downstairs area, on the platform, where you can climb aboard 13 original subway and elevated train cars dating to 1904. The museum's gift shop sells popular subway-map gifts.

DIME SAVINGS BANK   LANDMARK
Map p452 (9 DeKalb Ave at Fulton St Mall; ⊘8:30am-6pm Mon-Fri, 9am-3pm Sat; ⓢB/D, N/Q/R to DeKalb Ave) At a point where DeKalb Ave meets the Fulton St Mall sits the neo-classical Dime Savings Bank building from 1908. The interiors feature elaborate coffered ceilings and Corinthian columns crafted from red marble. It's now a working branch of the Chase bank, but you can still pop into the lobby for a gander. No pictures allowed.

START **ST GEORGE HOTEL**
END **JANE'S CAROUSEL**
DISTANCE **2 MILES**
DURATION **TWO HOURS**

Neighborhood Walk

Brownstones & Bridges

Studded with historic structures, the area around Brooklyn Heights is also a good spot for sublime views of Manhattan.

Start at the corner of Clark and Henry Sts, at the base of the 30-story 1 **St George Hotel**. Built between 1885 and 1930, it was once the city's largest hotel with 2632 rooms.

Two blocks to the north, at Orange and Hicks Sts, is 2 **Plymouth Church**. In the mid-19th century, Henry Ward Beecher led abolitionist sermons here, as well as 'mock auctions' to buy a slave's freedom.

Continue west on Orange and then south on Willow St. At 70 Willow, the yellow, 11-bedroom mansion served as 3 **Truman Capote's house** while he was writing *Breakfast at Tiffany's*.

Continue south, making a right on Pierrepont St, then following it as it bends to the left. The street turns into 4 **Montague Tce**, a one-block lane lined with old brownstones. Thomas Wolfe penned *Of Time and the River* at No 5.

From here, Remsen St travels west to reach the 5 **Brooklyn Heights Promenade**. This scenic park, with its staggering city views, was built by planner Robert Moses in 1942, as a way of placating locals irritated by the construction of the roaring expressway below.

Head north along the the Promenade, then north along Columbia Heights, following the road over the Brooklyn–Queens Expressway and down to the water at 6 **Fulton Ferry Landing**. George Washington made an important, hasty retreat here during the Battle of Long Island in 1776. At the pier, you'll find the 7 **Brooklyn Ice Cream Factory**, a good spot for a refuel.

From here, follow Water St under the 8 **Brooklyn Bridge** (completed 1883), and past the 9 **Empire Stores & Tobacco Warehouse**, two Civil War–era brick structures. The walk ends at Empire Fulton Ferry, part of Brooklyn Bridge Park and home to the gleaming 10 **Jane's Carousel**.

◉ Fort Greene & Clinton Hill

These appealing residential districts spread east and south from the Brooklyn side of the Manhattan Bridge (along the eastern side of Flatbush Ave). The neighborhoods are marked on the southwestern end by the **Williamsburgh Savings Bank Tower** (Map p448; 1 Hanson Pl at Flatbush Ave; S2/3, 4/5 to Atlantic Ave, D, N/R to Atlantic Ave-Pacific St), which was built in 1927 and for decades was the tallest building in Brooklyn. If you're lost, looking for the tower is a good way to regain your sense of direction. This is also where the Brooklyn Flea (p293) is held in the winter months.

If you're on the hunt for gorgeous 19th-century architecture, Washington and Clinton Aves in Clinton Hill are home to some beautiful clusters of post–Civil War row houses.

BROOKLYN ACADEMY OF MUSIC
ARTS CENTER

Map p448 (BAM; ☑718-636-4139; www.bam. org; 30 Lafayette Ave at Ashland Pl, Fort Greene; S2/3, 4/5, B, Q to Atlantic Ave) Founded in 1861, BAM is the country's oldest performing arts center and supplies New York City with its edgier works of modern dance, music and theater. The complex contains a 2109-seat opera house, an 874-seat theater and the four-screen Rose Cinemas. Its stage has showcased Mercer Cunningham retrospectives, contemporary African dance and avant-garde interpretations of Shakespeare.

Every fall, BAM hosts the Next Wave Festival, which presents an array of avant-garde works and artists talks. The on-site bar and restaurant, BAMcafé, stages free jazz, R&B and pop performances on weekends.

FORT GREENE PARK
PARK

Map p448 (btwn Myrtle & DeKalb Aves & Washington Park & Edward's St, Fort Greene; ⊘6am-1am; ⁂; SB, Q/R to DeKalb Ave) This 30-acre park sits on land that housed military forts during the Revolutionary War. In 1847, the area was designated Brooklyn's first park (a measure supported by newspaper editor Walt Whitman), and by 1867, Calvert Vaux and Frederick Olmsted were redesigning the place into the attractive hilltop landscape it is today. There are walkways, ball fields and a playground.

At the center of the park stands the Prison Ship Martyrs' Monument, supposedly the world's largest Doric column (it's 149ft high). Designed by Stanford White, it was built in 1905 to memorialize the 11,500 American prisoners of war who died in British prison ships during the Revolution.

◉ Boerum Hill, Cobble Hill & Carroll Gardens

Just south of Brooklyn Heights and Downtown Brooklyn, this cluster of tree-lined brownstone neighborhoods – Boerum Hill

WORTH A DETOUR

HARBOR DEFENSE MUSEUM

Beneath the breathtaking Verrazano-Narrows Bridge and located inside Fort Hamilton, military buffs will discover a small treasure trove of artifacts at the **Harbor Defense Museum** (www.harbordefensemuseum.com; 101st St & Fort Hamilton Pkwy; ⊘10am-4pm Mon-Fri, to 2pm Sat; ⁂; SR to Bay Ridge-95 St), the only army museum in New York City.

Built between 1825 and 1831, this arched brick fort is still an active army base (bring a photo ID to get in). The historic caponier, a freestanding bastion, houses the museum. The diverse collection includes helmets, weapons and uniforms from the Revolutionary War to WWII. There is also an array of vintage artillery. Take a guided tour if you want to learn how to load a 19th century cannon. (Interesting fact: future Confederate General Robert E Lee ran the fort in the 1840s.)

A few blocks west, you'll find the harbor-hugging, 2.5-mile-long Shore Parkway promenade. It's an ideal spot for a walk. North of Fort Hamilton is the old Italian district of Bay Ridge, where there are eateries and pubs along Third Ave, from 76th to 95th Sts.

To get here, take the R train to Bay Ridge–95 St and then walk half a dozen blocks to the southwest along 4th Ave. The museum is located in a small park adjacent to the Verrazano-Narrows Bridge.

(east of Court St), Cobble Hill (west of Court St) and Carroll Gardens (south of Degraw St), is short on attractions but full of great places to stroll, eat and shop.

In Boerum Hill, Smith St is a particularly enticing option. The roughly dozen-block stretch south of Atlantic Ave is filled with restaurants, bookshops, bars and neat boutiques – a more chilled-out alternative to the consumer craziness of Manhattan. Atlantic Ave is broader and busier, with bars, restaurants, Middle Eastern groceries and antique shops, all concentrated into the blocks between Boerum Pl and Third Ave.

To the south of Cobble Hill is Carroll Gardens, a long-time Italian neighborhood, which continues down to the Gowanus Expressway.

⊙ Red Hook

For more than a century, the Statue of Liberty has fixated on this gritty neighborhood of harbor warehouses and cracked brick streets. The neighborhood is really two in one. There is 'the Back,' the popular waterfront area, which channels a rakish, 1940s kind of vibe. (It inspired the 1954 Marlon Brando drama *On the Waterfront*.) And there's the district to the south, home to the Red Hook Houses, an austere series of public housing projects that date back to the 1930s.

The area around the Back has gentrified in recent years, and a shiny new Ikea housewares store now sits on the waterfront, as does a gourmet-foods-stuffed Fairway supermarket. In addition, cruise ships occasionally dock at the nearby cruise terminal. But Red Hook's remoteness – the closest subway stop is at least a dozen blocks away – has kept development at bay.

The area around the waterfront is a good spot for a chilled-out walk in good weather. It is best at the end of the day, when the sun starts to slip behind the Statue of Liberty.

The only way to get here is aboard the pokey B61 bus from Cobble Hill (which runs west on Atlantic Ave and then south along Columbia St), or via a long walk through a desolate industrial area from the Smith–9th Sts station of the F and G trains. Be careful at night.

FREE WATERFRONT MUSEUM   MUSEUM
Map p448 (☏718-624-4710; www.waterfront museum.org; 290 Conover St at Pier 44; ⊙4-8pm

Thu, 1-5pm Sat; 🚻; ⓈF to Smith St, 🚌B61 to Coffey St) The former Lehigh Valley Railroad Barge #79 (built 1914) was purchased for a dollar by its current owner, a juggler, who rescued it from its partially submerged state under the George Washington Bridge. Now it serves as a floating museum with exhibits and events. The museum is free, but if you leave a donation you get a temporary tattoo. It's not a huge attraction, but sufficiently odd to be interesting.

⊙ Gowanus

To the east of the elevated subway station at Smith–9th Sts, in an area surrounded by decrepit, industrial blocks, is the Gowanus Canal. A former creek named after Gouwane, a Canarsie Indian chief, it was here that ships to New York Harbor came to unload their goods. It was also where local industrial operations unloaded all kinds of untreated waste. Today, it has been declared a clean-up site by the Environmental Protection Agency. Despite its toxic status, the area is home to a number of artist studios and frequently attracts intrepid urban explorers in search of moody waterfront pictures.

In 2007, a baby minke whale – dubbed 'Sludgie' by the press – was founded swimming in the bay that leads to the canal. He beached himself shortly thereafter.

⊙ Park Slope

This is New York's most earnest baby-making center, a leafy neighborhood that draws professionals in search of 19th-century brownstones and family-friendly everything.

Most businesses are located along Seventh Ave, while more youthful bars line the stretch along Fifth Ave. The more ornate homes – in beaux arts, Romanesque Revival and neo-Gothic styles – can be found on Prospect Park West and Eighth Ave between Union and Ninth Sts.

OLD STONE HOUSE   CULTURAL BUILDING
Map p450 (☏718-768-3195; www.theoldstone house.org; Washington Park/JJ Byrne Playground, 3rd St at 5th Ave; suggested donation $3; ⊙11am-4pm Sat & Sun; 🚻; ⓈF, R to 4th Ave) This stone house is a replica of a 1699 Dutch farmhouse that was reconstructed by Robert

A WALK-THROUGH GREEN-WOOD CEMETERY

If you really want to enjoy a slice of scenic Brooklyn in total peace and quiet, make for **Green-Wood Cemetery** (Map p450; www.green-wood.com; 500 25th St at Fifth Ave; 🕒7:45am-6pm Oct-Apr, to 7pm May-Aug; [S]R to 25th St). A historic burial ground set on the borough's highest point, it covers almost 500 hilly acres. Its myriad tombs, mausoleums and patches of forest are connected by a looping network of roads and trails, making this a perfect spot for some aimless rambling.

Founded in 1838, the cemetery is the final resting place of all kinds of notable personalities. In fact, some 600,000 people are buried here – that's at least 530 miles worth, if you laid them head-to-toe. This includes inventor Samuel Morse, mobster Joey Gallo, abolitionist Henry Ward Beecher, and '80s graffitist and Brooklyn son Jean-Michel Basquiat.

The best spot in the cemetery is **Battle Hill**, the highest point, where the Continental Army fought off British troops during the 1776 Battle of Long Island. The event is commemorated by the 7ft statue of Minerva, the Roman goddess of wisdom, who waves to the Statue of Liberty in the distance. The hill is located in the northeast sector of the cemetery, off Battle Ave. Maestro Leonard Bernstein and Brooklyn Dodgers owner Charles Ebbets are both buried in the vicinity.

You can pick up a free map at the entrance. On Wednesdays at 1pm, there is a two-hour trolley tour (per person $15). Note the squawking green parakeets nesting atop the Gothic entryway – these guys apparently broke out of an airport crate in 1980 and have lived here ever since.

Tip: pack mosquito repellent in the summer.

Moses. There's a permanent exhibit devoted to the Battle of Long Island (what Brooklyn was known as c 1776) that includes period clothes and weapons. The original home also served as a club house for Brooklyn Superbas, a predecessor to the Brooklyn Dodgers.

MONTGOMERY PLACE — NEIGHBORHOOD

Map p450 (Montgomery Place btwn Prospect Park West & 8th Ave; [S]2/3, 4 to Grand Army Plaza) This shady, one-block street contains a coveted series of beaux arts row houses, most of which were built by Paris-educated Charles Pierrepont Henry Gilbert in the 1880s. The street is named for a British veteran who fought in the Revolutionary War.

Prospect Park

The creators of the 585-acre Prospect Park, Calvert Vaux and Frederick Olmsted, considered this an improvement over their other New York project, Central Park. Created in 1866, Prospect Park has many of the same features: a gorgeous meadow, a scenic lake and rambling hills that are straddled with leafy walkways. It receives roughly eight million visitors a year.

GRAND ARMY PLAZA — MONUMENT

Map p450 (Prospect Park, Prospect Park West & Flatbush Ave; 🕒6am-midnight; [S]2/3 to Grand Army Plaza, B, Q to 7th Ave) A large, landscaped traffic circle with a massive ceremonial arch sits at the intersection of Flatbush Ave and Prospect Park West. This marks the beginning of Eastern Parkway and the entrance to Prospect Park. Formally known as the Soldiers' and Sailors' Monument, the arch, which was built in the 1890s, is a memorial to Union soldiers who fought in the Civil War.

The *Quadriga*, the massive sculpture that rests on top of the archway, depicts Lady Columbia, a representation of the US, accompanied by two winged figures of Victory. On the north end, there is a small bust of John F Kennedy, the city's only official monument to the late President.

A greenmarket is held here from 8am to 4pm on Saturdays year-round.

[FREE] PROSPECT PARK LONG MEADOW — PARK

Map p450 (www.prospectpark.org; Prospect Park, near Prospect Park West & Eastern Parkway; 🕒6am-midnight; 👪; [S]B, Q to 7th Ave, 2/3 to Grand Army Plaza) The 90-acre Long Meadow, which is bigger than Central Park's Great Lawn, lies to the south of the park's formal entrance at Grand Army Plaza. It's a super strolling and lounging spot, filled with pick-up ball games and families flying kites. On the south end is the Picnic House, which has a shaded grove with picnic tables as well as public bathrooms

CHILDREN'S CORNER CHILDREN'S ACTIVITIES

Map p450 (Carousel & Zoo; ☎718-282-7789; www.prospectpark.org; Prospect Park at Lincoln Rd & Ocean Ave; carousel $2; ⏰noon-5pm Thu-Sun Apr-Oct; 👪; [S]B, Q to Prospect Park) Near Flatbush Ave, the Children's Corner contains a terrific 1912 carousel, originally from Coney Island, and the **Prospect Park Zoo** (Map p450; www.prospectparkzoo.com; Prospect Park at Lincoln Rd & Ocean Ave; adult/child $8/5; ⏰10am-5:30ampm Apr-Oct, to 4:30ampm Nov-Mar), featuring sea lions, baboons, wallabies and a small petting zoo. To the northeast of the carousel is the 18th century Lefferts Historic House, which has plenty of old-fashioned toys to goof around with.

AUDUBON CENTER BOATHOUSE BOATHOUSE

Map p450 (☎718-287-3400; www.prospectpark.org/audubon; Prospect Park, near Lincoln Rd & Ocean Ave; electric boats $8; ⏰noon-5pm Thu-Sun Apr-Nov, to 4pm Dec-Mar; 👪; [S]B, Q to Prospect Park) Sitting on a northern finger of Prospect Park Lake, the boathouse offers electric boat rides and paddle boats for rent during the summer. From here, there is a trailhead for 2.5 miles of woodsy nature trails (the route which takes you along Lullwater Creek is very scenic). Check the website for maps or ask at the boathouse.

[FREE] **PROSPECT PARK BANDSHELL** ARTS CENTER

Map p450 (www.prospectpark.org; Prospect Park, near 9th St & Prospect Park West; 👪; [S]F, G to 7 Ave) To the southwest of the park's Long Meadow, this band shell hosts free outdoor concerts during the summers. Performance calendars can be found online or at the Audubon Center Boathouse. South of this area, there are a number of ball fields.

Prospect Heights

Just across Flatbush Ave from Park Slope is the easygoing Prospect Heights. Once a home to Italian, Jewish and Irish residents, it began to attract African Americans and West Indians in the middle of the 20th century. Today, it draws a mix of young families and professionals who appreciate the proximity to Prospect Park. Most businesses are clustered along Vanderbilt and Washington Aves.

BROOKLYN MUSEUM OF ART MUSEUM

See p265.

BROOKLYN BOTANIC GARDEN GARDENS

Map p450 (www.bbg.org; 1000 Washington Ave at Crown St; adult/child $10/free, Tue & 10am-noon Sat free; ⏰8am-6pm Tue-Fri, 10am-6pm Sat & Sun mid-March–Oct, 8am-4:30pm Tue-Fri, 10am-4:30pm Sat & Sun Nov–Mar; 👪; [S]2/3 to Eastern Pkwy-Brooklyn Museum) One of Brooklyn's most picturesque attractions, this 52-acre garden is home to thousands of plants and trees, as well as a Japanese garden where river turtles swim alongside a Shinto shrine. The best time to visit is late April or early May, when the blooming cherry trees (a gift from Japan) are celebrated in Sakura Matsuri, the Cherry Blossom Festival.

A network of trails connect the Japanese garden to other popular sections devoted to native flora, bonsai trees, a wood covered in bluebells and a rose garden.

There are multiple entrances. The best one is at Washington Ave, south of the Brooklyn Museum, which is scheduled to be sporting a remarkable new visitors center in May of 2012. The structure, designed by Weiss/Manfredi, will feature a 'living' roof covered in 40,000 living plants.

[FREE] **BROOKLYN PUBLIC LIBRARY** LIBRARY

Map p450 (☎718-230-2100; www.brooklynpubliclibrary.org; 10 Grand Army Plaza btwn Flatbush & Eastern Pkwy; ⏰9am-9pm Mon-Thu, 10am-6pm Fri & Sat, 1pm-5pm Sun; 👪; [S]B, Q to 7th Ave, 2/3 to Eastern Pkwy-Brooklyn Museum) Brooklyn's Central Library is an art deco masterpiece from 1941 that contains over one million books, magazines and multimedia items. The limestone-covered building is shaped like an open book and there are 15 bronze panels above its 50ft-high entrance featuring literary characters like Tom Sawyer and Moby Dick. There is also a lobby cafe and a 3rd-floor computer center.

Bedford-Stuyvesant & Crown Heights

Bedford-Stuyvesant is New York City's largest African American district – it's where Notorious BIG grew up and film director

Spike Lee shot *Do the Right Thing*. The neighborhood takes up a sprawling swathe of central Brooklyn between Flushing and Atlantic Aves and incorporates everything from spruced-up historic districts to sleepy streets of ramshackle row houses to bleak public housing projects. The Stuyvesant Heights Historic District (corner Lewis Ave and Decatur St; A/C to Utica Ave), located near Bed-Stuy's southern limits, vies with Brooklyn Heights and Park Slope for most gorgeous late-19th-century brownstones.

South of Atlantic Ave, you'll find Crown Heights, another black enclave known for its resplendent West Indian Day parade (held every year on Labor Day.)

Parts of these neighborhoods bordering Bushwick and East New York can get sketchy. If you're keen on adventuring, ask around before setting out.

BROOKLYN CHILDREN'S MUSEUM   MUSEUM
(www.brooklynkids.org; 145 Brooklyn Ave at St Marks Ave, Crown Heights; admission $7.50; ⊙1-6pm Tue-Fri, 11am-6pm Sat & Sun Jul & Aug, 11am-5pm Wed-Fri, 10am-5pm Sat & Sun Sep-Jun; ⊛; ⓈC to Kingston-Throop Aves, 3 to Kingston Ave) A bright yellow, L-shaped structure houses this hands-on kid favorite. The collection contains almost 30,000 cultural objects (musical instruments, masks and dolls) and natural history specimens (rocks, minerals and a complete Asian elephant skeleton). Founded in 1899, it was the first museum made just for kids, and after an expansion in 2008, it is now two times its original size. The museum is located next to Brower Park and is about a mile from the Grand Army Plaza.

WEEKSVILLE HERITAGE
CENTER   HISTORIC SITE
(www.weeksvillesociety.org; 1698 Bergen St btwn Rochester & Buffalo Aves, Crown Heights; adult/child $5/free; ⊙tours 3pm Tue-Fri; ⓈA/C to Utica Ave) In 1838, a free African American by the name of James Weeks purchased a tract of land on the fringes of Brooklyn's settled areas to build a free black community of entrepreneurs, doctors, laborers and craftsmen. Over time, the village was absorbed into Brooklyn, but three of the historic wooden houses (aka the Hunterfly Road Houses) can be visited. If you're coming from the upper reaches of Manhattan, it's a bit of a trek – but for history buffs, it's worth it.

WYCKOFF HOUSE   HISTORIC BUILDING
(⊘718-629-5400; www.wyckoffassociation.org; 5816 Clarendon Rd btwn 59th St & Ralph Ave, East Flatbush; adult/child $5/free; ⊙guided tours 1pm & 3pm Tues-Fri, 11am, 1pm & 3pm Sat & Sun Apr-Oct, closed Sun Nov-Apr; ⓈA to Utica Ave, ▯B46 south to Clarendon Rd) Built in 1652, the Pieter Claesen Wyckoff House is New York City's oldest structure. A working farm until 1901, this Dutch Colonial H-frame house has shingled walls and split Dutch doors. It's located in the East Flatbush section of Brooklyn. Reservations required.

To get here take the A train to Utica Ave, then switch to the B46 bus headed south (in the direction of King's Highway). It's a 30-minute ride to Clarendon Rd. (If you pass King's Highway, you've gone too far.) Once you get off, it's a nine-block walk east to the home.

⊙ Coney Island & Brighton Beach

Located about an hour by subway from Lower Manhattan, these two beachside neighborhoods sit side by side, facing the Atlantic. Brighton Beach, to the east, is quieter, with coffee shops and grocery stands that display signs in Cyrillic and cater to the largely Ukrainian and Russian population. Coney Island, a mile to the west, is brassier, with carnival rides, boardwalk bars and a surreal parade of humanity.

The two communities are connected by a boardwalk that runs along the beach, the best see-and-be-seen spot in Brooklyn during the steamy summer months.

CONEY ISLAND   NEIGHBORHOOD
See p266.

NEW YORK AQUARIUM   AQUARIUM
Map p453 (www.nyaquarium.com; Surf Ave & W 8th St; adult/child $15/11, with 4-D theater show $19/15; ⊙10am-6pm Mon-Fri, to 7pm Sat & Sun May-Sep; ⊛; ⓈF, Q to W 8th St-NY Aquarium) This fun, kid-friendly aquarium offers an opportunity to peek at an ocean's worth of creatures. The shark and walrus feeding times are the big draw, and there are sea lion shows (free kisses if you dare). Admission on Fridays from 3pm to closing is by donation. Skip the overpriced '4-D' shows – basically, 3-D films with wind and other effects.

START **BRIGHTON BAZAAR**
END **RUBY'S**
DISTANCE **1.75 MILES**
DURATION **TWO HOURS**

Neighborhood Walk
On & Off the Boardwalk

➡ You'll see the best of Coney Island and Brighton Beach on this leisurely neighborhood jaunt.

Start by stocking up on snacks at the ❶ **Brighton Bazaar**, on the corner of Brighton Beach Ave and 11th St. This Russian market is a bounty of cheeses, caviar and blintzes.

Head west under the train tracks on ❷ **Brighton Beach Ave**, where a teaming array of shops dispense fresh fruit, fresh sausage, *matrushka* dolls and red-and-white tracks suits that say 'Russia.' Best window shopping ever.

At Brighton 1st St, head south to the ❸ **Boardwalk**. To your left you'll see a few beach-facing 'banquet halls.' Some of these serve mugs of *kvass* (a barley-based drink from the heartland).

Walk west on the Boardwalk and stop at the ❹ **New York Aquarium**, at W 8th St, to have a peak at the cute, whiskered sea lions or some toothy reef sharks.

From the Aquarium, you'll see the ❺ **Cyclone roller coaster** on the corner of Surf Ave and W 10th. This 1927 wood coaster is a creaking classic. It only takes two minutes to go around the 3000ft track but the clacking wood and scary dips can make it feel like forever.

One block to the west, you'll find ❻ **Deno's Wonder Wheel**, another Coney standout. Built in 1920 by the Eccentric Ferris Wheel Company and made from Bethlehem Steel, the 400,000 pound attraction is overhauled and repainted every year.

After the walk, treat yourself to a frank at ❼ **Nathan's Famous** on the corner of Surf and Stillwell Aves. See if you can beat the world record set by Joey Chestnut on July 4, 2011: he downed 62 dogs in 10 minutes at the annual hot dog eating contest.

Afterwards, head back to the Boardwalk, for a cold beer at ❽ **Ruby's**, a divey local mainstay.

BROOKLYN NEIGHBORHOOD WALK

Don't miss the sea horse tanks, full of fascinating and beautiful species. The aquarium closes 60 to 90 minutes earlier than the times posted above during the winter months (November to May).

◉ Williamsburg

WILLIAMSBURG   NEIGHBORHOOD
See p268.

◉ Bushwick

A couple of subway stops to the east of Williamsburg on the L train, the ramshackle blocks of Bushwick begin to appear. Now home to a mixed community of African Americans, as well as Mexican, Ecuadorean, Puerto Rican and Dominican immigrants, it was an important beer-brewing center in the late 19th and early 20th centuries. The stately homes of beer barons still line Bushwick Ave, some in decrepit condition.

In recent years, artists and musicians in search of cheap rents have begun to materialize in the area. As a result, the neighborhood's western fringes are already filling up with bars and industrial-chic restaurants. This area remains an industrial zone during the day but perks up on Friday and Saturday evenings when local bars and performance spaces come to life.

✖ EATING

A haven of all things high-end comfort, retro-vintage and bespoke, as well as plenty of ethnic joints that offer simple, unpretentious eats, Brooklyn is a place to bring your appetite. Not to mention your wallet.

✖ Brooklyn Heights, Downtown Brooklyn & Dumbo

ALMAR   ITALIAN $$
Map p452 (☑718-855-5288; 111 Front St btwn Adams & Washington Sts, Dumbo; mains $14-22; ⊘8am-10:30pm Mon-Thu, to 11pm Fri & Sat, 9am-4pm Sun; ⊕; ⓈF to York St, A/C/E to High St) A welcoming Italian eatery serves breakfast, lunch and dinner in a homey, wood-lined space in Dumbo. Alfredo's meatballs ($8) are top-notch, as is the rich and meaty lasagna Bolognese ($14). But if you're into seafood, don't miss the simple and delicious cavatelli with mussels, clams, shrimp and cherry tomatoes ($16) – it doesn't skimp

A TREE GROWS IN BROOKLYN

There are few phrases involving Brooklyn that are more used, lampooned or punned upon than 'a tree grows in Brooklyn.' It is constantly employed by the media, and even old television comedies (in an episode of *I Love Lucy*, Lucy tries to get her husband, Ricky, to star in a play called *A Tree Grows in Havana*).

All of these references are drawn from Betty Smith's bestselling 1943 novel *A Tree Grows in Brooklyn*, a poignant coming-of-age story that is now part of American popular culture. The book chronicles the life of Francie Nolan, a determined half-German, half-Irish girl living in squalid circumstances in the tenements of Williamsburg in the first couple of decades of the 20th century. Francie and her family live in an underheated tenement. They survive on stale bread. Often they go hungry. The kids comb the trash for scrap metal that they can sell to buy penny candy. There are references to the roaring elevated train, the clip-clop of horse-drawn carriages and the corrupt workings of politicians at Tammany Hall.

The story closely mirrors the life of its author (real name: Elisabeth Wehner), who was born in 1896 in Williamsburg, the daughter of working-class German immigrants. The book was a triumph for her in many respects. Not only was it critically acclaimed, but it was a rare feat for a female, working-class author to be embraced by the literary establishment. Above all, it serves as a compelling historical document, making frequent reference to the streets and landmarks of turn-of-the-20th century Williamsburg.

Want to get to know Brooklyn? Start with this book.

on the shellfish. There are muffins and coffee at breakfast and paninis at lunch. The small, inviting bar is an ideal spot to sip wine and nibble on olives.

GRIMALDI'S — PIZZERIA $

Map p452 (☎718-858-4300; www.grimaldisbrooklyn.com; 1 Front St cnr of Old Fulton St, Brooklyn Heights; pizzas $12-16; ⏰lunch & dinner; [S]A/C to High St) Legendary lines and pizzas are still dished up daily at this touristy pizza mecca. Thankfully, they live up to the hype: thin-crust pies are dabbed with San Marzano tomato sauce and topped with fresh mozzarella, and delivered bubbling to your table. They also make gooey calzones that could make a pacemaker skip a beat. Be prepared for long lines. Whole pies only.

The restaurant is in a new multilevel location after losing its former lease. Interestingly, a new pizza joint, Juliana's (www.julianaspizza.com) is scheduled to open next door sometime in 2012. And it will be run by Patsy and Carol Grimaldi, the original owners of Grimaldi's (they sold the business to Frank Ciolli, who has run it since 1998). Hopefully this means shorter lines all around. In the meantime, let the pizza wars begin!

BROOKLYN ICE CREAM FACTORY — ICE CREAM

Map p452 (www.brooklynicecreamfactory.com; Fulton Landing, Water & Old Fulton Sts, Brooklyn Heights; scoop $4, shake $7; ⏰noon-10pm Sun-Thu, to 11pm Fri & Sat; 👪; [S]A/C to High St) You can grab a cone or a milkshake within view of the Manhattan and Brooklyn Bridges at this shop located inside an old fireboat house. The Factory uses pure maple syrup in their maple walnut ice-cream flavor and the hot fudge is 72% pure cacao. Worth the price.

[TOP CHOICE] VINEGAR HILL HOUSE — AMERICAN $$

Map p452 (www.vinegarhillhouse.com; 72 Hudson Ave btwn Water & Front Sts, Vinegar Hill; mains $15-30; ⏰6-11pm Mon-Thu, to 11:30pm Fri & Sat, 11am-3:30pm & 5:30pm-11pm Sun; 🌿; [S]F to York St) Tucked into out-of-way Vinegar Hill, this homey spot is decked out in a charming array of thrift store bric-a-brac. But don't let the low-key decor fool you: chef Brian Leth cooks up an evolving menu that is bracingly fresh and unfussy, like homemade garganelli with escarole and preserved lemon or seared trout with hazelnuts and baby carrots. There is a wine list stocked with French vintages (from $36 per bottle), as well as retro cocktails (the John Collins is particularly refreshing).

This place is popular, especially in summer when the back patio is open. Show up near opening time if you don't want to wait.

JUNIOR'S — DINER $

Map p452 (www.juniorscheesecake.com; 386 Flatbush Ave cnr DeKalb Ave, Downtown Brooklyn; cheesecake slice $6; 👪; [S]B/D, N/Q/R to DeKalb Ave) If you want old-school Brooklyn with plenty of attitude, this is the place. And while some folks still come here for the food (which is forgettable), you should come here for one thing and one thing only: the cheesecake. Slices are rich, creamy and big enough to share.

CHEF'S TABLE — AMERICAN $$$

Map p452 (☎718-243-0050; www.brooklynfare.com/chefs-table; 200 Schermerhorn St btwn Hoyt & Bond Sts, Downtown Brooklyn; prix fixe from $135; [S]A/C, G to Hoyt-Schermerhorn) Cesar Ramirez's three-star Michelin eatery has the foodies frothing with a seafood-heavy tasting menu that features exotic items such as fried blowfish and fugu. With just 18 seats, tables are hard to come by so plan the trip around your reservation.

SUPERFINE — AMERICAN $

Map p452 (☎718-243-9005; 126 Front St cnr Pearl Pl, Dumbo; mains $14-22; ⏰lunch & dinner Tue-Fri & Sun, dinner Sat; [S]F to York St) This casual hangout is known for its Sunday brunches where Dumbonians sip Bloody Marys while catching bluegrass shows onstage. Windows line two sides, and the rumble of the subway on the Manhattan Bridge overhead puts a bumpy thrill into the meal. The menu covers Mediterranean, Mexican and American dishes. Try the grilled chicken sandwich with pancetta at lunch.

RIVER CAFÉ — AMERICAN $$$

Map p452 (☎718-522-5200; www.rivercafe.com; 1 Water St, Brooklyn Heights; fixed price dinner/brunch $125/55, lunch mains $24-30; ⏰lunch & dinner daily, brunch Sat & Sun; 🌿; [S]A/C to High St) Situated at the foot of the Brooklyn Bridge, this floating wonder offers beautiful views of downtown Manhattan – not to mention solidly rendered French-American cooking. Specialties include duck breast glazed with white truffle honey and oysters topped with lemon-pepper hollandaise, caramelized onions and bacon. Don't miss the apple tart. The atmosphere is sedate (jackets are required after 5pm) but incurably romantic.

🍴 Fort Greene, Clinton Hill & Bedford-Stuyvesant

PEACHES SOUTHERN COOKING **$$**

(www.peachesbrooklyn.com; 393 Lewis Ave, Bed-Stuy; mains $14-21; ⏲lunch & dinner; [S]A/C to Utica) The homey atmosphere and tasty Southern food make Peaches a Bed-Stuy favorite. The stone ground grits with blackened catfish ($14) is popular at all hours, while the French toast is in demand at brunch. The three-sides platter ($10) is a good veggie option; among other choices, you can put together a plate of sweet corn succotash, sautéed spinach and gooey mac 'n' cheese.

If there is a wait, head over to the bar and order a Brownstone Punch ($9), a dizzyingly fresh mix of fruit juice with light and dark rums and a splash of champagne.

NO 7 FUSION **$$**

Map p448 (☎718-522-6370; www.no7restaurant.co; 7 Greene Ave, Fort Greene; mains $17-24; ⏲5:30ampm-2am Tue-Fri, noon-2am Sat & Sun; 🍸; [S]C to Lafayette Ave) This intimate Fort Greene stalwart is all about vintage: there are wide-plank floors, a marble-topped bar and a cozy 20-seat dining area in the back. The short menu showcases the talents of chef Tyler Kord, featuring imaginative dishes such as seafood tortilla soup and broccoli tacos with feta, pine nuts and beans.

There's a saucy list of cocktails to choose from, too. Order the 'Whore Water' (tequila, Cointreau, watermelon, jalapeño, lime and Thai basil) at your own discretion.

[TOP CHOICE] **DOUGH** BAKERY **$**

(305 Franklin Ave cnr Lafayette Ave, Clinton Hill; doughnuts $2; ⏲7am-5pm; [S]G to Classon Ave) Situated on the border of Clinton Hill and Bed-Stuy, this small, out-of-the-way spot is a bit of a trek, but worth it if you have serious doughnut-ude. Puffy raised doughnuts are dipped in a changing array of glazes, including classic sugar, and exotic flavors like blood orange and hibiscus. Doughnut divinity for the tongue.

CHEZ LOLA BISTRO **$$**

Map p448 (www.chezlolabrooklyn.com; 387 Myrtle Ave btwn Clermont & Vanderbilt Aves, Fort Greene; mains $13-20; [S]A/C, G to Clinton-Washington Aves) This bright neighborhood spot – the menu advertises it as a 'bistro without borders' – serves up a solid mix of eats, including French onion soup ($7), a spicy salmon burger with shoestring fries ($12) and a changing selection of ravioli ($13). It's most popular at brunch for its fluffy pancakes and Croque Madames. In good weather, the outdoor patio is lovely.

🍴 Boerum Hill, Carroll Gardens & Red Hook

LUCALI PIZZERIA **$**

Map p448 (☎718-858-4086; 575 Henry St at Carroll St, Carroll Gardens; pizza $24, small calzone $10, toppings $3; ⏲dinner Wed-Mon; 👪; [S]F, G to Carroll St) One of New York's tastiest pizzas comes from this unlikely spot (it looks like a living room) run by Mark Iacono. Pizzas are all one size, with chewy crusts, fresh tomato sauce and super-fresh mozzarella. Toppings are limited, but the Brooklyn accent is for real. Cash only; BYO beer or wine.

[TOP CHOICE] **MILE END** DELI **$**

Map p448 (www.mileendbrooklyn.com; 97A Hoyt St, Boerum Hill; sandwiches $8-12; ⏲breakfast, lunch & dinner, brunch Sat & Sun) You can almost taste the smoked meats as you enter this new addition to Boerum Hill, which has exposed brick walls and a couple of communal tables. Mile End is small, like its portions, but big on flavors. Try a smoked beef brisket on rye with mustard ($12) – the bread is sticky soft and the meat will melt in your mouth. The only buzzkill is the extra $1.50 charge for a pickle – the sort of high-end shenanigan that must have old Brooklyn deli men spinning in their graves.

FRANKIES SPUNTINO ITALIAN **$$**

Map p448 (www.frankiesspuntino.com; 457 Court St btwn 4th Pl & Luquer St, Caroll Gardens; sweet sausage $16, braised lamb $19; ⏲lunch & dinner; [S]F, G to Carroll St) Frankies is a neighborhood magnet, attracting local couples, families and plenty of Manhattanites with hearty pasta dishes like cavatelli with hot sausage and pappardelle with braised lamb. But as a *spuntino* (snack joint), this place is more about the small plates, with a seasonal menu that boasts excellent fresh salads, cheeses, cured meats and heavenly crostinis.

FERDINANDO'S FOCACCERIA ITALIAN

Map p448 (☎718-855-1545; 151 Union St btwn Columbia & Hicks, Carroll Gardens; panelle $6, sandwiches $6-9, pastas $15-26; ⏲11am-8pm Mon-Thu, to 10pm Fri & Sat; ✍; [S]G, F to Carroll St) This real-deal Sicilian kitchen in Carroll Gardens has tiled floors and exposed brick walls, and has been dishing out delicious meals for generations. The *pannelle* (chick pea fritters) on a toasted sesame roll are the best you'll find this side of the Atlantic. Try the *pannelle* special, with a dollop of ricotta and Parmesan cheese – even better! Cash only.

PRIME MEATS GERMAN $$

Map p448 (www.frankspm.com; 465 Court St cnr Luquer St, Carroll Gardens; mains $17-32; ⏲10am-midnight Mon-Wed, to 1am Thu & Fri, 8am-1am Sat, to midnight Sun; [S]F, G to Carroll St) A pre-fab vintage spot in Carroll Gardens comes with lots of old-world flavor. The focus here is on house-cured and butchered meats and plenty of farm-to-table cooking. The menu is all late-19th-century German, featuring items like pickled fish and slow-braised beef sauerbraten with red cabbage. A list of hearty ales and retro cocktails keeps the theme going.

SAHADI'S SELF-CATERING

Map p452 (www.sahadis.com; 187 Atlantic Ave btwn Court & Clinton Sts, Boerum Hill; ⏲9am-7pm Mon-Sat; ✍; [S]2/3, 4/5 to Borough Hall) The smell of fresh roasted coffee and spices greets you as you enter this beloved Middle Eastern delicacies shop. The olive bar boasts two-dozen options and there are also enough breads, cheeses, nuts and hummus to fulfill the self-catering needs of a whole battalion.

SAUL FRENCH $$

Map p448 (☎718-935-9844; www.saulrestaurant.com; 140 Smith St btwn Dean & Bergen Sts, Boerum Hill; mains $24-37; ⏲dinner; [S]F to Bergen St) A veteran of French food temples like Le Bernardin and Bouley, chef Saul Bolton has been luring dedicated eaters to his Michelin-starred Boerum Hill eatery for a dozen years. The menu is compact and simple, with a focus on fresh produce and game meats (think confit of squab with roasted brussels sprouts), as well as fresh seafood. Reservations recommended.

CALEXICO REDHOOK MEXICAN $

Map p448 (www.calexicocart.com; 122 Union St btwn Columbia & Hicks Sts, Carroll Gardens; burritos $8; ⏲11:30am-11pm Mon-Sat, to 10pm Sun; ✍; [S]F, G to Carroll St) This casual spot near the Carroll Gardens/Red Hook border serves tasty (for New York) Mexican food, such as chipotle pork tacos and skirt steak burritos, as well as more modern items like chili-lime tofu. The beans and rice need work, but the meat dishes are very well rendered. Look for their namesake food trucks around the city.

FAIRWAY MARKET $

Map p448 (☎718-694-6868; 480-500 Van Brunt St, Red Hook; ⏲8am-10pm; ✍; [S]F, G to Carroll St, 🚌B61 to cnr Coffey & Van Brunt Sts) This sprawling supermarket offers an array of breads, cheeses, olives and smoked meats, as well as delicious pre-prepared foods. An on-site cafe (8am to 8pm) serves simple breakfasts and lunch, and offers excellent views of the Red Hook waterfront.

🍴 Park Slope & Prospect Heights

[TOP CHOICE] LOT 2 MODERN AMERICAN $$

Map p450 (www.lot2restaurant.com; 687 6th Ave btwn 19th & 20th Sts, Park Slope; mains $15-25, prix fixe Sunday supper adult/child $30/12 ; ⏲dinner Tues-Sat; [S]F to 7th Ave, R to Prospect Ave) This intimate rustic spot serves locally sourced, high-end comfort food in the southern end of Park Slope. The menu is small but big on flavors. Try the grilled cheese sandwich with creamy tomato soup ($10), crispy lamb belly with roasted cauliflower, squash puree and salsa verde ($21) or a juicy grass-fed burger with thick cut, duck-fat fries ($15). And don't miss the cocktails; the bartender whips up a stupendous Manhattan.

BAGEL HOLE BAKERY $

Map p450 (400 7th Ave btwn 12th & 13th Sts, Park Slope; bagel $2; ⏲6am-6pm Mon-Fri, to 5pm Sat, to 3pm Sun; ✍; [S]F, G to 7th Ave) Bagel Hole may look like a hole in the wall, but they make cushiony bagels that are chewy on the inside and taste even better with butter or a *schmear* (cream cheese). The toasted onion bagel is incredible. There are no tables, so pick your favorite to go and enjoy in nearby Prospect Park.

BARK HOT DOGS $

Map p450 (www.barkhotdogs.com; 474 Bergen St, Park Slope; hot dogs $4-7; ⏲noon-10pm Mon-Thu, to 2am Fri, 10am-2am Sat, to 10pm Sun; 👪;

Ⓢ4/5, N/R to Pacific St-Atlantic Ave) Excellent artisanal hot dogs will help you forget the 'dirty water dogs' plied by corner street vendors. Like everything else at Bark, these plump and juicy wieners come from local and organic sources and are served with all the trimmings. The pepper relish is a must, while the bacon-cheddar dog with pickled onion keeps sausage munchers howling for more.

FRANNY'S
PIZZERIA $$

Map p450 (www.frannysbrooklyn.com; 295 Flatbush Ave btwn St Marks & Prospect Pl, Park Slope; pizzas from $16; ◷5:30pm-11pm Mon-Fri, noon-11pm Sat & Sun; ◢; Ⓢ B, Q to 7th Ave) This busy (and rather pricey) modern spot in Park Slope serves bubbling thin-crust pizza baked in a brick oven, all decorated with a simple line-up of choice organic toppings such as buffalo mozzarella and oregano. There is an array of appetizers (such as cauliflower soup and wood-roasted sausage), as well as some well-rendered pastas.

CHERYL'S GLOBAL SOUL
CAFE $$

Map p450 (www.cherylsglobalsoul.com; 236 Underhill Ave btwn Eastern Pkwy & St Johns Pl, Prospect Heights; sandwiches $8-13, mains $13-24; ◷8am-4pm Mon, to 10pm Tue-Thu, to 11pm Fri & Sat; ◢⚑; Ⓢ2/3 to Eastern Pkwy-Brooklyn Museum) Around the corner from the Brooklyn Museum and the Brooklyn Botanic Garden, this homey brick-and-wood favorite serves up fresh, unpretentious cooking that draws on a world of influences. Expect everything from roasted tamarind chicken to exceptional homemade quiche to a long list of tasty sandwiches. There are veggie options, as well as kid-friendly peanut butter and jelly.

TOM'S RESTAURANT
DINER $

Map p450 (☏718-636-9738; 782 Washington Ave at Sterling Pl, Prospect Heights; ◷breakfast & lunch Mon-Sat; Ⓢ2/3 to Eastern Pkwy-Brooklyn Museum) Open since 1936, this diner looks like grandma's cluttered living room and delivers good, greasy-spoon cooking just three blocks from the Brooklyn Museum. Breakfast is served all day and it's a deal: two eggs, toast and coffee with home fries or grits comes to $4. Copious wall signs advertise specials – the blueberry-ricotta pancakes with lemon zest are the bomb. If you want to go old school, order an egg cream (milk, soda with chocolate syrup). Lines are loooong for weekend brunch.

CHUKO
JAPANESE $

Map p450 (www.barchuko.com; 552 Vanderbilt Ave cnr Dean St, Prospect Heights; ramen $12; ◷5:30pm-midnight Tue-Sun; ◢; Ⓢ B/Q to 7th Ave, 2/3 to Bergen St) This cozy wood-lined ramen shop brings a top-notch noodle game to Prospect Heights. Steaming bowls of al dente ramen are paired with one of several spectacularly silky broths, including an excellent pork bone and a full-bodied vegetarian. The rotating array of appetizers are *very* worthwhile. If the fragrant salt and pepper chicken wings are on the menu: Do. Not. Miss.

AL DI LÀ TRATTORIA
ITALIAN $$

Map p450 (www.aldilatrattoria.com; 248 5th Ave cnr Carroll St, Park Slope; ◷lunch & dinner; Ⓢ R to Union St) Run by a husband-and-wife team from northern Italy, this cheery Park Slope trattoria serves handmade pastas (like inventive red beet and ricotta ravioli) and belly warming classics (braised rabbit with buttery polenta). There are daily risottos, an excellent brunch (duck confit hash!) and a long list of Italian wines (from $32 per bottle).

SOUTHSIDE COFFEE
CAFE $

Map p450 (☏347-599-0887; 652 6th Ave btwn 19th & 20th Sts, Park Slope; Ⓢ F to 7th Ave, R to Prospect Ave) This little spot on the southern edges of Park Slope has gained a tweaky, diehard following for its tasty pastries and excellent coffee (which we order black, like our wear). The cappuccinos are of the artful sort, featuring designs in the foam, and there are fresh-baked cinnamon rolls on Sundays.

BLUE RIBBON SUSHI BROOKLYN
SUSHI $$$

Map p450 (☏718-840-0408; www.blueribbonrestaurants.com; 278 Fifth Ave btwn 1st St & Garfield Pl, Park Slope; sushi/sashimi dinner combo $33; ◷dinner; Ⓢ R to Union St) This warmly lit restaurant is a Brooklyn standard-bearer, delivering a long list of delectable Japanese specialties such as spicy blue crab rolls, gently-steamed *shumai* dumplings and raw whitefish served with scallions and cucumbers and doused in mustard miso. The menu changes regularly, but one standard feature is the excellent fried chicken – a good bet for the sushi intolerant. Blue Ribbon is crazy-popular: be prepared to wait for a table, especially on weekends.

🍴 Coney Island & Brighton Beach

Go Slavic on Brighton Beach Ave or hit Coney Island if you want that state-fair feel. For additional options at Coney Island, see Coney Island (p266).

[TOP CHOICE] VARENICHNAYA RUSSIAN $

Map p453 (☎718-332-9797; 3086 Brighton 2nd St, Brighton Beach; dumplings $6-7, mains $7-12; ⏰lunch & dinner; [S]B, Q to Brighton Beach) A small, family-run hideaway serves up consistently fresh dumplings from a variety of former Soviet Bloc countries. There are *pelmeni* (Siberian meat dumplings), *vareniki* (Ukrainian ravioli) and *mantis* (Uzbek lamb dumplings). The borscht is divine, as are the sturgeon and lamb kebabs. Bigger appetites will love the beef stroganoff served with kasha. On weekends, plan on waiting for a table.

TOTONNO'S PIZZERIA $$

Map p453 (☎718-372-8606; 1524 Neptune Ave cnr 16th St, Coney Island; large pizza $16-18; ⏰noon-8pm Wed-Sun; [✓]; [S]D/F, N/Q to Coney Island-Stillwell Ave) This old-school pizza parlor is open daily – as long as there's fresh dough. The toppings menu is slim (check the board above the open kitchen), but this is the kind of pie that doesn't need lots of overwrought decoration: coal-fired dough is topped with mozzarella first, followed by tomato sauce, so your crust never gets soggy. A place of pilgrimage, complete with real-deal New York attitude.

BRIGHTON BAZAAR SELF-CATERING $

Map p453 (1007 Brighton Beach Ave cnr 11th St, Brighton Beach; ⏰8am-10pm; [S]B, Q to Brighton Beach) A tantalizing local market is stuffed with out-of-the-oven breads, smoked meats and cheeses, as well as fresh-made crepes and shaved-beet salad. But the best bet is the ample buffet, full of pre-prepared Russian foods. The potato knishes are a standout, as are the sour cherry blintzes. Get here around lunchtime for the best selection.

CAFÉ GLECHIK RUSSIAN $$

Map p453 (☎718-616-0766; 3159 Coney Island Ave, Brighton Beach; cabbage rolls $11, kebabs $11-15, dumplings $7-9; ⏰breakfast, lunch & dinner; [S]B, Q to Brighton Beach) This chatty chew is known for the fact that globe-trotting chef Anthony Bourdain ate here on his TV show *No Reservations*. The dishes to get are the dumplings: *pelmeni* and *vareniki* with a wide assortment of stuffings. (Sour-cherry *vareniki* are the jam!) You'll also find classics like borscht, kebabs and hyper-sweet compote drinks. Cash only.

🍴 Williamsburg & Bushwick

[TOP CHOICE] ROBERTA'S PIZZERIA $$

Map p446 (www.robertaspizza.com; 261 Moore St near Bogart St, Bushwick; individual pizza $9-17, mains $13-28; ⏰11am-midnight; [✓]; [S]L to Morgan Ave) This hipster-saturated warehouse restaurant in Bushwick consistently produces some of the best pizza in New York. Service can be lackadaisical and the waits long (lunch is best), but the brick-oven pies are the right combination of chewy and fresh. The classic margherita is sublimely simple, while meat-lovers will appreciate the 'Beastmaser,' laden with Berkshire pork and jalapeños.

At lunch, the restaurant sells an off-the-menu 'working man's slice' – a massive block of Sicilian-style pizza – for $5. If you're on a budget, avoid the small (if well-rendered) pasta dishes. There is a wine list (from $30 per bottle) and a garden bar where you can enjoy a beer while you wait for your order. On weekends, there is brunch.

DRESSLER MODERN AMERICAN $$$

Map p446 (☎718-384-6343; www.dresslernyc.com; 149 Broadway btwn Bedford & Driggs Aves, Williamsburg; mains $26-35, bar menu $14-16; ⏰dinner Mon-Fri, lunch & dinner Sat & Sun; [S]J/M/Z to Marcy Ave) One of Williamsburg's top gastronomic destinations, the Michelin-starred Dressler serves a creative market-fresh mix of New American fare like crisp baby artichokes, bacon-wrapped monkfish and its famous oxtail ragout with herbed ricotta. The dining room is no less a work of art, with elaborately sculpted chandeliers, mosaic floors, a zinc bar and light box screens, all created by Brooklyn artisans.

A four-course chef's tasting is available for $85. If the main restaurant is too rich for your blood, hit the bar: a short menu has specialties like peeky-toe crab cakes and a juicy grilled hamburger for under $16.

MEATBALL SHOP ITALIAN $

Map p446 (☎718-551-0520; www.themeatballshop.com; 170 Bedford Ave btwn 7th & 8th Sts, Williamsburg; meatballs $7-9; ⏰noon-2am Sun-Wed, to 4am Thu-Sat; $ L to Bedford Ave) Hot and tasty balls keep a steady stream of eaters coming back to this Williamsburg newcomer, featuring vintage meat grinders on the dining room wall. Try the meatball smash, served on a brioche bun with spicy sauce, milky provolone and the 'family jewels' (a fried egg) – accompanied by a fresh and tasty green salad. If you have room, top it off with a homemade ice-cream sandwich.

MOMO SUSHI SHACK
JAPANESE $$

Map p446 (www.momosushishack.com; 43 Bogart St btwn Moore & Seigel, Bushwick; sushi rolls $5-10, mains $18; ⊘noon-3:30pm & 6pm-10:30pm Tue-Thu, to midnight Fri & Sat; ⊉; $ L to Morgan Ave) Three shared tables occupy this industrial-chic spot, where inventive Japanese tapas all come with instructions on how to eat them. Foodie preciousness aside, Momo's is staggeringly good, offering super-fresh classics and flamboyant contemporary creations, including sushi topped with truffle oil and tender dumplings presented with Anaheim chili confit. There are veggie options and a good list of sakes. Cash only.

BEST PIZZA
PIZZERIA $

Map p446 (http://best.piz.za.com; 33 Havemeyer St btwn 7th & 8th Sts, Williamsburg; slices from $3; ⊘noon-midnight, to 1am Sat; ⊉; $ L to Lorimer St, G to Metropolitan Ave) An unpretentious slice joint serves excellent plain cheese pizza, as well as a mind-blowingly delectable white ricotta slice, trimmed with sesame seeds and topped with caramelized onion. There's paper plate artwork on the walls, a boom box as sound system and a fridge with cold beer. Recommended.

CHAMPS
VEGETARIAN $

Map p446 (www.champsbakery.com; 176 Ainslie St at Leonard St; sandwiches $7-9, salads $6-10, pastries from $2; ⊘noon-9pm Mon-Sat, noon-6pm, Sun; ⊉; $ L to Lorimer, G to Metropolitan) This airy little vegan/vegetarian spot sells baked goods (including highly popular croissants), as well as an array of sandwiches and salads. The reasonable prices and all-day breakfasts keep things busy.

FETTE SAU
BARBECUE $

Map p446 (⊉718-963-3404; www.fettesaubbq.com; 354 Metropolitan Ave btwn Havenmeyer & Roebling Sts; pork ribs or brisket per pound $20; ⊘5pm-11pm Mon-Fri, noon-11pm Sat & Sun; $ L to Bedford Ave) Dry-rubbed, BBQ-craving Brooklynites descend en masse to the 'Fat Pig,' a cement-floored, wood-beamed space (formerly an auto body repair shop) that dishes up ribs, brisket and pastrami. Everything is smoked in-house and there is a range of accompaniments, but don't miss the burnt-end baked beans ($6), which are

---

THE BEST OF BROOKLYN PIZZA

New York is known for a lot of things: screeching subways, towering skyscrapers, bright lights. It's also known for its pizza, which comes in a variety of gooey, chewy, sauce-soaked varieties. Here is a list of some of the top places in the city to grab a pie or a slice:

DiFara Pizza (www.difara.com; 1424 Ave J cnr E 15th St; ⊘noon-4pm & 7-9pm Wed-Sat, 1-4pm & 7-9pm Sun; ⛭; $ B/Q to Avenue J) In operation since 1964 in the Midwood section of Brooklyn, this old-school slice joint is still lovingly tended to by proprietor Dom DeMarco, who makes the pies himself. Expect lines.

Totonno's (p283) The classic Coney Island pizzeria makes pies til the dough runs out.

Grimaldi's (p279) Legendary lines and legendary pizza with views of the Manhattan skyline.

Lucali (p280) Neapolitan-style pies started as a hobby for this noted Carroll Gardens pizzaiolo.

Franny's (p282) A contemporary eatery with an organic vibe serves simple pies in Park Slope.

Roberta's (p283) Divine pies with names like 'Banana Hammock' in Bushwick's artsy district.

If you want to try several pizzas in one go, sign up for an outing with Scott's Pizza Tours (p99), which will take you to the most vaunted brick ovens around the city by foot or by bus. Tours and times vary, check the website for tickets and details.

peppery, not-too-sweet and chock-full of meaty bits. There's a good choice of bourbon, whiskey and beer.

PIES-N-THIGHS
AMERICAN $

Map p446 (www.piesnthighs.com; 166 S 4th St at Driggs Ave; mains $6-13; ⏰breakfast, lunch & dinner, brunch on Sunday; Ⓢ J/M/Z to Marcy Ave, L to Bedford Ave) The menu here seems designed to soak up booze: fried chicken and a mean mac 'n' cheese. A fried chicken box ($13) includes cheese grits, collard greens or hush puppies. The best bet, however, is the chicken biscuit ($6), a puffy, fresh-baked biscuit stuffed with a fried breast and topped with hot sauce and honey.

CAFE EL PUENTE
DOMINICAN $

Map p446 (☑718-388-2416; 231 S 4th St btwn Havemayer & Roebling Sts, Williamsburg; lunch special $5-8, mains $6-15, whole roasted chicken $8; Ⓢ L to Bedford Ave, J/M/Z to Marcy Ave) An informal Dominican joint with steam tables serves up an array of Caribbean dishes, including gigantic portions of *mofongo* – mashed plantains and yuca, laced with pork, gravy and enough garlic to keep every vampire on *True Blood* at bay. The citrusy rotisserie chicken, served with rice and beans, is tops. Cheap lunch specials make this a deal.

BLUE BOTTLE COFFEE
CAFE $

Map p446 (www.bluebottlecoffee.net; 160 Berry St btwn 4th & 5th Sts, Williamsburg; coffee $4; ⏰7am-7pm Mon-Fri, 8am-7pm Sat & Sun) For the coffee connoisseurs, this top-of-the-line Williamsburg outpost (located in a former rope shop) uses a vintage Probat roaster on its beans. All drinks are brewed to order, so be prepared to wait a spell for your Kyoto iced. A small selection of baked goods includes coffee cake made with a chocolate stout from Brooklyn Brewery. Talk about locally sourced.

PETER LUGER STEAKHOUSE
STEAKHOUSE $$$

Map p446 (☑718-387-7400; www.peterluger.com; 178 Broadway near Driggs Ave, Williamsburg; porterhouse for two $88; ⏰lunch & dinner; Ⓢ J/M/Z to Marcy Ave) You are not here for the ambience (outdated) or the service (brusque), you are here for the steak. And New York's most storied steakhouse (in operation since 1887) serves up one hell of a tender porterhouse cut. The creamed spinach and the tomato salad are good, but skip the greasy German potatoes and sugary steak sauce.

If you've got the will and the space, Luger's also does a good hot fudge sundae. Walk it off on the nearby Williamsburg Bridge. Reservations recommended; cash only.

🍷 DRINKING & NIGHTLIFE

Dives. Cocktail lounges. And unassuming neighborhood joints. Brooklyn has got a bit of everything – including oodles of retro everything. (It's like everyone and their mother thought it'd be a good idea to resuscitate the 1920s.) Of the bunch, Williamsburg has the most hopping night scene.

📍 Fort Greene

DER SCHWARZE KÖELNER
BEER GARDEN

Map p448 (www.derschwarzekoelner.com; 710 Fulton St cnr Hanson Pl, Fort Greene; ⏰5pm-1am Mon-Thu, to 4am Fri-Sat, 2pm-1am Sun; Ⓢ C to Lafayette Ave) This casual beer garden with checkered floors, lots of windows and a lively, mixed crowd is located just a few blocks away from the Brooklyn Academy of Music. There are 18 beers on tap, all of which go swimmingly with a hot *brezel* (soft German pretzel). A variety of other snacks are served all night.

📍 Brooklyn Heights

FLOYD
BAR

Map p452 (131 Atlantic Ave btwn Henry & Clinton Sts, Brooklyn Heights; ⏰5pm-4am Mon-Thu, 4pm-4am Fri, 11am-4am Sat & Sun; Ⓢ 2/3, 4/5 to Borough Hall) This glass-front bar is home to young flirters who cuddle on tattered antique sofas while beer-swillers congregate around an indoor boccie court. A good local hang.

📍 Cobble Hill, Carroll Gardens & Red Hook

61 LOCAL
BEER GARDEN

Map p448 (www.61local.com; 61 Bergen St btwn Smith St & Boerum Pl, Cobble Hill; snacks $1-7, sandwiches $4-8; ⏰11am-midnight Sun-Thu, 11am-1am Fri & Sat; Ⓢ F, G to Bergen) A roomy brick-and-wood hall in Cobble Hill manages to be both chic and warm, with large communal tables, a mellow vibe and a good selection of craft beers (the Companion Wheat Wine Ale, made in nearby Williamsburg, is crisp and fresh). There's a simple menu of charcuterie and other snacks, including smoky ham sandwiches, fresh pickles and hummus dip.

ZOMBIE HUT — BAR

Map p448 (☎718-875-3433; 261 Smith St btwn Degraw and Douglass Sts, Carroll Gardens; 🕐5pm-2am Mon-Thu, 4pm-4am Fri-Sun; [S]F, G to Carroll St) It's forever a dead man's party at this hokey Carroll Gardens mainstay that serves up tall, strong, cocktails and a lively singles scene. A comfortable backyard is good for chit-chat or playing one of the free board games on hand.

SUNNY'S — BAR

Map p448 (☎718-625-8211; 253 Conover St btwn Beard & Reed Sts, Red Hook; 🕐8pm-2am Wed, to 4am Fri & Sat; [S]F, G to Carroll St, 🚌B61 to Coffey & Conover Sts) Way out in Red Hook, this super-inviting longshoreman bar – the sign says 'bar' – is straight out of *On the Waterfront*. Every Saturday at 10pm they host a foot-stomping bluegrass jam.

🍷 Park Slope

[TOP CHOICE] FREDDY'S — BAR

Map p450 (www.freddysbar.com; 627 Fifth Ave btwn 17th & 18th Sts, Park Slope; 🕐noon-4am; [S]R to Prospect Ave) Formerly located by the Atlantic Yards, developers for a sports arena used eminent domain to raze this old-time bar. But Freddy's didn't go without a fight: patrons chained themselves to the bar in protest. Thankfully, it relocated to Park Slope, where you can tip one back at the vintage mahogany bar while admiring the chains used in the protest. Donald, the co-owner, also makes crazy videos. Check out the one behind the bar of a cat drinking.

DER KOMMISSAR — BAR

Map p450 (www.derkommissar.net; 559 Fifth Ave & 15th St, Park Slope; 🕐noon-late; [S]F, G, R to 4th Ave, R to Prospect Ave) A long, narrow Park Slope bar has good tunes (the Beatles, not Falco), vintage films like Dr Strangelove, eight beers on tap, an extensive selection of schnapps, plus kick-ass Austrian sausages. Order a tasty Viennese with cheese ($6) with your favorite brew and the cook will squeeze a rubber chicken when your platter is ready.

GINGER'S — LESBIAN

Map p450 (www.gingersbarbklyn.com; 363 Fifth Ave at 5th St, Park Slope; 🕐5pm-4am Mon-Fri, 2pm-4am Sat & Sun; [S]F, G, R to 4th Ave-9th St) This bright blue-and-yellow lesbian watering hole comes complete with a jukebox, pool table, back deck and lots of regulars. There are daily happy-hour specials from 5pm to 8pm.

JACKIE'S FIFTH AMENDMENT — BAR

Map p450 (404 Fifth Ave at 7th St, Park Slope; 🕐8am-4am; [S]F, G, R to 4th Ave-9th St) A real-deal, classic dive in Park Slope with a padded bar, a spackled ceiling, colorful old-timers and cheap, cold buckets of beer.

EXCELSIOR — GAY

Map p450 (www.excelsiorbrooklyn.com; 390 Fifth Ave at 6th St, Park Slope; 🕐5pm-4am Mon-Fri, 2pm-4am Sat & Sun; [S]F, G, R to 4th Ave-9th St) This long-running Park Slope favorite has a cute and friendly crowd, a great jukebox and a refreshing back patio for summer months (and year-round smokers).

🍷 Coney Island & Brighton Beach

For another good boardwalk drinking joint, hit Ruby's (p267) in Coney Island.

LE SOLEIL DRAFT BARN — BEER GARDEN

Map p453 (☎718-934-6666; 3152 Brighton 6th St, on the boardwalk, Brighton Beach; [S]B, Q to Brighton Beach) Half a dozen beers on tap and more than 100 bottles to choose from make this boardwalk spot a notch above the rest. The food is forgettable, but the people-watching couldn't be any better in the summer months.

🍷 Williamsburg & Bushwick

[TOP CHOICE] COMMODORE — BAR

Map p446 (366 Metropolitan Ave cnr Havenmeyer St, Williamsburg; 🕐4pm-midnight Sun-Thu, to 1am Fri & Sat; [S]L to Lorimer St) This corner bar is a faux '70s recreation room with plenty of wood paneling and a few big booths to spread out in. Order a mint julep, a sloe gin fizz or the Commodore (piña colada with Amaretto) and play vintage arcade games for free. The cocktails are good and the atmosphere uncomplicated. Don't leave without sampling the food: they make the best damn barroom burger in Williamsburg. It gets crowded on weekends.

CLEM'S PUB

Map p446 (☎718-387-9617; 264 Grand St at Roebling St, Williamsburg; ⏲2pm-4am Mon-Fri, noon-4am Sat & Sun; [S]L to Bedford Ave, J/M/Z to Marcy Ave) This tidy Williamsburg pub keeps things chill. There's a long bar, friendly bartenders and a few outdoor tables that are perfect for summer people-watching. They also sell beer and a shot for only $5: choose between 'the Patriot' (Pabst Blue Ribbon and Jim Beam) and a 'Federale' (Tecate and Tequila).

MAISON PREMIERE COCKTAIL BAR

Map p446 (www.maisonpremiere.com; 298 Bedford Ave btwn 1st & Grand Sts, Williamsburg; ⏲4pm-4am Mon-Fri, noon-4am Sat & Sun; [S]L to Bedford Ave) We kept expecting to see Dorothy Parker stagger into this old-timey place, which features a chemistry-lab-style bar full of syrups and essences and suspendered bartenders to mix them all up. The cocktails are serious business: the epic list includes more than 20 absinthe drinks, various juleps, an array of specialty cocktails and a refreshing sweet-and-spicy 'Chilcano Reds.' A raw bar provides a long list of snacks on the half shell, all of them incredibly fresh.

PINE BOX ROCK SHOP BAR

Map p446 (www.pineboxrockshop.com; 12 Grattan St btwn Morgan Ave & Bogart St, Bushwick; ⏲4pm-2am Mon-Fri, 2pm-4am Sat, noon-2am Sun; [S]L to Morgan Ave) The cavernous Pine Box is a former Bushwick casket factory that has 16 drafts to choose from, as well as spicy, pint-sized Bloody Marys. Run by a friendly musician couple, the walls are filled with local artwork and a performance space in the back hosts regular gigs. Tasty bar snacks consist of hearty vegan empanadas.

RADEGAST HALL & BIERGARTEN BEER GARDEN

Map p446 (www.radegasthall.com; 113 N 3rd St at Berry St, Williamsburg; ⏲4pm-4am Mon-Fri, noon-4am Sat & Sun; [S]L to Bedford Ave) An Austro-Hungarian beer hall in Williamsburg offers up a huge selection of Bavarian brews as well as a kitchen full of munch-able meats. You can hover in the dark, woody bar area, or sit in the adjacent hall, which has a retractable roof and communal tables to feast at – perfect for plates full of pretzels and sausages.

ZABLOSKI'S BAR

Map p446 (☎718-384-1903; 107 N 6th St btwn Berry St & Wythe Ave, Williamsburg; ⏲2pm-4am; [S]L to Bedford Ave) This welcoming brick-lined spot in Williamsburg has cheap beer, chill bartenders, a pinball machine, a dart board and a pool table. Snag the table by the roll-down gate during happy hour and watch the street come alive at night.

METROPOLITAN GAY

Map p446 (559 Lorimer St at Metropolitan Ave, Williamsburg; ⏲3pm-4am; [S]L to Lorimer St, G to Metropolitan Ave) This low-key Williamsburg hangout draws a good blend of arty gays and lesbians with its cool staff, cheap drinks, outdoor patio and groovy DJs. During the summer, it's known for its Sunday backyard cookouts, and on Wednesday nights, it's all about the girls.

SPUYTEN DUYVIL BAR

Map p446 (www.spuytenduyvilnyc.com; 359 Metropolitan Ave btwn Havemayer & Roebling, Williamsburg; ⏲5pm-closing Mon-Fri, 1pm-closing Sat & Sun; [S]L to Lorimer St, G to Metropolitan Ave) This low-key Williamsburg bar looks like it was pieced together from a rummage sale. The ceilings are painted red, there are vintage maps on the walls and the furniture consists of tattered armchairs. But the beer selection is excellent, the locals from various eras are chatty and there's a decent sized patio with leafy trees that is open in good weather.

ALLIGATOR LOUNGE BAR

Map p446 (600 Metropolitan Ave btwn Lorimer & Leonard Sts, Williamsburg; ⏲3pm-4am Mon-Fri, 1pm-4am Sat & Sun; [S]L to Lorimer St, G to Metropolitan Ave) Buy a beer here and you get a free pizza – not a slice, but a fresh, personal-size pizza (toppings are a buck extra). This deal draws a mixed crowd of artsy and working-class locals – especially during happy hour when beers are $4 to $6. There's karaoke on Thursday and Friday nights. A deal.

HAREFIELD ROAD PUB

Map p446 (769 Metropolitan Ave btwn Graham Ave & Humboldt St, Williamsburg; ⏲noon-4am Mon-Fri, 11am-4am Sat & Sun; [S]L to Graham Ave)

A serene crowd can be found inside this East Williamsburg bar that sports a minimalist, medieval tavern kind of look. Other than a few wines served by the glass (from $6), its focus is beer, with over a dozen brews on tap ($4 to $6). There is also a long list of single malt scotches (from $10), and they serve paninis.

There's a small brick courtyard in back, and a very popular weekend brunch, served from 11am to 4pm.

☆ ENTERTAINMENT

BROOKLYN BOWL LIVE MUSIC

Map p446 (☎718-963-3369; www.brooklynbowl.com; 61 Wythe Ave btwn 11th & 12th Sts; lane rental per hr $40-50, shoe rental $4; ⌚6pm-2am Mon-Thu, to 4am Fri, noon-4am Sat, to 2am Sun; [S]L to Bedford Ave, G to Nassau Ave) This 23,000-sq-ft venue inside the former Hecla Iron Works Company combines bowling, microbrews, food and groovy live music. In addition to the live bands that regularly tear up the stage, there are NFL game days, karaoke and DJ nights – in fact, Questlove of the Roots can be found at the turntables on most Thursday nights. They also have bowling (p294).

MUSIC HALL OF WILLIAMSBURG LIVE MUSIC

Map p446 (www.musichallofwilliamsburg.com; 66 N 6th St btwn Wythe & Kent Aves, Williamsburg; [S]L to Bedford Ave) This popular Williamsburg music venue is *the* place to see indie bands in Brooklyn. (For many groups traveling through New York, this is their one and only spot.) It is intimate and the programming is solid. Recent sold out shows include local boy rappers Das Racist and alterna-crooner Aimee Mann.

KNITTING FACTORY LIVE MUSIC

Map p446 (☎347-529-6696; www.knittingfactory.com; 361 Metropolitan Ave at Havemayer St, Williamsburg; [S]G, L to Lorimer St) A long-time outpost for folk, indie and experimental music in New York, Williamsburg's Knitting Factory is where you go to see everything from cosmic space jazz to rock. The stage is small and intimate. A separate barroom has a soundproof window with stage views.

WARSAW LIVE MUSIC

Map p446 (www.warsawconcerts.com; Polish National Home, 261 Driggs Ave at Eckford St, Greenpoint; [S]L to Bedford Ave, G to Nassau Ave) A burgeoning New York classic, this stage is in the Polish National Home, with good views in the old ballroom, for bands ranging from indie darlings (The Dead Milkmen) to legends (George Clinton). Polish ladies serve $5 pierogis and $4 beers under the disco balls.

BAMCAFÉ LIVE MUSIC

Map p448 (☎718-636-4100; www.bam.org; 30 Lafayette Ave at Ashland Pl, Fort Greene; [S]D, N/R to Pacific St, B, Q, 2/3, 4/5 to Atlantic Ave) This high-ceilinged restaurant and lounge in the upstairs part of the Brooklyn Academy of Music is the spot to hit for free Friday and Saturday evening shows. The room is beautiful and the line-up is generally mellow, covering jazz, R&B, world music and experimental rock.

BAMcafé also hosts 'Eat Drink & Be Literary,' a weekly Thursday reading and dinner (per person including dinner $50). Past speakers have included novelists Jonathan Franzen, Julian Barnes and Jhumpa Lahiri.

BARBES LIVE MUSIC

Map p450 (☎347-422-0248; www.barbesbrooklyn.com; 376 9th St at Sixth Ave; suggested donation for live music $10; ⌚5pm-2am Mon-Thu, noon-4am Fri & Sat, noon-2am Sun; [S]F to 7th Ave) This bar and performance space, owned by two French musicians and longtime Brooklyn residents, has a world music vibe, offering eclectic music, ranging from Lebanese diva Asmahan to Mexican *bandas,* Venezuelan *joropos* and Romanian brass bands. There are readings and film screenings, too.

ZEBULON LIVE MUSIC

Map p446 (www.zebuloncafeconcert.com; 258 Wythe Ave, Williamsburg; [S]L to Bedford Ave) Ever arty and experimental, the Zeb is an unlikely tight space for reliably engaging shows of voodoo funk, dub, jazz and poetry – even Super Bowl parties come with a DJ spinning things you don't recognize. It's wee for its draw (we've seen an 18-piece band spilling off the stage), but there's alcohol and snacks.

BELL HOUSE LIVE MUSIC

Map p448 (www.thebellhouseny.com; 149 7th St, Red Hook; [S]F, G, R to 4th Ave-9th St) A big, old venue in the mostly barren neighborhood of Gowanus, the Bell House features live performances, DJ nights, indie rockers, burlesque parties and comedy. The handsomely converted warehouse has a spacious concert area, plus a friendly little bar in the front room with flickering candles, leather armchairs and a dozen beers on tap.

JALOPY LIVE MUSIC

Map p448 (www.jalopy.biz; 315 Columbia St at Woodhull St, Red Hook; [S]F, G to Carroll St) This fringe Carroll Gardens/Red Hook banjo shop has a fun DIY space with cold beer for its bluegrass, country and ukulele shows, including a feel-good Roots 'n' Ruckus show on Wednesday nights.

BARGEMUSIC CLASSICAL MUSIC

Map p452 (www.bargemusic.org; Fulton Ferry Landing, Brooklyn Heights; tickets $35; 👪; [S]A/C to High St) The chamber-music concerts held on this 125-seat converted coffee barge (built c 1899) are a unique, intimate affair. For over 35 years, it has been a beloved venue, with beautiful views of the East River and Manhattan. Performances of classical favorites are hosted four days a week throughout the year. Enjoy Beethoven as you gently float and bob on the river. There are free children's concerts on some Saturdays.

BROOKLYN ACADEMY OF MUSIC DANCE

Map p448 (BAM; www.bam.org; 30 Lafayette Ave at Ashland Pl, Fort Greene; [S]D, N/R to Pacific St, B, Q, 2/3, 4/5 to Atlantic Ave) At this performing arts complex, the Howard Gilman Opera House and Harvey Lichtenstein Theater host their share of ballet, modern and world dance performances. Among other groups, they've presented the Alvin Ailey American Dance Theater, the Mark Morris Dance Group and the Pina Bausch Dance Theater. This is also a good spot to catch experimental visiting troupes from all over the world.

BAM ROSE CINEMAS CINEMA

Map p448 (www.bam.org; 30 Lafayette Ave at Ashland Pl, Fort Greene; ticket $12; [S]D, N/R to Pacific St, B, Q, 2/3, 4/5 to Atlantic Ave) The gorgeous theater at the Brooklyn Academy of Music shows first-run, independent and foreign films in spaces blessed with comfy seating, great sight lines, big screens and a lovely, landmark design. You can also catch mini-festivals and revivals here.

BAM HOWARD GILMAN OPERA HOUSE OPERA

Map p448 (www.bam.org; 30 Lafayette Ave at Ashland Pl, Fort Greene; [S]D, N/R to Pacific St, B, Q, 2/3, 4/5 to Atlantic Ave) In addition to its excellent film, dance, music and theater programming, the Brooklyn Academy of Music regularly presents a small program of operas, with music by the Brooklyn Philharmonic, as well as live HD simulcasts of the Metropolitan Opera. The New York City Opera (p243) regularly performs here.

AMERICAN OPERA PROJECTS OPERA

Map p448 (www.operaprojects.org; 138 S Oxford St; [S]D, N/R to Pacific St, B, Q, 2/3, 4/5 to Atlantic Ave) Performing in venues around town, including the Lincoln Center's Juilliard School, this Brooklyn-based company is dedicated to bringing affordable and free productions to the masses, usually premiering new works by up-and-coming librettists. Smaller performances and libretto readings are held on-site.

ST ANN'S WAREHOUSE DANCE, THEATER

Map p452 (☎718-254-8779; www.stannswarehouse.org; 38 Water St btwn Main & Dock Sts, Dumbo; [S]A/C to High St) This avant-garde performance company took over an old spice mill and turned it into an exciting venue for the arts. Now the cavernous space regularly hosts innovative theater and dance happenings that attract the Brooklyn literati.

BROOKLYN PUBLIC LIBRARY READINGS

Map p450 (www.brooklynpubliclibrary.org; 10 Grand Army Plaza btwn Flatbush Ave & Eastern Pkwy, Prospect Heights; 👪; [S]2/3 to Grand Army Plaza) Located on the northeast edge of Brooklyn's Park Slope neighborhood, this grand library hosts a regular series of readings, including special events geared at the tots. Check their website for a schedule.

SHOPPING

Want it? Well, Brooklyn's got it. Williamsburg is chock full of home design shops, thrift stores, and hipster bookshops and boutiques. In South Brooklyn, you'll find some satisfying browsing (and good consignment) in the vicinity of Boerum and Cobble Hills. Atlantic Ave, running east to west near Brooklyn Heights, is sprinkled with antique stores. And Park Slope features a good selection of laid-back clothing shops.

RANDY DUCHAINE / ALAMY ©

MIKE HIPPLE / ALAMY ©

1. Brooklyn Flea (p293)

If you're looking for a quirky souvenir, try this market in Williamsburg, where 200 vendors sell antiques, craft items and vintage clothing.

2. Williamsburg (p268)

This bustling neighborhood is home to plenty of boutiques, bars and cafes.

3. Brooklyn Bridge Park (p264)

One of Brooklyn's newest sights, this park hosts Jane's Carousel, a vintage marvel from 1922 with 48 horses and 1200 lights.

TOP CHOICE BLACK GOLD
MUSIC

Map p448 (www.blackgoldbrooklyn.com; 461 Court St btwn 4th Pl & Luquer St, Carroll Gardens; ⊙6am-8pm Mon-Wed & Sat, to 9pm Thu & Fri, 10am-5pm Sun ; SF, G to Carroll St) Records, coffee, antiques and taxidermy await you in this tiny addition to the ever expanding Carroll Gardens Court St scene. Sample vintage vinyl on the turntable from John Coltrane to Ozzy Osborne and enjoy a damn good cup of coffee ($3.50), ground and brewed individually. Need a stuffed hyena from the Ozarks? Find one here.

SMITH + BUTLER
CLOTHING

Map p448 (www.smithbutler.com; 225 Smith St cnr Butler St, Caroll Gardens; ⊙noon-7pm; SF, G to Bergen St) This fashion shop in Caroll Gardens sells durable clothing that channels a nomadic Brooklyn biker vibe. It's a little pricey but has some really good finds for men and women (think hunting gear, gloves, wool scarves and plenty of plaids). The retro Captain America motorcycle helmets are the coolest, and they sell vintage cycles for the hard core.

THREE KINGS TATTOO
TATTOO

Map p446 (www.threekingstattoo.com; 572 Manhattan Ave btwn Driggs & Nassau Ave, Williamsburg; ⊙noon-10pm; SL to Bedford Ave, G to Nassau Ave) Because your vacation didn't happen unless you have a tattoo to prove it. If you were thinking of taking home a permanent keepsake from your trip to NYC, this would be the place to do it. Walk-ins welcome.

EVA GENTRY
CONSIGNMENT

Map p448 (www.evagentry.com; 389 Atlantic Ave btwn Hoyt & Bond Sts, Boerum Hill; SA/C, G to Hoyt-Schermerhorn, F to Bergen) This whitewashed, artfully arranged little boutique looks more like an art gallery than a consignment shop. But it's just the place to find gently worn designer brands by the likes of Marc Jacobs and Stella McCartney.

BEACON'S CLOSET (PARK SLOPE)
THRIFT STORE

Map p450 (☎718-230-1630; 92 Fifth Ave cnr Warren Street, Park Slope; ⊙noon-9pm Mon-Fri, 11am-8pm Sat & Sun; S2/3 to Bergen St) An excellent thrift shop stocked full of shoes, jewelry and bright vintage finds. It is the sister store of the bigger Beacon's Closet in Williamsburg (p294).

FLIRT
CLOTHING

Map p450 (www.flirt-brooklyn.com; 93 Fifth Ave btwn Park Pl & Prospect Pl, Park Slope; ⊙11am-7pm; SB/D, N/Q/R, 2/3, 4/5 to Atlantic Ave/Pacific St, G to Bergen St) The name says it all at this girlishly sexy Park Slope boutique, where a trio of stylish owners comes up with funky yet feminine creations such as custom-made skirts (pick your cut and fabric) and tiny tops in soft knits.

PS BOOKSHOP
BOOKS

Map p452 (www.psbnyc.com; 76 Front & Washington Sts, Dumbo; ⊙10am-8pm; SA/C to High St, F to York St) A new Dumbo favorite has aisles of used books full of lost treasures. This is a good shop with an excellent selection of art monographs, street books, children's books and vintage travelogues, as well as plenty of rare first editions.

POWERHOUSE BOOKS
BOOKS

Map p452 (www.powerhousebooks.com; 37 Main St, Dumbo; ⊙10am-7pm Mon-Fri, 11am-7pm Sat & Sun; SA/C to High St, F to York St) An important part of Dumbo's cultural scene, Powerhouse Books hosts changing art exhibitions, book-launch parties and weird and creative events in its 5000-sq-ft space. You'll also find intriguing books on urban art, photography and pop culture – all imprints of their namesake publishing house.

DESERT ISLAND COMICS
COMICS

Map p446 (www.desertislandbrooklyn.com; 540 Metropolitan Ave btwn Union Ave & Lorimer St, Williamsburg; ⊙noon-9pm Mon-Sat, to 7pm Sun; SL to Lorimer St, G to Metropolitan Ave) Desert Island is a indie comic-book shop located inside a former bakery in Williamsburg. Inside, you'll find hundreds of comics, graphic novels, local zines, prints and cards. They also sell original prints and lithographs by artists like Adrian Tomine and Peter Bagge.

SPOONBILL & SUGARTOWN
BOOKS

Map p446 (www.spoonbillbooks.com; 218 Bedford Ave at 5th St, Williamsburg; ⊙10am-10pm; SL to Bedford Ave) Williamsburg's favorite bookshop has an intriguing selection of art and coffee-table books, cultural journals, used and rare titles and locally made works not found elsewhere.

BOOK THUG NATION
BOOKS

Map p446 (www.bookthugnation.com; 100 N 3rd St btwn Berry St & Wythe Ave, Williamsburg; ⊙noon-9pm; SL to Bedford) This Williamsburg shop specializes in contemporary and classic literary fiction, and is a good source of cheap used tomes. It was founded by four street booksellers who moved into this tiny space to offer readers a wider variety of choices.

FUEGO 718 HANDICRAFTS

Map p446 (249 Grand St btwn Roebling St & Driggs Ave, Williamsburg; ⏲noon-8pm; [S]L to Bedford Ave) You'll find everything from kitsch to camp at Fuego 718. Mexican wrestlers, Peruvian *retablos,* Italian *milagros* – you name it, they probably have it. There is also an interesting selection of silk-screened prints, art and jewelry handcrafted by an array of Brooklyn and international designers.

LOVE BRIGADE CO-OP CLOTHING

Map p446 (www.lovebrigade.com; 230 Grand St btwn Roebling St & Driggs Ave, Williamsburg; ⏲noon-8pm Wed-Sun; [S]L to Bedford Ave) You'll find more than two dozen independent designers from all corners of the globe at this hyper-cute Williamsburg boutique. There are silk-screened tees, slouchy dresses and skinny jeans. Prices are reasonable.

ACADEMY ANNEX MUSIC

Map p446 (www.academyannex.com; 96 N 6th St btwn Berry St & Wythe Ave, Williamsburg; ⏲noon-9pm; [S]L to Bedford Ave) Serious vinyl vultures head to this Williamsburg mecca to browse bins stuffed full of rock, hip-hop, jazz, blues, electronica and world music. The annex also stocks an increasing number of CDs and some cassettes. Prices compare quite well with other shops, and the stock changes frequently.

ADOBE NEW YORK HOMEWARES

Map p446 (www.abode-newyork.com; 179 Grand St near Bedford Ave, Williamsburg; ⏲noon-7:30pm Mon & Wed-Sat, to 6pm Sun; [S]L to Bedford Ave) A contemporary home-furnishings

BROOKLYN MARKETS

When the weekend arrives, Brooklynites are out and about, strolling the stoop sales and hitting the markets. Here are a few good places to unearth something unusual (and enjoy a good bite while you're at it):

Brooklyn Flea (Map p448; www.brooklynflea.com; 176 Lafayette Ave btwn Clermont & Vanderbilt Aves, Fort Greene; ⏲10am-5pm Sat, Apr-Dec; 👪; [S]G to Clinton-Washington Aves) On the grounds of a school in Fort Greene, some 200 vendors sell their wares, ranging from antiques, records, vintage clothes, craft items and enticing food stalls stuffed with a smorgasbord of tasty treats. In winter, the market moves indoors to a gorgeous art deco space in the former Williamsburgh Savings Bank building at Flatbush near Atlantic Ave.

Brooklyn Flea (Map p446; www.brooklynflea.com; East River Waterfront btwn 6th & 7th Sts, Williamsburg; ⏲10am-5pm Sun, Apr-Dec; [S]L to Bedford Ave) On Sundays in the summer and fall, you can get more market action at this large outdoor space at the East River Waterfront in Williamsburg. You'll also find plenty of vintage furnishings, retro clothing and bric-a-bric, not to mention an array of lobster rolls, pupusas, tamales and chocolate. This area is also home to the popular Smorgasburg market on Saturdays in the summer, when food vendors from all over New York City descend on the area with tasty victuals.

DeKalb Market (Map p452; www.dekalbmarket.com; 138 Willoughby St at Flatbush Ave, Downtown Brooklyn; ⏲8am-10pm; [S]B/Q, R to Dekalb Ave, G, F, A/C, 2/3 to Fulton Mall) The latest and funkiest flea market in Brooklyn attracts shoppers who descend on more than 50 stalls inside and around a stack of repurposed shipping containers. There's handmade jewelry, trinkets, new and used clothing, doughnuts, cupcakes and even a community farm. Convenient.

Artists & Fleas (Map p446; www.artistsandfleas.com; 70 N 7th Ave btwn Berry St & Wythe Ave, Williamsburg; ⏲10am-7pm Sat & Sun; [S]L to Bedford Ave) In operation since 2003, this is a popular artists, designers and vintage market in Williamsburg, where you can find an excellent selection of crafty goodness.

Greenmarket (Map p450; Grand Army Plaza, Prospect Park West & Flatbush Ave; ⏲10am-5pm Sat; [S]2/3 to Grand Army Plaza) Open on Saturdays year-round, this greenmarket is a good spot to put together an impromptu picnic before heading into Prospect Park.

store for urban dwellers has great last-minute gifts – from designer knick-knacks and small furnishings to fancy salad forks by the likes of Sandy Chilewich and Tokyo Bay. There are gifts for the furry friends like a tepee for your cat.

BEACON'S CLOSET (WILLIAMSBURG) THRIFT STORE

Map p446 (www.beaconscloset.com; 88 N 11th St btwn Berry St & Wythe Ave, Williamsburg; 🕐11am-9pm Mon-Fri, to 8pm Sat & Sun; [S]L to Bedford Ave) Twenty-something groovers find this giant Williamsburg warehouse of vintage clothing part goldmine, part grit. Lots of coats, polyester tops and '90s-era tees are handily displayed by color, but the sheer mass can take time to conquer.

BROOKLYN INDUSTRIES CLOTHING

Map p446 (www.brooklynindustries.com; 162 Bedford Ave at 8th St, Williamsburg; 🕐11am-9pm Mon-Sat, noon-8:30pm Sun; [S]L to Bedford Ave) This is where the cool kids shop for hooded sweatshirts, silk-screened T-shirts and slinky knit dresses. It may be a chain but this one has the cachet of actually being in Brooklyn.

BUFFALO EXCHANGE CLOTHING

Map p446 (504 Driggs Ave at 9th St, Williamsburg; 🕐11am-7pm Mon-Sat, noon-8pm Sun; [S]L to Bedford Ave) A large new and used clothing shop is a go-to spot for Brooklynites on a budget – featuring clothes (designer and not), shoes, jewelry and accessories. It takes time to find the best pieces, so plan on spending some quality time here.

URBAN JUNGLE THRIFT SHOP

Map p446 (☎718-497-1331; 120 Knickerbocker Ave btwn Flushing Ave & Thames St, Bushwick; 🕐noon-7pm; [S]L to Morgan Ave) The selection is massive – OK, daunting – at this sprawling warehouse thrift shop on an industrial street in Bushwick. But the prices are low and the inventory is full of treasures from the '60s, '70s and '80s.

SPORTS & ACTIVITIES

For jet skiing, check the section on Coney Island (p266).

BROOKLYN BOWL BOWLING

Map p446 (www.brooklynbowl.com; 61 Wythe Ave btwn 11th & 12th Sts, Williamsburg; lane rental per hr $40-50, shoe rental $5; 🕐6pm-2am Mon-Thu, 6pm-4am Fri, noon-4am Sat, noon-2am Sun; [S]L to Bedford, G to Nassau Ave) This incredible alley is housed in the 23,000-sq-ft former Hecla Iron Works Company, which provided ornamentation for several NYC landmarks at the turn of the 20th century. There are 16 lanes surrounded by cushy sofas and exposed brick walls. In addition to bowling, you'll find plenty of music options as well.

ON THE MOVE CYCLING

Map p450 (☎718-768-4998; www.onthemovenyc.com; 400 Seventh Ave btwn 12th & 13th Sts, Park Slope; bike rentals per day incl helmet $35; 🕐11am-7pm Mon & Fri, noon-7pm Tue-Thu, 10am-6pm Sat, 11am-5pm Sun; [S]F to 7th Ave) A couple of blocks south from Brooklyn's Prospect Park, On the Move rents and sells all manner of bikes and gear. They are closed in inclement weather and cut back hours from October to March.

GOTHAM GIRLS ROLLER DERBY ROLLER DERBY

(☎888-830-2253; www.gothamgirlsrollerderby.com; $20 advance, $25-35 at the door; 🕐Apr-Nov; 👪) NYC's only all-female and skater-operated roller derby league is made up of four home teams: the Bronx Gridlock, Brooklyn Bombshells, Manhattan Mayhem and Queens of Pain. It also has two traveling teams: the All-Stars and the Wall Street Traitors. Matches are held all over the city, but naturally, we're partial to the Brooklyn Bombshells.

Bombers Anne Phetamean and Bitch Cassidy really know how to tear up the competition.

BROOKLYN CYCLONES BASEBALL

Map p453 (☎718-449-8497; www.brooklyncyclones.com; MCU Park, 1904 Surf Ave at 17th St, Coney Island; tickets $8-16; [S]D/F, N/Q to Coney Island-Stillwell Ave) The minor league team, part of the New York–Penn League, plays at a beachside park a few steps from the Coney Island boardwalk.

AUDUBON CENTER BOATHOUSE BOATING

Map p450 (☎718-287-3400; www.prospectpark.org/audubon; Prospect Park, entrance at Ocean Ave & Lincoln Rd; boat rides adult/child $8/4; 🕐noon-5:30pm Thu-Sun Apr-Sep, to 4:30pm Sat & Sun Oct-Mar; 👪; [S]B, Q to Prospect Park) A lovely Venetian-style boathouse offers electric boat rides and paddleboat rentals.

RED HOOK BOATERS KAYAKING

Map p448 (☎917-676-6458; www.redhookboaters.org; Louis Valentino Jr Pier Park, Coffey St; [S]F, G to Smith-9th Sts, 🚌B61 to Van Dyke St) This boathouse, located in remote Red Hook, offers free kayaking and canoeing out on the East River and in the Buttermilk Channel. Excursions are available two or three times weekly from May to October. Check the website or call before making the trip out.

BROOKLYN BOULDERS ROCK CLIMBING

Map p448 (www.brooklynboulders.com; 575 Degraw St at Third Ave, Boerum Hill; day pass $22; 🕒noon-10pm Mon-Thu, to midnight Fri & Sat, to 8pm Sun; [S]R to Union St) It's NYC's biggest indoor climbing arena for scaling aficionados and folks looking to reach new heights. Ceilings top out at 30ft inside this 18,000-sq-ft facility, and its caves, freestanding 17ft boulder and climbing walls offer numerous routes for beginners to experts. There are overhangs of 15°, 30° and 45°. Climbing classes are available.

GOWANUS DREDGERS CANOE CLUB BOATING

Map p448 (☎718-243-0849; www.gowanuscanal.org; cnr 2nd & Bond Sts, Gowanus Canal; suggested donation $5; [S]F, G to Carroll St or Smith-9th St) This unusual club will supply you with gear (a canoe and a map) for self-guided tours of the canal and the surrounding area. Participants are asked to help clean any garbage they might see on the way. April through October only. Reserve in advance.

KATE WOLLMAN RINK SKATING

Map p450 (www.prospectpark.org; Prospect Park, near Ocean & Parkside Aves; 👪; [S]B, Q to Prospect Park) The rink was closed during the 2011–2012 season due to construction on the Lakeside Center project (26 acres of parkland are being repurposed) and is scheduled to reopen as a year-round ice-skating facility in the 2012–2013 season. For details see the website.

PROSPECT PARK TENNIS CENTER TENNIS

Map p450 (www.prospectpark.org; Prospect Park, cnr Parkside & Coney Island Aves; 🕒7am-11pm; [S]F to Fort Hamilton Pkwy, Q to Parkside Ave) Open all year, this 11-court facility takes permits or sells single-use tickets on location from mid-May to mid-November. Hourly rates range from $36 to $74.

AREA YOGA CENTER YOGA

Map p448 (www.areayogabrooklyn.com; 2nd fl, 320 Court St, Cobble Hill; single class $11; 🕒classes 7am-8:15pm Mon-Fri, 8am-7pm Sat & Sun; [S]F, G to Carroll St) With a spa, a couple of shops and a yoga studio, Area conquers Brooklyn's Cobble Hill area for all things mind and body.

DYKER BEACH GOLF COURSE GOLF

(☎718-836-9722; cnr 86th St & Seventh Ave, Fort Hamilton/Dyker Heights; green fees before/after 3pm Mon-Fri $49/27, Sat & Sun $54/28, club rental $37; [S]R to 86th St) This scenic public course in Fort Hamilton is easiest to reach by subway. Call ahead about club rentals – they're sometimes not available. It's between Seventh and Tenth Aves, to the right, when approaching from the subway station.

BARCLAYS CENTER BASKETBALL

Map p450 (www.barclayscenter.com; cnr Flatbush & Atlantic Aves, Prospect Heights; [S]B/D, N/Q/R, 2/3, 4/5 to Atlantic Ave) The Dodgers still play baseball in Los Angeles but the New Jersey Nets – soon to become the Brooklyn Nets (rap star Jay-Z is a part-owner) – will be playing basketball at this rising new stadium sometime in late 2012 (if it opens on time). Check the website for updates.

Queens

LONG ISLAND CITY | ASTORIA | FLUSHING | CORONA | WOODSIDE

Neighborhood Top Five

1 Finding inspiration and provocation at **MoMA PS1** (p298), the Museum of Modern Art's cross-river sibling. From painting and sculpture to site-specifc installations, this cultural 'It kid' serves up some of the world's edgiest artwork, not to mention lectures, performances and an electric summer party series.

2 Reliving your favorite screen moments at the better-than-ever **Museum of the Moving Image** (p301).

3 Working up a sweat at aquatic wonderworld **New York Spa Castle** (p308).

4 Late-night Latino food truck crawling on **Roosevelt Ave** (p395).

5 Diving into the frenetic tide of Asian street life in Flushing.

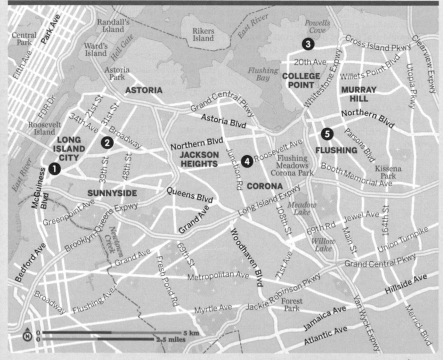

For more detail of this area, see Map p454 ➡

Explore Queens

Of the city's five boroughs, Queens is top dog in size and runner-up in head count. Anywhere else, it would be a major city in its own right. So where to begin? Assuming it's not Tuesday or Wednesday (when most of the galleries are closed), start your explorations with two days in Long Island City (LIC). It's packed with contemporary art musts like MoMA PS1, 5 Pointz and the lesser-known Fisher Landau Center for Art. Watch the sun set over Manhattan from Gantry Plaza State Park, and sip-and-sup in locally loved restaurants lining Vernon Blvd.

Spend a day or two exploring neighboring Astoria, taste-testing its ethnic delis and nosh spots, downing Czech beers at the Bohemian Hall & Beer Garden, and getting a cultural fix at the brilliant Museum of Modern Art and Noguchi Museum. Further out, Flushing (home to NYC's biggest Chinatown) also merits a full-day adventure, with enough hawker-style food stands, exotic grocery stores, kitschy malls and reflexology therapists to keep you purring for hours.

If it's hot and you feel like a splash, consider hitting the surf at up-and-coming Rockaway Beach. It has the city's best beach and finest fish taco.

Local Life

➜ **Hangouts** LIC locals relish cocktails, comfort food and gossip at El Ay Si (p304), while hipsters *sans* attitude down single-origin Joe and craft beers at Queens Kickshaw (p308).

➜ **Culture** Take an aerial tour of New York City without leaving the ground at the Queens Museum of Art (p301) – one of the city's true under-the-radar cultural gems.

➜ **Flushing** Snack on lamb dumplings in the Golden Shopping Mall (p304) basement, then fire up the palate at Hunan Kitchen of Grand Sichuan (p304) or Fu Run (p304).

Getting There & Away

➜ **Subway** Twelve lines service Queens. Useful lines from Manhattan include the N, Q, R and M to Astoria, the 7 to Long Island City, Jackson Heights, Sunnyside, Woodside, Corona and Flushing, and the A to Rockaway Beach. The E, J and Z trains reach Jamaica, while the G directly connects Long Island City to Brooklyn (including Williamsburg).

➜ **Train** Long Island Rail Road (LIRR) has a handy connection from Manhattan's Penn Station to Flushing.

➜ **Bus** Useful routes include the M60, which runs from La Guardia Airport to Harlem and Columbia University in Manhattan, via Astoria.

Lonely Planet's Top Tip

Don't miss the Fisher Landau Center for Art (p300) for modern art without the crowds and admission fee. Occupying two floors of an old parachute harness factory in Long Island City, the core of its stellar collection of painting, photography, sculpture and installation art spans the 1960s to the present day. The rotating exhibitions feature key works from A-listers like Robert Rauschenberg, Cy Twombly, Jenny Holzer and Jasper Johns. Get in quick before the secret is out.

✖ Best Places to Eat

➜ Sripraphai (p304)
➜ Fu Run (p304)
➜ Rockaway Taco (p301)
➜ Roosevelt Ave

For reviews, see p303 ➜

☉ Best Places to Chill Out

➜ Rockaway Beach (p301)
➜ New York Spa Castle (p308)
➜ Gantry State Park
➜ Bohemian Hall & Beer Garden (p308)

☉ Best Places for Culture Vultures

➜ MoMA PS1 (p298)
➜ Fisher Landau Center for Art (p300)
➜ SculptureCenter (p300)
➜ 5 Pointz (p300)

COREY WISE / LONELY PLANET IMAGES ©

TOP SIGHTS
MOMA PS1

Sorry, Gaga, but New York's true icon of edge is MoMA PS1. This smaller, hipper relative of Manhattan's Museum of Modern Art is a master at hunting down fresh, bold contemporary art and serving it up in a Berlin-esque, ex-school locale. Forget about pretty lily ponds in gilded frames. Here you'll be peering at videos through floorboards, schmoozing at DJ-pimped parties, and debating the meaning of nonstatic structures while staring through a hole in the wall. Expect over 50 exhibitions a year, exploring anything from Middle Eastern video art to giant mounds of thread. Nothing is predictable. Even a 2011 exhibition honoring the 10-year anniversary of 9/11 took a different route, ditching catastrophic images for an exploration of how the event has reshaped people's visual perceptions. Best of all, admission is free with your MoMA ticket – so hold on tight!

Roots, Radicals & PS1 Classics

Officially affiliated with MoMA in 2000, PS1 first hit the scene in the 1970s. This was the age of Dia, Artists' Space and the New Museum – new-gen spaces showcasing the growing tide of experimental, multimedia art flourishing in New York. In 1976, Alanna Heiss – a vocal supporter of art in alternative spaces – took possession of an abandoned school building in Queens and invited artists like Richard Serra, James Turrell and Keith Sonnier to create site-specific works in the empty classrooms. The end result was PS1's inaugural exhibition, *Rooms*. Remnants of the show live on in the space today, from Richard Art-

DON'T MISS...

- Temporary exhibitions
- Long-term installations
- Summer 'Warm Up' parties
- Saturday Sessions

PRACTICALITIES

- Map p454
- www.momaps1.org
- 22-25 Jackson Ave at 46th Ave
- suggested donation $10, admission for MoMA ticket holders free, Warm Up party admission $15
- 🕐noon-6pm Thu-Mon, Warm Up parties 2-9pm Sat Jul & Aug
- [S]E, M to 23rd St-Ely Ave; G to 21st; 7 to 45th Rd-Court House Sq

schwager's oval-shaped 'blimps' on the walls to Alan Saret's light-channeling *The Hole at P.S.1, Fifth Solar Chthonic Wall Temple*, on the north wing's 3rd floor. These creations are now part of the gallery's long-term installations, which also include Pipilotti Rist's video *Selbstlos im Lavabad* (Selfless in the Bath of Lava) – viewable through a floorboard in the lobby – and James Turrell's awe-inspiring *Meeting*, an open-top room where the sky is the masterpiece.

Summer 'Warm Up' Parties

It's not just the art that draws the crowds. Head in on Saturday afternoons from July to early September, and rock on at one of New York's coolest weekly music/culture events, Warm Up. It's a hit with everyone from verified hipsters to plugged-in music geeks, who spill into the MoMA PS1 courtyard to eat, drink, catch kooky performances and get their general groove on. The tunes are the main attraction, with a stellar line-up of top bands, experimental music and DJs each week. Featured artists have included Omar-S, Tanlines, NGUZUNGUZU and acid-house pioneer DJ Pierre. It's like one big block party, albeit with better music and art than your usual neighborhood slap-up. Not bad for $15. Linked to the fun is the annual YAP (Young Architects Program) competition, which sees emerging architects competing for the chance to transform the MoMA PS1 courtyard. Nabbing the prize in 2011 was Brooklyn's Interboro Partners, whose installation graced the space with a sexy, striking canopy of white sails and ropes. The initiative has now gone global, with an international edition held at Rome's Zaha Hadid–designed MAXXI museum.

Saturday Sessions

Another treat for culture vultures is the Saturday Sessions, taking place from 3pm to 5pm every second Saturday, January to late spring. Spanning lectures and film screenings to music performances and even architectural projects, the inspired lineup has included experimental comedy, postindustrial noise jams and Latin art-house dance. One week you might catch a symphony debut, another your taste buds might get involved, as was the case when artist Anne Apparu hosted an afternoon of sweet tea and 'inner-war' cookies (an original recipe meant to trigger collective meditations on violence and community). Expect to be titillated, provoked or just plain perplexed. Upcoming events are listed on the MoMA PS1 website.

BOOKSTORE

Expect further inspiration at Artbook (Map p454; www.artbook.com/artbookps1.html), the MoMA PS1 bookstore. Stock up on a solid selection of MoMA exhibition catalogues, coffee-table tomes, art theory titles and out-of-print fodder. You'll also find contemporary culture, film and performance titles; art, architecture and design journals; magazines; CDs and new media. We especially love the 'Where did you get that?' art-themed T-shirts. Signings, readings and other exhibition-based events take place here from time to time – scan the Artbook website for details.

Built in the Renaissance Revival style and dating back to the early 1890s, the MoMA PS1 building housed the first school in Long Island City. Low attendance forced its closure in 1963. A three-year, award-winning restoration by LA-based architect Frederick Fisher in the mid-1990s saw the addition of the building's outdoor galleries and main staircase.

SIGHTS

The Queens Visitor Center (www.discoverqueens.info; Queens Center Mall, 90-15 Queens Blvd; 🕐10am-6pm Mon-Fri, 11am-7pm Sat & Sun; [S]M, R to Woodhaven Blvd) **offers information on attractions and tours, while the Queens Council on the Arts** (☎347-505-3010; www.queenscouncilarts.org) **promotes art in the borough.**

For a more personalized introduction, Hunter College urban-geography professor Jack Eichenbaum leads many unusual **Walking Tours** (☎718-961-8406; www.geognyc.com; from $15) of Queens' ethnic neighborhoods, including a full-day walk/subway ride along the 7 train.

Long Island City

MOMA PS1 — GALLERY

See p298.

[TOP CHOICE] FISHER LANDAU CENTER FOR ART — MUSEUM

Map p454 (www.flcart.org; 38-27 30th St; admission free; 🕐noon-5pm Thu-Mon; [S]N/Q to 39th Ave) Surprisingly under the radar, this private art museum is a must for fans of modern and contemporary art. On any given visit you can expect to catch important works from some of the most iconic artists of the 20th and 21st centuries.

Co-designed by late British architect Max Gordon (designer of London's Saatchi Gallery), the space also hosts the Columbia University School of Visual Arts MFA Thesis Exhibition each May – a highly respected showcase for talented emerging artists.

NOGUCHI MUSEUM — MUSEUM

Map p454 (www.noguchi.org; 9-01 33rd Rd at Vernon Blvd; adult/child $10/free, by donation 1st Fri of the month; 🕐10am-5pm Wed-Fri, 11am-6pm Sat & Sun; [S]N/Q to Broadway) The art and the building here are the work of eponymous Japanese-American sculptor Isamu Noguchi, and both exude a Zen-like sensibility. Displayed in bare concrete galleries and an outdoor rock garden, the artist's abstract stone sculptures are a meditation on the struggle between nature and the manmade world.

The building itself was once a photo-engraving plant, located across the street from Noguchi's studio. Art aside, the space also hosts a small cafe and gift shop, the latter stocking Noguchi-designed lamps and furniture, as well as a small range of other mid-20th-century design pieces. The museum is a 10-block walk from the subway stop; there's also a shuttle bus (one way/round-trip $5/10) going four times each Sunday from the northeast corner of E 70th St and Park Ave in Manhattan. See the website for times.

SCULPTURECENTER — GALLERY

Map p454 (www.sculpture-center.org; 44-19 Purves St near 43rd Ave; suggested donation $5; 🕐11am-6pm Thu-Mon; [S]7 to 45th Rd-Court House Sq, E, M to 23rd St-Ely Ave, G to Long Island City-Court Sq) In a former trolley repair warehouse, down a dead-end street, SculptureCenter recalls Berlin with its collision of edgy art and industrial backdrop. Its two exhibition levels include a hangarlike main gallery and a cavernous underground space, providing an evocative backdrop for the gallery's rotating shows of both emerging and established artists. Expect anything from site-specific installations to video art.

5 POINTZ — GALLERY

Map p454 (Davis St; [S]7 to 45th Rd-Court House Sq, G to Long Island City-Court Sq, E, M to 23rd St-Ely Ave) One of the best collections of graffiti left anywhere in New York. Walk under the 7 subway tracks on Davis St, just south of Jackson Ave, to see the dazzling displays of wall-to-wall art on a cluster of industrial buildings.

[FREE] SOCRATES SCULPTURE PARK — ART

Map p454 (www.socratessculpturepark.org; Broadway at Vernon Blvd; 🕐10am-dusk; [S]N/Q to Broadway) Sculptures, installations and superb light shows define this 4.5-acre open-air space, right on the East River and close to Noguchi Museum. Try to time a visit around free events – like yoga and capoeira on summer Saturdays and movie screenings on Wednesdays from early July to late August; prescreening performances start at 7pm; films begin at sunset (food available).

GANTRY PLAZA STATE PARK — OUTDOORS

Map p454 (www.nysparks.com/parks; 4-09 47th Rd; [S]7 to Vernon Blvd-Jackson Ave) This design-savvy riverside park has cinematic views of Midtown (as seen in the 2005 film *The Interpreter*, with Sean Penn and Nicole Kidman), complete with four piers and public sunlounges for panoramic chilling. The restored, archlike gantries – in service until

WORTH A DETOUR

ROCKAWAY BEACH

Immortalized by the Ramones' 1977 song 'Rockaway Beach,' America's largest urban beach – and New York's best – is just a $2.25 trip on subway line A. Less crowded than Coney Island and well known for its surprisingly natural scenery and surf spots, it's now also home to a burgeoning summertime scene of hipsters, artists and locavore food options. At the heart of the revolution is the banging taco shack **Rockaway Taco** (www.rockawaytaco.com; 95-19 Rockaway Beach Blvd; ⏲11am-8pm; [S]A, S to Beach 98th St), whose guacamole-topped fish tacos are alone worth the trip out here. Close by on the boardwalk, concrete concession booths peddle treats from hipster staples like Brooklyn's Roberta's (p283) and Blue Bottle Coffee (p285).

Beyond the May-to-September scene of oiled bodies, surfboards and cruiser bikes is a natural wonderland that feels worlds away from New York's urban chaos. Much of the area is part of the 26,000-acre **Gateway National Recreation Area**, which encompasses several parks. One of these, toward the southern tip of the Rockaways, is **Jacob Riis Park**, named for an advocate and photographer of immigrants in the late 19th century; it's also home to Fort Tilden, a decommissioned coastal artillery installation from WWI.

Extending from near JFK international airport, the salty, marshy **Jamaica Bay Wildlife Refuge** is one of the most important migratory bird and wetland habitats along the eastern seaboard. In spring and fall, more than 325 bird species stop in to rest and snack, snapping up all sorts of briny sea creatures like clams, turtles, shrimp and oysters. Each season brings different visitors; spring features warblers and songbirds, and American woodcocks in late March. In mid-August shorebirds start to move south, landing here from Canada and fueling up for the trip to Mexico. Fall is when migrating hawks and raptors get mobile, along with ducks, geese, monarch butterflies and thousands and thousands of dragonflies. Birders and naturalists get the most action around the east and west ponds; these ponds are both about 1.5 miles in circumference and easily walkable, but wear mud resistant shoes, insect repellent and sunscreen, carry some water and watch out for poison ivy.

To get to the visitors center, exit at Broad Channel station, walk west along Noel Rd to Crossbay Blvd, turn right (north) and walk for about half a mile, and the center will be visible on the left side of the road.

1967 – are testament to the area's past as a loading dock for rail car floats and barges.

Dating back to 1936, the giant Pepsi-Cola sign at the park's northern end once topped a nearby Pepsi bottling plant, which has been since demolished.

Astoria

[TOP CHOICE] **MUSEUM OF THE MOVING IMAGE** MUSEUM

Map p454 (www.movingimage.us; 35th Ave at 36th St; adult/child $12/6, admission 4-8pm Fri free; ⏲10.30am-5pm Tue-Thu, to 8pm Fri, to 7pm Sat & Sun; 📶; [S]M, R to Steinway St) Fresh from a $65-million upgrade, this super-cool complex is now one of the world's top film, television and video museums. State-of-the-art galleries show off the museum's collection of 130,000-plus TV and movie artifacts, including Robert De Niro's wig from *Taxi Driver*, Robert Williams' space suit from *Mork & Mindy* and the creepy stunt doll used in *The Exorcist*.

Try your hand at film editing (including re-dubbing the 'We're not in Kansas anymore' scene from *The Wizard of Oz*), and get nostalgic over an impressive booty of vintage TVs, cameras and retro arcade games. The museum's temporary exhibitions are usually fantastic, as are the regular film screenings – check the website for details.

Flushing & Corona

QUEENS MUSEUM OF ART MUSEUM

Map p454 (QMA; www.queensmuseum.org; Flushing Meadows Corona Park; suggested donation adult/child $5/free; ⏲noon-6pm Wed-Sun, to 8pm Fri Jul & Aug; 📶; [S]7 to 111th St) Undergoing a massive expansion at the time of research, the QMA's most famous drawcard is the Panorama of New York City, a gobsmacking 9335-sq-ft miniature New York City, with all buildings accounted for and a 15-minute dusk-to-dawn light simulation of a New York day. The museum also hosts top-notch exhibitions of modern art, from contemporary photography to site-specific installations.

The QMA is housed in a historic building made for the '39 World's Fair (and once home to the UN), and you'll find a retro-fabulous collection of memorabilia from both the '39 and '64 fairs on display (with reproductions in the gift shop).

LOUIS ARMSTRONG HOUSE — CULTURAL BUILDING

Map p454 (www.louisarmstronghouse.org; 34-56 107th St; admission $10; ⏲10am-5pm Tue-Fri, noon-5pm Sat & Sun; [S]7 to 103rd St-Corona Plaza) At the peak of his career and with worldwide fame at hand, Armstrong chose Queens. Armstrong spent his last 28 years in this quiet Corona Heights home, now a museum and national treasure; he died here in 1971. Guides offer free 40-minute tours of his former abode, leaving on the hour (the last starts at 4pm).

Satchmo shared the house with his fourth wife, Lucille Wilson, a dancer at the Cotton Club. The tour offers an intimate glimpse into what was a happy life together, with entertaining anecdotes and a handful of home audio recordings. Armstrong's den, of which he was most proud, features a portrait of the great painted by none other than Benedetto (aka Tony Bennett).

FLUSHING MEADOWS CORONA PARK — OUTDOORS

Map p454 (www.nycgovparks.org/parks/fmcp; Grand Central Pkwy; [S]7 to Mets-Willets Point) The area's biggest attraction is this 1225-acre park, built for the '39 World's Fair and dominated by Queens' most famous landmark, the stainless steel **Unisphere** (Map

LOCAL KNOWLEDGE

QUEENS: THE NEW BROOKLYN

Julian Lesser, artist and publisher/editor of Queens magazine *Boro*, gives the low-down on his favorite New York borough (and why it should be your favorite, too).

The Best Thing About Queens

The cultural diversity. In Astoria alone you've got the original Greek population, plus everyone from Columbians and Brazilians to Egyptians. There's even a 'Little Egypt' on Steinway Ave, between Astoria Blvd and 30th Ave, with great kebab shops and strong coffee. Much of Queens is pretty mixed these days, but Flushing is incredibly Asian. The result is a really authentic shopping experience, with massive Asian grocery stores selling exotic looking fruits and every conceivable type of still-wriggling seafood. Planes fly low over Flushing so it's also cool if you're a plane-spotter.

Don't-Miss Eats

I love Brooklyn Bagel & Coffee Company (p303). They have amazing, huge bagels and a wide variety of cream cheeses. They create a new flavor every week for their customers to try. Don't miss the manchego and ricotta cheese grilled sandwich at Queens Kickshaw (p308). The Kickshaw team source a lot of their ingredients locally. In Long Island City, I love LIC Market (p303). It's like an intimate cafe but they do full service, and put a lot of love into the food. It's also handy if you're visiting MoMA PS1. A good dinner spot is El Ay Si (p304) – its tater tots (deep-fried potato balls) are super-addictive. It's also great for a lively late-night drink.

Cultural Picks

For cutting-edge contemporary art, spend an afternoon at MoMA PS1 and the nearby SculptureCenter (p300) in Long Island City. You could easily spend a few happy hours at the impressive Museum of the Moving Image (p301) in Astoria – it's a cool place to see props from classic films and TV shows. For a lesser-known treat, join one of the fascinating walking tours run by the Greater Astoria Historical Society (www.astorialic.org).

As told to Cristian Bonetto

p454) – it's the world's biggest globe, at 120ft high and weighing 380 tons. Facing it is the former New York City Building, now home to the highly underrated Queens Museum of Art.

Just south are three weather-worn, Cold War–era New York State Pavilion Towers, part of the New York State Pavilion for the 1964 World's Fair. If entering the park from the subway walkway, look for the 1964 World's Fair mosaics by Salvador Dali and Andy Warhol (just down from the pedestrian bridge from the subway). Also nearby is the **Arthur Ashe Stadium** (Map p454), and the rest of the USTA Billie Jean King National Tennis Center (p308). Head west on the pedestrian bridge over the Grand Central Pkwy to find a few more attractions, including the **New York Hall of Science** (Map p454; ☎718-699-0005; www.nyhallsci.org; 47-01 111th St; adult/child $11/8, 2-5pm Fri Sep-Jun free; 🕒daily Apr-Aug, closed Mon Sep-Mar, call or see website for hrs; [S]7 to 111th St). The park has grounds on its eastern and southern edges, too. The top-notch Astroturf soccer fields are popular for organized and pick-up soccer, and there's a pitch-and-putt golf course that's lit up for drunken golfers at night.

🍴 EATING

Spanakopita? Gal kua? Sopa de mariscos? If it exists, you can chomp on it in Queens. Head to Long Island City for locavore eateries, and to Astoria for anything from Greek to bagels – hot spots here include 30th Ave, Broadway (between 31st and 35th Sts) and 31st Ave. Steinway Ave between Astoria Blvd and 30th Ave is Astoria's 'Little Cairo.' Further east, Roosevelt Ave is perfect for a Latin food-truck crawl, while at the end of the 7 subway line lies Flushing, NYC's 'Chinatown without the tourists.'

For a clued-in exploration of the borough, join a weekend **World's Fare Food Tours** (www.worldsfaretours.com; tours $60-80) adventure, run by food writer Joe Stefano.

🍴 Long Island City & Astoria

VESTA TRATTORIA & WINE BAR — ITALIAN $$

Map p454 (www.vestavino.com; 21-02 30th Ave; mains $14-22; 🕒dinner Mon-Fri, brunch & dinner Sat & Sun; [S]N/Q to 30th Ave) Opened by childhood friends Giuseppe Falco and Leo Sacco, Vesta is one of those homely neighborhood secrets, with chatty regulars at the bar, local art on the walls and organic produce from a Brooklyn rooftop farm. The menu is simple and seasonal, with nourishing *zuppe* (soups), bubbling thin-crust pizzas and tasty mains of mostly pasta and risotto dishes.

Flavors and textures are well balanced, as in the *strozzapreti* pasta with Vidalia onions, roasted garlic and radicchio. Star of the popular weekend brunch is the Warm Bankie, a hangover-friendly slap-up of fried eggs with creamy polenta, asparagus, wild mushrooms and truffle oil.

LIC MARKET — CAFE $

Map p454 (www.licmarket.com; 21-52 44th Drive, Long Island City; mains $8-11; 🕒breakfast & lunch Mon-Fri, dinner Wed-Fri, brunch Sat & Sun; 📶; [S]E, M to 23rd St-Ely Ave; 7 to 45th Rd-Court House Sq) Everyone from local creatives to corporate high-flyers flock to this cool little cafe, pimped with local artwork and cooking pots. Breakfast winners include fresh pastries, Irish oatmeal, and eggs with home fries, while strictly seasonal lunch and dinner options span anything from Nantucket scallops to soulful risottos and game. The sandwiches are scrumptious and the coffee is strong and complex.

BROOKLYN BAGEL & COFFEE COMPANY — BAKERY $

Map p454 (www.brooklynbagelandcoffeecompany.com; 35-05 Broadway, Astoria; bagels from $1; [S]N/Q to Broadway; M, R to Steinway St) It may be in Queens, not Brooklyn, but there's little confusion about the caliber of bagels here. Ridiculously soft, dense and chewy, they come in a number of drool-inducing variations, including sesame, onion, garlic, and wholewheat oats and raisins. The cream cheeses are to-die-for, their changing repertoire of flavors including bacon, scallion and real-deal strawberry. Addictive personalities beware.

TAVERNA KYCLADES — GREEK $$

Map p454 (☎718-545-8666; www.tavernakyclades.com; 33-07 Ditmars Ave at 33rd St, Astoria; mains $12-26; [S]N/Q to Astoria-Ditmars Blvd) Kyclades is hands down our favorite spot for a decent Hellenic feed. Fresh seafood is its forte, shining through in simple classics like succulent grilled octopus and fried calamari. The grilled fish dishes are testament

to the adage that 'less is more,' while the *saganaki* (pan-fried cheese) is sinfully good. One dish not worth the price tag is the Kyclades Special.

For dinner later in the week, book in advance to avoid a long wait.

EL AY SI AMERICAN $$

Map p454 (www.elaysi.com; 47-38 Vernon Blvd btwn 47th Rd & 48th Ave, Long Island City; mains $9-19; ⏲dinner Wed-Sun, brunch Sat & Sun; [S]7 to Vernon Blvd-Jackson Ave) Good-lovin' comfort grub, camaraderie and Gen-X anthems lurk behind the velvet drapes at this feel-good, bar-style nosh spot. Squeeze in at the bar or score yourself a booth for fresh, lip-licking numbers like jalapeño sweet corn fritters, tequila-lime fire-grilled shrimps and one seriously good wild boar shepherd's pie. Get in early or prepare to wait.

🍴 Woodside

[TOP CHOICE] **SRIPRAPHAI** THAI $

Map p454 (www.sripraphairestaurant.com; 64-13 39th Ave; mains $9-22; ⏲closed Wed; [S]7 to 69th St) If you think NYC is a dud at Southeast Asian food, prepare to eat your words (and everything in sight) at this ever-packed Thai legend. The grub is fresh, cheap, authentic and delicious. Must-haves include crispy ground catfish topped with green mango salad and cashews, and the fried soft shell crab with shredded green mango sauce. Go early or prepare to wait. Cash only.

WORTH A DETOUR

JACKSON HEIGHTS

All riders on the 'International Express' 7 train ought to stop off at the 74th St–Broadway stop. It's famously home to many Indians – with many curry and Bollywood DVD shops to suit – as well as other ethnic groups including Bangladeshi, Vietnamese, Korean, Mexican, Colombian and Ecuadorian. It's here that you'll also find food-blogger favorite **Tawa's Nepali Hut** (Map p454; 37-38 72nd St, Jackson Heights; dishes $4-8; [S]7 to 74th St-Broadway), a super-authentic Nepalese bolthole serving up snack-friendly *alu dum* (curried fried potatoes) and *roti sel* (deep-fried rice flour rings), delicate chicken curry *momas* (Nepalese dumplings) and nongamey goat curry.

🍴 Flushing & Corona

FU RUN CHINESE $

Map p454 (40-09 Prince St, Flushing; [S]7 to Flushing-Main St) Fu Run has a cult following for very good reason: its northeast Chinese cooking is extraordinary. Reconfigure your understanding of the country's flavors over sauerkraut-laced pork dumplings, mixed vegetable with green bean sheet jelly or the unforgettable Muslim lamb chop (deep-fried ribs dressed in dried chilies, and cumin and sesame seeds).

When done, push the boundaries further with its famed *ba si* (deep-fried cubes of sweet potato, taro and apple coated in molten caramel). It's Chinese, Jim, but not as we know it.

GOLDEN SHOPPING MALL CHINESE $

Map p454 (41-28 Main St, Flushing; meals from $2.50; [S]7 to Flushing-Main St) You're not in Kowloon, though you'd be forgiven for thinking so. A heaving, chaotic jumble of airborne noodles, hanging ducks and greasy Laminex tables, Golden Mall's basement food court serves up some of the city's best Asian hawker-style grub. Indeed, this headily scented warren – entered directly from the street – gives new meaning to the term 'cheap thrill.'

Don't be intimidated by the lack of English menus. Most stalls have at least one English speaker, and the constant flow of regulars is usually happy to point out their personal favorites, whether it's Lanzhou hand-pulled noodles or spicy pig ears. Two musts are the lamb dumplings from Xie Family Dishes (stall 38) – best dipped in a little black vinegar, soy sauce and chili oil – and the spicy cumin lamb burger at Xi'an Famous Foods next door.

HUNAN KITCHEN OF GRAND SICHUAN CHINESE $$

Map p454 (www.thegrandsichuan.com; 42-47 Main St, Flushing; mains $9-23; [S]7 to Flushing-Main St) Work up a sweat at this respectable Flushing restaurant, best known for its fiery specialties from Hunan, a province in south-central China. Standout dishes include a deliciously salty white pepper smoked beef, tender chicken with hot red

ROOSEVELT AVE FOOD-TRUCK CRAWL

When it comes to sidewalk grazing, it's hard to beat Roosevelt Ave and its army of late-night Latino food trucks, carts and stalls. Just one stroll from 90th St to 103rd St will have you sipping on *champurrados* (a warm, thick, corn-based chocolate drink), nibbling on a *cemita* (a Mexican sandwich) and making a little more room for some Ecuadorian fish stew. It's a cheap, authentic and quintessentially Queens experience. Hungry? Then set off on a taste-testing mission to find the best of Roosevelt Ave's culinary wonders.

Maravillas Restaurant (37-64 90th St at Roosevelt Ave; S 7 to 90th St-Elmhurst Ave) is a hit with karaoke-singing Mexican cowboys. Ditch the indoor section for the sidewalk counter. The menu is in Spanish but ask for an El Pastor ($2) and an Arabes ($3), both types of taco topped with succulent shaved pork marinated in chili costeño (a type of hot chili), tomato, fresh oregano, fresh orange and pineapple juice, garlic and achiote. Wash it all down with a *champurrado*.

From Maravillas, head back to Roosevelt Ave, cross onto the avenue's south side, and head one block east to the intersection of Benham St. Here you'll find the legendary food truck **Tia Julia** (Benham St at Roosevelt Ave; ⊙10am-5am; S 7 to 90th St-Elmhurst Ave), justifiably famous for its *cemitas* ($7).

A few steps further east along Roosevelt Ave sits the unmarked food stall **El Coyote Dormilon** (Roosevelt Ave btwn Benham & Aske Sts; ⊙8pm-4am; S 7 to 90th St-Elmhurst Ave). The coyote might be snoozing, but the vendor is up and at it, busily turning masa from her bucket into warm, super-fresh tortillas. (Note: fresh masa and a tortilla press are a good sign at any stall.) Quesadillas ($3) are the speciality here – try the distinctive *cuitlacoche* (fungus) and *quesillo* (stringy, cow's milk cheese) combo. It's seriously fine.

Keep strolling along Roosevelt Ave to Warren St. Parked along the street is a line of mega food trucks, including the brilliant **Hornado Ecuatoriano** (Warren St at Roosevelt Ave; S 7 to Junction Blvd). If you dare, try the *guatita* (a steamy Ecuadorian dish of tender tripe cooked in a mild, curry-style peanut sauce; $9). The food on Warren St is more expensive but also more substantial.

Another Warren St star is **El Guayaquileño** (Warren St btwn Roosevelt Ave & 40th Rd; ⊙8am-10.30pm Sun-Thu, to around 4am Fri & Sat; S 7 to Junction Blvd), famous for its Ecuadorian fish stew made of yuka, tuna, cilantro, onion, lemon, cumin and toasted corn kernels. It's flavorsome, wonderfully textured and a meal in itself. I hat said, leave room for the *bollos de pescado* (mashed green plantain with tuna, steamed in a banana leaf and served with tomato and chopped onion; $9).

If you're a Latino food-truck virgin, or simply enjoy food-hunting with other curious food lovers, consider doing the **Queens Midnight Street Crawl** (www.jeffreytastes.com; tour $48), a casual, late-night tour of the area's street-food gems led by Queens food buff and blogger Jeff Orlick. Either way, *¡buen provecho!*

---

pepper, and an incredibly flavorsome lamb with cumin flavor. If you're in a large group, order the house speciality BBQ duck, Hunan style.

TORTILLERIA NIXTAMAL   MEXICAN $

Map p454 (www.tortillerianixtamal.com; 104-5 47th Ave, Corona; dishes $2.50-10; ⊙11am-6pm Mon-Wed, to 10pm Thu-Sun; S 7 to 103rd St-Corona Plaza) A mile west of the Queens Museum of Art sits this lo-fi foodie staple. Looking like a big bright workshop, its red-and-yellow picnic benches are perpetually packed with peckish immigrant families and roving gastronomes. The secret weapon is the Rube Goldbergian machine, which transforms additive-free masa into super-tasty tacos and tamales.

The guys here are purists: tacos are no-fuss and authentic, with a simple garnish of cilantro, onion and lime. One fusion exception is the 'Italiano' tamale (sausage, peppers and fresh mozzarella), created in honor of the neighborhood's old-school locals. Wash it all down with a Mexican Coke while cheering on El Tricolor.

1. Noguchi Museum (p300)
This museum highlights the Zen-like art of Japanese-American Isamu Noguchi.

2. Queensboro Bridge
Woody Allen's movie, *Manhattan*, featured views of this bridge, which links Queens with Manhattan.

3. Flushing Meadows Corona Park (p302)
Queens' most famous landmark is the park's huge, stainless steel Unisphere.

IMAGESTATE / ALAMY ©

GRANT FAINT / GETTYIMAGES ©

🍷 DRINKING & NIGHTLIFE

BOHEMIAN HALL & BEER GARDEN
BEER HALL

Map p454 (www.bohemianhall.com; 29-19 24th Ave btwn 29th & 31st Sts, Astoria; [S]N/Q to Astoria Blvd) Easily one of NYC's great happy-drinking grounds, this outdoor beer garden is especially brilliant when the weather is warm. The mouthwatering list of cold Czech imports on draft are served with Czech accents, as are the potato dumplings and burgers. Some warm nights, folk bands set up (with occasional cover charge of $5 or so); arrive early to ensure a spot.

The building itself dates from 1919, when it housed the Bohemian Citizen's Benevolent Society (founded for Czech immigrants in 1892).

QUEENS KICKSHAW
CAFE, BAR

Map p454 (www.thequeenskickshaw.com; 40-17 Broadway, Astoria; ⏲7.30am-1am Mon-Fri, 9am-1am Sat & Sun; 📶; [S]M, R to Steinway St) If Queens is the 'new Brooklyn,' this Astoria hangout is the giveaway: think recycled bar, indie folk tunes, and communal tables lined with wi-fi–ing Macheads. Brainstorm over a single-origin brew, or loosen up with a craft ale or vino. Gut liners include fantastic grilled sandwiches (try the Gouda, with black bean hummus, guava jam and pickled jalapeños). Cash only.

CREEK
BAR

Map p454 (www.creeklic.com; 10-93 Jackson Ave at 49th Ave, Long Island City; [S]7 to Vernon Blvd-Jackson Ave) Good for a see-what-happens evening, this local bar has a burrito grill in the back and open-mic and comedy nights, plus films and live performances held in the makeshift theater upstairs. The crowd is a lively mix of Queens-forever locals and newbie pioneers. Occasional live shows tend to favor the distortion pedal.

🏃 SPORTS & ACTIVITIES

NEW YORK SPA CASTLE
DAY SPA

Map p454 (www.nyspacastle.com; 131-10 11th Ave, College Point; adult/child weekdays $35/20, weekend $45/25; ⏲6am-midnight; 📶; [S]7 to Flushing-Main St) Based on a Korean bathhouse, this five-story, 100,000-sq-ft-spa complex is a bubbling, steaming dream of mineral and massage pools, 'healing' saunas, steam rooms, waterfalls and poolside cocktails. There's a food court, massage treatments (from $40) and a gym ($5), as well as a free shuttle bus service to/from Flushing–Main St subway station on the 7 train. Avoid the place on weekends as it gets packed.

USTA BILLIE JEAN KING NATIONAL TENNIS CENTER
SPECTATOR SPORTS

Map p454 (☎718-760-6200; www.usta.com; Flushing Meadows Corona Park, Queens; [S]7 to Mets-Willets Pt) The US Open takes place in late August; tickets usually go on sale at Ticketmaster in April or May, but are hard to get for marquee games. General admission to early rounds is easier; running about $80 (top bleachers on Court 7 can take in five matches at once). Scan the USTA website in January/February for updates.

The USTA has 30 outdoor courts and an indoor tennis center with 12 courts (per hour outdoor court $20 to $32, indoor court $20 to $65) that can be hired. Reservations can be made up to two days in advance. Hourly lessons are $90 to $120.

LONG ISLAND COMMUNITY BOATHOUSE
KAYAKING

Map p454 (www.licboathouse.org; 31st Ave, Hallets Cove; ⏲free kayaking 1-5pm Sun mid-May–mid-Oct; [S]N/Q to Broadway) This boathouse regularly offers free walk-up kayaking, as well as other trips from its other boathouse at Anable Basin, including Friday Night 'Chill Paddles' and more adventurous (and demanding) Saturday paddles.

ASTORIA POOL
SWIMMING

Map p454 (www.nycgovparks.org/parks/astoriapark; Astoria Park, cnr 19th St & 23rd Dr, Astoria; ⏲11am-7pm late Jun-early Sep; [S]N/Q to Astoria Blvd) This Works Progress Administration Olympic-size outdoor pool, built in 1936, is an art-deco wonder with views of Manhattan and the Triborough Bridges. It's also the city's biggest. Crowds break 1000 on shiny summer days.

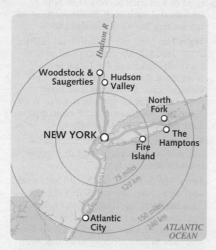

Day Trips from New York City

The Hamptons p310

New York's version of Malibu is a star-studded coastline with opulent mansions and see-and-be-seen parties, but under the Hollywood veneer lies a constellation of quiet fishing communities.

Fire Island p314

This favored gay getaway roars with dancing drag queens and a carefree summer club scene. Quieter nooks can be scouted for a spot of kayaking.

North Fork p316

Long Island's vineyards hold their own with a delightful assortment of reds, whites and – the local specialty – ice wine.

Hudson Valley p318

The gorgeous landscapes of Dutchess County are fit for a king; ogle mind-blowing art installations in the Lower Hudson then head north to learn about American nobles, the Roosevelts.

Woodstock & Saugerties p321

Supplement your pilgrimage to hippiedom with a round of antiquing and quiet walks in protected parks.

Atlantic City p322

Visit the land that inspired the Monopoly board; strut along the Boardwalk and try your luck at one of the ostentatious casinos.

The Hamptons

Explore

You'll still catch glimpses of the fishers' lifestyle and artistic hideaways that once made the Hamptons such a tranquil delight, but for most of the summer this little jut of land becomes a frenetic scene mobbed with jet-setters, celebrities and throngs of curious wannabes. Luckily there's still plenty of opportunity for outdoor activity, from kayaking to mountain biking – and yes, even a few untrammeled beaches.

There's no shortage of boutique shops, trendy eateries and celeb-heavy clubs in summer, and absolutely everything costs a pretty penny out here, with most inns charging well over $300 a night. Summer is high season; prices do drop a wee bit and traffic jams disappear about a month after Labor Day. This lessening of crowds, combined with the balmy weather of the fall harvest season, make autumn the most likely time for an unhurried visit.

The Best...

➡ **Sight** Southampton Historical Museum (p312)

➡ **Place to Eat** Lobster Roll (p313)

➡ **Place to Drink** Dune (p313)

Top Tip

Those in search of summer solitude should plan a visit on a weekday, as the weekends are stuffed to the gills with New Yorkers looking for a sea breeze instead of stifling urban heat.

Getting There & Away

Car Take the Midtown Tunnel out of Manhattan onto I-495/Long Island Expressway. Follow this for about 1½ hours to exit 70 to Sunrise Hwy East/Rte 24. After about 10 miles merge onto Montauk Hwy/Rte 27, which goes directly to Southampton. Continue along Rte 27 to get to all towns east of there.

Bus The Hampton Jitney (☑800-936-0440, 283-4600; www.hamptonjitney.com; 1-way/round-trip $30/53) is a 'luxury' express bus. Its Montauk line departs from Manhattan's East Side: 86th St between Lexington and Third Aves (in front of Victoria's Secret), then 69th St, 59th St and 40th St. It makes stops at villages along Rte 27 in the Hamptons.

Train The Long Island Rail Road (LIRR; ☑718-217-5477; www.mta.nyc.ny.us/lirr; 1-way off-peak/peak $16.75/23) leaves from Penn Station in Manhattan, and Hunterspoint Ave Station and Jamaica Station in Queens, making stops in West Hampton, Southampton, Bridgehampton, East Hampton and Montauk.

You can buy tickets in advance online and reserve round-trip trips in summer (a boon on Sunday night).

Ferry The South Ferry (☑749-1200; www.southferry.com; Rte 114, North Haven) runs between Sag Harbor and Shelter Island every 10 to 15 minutes daily between 5:45am and 1:45am, June 1 to Labor Day; and 9am to 5pm Monday to Friday, 9am to 1pm Saturday between Labor Day and May 30.

Need to Know

➡ **Area Code** 631

➡ **Location** 100 miles east (East Hampton); 2½-hour drive

➡ **Information** Southampton Chamber of Commerce (☑283-0402; 76 Main St; ☺9am-5pm, Mon-Fri), Windmill Information Center (☑692-4664; Long Wharf at Main St; ☺9am-4pm Sat & Sun)

⊙ SIGHTS

The Hamptons is actually a series of villages, most with 'Hampton' in the name. Those at the western end – or 'west of the canal,' as locals call the spots that are on the other side of the Shinnecock Canal – include Hampton Bays, Quogue and Westhampton. They are less frenzied than those to the east, which start with the village of Southampton.

Southampton

Southampton is an old-moneyed and rather conservative spot compared to some of its neighbors. It's home to sprawling old mansions, a main street with no 'beachwear' allowed, and some lovely beaches.

Upstate New York

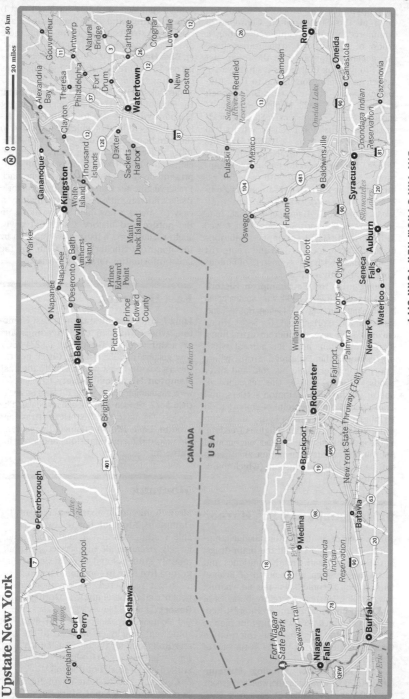

50 km
20 miles

N

CANADA
USA

Lake Ontario

Lake Erie

Niagara Falls
Fort Niagara State Park
Seaway Trail
QEW
78
104
18
Tonawanda Indian Reservation
Edie Canal
Medina
98
19
Brockport
Hilton
490
Rochester
Fairport
Palmyra
Newark
Williamson
Wolcott
New York State Thruway (Toll)
90
63
Batavia
20
Buffalo

Lyons
Clyde
Seneca Falls
Waterloo
Auburn
90
Skaneateles Lake
20
Syracuse
81
Onondaga Indian Reservation
Baldwinsville
481
Fulton
Oswego
104
Pulaski
Mexico
81
Salmon River Reservoir
Redfield
13
Camden
Oneida Lake
Rome
26
12
Oneida
Canastota
90
Cazenovia

New Boston
Watertown
12
Croghan
Lowville
Carthage
26
3
Natural Bridge
Antwerp
Fort Drum
37
Philadelphia
Theresa
11
Clayton
Alexandria Bay
Gouverneur

Dexter
Sackets Harbor
12E
Thousand Islands
12
Kingston
Wolfe Island
Gananoque
Yarker

Main Duck Island
Amherst Island
Bath
Deseronto
Napanee
Napanee
Prince Edward Point
Prince Edward County
Picton
Belleville
Trenton
Brighton
401
Colborne

Lake Rice
Peterborough
Pontypool
7
Greenbank
Lake Scugog
Port Perry
Oshawa

Pick up maps and brochures about the town at the Southampton Chamber of Commerce, which is squeezed among a group of high-priced artsy-crafty shops and decent restaurants. In the town, just past Stonybrook College, is a small Native American reservation, home to the tiny **Shinnecock Museum** (☎287-4923; Montauk Hwy; adult/under 6yr $5/3; ☺11am-4pm Fri-Sun), dedicated to preserving local Native art. Its two permanent collections – *A Walk With the People,* a set of large murals, and *My Spirit Dances Forever,* two-dozen bronze sculptures – are interspersed with traveling exhibitions. The **Parrish Art Museum** (☎631-283-2118; www.parrishart.org; 25 Jobs Lane; adult/child $5/3; ☺11am-5pm Mon-Sat, 1pm-5pm Sun late May-early Sep, closed Tue & Wed early Sep to late May) has quality exhibitions featuring great local artists and a cute gift shop stacked with glossy posters of famous Long Island landscapes.

Don't miss the **Southampton Historical Museum** (☎283-2494; www.southamptonhistoricalmuseum.org; 17 Meeting House Lane; admission $4; ☺11am-4pm Tue-Sat), which encompasses several different attractions: Rogers Mansion, built for a local whaling captain; the Pelletreau Store, where a former jeweler made his gold and silver goods; Whaley House, the residence of one of the first Southampton settlers; and Conscience Point, the point of embarkation for pilgrims coming from Lynn, Massachusetts, in search of wider religious freedom. These attractions are spread out around Southampton, but information about each can be found at the museum (which maintains the sites).

Bridgehampton & Sag Harbor

To the east of Southampton, Bridgehampton has the shortest of all the main drags, but it's packed with trendy boutiques and restaurants. Seven miles north of Bridgehampton on Peconic Bay is the old whaling town of Sag Harbor. There are bunches of historic homes and points of interest here and you can pick up a walking-tour map of historic sites at the Windmill Information Center (p310) on Long Wharf at the end of Main St.

The **Sag Harbor Whaling Museum** (☎725-0770; www.sagharborwhalingmuseum.org; 200 Main St at Garden St; adult/child $5/4; ☺10am-5pm Mon-Sat, 1-5pm Sun May 17-Oct 1) is fascinating, and the village's tiny Cape Cod–style streets are a joy to stroll; there are several excellent restaurants to discover. **Bike Hampton** (☎725-7329; 36 Main St; hire per day $35-45) rents bicycles and sells maps of cycling trails.

A quick ferry ride on the South Ferry from the edge of North Haven, which borders Sag Harbor, will take you to sleepy Shelter Island, nearly a third of which is dedicated to the **Mashomack Nature Preserve** (☎749-1001), dotted with hiking trails. Take precautions while hiking – ticks are an ever-present problem. Outside the Mashomack Preserve, Shelter Island abounds in historic B&Bs and romantic restaurants, making it easy to spend a few days here soaking up the nature and history. Check out www.shelter-island.org, a listings website run by the nonprofit Shelter Island Club, for the latest information on what's available.

East Hampton

Long Island's trendiest town is East Hampton, where you can catch readings and art exhibitions at **Guild Hall** (☎324-0806; www.guildhall.org; 158 Main St). Check out the town's colonial past with a visit to the **East Hampton Historical Society** (☎324-6850; www.easthamptonhistory.org; 101 Main St; adult/child $4/2; ☺noon-5pm Sat summer only). The Society tends to five historical attractions around East Hampton, including several old colonial farms, mansions and a marine museum.

Montauk

More honky-tonk than the rest of the Hamptons, Montauk has relatively reasonable restaurants and a louder bar scene, largely because all the service personnel (mainly students and new Mexican immigrants) live here in communal housing.

To get pampered, book a room at the beachfront, spa-equipped **Gurney's Inn Resort** (☎668-2345; www.gurneysinn.com; 290 Old Montauk Hwy, Montauk; r $250-600). For some real beachy eatin', head to the Lobster Roll (look for the big blue 'Lunch' sign) for – what else? – a rich lobster-meat salad stuffed into a fresh hot-dog roll.

Covering the eastern tip of the South Fork is **Montauk Point State Park** (☎668-

3781), with its impressive Montauk Lighthouse. You can camp in the sand nearby at windswept **Hither Hills State Park** (☑668-2554, 456-2267; http://nysparks.state.ny.us/parks), a fantastic nature spot that offers a bit of everything: year-round fishing for anglers and special permits to fish at night; beach camping; the unique 'walking dunes' in Napeague Harbor (at the east end of the park); and lots of open woodlands to tramp though (and you can bring your dog, too). You can also try pitching a tent at **Cedar Point Park** (☑244-7275) in the Springs section of East Hampton on the calm Northwest Harbor. Just be sure to call ahead, as sites tend to fill up fast.

Montauk retains a strong fishing tradition and there are many opportunities to cast a line here. You can contract charter boats at the dock for a day of fishing or jump on one of the party cruises (about $50 to $85 per person for a half day). Captain Fred E Bird's **Flying Cloud** (☑668 2026; www.montaukflyingcloud.com; 67 Mulford Ave) comes highly recommended for fluke fishing May to September and sea bass, porgies and striper fishing September to November.

EATING

BLUE SKY MEDITERRANEAN LOUNGE   MEDITERRANEAN **$$**
(☑725-1810; www.blueskysagharbor.com; 63 Main St; mains $10-28) Unwind over a glass of wine and a bowl of pasta at Blue Sky Mediterranean Lounge on Main St.

DELLA FEMINA   MODERN AMERICAN **$$**
(☑329-6666; www.dellafemina.com; 99 N Main St, East Hampton; mains $18-35; ⊘6-11pm Fri & Sat, 6-10pm Sun-Thu) An East Hampton standby is Della Femina, owned by flamboyant Jerry Della Femina, who throws a massive beach party every July 4.

LOBSTER ROLL   SEAFOOD **$**
(☑631-267-3740; Rte 27; mains $10-12; ⊘11:30am-10pm summer) On Rte 27, between the towns of Amagansett and Montauk, a few roadside fish shacks like this institution pop up. With its distinctive 'Lunch' sign, the Lobster Roll serves the namesake sandwich as well as fresh steamers and fried clams.

AMAGANSETT FARMERS MARKET   MARKET **$**
(☑631-267-6600; Main St, Amagansett; ⊘9am-5pm May-Oct) Fresh flowers for the porch table, corn for the beach clambake and something surprising for the afternoon luncheon – the sophisticated farm stand caters to all the locals' needs.

NICK & TONI'S   ITALIAN **$$**
(☑324-3550; 136 N Main St; mains $18-30) Flawless Italian restaurant styled to look like an old Tuscan farmhouse.

SCOOP DU JOUR   ICE CREAM **$**
(☑329-4883; 35 Newton Ln; ice cream $4-8) Popular ice-cream parlor.

TURTLE CROSSING   BARBECUE **$$**
(☑324-7166; 221 Pantigo Rd; mains $10-25; ⊘summer only) A barbecue-inspired joint great for kids.

🍸 DRINKING & NIGHTLIFE

Nightlife is a seasonal and somewhat transient affair in sandy Southampton. The local youngsters gravitate to the beach bars in East Quogue, an enclave about 15 minutes' drive from Southampton.

As well as the clubs listed here, many others open in May and shut in September, moving from year to year depending on where they can find leasable space. The hippest nightclubs generally open Thursday to Sunday between late May/early June and Labor Day (first weekend of September).

GOLDEN PEAR   CAFE
(☑283-8900; www.goldenpear.com; 99 Main St; snacks & meals $5-18; ⊘7:30am-5pm) If clubbing is not your thing but socializing is, pull up to Golden Pear to have a cappuccino and rub shoulders with the jet set and the locals.

PINK   CLUB
(☑287-9888; www.pinkelephantclub.com; 281 County Rd/Rte 27, near N Main St) Trendy Pink – formerly the Pink Elephant – is a local mainstay and an offshoot of the Manhattan club of the same name.

DUNE   CLUB
(☑283-0808; www.dunesouthampton.com; 1181 North Sea Rd; ⊘10pm-4am Sun-Thu summer only) Another local mainstay in Southampton.

SLEEPING IN THE HAMPTONS

High season in the Hamptons is late May to mid-September.

1708 House (☎287-1708; www.1708house.com; 126 Main St, Southampton; r $195-495) History buffs might gravitate toward this local standout. It's in central Southampton and prides itself on its turn-of-the-century charm.

American Hotel (☎725-3535; www.theamericanhotel.com; Main St, Sag Harbor; r low season $200-300, high season $300-400) An old-world hotel (but excellent and modern), it has a popular downstairs restaurant and bar that has continued to be a center of the social scene for many years. An ideal choice for any lover of European elegance and efficiency, you'll find fine accommodations all set in a superb location.

Memory Motel (☎668-2702; 692 Montauk Hwy, Montauk; r $95-120) For a kitschy 'bargain,' try staying at the Memory Hotel, a scruffy but comfortable spot where Mick Jagger often stayed in the 1970s and where he was inspired to write the Rolling Stones song of the same name. Better yet, unless you are a hardcore Stones fan, you may just want a drink at the bar – the dusty accommodations aren't for the fainthearted.

RED BAR BRASSERIE   BISTRO
(☎283-0704; 210 Hampton Rd; mains $15-28) A great place for romance and candlelight, the Red Bar Brasserie is another place where you can rub shoulders with the jet set and the locals.

75 MAIN   LIVE MUSIC
(☎283 7575; 75 Main St; mains $12-30) Head here for daily happy hours and a live band at night.

In Bridgehampton new nightclubs blow in and bow out every season. Two good stalwart places to get a drink are **World Pie** (☎537-7999; 2402 Montauk Hwy; mains $12-18) – a great pizza joint/bar with outside seating – and **Almond** (☎537-8885; www.almondrestaurant.com; 1970 Montauk Hwy; mains $12-39), a trendy boîte (it's not a bad idea to call ahead for a table).

Fire Island

Explore

Infamous Fire Island – a staple summer getaway of New York's gay community – is a skinny barrier island of sand that runs parallel to Long Island. Along its scant 50 miles, you'll find tiny towns, wild dunes, pine forests, hiking trails and plenty of postcard-worthy beach moments along the soft white sands.

The island is federally protected as the **Fire Island National Seashore** (☎631-289-4810; www.nps.gov/fiis) and much of the land strip is a no-go zone for cars, which fosters a serene environment while adding to the area's rugged charm. In summer, expect hamlets jam-packed with roaring nightclubs next to neighboring stretches of sand where you'll find nothing but pitched tents and deer – quite an odd juxtaposition.

The Best...

➡ **Sight** Sunken Forest (p316)
➡ **Place to Eat** CJ's (p316)
➡ **Place to Drink** Houser Bar (p316)

Top Tip

If you're visiting during a summer weekend, make sure to skip out early on Sunday (before 3pm) or spend the night and leave Monday – the line for the ferry on Sunday evenings is impossible.

Getting There & Away

Car Take the Midtown Tunnel out of Manhattan onto I-495/Long Island Expressway. For Sayville ferries (to The Pines, Cherry Grove and Sunken Forest), get off at exit 57 on to the Vets Memorial Hwy. Make a right on Lakeland Ave and take it to the end, following signs for the ferry. For Davis Park Ferry from Patchogue (to Watch Hill), take the Long Island

Expressway to exit 63 southbound (North Ocean Ave). For Bay Shore ferries (all other Fire Island destinations), take the Long Island Expressway to exit 30E, then get onto the Sagtikos Parkway to exit 42 south, to Fifth Ave terminal in Bay Shore. To get to Robert Moses State Park by car, take exit 53 off the Long Island Expressway and travel south across the Moses Causeway.

Train The Long Island Rail Road (LIRR; p388) makes stops in both Sayville and Bay Shore.

Ferry The LIRR has a connecting summer-only shuttle service to the Fire Island Ferry Service (☑665-3600; Bay Shore), Sayville Ferry Service (☑589-0810) and Davis Park Ferry (☑475-1665). Visit www.fireisland ferries.com for more information.

Need to Know

➔ **Area Code** 631

➔ **Location** 60 miles east; two hours (including ferry ride)

➔ **Information** Fire Island Information (www.fireisland.com), South Bay Water Taxi (☑665 8885; www.fireislandwatertaxi.com; 133 Ocean Ave; fares $10-20)

◉ SIGHTS

Robert Moses State Park (☑669-0449; www.nysparks.state.ny.us), the only part of the island that's accessible by car, lies at the westernmost end and features wide, soft-sand beaches with mellower crowds than those at Jones Beach. It's also home to the **Fire Island Lighthouse** (☑681-4876), which houses a history museum. Walk way east along the shore here and you'll stumble upon a lively nude beach.

The gemlike parts of Fire Island, though, are found further east, in the tranquil, car-free villages. Davis Park, Fair Harbor, Kismet, Ocean Bay Park and Ocean Beach combine small summer homes with tiny

---

DETOUR: JONES BEACH

The offerings of **Jones Beach State Park** (☑516-785-1600; http://nysparks.state.ny.us; 1 Ocean Parkway) are simple: 6½ miles of clean sand covered with bodies. The character of the beach differs depending on which 'field' you choose – 2 is for the surfers and 6 is for families, and there's a gay beach followed by a nude beach way east – but it's a definite scene no matter where you choose to head. The ocean gets quite warm by midsummer and there are plenty of lifeguards. In between sunning and riding waves you might also hop into one of the two massive on-site pools for a swim; play shuffleboard or basketball on beachside courts; stroll the two-mile boardwalk; visit the still waters of the bay beach; or, at **Castles in the Sand** (☑516-785-1600; admission $1; ☉10am-4pm Sat & Sun Memorial Day-Labor Day), learn how builder Robert Moses transformed Long Island with the creation of Jones Beach in the 1940s.

Biking and running are allowed along a four-mile path that stretches through the park, and there are places to rent bikes along the beach. When the sun goes down, you can grill at one of the many barbecues in the sand, grab burgers at the few local restaurants near the beach, or head to the **Jones Beach Theater** (☑516-221-1000; www.jonesbeach.com), where al fresco concerts under the stars feature famous pop stars from the '80s and '90s, as well as classics like Eric Clapton and James Taylor.

Jones Beach is about 33 miles east of NYC, and it takes roughly 45 minutes to arrive using public transportation. The **Long Island Rail Road** (LIRR; ☑718-217-5477; www.mta.nyc.ny.us/lirr; round-trip $16.50) offers round trips from Manhattan's Penn Station and Brooklyn's Flatbush Ave Station (transfer required at Jamaica) to Freeport Station on Long Island; a free shuttle bus runs from the station to the beach between Memorial Day Weekend and Labor Day. If you have your own vehicle take the Midtown Tunnel from Manhattan onto I-495/Long Island Expressway (LIE); turn off exit 38 to the eastbound Northern State Parkway, then look for exit 33 for the Wantagh Parkway. That goes straight to Jones Beach State Park. (You can also take the LIE to exit 31S for the Cross-Island Parkway and then exit 25A onto the Southern State Parkway to get to the Wantagh Parkway.)

SLEEPING ON FIRE ISLAND

Grove Hotel (☑597-6600; www.grovehotel.com; Cherry Grove; r $75-500) With beachy, basic rooms, the Grove Hotel offers the main source of entertainment at its nightclub.

Madison Fire Island (☑597-6061; www.themadisonfi.com; The Pines; r $200-775) Fire Island's first 'boutique' hotel, which rivals anything Manhattan has to offer in terms of amenities, has killer views from a rooftop deck and a gorgeous pool (and pool boys).

Otis Pike Fire Island Wilderness (☑289-9336; campsite $25) Reservations are a must, as sites fill up a year in advance.

towns that have grocery stores, bars, nightclubs and restaurants – just keep in mind that almost everything in every town shuts down a couple of weeks after Labor Day. You can rely on the South Bay Water Taxi service to shuttle you between villages.

Perhaps the most infamous villages are those that have evolved into gay destinations: **Cherry Grove** (www.cherrygrove.com) and the **Pines** (www.thepinesfireisland.com). While day trips are easy to Fire Island, staying for a night or two on this car-free oasis, where boardwalks serve as pathways between the dunes and homes, is wonderful.

If you want to skip the scene altogether and just get back to nature, enjoy a hike through the **Sunken Forest**, a 300-year-old forest, with its own ferry stop (called Sailor's Haven). It's not easily accessible in the winter season after the ferry shuts down. At the eastern end of the island, the 1300-acre preserve of **Otis Pike Fire Island Wilderness** includes a beach campground at Watch Hill; just beware of the fierce mosquitoes and overly inquisitive deer.

✖ EATING & DRINKING

CJ'S   AMERICAN $$
(☑583-9890; www.cjsfireisland.com; 479 Bay Walk, Atlantique; mains $10-30) Open year-round, CJ's is raucous and fun and a great place to wait for your ferry. It's packed on summer weekend nights, so get here early.

ALBATROSS   BURGERS $$
(The Tross; ☑583-5697; btwn Bayview & Denhoff Sts, Ocean Beach; mains $12-18) Outdoor patio dining, perfect for people-watching; appeals to locals and summer visitors alike.

HOUSER BAR   BAR
(☑583-7805; 781-85 Evergreen Walk; mains $8) Houser's is not just a bar, it's a complex. As well as being a popular watering hole, it's also a hotel and a restaurant. All three are popular, especially the bar on weekends.

☆ ENTERTAINMENT

KISMET INN & MARINA   BAR
(☑583-5592; Oak Walk) Nightly sunset social hour.

THE DOCK   BAR
(☑583-5200; Bay Walk) Stop by for 'The Sixers,' a nightly gathering to watch the sunset.

North Fork

Explore

Once synonymous with beachy hideaways, Long Island is now famous for its great grapes. Over the past three decades what was one lone winery has become a thriving industry that takes up more than 3000 acres of land. Most vineyards are at the East End's **North Fork**, where you can follow the green 'wine trail' signs along Rte 25 once you pass Riverhead. **South Fork** has Duck Walk Vineyards and **Wölffer Estate Vineyards** (☑537-5106; Sagaponack, South Fork), and you can explore them if you choose before continuing on to the North Fork via Shelter Island and two ferries.

The Best...

➡ **Sight** Tasting Room
➡ **Place to Eat** Polish Town (p318)
➡ **Place to Drink** At the wineries (take your pick!)

Top Tip

The North Folk wineries are an easy DIY adventure. Consider taking the train out to Long Island and renting a car out there – prices are cheaper than in Manhattan and you'll save time, gas and frustration.

Getting There & Away

Bus The Hampton Jitney (☑362-8400; www.hamptonjitney.com) picks up passengers at 86th St in Manhattan between Lexington and Third Aves, and also 69th, 59th and 44th Sts. It makes stops in 10 North Fork villages.

Car Take the Midtown Tunnel out of Manhattan, which will take you onto I-495/Long Island Expressway. Take this until it ends, at Riverhead, and follow signs onto Rte 25. Stay on Rte 25 for all points east.

Train The Long Island Rail Road (LIRR; ☑217-5477; http://mta.nyc.ny.us/lirr; one-way off-peak/peak $18.25/25) has a North Fork line, usually called the Ronkonkoma Branch, with trips leaving from Penn Station and Brooklyn. Make sure the stop at the end of your line is Greenport.

Ferry To get from the North Fork to the South Fork (or vice versa), take the North Ferry (☑631-749-0139; www.northferry.com) and South Ferry (p310) services to and from Shelter Island.

Need to Know

➡ **Area Code** 631
➡ **Location** 100 miles east; 2¼-hour drive
➡ **Information** Long Island Wine Council (☑631-369-5887; www.liwines.com; 104 Edwards Ave)

⊙ SIGHTS

Harvest time is in fall, which, combined with colorful foliage and pumpkin-picking opportunities, makes it an ideal time to visit North Fork (although most places remain open year-round). If driving yourself doesn't appeal, consider a wine-tour option. **Vintage Tours** (☑631-765-4689; www.vintagetour1.com) will shepherd you around in a van. **North Fork Trolley Co** (☑631-369-3031; www.northforktrolley.com) has converted trolleys for its tours, and you can even hit the vineyards on a bike with **Adventure Cycles & Sports** (☑516-755-2453; www.go rideabike.com).

Wineries are generally open from 11am to 5pm, with closing time extended by an hour in summer, but not all have tours or tastings every day. If you want to taste the wine without the travel, head straight to the **Tasting Room** (☑631-765-6404; 2885 Peconic Lane). You can sit in the 1860 store, with its original tin ceiling, tin walls and wood floors, and sip on the best from all the local vineyards.

A drive along the back roads of the North Fork affords some beautiful, unspoiled vistas of farms and rural residential areas. If you're too bushed to make the trip out and back in one day (a doable, but tiring, prospect), you'll find plenty of classic inns where you can rest your head for the night.

Several wineries offer full-scale tours of their facilities. The following are just some of the wineries offering tastings:

BEDELL CELLARS   WINE TASTING

(☑631-734-7537; Main Road, Rte 25, Cutchogue) A family-owned and operated estate that prides itself in sustainable harvesting and production practices. With over 30 years of experience, this is one of the most established wineries in the region, and is often considered the benchmark for North Fork grape growing. Don't miss the tasting room – one of the best on the Eastern Seaboard.

DUCK WALK VINEYARDS   WINE TASTING

(☑726-7555; Southampton, South Fork) Proudly boasting an array of award-winning wines, Duck Walk is the brainchild of one of the founders of Long Island's small wine industry. The first location, housed in a chateau-style building, is in Water Mill, the second location is on the North Fork encircled by acres upon acres of white grapes. Live weekly jam sessions are a popular occurrence.

SLEEPING AT THE NORTH FORK WINERIES

Jedediah Hawkins Inn (☑722-2900; www.jedediahhawkinsinn.com; 400 S Jamesport Rd; r $300-900) Handsomely outfitted with period pieces.

Quintessentials B&B Spa (☑259-0939, 477-9400; www.quintessentialsinc.com; 8585 Main Rd; r $175-275) A Victorian place in East Marion that's outfitted with a full-service spa, plush quarters and peaceful, flowering grounds.

Red Barn B&B (☑722-3695; www.redbarnbandb.com; 733 Herricks Lane; r $195-295) A cozy, antique-filled inn in Jamesport.

PINDAR VINEYARDS   WINE TASTING
(☑734-6200; Peconic) An iconic spot for vino guzzling, Pindar retains the original flavor of North Fork wine, for it was here that the island's boutique industry began back in 1979. What was once a mere 30 acres of farmland has blossomed into vineyards and orchards as far as the eye can see (500 acres and counting) – guided tours and weekend live music (in summer) are the norm.

✖ EATING

If you do wind up driving out, a stop in **Riverhead** is worthwhile for its **Polish town**, a tiny, insular community of Polish immigrants with various ethnic bakeries and eateries, such as the **Euro Deli** (☑727-1635; 517 Pulaski St; $5-20), that are loaded with fresh kielbasa and European cheeses. In nearby Greenport, the **Scrimshaw Restaurant** (☑477-8882; Preston's Wharf; mains $12-30) draws in crowds with its Asian-American fusion fare and nautical setting, or you can drink and eat in classic pub fashion at **Digger's** (☑369-3200; 58 W Main St; mains $10-20).

Hudson Valley

Explore

Winding roads along the Hudson River take you by picturesque farms, Victorian cottages, orchards and mansions built by New York's elite. Painters of the Hudson River School romanticized these landscapes – you can see their work at art museums in the area. Autumn is a beautiful time for a trip up this way, either by car or train (though having a car makes site-hopping much easier); cyclists also love the beauty and challenge of riding through the area. The Lower Hudson is largely the domain of must-see museums that have the liberty of occupying vast tracts of space, while the Upper Hudson sheds an interesting light on the life of one of America's best-known presidential families, the Roosevelts.

The Best...

➡ **Sights** Dia Beacon (p320) and Storm King Art Center (p320)

➡ **Place to Eat** Culinary Institute of America (p320)

➡ **Place to Sleep** Storm King Lodge (p319)

Top Tip

Foodies who want a bit of choice should gravitate towards Poughkeepsie, which has a thriving academic population and a reasonably diverse eating scene.

Getting There & Away

Car From Manhattan, take the Henry Hudson Parkway across the George Washington Bridge (I-95) to Palisades Parkway. Head for the New York State Thruway to Rte 9W or Rte 9, the principal scenic river routes. You can also take the Taconic State Parkway north from Ossining, a pretty road in autumn.

Bus Short Line Buses (☑212-736-4700; www.shortlinebus.com) runs regular trips to Hyde Park (round-trip $46) and Rhinebeck ($50).

Train While Amtrak (☑212-582-6875, 800-872-7245; www.amtrak.com) connects with several communities on the Hudson River's eastern shore, your best and cheapest bet from New York City is the commuter train line Metro-North (☑800-638-7646, 212-532-4900; http://mta.info; one-way off-peak $9-16), which departs from Grand Central Terminal (take the Hudson Line). On weekends, Metro-North runs special summer and autumn tourist packages that include train fare and transportation to and from specific sites such as Hyde Park and the Vanderbilt Mansion.

Need to Know

➡ **Area Code** 845

➡ **Location** 95 miles north (Hyde Park); 1¾-hour drive

➡ **Information** Dutchess County Tourism (☑800-445-3131; www.dutchessny.gov; 3 Neptune Rd), Hudson Valley Network (www.hvnet.com) and Hudson Valley Tourism (☑800-232-4782; www.hudsonvalley.org)

 SIGHTS

Upper Hudson

The largest town on the Hudson's east bank, **Poughkeepsie** (puh-*kip*-see) is famous for **Vassar**, a private liberal-arts college that admitted only women until 1969. Its modern **Francis Lehman Loeb Art Center** (☑845-437-5632; Poughkeepsie; admission free; ☾10am-5pm Tue-Sat, 1-5pm Sun) features paintings of the Hudson River School and

contemporary work. The office of Dutchess County Tourism has regional information.

Hyde Park has long been associated with the Roosevelts, a prominent family since the 19th century. The **Franklin D Roosevelt Library & Museum** (☑845-229-8114; www.fdrlibrary.marist.edu; 511 Albany Post Rd/Rte 9, Hyde Park; admission museum $7, museum & house $14; ☾9am-5pm) features exhibits on the president who created the New Deal and led the USA into WWII. Eleanor Roosevelt's cottage, **Val-Kill** (☑845-229-9115; www.nps.gov/elro; Albany Post Rd, Hyde Park; admission $8; ☾9am-5pm daily May-Oct, Thu-Mon Nov-Apr), was her retreat from Hyde Park, her mother-in-law and FDR himself. The **Vanderbilt Mansion** (☑800-967-2283; www.nps.gov/vama; Rte 9, Hyde Park; admission $8; ☾9am-5pm), a national historic site two miles north on Rte 9, is a spectacle of lavish beaux arts and eclectic architecture. A combination ticket ($21) is available for the three sites; reservations are recommended.

There are plenty of other grand mansions to explore nearby, such as **Kykuit** (☑914-631-9491; Pocantico Hills, Tarrytown; adult/child $22/18; ☾tours 9:45am, 1:45pm & 3pm), a Rockefeller home with antique carriages and gardens in **Tarrytown**, along with the Gothic Revival mansion **Lyndhurst Castle** (☑914-631-4481; www.lyndhurst.org; Rte 9, Tarrytown; castle/grounds $12/6; ☾grounds open daily dusk-dawn). **Olana** (☑518-828-0135; www.olana.org; Rte 9G, Hudson; house & gallery tour adult/child $9/8; ☾grounds 8am-sunset daily, tours 10am-5pm Tue-Sun), built with Moorish touches by Hudson River School artist Frederic Church, is in Hudson. **Springwood** (☑800-967-2283; Albany Post Rd, Hyde Park; admission $14; ☾9am-5pm), in Hyde Park, was FDR's boyhood country home.

SLEEPING ON THE HUDSON

Cheap motel chains in Poughkeepsie are clustered along Rte 9, south of the Mid-Hudson Bridge.

Copper Penny Inn (☑845-452-3045; www.copperpennyinn.com; 2406 New Hackensack Rd, Poughkeepsie; r $139-229) This old, 1860s farmhouse has been lovingly converted into a casual B&B with four rooms – all sporting unique design details. Sun pours through the ample windows casting rays of light upon the charming collection of eclectic furniture and antiques.

Storm King Lodge (☑845-534-9421; www.stormkinglodge.com; 100 Pleasant Hill Rd, Mountainville; r $160-195) Once a carriage home for a large farming estate, the charming Storm King Lodge is a stately structure from the 1800s that's filled to the brim with tasteful furnishings like cozy quilts, deep leather parlor chairs, fresh flowers and thick slats of shiny wood running across the creaky floors.

Lower Hudson

The area around Beacon offers a great opportunity to combine a nature trip with an art outing; it's home to two fantastic museums and two unspoiled nature parks.

Storm King Art Center (☎534-3115; www.stormking.org; Old Pleasant Hill Rd; admission $10) in Mountainville, on the west side of the Hudson River, is a giant open-air museum on 500 acres, part sculpture garden and part sculpture landscape. The spot was founded in 1960 as a museum for painters, but it soon began to acquire larger installations and monument works that were placed outside, in natural 'rooms' created by the land's indigenous breaks and curves. There's a small museum on site, formerly a 1935 residence designed like a Norman château, and plenty of picnic sites that visitors are encouraged to use (besides vending machines, there's no food sold here).

Open only from April through November, Storm King changes with the seasons. The entrance has five tall columns, surrounding the figure of a slim girl (flashing a thumbs-up sign), and leads to a sweeping trail of huge maples, guarded by three towering structures by Mark di Suvero. Across the expanse of meadow is the Storm King Wall, artist Andy Goldsworthy's famously sinuous structure that starts with rocks, crescendos up and across some hills, encompasses a tree, then dips down into a pond, slithering out the other side and eventually disappearing into the woods. Other permanent pieces were created by Alexander Calder, Henry Moore, Richard Serra and Alice Aycock, to name a few.

Another attraction on the east side of the Hudson River is the town of **Beacon** – a once scruffy waterfront village that's trying to spruce itself up with one very worthwhile stop: **Dia Beacon** (☎440-0100; www.diaart.org; ☉11am-6pm Thu-Mon mid-April–mid-Oct, to 4pm Fri-Mon mid-Oct–mid-Apr; admission $10), an outpost of NYC's Dia Center for the Arts. The Dia Beacon is in a former factory (there are plenty of abandoned ones on the outskirts of town) and is filled with huge Richard Serra ironwork pieces, as well as ever-changing installations on loan from the Manhattan Dia outpost.

For hikers, **Harriman State Park** (☎845-786-5003; http://nysparks.state.ny.us/parks), on the west side of the Hudson, spans 72 sq miles and provides swimming, hiking, camping and a visitors center. Adjacent **Bear Mountain State Park** (☎845-786-2701; http://nysparks.state.ny.us/parks; ☉8am-dusk) offers great views from its 1305ft peak. The Manhattan skyline looms beyond the river and surrounding greenery. You can enjoy hiking in summer, wildflowers in spring, gold foliage in fall and cross-country skiing in winter.

✖ Eating

CULINARY INSTITUTE OF AMERICA ITALIAN, FRENCH $$$
(☎800-285-4627; www.ciachef.edu; 1946 Campus Drive, Hyde Park) Trains future chefs and can satisfy anyone's gastronomic cravings.

DETOUR: LONG BEACH

Beautiful Long Beach, 30 miles from New York City (and much closer than either Jones Beach or Fire Island), is one of the best stretches of sand you can find. It's easily accessible by train and has clean beaches, a hoppin' main strip with shops and eateries within walking distance of the ocean, a thriving surfing scene and many city hipsters. **Lincoln Beach**, at the end of Lincoln Blvd, is the main spot for surfing; you can rent bikes at **Buddy's** (☎516-431-0804; 907 W Beech St; bike hire per 3hr $20).

There's plenty of good eats in the town around the beach. Stroll around and find whatever takes your fancy, or make a beeline for **Kitchen Off Pine Street** (☎516-431-0033; 670 Long Beach Blvd; mains $6-12; ☉lunch & dinner Tue-Sun). For more info contact the **City of Long Beach** (☎516-431-1000; www.longbeachny.org; 1 W Chester St; ☉9am-4pm Mon-Fri). To get here by train, use the Long Island Rail Road (p388), which goes directly to Long Beach from both Penn Station and Flatbush Ave in Brooklyn.

CUP & SAUCER TEA ROOM CAFE $
(☎831-6287; www.thecupandsaucertearoom.
com; 165 Main St, Beacon; light meals $4-12)

ST ANDREW'S CAFE CAFE $$$
(☎471-6608; Hyde Park; dinner around $30) Casual, but reservations are required.

ways (☎800-858-8555; www.trailwaysny.
com; average round-trip $115).

Need to Know
→ **Area Code** 845
→ **Location** 110 miles north (Saugerties)
→ **Information** Woodstock Guild
(☎679-2079; www.woodstockguild.org;
Woodstock; 9am-5pm Mon-Fri)

Woodstock & Saugerties

Explore
In the southern Catskills, the town of **Woodstock** symbolizes the tumultuous 1960s, when young people questioned authority, experimented with freedom and redefined popular culture. Today it's a combination of quaint and hip – an artists' colony full of young urbanites. The Woodstock Guild is a good source for finding out the latest goings-on in the arts and culture scene, such as the annual Woodstock Film Festival in October, which attracts film fans from all over.

The Best...
→ **Sight** Woodstock
→ **Place to Eat** Miss Lucy's Kitchen (p322)
→ **Place to Sleep** Kate's Lazy Meadow Motel (p322)

Top Tip
Bring an empty bag with you – the antiquaries are tempting, and we can almost guarantee that you'll end up bringing home a li'l something from a bygone era.

Getting There & Away
Car Take the New York State Thruway (via the Henry Hudson Hwy north from Manhattan) or I-87 to Rte 375 for Woodstock, Rte 32 for Saugerties or Rte 28 for other points.

Bus Frequent buses to Kingston, the Catskills' gateway town, as well as to Saugerties, Flagstop and Woodstock are operated by Adirondack Pine Hill Trail-

◉ SIGHTS

Woodstock is most famous for the 1969 music festival of the same name. There's just one problem – it didn't happen here. The concert was in **Bethel**, a small town about 40 miles southeast. But no matter; Woodstock has embraced its hippie ethos tightly, as you'll see from the offbeat and quirky Tinker St shops and organic cateries, all decorated in vibrant hues. In summer, the locals assemble at the town square (which is, of course, a peace sign) for a drum circle from 4pm to 6pm on Sundays. They chant and dance with long-ago abandon. Just a few miles northeast you'll find **Saugerties**, with its own attractive downtown area and a smaller offering of galleries, cafes and eateries. Hands down, the best place to stay is the Saugerties Light House (p322) – once a working structure, now restored and gorgeous to behold across Esopus Creek (you have to be boated out).

In between these two towns lies a hidden art installation that takes a bit of work to find but is well worth the effort. **Opus 40** (☎246-3400; www.opus40.org; 50 Fite Rd; adult/child $10/$3; ⊙11am-6pm Thu-Sun) is the sculpture put together by artist Harvey Fite, who bought an old slate quarry in the 1930s and made it his permanent studio. Over decades, he coaxed deep canyons and shapes out of the abandoned quarry, moving and shifting tons and tons of flinty blue stones and creating a living, flowing outdoor art installation. It sometimes opens on a Monday from late May to early October.

South of Saugerties, Rte 28 crosses the Catskills west of Woodstock, then winds past the Ashokan Reservoir and through the 'French Catskills.' Along this way are excellent restaurants, camping, inexpensive lodging, antique shops and character galore.

Nearby **Fleischmanns** is a door to a bygone era (the town is named after the yeast manufacturer who used to have a factory here). The woodsy hamlet is a favorite summer retreat for Orthodox Russian Jews, who in their heavy, traditional garb shop for antiques alongside locals.

Bethel, which was all but forgotten after its cataclysmic three-day concert in 1969, is now home to the fantastic **Bethel Woods Performing Arts Center** (866-781-2922; www.bethelwoodscenter.org; 200 Hurd Rd). The center, which hosts frequent outdoor concerts in summer, also has the **Bethel Woods Museum** (adult/child $13/9; 10am-5pm Thu-Sun Apr-May, to 7pm daily Jun-Aug, to 5pm Thu-Sun Sep-Dec, closed Jan-Mar), dedicated to the hippie movement and the 1960s. Woodstock's rabble-rousing spirit lives on in the museum's evocative pictures and multimedia exhibits.

Three-hundred miles of fantastic hiking can be found in the **Catskill Forest Preserve**, a huge swath of land that contains the vital watershed feeding New York City's ravenous thirst. It's also great for camping. **The NY/NJ Trail Conference** (212-685-9699; www.nynjtc.org) has maps and information. For winter skiing head north along Rtes 23 and 23A to **Windham Mountain** (518-734-4300; www.skiwindham.com), a family-friendly resort that embraces ecofriendly practices to the fullest extent, using energy from its snow-making machines to heat mountain lodges and condos, and buying wind offsets to reduce its carbon footprint. In summer, it runs all sorts of fun, family outdoor activities (golf, spa treatments and mountain-biking anyone?). Nearby **Belleayre Resort** (254-5601, 800-942-6904; www.belleayre.com) is a state-run

facility that has great winter skiing and is open for hiking in summer.

For a lazy outdoor day, head to **Phoenicia** to go inner-tubing down the Esopus Creek, which flows near Rte 28. **Town Tinker** (688-5553; www.towntinker.com; Bridge St, Phoenicia; per tube $10) will provide life jackets, tubes and transport back to your car.

✕ EATING

CAFE TAMAYO   AMERICAN **$$**
(845-246-9371; www.cafetamayo.com; 89 Partition St, Saugerties; mains $16-34; dinner Fri & Sat, Sun from May-Oct) Housed in an old 1864 tavern with wedding cake ceilings and tranquil outdoor seating, Cafe Tamayo serves prix-fixe menus of Hudson Valley–sourced American food with ethnic influences, including an asparagus risotto, braised rabbit and a to-die-for chocolate pot de creme. After dinner, retreat upstairs to one of the four simple, vintage rooms (r $110-190).

FEZ   MOROCCAN **$$**
(845-247-7198; 71 Partition St; mains $14-18; Wed-Sun) For an atmospheric trip to Morocco, duck into Fez to dine on pistachio chicken breast, savory tagines, couscous and kebabs among deep orange walls and a lively vibe.

MISS LUCY'S KITCHEN   CAFE **$$**
(845-246-9240; www.misslucyskitchen.com; 90 Partition St, Saugerties; mains $17-24; lunch & dinner Wed-Sun) A delightful cafe whose warm-mustard and exposed-brick walls are lined with old books and aprons, Miss Lucy's Kitchen exudes a homey, feel-good cheerfulness that belies the fact that it doesn't mess around with its comfort food, like a cassoulet, grilled lamb chops or a vegetarian strudel.

SLEEPING IN WOODSTOCK & SAUGERTIES

Kate's Lazy Meadow Motel (688-7200; www.lazymeadow.com; 5191 Rte 28, Mt Temper; r $150-275) A hip, kitschy inn owned by Kate Pierson of the B-52s.

Saugerties Lighthouse (247-0656; www.saugertieslighthouse.com; r $165-180) Unique sleep at the lighthouse. Book in advance.

Atlantic City

Explore

All aboard the late-night express! Atlantic City may be rowdy and slightly tacky, but it has undeniable 'bad boy' allure that many New Yorkers just can't resist. Sure, they may sniff and roll their eyes at the over-the-top cheesiness, but just check out how many buses are running non-stop between New York and Atlantic City – not to mention the new train service, ACES, which travels on weekends.

Looking at the raucous and ritzy Atlantic City of today, it's hard to believe that in the early 1900s it was nothing but a genteel seaside resort. Nowadays you'll rub elbows with a wide gamut of folks when you visit New Jersey's Sin City. The all-you-can-eat buffets appeal to retirees, ex-cons, students and others in need of a good meal. But there are also flashy businesspeople, a politician or two, lots of high rollers flashing their cash, and even celebrities – usually in town because they're performing at one of the many high-end hotels along the strip.

The Best...

➡ **Sight** Trump Taj Mahal (p324)
➡ **Place to Eat** Knife and Fork Inn (p324)
➡ **Casino** Borgata Hotel Casino & Spa (p324)

Top Tip

Last-minute deals are a dime a dozen in AC – check websites and flash sales one or two days before you want to visit and you can usually score slashed hotel rates if you plan on spending the night.

Getting There & Away

Car Leave Manhattan via one of the Hudson River crossings (Holland Tunnel, Lincoln Tunnel or George Washington Bridge). Take the NJ Turnpike to the Garden State Parkway; Atlantic City is exit 38 off the parkway. The Atlantic City Expressway runs directly to Atlantic City from Philadelphia.

Bus Greyhound (☏231-2222; www.greyhound.com), Academy (☏442-7272; www.academybus.com) and New Jersey Transit (☏762-5100; www.njtransit.com) buses run from Port Authority Bus Terminal. Gray Line (☏397-2620; www.grayline.com) operates from 900 Eighth Ave between W 53rd and 54th Sts in Midtown. A casino will often refund the fare (in chips, coins or coupons) if you get a bus

directly to its door. Fares are cheaper Monday to Thursday.

Train New Jersey Transit (☏762-5100; www.njtransit.com) has an express train to Atlantic City on weekends (the ACES train). During the week, a NJ Transit train trip requires two connections and is about twice the cost of a bus trip. Amtrak (☏872-7245; www.amtrak.com) offers weekday trains with a stop in Philly.

Need to Know

➡ **Area Code** 609
➡ **Location** 130 miles south of NYC
➡ **Information** Visitor Information Center (☏449-7130; www.atlanticcitynj.com; Garden State Parkway; ◷9am-4pm) Under the giant tepee in the middle of the Atlantic City Expressway.

⊙ SIGHTS

If you're a gambler, you can't beat the selection of nearly 1000 blackjack tables and more than 30,000 slot machines in town. As in Las Vegas, the hotel-casinos have themes, from the Far East to Ancient Rome, but the scale is much smaller on the New Jersey boardwalk. Inside the casinos you'll find clanging slot machines, flashing lights and gluttonous all-you-can-eat buffets. Donald Trump has a large presence in Atlantic City, of course – there's **Trump's Marina Resort** (☏441-2000; Huron Ave), with an art deco theme; **Trump Plaza Casino Hotel** (☏441-6000; Mississippi Ave at the Boardwalk); and the **Trump Taj Mahal** (☏609-449-1000; www.trumptaj.com; 1000 Boardwalk; ◷24hr), where nine two-ton limestone elephants welcome visitors and 70 bright minarets crown the rooftops.

Even now, with the US experiencing some economic doldrums, business is good in Atlantic City – maybe because more people are willing to take a quick flutter at the tables in the hopes it'll change their luck. Two major changes to occur in recent years include the large-scale overhaul of the classic **Borgata Hotel Casino & Spa** (p324), which now has multiple bars, 16 restaurants, tricked-out suites and a 2400-seat entertainment plaza, where the likes of John Legend play.

SLEEPING IN ATLANTIC CITY

Rates at the following places fluctuate hugely, from around $85 to $800 a night, depending on weekend events, time of year, vacancy etc.

Borgata Hotel Casino & Spa (☑866-692-6742; One Borgata Way; r from $109) A swirling tower looming over the shores of the AC, Borgata is one of the favorite spots around for a getaway from the Big Apple. Despite the name, there's nothing particularly Italian about the hotel-cum-casino; in fact, it feels like quite the homage to American comfort with extra-large beds and overstuffed furniture in rooms stocked with catalog details that feel unobtrusively modern.

Trump Taj Mahal (☑449-1000; 1000 Boardwalk; r from $129) Bearing no resemblance to the actual Taj Mahal, this palatial casino rivals those on Vegas' central strip with gaming tables and slots as far as the eye can see under gaudy chandeliers. Upstairs in the sky-scraping tower, expect rooms and suites with scarlet accent walls and mirrors over the California king-sized beds.

Oh, and let's not forget the massive Borgata Casino, which has hundreds of different card games and slot machines available to divest you of your cash.

Harrah's (one of the friendliest in town for newbie dice throwers) is upgrading, too: a 44-story waterfront tower with a glass-domed tropical oasis has gone up in the last couple of years. The southernmost casino, **Atlantic City Hilton** (☑340-7111; Boston Ave at the Boardwalk), has over 500 hotel rooms. **Caesar's Atlantic City** (☑348-4411; Arkansas Ave at the Boardwalk) contains 1000 rooms and the **Tropicana Casino & Entertainment Resort** (☑340-4000; Iowa Ave at the Boardwalk) is even bigger, plus it has a slew of nightclubs inside.

If you're not so much into blackjack, check out the **Absecon Lighthouse** (☑449-1360; www.abseconlighthouse.org; cnr Rhode Island & Pacific Aves; adult/child $7/4; ☺10am-5pm daily Jul-Aug, 11am-4pm Thu-Mon Sep-Jun), which dates from 1857 and, at 171ft high, ranks as the tallest in New Jersey and the third tallest in the country. It's been restored to its original specifications (including the Frensel lens) and you can climb the 228 steps to the top for phenomenal views.

EATING

Good food can be found away from the casinos. A few blocks inland from the Boardwalk, **Mexico Lindo** (☑345-1880; 2435 Atlantic Ave; mains $7-12; ☺8am-10pm), a low-key joint, is a favorite among expat Mexicans, while **Angelo's Fairmount Tav-**ern (☑344-2439; www.angelosfairmounttavern.com; Mississippi Ave at Fairmount Ave; mains $13-20; ☺11:30am-3pm & 5-11pm Mon-Fri, 4:30-11pm Sat-Sun) is a beloved, family-owned Italian restaurant. The outdoor patio makes a nice spot to take in the sunset and have a pint and a burger.

If you've got a car, try **Hannah G's** (☑823-1466; www.hannahgs.com; 7310 Ventnor Ave; mains $5-13; ☺7am-2pm Mon-Sun), an excellent breakfast and lunch spot in nearby Ventnor. **Ventura's Greenhouse Restaurant** (☑822-0140; www.venturasgreenhouse.com; 106 Benson Ave; mains $12-25; ☺11am-midnight Sun-Thu, 11am-1am Fri-Sat), in next-door Margate City, is an Italian restaurant loved by locals. To go upscale, try the **Knife and Fork Inn** (☑344-1133; www.knifeandforkinn.com; 29 South Albany Ave; mains $11-35), once a private gentlemen's club in 1912, now open to all.

☆ ENTERTAINMENT

Each of the casinos offers a full schedule of entertainment, but there is some life outside the gambling dens. Built in 1870, Atlantic City's **Boardwalk** was the first in the world. Enjoy a walk or a hand-pushed **rolling chair ride** (you'll be charged by the block, and tips are expected) and drop in on the informative **Atlantic City Historical Museum** (☑347-5839; www.acmuseum.org; Garden Pier; ☺10am-4pm), run by a quirky old-timer.

The **Steel Pier** amusement area, directly in front of the Trump Taj Mahal, belongs to Donald Trump's empire. It used to be the place where the famous diving horse plunged into the Atlantic before crowds of spectators, but today it's a collection of small amusement rides, games of chance, candy stands and 'the biggest Go-Kart track in South Jersey!'

The Visitor Information Center can provide you with maps and accommodation deals, as can the various other information booths on or near the Boardwalk.

Sleeping

Like the student with their hand up at the front of the class, NYC just seems to know how to do everything well, and its lodging scene is no exception. Brilliant minds have descended upon the 'city that never sleeps' to create some of the most inventive and memorable spaces for those who might just want to grab a bit of shut-eye during their stay.

Booking Accommodations

In New York City, the average room rate is well over $300. But don't let that scare you, there are great deals to be had – almost all of which can be found through savvy online snooping.

When hunting for the best deals it's best to launch a two-pronged approach: if you don't have your heart set on a particular property, then check out discount juggernauts like Expedia (www.expedia.com), Orbitz (www.orbitz.com) and Priceline (www.priceline.com). For those who do have an inkling as to where they'd like to stay – it might sound simple – but it's best to start at your desired hotel's website. These days it's not uncommon to find deals and package rates directly on the site of your accommodation of choice.

Also worth checking out are the slew of members-only websites, like Jetsetter (www.jetsetter.com) that offer discounted rates and 'flash sales' (limited time only sales akin to Groupon) for their devotees. Flash sales are a great way to scoop up discounted beds when planning a holiday at the last minute.

Room Rates

Unlike other popular destinations throughout the world, New York City doesn't have a 'high season' in the common way that beach destinations do. Sure, there are busier times of the year when it comes to tourist traffic, but at over 51 million visitor per annum, the Big Apple never needs to worry when it comes to filling up beds. As such, room rates fluctuate based on availability; in fact, most hotels have a booking algorithm in place that spits out a price quote relative to the number of rooms already booked on the same night, so the busier the evening the higher the price goes.

If you're looking to find the best room rates, then flexibility is key – weekdays are often cheaper, and you'll generally find that accommodations in winter months have smaller price tags. If you are visiting over a weekend, try for a business hotel in the Financial District, which tends to empty out when the workweek ends.

Beyond Hotels & Hostels

We can all thank little Plaza-dweller Eloise for conjuring up fanciful dreams of hanging one's hat in a luxury New York City hotel room, but these days, finding a place to sleep in the city that never does is hardly restricted to the traditional spectrum of lodging.

Websites like Airbnb (www.airbnb.com) are providing a truly unique – and not to mention economical – alternative to the wallet-busting glitz and glam. Selling 'unique spaces' to tourists looking for their home away from home, sites like Airbnb offer locals the opportunity to rent out their apartments while they're out of town, or lease a space (be it a bedroom or pull-out couch) in their home. Airbnb is an undeniable hit in NYC, where space comes at a premium and obscenely high real estate prices act as quite the incentive for locals to supplement their housing income.

Lonely Planet's Top Choices

Ace Hotel New York City (p337) A hipster funhouse for all wallet sizes comes with too-cool-for-school digs, DJs spinning beats in the lobby next to hand-crafted coffee.

Hôtel Americano (p333) This designer's dream is the boutique sleep of the future stocked with an international assortment of upscale treats.

Greenwich Hotel (p329) Personal touches (from Moroccan tiles to Japanese lanterns) reign supreme at Robert De Niro's pet project.

Surrey (p342) Synonymous with the term 'luxury,' the Surrey spares no expense – think Egyptian cotton, Pratesi robes and room service by one of the top restaurants in town.

Andaz Fifth Avenue (p337) A boutique homage to NYC's jetsetterdom is impossibly chic yet wonderfully unpretentious.

Gramercy Park Hotel (p336) A grande dame with a sassy facelift offers keys to the coveted park below.

Best by Budget

$

Harlem Flophouse (p345)
Pod Hotel (p341)
East Village Bed & Coffee (p332)
Sugar Hill Harlem (p345)

$$

Nu Hotel (p346)
Country Inn the City (p343)
Bubba & Bean Lodges (p342)
B&B On the Park (p346)
Cosmopolitan Hotel (p330)
Gild Hall Wall Street (p329)

$$$

Greenwich Hotel (p329)
Setai Fifth Avenue (p338)
Chatwal New York (p338)
Pierre (p337)

Best for Views

Standard (p333)
Carlyle (p343)
Aloft New York Brooklyn (p346)
Setai Fifth Avenue (p338)
Z Hotel (p347)

Best for Families

Hotel Beacon (p343)
70 Park (p339)
Hotel Gansevoort (p333)
Belvedere Hotel (p341)
Bubba & Bean Lodges (p342)
Nu Hotel (p346)

Best Boutique Digs

Library Hotel (p338)
Bowery Hotel (p332)

Best for Honeymooners

Crosby Street Hotel (p330)
Carlyle (p343)
Country Inn the City (p343)
Plaza (p338)

Best for Jetsetters

Standard (p333)
Dream Downtown (p333)
SoHo House (p334)
Hotel Gansevoort (p333)

NEED TO KNOW

Prices
Prices in the guide represent the standard range in rates at each establishment regardless of the time of year.

$	less than $150
$$	$150 to $350
$$$	more than $350

Check-In & Check-Out
Expect check-in to always be mid-afternoon and check-out to be in the late morning. Early check-ins are rare, though high-end establishments can usually accommodate requests with notice.

Reservations
Reservations are essential. Walk-ins are practically impossible and rack rates are almost always unfavorable relative to online deals.

Websites
➡ **Lonely Planet** (hotels.lonelyplanet.com) Accommodation reviews and bookings.
➡ **Playbill** (www.playbill.com) Select rates on Manhattan hotels.
➡ **Kayak** (www.kayak.com) Simple all-purpose search engine.

Tipping
Tip your maid $3 to $5 per night. Porters should receive a dollar or two, and other service staff should also be tipped accordingly.

Breakfast
Breakfast is not included in the price of the room unless specified in the review.

SLEEPING

Where to Stay

Neighborhood	For	Against
Lower Manhattan & the Financial District	Convenient to Tribeca's night scene and ferries. Cheap weekend rates at business hotels.	Although elegant, the area can feel impersonal, corporate and even a bit desolate after business hours.
SoHo & Chinatown	Shop to your heart's content right on your doorstep.	Crowds (mostly tourists) swarm the commercial streets of SoHo almost all day.
East Village & Lower East Side	Funky and fun, the area feels the most quintessentially 'New York' to visitors.	Not tons to choose from when it comes to hotel sleeps.
Greenwich Village, Chelsea & the Meatpacking District	Brilliantly close-to-everything feel in a thriving, picturesque part of town.	Space is at a premium, so penny-pinchers need not apply. Rooms can sometimes be on the small side, even for NYC.
Union Square, Flatiron District & Gramercy	Convenient subway access to anywhere in the city. You're also steps away from the Village and Midtown in either direction.	Prices are high and there's not much in the way of neighborhood flavor.
Midtown	In the heart of the postcard's version of NYC: skyscrapers, museums, shopping and Broadway shows.	One of the most expensive areas in the city. Can often feel touristy and impersonal.
Upper East Side	You're close to top-notch museums and Central Park.	Wallet-busting prices are common; and you're not particularly central.
Upper West Side & Central Park	Convenient access to Central Park and the Museum of Natural History.	Tends to swing a bit too far in the familial direction if you're looking for a livelier scene.
Harlem & Upper Manhattan	Your dollar stretches a lot further up here and there's some great eating.	You'll be commuting down to the action.
Brooklyn	Palpable neighborhood vibe, safely removed from the droves of tourists.	Less convenient to attractions, and transportation can be a challenge.
Queens	Much cheaper than Manhattan. Digs in Long Island City are only a subway stop away from Midtown.	Prevailing industrial setting makes the area far less charming than Manhattan and Brooklyn.

Lower Manhattan & the Financial District

It used to be all business all the time in the financial district around Wall Street, but these days you'll find condos, hotels, restaurants, bars and even a few nightclubs in the cozy enclave at the southern tip of Manhattan. On weekdays it fills with workers, and in summer it's particularly lively as crowds en route to the Statue of Liberty and Battery Park wander the crooked lanes dating from the days of New Amsterdam.

Nearby Tribeca's a hot spot for hip hotel eateries inside the likes of Smyth Tribeca, the latest boutique offering from the brains behind Gild Hall. As of research time, developers were putting the finishing touches on a super-luxe Andaz hotel at 75 Wall St that's sure to set a new standard for business-class opulence.

[TOP CHOICE] GREENWICH HOTEL BOUTIQUE HOTEL $$$

Map p416 (☎212-941-8900; www.greenwichhotelny.com; 377 Greenwich St btwn N Moore & Franklin Sts; r from $495; 📶🏊; [S]1 to Franklin St; A/C/E to Canal St) From the plush drawing room (complete with crackling fire), to the lantern-lit pool inside a reconstructed Japanese farmhouse, nothing about Robert De Niro's Greenwich Hotel is generic. Each of the 88 individually designed rooms feature floor-to-ceiling French doors opening to the flower-filled courtyard; dark, aged wood across the floors; and opulently tiled Carrara marble or Moroccan tiled bathrooms.

ANDAZ WALL ST HOTEL

Map p416 (☎212-590-1234; http://andaz.hyatt.com; 75 Wall St at Water St; 📶; [S]2/3 to Wall St) The new favorite of hip downtown business types, the 253-room Andaz take sleek and handsome, and gives it a relaxed, new-school vibe. Guests are checked-in on hand-held tablets, and treated to complimentary wi-fi, local calls, minibar soda and snacks, and wine in the lobby. Rooms are spacious, contemporary and elegantly restrained, with 7ft-high windows, oak floors, Zen-like soak tubs, and sublimely comfortable beds.

Sip on well-crafted cocktails at Bar Seven Five, nosh at farm-to-table restaurant Wall & Water, then work it all off at the 24-hour fitness center.

GILD HALL WALL STREET BOUTIQUE HOTEL $$

Map p416 (☎212-232-7700; www.wallstreetdistrict.com; 15 Gold St; r from $225; 📶) Boutique and brilliant, Gild Hall's entryway leads to a bi-level library and champagne bar that oozes hunting lodge chic. Rooms fuse Euro elegance and American comfort, with high tin ceilings, glass-walled balconies, Sferra linens, and mini-bars stocked with Dean & Deluca treats. Hermès designed the leather headboards on the king-size beds, which work perfectly in their warmly hued, minimalist surroundings.

SMYTH TRIBECA BOUTIQUE HOTEL $$$

Map p416 (☎212-587-7000; www.thompsonhotels.com; 85 W Broadway; r $259-459; 📶; [S]A/C, 1/2/3 to Chambers St) Another Thompson boutique hotel, with the same combo of luxury and laid-back hipness that you'll find at sister locations Gild Hall, 6 Columbus, 60 Thompson, and Thompson LES. Sexy Chesterfields and tartan rugs define the lobby, while the sound-proofed rooms are a soothing combo of charcoal carpets, walnut paneling, white Sferra linen and red Saarinen Womb chairs for a splash of color.

Extra in-house perks include a buzzing French bistro, two bars and a fitness center. Wi-fi is a cheeky $15 per 24 hours.

DUANE STREET HOTEL BOUTIQUE HOTEL $$

Map p416 (☎212-964-4600; www.duanestreethotel.com; 130 Duane St at Church St; r $215-429; 📶; [S]A/C, 1/2/3 to Chambers St) Fancy your own minimalist Manhattan loft? Then check into one of these sparsely decorated rooms with bright accent walls, large comfy beds and splashes of sleek furniture. Light sleepers may not enjoy the street traffic noise at night, but aside from that, Duane Street's a find, with easy walking access to Tribeca restaurants and bars, the World Trade Center and Brooklyn Bridge.

Wi-fi is complimentary and guests have complimentary access to a nearby Equinox gym.

WALL STREET INN LUXURY HOTEL $$$

Map p416 (☎212-747-1500; www.thewallstreetinn.com; 9 S William St; r incl breakfast from $275; 📶) The sedate stone exterior of this inn belies its warm, Colonial-style interior. Beds are big and plush, and rooms have glossy wood furnishings and long drapes. The bathrooms are full of nice touches, like Jacuzzis in the deluxe rooms and tubs in the others.

The building is a piece of history, too – the 'LB' tile in the entry dates from the previous tenants, the Lehman Brothers banking company.

COSMOPOLITAN HOTEL HOTEL $$

Map p416 (⌨212-566-1900; www.cosmohotel. com; 95 W Broadway at Chambers St; d from $200; 🛜) Cosmo is a hero if you'd rather save your bills for the area's chic eateries and boutiques. The 130-room hotel isn't much to brag about – clean, carpeted rooms with private bathrooms, a double bed or two, and IKEA-knock-off furnishings. But it's clean and comfortable, with major subway lines at your feet, plus all of Tribeca, Chinatown and Lower Manhattan a walk away.

🛏 SoHo & Chinatown

Visitors love the likes of SoHo's posh streets and hoteliers have taken note. There are a lot of great accommodation options to choose from along these Euro-fied lanes, but they come at quite a cost. Is it worth it? Totally. You'll have some of the world's best shopping, drinking and dining at your doorstep, and you're a short subway hop or taxi ride from some of Manhattan's other great neighborhoods.

Slightly cheaper digs await those that don't mind being a couple of avenues over in the borderlands of some of the area's other districts like Nolita and Chinatown.

CROSBY STREET HOTEL BOUTIQUE HOTEL $$$

Map p418 (⌨212-226-6400; www.firmdale hotels.com; 79 Crosby St near Spring St; r from $500; 🚇6 to Lafayette St, R/W to Prince St) Step into Crosby Street for afternoon tea and you'll never want to leave. It's not just the clotted cream and raisiny scones that will grab you, but the fun and upbeat lobby (with mauve sofas and striking artwork), the whimsical striped chairs in the bar and the unique rooms. Some are a stark black and white (dotted and striped walls and bedspreads that somehow go together) and others as pretty as an English garden.

NOLITAN HOTEL HOTEL $

Map p418 (⌨212-925-2555; www.nolitanhotel. com; 30 Kenmare St btwn Elizabeth & Mott Sts; r from $143; 🚇J to Bowery, 4/6 to Spring St; B/D to Grand St) Set behind a memorable facade of floating postive-negative Tetris bricks, the Nolitan is a great find situated between two of the most popular New York neighborhoods: SoHo and the Village. Tuck into a good book in the inviting lobby lounge, or head upstairs to your stylish pad that feels like it's waiting to be photographed in the next CB2 catalog. Pets are catered to with alacrity.

THE JAMES NEW YORK HOTEL $$$

Map p418 (⌨212-465-2000; www.jameshotels. com/new-york.aspx; 27 Grand St btwn Ave of the Americas & Thompson St; r from $999; 🚇A/C/E, 1/2 to Canal St; A/C/E to Spring St) The James plays with a variety of architectural elements in each of the hotel's different spaces, and somehow they all seem to work beautifully. The public areas – especially the designated lobbies – use the generous amounts of natural light as the midday sun pours through the tooth-white drapery. Unusually grassy pockets add an element of pleasant surprise to the outside zones that squat under skyscraping slabs of concrete. At night, after the curtains close, the wooden slatting and dark-wood furniture make the rooms feel wonderfully cozy.

THOMPSON LES BOUTIQUE HOTEL $$

Map p424 (⌨212-204-6485; www.thompsonles. com; 190 Allen St near Stanton St; r from $249; 🚇F/V to Lower East Side-2nd Ave) Another high-end offering from the brains trust behind boutique beauties Gild Hall and 6 Columbus, Thompson LES has 18 floors of industrial, loft-like rooms with exposed concrete walls, beds with lightboxes for headboards and a 'sensuality kit' in the honor bar. Views from the rooms are fantastic, but nothing beats the scenic sweep from the rooftop bar (for guests only).

MONDRIAN SOHO HOTEL $$

Map p418 (⌨212-389-1000; www.mondriansoho. com; 9 Crosby St btwn Howard & Grand Sts; r from $249; 🚇4/6, N/Q/R, J/Z to Canal St) The trademark Mondrian playfulness now inhabits over 250 rooms at the beautiful downtown property. The designs have dabbled with fairy-tale color schemes while tricking the senses with an eclectic assortment of oddly texturized *objets d'art*. Creamy whites and purple-y blues reign on the upper levels, giving guests the impression that they're staring out at the city from upon a cloud. Don't miss **Imperial No Nine** – just off of the lobby – where succulent seafood meals are served under a maelstrom of ficus leaves and crystal chandeliers.

TRUMP SOHO NEW YORK HOTEL **$$$**

Map p418 (☎212-842-5500; 246 Spring St btwn Ave of the Americas & Varick St; r from $319; [S]A/C/E to Spring St; 1/2 to Canal St; 1/2 to Houston St) Classic American luxury comes in the form of carefully appointed rooms with oversized beds, super-plush rugs and spacious bathrooms sporting the latest in futuristic fixtures. A highly acclaimed spa and a handful of high-end restaurants round out the Trump Soho's offerings – it's hard to find a reason to leave the glass-encased premises once you've settled in!

MERCER BOUTIQUE HOTEL **$$$**

Map p418 (☎212-966-6060; www.mercerhotel.com; 147 Mercer St at Prince St; r from $350; [S]N/R/W to Prince St) Right in the heart of SoHo's brick lanes, the grand Mercer is where stars sleep. Above the leisurely lobby full of fat, plush sofas, the 75 rooms offer a slice of chic loft life in a century-old warehouse. Flat-screen TVs, dark-wood floors and white-marble, mosaic-tile bathrooms (some with square tubs under a skylight) add a modern touch to rooms that sport the building's industrial roots – with giant oval windows, steel pillars and exposed-brick walls.

BLUE MOON HOTEL BOUTIQUE HOTEL **$$$**

Map p424 (☎212-533-9080; www.bluemoon-nyc.com; 100 Orchard St btwn Broome & Delancey Sts; r from $250; [S]F/V to Lower East Side-2nd Ave) You'd never guess that this quaint, welcoming brick guesthouse – full of festive yellows, blues and greens – was once a foul tenement back in the day (the day being 1879). Except for a few ornate touches, like original wood shutters, wrought-iron bed frames and detailed molding, Blue Moon's clean, spare rooms are entirely modern and comfortable, with big beds, great views from large windows and elegant marble baths.

GEM HOTEL BOUTIQUE HOTEL **$$**

Map p424 (☎212-358-8844; www.thegemhotel.com; 135 Houston St at Forsyth St; r from $180; 📶; [S]F to 2nd Ave; J to the Bowery; 4/6 to Bleecker St) Renovated from a former Howard Johnson hotel, the Gem still has the plain, boxy exterior of the well-known chain, but it's done away with the bland inside, replacing it with cheery white linens, colorful comforters and tiny desks. Rooms are small, each with a private bath, and you'll get nice Gilchrist & Soames amenities, but expect some noise to filter up from the street outside.

SOLITA SOHO HOTEL **$**

Map p418 (☎212-925-3600; www.solitasohohotel.com/; 159 Grand St btwn Centre & Lafayette Sts; r $129; [S]6 to Canal St) A new addition to the downtown scene, Solita is great for anyone who wants to soak up the flavor of Chinatown and Little Italy. Part of the Clarion chain, the Solita's got no surprises: a clean, functional lobby accessed through a glass-topped portico on the street, and smallish, slightly octagonal black-and-white rooms with wide beds (plump beige duvets and big pillows), private baths and a tiny desk. Its price says budget, but the service and amenities are boutique.

60 THOMPSON BOUTIQUE HOTEL **$$$**

Map p418 (☎212-431-0400; www.60thompson.com; 60 Thompson St btwn Broome & Spring Sts; s/d $360/425; 📶) Built from scratch in 2001, the snazzy 100-room 60 Thompson is definitely a place to be seen, either in the futurist Thai restaurant Kittichai, or swirling cocktails on the rooftop Thom Bar. Rooms are small but comfy: beds have goose-down duvets and leather headboards, and you can watch DVDs on the flat-screen TVs from a wing-backed seat or creamy tweed sofa. If the price is within reach, the extra-luxurious suites provide a lot more space and comfort. Wi-fi and high-speed internet are free hotel-wide.

HOTEL ON RIVINGTON BOUTIQUE HOTEL **$$**

Map p424 (THOR; ☎212-475-2600; www.hotelonrivington.com; 107 Rivington St btwn Essex & Ludlow Sts; r from $160; 📶; [S]F to Delancey St; J/M/Z to Essex St; F to 2nd Ave) Opened in 2005, the 20-floor THOR – that's the hotel acronym, not the viking – looks like a shimmering new-Shanghai building towering over 19th century tenements. The 'unique' rooms have enviable views over the East River and downtown's sprawl, along with hanging flat-screen TVs. The standard rooms have one glass wall with a view (instead of three) and are a tighter squeeze.

OFF-SOHO SUITES BUDGET HOTEL $

Map p424 (☎212-979-9815; www.offsoho.com; 11 Rivington St btwn Chrystie & Bowery Sts; r $119; [S]J/M/Z to Bowery) There's more grit than glam in Off-Soho Suites' 40 unpretentious rooms, which sleep four and contain fully functional kitchenettes (including microwave, stove, oven and generously stocked shelves). The location is unbeatable – right between Nolita, Chinatown and the Lower East Side – which mitigates the rather shabby decor in some of the older rooms. It's not hip or happening, but it's fun, functional and easy on the wallet.

East Village & Lower East Side

Statement-making structures have been cropping up in these once grittier neighborhoods giving the area a fun, world-in-one feel that still remains distinctly New York in style. Visitors seeking that true city feel will be perfectly happy taking up residence along these low-numbered streets, especially if you've got the dime for a room at the Bowery or Cooper Square hotels. Stay west if subway convenience is a primary concern – underground transport quickly thins as you head east, especially beyond First Ave.

BOWERY HOTEL BOUTIQUE HOTEL $$$

Map p422 (☎212-505-9100; www.thebowery hotel.com; 335 Bowery btwn 2nd & 3rd Sts; r from $325; 📶) Pick up your old-fashioned gold room key with its red tassel in the dark, hushed lobby – filled with antique velvet chairs and faded Persian rugs – then follow the mosaic floors to your room. There you can dock your iPod, use the wi-fi, check out the 42in plasma, watch some DVDs, or raid your bathroom goodies (courtesy of CO Bigelow, the Greenwich Village apothecary). Rooms have huge factory windows with unobstructed views, simple white spreads with red piping, and elegant four-poster beds. The Bowery's zinc-topped bar, outside garden patio, and rustic Italian eatery, Gemma's, are always packed.

STANDARD COOPER SQUARE HOTEL $$

Map p422 (☎212-475-5700; www.standard hotels.com/eastvillageny; 25 Cooper Sq btwn the Bowery & 4th St; from $245; 📶; [S]N/R to 8th St-NYU; 4/6 to Bleecker St; 4/6 to Astor Pl) Rising above the East Village like an unfurled sail, Cooper Square's gleaming, white structure has caused controversy since day one. Visitors are entranced by the futuristic, white-walled rooms with sweeping East Village views (and either love or hate the dark hallways and chic lobby with greenish glass walls). The hotel's strikingly out of place in low-rise East Village – even with the ersatz graffiti wall its designers placed at the entrance. For a more authentic glimpse at the old East Village, head to the outdoor patio bars. From there you can look right into the apartments in neighboring tenements – a mere 29in away.

EAST VILLAGE BED & COFFEE B&B $

Map p422 (☎212-533-4175; www.bedandcoffee.com; 110 Ave C btwn 7th & 8th Sts; r with shared bath from $115; ❄📶) Owner Anne has turned her family home into a quirky, arty, offbeat B&B with colorful, themed private rooms (one shared bathroom per floor) and great amenities, like free bikes, free wi-fi, and wonderful insider tips on the best the East Village has to offer. Anne's dogs roam the first two floors, but the upper ones are pet free. Each floor has shared common and kitchen space, and guests get keys so they can come and go (no curfew). Reservations are required; book early as it fills fast.

EAST VILLAGE B&B B&B $

Map p422 (☎212-260-1865; evbandb@juno.com; Apt 5-6, 244 E 7th St btwn Aves C & D; r $100-150; [S]F/V to Lower East Side-2nd Ave) A popular oasis for Sapphic couples who want peace and quiet in the midst of the noisy East Village scene. Its three rooms (two black-and-white and one red) are way stylish – bold linens, modern art, gorgeous wooden floors – and the shared living-room space is filled with light, beautiful paintings from around the globe, exposed brickwork and a big-screen TV. As it's beyond Ave A, though, it's a particularly long walk to the subway station.

Greenwich Village, Chelsea & the Meatpacking District

Real estate in the desirable West Village is the highest in the city, and this plays out in hotel tariffs as well. Staying here,

however, is well worth opening your wallet a bit wider as you'll be treated to a wonderful neighborhood vibe at some of the more memorable properties in town.

Just a few blocks up in Chelsea, you'll find a spike in new development with a horde of swankified properties promising cutting-edge design befitting the pages of a Scandinavian design magazine. Prices are surprisingly competitive, so you'll get a lot of substance for your buck. Nights in Chelsea will ensure convenient (read: walkable) access to Broadway's lights and boutique shopping and eating downtown.

HÔTEL AMERICANO — HOTEL $$

Map p430 (☎212-216-0000; www.hotel-americano.com; 518 W 27th St btwn 10th Ave & 11th Ave; r from $255 ; [S]A/C/E to 23 St) Design geeks will go giddy when they walk into one of Hôtel Americano's perfectly polished rooms. It's like sleeping in a bento box, but the food's been replaced by a carefully curated selection of minimalist and muted furniture. Oh, and that thing hanging from the ceiling that looks like a robot's head? It's a dangly fireplace, of course. You'll also have everything from Turkish towels to Japanese washing cloths, and all controls are activated by your personal iPad. When you're ready to venture from your museum-eqsue cocoon, explore surrounding Chelsea on a guest bike.

STANDARD — BOUTIQUE HOTEL $$$

Map p426 (☎877-550-4646, 212-645-4646; www.standardhotels.com; 848 Washington St at 13th St; r from $325; [S]A/C/E to 14th St; L to 8th Ave) Hipster hotelier André Balazs has built a wide, boxy, glass tower that straddles the High Line, an old elevated train track recently turned into a public park. It's an exhibitionist's delight, and plenty of Standard visitors seem to like the thrill of parading in front of their floor-to-ceiling windows in a towel (or less). (Judging by the crowds who gather below on the High Line, voyeurism is alive and well in New York.) Every room has sweeping Meatpacking District views and fills with cascading sunlight that makes the Standard's glossy, wood-framed beds and marbled bathrooms glow in a particularly homey way. Discounted rooms are often available online only, especially for off-season months.

HOTEL GANSEVOORT — LUXURY HOTEL $$$

Map p426 (☎212-206-6700; www.hotelgansevoort.com; 18 Ninth Ave at 13th St; r from $325; 📶🏊; [S]A/C/E, 1/2/3 to 14th St; L to 8th Ave) Coated in zinc-colored panels, and booming up top where rooftop bar Plunge attracts block-long lines (and guests swim in the skinny pool overlooking the Hudson River), the 14-floor Gansevoort has been a swank swashbuckler of the Meatpacking District since it opened in 2004. Rooms are luscious and airy, with fudge-colored suede headboards, plasma-screen TVs and illuminated bathroom doors. Rooms with the best views and private balconies go for upwards of $800.

DREAM DOWNTOWN — HOTEL $$

Map p430 (☎212-229-2559; www.dreamdowntown.com; 355 W 16th St btwn Eighth & Ninth Aves; r $199-499; [S]A/C/E to 14 St; L to 8 Ave; 1/2 to 18 St) The newest link in the chain from the Dreamteam is looming behemoth that sinks its circle-themed footprint deep in the heart of Chelsea. The metallic facade is punctuated by portholes that look like windows of Captain Nemo's would-be space vessel; a generous smattering of ellipses echo throughout, including bedroom walls and the subtle tiling of the lap pool – a refreshing oasis on unbearable summer days. Ample public space is also a priority here, which takes the shape of several cocktail lounges and restaurants that attract weekenders in the know.

CHELSEA PINES INN — B&B $$

Map p426 (☎888-546-2700, 212-929-1023; www.chelseapinesinn.com; 317 W 14th St btwn Eighth & Ninth Aves; r from $159; [S]A/C/E to 14th St; L to 8th Ave) With its five walk-up floors coded to the rainbow flag, the 26-room Chelsea Pines is serious gay-and-lesbian central, but guests of all stripes are welcome. It helps to be up on your Hitchcock beauties, as vintage movie posters not only plaster the walls but rooms are named for starlets like Kim Novak, Doris Day and Ann-Margret. There's a sink in the walk-in closet of standard rooms, with clean bathrooms down the hall. The small cafe downstairs has free wi-fi access, and opens to a tiny courtyard out back. There's plenty of advice on cruising, partying and eating by the lively staff, and breakfast is included in the rate.

MARITIME HOTEL BOUTIQUE HOTEL **$$$**

Map p430 (☎212-242-4300; www.themaritimehotel.com; 363 W 16th St btwn Eighth & Ninth Aves; r $229-725; [S]A/C/E to 14th St; L to 8th Ave) Originally the site of the National Maritime Union headquarters (and more recently a shelter for homeless teens), this white tower dotted with portholes has been transformed into a marine-themed luxury inn by a hip team of architects. It feels like a luxury *Love Boat* inside, as its 135 rooms, each with their own round window, are compact and teak-paneled, with gravy in the form of 20in flat-screen TVs and DVD players. The most expensive quarters feature outdoor showers, a private garden and sweeping Hudson views.

CHELSEA LODGE B&B **$$**

Map p430 (☎212-243-4499; www.chelsealodge.com; 318 W 20th St btwn Eighth & Ninth Aves; s/d $134/144; [S]A/C/E to 14th St; 1 to 18th St) Housed in a landmark brownstone in Chelsea's lovely historic district, the European-style, 20-room Chelsea Lodge is a super deal, with homey, well-kept rooms. Space is tight, so you won't get more than a bed, with a TV (with cable) plopped on an old wooden cabinet. There are showers and sinks in rooms, but toilets are down the hall. Six suite rooms have private bathrooms, and two come with private garden access.

SOHO HOUSE BOUTIQUE HOTEL **$$$**

Map p426 (☎212-627-9800; www.sohohouseny.com; 29-35 Ninth Ave btwn 13th & 14 Sts; from $600; [S]L to Eighth Ave; A/C/E, 1/2/3 to 14 St) Well over a decade in age now, Soho House loves to flaunt their members-only attitude to the eager legions of wannabe jetsetters who hover around the Meatpacking District. For visitors with deep pockets, however, you can shack up here and enjoy all the amenities available only to those whose names appear on the almighty list. Beautifully decorated parlors, a private screening room and a glorious rooftop pool await.

JANE HOTEL HOTEL **$$**

Map p426 (☎212-924-6700; www.thejanenyc.com; 113 Jane St btwn Washington St & West Side Hwy; r with shared bath from $99; 📶) The claustrophobic will want to avoid the Jane's tiny 50ft rooms, but if you can stomach living like a luxury sailor, check into this recently renovated gem. The Jane was once a home for downtrodden seamen, and as recently as 2007 still had washed-up navvies living in its tiny rooms. Now it's outfitted for modern travelers, with air-con, wi-fi, iPod docks and a gorgeous communal lobby/lounge that looks like it belongs in a five-star hotel. The small cabin rooms have shared bathrooms; the more expensive captain's quarters come with private commodes.

NOMAD HOTEL BOUTIQUE HOTEL **$$**

(☎212-796-1500; www.thenomadhotel.com; 1170 Broadway at 28th St; r from $445; [S]N/R to 28th St) Crowned by a copper turret, this beaux art dream of design is one of the city's hottest new addresses, where a vagabond-chic aesthetic permeates every hardwood-ed nook in the bedrooms upstairs (clawfoot tubs!). Don't miss Atrium, the brilliant restaurant just beyond the lobby, where delicate recipes blend the freshest ingredients in a variety of slow-cooked dishes with exceptionally flavorful results (the horseradish hamachi and the oversized scallops are truly divine).

LAFAYETTE HOUSE BOUTIQUE HOTEL **$$$**

Map p418 (☎212-505-8100; www.lafayettenyc.com; 38 E 4th St btwn Fourth Ave & Lafayette St; r from $350; [S]B/D/F/V to Broadway-Lafayette St; 6 to Bleecker St) A former townhouse that's been turned into homey, spacious suites (each with a working fireplace), Lafayette House feels very Victorian. Suites have big beds, a desk, thick drapes and old-fashioned armoires. Bathrooms are large, with claw-footed tubs, and some rooms have mini-kitchenettes. The only drawback might be the occasional bit of noise from the bar next-door, although as a plus you can also order room service from its kitchen. Light sleepers should ask for rooms away from the street to avoid any problem.

WEST ELEVENTH TOWNHOUSE B&B **$$**

Map p426 (☎212-675-7897; www.west-eleventh.com; 278 W 11th St btwn 4th & Bleecker Sts; r from $242; [S]1 to Christopher St; A/C/E, F/V to W 4th St-Washington Sq) Ring bell 11 when you show up at this gracious West Village townhouse, which offers five spacious suites – more like small apartments than hotel rooms – with tiny kitchenettes, cozy living areas with artfully decorated nooks and crannies, and handsome four-poster beds. The location is fantastic – in the heart of the Village – but a narrow, steep staircase (no lift), creaky floors and some outdated plumbing come with the territory.

INCENTRA VILLAGE HOUSE
B&B $$

Map p426 (☎212-206-0007; www.incentravillage.com; 32 Eighth Ave btwn 12th & Jane Sts; r from $169; [S]A/C/E to 14th St; L to 8th Ave) An easy walk to Chelsea clubs, these two red-brick, landmark townhouses were built in 1841 and later became the city's first gay inn. Today, the 12 rooms get booked way in advance by many queer travelers; call early to get in on its gorgeous Victorian parlor and antique-filled, serious-Americana rooms (one is fully red-white-and-blue, with a possibly stunned George Washington watching over the brass bed). The Garden Suite has access to a small garden in back and there's wi-fi access in the parlor.

VILLAGE GUEST HOUSE
B&B $

Map p426 (☎646-257-0268; www.villageguesthousenyc.com; 123 Washington Pl near Sheridan Sq; r $150; [S]1 to Christopher St; A/C/E to West 4th St) On a tree-lined block, just a few minutes away from Washington Square Park, sits the Village Guest House, with six cozy apartment rooms to rent, each with private baths, wi-fi, and queen or king beds. The owners live on-site and lovingly maintain their 1831 Federalist building, decorated with appropriate historical flourishes and protected by a strict no-smoking policy. In off-season, online bookings can drop to $100 a night. Email is the best way to reach owner Colleen, or call her assistant Humphrey at the listed number. Some of the rooms are in their annex property a block away at 17 Barrow St.

INN ON 23RD ST
B&B $$

Map p430 (☎212-463-0330; www.innon23rd.com; 131 W 23rd St btwn Sixth & Seventh Aves; r from $179; [S]F/V, 1 to 23rd St) Housed in a lone 19th-century, five-story townhouse on busy 23rd St, this 14-room B&B is a Chelsea gem. Bought in 1998 and extensively renovated by the Fisherman family (who wisely installed an elevator), the rooms are big and welcoming, with fanciful fabrics on big brass or poster beds and TVs held in huge armories. There's an honor-system bar and an ol' piano for you to play boogie-woogie on in the lounge, and a 2nd-floor, all-Victorian library that doubles as a breakfast room.

COLONIAL HOUSE INN
B&B $

Map p430 (☎800-689-3779, 212-243-9669; www.colonialhouseinn.com; 318 W 22nd St btwn Eighth & Ninth Aves; r $130-350; [S]C/E to 23rd St) Friendly and simple, this 20-room gay inn is tidy but a bit worn and small. Most rooms have small walk-in closets (with a small TV and refrigerator) and sinks. When the weather is nice, the rooftop deck sees some nude sunbathing. The smaller rooms have shared baths, while the deluxe suite has a private bath and private access to the back garden.

CHELSEA HOTEL
HISTORIC HOTEL $$

Map p430 (☎212-243-3700; www.hotelchelsea.com; 222 W 23rd St btwn Seventh & Eighth Aves; r/ste from $129/585; [S]C/E, 1/2 to 23rd St) Immortalized by poems, overdoses (Sid Vicious did the deed here, after allegedly killing Nancy Spungen) and Ethan Hawke's novel writing, the one-of-a-kind Chelsea is more of a landmark than anything else. Although temporarily closed at the time of research, you can usually enjoy the mix-match of rooms lovingly showing off their decades – most are huge, with ruby-red carpets or dripdrop designs on rugs over wooden floors. Some have kitchenettes and separate living rooms. There's always a few eccentrics hanging around, even though most of the longtime Chelsea dwellers were booted out. In off-season, online rates go as low as $99 for rooms with shared bathrooms.

CHELSEA HOSTEL
HOSTEL $

Map p430 (☎212-647-0010; www.chelseahostel.com; 251 W 20th St btwn Seventh & Eighth Aves; dm $38-68, s $70-95, d from $95; [S]A/C/E, 1/2 to 23 St; 1/2 to 18 St) Occupying some serious real estate in the desirable Chelsea neighborhood, this old bastion of backpackerdom is a good pick if location ranks at the top of your list. Walkable to the Village and Midtown, Chelsea Hostel capitalizes on its convenience with somewhat steep prices, but it's kept clean (even a tad sterile at times) and there's access to common rooms and kitchens where other budget travelers often meet and hang.

🛏 Union Square, Flatiron District & Gramercy

A lot of visitors like to stay amid the glitzy lights of Times Square because of its convenient position to the many different hotspots around the city, but consider for a second that Union Sq and its neighbors are just as good. A quick

glance at the subway map will show a handful of lines that crisscross in this busy downtown hub – you're a straight shot to Lower Manhattan and the museums on the Upper East Side, and the adorable nooks in the Village are at your doorstep. Try the area's cache of inns, boutique digs and rather romantic options that are something a bit more subdued than the Vegas-esque lights of Broadway.

GRAMERCY PARK HOTEL BOUTIQUE HOTEL **$$$**
Map p432 (☎212-475-4320; www.gramercyparkhotel.com; 2 Lexington Ave at 21st St; r from $350; [S]6 to 23rd St) Formerly a grand old dame, the Gramercy's had a major facelift and emerged looking young and sexy. Dark wood paneling and sumptuous red suede rugs and chairs greet you in the lobby, while the rooms – overlooking nearby Gramercy Park – have customized oak furnishings, 400-count Italian linens, and big, feather-stuffed mattresses on sprawling beds. Colors are rich and alluring, fit for a Spanish grandee. The largest rooms – sprawling suites with French doors dividing living and sleeping areas – start at $800. Be sure to visit the celebrity-studded Rose and Jade bars, the guest-only rooftop terrace, and Maialino (p167), the on-site rustic Italian eatery run by Danny Meyer.

HOTEL GIRAFFE BOUTIQUE HOTEL **$$$**
Map p434 (☎877-296-0009, 212-685-7700; www.hotelgiraffe.com; 365 Park Ave S at 26th St; r $339-475; [S]N/R/W, 6 to 23rd St) Up a notch in posh from most of the boutiques this far south, the new 12-floor Giraffe earns its stripes, or dots, with sleek, modern rooms and a sunny rooftop area for drinks or tapas. Most of the 72 rooms have small balconies. All come with flat-screen TVs and DVD players, granite work desks and automatic black-out shades to open and shut the (big) windows from your bed. Corner suites add a living room with pull-out sofa.

W NEW YORK UNION SQUARE HOTEL **$$$**
Map p432 (☎212-253-9119, 888-625-5144; www.whotels.com; 201 Park Ave S at 17th St; r $389; [S]L, N/Q/R/W, 4/5/6 to 14th St-Union Sq) The ultra-hip W demands a black wardrobe and credit card. The standard rooms aren't big, but – set in a 1911, one-time insurance building – benefit from high ceilings, and are decked out with all the modern bells and whistles (flat-screens, iPod docks, wi-fi and so on). The suites – wow and extreme wow – are spectacular, with huge bathtubs and free fuzzy robes and slippers to pad around in.

INN AT IRVING PLACE B&B **$$$**
Map p432 (☎800 685 1447, 212 533 4600; www.innatirving.com; 56 Irving Pl btwn 17th & 18th Sts; r $379; [S]L, N/Q/R/W, 4/5/6 to 14th St-Union Sq) Richly Victorian, this intimate and exquisite 11-room red-brick townhouse dates from 1834 and is stuffed with period pieces and rosy patterns of days past. The spacious rooms have massive four-poster beds, plump easy chairs, cozy sofas and handsome armories set atop dark-wood floors. Breakfast is served in the atmospheric Lady Mendl parlor.

WYNDHAM GARDEN HOTEL **$$**
Map p432 (☎212-243-0800; www.wyndham.com; 37 W 24th St btwn Fifth & Sixth Aves; r $159-269; [S]N/R, 4/5/6 to 14th St) Nearly equal distance between Chelsea and Union Square, the Wyndham's colorful checked entrance fits in with the surrounding, unique neighborhoods. The whimsy disappears once you're inside – it's beige walls, taupe carpet and plain work stations is just what you'd expect from a chain hotel (but one that caters to business folk). Still, it's a fantastic location, and the rooms are as clean as a whistle.

CHELSEA INN B&B **$$**
Map p432 (☎212-645-8989; www.chelseainn.com; 46 W 17th St btwn Fifth & Sixth Aves; r from $100; 🛜; [S]A/C/E to 14th St; 1 to 18th St) Made up of two adjoining 19th century townhouses, this funky-charming hide-away (a four-story walk-up) has small but comfortable rooms that look like they were furnished entirely from flea markets or grandma's attic. It's character on a budget, just a bit east of the most desirable part of its namesake 'hood. Most of the rooms have private baths; the two rooms that go for the lowest prices share a bathroom.

HOTEL 17 BUDGET HOTEL **$**
Map p432 (☎212-475-2845; www.hotel17ny.com; 225 E 17th St btwn Second & Third Aves; r $89-150; [S]N/Q/R/W, 4/5/6 to 14th St-Union Sq; L to 3rd Ave) Right off Stuyvesant Sq on a leafy residential block, this popular eight-floor townhouse has old–New York charm with cheap prices – plus Woody Allen shot a frightening dead-body scene here for his film *Manhattan Murder Mystery* (1993). Only four of the

120 rooms have private bathrooms (all are free of the film's dead bodies). Rooms are small, with traditional, basic furnishings (gray carpet, striped wallpaper, chintzy bedspreads, burgundy blinds) and lack much natural light. If this place is booked, ask about its sister property, **Hotel 31** (Map p434; ☎212-685-3060; www.hotel31.com; 120 E 31st St btwn Lexington & Park Aves; [S]N/R/W, 6 to 28th St).

JAZZ ON THE TOWN HOSTEL **$**

Map p432 (☎212-228-2780; www.jazzhostels.com; 307 E 14th St btwn First & Second Aves; dm $34-42; [S]L to 1st Ave) Affiliated with the Jazz on the Park Hostel (p344), this crammed, four-floor walk-up is, despite the smiles, a by-the-numbers hostel with functional, slightly depressing dorm rooms of four or six beds; one dorm is females only. There's a rooftop deck with artificial turf and seats overlooking loud 14th St. There are a few computers to check email, a storage room and laundry facilities.

Midtown

If you want to be in the heart of the action, consider Midtown East, which encompasses the area around Grand Central Terminal and the UN. It's not as crazy and eclectic as Midtown West, but options are endless and prices and conditions range from $75 cheapies with shared toilets down the hall to thousand-dollar suites with private terraces overlooking the city's blinking lights.

Light sleepers beware – Midtown West is a 24-hours-a-day kind of place. Better bring your eyeshades. If the idea of sleeping under the neon sun of Times Sq excites rather than depresses you, Midtown West is your perfect location. It's go-go-go all day and night long, thanks to the juxtaposition of Broadway and its fantastic theater with the heart of Manhattan's business district. To top it off, Hell's Kitchen's Ninth Ave has a huge range of restaurants with cuisines from all over the world.

[TOP CHOICE] **ANDAZ FIFTH AVENUE** BOUTIQUE HOTEL **$$**

Map p434 (☎212-601-1234; http://andaz.hyatt.com; 485 Fifth Ave at 41st St; d: $355-595; 📶; [S]S, 4/5/6 to Grand Central-42nd St; 7 to Fifth Ave) Uber-chic yet youthful and relaxed, the Andaz ditches stuffy reception desks for hip, mobile staff who check you in on tablets in the art-laced lobby. The hotel's 184 rooms are contemporary and sleek, with NYC-inspired details like 'Fashion District' rolling racks and subway-inspired lamps. We especially love the sexy, spacious bathrooms, complete with rain showers, black porcelain foot baths and CO Bigelow amenities.

There's a 'secret' basement bar pouring limited-edition spirits, a locavore-focused restaurant (you can watch the chefs in action at the 2nd-floor showroom kitchen), and regular talks by guest artists and curators. And if that wasn't enough, there's free vino from 6pm in the book-lined lobby lounge.

PIERRE LUXURY HOTEL **$$$**

Map p434 (☎212-838-8000; www.tajhotels.com; 2 E 61st St at Fifth Ave; r from $595; 📶; [S]N/Q/R to 5th Ave-59th St) Opulent, historic and obscenely romantic, the Pierre is a destination it itself. The lobby looks like a Gilded Age period piece, the on-site restaurant (La Caprice) is imported from London, and the spacious rooms (in muted tones with delicate accent colors) beckon with wide beds, sweeping views of Central Park (at the hotel's front door) and decadent, full-size bathrooms.

The Pierre's 49 suites have gracious sitting areas – some with fireplaces and antique desks for business – that are both lavish and tranquil, and the on-site spa beckons with treatments based on traditional Indian teachings, herbs and oils.

ACE HOTEL NEW YORK CITY BOUTIQUE HOTEL **$$**

Map p434 (☎212-679-2222; www.acehotel.com/newyork; 20 W 29th St btwn Broadway & Fifth Ave; r from $99-369; 📶) A hit with social media types and cashed-up creatives, the Ace's standard and deluxe rooms are best described as upscale bachelor pads – plaid bedspreads, quirky wall stencils, leather furnishings and fridges. Some even have Gibson guitars and turntables. For cool kids with more 'cred' than 'coins,' there are 'cheap' and 'bunk' rooms (with bunk beds), which are yours for $159 and $139 in winter.

The vibe here is upbeat and fun, with two designer shops; a cozy, hipster-packed lobby serving up live bands and DJs; superlative espresso bar Stumptown (p198) and two of the area's top nosh spots – carnivorous the Breslin and seafood-centric John Dory Oyster Bar (p195).

SETAI FIFTH AVENUE LUXURY HOTEL **$$$**

Map p434 (www.capellahotels.com/newyork; 400 Fifth Avenue at 36th St; r from $545; ᯤ; [S]N/Q/R to 34th St-Herald Sq) Rooms at the luxurious, skyscraping Setai are more akin to suites (the smallest is a generous 400 sq ft). Understatedly chic, all feature neutral hues, handsome wood paneling, Duxiana mattresses and Nespresso machines. The marble-floor bathrooms are equally impressive, with deep soaking tub and TV-embedded mirror. Local calls and garment pressing are complimentary, as is early check-in or late check-out.

We also love the luxe spa, good-sized gym, and live nightly jazz (direct from the Lincoln Center) in the bar. Super-centrally located, the 214-room hotel is also home to Michael White's Michelin-starred restaurant Ai Fiori.

FOUR SEASONS LUXURY HOTEL **$$$**

Map p434 (☎212-758-5700, 800-819-5053; www.fourseasons.com/newyorkfs; 57 E 57th St btwn Madison & Park Aves; r $650; ᯤ; [S]N/Q/R to Fifth Ave-59th St) Housed in a 52-floor tower designed by IM Pei, this five-star chain delivers seamless luxury. Even the smallest of the 368 neutrally hued rooms are generously sized, with spacious closets and 10in plasma TVs in the full-marble bathrooms. The views over Central Park from the 'Park View' rooms are practically unfair.

Then there's the impeccable service, Joël Robuchon's Michelin-starred **L'Atelier**, the luxury spa and the 24-hour fitness center. It's a hard life, but someone's got to live it.

CHATWAL NEW YORK LUXURY HOTEL **$$$**

Map p438 (☎212-764-6200; www.thechatwalny.com; 130 W 44th St btwn Sixth Ave & Broadway; r $450-795; ᯤ🏊; [S]N/Q/R, S, 1/2/3, 7 to Times Sq-42nd St) A restored art deco jewel in the heart of the Theater District, the Chatwal is as atmospheric as it is historic; the likes of Fred Astaire and Irving Berlin once supped, sipped and sung in its Lambs Club restaurant/bar. Vintage Broadway posters adorn the uber-luxe guestrooms, inspired by steamer cabin trunks and featuring 42-inch plasma screens and 400-thread linen counts.

Restored by master architect Thierry Despont, the beaux arts building itself is the work of Stanton White, creator of Washington Square Arch. The hotel is also home to a soothing, luxury spa.

LIBRARY HOTEL BOUTIQUE HOTEL **$$$**

Map p434 (☎212-983-4500, 877-793-7323; www.libraryhotel.com; 299 Madison Ave at 41st St; r $399-699; ❄ᯤ; [S]S, 4/5/6, 7 to Grand Central-42nd St) Each floor at this discreetly elegant hotel is dedicated to one of the 10 major categories of the Dewey Decimal System: Social Sciences, Literature, Philosophy and so on, with a total of 6000 volumes split up between quarters. The decor is equally bookish, with mahogany paneling, hushed reading rooms and a gentlemen's club atmosphere.

The 'petit' rooms are cunningly designed with all the amenities of the larger suites, but they are only just big enough for one adult. There's a rooftop deck bar, as well as complimentary wine and cheese between 5pm and 8pm. Rates drop dramatically in January.

YOTEL HOTEL **$$**

Map p438 (☎646-449-7700; www.yotel.com; 570 Tenth Ave at 41st St; r from $150; ᯤ; [S]A/C/E to 42nd St-Port Authority Bus Terminal; 1/2/3, N/Q/R, S, 7 to Times Sq-42nd St) Part futuristic spaceport, part Austin Powers set, this uber-cool 669-room option bases its rooms on airplane classes: Premium Cabin (Economy), First Cabins (Business) and VIP Suites (First); the suites come with rotating bed and private terrace with hot tub. Small but cleverly configured, Premium cabins include automated adjustable beds, while all cabins feature floor-to-ceiling windows with killer views, slick bathrooms and iPod connectivity.

You'll find coffee, tea, microwaves and fridges in the communal 'galleys'; there are DJ-spun tunes on weekends in the Club Lounge; and Latin-Asian dishes are served in the sumo wrestling ring inspired Dohyo restaurant/bar. There's also a gym and a designer outdoor terrace with a stunning skyscraper backdrop.

PLAZA LUXURY HOTEL **$$$**

Map p434 (☎212-759-3000, 800-759-3000; www.theplaza.com; 768 Fifth Ave at Central Park South ; ᯤ; [S]N/R to Fifth Ave-59th St) The palatial Plaza looks ever more incredible after its $400 million facelift. Suitably set in a landmark French Renaissance-style building, its 282 guestrooms are a suitably regal affair, with sumptuous Louis XV-style furniture and 24-carat gold-plated bathroom faucets.

Among the hotel's long list of luxe drawcards is the fabled Palm Court, which is famed for its stained-glass ceiling and afternoon tea. Add white-gloved butler service, a wine-therapy Caudelié Spa, luxury retail and dining options, and you too can expect to develop a royalty complex.

IVY TERRACE B&B **$$**

Map p434 (☎516-662-6862; www.ivyterrace.com; 58th St btwn Second & Third Aves; r $269-325; 📶; [S]4/5/6 to 59th St; N/Q/R to Lexington Ave-59th St) Especially popular with couples, Ivy Terrace is a seriously charming B&B. The spacious, Victorian-inspired rooms cozily combine elegant drapes, antique furniture (the Rose Room features a canopy bed), hardwood floors and kitchens with breakfast supplies. One of the suites even has a flagstone balcony. There's a three night minimum stay (sometimes five to seven nights), and no elevator.

Its location is just east of the Midtown fray but close to Bloomingdales and the mega shopping strips of Madison and Fifth Aves.

RITZ-CARLTON LUXURY HOTEL **$$$**

Map p438 (☎212-308-9100, 866-671-6008; www.ritzcarlton.com; 50 Central Park South btwn Sixth & Seventh Aves; r $595-995; 📶; [S]N/Q/R to 57th St-7th Ave; F to 57th St) Pure, unadulterated luxury: this landmark building comes with views of Central Park so giant you almost can't see New York. All 261 rooms feature French colonial undertones, with tasseled armchairs, beautiful inlaid-tile bathrooms and loads of space for your countless Louis Vuitton cases, dahhhling. Park view rooms come with a *Birds of New York* field guide set by a telescope.

Laurent Tourondel's BLT Market mixes classic French and American cuisine for Ritz diners (only fresh upstate-NY ingredients, of course) and the high-end spa will pamper, polish and preen you with La Prairie products.

WALDORF-ASTORIA LEGENDARY CHAIN **$$**

Map p434 (☎800 925 3673, 212 355 3000; www.waldorfastoria.com; 301 Park Ave btwn 49th & 50th Sts; r $289-514; [S]6 to 51st St; E, F to Lexington Ave-53rd St) An attraction in itself, the 416-room, 42-floor legendary hotel is an art deco landmark. It's massive, occupying a full city block – with 13 conference rooms, and shops and eateries keeping the ground floor buzzing with life. Elegant rooms conjure some old-world fussiness, with rose petal rugs and embossed floral wallpaper. Staff tell us three-quarters of daily visitors come just to look. Plenty to gawk at: the *Wheel of Life* mosaic tile entry (at the Park Ave entrance) features nearly 150,000 tiles.

LONDON NYC LUXURY HOTEL **$$$**

Map p438 (☎212-307-5000, 866-690-2029; www.thelondonnyc.com; 151 W 54th St btwn Sixth & Seventh Aves; ste from $389 ; ❄📶; [S]B/D, E to 7th Ave) This luxe hotel salutes the British capital in sophisticated ways, including a silk-stitched tapestry of Hyde Park (or is it Central Park?) in the lobby, and a Michelin-starred restaurant by Gordon Ramsay. But the real draw are the huge, plush rooms – all called suites, and all with separate bedroom and living area. In winter, online prices drop to the high $200s.

Suites are subdued and sophisticated, with luxe touches including parquet floors, 2000-thread-count linens and spacious bathrooms with showers for two. Amenities include an equally sleek gym.

70 PARK HOTEL **$$$**

Map p434 (☎212-973-2400, 877-707-2753; www.70parkave.com; 70 Park Ave at 38th St; r $339-479; 📶; [S]S, 4/5/6, 7 to Grand Central-42nd St) Beyond the plush and cozy lobby lounge, complete with limestone fireplace, this recently renovated slumber number offers 205 slinky rooms packed with state-of-the-art technology (including great sound systems); comfy plush beds; and a palate of black, white, purple and chrome. Adjoining rooms can be turned into large suites for families. Pets are welcome, and staff are friendly.

ROYALTON BOUTIQUE HOTEL **$$**

Map p434 (☎800-635-9013, 212-869-4400; www.royalton.com; 44 W 44th St btwn Fifth & Sixth Aves; d $250-450; 📶; [S]B/D/F/M to 42nd St) This modern-classic creation by Ian Schrager and Philippe Starck makes a grand introduction with its mahogany-rich, African art-laced lobby. Up the dark hallways are mid-size rooms with short, wide beds and soft, muted, pastel-hued furnishings. Some rooms have circular 'soaking tubs,' deluxe rooms feature a fireplace, and there's an iPad in every room. There's a fitness center to boot.

IROQUOIS
HOTEL $$$

Map p438 (☎info 800-332-7220, info 212-840-3080; www.iroquoisny.com; 49 W 44th St, Midtown West; d $230-500; 📶; [S]B/D/F/M to 42nd St-Bryant Park) Steeped in history (James Dean lived in room 803 from 1951 to 1953), this classic 114-room hotel oozes Old New York charm and an enviable location in the heart of Midtown.

It's a wonderfully atmospheric place, complete with a small oak library, intimate cocktail salon Lantern's Keep, and superb French-inspired restaurant Triomphe (the latter attracting a loyal pretheater crowd). Some rooms on the top three of its dozen floors face the Chrysler Building through a canyon of Midtown buildings. Softly colored, with classic wooden furniture, all rooms have goose-down pillows and small, Italian marble bathrooms. There's a small fitness center and complimentary shoe shine service. Jimmy Dean must have dug that.

STRAND
BOUTIQUE HOTEL $$

Map p438 (☎212-448-1024; www.thestrandnyc.com; 33 W 37th St btwn Fifth & Sixth Aves; d from $249; 📶; [S]B/D/F/M, N/Q/R to 34th St-Herald Sq) This gleaming boutique option is a stone's throw from the Empire State Building, Bryant Park, Macy's, Grand Central and other Midtown icons. The eye-catching lobby features a two-story cascading waterfall and a tinkling piano bar, while even the standard rooms are large enough for a settee and a plush chair, giving them a suite-like feel.

Topping it all off (literally) is an all-weather rooftop bar with a view to die for.

BRYANT PARK HOTEL
BOUTIQUE HOTEL $$$

Map p434 (☎212-869-0100, 877-640-9300; www.bryantparkhotel.com; 40 W 40th St btwn Fifth & Sixth Aves; d $324-519; 📶; [S]B/D/F/M to 42nd St-Bryant Park; 7 to 5th Ave) Looming to the south of cosmopolitan Bryant Park, this modish 130-room hotel (complete with red-leather elevator) dishes out bare-bone minimalist rooms, most with huge views and all with high-tech sound system, flat-screen TV, travertine bathroom, full-size soaking tubs and cashmere robes. If you can, opt up for a suite that faces the park (higher-priced ones have terraces).

Originally the American Standard Building (1934), this black-and-gold tower hotel also features a small fitness center, a sexy, vaulted underground bar, and an uber-sleek sushi restaurant with the odd celebrity diner.

6 COLUMBUS
BOUTIQUE HOTEL $$$

Map p438 (☎212-204-3000; www.thompsonhotels.com; 6 Columbus Circle; d $231-498; 📶; [S]A/C, B/D, 1 to 59th St-Columbus Circle) Flashback to the 1960s at this ultra-mod boutique hotel, brought to you by the owners of downtown 'It' spots Smyth Tribeca, Gild Hall, Thompson LES and 60 Thompson. Rooms are small but fun, with retro-cool detailing and high-tech hook-ups like LCD TVs and iPod docks. The uber-cool, intimate rooftop bar is outstanding for a twlight toast.

Then there's the location; steps from Central Park, next to Time Warner and backed by a major subway hub.

CHAMBERS
BOUTIQUE HOTEL $$$

Map p434 (☎866-204-5656, 212-974-5656; www.chambersnyc.com; 15 W 56th St btwn Fifth & Sixth Aves; r $350; 📶; [S]F to 57th St; N/Q/R to 5th Ave-59th St) Chambers is chic and intimate, its mezzanine lounge pimped with anime-inspired wall art and area-rugs. Its 77 rooms are simple yet elegant, with plush cushions on wood-frame beds, and concrete-floor bathrooms featuring giant showerheads. The on-site restaurant Ma Peche is helmed by culinary genius David Chang of Momofuku fame, and Fifth Ave's upmarket department stores are a bag swing away.

NIGHT
BOUTIQUE HOTEL $$$

Map p438 (☎212-835-9600; www.nighthotelny.com; 132 West 45th St btwn Sixth & Seventh Aves; r from $329; 📶; [S]B/D/F/M to 47th-50th Sts-Rockefeller Center) Dark, decadent and delicious, sleeping at Night feels like stepping into an Anne Rice novel. From the rocker-glam entrance, draped in crushed velvet, to the sleek-and-sexy black and white rooms (complete with gothic lettering on the carpets), celebrated hotelier Vikram Chatwal's stark, two-toned establishment stands out all the more in the glare of Times Sq's neon. Rooms are small but comfy.

Wi-fi will set you back $10 per 24 hours.

DREAM
BOUTIQUE HOTEL $$$

Map p438 (☎212-247-2000, 866-437-3266; www.dreamny.com; 210 W 55th St btwn Broadway & Seventh Ave; r $299-509; 📶; [S]N/Q/R to 57th St-7th Ave) Dream is glossy, glam and just a little crazy. The lobby features a two-story aquarium filled with tropical fish and a giant three-figure statue culled from a Connecticut Russian restaurant; its fabulous rooftop hangout, Ava, draws the odd celebrity, and its minimal all-white rooms come with glowing blue lights and high-tech floating TV screens.

INK48
BOUTIQUE HOTEL $$

Map p438 (☎212-757-0088; www.ink48.com; 653 11th Ave at 48th St; d $272-480; 📶; [S]C/E to 50th St) The Kimpton hotel chain has braved Midtown's wild far west with Ink48, perched on the subway-starved edge of Manhattan. Occupying a converted printing house, the compensation is sweet: stellar skyline and Hudson River views; chic contemporary rooms; a boutique spa and restaurant; and a stunning rooftop bar. Topping it off is easy walking access to Hell's Kitchen's thriving restaurant scene.

POD HOTEL
HOTEL $$

Map p434 (☎212-355-0300; www.thepodhotel.com; 230 E 51st St btwn Second & Third Aves; r from $129; 📶) A dream come true for folks who would like to live inside their iPod – or at least curl up and sleep with it – this affordable hot spot has a range of room types, most barely big enough for the bed. 'Pods' have bright bedding, tight workspaces, flatscreen TVs, mp3 docking stations and 'rain' showerheads.

HOTEL ELYSÉE
BOUTIQUE HOTEL $$$

Map p434 (☎212-753-1066; www.elyseehotel.com; 60 E 54th St btwn Madison & Park Aves, Midtown East; r $259-595; 📶; [S]E/M to Lexington Ave-53rd St; 6 to 51st) Impeccably refined and lavished with antiques and classic detailing, this intimate hotel has been bedding the famous and fabulous since 1926. Come evening, star spot over complimentary wine and cheese in the lounge, or in the deco-glam Monkey Bar restaurant, co-owned by Vanity Fair editor Graydon Carter and featured in both *Mad Men* and *Sex and The City*.

There's no gym on-site but passes to NY Sports Club are complimentary.

STAY
BOUTIQUE HOTEL $$

Map p438 (☎212-768-3700, 800-336-4110; www.stayhotelny.com; 157 W 47th St btwn Sixth & Seventh Aves; d $249-565; 📶; [S]A/C/E to 42nd St-Port Authority Bus Terminal; N/Q/R, S, 1/2/3, 7 to Times Sq-42nd St) Stay offers 'location, location', but little space. Standard rooms are teeny-tiny, but comfortable nonetheless (an upgrade will snag you a larger room with a closet). All have wi-fi, iPod docks, flatscreens and Gilchrist & Soames amenities. There's no gym but passes to NY Sports Club are free. We love the adjoining bar/restaurant, Aspen Social Club, decked out like a cozy Colorado ski club.

CASABLANCA HOTEL
BOUTIQUE HOTEL $$

Map p438 (☎212-869-1212, 888-922-7225; www.casablancahotel.com; 147 W 43rd St btwn Sixth Ave & Broadway; r $249-400; 📶; [S]S, N/Q/R, 1/2/3, 7 to Times Sq-42nd St) Low-key, tourist-oriented and only steps away from Times Square, the popular 48-room Casablanca pages North Africa with its tiger statues, Moroccan murals, framed tapestries and a 2nd-floor lounge named Rick's Cafe, after the movie. Rooms are small but pleasant and comfortable, with sisal-like carpets and a window-side seating area. You'll also find free internet, all-day espresso and wine at 5pm.

HOTEL METRO
HOTEL $$

Map p438 (☎212-947-2500; www.hotelmetronyc.com; 45 W 35th St btwn Fifth & Sixth Aves; r $140-495; 📶; [S]B/D/F/M, N/Q/R to 34th St-Herald Sq) Imbued with a faint whiff of 1930s art deco, the 181-room, 13-floor Metro offers somewhat plain but undeniably comfortable rooms, with caramel color schemes, flatscreen TVs and more thinking space than most hotels in its price range. Perks include free breakfast, a fitness center, and a rooftop bar with impressive views of the Empire State Building.

414 HOTEL
HOTEL $$

Map p438 (☎212-399-0006; www.414hotel.com; 414 W 46th St btwn Ninth & Tenth Aves; r incl breakfast from $200; [S]A/C/E to 42nd St-Port Authority Bus Terminal) Set up like a guesthouse, this affordable, friendly option offers 22 tidy rooms a couple of blocks west of Times Sq. Rooms are simply yet tastefully decorated, with cable TV and private bathroom; those facing the leafy inner courtyard are the quietest. The courtyard itself is the perfect spot to enjoy your complimentary breakfast in the warmer months.

BELVEDERE HOTEL HOTEL $$

Map p438 (☎212-245-7000, 888-468-3558; www.belvederehotelnyc.com; 319 W 48th St btwn Eighth & Ninth Aves; r $399; 📶; [S]C/E to 50th St) Open since 1928, the 334-room Belvedere's roots (and facade) are art deco originals, even if the makeover is a modern take on the era's glory. True to its vintage, it's built on a luxurious scale, its bathrooms bigger than many boutique hotel rooms. Rooms are classically decorated, with handy mini-kitchenettes to boot.

GERSHWIN HOTEL HOTEL $$

Map p434 (☎212-545-8000; www.gershwinhotel.com; 7 E 27th St at Fifth Ave; dm/d/ste from $45/109/299; 📶; [S]N/R, 6 to 28th St) This raffish, pop art-themed veteran (with original Warhol soup can painting in the lobby) is part hostel, part hotel and part gallery. No-frills dorms with two, four or six bunks (apparently a common place for up-and-coming models to bed down) all have private bathrooms. The private rooms and family suites are small and retro ('70s-style quilt anyone?), but clean and cheap.

HOTEL 373 HOTEL $$

Map p434 (☎888-382-7111, 212-213-3388; www.hotel373.com; 373 Fifth Ave at 35th St; r $149-329; 📶; [S]N/Q/R, B/D/F/M to 34th St-Herald Sq) The claustrophobic among us will not appreciate Hotel 373's cunning, multi-use furnishings and teeny-tiny little rooms, but those who like a great deal will understand that an affordable *and* clean, fun, fabulous hotel just steps from the Empire State Building always has a drawback somewhere.

ECONO LODGE BUDGET HOTEL $$

Map p438 (☎212-246-1991; www.econolodge.com; 302 W 47th St at Eighth Ave; d $150-279; 📶; [S]C/E to 50th St; N/R to 49th St) A budget option steps away from the Times Sq action, Econo Lodge has a small, no-frills lobby that leads to small, no-frills rooms. Some have double beds and can hold four, and others are kings, with just enough room to squeeze in an armoire and decent-sized bathroom. A modest continental breakfast is included in the price.

When the rates come down in off-season, the prices are more in line with the hotel's offerings.

Upper East Side

The Upper East Side contains some of the wealthiest zip codes in the country, so accommodations aren't cheap. But that's the price you pay for being walking distance from some of New York's grandest cultural attractions.

[TOP CHOICE] **BUBBA & BEAN LODGES** B&B $$

Map p440 (☎917-345-7914; www.bblodges.com; 1598 Lexington Ave btwn 101st & 102nd Sts; r from $180; 📶; [S]6 to 103rd St) Owners Jonathan and Clement have turned a charming Manhattan townhouse into an excellent home-away-from-home (named after their Boston Terriers, Bubba and Bean). The five guest rooms are simply furnished, with crisp, white walls, hardwood floors and navy linens, providing the place with a modern, youthful feel. All units are equipped with private bathrooms as well as kitchenettes with cookware.

1871 HOUSE HISTORIC HOTEL $$

Map p440 (☎212-756-8823; www.1871house.com; 130 E 62nd St btwn Park & Lexington Aves; r $265-445; 📶; [S]N/R/W to Lexington Ave-59th St) Named for the year it was built, this historic home now serves as a quaint five-room inn. Each unit (including two multi-room suites) is like a miniapartment, with a kitchenette, private bath, queen beds, working fireplace and period-style furnishings. All the rooms are light-filled, with airy 12ft ceilings, while the suites, on the upper floors, can sleep up to five.

This is a great value place for the neighborhood. But note that this is a characterful, vintage structure: there is no elevator, the floors are a bit creaky, and in winter, heat is provided by steam radiators.

SURREY LUXURY HOTEL $$$

Map p440 (☎212-288-3700; www.thesurrey.com; 20 E 76th St near Madison Ave; d $350-800, ste $620-1800; 📶; [S]6 to 77th St) This steely Upper East Side gem – literally, everything is decorated in silvery shades of grey – is all about luxury. The staff is attractive, the vibe is cool and the walls are decorated by name-brand contemporary artists like Chuck Close. In addition, the roomy 'salons' (aka 'guest rooms') are equipped with Duxiana beds decked out in Egyptian-cotton linen.

Bigger one-bedroom suites are armed with soaking tubs and fireplaces, while the truly palatial two-bedroom units are no doubt equipped with their own zip codes. All 190 guest rooms are stocked with Pratesi robes and custom-made bath amenities. There is a spa and a fantastic rooftop terrace, but the best part is the room service, which is supplied by Café Boulud (p220) downstairs.

CARLYLE
LUXURY HOTEL **$$$**

Map p440 (☎212-744-1600; www.thecarlyle.com; 35 E 76th St btwn Madison & Park Aves; r from $450; ☎; S6 to 77th St) Since its 1930 opening, the 188-room Carlyle has been known as a bastion of demure elegance. And while the hotel has been updated several times since then, the original deco design shines through, especially in the gleaming black-and-white marble lobby. Guest rooms remain traditional, with Louis XVI–style furnishings, but include modern amenities like whirlpool tubs and Yves Delorme linens.

It probably comes as little surprise that notable guests here have included John and Jacqueline Kennedy, as well as Princess Diana. There is a spa, a salon, a restaurant and a cafe – but don't miss Bemelmans Bar (p224) with its delightfully retro feel.

FRANKLIN
HOTEL **$$**

Map p440 (☎800-607-4009, 212-369-1000; www.franklinhotel.com; 164 E 87th St btwn Lexington & Third Aves; d $200-490; ☎; S4/5/6 to 86th St) Fronted by a classic red-and-gold awning, this long-time spot channels a 1930s feel – starting with the vintage elevator. As with many old-timey New York spots, the rooms and bathrooms are tiny. But the decor is modern, the staff is congenial and the location couldn't be more ideal – walking distance from Central Park and many museums.

In addition, wine and cheese is served in the evenings and a robust continental breakfast is laid out every morning. Rooms facing the back are quieter.

AFFINIA GARDENS
APARTMENT **$$**

Map p440 (www.affinia.com; 215 E 64th St btwn Second & Third Aves; ste $250-500, 2-br ste $600-1000; ☎⊛; SF to Lexington Ave-63rd St; 6 to 68th St-Hunter College) Located just four blocks from Central Park, this expansive hotel (part of the Affinia chain) has 129 roomy suites with full kitchens, some of which are available with furnished 600-sq-ft patios.

Junior, one- and two-bedroom suites (the latter sleeps up to six) range between 400 and 950 sq ft – a hefty amount of real estate as far as Manhattan is concerned.

Comfortable, modern units come with fluffy white bed spreads, pillow menus and chunky couches. There is also a fitness center.

🛏 Upper West Side & Central Park

TOP CHOICE COUNTRY INN
THE CITY
HISTORIC INN **$$**

Map p442 (☎212-580-4183; www.countryinnthecity.com; 270 W 77th St btwn Broadway & West End Aves; apt $220-350; ☎; S1 to 79th St) Just like staying with your big-city friend – if, that is, your big-city friend happens to own a landmark 1891 limestone townhouse on a picturesque tree-lined block. Country Inn has four roomy, self-contained apartments, each of which comes with sparkling wood floors, four-poster beds, cherry-wood furnishings and other decorative, antique pieces, conveying a late 19th-century feel (down to the crown moldings). The decor is tasteful without being fusty. And each of the units come with private bath and kitchenette (in addition to some welcome food supplies). There's a three-night minimum. Winter rates drop considerably.

ON THE AVE
BOUTIQUE HOTEL **$$$**

Map p442 (☎212-362-1100; www.ontheave.com; 2178 Broadway at 77th St; r from $225; ☎; S1 to 77th St) This modern hotel has 282 casually elegant rooms decked out in warm earth tones. Niceties include plush bedding, suede headboards, roomy (for New York) bathrooms, coffee makers and flat-screen TVs. The 23 suites, all located on the top floors, come with furnished private terraces and extravagant Manhattan views. The service is congenial and the location, ideal. An excellent value.

HOTEL BEACON
HOTEL **$$**

Map p442 (☎212-787-1100, reservations 800-572-4969; www.beaconhotel.com; 2130 Broadway btwn 74th & 75th St; d $230-300, ste $300-450; ☎⊛; S1/2/3 to 72nd St) Adjacent to the Beacon Theatre (p242), this family favorite offers a winning mix of attentive service, comfortable rooms and convenient location. The Beacon has 260 units (including one- and two-bedroom suites) decorated in muted shades of Pottery Barn green. The units are well maintained and quite roomy – and all come with coffee makers and kitchenettes. Upper stories have views of Central Park in the distance. A good deal all around.

HOTEL BELLECLAIRE HOTEL **$$**

Map p442 (☎212-362-7700; www.hotelbelleclaire.com; 250 W 77th St at Broadway; d $129-359, Broadway King $220-480, ste $310-600; 📶; [S]1 to 79th St) A landmark beaux arts building designed by architect Emory Roth in 1903 houses a 230-room hotel that is a good value for the location. Contemporary rooms come in a variety of sizes and configurations, with some units bigger or with better daylight than others. Some rooms face interior alleyways.

The expansive 'Broadway King' rooms are the best. The hotel has plenty of literary lore: famous guests include Mark Twain and Russian writer Maxim Gorky. Gorky, incidentally, was thrown out in 1906 when it was discovered that his female companion was not his wife.

JAZZ ON THE PARK HOSTEL HOSTEL **$**

Map p442 (☎212-932-1600; www.jazzhostels.com; 36 W 106th St btwn Central Park West & Manhattan Ave; dm $35-45, d $85-115; 📶; [S]B, C to 103rd St) This flophouse-turned-hostel right off of Central Park is generally a good bet, with clean dorms sporting four to 12 bunks in co-ed and single-sex configurations. Public spaces include a cafe/TV lounge, three terrace sitting areas and a basement lounge. The snack bar serves hamburgers-and-hot-dog fare. Plus, there's locked luggage areas and lockers.

INN NEW YORK CITY HISTORIC INN **$$$**

Map p442 (☎212-580-1900, 800-660-7051; www.innnewyorkcity.com; 266 W 71st St at West End Ave; ste $475-645; 📶; [S]1/2/3 to 72nd St) Four massive, quirky suites occupy a whole floor in this 1900 townhouse, which channels a private university club kind of vibe. Rooms feature handsome chestnut furnishings, featherbeds topped in down comforters, Jacuzzi tubs, stained glass panels and flowery carpeting. The Opera Suite (complete with piano) has a small outdoor terrace and the Spa suite comes with a sauna.

LUCERNE HOTEL **$$**

Map p442 (☎212-875-1000; www.thelucernehotel.com; 201 W 79th St cnr Amsterdam Ave; d $200-425, ste $400-625; 📶👪; [S]B, C to 81st St) This unusual 1903 structure breaks away from beaux arts in favor of the baroque, with an ornately-carved terracotta-colored facade. Inside is a stately 197-room hotel, ideal for couples and families with children (Central Park and the American Museum of Natural History are a stone's throw away). Nine types of guest rooms evoke a contemporary Victorian look. Think: flowered bedspreads, scrolled headboards and plush pillows with fringe.

Larger rooms have kitchenettes and some of the smaller rooms can be connected to make one big suite. Service is courteous and there is a nice Mediterranean restaurant on-site.

HOSTELLING INTERNATIONAL NEW YORK HOSTEL **$**

Map p442 (HI; ☎212-932-2300; www.hinewyork.org; 891 Amsterdam Ave at 103rd St; dm $32-40, d from $135; 📶) This red-brick mansion from the 1880s once served as headquarters to the 'Association for the Relief of Respectable, Aged, Indigent Females,' a home for war widows. For the last two decades its halls have housed HI's 672 well-scrubbed bunks. It's rather 19th century industrial, but benefits include good public areas, a backyard, a communal kitchen and a cafe. There are private rooms with private bathrooms, too, as well as lockers for rent. The hostel is alcohol-free.

EMPIRE HOTEL HOTEL **$$$**

Map p442 (☎212-265-7400; www.empirehotelnyc.com; 44 W 63rd St at Broadway; r from $225; 📶🏊; [S]1 to 66th St-Lincoln Center) This old hotel was remade a few years back, complete with canopied pool deck, sexy rooftop bar and a dimly-lit lobby lounge studded with zebra-print settees. The 422 rooms come in various configurations, and feature brightly-hued walls with plush dark leather furnishings.

It's a big hotel, so you're not going to get personalized service, but the location is excellent and the brilliant red Empire Hotel sign on the roof makes the perfect backdrop for Instagram pictures.

HOTEL NEWTON HOTEL **$$**

Map p442 (☎212-678-6500; www.newyorkhotel.com/newton; 2528 Broadway btwn 94th &

95th Sts; d $120-350; 🛜; Ⓢ1/2/3 to 96th St) The Newton isn't going to win any interior design awards. (Hello, flowery 1980s bedspreads!) But it's super clean and well managed, making it a solid budget option. The 105 guest rooms are small, but tidy, and come stocked with TVs, mini-refrigerators, coffee makers and microwaves. The bathrooms are all well maintained. Larger 'suites' are roomier and feature a sitting area.

JAZZ ON AMSTERDAM AVE — HOSTEL $

Map p442 (📞646-490-7348; www.jazzhostels. com; 201 W 87th St at Amsterdam Ave; dm $44, r $100; 🛜; Ⓢ1 to 86th St) The same company that runs other Jazz hostels around New York and in other cities, recently opened this 30-bed hostel with a smattering of private rooms. Housed in a converted apartment building, the rooms are simply furnished and standard hostel amenities include linens, towels, luggage storage and wi-fi in the lobby.

Overall, it's a decent, if Spartan, set up. The down side: it gets noisy and not all floors have been renovated. The plus: the location couldn't be better.

🛏 Harlem & Upper Manhattan

HARLEM FLOPHOUSE — GUESTHOUSE $

Map p444 (📞347-632-1960; www.harlemflop house.com; 242 W 123rd St btwn Adam Clayton Powell Jr & Frederick Douglass Blvds, Harlem; r with shared bath from $125; 🛜; ⓈA/C, B/D, 2/3 to 124th St) This lovely four-room, 1890s townhouse conjures up the Jazz Age, with brass beds, polished wood floors and vintage radios (set to a local jazz station). It feels like a trip to the past – which means shared bathrooms, no air-con and no TVs. But for the real-deal retro ambience, it can't be beat.

The owner is a helpful source of information on the neighborhood. Note that there is a friendly house cat.

TOP CHOICE ALOFT HARLEM — BOUTIQUE HOTEL $$

Map p444 (📞212-749-4000; www.alofthotel. com; 2296 Frederick Douglass Blvd btwn 123rd & 124th Sts, Harlem; d $150-420; 🛜; ⓈA/C, B/D, 2/3 to 125th St) A trendy new hotel designed for younger travelers channels a W Hotel vibe but at a far cheaper price. The 124

guest rooms are snug (285 sq ft) but chicly appointed, with crisp white linens, fluffy comforters and brightly-accented pillows. The modern bathrooms are small (no tubs), but are highly functional and feature amenities courtesy of Bliss.

A basement lounge with pool tables can get boisterous, but it'll be stumbling distance to your room. All around, it's convenient (the Apollo Theater and the bustling 125th St commercial district are nearby) and a good deal.

MOUNT MORRIS HOUSE B&B — B&B $$

Map p444 (📞917-478-6214; www.mountmor rishouse.com; 12 Mt Morris Park W btwn 121st & 122nd Sts, Harlem; ste $175-375; 🛜; Ⓢ2/3 to 116th St) This small inn is housed in a stunning Gilded Age townhouse from 1888 and boasts four extravagantly roomy megasuites: the Sage, Jade, Terracotta and Loft rooms. Each is appointed in period-style furnishings, with four-poster beds, Persianstyle rugs and brocaded settees, as well as fireplaces and vintage bathtubs. Breakfasts are varied and bountiful – and served, without fail, at 8:30am.

The B&B is an easy walk to 125th street and is located a stone's throw from the playgrounds at Marcus Garvey Park. Cash preferred.

102 BROWNSTONE — HOTEL $$

Map p444 (📞212-662-4223; www.102brown stone.com; 102 W 118th St btwn Malcolm X & Adam Clayton Powell Jr Blvds; r from $120; 🛜; ⓈA/C, B, 2/3 to 116th St) This intimate five-room guesthouse is a charming and convenient spot for travelers who want to explore the city but come to a little peace and quiet at the end of the day. All of the units have antique-style furnishings, private bathrooms and minifridges. The Zen suite – decorated in lemony tones – has a full kitchen and a Jacuzzi bath.

SUGAR HILL HARLEM — B&B $

Map p444 (📞212-234-5432, 917-464-3528; www. sugarhillharleminn.com; 460 W 141st St btwn Amsterdam & Convent Aves, Sugar Hill; r $125-310; ⓈA/C, B/D to 145th St) An airy townhouse has been restored to its turn-of-the-century splendor, with suites named after African American jazz greats. Well-appointed rooms feature antique-style furnishings but are equipped with modern touches like TVs and hair dryers. All units come with their own bathrooms (not necessarily en suite) and most have massive bay windows that admit lots of light; a couple have kitchens.

There is a nice garden, but no elevator (the building is three stories tall). A few additional guest rooms are located in a second renovated townhouse around the corner on Convent Ave.

Brooklyn

A short train ride across the East River and you'll find bigger and (sometimes) brighter rooms – and a lot more bang for your buck. Note, though, that Brooklyn is more than 70 sq miles and transport within the borough can be a challenge, so pick an area (north or south) that offers the best proximity to the sights you want to see.

North Brooklyn includes the hipster enclaves of Williamsburg and Bushwick, as well as the residential district of Bedford-Stuyvesant. South Brooklyn is awash in B&Bs and sleek spots. It covers downtown, Brooklyn Heights, Cobble Hill, Carroll Gardens, Park Slope and beyond.

NU HOTEL — HOTEL $$

Map p452 (☎718-852-8585; www.nuhotelbrooklyn.com; 85 Smith St, Downtown Brooklyn; d incl breakfast from $199; [wi-fi]; [S]F, G to Bergen St) The 93 rooms in this downtown Brooklyn hotel are of the stripped-down variety, featuring lots of crisp whiteness (sheets, walls, duvets). Furnishings are made from recycled teak and the floors are cork. Units come in several configurations, but families will dig the 'Nu Friends' suite, stocked with a queen bed and a bunk that sleeps two.

There is a small lounge and bikes are available. Note that while the hotel's big-paned windows are great for light, they're lousy for noise filtering. Ask for a room away from busy Atlantic Ave if you are a light sleeper.

B&B ON THE PARK — B&B $$

Map p450 (☎718-499-6115; www.bbnyc.com; 113 Prospect Park West btwn 6th & 7th Sts, Park Slope; r $225-325; [wi-fi]; [S]F to 7th Ave) Located in Park Slope, this beautiful Victorian B&B has five rooms splashed out in Persian-style rugs, potted plants and poster beds covered in pillows. It all goes well with the meticulously maintained vintage architecture, which includes wall moldings, gas-operated fireplaces and the original wood floors. The rooms are big and individually decorated. Breakfast is huge, and there's a garden out back. Cash or check only.

ALOFT NEW YORK BROOKLYN — BOUTIQUE HOTEL $$

Map p452 (☎718-256-3833; www.aloftnewyorkbrooklyn.com; 216 Duffield St btwn Willoughby & Fulton Sts, Downtown Brooklyn; d $125-$299; [wi-fi]; [S]2 to Hoyt St) A cheery, modern boutique in downtown, Aloft is walking distance from the sights in Cobble Hill and Carroll Gardens. Its 176 rooms are simple and cozy, with 9ft ceilings, minimalist furnishings, bright pillows and plenty of wood trim. Bath amenities are by Bliss. But the best feature is the dizzying rooftop lounge that is open til 4am on weekends.

HOTEL LE BLEU — HOTEL $$

Map p448 (☎718-625-1500; www.hotelbleu.com; 370 4th Ave, Park Slope; d incl breakfast $169-349; [P][wi-fi]) Situated on a charmless, industrial road on the edge of Park Slope, this hotel nonetheless manages to pull off 48 attractive units in a sleek palette of brown, white and blue. (It's not 'Le Bleu' for nothing.) Rooms are chock full of amenities, including bathrobes and coffeemakers, and the rate includes a light breakfast.

If you're a stickler for privacy, note that the bathrooms have transparent shower walls that look onto the room. During off-peak periods, the low prices make this a deal.

BLUE PORCH — B&B $

off Map p450 (☎718-434-0557; www.blueporchnyc.com; 15 DeKoven Court at Foster Ave & Rugby Rd, Ditmas Park; r $150; [wi-fi]; [S]B, Q to Newkirk Ave) A lovely 1904 Victorian with two bright, airy guest rooms is located in the sleepy district of Ditmas Park (south of Prospect Park). The bathrooms are beautifully kept, the rooms have polished wood floors and the continental breakfasts are generous. It's a good deal if you don't mind the 40-minute trip into Manhattan. A two-night minimum is required.

From the subway stop at Newkirk Ave, walk south (away from Manhattan) to Foster Ave and make a left on Rugby Rd. The inn lies in the first cul-de-sac to the left.

HOTEL LE JOLIE — BOUTIQUE HOTEL $$

Map p446 (☎718-625-2100; www.hotellejolie.com; 235 Meeker Ave btwn Union Ave & Lorimer St, Williamsburg; d $150-400; [wi-fi]; [S]L to Bedford Ave) An unremarkable 54-room hotel sits alongside the Brooklyn Queens Expressway (leading some locals to call it 'Le Hotel BQE'), but it's comfortable and reasonable. Rooms are sleek, with beds sporting monolithic *2001: A Space Odyssey*–like headboards. There are iPod docks and flat-screen TVs. But the real deal here is the proximity to Bedford Ave.

Rooms on the upper stories with Manhattan views are best.

NEW YORK LOFT HOSTEL HOSTEL $

Map p446 (☎718-366-1351; www.nylofthostel.com; 249 Varet St btwn Bogart & White Sts, Bushwick; dm $35, r $210; 📶; [S]L to Morgan Ave) This renovated 1913 warehouse building in Bushwick is a good choice for urban pioneers. Spacious, brick-lined dorms come in configurations of eight to 16. There's also a private room for three that comes with shared bath. Amenities include a communal kitchen, a large patio area with picnic tables and a small terrace with a hot tub.

The reception rents cell phones and iPads for $10 a day. It's not the prettiest part of Brooklyn, but there are plenty of good restaurants and bars nearby. A good place to get your hipster on.

AKWAABA MANSION INN B&B $$

(☎718-455-5958, 866-466-3855; www.akwaaba.com; 347 MacDonough St btwn Lewis & Stuyvesant Aves, Bedford-Stuyvesant; r $175-190; 📶; [S]A/C to Utica Ave) Sitting on a tree-lined block of tidy, century-old townhouses in Bedford Stuyvesant, this graceful B&B is tucked into a sprawling mansion built by a local beer baron back in 1860. Period design flourishes include brass beds, marble fireplaces, the original parquet floors and a screened-in wrap-around porch – the perfect spot to settle in with a book.

African textiles and vintage photographs add a personal touch. The mansion has four roomy suites, each with private bathroom, while a couple of the units have Jacuzzi tubs for two.

HOTEL WILLIAMSBURG BOUTIQUE HOTEL $$$

Map p446 (☎718-218-7500; www.hwbrooklyn.com; 160 N 12th St btwn Bedford Ave & Berry St, Williamsburg; d $275-675; 📶🏊; [S]L to Bedford; G to Nassau) This hipster hotel on the fringes of Williamsburg was a work in progress at press time and like the second Death Star in the *Empire Strikes Back*, not fully operational. (It opened, behind schedule, in late 2011.) It's insufferably chic, with tiny, minimalist rooms with glass-walled bathrooms – a stunning opportunity to see your traveling companion on the pooper.

There is a large pool surrounded by design-conscious loungers, a too-cool-for-school vinyl library, two bars and a restaurant. Overall an attractive spot, but pricey given the less-than-convenient location.

🛏 Queens

This sprawling borough still lags behind Manhattan and Brooklyn in terms of boutique and B&B charmers, but it beats everybody when it comes to chain hotels offering great deals.

Z HOTEL BOUTIQUE HOTEL $$

Map p454 (☎212-319-7000, 877-256-5556; www.zhotelny.com; 11-01 43rd Ave at Eleventh St, Long Island City; r $165-405; 📶; [S]F to 21st-Queensbridge; E, M to 23rd St-Ely Ave) Its location might scream 'industrial wasteland,' but every room at this design-savvy newbie delivers jaw-dropping views of Manhattan. The 100 rooms themselves are impressive, decked out in dark, contemporary shades, and NYC-themed stencil and designer fixtures. More astounding views (and a pizza oven) await at the rooftop bar, while the downstairs restaurant/bar is a salt-of-the-earth combo of American comfort food and Sunday football games.

Wi-fi is free, as are local and international calls. Rumor has it that online rates occasionally drop as low as $99 per night.

RAVEL BOUTIQUE HOTEL $$

Map p454 (www.ravelhotel.com; 8-08 Queens Plaza South at Vernon Blvd, Long Island City; d $140-190; [P]📶; [S]F to 21st St-Queensbridge) The industrial location may feel a little desolate, but this Long Island City option is two short subway stops from Midtown. Rooms may not be as boutique-luxe as the hotel claims, but all are smart and contemporary, with vibrant accents, plush bedding and bathrooms featuring rainforest showers (the super-spacious superior rooms have soaking tubs). The sleek rooftop restaurant/bar offers breathtaking Manhattan views.

VERVE HOTEL HOTEL $

Map p454 (☎718-786-4545; www.ascendcollection.com; 40-03 29th St at 40th Ave, Long Island City; d $122-242; [P]📶; [S]N/Q to 39th Ave) It won't knock your socks off from the outside, but this Long Island City hotel – part of the

Ascend chain – has several things going for it, including a parking garage (if you must drive), a nearby subway stop, great Manhattan views, proximity to Astoria and many LIC attractions, and surprisingly tasteful rooms.

Fitted up in gentle maroon and beige tones, the rooms are big and breezy, some with a hot tub tucked into the corner. Larger suites have separate sitting rooms.

COUNTRY INN & SUITES HOTEL **$**
Map p454 (☎718-729-0111, 800-596-2375; www.countryinns.com; 40-34 Crescent St btwn 40th & 41st Aves, Long Island City; r $76-159; 📶; [S]F to 21st St; N/Q to 39th Ave) An easy schlep to Manhattan and extra-large rooms – some with kitchens and living room areas – keeps this chain hotel full year-round. Prices drop below $100 in off months, and even in peak season are still a bargain for NYC. And while it won't rate high for flair (think cookie-cutter furnishings), it's clean, has good beds, and breakfast is included.

MARCO LAGUARDIA HOTEL & SUITES BUSINESS HOTEL **$$**
Map p454 (☎718-445-3300; www.marcolaguardiahotel.com; 137-07 Northern Blvd at Farrington St, Flushing; r $150-199; 📶; [S]7 to Flushing-Main St) For travelers whose main focus is Queens – be it the Mets at Citi Field, tennis at Flushing Meadows or taste-testing the borough's ethnic eateries – this is a convenient and welcoming choice. Located near LaGuardia Airport (free shuttle service) and JFK, it's a 30-minute ride into Manhattan on the 7 line.

Rooms are designed with business travelers in mind – space aplenty, desks with free wi-fi, 24-hour business center, gym and room service.

Understand
New York City

New York City Today

Now more than ever, New York City continues to fulfill its destiny as a shining beacon of progress. Human rights are challenged and championed – marriage laws extended to all, as thousands march for fiscal reform. The latest social trends continue to change the landscape as well, from the dinner plate to the worldwide web. And – already towering above the city that never sleeps – is a brand new tower, designed to be the tallest in America, that's both a symbol of a hopeful future and a reminder of a painful past.

Best on Film

Annie Hall (1977) Oscar-winning romantic comedy by the king of New York neuroses, Woody Allen.

Manhattan (1979) Allen's at it again with tales of twisted love set among NYC's concrete landscape.

Taxi Driver (1976) Scorsese's tale of a troubled taxi driver and Vietnam vet.

West Side Story (1961) A modern-day *Romeo and Juliet* set on the gang-ridden streets of New York.

Best in Print

The Amazing Adventures of Kavalier & Clay (Michael Chabon; 2000) Beloved Pulitzer-winning novel that touches upon Brooklyn, escapism and the nuclear family.

A Tree Grows in Brooklyn (Betty Smith; 1943) An Irish-American family living in the Williamsburg tenements at the beginning of the 20th century.

Down These Mean Streets (Piri Thomas; 1967) Memoirs of tough times growing up in Spanish Harlem.

Invisible Man (Ralph Ellison; 1952) Poignant prose exploring the situation of African Americans in the early 20th century.

The Age of Innocence (Edith Wharton; 1920) Tales and trials of NYC's social elite in the late 1800s.

Occupy Wall Street

Inspired by the revolutionary spirit in Tunisia and Egypt, thousands took to the Financial District's Liberty Sq on 17 September, 2011, to take a stand against the nation's division of personal wealth, and how the so-called '99%' are at the mercy of the rule-writing, wealthiest '1%.' Known as Occupy Wall Street, the movement is largely a byproduct of the Global Economic Crisis that saw the bankruptcy and closure of several heavyweight money movers – most headquartered in New York City. And in true NYC fashion, the protests have since spread like wildfire through the rest of the country (100 cities and counting) and beyond. For more information, see www.occupywallst.org.

Start-Up, Up & Away!

The dot-com days may be long over, but social media is still raking in the chips. In New York City, America's networking hive, there are many busy bees at work crafting web-based businesses that are revolutionizing the transference of the almighty dollar. Humans have been connecting with one another for almost a decade on Facebook, and now a wave of New York–based start-ups are giving people a new way of engaging with a variety of consumables from packaged vacations to medical supplies, and everything in between. Exclusive web clubs, 24-hour flash sales, and dynamic cross-media synergy have taken the virtual world by storm, and most of them are based here.

Marriage Is So Gay

New York has long been the hub of gay rights in America, and on June 24, 2011, the state government granted a major boon to the LGBT community when it legalized marriage between two persons of the same gender in the Marriage Equality Act. It had been a long, arduous fight full of divisive political maneuvers, but the promise of minting gay and lesbian couples has begun – in earnest – to clear the dark cloud of limited liberties over the rest of the nation. And in the meantime, economic pundits predict that the state will receive an additional $200 million in tourist funds fueled by rainbow-flag-toting travelers looking to get hitched.

Freedom Tower

A great day of solemn remembrance occurred on September 11, 2011 – 10 years after the tragic terrorist attacks that caused the felling of the twin towers. Thousands gathered at Ground Zero to honor the dead, surrounded by the foundations of many new buildings – the soon-to-be monuments that will take the place of the Twin Towers. After years of planning, the centerpiece – the Freedom Tower, as it's commonly known – is nearing completion. In 2014, its target opening date, the building will be America's tallest, with observation decks on the 100th, 101st and 102nd floors.

At the time of research, tickets for the tumbling waterfalls of the 9/11 Memorial must be booked online in advance due to the ongoing construction in the surrounding area. Same-day access can be scored when purchasing a ticket to the WTC Tribute Visitor Center.

New Eats, Old Drinks

Gourmet food trucks and pop-up restaurants remain stalwarts of the city's hip eating scene, but so-called 'new American' fare is the true darling of the dinner plate. A gourmet spin on traditional comfort food – or peasant food, if you will – the long-established movement seeks to fuse repast standards with a lofty dedication to market-fresh produce and seasonal ingredients. Many of the city's most critically acclaimed chowhouses (the brainchildren of the city's brigade of celebrity chefs) offer souped-up versions of family recipes – a tribute to New York's immigrant citizenry.

While 'new American' holds sway over the cuisine scene, the situation behind the bar is thoroughly old-fashioned. Ironically inspired by the years when public tipples were obsolete, the city's penchant for speakeasy-style digs comes in several iterations: entrances through secret doors, barkeeps in period clothing (slacks and suspenders!) and delicious mixed beverages stirred with utmost care.

if New York City were 100 people

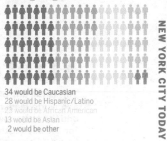

34 would be Caucasian
28 would be Hispanic/Latino
23 would be African American
13 would be Asian
2 would be other

housing
(% of population)

67.5
Renters

0.05
Homeless
(documented)

32
Homeowners

population per sq mile

MANHATTAN   NEW YORK STATE

≈ 5,000 people

History

This is the tale of a city that never sleeps, of a kingdom where tycoons and world leaders converge, of a place that's seen the highest highs and the most devastating lows. Yet through it all, it continues to reach for the sky (both figuratively and literally). And to think it all started with $24 and a pile of beads...

NYC's Top Historical Sights

Ellis Island (Lower Manhattan)

Frick Collection (Upper East Side)

Gracie Mansion (Upper East Side)

Jane's Carousel (Brooklyn)

Morris-Jumel Mansion Museum (Harlem & Upper Manhattan)

LIVING OFF THE LAND

Long before the days of European conquest, the swath that would eventually become NYC belonged to Native Americans known as the Lenape – 'original people' – who resided in a series of seasonal campsites. They lived up and down the eastern seaboard, along the signature shoreline, and on hills and in valleys sculpted by glaciers after the Ice Age left New York with glacial debris now called Hamilton Heights and Bay Ridge. Glaciers scoured off soft rock, leaving behind Manhattan's stark rock foundations of gneiss and schist. Around 11,000 years before the first Europeans sailed through the Narrows, the Lenape people foraged, hunted and fished the regional bounty here. Spear points, arrowheads, bone heaps and shell mounds testify to their presence. Some of their pathways still lie beneath streets such as Broadway. In the Lenape language of Munsee, the term Manhattan may have translated as 'hilly island.' Others trace the meaning to a more colorful phrase: 'place of general inebriation.'

1524: A RUDE AWAKENING

The Lenape people lived undisturbed until explorers muscled in, firstly by way of the French vessel *La Dauphine,* piloted by Florentine explorer Giovanni da Verrazano. He explored the Upper Bay in 1524, deemed it a 'very beautiful lake,' and while anchored at Staten Island, he attempted to kidnap some of the Native Americans he encountered. This began several

TIMELINE	c AD 1500	1625–26	1646
	About 15,000 Native Americans live in 80 sites around the island, including the Iroquois and the Algonquins people, who fought among themselves before clashing with Europeans.	As the population of New Amsterdam reaches 200, the Dutch West India Company imports slaves from Africa to New Amsterdam to work in the fur trade and construction.	The Dutch found the village of Breuckelen on the eastern shore of Long Island, naming it after Breuckelen in the Netherlands; it will remain an independent city until 1898.

decades of European explorers raiding Lenape villages, and cultivated the Lenape's deep mistrust of outsiders. By the time the Dutch West India Company employee Henry Hudson arrived in 1609, encounters with Native Americans were often dichotomized into two crude stories that alternated between 'delightful primitives' and 'brutal savages.'

BUYING MANHATTAN

The Dutch West India Company sent 110 settlers to begin a trading post here in 1624. They settled in Lower Manhattan and called their colony New Amsterdam, touching off bloody battles with the unshakable Lenape. It all came to a head in 1626, when the colony's first governor, Peter Minuit, became the city's first – but certainly not the last – unscrupulous real estate agent by purchasing Manhattan's 14,000 acres from the Lenape for 60 guilders ($24) and some glass beads.

PEG LEG, IRON FIST

After the island's purchase, the colony quickly fell into disrepair under the governance of Willem Kieft. Then Peter Stuyvesant stepped in and busily set about fixing the demoralized colony, making peace with the Lenape, establishing markets and a night watch, repairing the fort, digging a canal (under the current Canal St) and authorizing a municipal wharf. His vision of an orderly and prosperous trading port was partially derived from his previous experience as governor of Curaçao – and the burgeoning sugar economy in the Caribbean helped to inspire an investment in slave trading that soon boosted New Amsterdam's slave workforce to 20% of the population. After long service, some were partially freed and given 'Negroe Lots' near today's Greenwich Village, the Lower East Side and City Hall. The Dutch West India Company encouraged the fruitful connection to plantation economies on the islands, and issued advertisements and offered privileges to attract merchants to the growing port. Although these 'liberties' did not at first extend to the Jews who fled the Spanish Inquisition, the Dutch West India Company turned Stuyvesant's intolerance around. By the 1650s, warehouses, workshops and gabled houses were spreading back from the dense establishments at the river's edge on Pearl St.

But by 1664, the English showed up in battleships, ready for a nasty fight. Stuyvesant was tired, though, and avoided bloodshed by surrendering without a shot. King Charles II promptly renamed the colony after his brother the Duke of York. New York became a prosperous British port and its population rose to 11,000 by the mid-1700s. The

NYC Names & their Dutch Origins

Gramercy:
Kromme Zee
('crooked lake')

Coney Island:
Konijneneiland
('rabbits island')

Yonkers: jonker
('squire')

Bowery: bouwerij
(old-fashioned
word for 'farm')

Bronx: named for
Jonas Bronck

1754	1776	1784	1791
The first institution of higher learning, King's College, is founded by royal charter from George II. After the American Revolution, it's reborn as Columbia University.	American colonies sign the Declaration of Independence on July 4. Figures who helped create this document include John Hancock, Samuel Adams, John Adams and Benjamin Franklin.	Alexander Hamilton founds America's first bank, the Bank of New York, with holdings of $500,000. It will become the first corporate stock to be traded on the New York Stock Exchange.	Bill of Rights adopted as constitutional amendments articulating citizens' rights, including freedom of speech and the right to bear.

honeymoon, however, was short lived as New York grew in prominence as the change point in the exchange of slaves and good between worlds.

TAX & PRESS

Evidence of the rising tension could be found in the colonial press, as John Peter Zenger's *New York Weekly Journal* flayed the king and royal governor so regularly that the authorities tried to convict Zenger for seditious libel. He was acquitted, though, and that was the beginning of what we know today as 'freedom of the press.'

Meanwhile, some 2000 New Yorkers continued to resist their involuntary servitude. At the same time trade with the Caribbean accelerated and wharves lined the East River to accommodate the bulging merchant ships. By the 18th century, the economy was so robust the locals were improvising ways to avoid sharing the wealth with London. Smuggling to dodge various port taxes was commonplace, and the jagged coastline, full of coves and inlets, hid illegal activity well. And so New York was a hotbed of hotheads and tax dodgers, and provided the stage for the fatal confrontation with King George III.

REVOLUTION & WAR

Patriots clashed in public spaces with Tories, who were loyal to the king, while Lieutenant Colonel Alexander Hamilton, an intellectual, became a fierce anti-British organizer. Citizens fled the scene, sensing the oncoming war, and revolutionary battle began in August of 1776, when General George Washington's army lost about a quarter of its men in just a couple of days. He retreated, and fire encompassed much of the colony. But soon the British left and Washington's army reclaimed their city. After a series of celebrations, banquets and fireworks at Bowling Green, General Washington bade farewell to his officers at what is now the Fraunces Tavern Museum and retired as commander-in-chief.

But in 1789, to his surprise, the retired general found himself addressing crowds at Federal Hall, gathered to witness his presidential inauguration. Alexander Hamilton, meanwhile, began rebuilding New York and became Washington's secretary of the treasury, working to establish the New York Stock Exchange. But people distrusted a capitol located adjacent to the financial power of Wall St merchants, and New Yorkers lost the seat of the presidency to Philadelphia shortly thereafter.

1789	1795	1811	1825
Following a seven-day procession from his home in Mount Vernon, George Washington is inaugurated at Federal Hall as the country's first president.	Just two years after turning away refugees from a Yellow Fever epidemic in Philadelphia, New York finds itself in the midst of its own outbreak, which kills nearly 750 people.	Manhattan's grid plan is developed by Mayor DeWitt Clinton, which leads to reshaping the city by leveling hills, filling in swamps and laying out plans for future streets.	The Erie Canal, considered one of the greatest engineering feats of the era, is ceremoniously completed, greatly influencing trade and commerce in New York.

POPULATION BUST, INFRASTRUCTURE BOOM

There were plenty of setbacks at the start of the 19th century: the bloody Draft Riots of 1863, massive cholera epidemics, rising tensions among 'old' and new immigrants, and the serious poverty and crime of Five Points, the city's first slum, located where Chinatown now lies. Eventually, though, the city was prosperous and found resources to build mighty public works. A great aqueduct system brought Croton Water to city dwellers, relieving thirst and stamping out the cholera that was sweeping the town. Irish immigrants helped dig a 363-mile 'ditch' – the Erie Canal – linking the Hudson River with Lake Erie. The canal's chief backer, Mayor DeWitt Clinton, celebrated the waterway by ceremonially pouring a barrel of Erie water into the sea. Clinton was also the mastermind behind the modern-day grid system of Manhattan's street layout – a plan created by his commission to organize the city in the face of an oncoming population explosion.

And there was yet another grand project afoot – one to boost the health of the people crammed into tiny tenement apartments – in the form of an 843-acre public park. Begun in 1855 in an area so far uptown that some immigrants kept pigs, sheep and goats there, Central Park was both a vision of green reform and a boon to real-estate speculation. As much as Central Park promised a playground for the masses, the park project also offered work relief for the city when the Panic of 1857 (one of the city's periodic financial debacles) shattered the nation's finance system.

Another vision was realized by German-born engineer John Roebling, who sought a solution to a series of winter freezes that had shut down the ferry system connecting downtown Manhattan to Brooklyn, then an independent city. He designed a soaring symphony of spun wire and Gothic arches to span the East River, and his Brooklyn Bridge accelerated the fusion of the neighboring cities.

New York City was the first capital of the United States – George Washington took his first presidential oath at Federal Hall in 1789.

19TH-CENTURY CORRUPTION & IMMIGRATION

Out of such growth and new prosperity came the infamous William 'Boss' Tweed – a powerful and charming politician who had served in the US House of Representatives and had become the leader of the political organization Tammany Hall, which basically looked out for the wealthy. He soon took charge of the city treasury and spent years embezzling funds – perhaps up to $200 million – which put the city in debt and contributed to citizens' growing poverty. His crimes were highlighted by Thomas Nast's biting caricatures in the 1870s, and Boss was eventually caught and thrown in jail, where he died.

1853
The State Legislature authorizes the allotment of public lands, which removes 17,000 potential building sites from the real-estate market for what will later become Central Park.

1861–65
American Civil War erupts between North and South. The war's end on April 9, 1865, is marred by President Lincoln's assassination five days later.

Central Park (p229)

By the turn of the 20th century, elevated trains carried a million people a day in and out of the city. Rapid transit opened up areas of the Bronx and Upper Manhattan, spurring mini building booms in areas near the lines. At this point, the city was simply overflowing with the masses of immigrants arriving from southern Italy and Eastern Europe, who had boosted the metropolis to around three million. The journey from immigrant landing stations at Castle Garden and Ellis Island led straight to the Lower East Side. There, streets reflected these myriad origins with shop signs in Yiddish, Italian, German and Chinese. Ethnic enclaves allowed newcomers to feel comfortable speaking their home languages, buy both familiar and New World staples from pushcart peddlers and worship varied versions of the Christian and Jewish faiths.

CLASS LESSONS

All sorts of folks were living in squalor by the late 19th century, when the immigration processing center at Ellis Island opened, welcoming one million newcomers in just its first year. They crammed into packed tenements, shivered in soup lines and shoveled snow for nickels. Children collected rags and bottles, boys hawked newspapers, and girls sold flowers to contribute to family income. Family budgets were so meager that it was common to pawn the sheets to raise food money before a payday.

Meanwhile, newly wealthy folks – boosted by an economy jump-started by financier JP Morgan, who bailed out sinking railroads and led to New York being the headquarters of Standard Oil and US Steel – began to build increasingly splendid mansions on Fifth Ave. Modeled on European chateaux, palaces such as the Vanderbilt home, on the corner of 52nd St and Fifth Ave, reached for new summits of opulence. Tapestries adorned marble halls, mirrored ballrooms accommodated bejeweled revelers, and liveried footmen guided grand ladies from their gilded carriages in a society where Astors, Fricks and Carnegies ruled. Reporter and photographer Jacob Riis illuminated the widening gap between the classes by writing about it in the *New York Tribune* and in his now-classic 1890 book, *How the Other Half Lives,* eventually forcing the city to pass much-needed housing reforms.

1898: BOROUGHS JOIN MANHATTAN

After years of governmental chaos caused by the 40 independent municipalities around the New York area, a solution came in 1898: the ratifying of the Charter of New York, which joined the five boroughs of Brooklyn, Staten Island, Queens, the Bronx and Manhattan into the

1863	1870	1883	1886
The Civil War Draft Riots erupt in New York, lasting for three days and ending only when President Lincoln dispatches combat troops from the Federal Army to restore order.	After four years of lobbying for a national institution of art by a civic group, the Metropolitan Museum of Art is founded by a group of local leaders, philanthropists and artists.	The Brooklyn Bridge, which was built at a cost of $15.5 million (and 27 lives) opens; 150,000 people walk across its span at the inaugural celebration.	The Statue of Liberty's pedestal is completed, allowing the large lady to be presented to New York at a dedication ceremony that takes place before thousands of citizens.

largest city in America. The move brought even more development, this time in the form of skyscrapers that made good use of the steel industry and spawned many building contests to see who could reach higher into the sky. New York was home to nearly 70 skyscrapers by 1902.

FACTORY TRAGEDY, WOMEN'S RIGHTS

Wretched factory conditions – low pay, long hours, abusive employers – in the early 20th century were illuminated with a tragic event in 1911. It was the infamous Triangle Shirtwaist Company fire, in which rapidly spreading flames caught onto the factory's piles of fabrics and killed 146 of 500 women workers who were trapped behind locked doors. The event led to sweeping labor reforms after 20,000 female garment workers marched to City Hall. At the same time, suffragists held street-corner rallies to obtain the vote for women. Nurse and midwife Margaret Sanger opened the first birth-control clinic in Brooklyn, where 'purity police' promptly arrested her. After her release from jail in 1921, though, she formed the American Birth Control League (now Planned Parenthood), providing services for young women and researching methods of safe birth control.

THE JAZZ AGE

All this sassiness paved the way for what came to be known as the Jazz Age, when Prohibition outlawed the sale of alcohol, encouraging bootlegging and speakeasies, not to mention organized crime. Congenial mayor James Walker was elected in 1925, Babe Ruth reigned at Yankee Stadium and the Great Migration from the South led to the Harlem Renaissance, when the neighborhood became the center of African American culture and society. It produced poetry, music, painting and an innovative attitude that continues to influence and inspire. Harlem's daring nightlife in the 1920s and '30s attracted the flappers and gin-soaked revelers that marked the complete failure of Prohibition. Indeed, the Jazz Age seems to have taught women to smoke, drink and dance at speakeasies, a foretaste of the liberated nightlife that New Yorkers still enjoy today.

HARD TIMES

The fun times were not to last. The stock market crashed in 1929, beginning the Great Depression of the 1930s, which the city dealt with

---

NYC's Tallest Building

Woolworth Building (1913–1930)

Chrysler Building (1930–31)

Empire State Building (1931–1972 & 2001–present day)

World Trade Center (1972–2001)

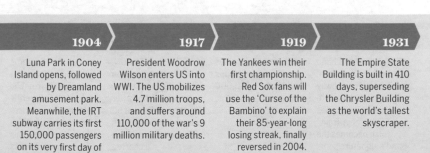

1904	**1917**	**1919**	**1931**
Luna Park in Coney Island opens, followed by Dreamland amusement park. Meanwhile, the IRT subway carries its first 150,000 passengers on its very first day of operation.	President Woodrow Wilson enters US into WWI. The US mobilizes 4.7 million troops, and suffers around 110,000 of the war's 9 million military deaths.	The Yankees win their first championship. Red Sox fans will use the 'Curse of the Bambino' to explain their 85-year-long losing streak, finally reversed in 2004.	The Empire State Building is built in 410 days, superseding the Chrysler Building as the world's tallest skyscraper.

through a combination of grit, endurance, rent parties, militancy and a slew of public-works projects. The once-grand Central Park blossomed with shacks, derisively called Hoovervilles, after the president who refused to help the needy. But Mayor Fiorello LaGuardia found a friend in President Franklin Roosevelt, and worked his Washington connections to great effect to bring relief money – and subsequent prosperity – home.

WWII brought troops galore to the city, ready to party down to their last dollar in Times Sq, before being shipped off to Europe. Converted to war industries, the local factories hummed, staffed by women and African American workers who had rarely before had access to these good unionized jobs. The explosion of wartime activity led to a huge housing crunch, which brought New York its much-imitated and tenant-protecting Rent Control Law.

But there were few evident controls on business, as Midtown bulked up with skyscrapers after the war. The financial center marched north, while banker David Rockefeller and his brother, Governor Nelson Rockefeller, dreamed up the Twin Towers to revitalize downtown.

ENTER ROBERT MOSES

Working with LaGuardia to usher the city into the modern age was Robert Moses, an urban planner who would influence the physical shape of the city more than anyone else in the 20th century – either wonderfully or tragically, depending on whom you ask. He was the mastermind behind the Triborough Bridge, Jones Beach State Park, the Verrazano-Narrows Bridge, the West Side Hwy and the Long Island parkway system – not to mention endless highways, tunnels and bridges, which shifted this mass-transit area into one largely dependent on the automobile. His vision was one of doing away with intimate neighborhoods of brownstones and townhouses and of creating sweeping parks and soaring towers. The approach got preservationists fired up and their efforts to stop him from bulldozing neighborhoods led to the Landmarks Preservation Commission being formed in 1965. His years of work were documented in the 1974 Pulitzer Prize–winning book *The Power Broker,* by Robert Caro, which portrayed Moses as an antipreservationist who had callously removed huge numbers of residents to make way for development. He responded with the following statement: 'I raise my stein to the builder who can remove ghettos without removing people as I hail the chef who can make omelets without breaking eggs.'

1941	1941–45	1945	1954
Duke Ellington's band leader Billy Strayhorn, inspired by the subway line that leads to Harlem, composes 'Take the A Train,' which becomes the band's signature song.	WWII: America deploys 16 million troops and suffers 400,000 deaths.	The UN, headquartered on Manhattan's east side, is established after representatives of 50 countries meet in San Francisco to agree on a charter.	The Supreme Court rules that segregation in public schools is 'inherently unequal' and orders desegregation 'with all deliberate speed.' This spurs the civil rights movement.

BEATS & GAYS

The '60s ushered in an era of legendary creativity and anti-establishment expression, with many of its creators centered right downtown in Greenwich Village. One movement was Abstract Expressionism, a large-scale outbreak of American painters – Mark Rothko, Jackson Pollock, Lee Krasner, Helen Frankenthaler and Willem de Kooning among them – who offended and intrigued with incomprehensible squiggles and blotches and exuberant energy. Then there were the writers, such as Beat poets Allen Ginsberg and Jack Kerouac or novelist/playwright Jane Bowles. They gathered in Village coffeehouses to exchange ideas and find inspiration, which were often found in the form of folk music from some burgeoning big names, such as Bob Dylan. It all created an environment that was ripe for rebellion – a task that gay revelers took on with gusto, finding their political strength and voice in fighting a police raid at the Stonewall Inn in 1969. The Stonewall Riots, as they are now known, showed the city and the world that the lesbian and gay community would not accept being treated as second-class citizens.

> New York City has 722 miles of subway tracks.

'DROP DEAD'

By the early 1970s, deficits had created a serious fiscal crisis, demoting elected Mayor Abraham Beame to a figurehead, and turning over the city's real financial power to Governor Carey and his appointees. President Ford's refusal to lend federal aid – summed up nicely by the *Daily News* headline 'Ford to City, Drop Dead!' – marked the nadir of relationships between the US and the city it loved to hate. As massive layoffs decimated the city's working class, untended bridges, roads and

---

THREE WOMEN WHO CHANGED NEW YORK

Margaret Sanger (1879–1966) A nurse, midwife and activist who opened the first birth-control clinic in the country in NYC in 1916. She founded the American Birth Control League, which would later become Planned Parenthood.

Jane Jacobs (1917–2006) Sprung into action against Robert Moses' plan to clear a huge tract of her neighborhood for public housing. She defended preservation and inspired the creation of the Landmarks Preservation Commission (the first such US group).

Christine Quinn (b 1967) The first woman – and open lesbian – to become City Council Speaker in 2006, breaking boundaries of both gender and sexuality, as the second-most powerful official (after the mayor) in NYC.

1963

The original Penn Station is demolished to build Madison Square Garden; public outcry leads to the foundation of the Landmarks Preservation Commission.

1965–75

US involvement in the Vietnam War tears the nation apart as 58,000 Americans die, along with four million Vietnamese and 1.5 million Laotians and Cambodians.

RICHARD CUMMINS / LONELY PLANET IMAGES ©

Madison Square Garden (p205)

parks reeked of hard times. Even the bond raters turned their thumbs down on New York's mountain of debt.

But the traumatic '70s – which reached a low point in 1977 with a citywide blackout and terrorizing serial killer Son of Sam – actually drove down rents for once. It helped to nourish an exciting alternative culture that staged performances in abandoned schools, opened galleries in unused storefronts and breathed new life into the hair-dye industry. The fees from shooting the movie *Fame* at PS 122 at 9th St and First Ave, for example, helped pay for the renovation of the still-popular performance space. Green-haired punks turned former warehouses into pulsing meccas of nightlife, transforming the former industrial precincts of SoHo and Tribeca. Immortalized in Nan Goldin's famous photographic performance piece *The Ballad of Sexual Dependency,* this renaissance bent gender roles into pretzels and turned the East Village into America's center of tattooing and independent filmmaking.

Forgotten-NY.com is Queens native Kevin Walsh's compendium of historic NYC, with not-found-elsewhere tales about everything from old subway stations to cemeteries.

OUT OF THE ASHES

Meanwhile, in South Bronx, a wave of arson reduced blocks of apartment houses to cinders. But amid the smoke, an influential hip-hop culture was born both here and in Brooklyn, fueled by the percussive rhythms of Puerto Rican salsa. Rock Steady Crew, led by 'Crazy Legs' Richie Colon, pioneered athletic, competitive break-dancing. Kool DJ Herc spun vinyl for break beat all-night dance parties, drawing on his Jamaican apprenticeship in appropriated rhythms. Afrika Bambaataa, another founding DJ of hip-hop, formed Zulu Nation, to bring DJs, break-dancers and graffiti writers together to end violence. Daring examples of the latter dazzled the public with their train-long graphics. Perhaps the best-known 'masterpiece' belied the graf writers' reputation as vandals: Lee 163, with the Fab 5 crew, painted a whole car of trains with the message 'Merry Christmas, New York.' Some of these maestros of the spray can infiltrated the art world, most notably Jean-Michel Basquiat, once known by his tag 'Samo,' who hung with Andy Warhol and sold with the big boys in the go-go art world of the 1980s.

Some of the easy money snagged in the booming stock markets of the 1980s was spent on art, but even more was blown up the noses of young traders. While Manhattan neighborhoods struggled with the spread of crack cocaine, the city reeled from the impact of addiction, citywide crime and an AIDS epidemic that cut through communities. Mayor Edward Koch could barely keep the lid on the city as homelessness burgeoned and landlords converted cheap, old single-room hotels into luxury apartments. Squatters in the East Village fought back when po-

1969	1973	1976–77	1977
American astronauts land on the moon, fulfilling President Kennedy's 1961 promise to accomplish this feat within a decade.	In Roe v. Wade, the Supreme Court legalizes abortion. Today, this decision remains controversial and socially divisive.	David Berkowitz, the 'Son of Sam' killer, says a demon in a dog told him to commit a string of murders around the city. He kills six and wounds seven others.	Following a lightning strike at a power substation, a summer blackout leaves New Yorkers in the dark for 24 sweltering hours, which leads to rioting around the city.

lice tried to clear a big homeless encampment, leading to the Tompkins Square Park riots of 1988. Hard to imagine that just a few years later, Manhattan would yet again become the shiny apple of prosperity's eye.

DOT-COM DAYS

A *Time* magazine cover in 1990 sported a feature story on 'New York: The Rotting Apple.' Still convalescing from the real-estate crash at the end of the 1980s, the city faced crumbling bridges and roads, jobs leaking south and Fortune 500 companies hopping the rivers to suburbia. And then the dot-com market roared in, turning geeks into millionaires and the New York Stock Exchange into a speculator's fun park. Buoyed by tax receipts from IPO (initial public offering) profits, the city launched a frenzy of building, boutiquing and partying unparalleled since the 1920s.

With pro-business, law-and-order Rudy Giuliani as mayor, the dingy and destitute were swept from Manhattan's yuppified streets to the outer boroughs, leaving room for Generation X to score digs and live the high life. Abrasive, aggressive and relentless, Mayor Giuliani grabbed headlines with his campaign to stamp out crime, even kicking the sex shops off notoriously seedy 42nd St. The energetic mayor succeeded in making New York America's safest large city, by targeting high-crime areas, using statistics to focus police presence, and arresting subway fare-evaders, people committing a minor infringement of city law but who often had other charges pending. So, in the 1990s, crime dropped, powering a huge appetite for nightlife in the city that never sleeps. Restaurants boomed in the spruced-up metropolis, Fashion Week gained global fame and *Sex and the City* beamed a vision of sophisticated singles in Manolos around the world.

Meanwhile, to the delight of unionized plumbers, electricians and carpenters, real-estate prices sizzled, setting off a construction spree of new high-rises, converted warehouses and rejuvenated tenements. Throwing off the uncertainty of the era of David Dinkins, a cautious politician who was NYC's first African American mayor, New Yorkers flaunted the new wealth. Areas of the Lower East Side that housed artist storefront galleries in the 1970s and '80s morphed overnight into blocks of gentrified dwellings with double-door security and maintenance charges equal to normal humans' take-home pay.

Those left behind seldom seemed to bother Mayor Giuliani. No new housing for ordinary people was built, but plenty of solid apartment stock disappeared from their rent rolls, as landlords converted rentals into pricey cooperative buildings. And yet the city's population grew

1980	1988	1989	2001
Gunman Mark David Chapman kills John Lennon in front of his home at the Dakota. Five years later, the Strawberry Fields memorial to Lennon is dedicated nearby in Central Park.	Crowds of squatters, who had turned the East Village's Tompkins Square Park into a massive homeless encampment, riot when cops attempt to forcibly remove them.	The 1960s-era Berlin Wall is torn down, marking the end of the Cold War between the US and the USSR (now Russia). The USA becomes the world's last remaining superpower.	On September 11, terrorist hijackers fly two planes into the Twin Towers, destroying the World Trade Center and killing nearly 2800 people.

and grew as ambitious young graduates flocked to the financial center. At the new Ellis Island – JFK airport – customs officials greeted wave after wave of Southeast Asians, South Americans and other immigrants who were willing to double up in cramped quarters in the outer boroughs. Still, things were faltering in New York at the dawn of the new millennium, and when that fateful day came in 2001, it forever changed the perspective of both the city and the world.

History on the Pages

The Historical Atlas of New York City: A Visual Celebration of 400 Years of New York City's History (Eric Homberger, 1998)

Gotham: A History of New York City to 1898 (Edwin G Burrows and Mike Wallace, 2003)

The Restless City: A Short History of New York from Colonial Times to the Present (Joanne Reitano, 2006)

Taxi! A Social History of the New York City Cabdriver (Graham Russell Gao Hodges, 2007)

New York (James Rutherford, 2009)

SEPTEMBER 11

September 11, 2001, was the day terrorists flew two hijacked planes into the World Trade Center's Twin Towers, turning the whole complex into dust and rubble and killing nearly 2800 people. Downtown Manhattan took months to recover from the ghastly fumes wafting from the ruins of the World Trade Center as forlorn missing-person posters grew ragged on brick walls. While recovery crews coughed their way through the debris, the city braved constant terrorist alerts and an anthrax scare to mourn the dead. Shock and grief drew people together, uniting the oft-fractious citizenry in a determined effort not to succumb to despair. Before the year was out, community groups were already gathering together in 'Imagine New York' workshops, to develop ideas for renewal and a memorial at the World Trade Center site.

THE NOUGHTS IN NEW YORK

The 10 years after 9/11 were a period of rebuilding – both physically and emotionally. In 2002, Mayor Michael Bloomberg began the unenviable task of picking up the pieces of a shattered city that had thrust all its support behind his predecessor, longtime controversial Mayor Rudy Giuliani, whose popularity rose after his reaction to September 11. Wrangling for his own rep, Bloomberg found his critics during his four-year campaign to build a huge sports arena atop the West Side Hwy, in order to bring the Jets back from Jersey and score a bid for the 2012 Olympic Games. All three failed after state capital Albany said 'no' to a $2.2 billion project (to the cheer of many a New Yorker fearing traffic build-up and cost), but Bloomberg didn't take a dent in the 2005 elections, comfortably topping Bronx Democrat Fernando Ferrer.

Much to Bloomberg's pleasure, however, New York did see a ton of renovation and reconstruction, especially after the city hit its stride with spiking tourist numbers in 2005. The MoMA was completely refurbished and by the latter part of Bloomberg's second term as mayor,

2002	2005	2008–9	2010
Gambino crime family boss John Gotti (the Dapper Don), dies of cancer in prison, while serving a sentence for murder, racketeering, tax evasion and other charges.	Following a feverish bid by the group NYC 2012, founded by local rich guy Daniel Doctoroff, the city loses its bid for the 2012 Olympics.	Barack Obama becomes the first African American president. Later, the stock market crashes due to mismanagement by major American financial institutions.	Mayor Michael Bloomberg is sworn into a third term after winning an election that he personally made possible by abolishing the local term-limits law.

the entire city seemed to be under construction, with luxury high-rise condos sprouting up in every neighborhood.

Soon the economy buckled under its own weight in what has largely become known as the global financial crisis. The city was paralyzed as the cornerstones of the business world were forced to close shop. Although much less hit than many pockets of the country, NYC still saw a significant dip in real-estate prices and many cranes turned to frozen monuments of a broken economy. Bloomberg amended the local constitution to allow for a third term, which he won in 2009 – but not by a landslide.

In 2011, the city celebrated the 10th anniversary of the 9/11 attacks with the opening of a remembrance center and as a half-built Freedom Tower – a new corporate behemoth – loomed overhead.

2011

The second phase of the High Line opens, effectively doubling its size. A third portion will encourage the redevelopment of industrial land in the West 30s.

COREY WISE / LONELY PLANET IMAGES ©

2013

Expected date of completion for One World Trade Center, commonly known as the Freedom Tower, erected on the land where the Twin Towers once stood

The High Line (p130)

The NYC Table

Unlike California, the South or even the Southwest, New York is never really referred to as having one defining cuisine. Ask for some 'New York food' and you could wind up getting anything from a hot dog to contemporary Jewish sharing plates or a $190 Gallic-inspired tasting menu at Le Bernardin.

Cuisine in this multicultural town is global by definition and constantly evolving by its very nature. That said, it's the edibles with the longest histories that folks usually have in mind when they refer to New York City specialties. Those at the top of the list – bagels and slices of pizza – were introduced by Eastern European Jews and Italians, because those groups were among the earliest wave of immigrants here. But it doesn't end there, with egg creams, cheesecake and spot-hitting hot dogs also uncontested staples of a New York feed.

FOOD SPECIALTIES

Hot Dogs

A derivative of sausage and one of the oldest forms of processed food, the hot dog goes back thousands of years, making its way to New York via various European butchers in the 1800s. One, Charles Feltman of Germany, was apparently the first to sell them from pushcarts along the Coney Island seashore. But Nathan Handwerker, originally an employee of Feltman's, opened his own shop across the street, offering hot dogs at half the price of those at Feltman's and putting his former employer out of business. Today, the original and legendary Nathan's still stands in Coney Island, while its empire has expanded on a national scale. And there is barely a New York neighborhood that does not have at least a few hot-dog vendors on its street corners, although some locals would never touch one of those 'dirty-water dogs,' preferring the new wave of chi-chi hot-dog shops that can be found all over town. Enjoy yours, wherever it's from, with 'the works': smothered with spicy brown mustard, relish, sauerkraut and onions.

Bagels

Bagels may have been invented in Europe, but they were perfected around the turn of the 19th century in New York City – and once you've had one here, you'll have a hard time enjoying one anywhere else. It's a straightforward masterpiece: a ring of plain-yeast dough that's first boiled and then baked, either left plain or topped with various finishing touches, from sesame seeds to chocolate chips. 'Bagels' made in other parts of the country are often just baked and not boiled, which makes them nothing more than a roll with a hole. And even if they do get boiled elsewhere, bagel-makers here claim that it's the New York water that adds an elusive sweetness never to be found anywhere else. Which baker creates the 'best' bagel in New York is a matter of (hotly contested) opinion, but most agree that Manhattan's Ess A Bagel and Absolute Bagel, Brooklyn's Bagel Hole and Queens' Brooklyn Bagel & Coffee Company rank pretty high. The most traditionally New York way to order one is by asking for a 'bagel and a

There's a plethora of books about NYC's culinary history. Top reads include William Grimes' *Appetite City: A Culinary History of New York*, Arthur Schwartz's *New York City Food: An Opinionated History and More Than 100 Legendary Recipes*, and *Gastropolis: Food & New York City*, edited by Annie Hauck Lawson & Jonathan Deutsch.

Bargain-savvy gastronomes love the biannual NYC Restaurant Week. Taking place in January to February and June to July, it sees many of the city's restaurants (including some of its best) serving up three-course meals at cut prices. Check www.nycgo.com/restaurantweek for details and reservations.

schmear,' which will yield you said bagel with a small but thick swipe of cream cheese. Or splurge and add some lox – thinly sliced smoked salmon – as was originally sold from pushcarts on the Lower East Side by Jewish immigrants back in the early 1900s.

Pizza

Pizza is certainly not indigenous to Gotham. But New York–style pizza is a very particular item and the first pizzeria in America, opened in 1905, was Lombardi's in Manhattan's Little Italy.

While Chicago-style pizza is 'deep dish' and Californian tends to be light and doughy, New York prides itself on pizza with a thin crust and an even thinner layer of sauce – and slices that are triangular (unless they're Sicilian-style, in which case they're rectangular). Pizza made its way over to New York in the 1900s through Italian immigrants and its regional style soon developed with a thin crust that allows for faster cooking time in a city where everyone's always in a hurry. Today there are pizza parlors about every 10 blocks, especially in Manhattan and most of Brooklyn, where you'll find standard slices for $3. The style at each place varies slightly – some places touting cracker-thin crust, others offering slightly thicker and chewier versions, and many selling nouveau styles with everything from shrimp to cherries on top.

Egg Creams

Now don't go expecting eggs or cream in this frothy, old-school beverage – just milk, seltzer water and plenty of chocolate syrup (preferably the classic Fox's U-Bet brand, made in Brooklyn). When Louis Auster of Brooklyn, who owned soda fountains on the Lower East Side, invented the treat back in 1890, the syrup he used was indeed made with eggs and he added cream to thicken the concoction.

The name stuck, even though the ingredients were modified, and soon the drink was were a staple of every soda fountain in New York. While Mr Auster sold them for 3¢ apiece, today they'll cost you anywhere from $1.50 to $4, depending on where you find one – which could be from old-school institutions such as Katz's Delicatessen in the Lower East Side or Tom's Restaurant in Brooklyn.

New York–Style Cheesecake

Sure, cheesecake, in one form or another, has been baked and eaten in Europe since the 1400s. But New Yorkers, as they do with many things, have appropriated its history in the form of the New York–style cheesecake.

Immortalized by Lindy's restaurant in Midtown, which was opened by Leo Lindemann in 1921, the particular type of confection served there – made of cream cheese, heavy cream, a dash of vanilla and a cookie crust – became wildly popular in the '40s. Today, you'll find this local favorite on many dessert menus, whether you're at a Greek diner or haute-cuisine hot spot. One of the city's best is the homemade strawberry cheesecake at Sarge's Deli in Midtown East – an absurdly rich, guilt-inducing revelation.

URBAN FARM TO TABLE

Having perfected the fast, New York City is rediscovering the slow. In recent years, a growing number of city rooftops, backyards and community gardens have been transformed into urban farms, turning America's biggest concrete jungle into an unlikely food bowl. While you can expect to find anything from organic tomatoes atop Upper

City Harvest (www.cityharvest.org) is a non-profit organization that distributes unused food to over 300,000 struggling New Yorkers each week. A whopping 83,000 pounds of food is rescued weekly from city restaurants, bakeries and catering companies.

East Side delis to beehives on East Village tenement rooftops, the current queen of the crop is Brooklyn Grange (www.brooklyngrangefarm. com) – a one-acre organic farm atop a Long Island City warehouse. Growing everything from carrots and beans to 40 varieties of tomatoes, it's purportedly the world's biggest rooftop farm and the brainchild of young farmer Ben Flanner. Obsessed with farm-to-table eating, this former E*Trade marketing manager kick-started NYC's rooftop revolution in 2009 with the opening of its first rooftop soil farm – Eagle Street Rooftop Farm – in nearby Greenpoint. Flanner's collaborators include some of the city's best-known restaurateurs, whose menus at hot spots like Brooklyn's Marlow & Sons, Diner and Roberta's make a point of showcasing this sustainable, homegrown produce. Helping propel this greening of New York's culinary scene is Mayor Michael Bloomberg, whose ecofriendly development plan for the city, PlaNYC 2030, includes an appetizing tax break for those who install green roofs.

DRINKS SPECIALTIES

Cocktails

New York City is a master of mixed libations. After all, this is the home of Manhattans, legendary speakeasies and Cosmo-clutching columnists with a passion for fashion. Legend has it that its namesake drink Manhattan – a blend of whiskey, sweet vermouth and bitters – began life on the southeast corner of 26th St and Madison Ave, at the long-gone Manhattan Club. The occasion was a party in 1874, thrown by Jennie Churchill (mother of British Prime Minister Winston) to celebrate Samuel J Tilden's victory in the New York gubernatorial election. Inspired, one of the barmen decided to create a drink to mark the occasion, naming it in honor of the bar.

Another New York classic was born that very year – the summer-centric Tom Collins. A mix of dry gin, sugar, lemon juice and club soda, the long drink's name stems from an elaborate hoax in which hundreds of locals were informed that a certain Tom Collins had been sullying their good names. While many set out to track him down, clued-in bartenders relished the joke by making the drink and naming it for the fictitious troublemaker. When the aggrieved stormed into the bars looking for a Tom Collins, they were served the drink to cool their tempers.

These days, NYC's kicking cocktail scene is big on rediscovered recipes, historical anecdotes and vintage speakeasy style. Once obscure bartenders like Harry Johnson and Jerry Thomas are now born-again legends, their vintage concoctions revived by a new generation of braces-clad mixologists. Historic ingredients like Crème de Violette, Old Tom gin and Batavia Arrack are back in vogue, as are single-spirit establishments, among them tequila- and mezcal-focused Mayahuel in the East Village and the self-explanatory Rum House in Midtown. The latter is known for its stash of the legendary Black Tot – a rare, last-consignment rum produced by the Royal British Navy (and yours for around $250 a pour).

Brooklyn Amber

The city's growing obsession with all things locavore includes its liquid amber. Beer brewing was once a thriving industry in the city – by the 1870s, Brooklyn boasted a belly-swelling 48 breweries. Most of these were based in Williamsburg, Bushwick and Greenpoint, neighborhoods packed with German immigrants with extensive brewing know-how. By the eve of Prohibition in 1919, the borough was one of the country's

NYC Master Chef Cookbooks

The Babbo Cookbook (Mario Batali)

Asian Flavors of Jean-Georges (Jean-Georges Vongerichten)

Urban Italian (Andrew Carmellini & Gwen Hyman)

Momofuku (David Chang & Peter Meehan)

The first public brewery in America was established by colonial governor Peter Minuit (1580–1638) at the Market (Marckvelt) field in what is now known as the Financial District in Lower Manhattan. Minuit is credited with 'purchasing' Manhattan from the native Lenape people in May 1626.

THE COFFEE LOWDOWN

Adam Craig, co-owner of specialty coffee shop Culture Espresso (p198), in Midtown talks about coffee.

What drove you to open a coffee shop in Manhattan?

Back home in Australia, great coffee is almost a birthright. While Brooklyn has a few good coffee shops, much of the joe across NYC is low grade. Beans are often roasted and stored in warehouses for three to six months, meaning that by the time they're used, they're stale. Also, a lot of people making the coffee here don't often have a real respect for it. The machines get dirty and they're not cleaned.

Culture Espresso aside, what are your coffee shop recommendations?

In Manhattan, definitely try Ninth Street Espresso (Map p442) in the East Village, Third Rail (240 Sullivan St) in the West Village and Stumptown (p198) in Midtown. In Brooklyn, top specialty spots include my former cafe Variety in Greenpoint, Cafe Peddler in Carroll Gardens, and Williamsburg's pioneering Cafe El Beit. Williamsburg is also home to San Franciscan roaster Blue Bottle Coffee (p285). In Astoria, Queens, head to Queens Kickshaw (p308).

What do the coffee cognoscenti drink?

Most commonly, espresso-machine drinks made using single-origin coffee; coffee sourced from a specific geographic region. African-sourced coffee is a little more citrus-like, South American varieties are nuttier and more full-bodied, while Asian coffee often has 'blueberry' and 'chocolate' coming through. Non-espresso drinks include the light-bodied 'pour over,' in which coffee is extracted through a cone over two-and-a-half to three minutes, and the 'Chemex coffee,' another filtered variety whose tea-like consistency highlights the subtler nuances of the beans.

And on a hot day?

Wised-up New Yorkers opt for a 'cold brew,' prepared using two different methods. The first, known as 'full immersion,' is made by steeping coarsely ground coffee in water for 16 hours to create a concentrate. The concentrate is then brought back with water to create a drink that's full-bodied, chocolatey and low in acidity. The second method, called 'Kyoto cold drip,' sees coffee passed through a ceramic filter at about one drop every two seconds for 16 to 18 hours. The result, served on ice, is super concentrated and akin to drinking cognac.

leading beer peddlers, as famous for kids carrying growlers (beer jugs) as for its bridges and hot dogs. By the end of Prohibition in 1933, most breweries had shut shop. And while the industry rose from the ashes in WWII, local flavor gave in to big-gun Midwestern brands.

Fast-forward to today and Brooklyn is once more a catchword for a decent brewski as a handful of craft breweries put integrity back on tap. Leading the charge is Brooklyn Brewery (p269), whose seasonal offerings include its Post Road Pumpkin Ale (available August to November) and a luscious Black Chocolate Stout (a take on Imperial Stout, available October to March). The brewery's top comrades-in-craft are Sixpoint Craft Ales (www.sixpoint.com) and Kelso of Brooklyn (www.kelsoofbrooklyn.com), both of which also offer year-round classics and seasonal treats. Beer nuts can savor the flavor across the city, at craft-versed drinking holes like Brooklyn's Prime Meats and 61 Local, and Manhattan's Keg 229.

The Arts

The spectacles of Broadway. The gleaming white-box galleries of Chelsea. Joints playing jazz, music halls blaring moody indie rock and opera houses that stage melodramatic tales about star-crossed lovers. For more than a century, NYC has been the capital of cultural production in the US. And while gentrification has pushed many artists out to the city's fringes and beyond, New York nonetheless remains a vital center for the visual arts, music, theater, dance and literature. And for the visitor, there's an endless stream of things to see and do.

THE BIRTH OF AN ARTS CENTER

When it comes to almost all facets of the arts, New York really got its sea legs in the early 20th century, when the city attracted and retained a critical mass of thinkers, artists, writers and poets. It was at this time that the homegrown art scene began to take shape. In 1905, photographer Alfred Stieglitz opened 'Gallery 291,' a Fifth Ave space that provided a vital platform for American artists and helped establish photography as a credible art form.

In the 1940s, an influx of cultural figures fleeing the carnage of WWII saturated the city with fresh ideas – and NYC became an important cultural hub. Peggy Guggenheim established the Art of This Century gallery on 57th St, a space that helped launch the careers of painters like Jackson Pollock, Willem De Kooning and Robert Motherwell. These Manhattan-based artists came to form the core of the Abstract Expressionist movement – also known as the New York School – creating an explosive and rugged form of painting that changed the course of modern art as we know it.

On any given week, New York is home to countless art exhibits, installations and performances. Get a comprehensive listing of happenings at www.artcat. com and www. nyartbeat.com.

An American Avant-Garde

The Abstract Expressionists helped establish New York as a global arts center, then another generation of artists carried the ball. In the 1950s and '60s, Robert Rauschenberg, Jasper Johns and Lee Bontecou began creating sculpture constructions, from welded steel to taxidermy goats. By the mid-'60s, pop art – a movement that utilized the imagery and production techniques of popular culture – had taken hold, with Andy Warhol at the helm.

By the '60s and '70s, when New York's economy was in the dumps and much of SoHo lay in a state of decay, the city became a hotbed of conceptual and performance art. Gordon Matta-Clark sliced up abandoned buildings with chainsaws and the artists of Fluxus staged happenings on downtown streets. Carolee Schneeman organized performances that utilized the human body. At one famous 1964 event, she had a crew of nude dancers roll around in an unappetizing mix of paint, sausages and dead fish in the theater of a Greenwich Village church. It was art on the cutting edge.

Art in the Present

Today, the arts scene is mixed and wide-ranging. The major institutions – the Metropolitan Museum of Art, the Museum of Modern Art, the Whitney Museum, the Guggenheim Museum and the Brooklyn Museum – show major retrospectives covering everything from Renaissance portraiture to contemporary installation. The New Museum, on the Lower East Side, is more daring. And countless smaller institutions, like the Bronx Museum, El Museo del Barrio and the Studio Museum in Harlem, focus on narrower pieces of art history. (Don't underestimate these latter places. They may be small, but the programming is excellent.)

The gallery scene is equally diffuse, with more than 800 galleries showcasing all kinds of art all over the city. The blue chip dealers can be found clustered in Chelsea and the Upper East Side. Spaces that showcase emerging and mid-career artists have settled into the Lower East Side. And the most experimental happenings generally take place in Bushwick, in old warehouses and basements.

Graffiti & Street Art

Contemporary graffiti as we know it – the hyper-saturated text pieces that boast a writer's nickname – was a phenomenon that was cultivated in New York. In the 1970s, the graffiti-covered subway train became a potent symbol of the city and work by figures like Dondi, Blade and Lady Pink became known around the world. In addition, fine artists such as Jean-Michel Basquiat, Kenny Scharf and Keith Haring began incorporating elements of graffiti into their work.

The movement received new life in the late 1990s when a new generation of artists – many with art school pedigrees – began using materials such as cut paper and sculptural elements (all illicitly). Well-known New York City artists working in this vein include John Fekner, Stephen 'Espo' Powers, Swoon and the twin-brother duo Skewville. A good spot to see graffiti is the Brooklyn side of the Williamsburg Bridge.

A RICH MUSIC LEGACY

This is the city where jazz players like Ornette Coleman, Miles Davis and John Coltrane pushed the limits of improvisation in the '50s. It's where various Latin sounds – from cha-cha-cha to rumba to mambo – came together to form the hybrid we now call *salsa*, where folks singers like Bob Dylan and Joan Baez crooned protest songs in coffeehouses, and where bands like the New York Dolls and the Ramones tore up the stage in Manhattan's gritty downtown. It was the ground zero of disco. And it was the cultural crucible where hip-hop was nurtured and grew – then exploded.

The city remains a magnet for musicians to this day. The local indie rock scene is especially vibrant: groups like the Yeah Yeah Yeahs, LCD Soundsystem, Animal Collective and Clap Your Hands Say Yeah all emerged out of New York. Williamsburg is at the heart of the scene – two neighborhoods with copious clubs and bars, as well as indie record labels and internet radio stations. The best venues for rock include the Music Hall of Williamsburg and the Brooklyn Bowl (bowling and music in one place!) – as well as Bowery Ballroom in Manhattan.

All That Jazz

Jazz, too, remains a juggernaut – from the traditional to the experimental. The best bets for jazz are the Village Vanguard (p151) and the Jazz Standard (p242). For more highbrow programming, there's Jazz at Lincoln Center, which is run by trumpeter Wynton Marsalis and features a wide array of solo outings by important musicians, as well as tribute concerts to figures such as Dizzy Gillespie and Thelonious Monk.

Brooklyn has a hopping indie music scene, with local bands performing regularly in Williamsburg and Bushwick. To hear the latest sounds, log on to www.newtown radio.com.

INDIE

A NEW YORK HIP-HOP PLAYLIST

NYC is the cradle of hip-hop. Classics from artists from the city include the following:

'Rapper's Delight,' by the Sugarhill Gang (1979) The single that launched the commercial birth of hip-hop, from a trio of New York–New Jersey rappers.

'White Lines,' by Grand master Flash and the Furious Five (1983) The ultimate '80s party song from a Bronx group.

'It's Like That,' by Run DMC (1983) That's the way it is for the legendary Queens trio.

'Fat Boys,' by the Fat Boys (1984) Brooklyn's ultimate beat-boxers.

'No Sleep 'Til Brooklyn,' by the Beastie Boys (1986) An NYC trio who bravely fought for their right to party.

'Ain't No Half Steppin','by Big Daddy Kane (1988) Mellifluous rhymes from a Brooklyn master.

'Shoop,' by Salt-n-Pepa (1994) The Queens of Rap hail from Queens.

'Juicy,' by Notorious BIG (1994) One of rap's most iconic figures grew up in Bed-Stuy, Brooklyn.

'In Da Club,' by 50 Cent (2003) This global party hit was produced by a rapper from South Jamaica, Queens.

'99 Problems,' by Jay-Z (2004) One of Bed-Stuy's bright stars is now a major music mogul.

Countless other venues around the city cater to a world of tastes: cabaret, bluegrass, country, Latin rap, R&B, Mexican regional music and Colombian *cumbias*. Your ears will never be starved for attention.

Classical & Opera

You'll find the classics at Lincoln Center. Here, the Metropolitan Opera puts on a wide array of well-known operas, from Verdi's *Aida* to Mozart's *Don Giovanni*. It is also here that the legendary New York Philharmonic is based (the symphony that was once directed by one of the 20th century's great maestros, Leonard Bernstein). In any given season, you can hear an array of masterworks being performed. Carnegie Hall, the Merkin Concert Hall and the Frick Collection also offer wonderful – and more intimate – spaces to enjoy great classical music.

For more avant-garde fare, try the New York City Opera, the Center for Contemporary Opera and the Brooklyn Academy of Music (BAM) – the latter is now one of the city's vital opera and classical music hubs. Another excellent venue, featuring highly experimental work, is St Ann's Warehouse in Brooklyn.

For comprehensive coverage of the American jazz scene, log on to www.jazztimes. com, which features plenty of stories about all the established and rising New York acts.

ON BROADWAY

In the early 20th century, clusters of theaters settled into the area around Times Square and began producing popular plays and suggestive comedies – a movement that had its roots in early vaudeville. By the 1920s, these messy works had evolved into on-stage spectacles like *Show Boat*, an all-out Oscar Hammerstein production about the lives of performers on a Mississippi steamboat. In 1943, Broadway had its first runaway hit – *Oklahoma!* – that remained on stage for a record 2212 performances.

Today, Broadway musicals are a major component of cultural life in New York – shown in one of 40 official Broadway theaters, the lavish early 20th-century jewels that surround Times Square. If you're on a budget, look for off-Broadway productions. These tend to be more intimate and inexpensive, and are often just as good.

For the cheapest tickets (mostly on the day of the performance), visit the TKTS Booths in Midtown (p178) and Lower Manhattan (p57).

OTHER PERFORMANCE

From Shakespeare to David Mamet to rising experimental playwrights like Suzan-Lori Parks, New York has plenty of offerings when it comes to the stage. In addition to Broadway, the Lincoln Center theaters are hubs for works by modern and contemporary playwrights. The Joseph Papp Public Theater, BAM, Performance Space 122 and St Ann's Warehouse all offer edgier programming. Numerous festivals, such as the Fringe Festival (p27), also show new work.

Dance

For nearly 100 years, the city has been at the center of American dance. The American Ballet Theatre (ABT), led by the fabled George Balanchine, was founded here in 1949. The company promoted the idea of cultivating American talent, hiring native-born dancers and putting on works by choreographers such as Jerome Robbins, Twyla Tharp and Alvin Ailey. The company still performs in New York and around the world.

But the city is perhaps best known for nurturing a generation of modern dance choreographers – figures like Martha Graham, who were challenging traditional notions of dance with boxy, industrial movements on bare, almost abstract sets. (No flittering ballerinas here.) The boundaries were pushed ever further by Merce Cunningham, who disassociated dance from music. Today, companies like Elizabeth Streb's Extreme Action company are pushing dance to its physical and gymnastic limits.

Lincoln Center and BAM host regular performances, and up-and-coming acts can be seen at the Kitchen (p152), Joyce Theater (p153), the Dance Theater Workshop (p153) and the Baryshnikov Arts Center.

At http://theater. nytimes.com, you can use the 'Show Tuner' app to find theatrical works that suit your taste and mood. They also keep comprehensive theater listings.

New York in Letters

The city that is home to the country's biggest publishing houses has also been home to some of its best-known writers. In the 19th century, Herman Melville (*Moby Dick*), Edith Wharton (*The House of Mirth*) and Walt Whitman (*Leaves of Grass*) all congregated here. But – as with all things New York City – things really got cooking in the early part of the 20th century. There were the liquor-fueled literary salons of poet-communist John Reed in the 1910s, the acerbic wisecracks of the Algonquin Round Table in the 1920s and the thinly-veiled novels of Dawn Powell in the '40s, a figure whose work often critiqued New York's media establishment.

The 1950s and '60s saw the rise of writers who began to question the status quo, be it literary or political. Poet Langston Hughes examined the condition of African Americans in Harlem and Beat poets like Allen Ginsburg rejected traditional rhyme in favor of free-flowing musings. The last decades of the 20th century offered myriad styles, including chronicler of the greed- and coke-fueled '80s (Jay McInerney) to voices from underrepresented corners of the city (Piri Thomas, Audre Lorde).

These days, New York writers continue to cover a vast array of realities in their work – from zombies (Colson Whitehead) and postmodern narrative techniques (Jennifer Egan), to the crazy impossibility that is New York (Michael Chabon). Hint: pick up a copy of *The Amazing Adventures of Kavalier & Clay*.

The New York Public Library and BAM both host widely-attended lectures and readings.

Architecture

New York's architectural history is a layer cake of ideas and styles – one that is literally written on the city's streets. Humble colonial farmhouses and graceful Federal-style buildings can be found alongside ornate beaux arts palaces from the early 20th century. There are the revivals (Greek, Gothic, Romanesque and Renaissance) and the unadorned forms of the International Style. And, in recent years, there has been the addition of the torqued forms of deconstructivist architects. For the architecture buff, it's a bonanza.

COLONIAL FOUNDATIONS

New York's architectural roots are modest. Early Dutch colonial farmhouses were all about function: clapboard wooden homes with shingled, gambrel roofs were positioned to take advantage of daylight and retain heat in winter. A number of these have somehow survived to the present. The most remarkable is the Pieter Claesen Wyckoff House in East Flatbush, Brooklyn. Originally built in 1652 (with additions made over the years), it is the oldest house in the entire city.

After the Dutch colony of New Netherlands became the British colony of New York in 1664, architectural styles moved to Georgian. Boxy brick and stone structures with hipped roofs began to materialize. In the northern Manhattan district of Inwood, the Morris-Jumel Mansion from 1765 is an altered example of this: the home was built in the Georgian style by Roger Morris, then purchased by Stephen Jumel, who added a neo-Classical facade in the 19th century. Another British colonial building of interest is the Fraunces Tavern, near the South Street Seaport, where George Washington bid an emotional farewell to the officers who had accompanied him throughout the American Revolution. Today the structure contains a museum and a restaurant.

On the ceremonial end is St Paul's Chapel, just south of City Hall Park. Built in the 1760s, it's the oldest surviving church in the city, and it's considered the oldest building in NYC still in continuous use. Its design was inspired by the much bigger St Martin-in-the-Fields church in London.

AIA Guide to New York, 5th Edition. A comprehensive guide to the most significant buildings in the city.

ARCHITECTURE IN THE EARLY REPUBLIC

In the early 1800s, architecture grew lighter and more refined. The so-called Federal style employed classical touches – slim, columned entrances, triangular pediments at the roof line and rounded fanlights over doors and windows. Some of the best surviving examples of these are tied to municipal government. City Hall, built in 1812, owes its French form to émigré architect Joseph François Mangin and its Federal detailing to American-born John McComb Jr. The interior contains an airy rotunda and curved cantilevered stairway.

Uptown, on the Upper East Side, Gracie Mansion (1799), the official residence of New York City's mayor since 1942, offers a fine example of a Federal residence, with its broad, river-view porch and leaded glass sidelights.

This stretch of riverfront was once lined with buildings of the sort – a sight that impressed Alexis de Tocqueville during his tour of the United States in the early 19th century.

Other Federal-style specimens include the James Watson House (1793), at 7 State Street right across from Battery Park, and the Merchant's House Museum (1832), in Greenwich Village. The latter still contains its intact interiors.

THE GREEK REVIVAL

Following the publication of an important treatise on Greek architecture in the late 1700s, architects began to show a renewed interest in pure, Classical forms. In the US, a big instigator of this trend was Minard Lafever, a New Jersey-born carpenter-turned-architect-turned-author-of-pattern-books. By the 1830s, becolumned Greek Revival structures were going up all over New York.

Manhattan contains a bevy of these buildings, including the gray granite St Peter's Church (1838) and the white-marble Federal Hall National Memorial (1842) – both of which are located in the Financial District. In Greenwich Village, a row of colonnaded homes built on the north side of Washington Square (Numbers 1–13) in the 1820s are fine residential interpretations of this style.

GOTHIC REVIVAL & ROMANESQUE

Starting in the late 1830s, the simple Georgian and Federalist styles started to give way to more ornate structures that employed Gothic and Romanesque elements. This was particularly prominent in church construction. An early example of this was the Church of the Ascension (1841) in Greenwich Village – an imposing brownstone structure studded with pointed arches and a crenelated tower. The same architect – Richard Upjohn – also designed downtown Manhattan's Trinity Church (1842) in the same style. In this category, the Church of St Ann & the Holy Trinity, at 157 Montague St in Brooklyn Heights, is also worthwhile. Interestingly, it was designed by Lafever (who, when he wasn't doing Greek Revival, was going neo-Goth).

By the 1860s, these places of worship were growing in size and scale. Among some of the most resplendent are St Patrick's Cathedral (1853–1879), which took over an entire city block at Fifth Ave and 51st St, and the perpetually under construction Cathedral Church of St John the Divine (1911–41), in Morningside Heights. The style was so popular that one of the city's most important icons – the Brooklyn Bridge (1870–83) – is built in a Gothic Revival style. It boasts heavy stone towers and pointed arches – a symbol of the city itself.

Romanesque elements (such as curved arches) can be spotted on structures all over the city. Some of the most famous include the Joseph Papp Public Theater (formerly the Astor Library) in Greenwich Village, built between 1853 and 1881, and the breathtaking Temple Emanu-El (1927–29) on Fifth Ave on the Upper East Side.

For a comprehensive history on the design and construction of one of NYC's most iconic structures, pick up John Tauranac's *The Empire State Building: Making of a Landmark*.

THE BEAUTY OF BEAUX ARTS

At the turn of the 20th century, New York entered a gilded age. Robber barons such as JP Morgan, Henry Clay Frick and John D Rockefeller – awash in steel and oil money – built themselves lavish manses. Public buildings grew ever more extravagant in scale and ornamentation.

Architects, many of whom trained in France, came back with European ideals of design. Gleaming white limestone began to replace all the brownstone, first stories were elevated to allow for dramatic staircase entrances and buildings began to be laced with sculptured keystones and Corinthian columns. For a while, it seems that nothing was built in New York unless it was in the beaux arts style.

McKim Mead & White's Villard Houses, from 1884 (now the Palace Hotel), show the movement's early roots. Loosely based on Rome's Palazzo della Cancelleria, they channeled the symmetry and elegance of the Italian Renaissance. Other classics include the central branch of the New York Public Library (1911) designed by Carrère and Hastings, the 1902 extension of the Metropolitan Museum of Art by Richard Morris Hunt, and Warren & Wetmore's stunning Grand Central Station (1913), which is capped by a statue of Mercury, the god of commerce.

Esteemed New York architecture critic Ada Louise Huxtable gathers some of her most important essays in the book *On Architecture: Collected Reflections on a Century of Change.*

REACHING SKYWARD

By the time New York settled into the 20th century, elevators and steel-frame engineering had allowed the city to grow up – literally. This period saw a building-boom of skyscrapers, starting with Cass Gilbert's neo-Gothic 57-storey Woolworth Building (1913). To this day it remains one of the 50 tallest buildings in the United States.

Others soon followed. In 1930, the Chrysler Building, the 77-storey art deco masterpiece designed by William Van Alen, became the world's tallest structure. The following year, the record was broken by the Empire State Building, a clean-lined art deco monolith crafted from Indiana limestone. Its spire was meant to be used as mooring mast for dirigibles – an idea that made for good publicity, but which proved to be impractical and unfeasible.

MODERNISM & BEYOND

During WWII, the city became the center of everything. Displaced European architects and other thinkers landed here in advance of the Nazi invasion. When the war was over, many chose to remain in the US, creating a lively dialogue between American and European architects. This was a period when urban planner Robert Moses was furiously rebuilding vast swathes of New York (to the detriment of many neighborhoods) and designers and artists became obsessed with the clean, unadorned lines of the International Style.

Public Art: New York by Jean Parker Phifer, with photos by Francis Dzikowski, is an informative guide to the city's public monuments.

One of the earliest projects in this vein were the UN buildings (1947–52), the combined effort of a committee of architects, including the Swiss-born Le Corbusier, Brazil's Oscar Niemeyer and America's Wallace K Harrison. The Secretariat employed New York's first glass curtain wall – which looms over the ski-slope curve of the General Assembly. Other significant Modernist structures from this period include Gordon Bunshaft's Lever House (1950–52), a floating, glassy structure on Park Ave and 54th St, and Mies van der Rohe's austere, 38-storey Seagram Building (1956–59), located just two blocks to the south.

While these designs remain elegant, the glut in glass-box architecture resulted in a million lookalike buildings. By the late 20th century, some architects began to rebel against the hard-edged nature of Modernist design. In 1984, Philip Johnson – a figure who created more than his share of glass boxes over the course of his career – produced the pink granite AT&T Building (now the Sony Building), capping its roofline with a scrolled, neo-Georgian pediment. It's not universally loved, but it can most certainly be picked out of the crowd.

NEW YORK'S MUST-SEE BUILDINGS

Chrysler Building (p183) Manhattan's most elegant skyscraper boasts steel ornamentation inspired by the automobile, including gargoyles that are shaped like retro hood ornaments.

Beekman Tower (Map p416) Frank Gehry has added a luminous, undulating skyscraper to Manhattan's downtown skyline. (Too bad the rippling effect was not continued on the back side of the building.)

Cooper Union for the Advancement of Science & Art (7 East 7th St, NoHo) A steel mass that looks as if it were about to split in two from some unseen seismic force. With this structure, New York stepped firmly into the future.

Grand Central Terminal (p187) A classic beaux arts stunner, with an airy concourse capped by vaulted ceilings decorated with an astronomical pattern.

Morris-Jumel Mansion (p258) Harkening back to the colony, this whitewashed Georgian/Federal building recalls a time when northern Manhattan was nothing but rolling estates.

Empire State Building (p185) Like a martini, a good steak and jazz, this Depression-era skyscraper never ever gets old.

Temple Emanu-el (p218) This imposing Romanesque synagogue on the Upper East Side has ceilings that are painted in gold.

New Museum of Contemporary Art (p103) A stacked-cube structure by SANAA has a translucent aluminum exterior that is all kinds of sexy (even if the galleries have a detention-center vibe).

New York Times Tower (Map p438) Renzo Piano's ceramic tube-draped tower may look bland in the daylight, but at dusk, when the interior lights can be seen from the street, it's as if the grey lady is shedding her clothes.

Whitney Museum of American Art (p217) Modernism doesn't get more brutal than this: Marcel Breuer's inverted staircase structure looks like the very well-designed lair of an action movie baddie. Bring it on.

BRING ON THE STARCHITECTS

The types of non-rectilinear deconstructivist buildings (as in Frank Gehry's billowy museum in Bilbao) that began to appear in other parts of the world in the mid-1990s were late getting to New York. Between the tight spaces, expensive real estate and labyrinthine nature of zoning and construction, it is a wonder that anything gets built at all. A prime example of this is the former World Trade Center site, where Daniel Libeskind's twisting, angular tower has been replaced by a boxier architecture-by-committee glass obelisk. And Santiago Calatrava's luminous design for the local transportation hub remains little more than a very ethereal rendering.

That said, the last five years have begun to see the arrival of some daring additions. The earliest of these was Norman Foster's Hearst Tower (2006) at Eighth Ave and 57th St, a glass tower that zigzags its way out of an art deco sandstone structure built in the 1920s. Others have followed, including Renzo Piano's New York Times Building (2007), a 52-storey building armored in ceramic rods, and Gehry's IAC Building (2007), a billowing white-glass structure that the locals like to compare to a wedding cake. (The High Line Park, by the way, offers excellent views of the Gehry Building, from the vicinity of 18th and 19th Sts.)

In 2009, the city saw the completion of various notable structures. These include Jean Nouvel's 100 Eleventh Ave, a Chelsea apartment building that boasts of an exuberant arrangement of angled windows, and Cook + Fox's Bank of America Tower at Bryant Park, an elegant, torqueing structure that has broken away from the boring corporate headquarters trend. The year's most avant-garde building, however, came courtesy of California architect Thom Mayne of Morphosis, whose academic center for the Cooper Union in the Village resembles nothing less than an earthquake in motion.

Gehry added another of his rippling forms to the city skyline in 2011 – the Beekman Tower, in downtown Manhattan. But all eyes will now be on the rising structures at the former World Trade Center site in downtown Manhattan. Whether it will be critically acclaimed or beloved remains to be seen. But the structures are certainly in keeping with New York, a city that is continually rebuilding its past.

Painting the Town Pink

New York City is out and damn proud. It was here that the Stonewall Riots took place, that the modern gay rights movement bloomed and that America's first Pride march hit the streets. Yet even before the days of 'Gay Lib', the city had a knack for all things queer and fabulous, from Bowery sex saloons and Village Sapphic poetry to drag balls in Harlem. It hasn't always been smooth sailing, but it's always been one hell of a gripping ride.

BEFORE STONEWALL
Subversion in the Villages

By the 1890s, New York City's rough-and-ready Lower East Side had established quite a reputation for scandalous 'resorts' – dancing halls, saloons and brothels – frequented by the city's 'inverts' and 'fairies'. From Paresis Hall at 5th St and Bowery to Slide at 157 Bleecker St, these venues offered everything from cross-dressing spectaculars and dancing to backrooms for same-sex shenanigans. For closeted middle-class men, these dens were a secret thrill – places reached undercover on trains for a fix of camaraderie, understanding and uninhibited fun. For curious middle-class straights, they were just as enticing – salacious destinations on voyeuristic 'slumming tours.'

As New York strode into the 20th century, writers and bohemians began stepping into Greenwich Village, lured by the area's cheap rents and romantically crooked streets. The area became known for unconventionality and free thinking, which turned the Village into an Emerald City for gays and lesbians, a place with no shortage of bachelor pads, more tolerant attitudes and – with the arrival of Prohibition – an anything-goes speakeasy scene. A number of gay-owned businesses lined MacDougall St, among them the legendary Eve's Hangout at number 129. A tearoom run by Polish Jewish immigrant Eva Kotchever (Eve Addams), it was famous for two things: poetry readings and a sign on the door that read 'Men allowed but not welcome.' There would have been little chance of welcome drinks when police raided the place in June 1926, charging Eve with 'obscenity' for penning her Lesbian Love anthology, and deporting her back to Europe. Three years later, Eve was honored by a Greenwich Village theater group, who staged a theatrical version of her book at Play Mart, a basement performance space on Christopher St.

GLBT IN HISTORY

1927
New York State amends a public-obscenity code to include a ban on the appearance or discussion of gay people onstage in reaction to the increasing visibility of gays on Broadway.

1966
On April 21, gay rights organization Mattachine Society stages a 'Sip-In' at the city's oldest gay drinking hole, Julius Bar, challenging New York's ban on serving alcohol to GLBT people.

1969
Eight police officers raid the Stonewall Inn in Greenwich Village in the early hours of June 28, sparking a mass riot that lasts several days and gives birth to the modern gay rights movement.

1987
ACT UP is founded to challenge the US government's slow response in dealing with AIDS. The activist group stages its first major demonstration on March 24 on Wall St.

2011
New York's Marriage Equality Act comes into effect at 12.01am on July 24. A lesbian couple from Buffalo take their vows just seconds after midnight in Niagara Falls.

Divas, Drag & Harlem

While Times Square had also developed a reputation for attracting gay men – many of them working in the district's theaters, restaurants and speakeasy bars – the hottest gay scene in the 1920s was further north in Harlem. The neighborhood's flourishing music scene included numerous gay and lesbian performers, among them Gladys Bentley and Ethel Waters. Bentley – who was as famous for her tuxedos and girlfriends as she was for her singing – had moved her way up from one-off performances at cellar clubs and tenement parties to headlining a revue at the famous Ubangi Club on 133rd St, where her supporting acts included a chorus line of female impersonators.

Even more famous were Harlem's drag balls, which had become a hit with both gay and straight New Yorkers in the Roaring Twenties. The biggest of the lot was the Hamilton Lodge Ball, organized by Lodge #710 of the Grand United Order of Odd Fellows and held annually at the swank Rockland Palace on 155th St. Commonly dubbed the Faggot's Ball, it was a chance for both gay men and women to (legally) cross-dress and steal a same-sex dance, and for fashionable 'normals' to indulge in a little voyeuristic titillation. The evening's star attraction was the beauty pageant, which saw the drag-clad competitors compete for the title of 'Queen of the Ball.' Langston Hughes proclaimed it the 'Spectacles of color' and the gay writer was one of many members of New York's literati to attend the ball. It was also attended by everyone from prostitutes to high-society families, including the Astors and the Vanderbilts. Even the papers covered the extravaganza, its outrageous frocks the talk of the town.

America's first gay-rights rally was held in New York City in 1964. Organized by the Homosexual League of New York and the League for Sexual Freedom, the picket took place outside the Army Induction Center on Whitehall Street, where protestors demanded an end to the military's anti-gay policies.

STONEWALL REVOLUTION

Alas, the relative transgression of the early 20th century was replaced with a new conservatism in the following decades, as the Great Depression, WWII and the Cold War took their toll. Conservatism was helped along by senator Joseph 'Joe' McCarthy, who declared that homosexuals in the State Department threatened America's security and children. Tougher policing aimed to eradicate queer visibility in the public sphere, forcing the scene further underground in the 1940s and '50s. Although crackdowns on gay venues had always occurred, they became increasingly common.

When, in the early hours of June 28, 1969, eight police officers raided the Stonewall Inn – a gay-friendly watering hole in Greenwich Village – patrons did the unthinkable: they revolted. Fed up with both the harassment and corrupt officers receiving payoffs from the bars' owners (who were mostly organized crime figures), they began bombarding the officers with coins, bottles, bricks and chants of 'Gay power' and 'We shall overcome'. They were also met by a line of high-kicking drag queens and their now legendary chant, 'We are the Stonewall girls, we wear our hair in curls, we wear no underwear, we show our pubic hair, we wear our dungarees, above our nelly knees...' Although police reinforcements dispersed the crowd, the protestors were back more resolute and in greater numbers in the following days.

In the days of raids and outward gay oppression, undercover police were better known as Betty Badge, Lily Law or Alice Blue Gown in gay parlance.

Their collective anger and solidarity was a turning point, igniting intense and passionate debate about discrimination and forming the catalyst for the modern gay rights movement, not just in New York, but across the US and in countries from the Netherlands to Australia. A year later, on June 28, 1970, America's first gay march took place in the city. Departing from Christopher St, its planned end point was 14th St, but verbal abuse from more hostile members of the public strengthened the marchers' resolve, leading them up to 34th St and on to Central Park. In June 1999, the Stonewall Inn building, Christopher St and the surrounding streets were declared a National Historic Landmark.

IN THE SHADOW OF AIDS

While the Stonewall riots set the wheels in motion for slow but resolute positive change, LGBT activism intensified as HIV and AIDS hit world headlines in the early 1980s. Faced with ignorance, fear and the moral indignation of those who saw AIDS as a 'gay cancer,' activists like writer Larry Kramer set about tackling what was quickly becoming an epidemic. Out of his efforts was born ACT UP (AIDS Coalition to Unleash Power) in 1987, an advocacy group set up to fight the perceived homophobia and indifference of then President Ronald Reagan, as well as to end the price gouging of AIDS drugs by pharmaceutical companies. One of its boldest protests took place on September 14, 1989, when seven ACT UP protestors chained themselves to the VIP balcony of the New York Stock Exchange, demanding pharmaceutical company Burroughs Wellcome lower the price of AIDS drug AZT from a prohibitive $10,000 per patient per annum. Within days, the price was slashed to $6400 per patient.

A Chorus Line was the first musical to highlight a gay narrative. The show debuted at the Shubert Theatre in 1975, running for 15 years.

The epidemic itself had a significant impact on New York's artistic community, with some of its most brilliant creative talent lost to the disease. Among its most high-profile victims were artist Keith Haring, photographer Robert Mapplethorpe and fashion designer Halston. Yet out of this loss grew a tide of powerful AIDS-related plays and musicals that would not only win broad international acclaim, but would become part of America's mainstream cultural canon. Among these are Tony Kushner's political epic *Angels in America* and Jonathan Larson's rock musical *Rent*, the latter a contemporary reinterpretation of Puccini's opera *La Bohème*. Both works would win Tony Awards and the Pulitzer Prize.

MARRIAGE & THE NEW MILLENNIUM

The GLBT fight for complete equality took two massive steps forward in 2011. On September 20, a federal law banning GLBT military personnel from serving openly – the so-called 'Don't Ask, Don't Tell' policy – was repealed after years of intense lobbying. Three months earlier persistence had led to an even greater victory – the right to marry. It was on June 15, by a margin of 80 to 63, that the New York State Assembly passed the Marriage Equality Act. On 24 June, the very eve of New York City Gay Pride, it was announced that the Act would be considered as the final bill of the legislative session. Considered and amended, the bill was approved by a margin of 33 to 29 and signed into law at 11.55pm by New York Governor Andrew Cuomo. The Senate had rejected a similar bill by a margin of 24 to 38 in December 2009.

Queer Screen Classics

The Boys in the Band (1970)

Torch Song Trilogy (1988)

Paris is Burning (1990)

Jeffrey (1995)

Angels in America (2003)

Divided Opinion

The 2011 victory ignited immediate jubilation in the state's capital Albany, in the surrounding streets and on New York City's Christopher St, where 42 years earlier, angry crowds had begun the fight for equal rights. In the Twitter-sphere, celebrities shared their own elation, from Kathy Griffin's 'Tonight we're all New Yorkers! Straight & gay alike, let's all celebrate marriage #equality. The right side of history!' to Lady Gaga's 'The revolution is ours to fight for love, justice+equality. Rejoice

GLBT Reads

Dancer from the Dance (Andrew Holleran)

Last Exit to Brooklyn (Hubert Selby)

Another Country (James Baldwin)

City Boy (Edmund White)

NY, and propose.' Veteran comedian Steve Martin got in on the act too, proposing to fellow actor Alec Baldwin. Baldwin, one of several high-profile New Yorkers who had voiced support for the bill, replied: 'Ok. But if you play that effing banjo after eleven o'clock...'

Less elated were those who had condemned the proposed bill. Among the most prolific of these were New York State Senator Rubén Díaz, the only Democratic senator to oppose the bill, and New York Archbishop Timothy Dolan, who had described the bill as an 'ominous threat' to society. Equally devastated was Maggie Gallagher, then chairperson of the National Organization for Marriage (NOM), a non-profit organization established in 2007 to fight same-sex marriage. Yet even their disapproval could not tarnish the history-making day of July 24, 2011, when the Marriage Equality Act officially kicked in and Buffalo grandmothers Kitty Lamert, 54, and Cheryle Rudd, 53, became New York's first wedded same-sex couple.

NYC on Screen

New York City has a long and storied life on screen. It was on these streets that a bumbling Woody Allen fell for Diane Keaton in *Annie Hall*, that Meg Ryan faked her orgasm in *When Harry Met Sally* and that Sarah Jessica Parker philosophized about the finer points of dating and Jimmy Choos in *Sex and the City*. To fans of American film and television, traversing the city can feel like one big déjà vu of memorable scenes, characters and one-liners.

HOLLYWOOD ROOTS & RIVALS

Believe it or not, America's film industry is an East Coast native. Fox, Universal, Metro, Selznick and Goldwyn all originated here in the early 20th century, and long before Westerns were shot in California and Colorado, they were filmed in the (now former) wilds of New Jersey. Even after Hollywood's year-round sunshine lured the bulk of the business west by the 1920s, 'Lights, Camera, Action' remained a common call in Gotham.

The Kaufman Astoria Legacy

The heart of the local scene was Queens' still-kicking Kaufman Astoria Studios. Founded by Jesse Lasky and Adolph Zukor in 1920 as a one-stop shop for their Famous Players–Lasky Corporation, the complex would produce a string of silent-era hits, among them *The Sheik* (1921) and *Monsieur Beaucaire* (1924), both starring Italian-born heartthrob Rudolph Valentino, and *Manhandled* (1924), starring early silver-screen diva Gloria Swanson. Renamed Paramount Pictures in 1927, the studios became known for turning Broadway stars into big-screen icons, among them the Marx Brothers, Fred Astaire and Ginger Rogers, the latter making her feature-film debut as a flapper in *Young Man of Manhattan* (1930).

Despite Paramount moving all of its feature film shoots to Hollywood in 1932, the complex – renamed Eastern Services Studio – remained the home of Paramount's newsreel division. Throughout the 1930s, it was also known for its 'shorts,' which launched the careers of homegrown talent like George Burns, Bob Hope and Danny Kaye. After a stint making propaganda and training films for the US Army between WWII and 1970, what had become known as the US Signal Corps Photographic Center was renamed the Kaufman Astoria Studios by George S Kaufman (the real estate agent, not the playwright) in 1983. Modernized and expanded, the studio has gone on to make a string of flicks, including *All that Jazz* (1979), *Brighton Beach Memoirs* (1986), *The Stepford Wives* (2004) and *Men in Black III* (2012). It was here that the Huxtables lived out their middle-class Brooklyn lives in '80s TV sitcom *The Cosby Show,* and it's still here that small-screen favorites *Sesame Street* and *Gossip Girl* are taped.

Beyond Astoria

But Kaufman Astoria Studios is not alone, with numerous film and TV studios across New York City. Slap bang in the historic Brooklyn Navy Yard, the 15-acre Steiner Studios is the largest studio complex outside Hollywood. Its film credits to date include *The Producers* (2005), *Revolutionary Road* (2008), *Sex & the City* 1 and 2 (2008, 2010), and *Mr Popper's Penguins* (2011). The studios have also been used for numerous TV shows, among them *Pan Am* and Martin Scorsese's critically acclaimed gangster drama *Boardwalk Empire*. Back in Queens you'll find the city's other big gun, Silvercup Studios. Its list of features include NYC classics like Francis Ford

Metro Goldwyn Mayer's famous 'Leo the Lion' logo was designed by Howard Dietz. His inspiration was the mascot of New York's Columbia University, where the publicist had studied journalism. Leo's famous roar was first added to films in 1928.

Coppola's *The Godfather: Part III* (1990) and Woody Allen's *Broadway Danny Rose* (1984) and *The Purple Rose of Cairo* (1985). Its TV gems include mafia drama *The Sopranos* and the equally lauded comedy *30 Rock*, the latter starring Tina Fey as a TV sketch writer and Alec Baldwin as a network executive at the Rockefeller Center.

In reality, the Rockefeller Center is home to the NBC TV network, its long-running variety show *Saturday Night Live* the real inspiration behind Fey's *30 Rock* project. Other media networks dotted across Manhattan include the Food and Oxygen Networks, both housed in the Chelsea Market, as well as Miramax and Robert De Niro's Tribeca Productions, the latter two based in the Tribeca Film Center.

Beyond the studios and headquarters are some of the top film schools – New York University's (NYU) Tisch Film School, the New York Film Academy, the School of Visual Arts, Columbia University and the New School. But you don't have to be a student to learn, with both the Museum of the Moving Image in Astoria, Queens, and the Paley Center for Media in Midtown Manhattan acting as major showcases for screenings and seminars about productions both past and present.

The infamous subway grill scene in *The Seven Year Itch* (1955) – in which Marilyn Monroe enjoys a dress-lifting breeze – was shot at 586 Lexington Ave, outside the since-demolished Trans-Lux 52nd Street Theatre.

LIGHTS, LANDMARKS, ACTION!

Downtown Drama to Midtown Romance

It's not surprising that NYC feels strangely familiar to many first-time visitors – the city itself has racked up more screen time than most Hollywood divas put together and many of its landmarks are as much a part of American screen culture as its red-carpet celebrities. Take the Staten Island Ferry, which takes bullied secretary Melanie Griffiths from suburbia to Wall St in *Working Girl* (1988); Battery Park, where Madonna bewitches Aidan Quinn and Rosanna Arquette in *Desperately Seeking Susan* (1985); or the New York County Courthouse, where villains get their just deserts in *Wall St* (1987) and *Goodfellas* (1989), as well as in small-screen classics like *Cagney & Lacey*, *NYPD Blue* and *Law & Order*. The latter show, famous for showcasing New York and its characters, is honored with its own road – Law & Order Way – which leads to Pier 62 at Chelsea Piers.

Few landmarks can claim as much screen time as the Empire State Building, famed for its spire-clinging ape in *King Kong* (1933, 2005), as well as for the countless romantic encounters on its observation decks. One of its most famous scenes is Meg Ryan and Tom Hanks' after-hours encounter in *Sleepless in Seattle* (1993). The sequence – which uses the real lobby but a studio-replica deck – is a tribute of sorts to *An Affair to Remember* (1959), which sees Cary Grant and Deborah Kerr make a pact to meet and (hopefully) seal their love atop the skyscraper.

In 1965, an up-and-coming Barbra Streisand filmed a short segment for her TV special *My Name is Barbra* at Bergdorf Goodman. Arriving at night, she gallivants through the upmarket department store, camping it up for the camera while singing *Second Hand Rose*, a tongue-in-cheek reference to her love of thrift-store threads.

Sarah Jessica Parker is less lucky in *Sex and the City* (2008), when a nervous Chris Noth jilts her and her Vivienne Westwood wedding dress at the New York Public Library. Perhaps he'd seen *Ghostbusters* (1984) a few too many times, its opening scenes featuring the haunted library's iconic marble lions and Rose Main Reading Room. The library's foyer sneakily stands in for the Metropolitan Museum of Art in *The Thomas Crown Affair* (1999), in which thieving playboy Hugh Grant meets his match in sultry detective Rene Russo. It's at the fountain in adjacent Bryant Park that DIY sleuth Diane Keaton debriefs husband Woody Allen about their supposedly bloodthirsty elderly neighbor in *Manhattan Murder Mystery* (1993). True to form, Allen uses the film to showcase a slew of New York locales, among them the National Arts Club in Gramercy Park and one of his own former hangouts, Elaine's at 1703 Second Ave. It's here, at this since-closed Upper East Side restaurant,

FILM CLASSICS SHORTLIST

It would take volumes to cover all the films tied to Gotham, so fire up the imagination with the following classics.

Taxi Driver (Martin Scorsese, 1976) Starring Robert De Niro, Cybill Shepherd and Jodie Foster. De Niro is a mentally unstable Vietnam War vet whose violent urges are heightened by the city's tensions. It's a funny, depressing, brilliant classic that's a potent reminder of how much grittier this place used to be.

Manhattan (Woody Allen, 1979) Starring Woody Allen, Diane Keaton and Mariel Hemingway. A divorced New Yorker dating a high-school student (the baby-voiced Hemingway) falls for his best friend's mistress in what is essentially a love letter to NYC. Catch romantic views of the Queensboro Bridge and the Upper East Side.

Summer of Sam (Spike Lee, 1999) Starring John Leguizamo, Mira Sorvino and Jennifer Esposito. Spike Lee puts NYC's summer of 1977 in historical context by weaving together the Son of Sam murders, the blackout, racial tensions and the misadventures of one disco-dancing Brooklyn couple, including scenes at CBGB and Studio 54.

Angels in America (Mike Nichols, 2003) Starring Al Pacino, Meryl Streep and Jeffrey Wright. This movie version of Tony Kushner's Broadway play recalls 1985 Manhattan: crumbling relationships, AIDS out of control and a closeted Roy Cohn – advisor to President Ronald Reagan – doing nothing about it except falling ill himself. Follow characters from Brooklyn to Lower Manhattan to Central Park.

Party Monster (Fenton Bailey, 2003) Starring Seth Green and Macauley Culkin, who plays the famed, murderous club kid Michael Alig, this is a disturbing look into the drug-fueled downtown clubbing culture of the late '80s. The former Limelight club is featured prominently.

Precious (Lee Daniels, 2009) Based on the Novel Push by Sapphire. This unflinching tale of an obese, illiterate teenager who is abused by her parents takes place in Harlem, offering plenty of streetscapes and New York–ghetto 'tude.

that Keaton explains her crime theory to Allen and dinner companions Alan Alda and Ron Rifkin. The restaurant was a regular in Allen's films, also appearing in *Manhattan* (1979) and *Celebrity* (1998).

Across Central Park – whose own countless scenes include Barbra Streisand and Robert Redford rowing on its lake in clutch-a-Kleenex *The Way We Were* (1973) – stands the Dakota Building (1 W 72nd St at Central Park West), used in the classic thriller *Rosemary's Baby* (1968). The Upper West Side is also home to Tom's Restaurant (Broadway at 112th St), whose facade was used regularly in *Seinfeld*. Another neighborhood star is the elegant Lincoln Center, where Natalie Portman slowly loses her mind in the psychological thriller *Black Swan* (2010), and where love-struck Brooklynites Cher and Nicolas Cage meet for a date in *Moonstruck* (1987). The Center sits on what had previously been a rundown district of tenements, captured in Oscar-winning gangland musical *West Side Story* (1961).

Dancing in the Streets

Knives make way for leotards in the cult musical *Fame* (1980), in which New York High School of Performing Arts students do little for the city's traffic woes by dancing on Midtown's streets. The film's graphic content was too much for the city's Board of Education, who banned shooting at the real High School of Performing Arts, then located at 120 W 46th St. Consequently, filmmakers used the doorway of a disused church on the opposite side of the street for the school's entrance, and Haaren Hall (Tenth Ave and 59th St) for interior scenes.

In 2011, a record-breaking 23 TV series were being filmed in NYC. The city's TV industry, worth $5 billion, supports over 100,000 jobs and over a third of professional actors in the country are based here.

NYC Film Festivals

Dance on Camera
(January)

New York International Children's Film Festival
(March)

Tribeca Film Festival (April)

Human Rights Watch International Film Festival (June)

NewFest: LGBT Film Festival (July)

New York Film Festival (September/ October)

Fame and *West Side Story* are not alone in turning Gotham into a pop-up dance floor. In *On the Town* (1949), starstruck sailors Frank Sinatra, Gene Kelly and Jules Munshin look straight off a Pride float as they skip, hop and sing their way across this 'wonderful town,' from the base of Lady Liberty to Rockefeller Plaza and the Brooklyn Bridge. Another wave of campness hits the bridge when Diana Ross and Michael Jackson cross it in *The Wiz* (1978), a bizarre take on the Wizard of Oz, complete with munchkins in Flushing Meadows Corona Park and an Emerald City at the base of the WTC Twin Towers. That same year, the bridge provided a rite of passage for a bellbottomed John Travolta in *Saturday Night Fever* (1978), who leaves the comforts of his adolescent Brooklyn for the bigger, brighter mirror balls of Manhattan. Topping them all, however, is the closing scene in Terry Gilliam's *The Fisher King* (1991), which sees Grand Central Terminal's Main Concourse turned into a ballroom of waltzing commuters.

Location Tours

The best way to find all the spots you want to see is to take a movie- or TV-location guided tour, such as On Location Tours (p394), which takes you to spots where your favorite films and TV shows were filmed, including *The Devil Wears Prada*, *Spider-Man*, *How I Met Your Mother* and more. Or you can do it yourself after visiting the Mayor's Office of Film Theatre & Broadcasting (www.nyc.gov/film) website to check out the interactive 'Scenes from the City' map and download the 'Made in NY: Walking Tours of Film and TV Locations in New York City' podcasts.

Survival Guide

Transportation

GETTING TO NEW YORK CITY

With its three bustling airports, two train stations and a monolithic bus terminal, New York City rolls out the welcome mat for the more than 50 million visitors who come to take a bite out of the Big Apple each year.

Direct flights are possible from most major American and international cities. Figure six hours from Los Angeles, seven hours from London and Amsterdam, and 14 hours from Tokyo. Consider getting here by train instead of car or plane to enjoy a mix of bucolic and urban scenery en route, without unnecessary traffic hassles, security checks and excess carbon emissions.

Flights, tours and rail tickets can be booked online at lonelyplanet.com/bookings.

John F Kennedy International Airport

John F Kennedy International Airport (JFK; ☑718-244-4444; www.panynj. gov), 15 miles from Midtown in southeastern Queens, has eight terminals, serves 45 million passengers annually and hosts flights coming and going from all corners of the globe. Major renovations have been in progress for several years, including the AirTrain link with the subway (and free service between terminals).

If you go with Jet Blue, you fly from the gorgeous ex-TWA terminal (now Terminal 5), designed by Finnish architect Eero Saarinen in 1962.

Taxi

A yellow taxi from Manhattan to the airport will use the meter; prices (often about $55) depend on traffic – it can take 45 to 60 minutes. From JFK, taxis charge a flat rate of $45 to any destination in Manhattan (not including tolls or tip); it can take 45 to 60 minutes for most destinations in Manhattan.To/from a destination in Brooklyn, the metered fare should be about $35 to $45.

Car Service

Car services have set fares from $45. Note that the Williamsburg, Manhattan, Brooklyn and Queensboro-59th St Bridges have no toll either way, while the Queens-Midtown Tunnel and the Brooklyn-Battery Tunnel cost $6.50 going into Manhattan.

Private Vehicle

If you're driving from the airport, either go around Brooklyn's south tip via the Belt Parkway to US 278 (the Brooklyn-Queens Expressway; BQE), or via US 678 (Van Wyck Expressway) to US 495 (Long Island Expressway; LIE), which heads into Manhattan via the Queens-Midtown Tunnel (all tunnels are free leaving Manhattan). Often the Manhattan or Wil-

liamsburg Bridges are just as easy to use – and free.

Express Bus

The New York Airport Service Express Bus costs $15.50.

Subway

Take either the A line (bound for Rockaway Beach) to Howard Beach–JFK Airport station, or the E, J or Z line or the Long Island Rail Road to Sutphin Blvd–Archer Ave (Jamaica Station), where you can catch the AirTrain to JFK. (The E express from Midtown has the fewest stops.) The overpriced AirTrain finishes the tail end of a long trip for $5 one way; you can use a MetroCard to swipe yourself in. Expect it to take at least 90 minutes from Midtown.

LaGuardia Airport

Used mainly for domestic flights, **LaGuardia** (LGA; ☑718-533-3400; www.panynj. gov) is smaller than JFK but only eight miles from midtown Manhattan; it sees about 26 million passengers per year. It has been open to commercial use since 1939, making it considerably older, too. US Airways and Delta have their own terminals.

Taxi

A taxi to/from Manhattan costs about $40 for the approximately half-hour ride.

CLIMATE CHANGE & TRAVEL

Every form of transport that relies on carbon-based fuel generates CO_2, the main cause of human-induced climate change. Modern travel is dependent on airplanes, which might use less fuel per kilometer per person than most cars but travel much greater distances. The altitude at which aircraft emit gases (including CO_2) and particles also contributes to their climate change impact. Many websites offer 'carbon calculators' that allow people to estimate the carbon emissions generated by their journey and, for those who wish to do so, to offset the impact of the greenhouse gases emitted with contributions to portfolios of climate-friendly initiatives throughout the world. Lonely Planet offsets the carbon footprint of all staff and author travel.

Car Service

A car service to LaGuardia costs $35.

Express Bus

The New York Airport Service Express Bus costs $10 to $13.

Private Vehicle

The most common driving route from the airport is along Grand Central Expressway to the BQE (US 278), then to the Queens-Midtown Tunnel via the LIE (US 495). Downtown-bound drivers can stay on the BQE and cross (free) via the Williamsburg Bridge.

Subway/Bus

It's less convenient to get to LaGuardia by public transportation than the other airports. The best subway link is the 74th St–Broadway station (7 line, or the E, F, G, R, V lines at the connecting Jackson Hts–Roosevelt Ave station) in Queens, where you can take the Q33, Q47 or Q48 bus to the airport (about 30 minutes by bus). You can also take the 4/5/6 line to connect to the M60 bus, which runs east along Harlem's 125th St and often takes more than an hour in traffic.

Newark Liberty International Airport

Don't write off New Jersey when looking for airfares to New York. About the same distance from Midtown as JFK (16 miles), **Newark's airport** (EWR; ☑973-961-6000; www.panynj.gov) brings many New Yorkers out for flights (there's around 36 million passengers annually). It became the metropolis' first major airport in 1928.

Car Service/Taxi

A car service runs about $45 to $60 for the 45-minute ride from Midtown – a taxi is roughly the same. You'll have to pay $8 to get into NYC through the Lincoln (at 42nd St) and Holland (at Canal St) Tunnels and, further north, the George Washington Bridge, though there's no charge going back through to NJ. There are a couple of cheap tolls on New Jersey highways, too, unless you ask your driver to take Highway 1 or 9.

Subway/Train

Public transportation to Newark is convenient, but a bit of a rip-off. NJ Transit runs rail service (with an AirTrain connection) between Newark airport (EWR) and New York's Penn Station for a shocking $12.50 each way (hardly worth it if you're traveling with a couple of others). The trip uses a commuter train, takes 25 minutes and runs every 20 or 30 minutes from 4:20am to about 1:40am. Hold onto your ticket, which you must show upon exiting at the airport. A clumsier, 'stick-it-to-the-man' alternative is riding NJ Transit from New York's Penn Station to Newark's Penn Station ($4 one way), then catching bus 62 (every 10 or 20 minutes) for the 20-minute ride to the airport ($1.35).

Express Bus

The Newark Liberty Airport Express has a bus service between the airport and Port Authority Bus Terminal, Bryant Park and Grand Central Terminal in Midtown ($15 one way). The 45-minute ride goes every 15 minutes from 6:45am to 11:15pm (and every half hour from 4:45am to 6:45am and 11:15pm to 1:15am).

Bus

For long-distance bus trips, you'll leave and depart from the world's busiest bus station, the **Port Authority Bus Terminal** (☑212-564-8484; www.panynj.gov; 41st St at Eighth Ave), which sees nearly 60 million passengers pass through each year. Bus companies leaving from here include the following:

Greyhound (☑800-231-2222; www.greyhound.com) Connects New York with major cities across the country.

New Jersey Transit (☑800-772-2287; www.njtransit.com) Serves New Jersey; its 319 bus goes 10 or 12 times daily to Atlantic City (round trip $39).

Peter Pan Trailways

(☎800-343-9999; www.peter panbus.com) Daily express service to Boston (one-way/round-trip $14/28), Washington, DC ($17/34) and Philadelphia ($9/18).

ShortLine Bus

(☎20 1-529-3666, 800-631-8405; www.shortlinebus.com) Goes to northern New Jersey and upstate New York (Rhinebeck for $25.30, Woodbury Common for $21).

Budget Buses

A growing number of budget bus lines operate from locations just outside **Penn Station** (☎212-582-6875, 800-872-7245; W 33rd St btwn Seventh & Eighth Aves):

BoltBus (☎877-265-8287; www.boltbus.com) Notable for its free wi-fi, BoltBus travels from New York to Philadelphia, Boston, Baltimore and Washington, DC (all from $8). Buses to DC and Baltimore leave from the northeast corner of 33rd and Seventh Ave; buses to Philadelphia and Boston leave from 34th St and Eighth Ave, northwest corner.

Megabus (☎1877-462-6342; http://us.megabus.com) Also offering free wi-fi, Megabus travels between New York and Boston (from $1), Washington, DC (from $1) and Toronto ($39), among other destinations.

Vamoose (☎212-695-6766, 877-393-2828; www.vamoose bus.com) Sends buses to Arlington, Virginia (one-way $30), near Washington, DC. Buses leave from 255 W 31st St.

Chinatown Buses

Crazy and cheap, Chinatown buses depart from pushy 'sidewalk terminals' at various points around Canal St to Boston, Philadelphia, Washington, DC, and other areas on the East Coast. There are no seat reservations; often on weekends you may have to wait for the next bus, an hour later.

Fung Wah (☎212-925-8889; www.fungwahbus.com; 139 Canal St at Bowery) Fung Wah offers hourly departures to Boston ($15) from 7am to 10pm or 11pm.

2000 New Century

(www.2001bus.com; Allen St btwn Broome & Grand Sts) 2000 New Century goes almost half-hourly from 7am to 11pm to Philadelphia ($12) and a bit less often to DC ($20).

Train

Penn Station (☎212-582-6875, 800-872-7245; W 33rd St btwn Seventh & Eighth Aves)

Amtrak (☎800-872-7245; www.amtrak.com) Trains leave from Penn Station, including the Metroliner and Acela Express services to Princeton, NJ, and Washington, DC (note that both these express services will cost twice as much as a normal fare). All fares vary, based on the day of the week and the time you want to travel. There is no baggage-storage facility at Penn Station.

Long Island Rail Road (LIRR; ☎718-217-5477; www.mta.nyc.ny.us/lirr; round-trip $14) The Long Island Rail Road serves some 280,000 commuters each day, with services from Penn Station to points in Brooklyn and Queens, and on Long Island. Prices are broken down by zones. A peak-hour ride from Penn Station to Jamaica Station (en route to JFK via AirTrain) costs $8.25 if you buy it online (or a whopping $15 onboard!).

New Jersey Transit (☎800-772-2287; www.njtransit.com) Also operates trains from Penn Station, with services to the suburbs and the Jersey Shore.

New Jersey PATH (☎800-234-7284; www.panynj.gov/path) Another option for getting into NJ's northern points, such as Hoboken and Newark. Trains ($1.75) run from Penn Station along the length of Sixth Ave, with stops at 33rd, 23rd, 14th, 9th and Christopher Sts, as well as at the reopened World Trade Center site.

Metro-North Railroad (☎212-532-4900; www.mta.info/mnr) The last line departing from Grand Central Terminal, the Metro-North Railroad serves Connecticut, Westchester County and the Hudson Valley.

Boat

If you're arriving in NYC by yacht, there are ports at an exclusive boat slip at the World Financial Center and a long-term slip at the **79th St Boathouse** on the Upper West Side.

GETTING AROUND NEW YORK CITY

Once you've arrived in NYC, getting around is fairly easy. The 660-mile subway system is cheap and (reasonably) efficient and can whisk you to nearly every hidden corner of the city. There are also buses, ferries, trains, pedicabs and those ubiquitous yellow taxis (though don't expect to see many available when it's raining) for zipping around and out of town when the subway simply doesn't cut it.

The sidewalks of New York, however, are the real stars in the transportation scheme - this city is made for walking. Increasingly, it's also made for bicycles, with the addition of hundreds of miles of new bike lanes and greenways over the last few years.

Subway & Buses

The New York subway's 660-mile system, run by the **Metropolitan Transportation Authority** (MTA; 718-330-1234; www.mta.info), is iconic, cheap ($2.50 for a SingleRide, $2.25 if using MetroPass), round-the-clock and easily the fastest and most reliable way to get around the city. It's also safer and (a bit) cleaner than it used to be (and now has overly cheerful automated announcements on some lines).

It's a good idea to grab a free map, available from any attendant. When in doubt, ask someone who looks like they know what they're doing. They may not, but subway confusion (and consternation) is the great unifier in this diverse city. And if you're new to the underground, never wear headphones when you're riding, as you might miss an important announcement about track changes or skipped stops.

Metrocards for Travelers

New York's classic subway tokens now belong to the ages: today all buses and subways use the yellow-and-blue **MetroCard** (718-330-1234; www.mta.info/metrocard), which you can purchase or add value to at one of several easy-to-use automated machines at any station. You can use cash or an ATM or credit card. Just select 'Get new card' and follow the prompts.

There are two types of MetroCard. The 'pay-per-ride' is $2.25 per ride, though the MTA tacks on an extra 7% bonus on Metro-Cards over $10. (If you buy a $20 card, you'll receive $21.70 worth of credit.) If you plan to use the subway quite a bit, you can also buy an 'unlimited ride' card ($29 for a seven-day pass). These

---

SUBWAY CHEAT SHEET

A few tips for understanding the madness of the New York underground follows:

Numbers, Letters, Colors

Color-coded subway lines are named by a letter or number, and most carry a collection of two to four trains on their tracks. For example, the red-colored line in Manhattan is the 1, 2, 3 line; these three separate trains follow roughly the same path in Manhattan, then branch out in the Bronx and Brooklyn.

Express & Local Lines

A common mistake is accidentally boarding an 'express train' and passing by a local stop you want. Know that each color-coded line is shared by local trains and express trains; the latter make only select stops in Manhattan (indicated by a white circle on subway maps). For example, on the red line, the 2 and 3 are express, while the slower 1 makes local stops. If you're covering a greater distance – say from the Upper West Side to Wall St – you're better off transferring to the express train (usually just across the platform from the local) to save time.

Getting in the Right Station

Some stations – such as SoHo's Spring St station on the 6 line – have separate entrances for downtown or uptown lines (read the sign carefully). If you swipe in at the wrong one – as even crusty locals and certain LP researchers do on occasion – you'll either need to ride the subway to a station where you can transfer for free, or just lose the $2.25 and re-enter the station (usually across the street). Also look for the green and red lamps above the stairs at each station entrance; green means that it's always open, while red means that particular entrance will be closed at certain hours, usually late at night.

Lost Weekend

All the rules switch on weekends, when some lines combine with others, some get suspended, some stations get passed, others get reached. Locals and tourists alike stand on platforms confused, sometimes irate. Check the www.mta.info website for weekend schedules. Sometimes posted signs aren't visible until after you reach the platform.

WALKING

Screw the subway and the cabs and buses, the personal jet-pack and the hot-air balloon you packed in your bag – get on your feet and go green. New York, down deep, can't be seen until you've taken the time to hit the sidewalks: the whole thing, like Nancy Sinatra's boots, is made for pedestrian transport. Broadway runs the length of Manhattan, about 13.5 miles. Crossing the East River on the pedestrian planks of the Brooklyn Bridge is a New York classic. Central Park trails can get you to wooded pockets where you can't even see or hear the city.

For some self-guided walking tours, see the neighborhood walks in the individual Explore chapters.

cards are handy for travelers – particularly if you're jumping around town to a few different places in one day.

Note that the MetroCard works for buses as well as subways (and offers free transfers between them).

Taxi

Hailing and riding in a cab are rites of passage in New York – especially when you get a driver who's a neurotic speed demon, which is often. (A word of advice: don't forget to buckle your seatbelt.) Still, most taxis in NYC are clean and, compared to those in many international cities, pretty cheap.

The **Taxi Limousine & Commission** (TLC; ☎311), the taxis' governing body, has set fares for rides (which can be paid with credit or debit card). It's $2.50 for the initial charge (first one-fifth of a mile), 40¢ each additional one-fifth mile as well as per 60 seconds of being stopped in traffic. There is also a $1 peak surcharge (weekdays 4pm to 8pm), and a 50¢ night surcharge (8pm to 6am), plus a new NY State surcharge of 50¢ per ride. Tips are expected to be 10% to 15%, but give less if you feel in any way mistreated – and be sure to ask for a receipt and use it to note the driver's license number.

The TLC keeps a Passenger's Bill of Rights, which gives you the right to tell the driver which route you'd like to take, or ask your driver to stop smoking or turn off an annoying radio station. Also, the driver does not have the right to refuse you a ride based on where you are going.

To hail a cab, look for one with a lit (center) light on its roof. It's particularly difficult to score a taxi in the rain, at rush hour and around 4pm, when many drivers end their shifts.

Private car services are a common taxi alternative in the outer boroughs. Fares differ depending on the neighborhood and length of ride, and must be determined beforehand, as they have no meters. Though these 'black cars' are quite common in Brooklyn and Queens, never get into one if a driver simply stops to offer you a ride – no matter what borough you're in. A couple of car services in Brooklyn include **Northside** (☎718-387-2222; 207 Bedford Ave) in Williamsburg and **Arecibo** (☎718-783-6465; 170 Fifth Ave at Degraw St) in Park Slope.

Ferry

New York Water Taxi (☎212-742-1969; www.nywatertaxi.com; hop-on-hop-off service 1-day $26) has a fleet of zippy yellow boats that provide an interesting alternative way of getting around. Boats run along several different routes, including a hop-on, hop-off weekend service around Manhattan and Brooklyn. NY Water Taxi also runs year-round commuter service connecting a variety of locations in Manhattan, Queens and Brooklyn.

Another bigger, brighter ferry (this one's orange) is the commuter-oriented **Staten Island Ferry** (Map p416; www.siferry.com; Whitehall Terminal at Whitehall & South Sts; fare free; ⌚24hr; [S]1 to South Ferry), which makes constant free journeys across New York Harbor.

Train

Long Island Rail Road, New Jersey Transit and New Jersey PATH all offer useful services (p388) for getting around NYC and surrounds.

Directory A–Z

Business Hours

Nonstandard hours are listed in specific reviews throughout the neighborhood chapters in the Explore section of this guide. Standard business hours are as follows:

Banks 9am-6pm Mon-Fri, some also 9am-noon Sat

Businesses 9am-5pm Mon-Fri

Restaurants Breakfast is served from 6am to noon, lunch goes from 11am to around 3pm, and dinner stretches between 5pm and 11pm. The popular Sunday brunch (often served on Saturdays too) lasts from 11am until 4pm.

Bars & Clubs 5pm-2am

Entertainment 6pm-midnight

Shops 10am to around 7pm on weekdays, 11am to around 8pm Saturdays, and Sundays can be variable – some stores stay closed while others keep weekday hours. Stores tend to stay open later in the neighborhoods downtown.

Customs Regulations

US customs allows each person over the age of 21 to bring 1L of liquor and 200 cigarettes duty free into the USA (smokers take note: cigarettes cost around $8 a pack here in the big city,

so take advantage of those duty-free shops). Agricultural items including meat, fruits, vegetables, plants and soil are prohibited. US citizens are allowed to import, duty free, up to $800 worth of gifts from abroad, while non-US citizens are allowed to import $100 worth. If you're carrying more than $10,000 in US and foreign cash, traveler's checks, money orders etc, you need to declare the excess amount. There is no legal restriction on the amount that may be imported, but undeclared sums in excess of $10,000 will probably be subject to investigation. If you're bringing prescription drugs, make sure they're in clearly marked containers; and leave the illegal narcotics at home. For updates, check www.cbp.gov.

Discount Cards

The following discount cards offer a variety of passes and perks to some of the city's must-sees. Check the websites for more details.

Downtown Culture Pass (www.downtownculturepass.org)

New York CityPASS (www.citypass.com)

Explorer Pass (www.nyexplorerpass.com)

The New York Pass (www.newyorkpass.com)

Electricity

The US electric current is 120V, 60Hz AC. Outlets are made for flat two-prong plugs (which often have a third, rounded prong for grounding). If your appliance is made for another electrical system (eg 220V), you'll need a step-down converter, which can be bought at hardware stores and drugstores for around $25 to $60. Most electronic devices (laptops, camera-battery chargers etc) are built for dual-voltage use, however, and will only need a plug adapter.

The website www.kropla.com provides useful information on electricity and adapters.

120V/60Hz

120V/60Hz

Embassies & Consulates

The presence of the UN in New York City means that nearly every country in the world maintains diplomatic offices in Manhattan. You can check the local *Yellow Pages* under 'consulates' for a complete listing.

Australian Consulate (☎212-351-6500; www.australianntc.org; 34th fl, 150 E 42nd St; ☻8:30am-5pm Mon-Fri; ⓢ4/5/6 to Grand Central-42nd St)

Brazilian Consulate (☎917-777-7777; www.brazilny.org; 21st fl, 1185 Sixth Ave; ☻10am-noon & 2:30am-4pm Mon-Fri; ⓢB/D/F/V to 47th-50th Sts-Rockefeller Ctr)

Canadian Consulate (www.canada-ny.org; 1251 Sixth Ave; ☻8:45am-5pm Mon-Fri; ⓢB/D/F/V to 47th-50th Sts-Rockefeller Ctr)

French Consulate (☎212-606-3680; www.consulfrance-newyork.org; 934 Fifth Ave; ☻9am-1pm Mon-Fri; ⓢ6 to 77th St)

German Consulate (☎212-610-9700; www.germany.info;

871 UN Plaza at 49th St & First Ave; ☻9am-noon Mon-Fri; ⓢ4/5/6 to Grand Central-42nd St)

Indian Embassy (☎212-774-0600; www.indiacgny.org; 3 E 64th St; ☻9am-5:30pm Mon-Fri; ⓢ6 to 68th St-Hunter College)

Japanese Consulate (☎212-371-8222; www.ny.us.emb-japan.go.jp; 299 Park Ave btwn 48th & 49th Sts; ☻9am-5:30pm Mon-Fri; ⓢ6 to 51st St; E, V to Lexington Ave-53rd St)

UK Consulate (☎212-745-0200; 845 Third Ave btwn 51st & 52nd Sts; ☻9am-5pm Mon-Fri; ⓢ6 to 51st St; E, V to Lexington Ave-53rd St)

Emergency

Police, Fire, Ambulance (☎911)

Poison Control (☎800-222-1222)

Internet Access

It is rare to find accommodation in New York City that does not offer a way for guests to connect to the internet – a log-in fee is often required.

New York Public Library (www.nypl.org/branch/local) Offers free internet access for laptop toters and half-hour internet access via public terminals at almost all of its locations around the city.

NYC Wireless (www.nycwireless.net) A local free-wi-fi activist group that has an online map of free access points, which requires sign-in. Other public areas with free wi-fi include the following:

Columbia University (Map p444; www.columbia.edu; Broadway at 116th St; ⓢ1 to 116th St-Columbia University)

South Street Seaport (Map p416; ☎212-732-7678; www.southstreetseaport.com; Pier 17 btwn Fulton & South Sts; ☻10am-9pm Mon-Sat, 11am-8pm Sun)

Internet kiosks can also be found at the scatter of **Staples** (www.staples.com) and **FedEx Kinko** (www.fedexkinkos.com) locations around the city.

Legal Matters

If you're arrested, you have the right to remain silent. There is no legal reason to speak to a police officer if you don't wish to – especially since anything you say 'can and will be used against you' – but never walk away from an officer until given permission. All persons who are arrested have the legal right to make one phone call. If you don't have a lawyer or family member to help you, call your consulate. The police will give you the number upon request.

Medical Services

Before traveling, contact your health-insurance provider to find out what types of medical care it will cover outside your hometown (or home country). Overseas visitors should acquire travel insurance that covers medical situations in the US, as non-emergency care for uninsured patients can be very expensive. For non-emergency appointments at hospitals, you'll need proof of insurance or cash. Even with insurance, you'll most likely have to pay up front for non-emergency care.

Clinics

Bolte Medical Urgent Care Center (☎212-588-9314; www.boltemedical.com; 141 E 55th St at Lexington Ave; ⓢ6 to 51st St; E, V to Lexington Ave-53rd St) This clinic offers same-day appointments for illness diagnosis.

Callen-Lorde Community Health Center (☎212-271-7200; www.callen-lorde.org; 356 W 18th St btwn Eighth & Ninth Aves; [S]A/C/E, L to 8th Ave-14th St) This medical center, dedicated to the LGBT community and people living with HIV/AIDS, serves people regardless of their ability to pay.

Duane Reade Walk-in Medical Care (www.drwalkin.com) The drugstore chain's walk-in clinic. Hospital-affiliated doctors are available to offer diagnosis and treatment.

New York County Medical Society (☎212-684-4670; www.nycms.org) Makes doctor referrals by phone, based on type of problem and language spoken.

Planned Parenthood (☎212-965-7000; www.plannedparenthood.org; 26 Bleecker St; [S]B/D/F/V to Broadway-Lafayette St; 6 to Bleecker St) Provides birth control, STD screenings and gynecological care.

Travel MD (☎212 737 1212; www.travelmd.com) Care specifically for visitors to NYC; hotel appointments can be made.

Emergency Rooms

Emergency services can be slow (unless your medical condition is absolutely dire); a visit should be avoided if other medical services can be provided to mitigate the situation.

Bellevue Hospital Center (☎212-562-1000; 462 First Ave at 27th St; [S]6 to 28th St)

Lenox Hill Hospital (☎212-434-2000; 100 E 77th St at Lexington Ave, Upper East Side; [S]6 to 103rd St)

Mount Sinai Hospital (☎212-241-6500; 1190 Fifth Ave btwn 98th & 101st St; [S]6 to 103rd St)

New York-Presbyterian Hospital (☎212-305-6204; 622 168th St at Ft Washington Ave; [S]A/C, 1 to 168th St)

St Vincent's Medical Center (☎212-604-7000; 153 W 11th St at Greenwich Ave; 🕐24hr; [S]1/2/3, F to 14th St; L to 6th Ave)

Pharmacies

New York is bursting with 24-hour 'pharmacies,' which are handy all-purpose stores where you can buy over-the-counter medications anytime; the pharmaceutical prescription counters have more limited hours. Check websites for locations; major pharmacy chains include the following:

CVS (www.cvs.com)

Duane Reade (www.duanereade.com)

Rite Aid (www.riteaid.com)

Walgreens (www.walgreens.com)

Money

US dollars are the only accepted currency in NYC. While debit and credit cards are widely accepted, it's wise to have a combination of cash and cards.

ATMs

Automatic teller machines are on practically every corner. You can either use your card at banks – usually in a 24-hour-access lobby, filled with up to a dozen monitors at major branches – or you can opt for the lone wolves, which sit in delis, restaurants, bars and grocery stores, charging fierce service fees that go as high as $5.

Most New York banks are linked by the New York Cash Exchange (NYCE) system, and you can use local bankcards interchangeably at ATMs – for an extra fee if you're banking outside your system.

Changing Money

Banks and moneychangers, found all over New York City (including all three major airports), will give you US currency based on the current exchange rate.

American Express (☎212-421-8240, for locations 800-221-728; Park & 53rd; 🕐9am-5pm Mon-Fri) Many branches about town, including this one at Park Ave & 53rd.

Travelex (☎212-265-6049; 1590 Broadway at 48th St; 🕐9am-7pm Mon-Sat, 9am-5pm Sun) Features currency exchange at eight locations in the city, including this Times Sq office.

Credit Cards

Major credit cards are accepted at most hotels, restaurants and shops throughout New York City. In fact, you'll find it difficult to perform certain transactions, such as purchasing tickets to performances and renting a car, without one.

Stack your deck with a Visa, MasterCard or American Express, as these are the cards of choice here. Places that accept Visa and MasterCard also accept debit cards, which deduct payments directly from your checking or savings account. Be sure to check with your bank to confirm that your debit card will be accepted in other states or countries – debit cards from large commercial banks can often be used worldwide.

If your cards are lost or stolen, contact the company immediately. The following are toll-free numbers for the main credit-card companies:

American Express (☎800-528-4800)

Discover (☎800-347-2683)

MasterCard (☎800-826-2181)

Visa (☎800-336-8472)

Tipping

See p32 for tips on tipping.

Organized Tours

There are dozens upon dozens of organized tours around the city. The following are a few favorites; consult the Explore chapters for additional recommendations.

Big Apple Greeter Program (☎212-669-8159; www.bigapplegreeter.org; tours free) If you find NYC a bit overwhelming – and who wouldn't? – call to set up an intimate stroll, in the neighborhood of your choice, led by a local volunteer who just can't wait to show off his or her city to you. You'll be matched with a guide who suits your needs, whether that means speaking Spanish or American Sign Language, or knowing just where to find the best wheelchair-accessible spots in the city.

Bike the Big Apple (☎877-865-0078; www.bikethebigapple.com; tours incl bike & helmet $70-80) Bike the Big Apple, recommended by NYC & Company (the official tourism authority of New York City and operators of www.nycgo.com), offers five set tours. Its most popular is the six-hour Back to the Old Country – the Ethnic Apple Tour, 12 miles of riding that covers Williamsburg, Roosevelt Island and the east side of Manhattan. Other tours visit the Bronx' Little Italy, city parks, Brooklyn chocolate shops and Manhattan at night.

Circle Line Boat Tours (Map p438; ☎212-563-3200; www.circleline42.com; 42nd St at Twelfth Ave; tours $20-29.50; [S]A/C/E to 42nd-Port Authority) The classic Circle Line – whose local 1970s TV-commercial song is now the stuff of kitschy nostalgia – guides you through all the big sights from the safe distance of a boat that circumnavigates the five boroughs. It's got a bar on board and has a bit of a party reputation (especially its two-hour evening cruise); other options include a three-hour day trip and an abbreviated 75-minute journey.

Foods of New York (☎212-239-1124; www.foodsofny.com; tours $40-75) The official foodie tour of NYC & Company offers various three-hour tours that help you eat your way through gourmet shops in either Chelsea or the West Village. Prepare thyself for a moving feast of French bread, fresh Italian pasta, sushi, global cheeses, real New York pizza, local fish and freshly baked pastries.

Gray Line (☎212-397-2620; www.newyorksightseeing.com; tours $50-75) The most ubiquitous guided tour in the city, Gray Line is responsible for bombarding New York streets with the red double-decker buses that locals love to hate. Really, though, for a comprehensive tour of the big sights, it's a great way to go. The company offers nearly 30 different options, the best being both the popular hop-on, hop-off loops of Manhattan. Tours are available in various languages.

Liberty Helicopter Tours (Map p438; ☎212-967-6464; www.libertyhelicopters.com; Twelfth Ave at 30th St & Pier 6, East River; per person for 15 mins $150; [S]A/C/E to 34th St-Penn Station) Enjoy a bird's-eye view of the city in a very Donald Trump sort of way as a helicopter whisks you high above the skyscrapers. Just get ready to shell out for the privilege.

Municipal Art Society (☎212-935-3960; www.mas.org; 457 Madison Ave; tours adult $15) Various scheduled tours focusing on architecture and history.

New York Gallery Tours (Map p430; ☎212-946-1548; www.nygallerytours.com; 526 W 26th St at Tenth Ave; tours $20; [S]C/E to 23rd St) You know you're supposed to check out the array of amazing modern-art galleries in Chelsea. But where to begin? This excellent guided tour – with additional gay and lesbian tours that focus on a 'queer aesthetic' – takes you to a slew of galleries and provides helpful commentary along the way.

On Location Tours (☎212-209-3370; www.screentours.com; tours $15-45) Face it: you want to sit on Carrie Bradshaw's apartment stoop and visit the design studio from *Will & Grace*. This company offers four tours – covering *Sex and the City*, *The Sopranos*, general TV and movie locations, and movie locations in Central Park – that let you live out your entertainment-obsessed fantasies. A couple of the tours are also available in German.

Strayboots (☎877-787-2929; www.strayboots.com; tours from $12) Self-guided hybrid tours that fuse interesting urban info and a scavenger-hunt element to help New York neophytes find their way around the neighborhood of their choice. Go at your own pace as you text in your answers to central command to receive your next clue. At the time of research a savvy, tailor-made app was in the works.

Wildman Steve Brill (☎914-835-2153; www.wildmanstevebrill.com; sliding scale up to $15) New York's best-known naturalist – betcha didn't know there were any! – has been leading folks on foraging expeditions through city parks for more than 20 years. He'll trek with you through

Central Park, Prospect Park, Inwood Park and many more, teaching you to identify natural riches including sassafras, chickweed, ginkgo nuts, garlic and wild mushrooms along the way. It's wild.

Post

Visit the **US Post Office** (www.usps.com) website for up-to-date information about postage prices and branch locations throughout the city.

Public Holidays

Following is a list of major NYC holidays and special events. These holidays may force the closure of many businesses or attract crowds, making dining and accommodations reservations difficult.

New Year's Day January 1

Martin Luther King Day Third Monday in January

Presidents' Day Third Monday in February

Easter March/April

Memorial Day Late May

Gay Pride Last Sunday in June

Independence Day July 4

Labor Day Early September

Rosh Hashanah and Yom Kippur Mid-September to mid-October

Halloween October 31

Thanksgiving Fourth Thursday in November

Christmas Day December 25

New Year's Eve December 31

Safe Travel

Crime rates in NYC are still at their lowest in years. There are few neighborhoods remaining where you might feel apprehensive, no matter what time of night it is (and they're mainly in the outer boroughs). Subway stations are generally safe, too, though some in low-income neighborhoods, especially in the outer boroughs, can be dicey. There's no reason to be paranoid, but it's better to be safe than sorry, so use common sense: don't walk around alone at night in unfamiliar, sparsely populated areas, especially if you're a woman. Carry your daily walking-around money somewhere inside your clothing or in a front pocket rather than in a handbag or a back pocket, and be aware of pickpockets particularly in mobbed areas, like Times Sq or Penn Station at rush hour.

Taxes

Restaurants and retailers never include the sales tax – which is 8.875% – in their prices, so beware of ordering the $4.99 lunch special when you only have $5 to your name. Several categories of so-called 'luxury items,' including rental cars and dry-cleaning, carry an additional city surcharge of 5%, so you wind up paying an extra 13.875% in total for these services.

Clothing and footwear purchases under $110 are tax-free; anything over that amount has a state sales tax of 4.375%. Hotel rooms in New York City are subject to a 14.75% tax, plus a flat $3.50 occupancy tax per night. Since the US has no nationwide value-added tax (VAT), there is no opportunity for foreign visitors to make 'tax-free' purchases.

Telephone

Phone numbers within the USA consist of a three-digit area code followed by a seven-digit local number. If you're calling long distance, dial 1 + the three-digit area code + the seven-digit number. To make an international call from NYC, call 011+ country code + area code + number. When calling Canada, there is no need to use the 011.

Area Codes in NYC

No matter where you're calling within New York City, even if it's just across the street in the same area code, you must always dial 1 + the area code first.

Manhattan 212, 646

Outer boroughs 347, 718, 929

All boroughs (usually cell phones) 917

Cell Phones

Most US cell phones besides the iPhone operate on CDMA, not the European standard GSM – make sure you check compatibility with your phone service provider. North Americans should have no problem, though it is best to check with your service provider about roaming charges.

If you require a cell phone, you'll find many store fronts – most run by Verizon, T-Mobile or AT&T – where you can buy a cheap phone and load it up with prepaid minutes, thus avoiding a long-term contract.

Operator Services

Local directory 411

Municipal offices and information 311

National directory information 1-212-555-1212

Operator 0

Toll-free number information 800-555-1212

Time

New York City is in the Eastern Standard Time (EST) zone – five hours behind Greenwich Mean Time, two hours ahead of Mountain Standard Time (including Denver, Colorado) and three hours ahead of Pacific Standard Time (San Francisco

PRACTICALITIES

Newspapers & Magazines

There are scads of periodicals to choose from. What else would you expect from one of the media capitals of the world? Newspapers include the following:

New York Post (www.nypost.com) The *Post* is known for screaming headlines, conservative political views and its popular Page Six gossip column.

New York Times (www.nytimes.com) 'The gray lady' has become hip in recent years, adding sections on technology, arts and dining out.

Village Voice (www.villagevoice.com) Owned by national alternative-newspaper chain New Times, the legendary *Voice* has less bite but still plenty of bark. It's home to everyone's favorite gossip columnist, Michael Musto.

Wall Street Journal (www.wallstreetjournal.com) This intellectual daily focuses on finance, though its new owner, media mogul Rupert Murdoch, has ratcheted up the general coverage to rival that of the *Times*.

Magazines that give a good sense of the local flavor include the following:

New York Magazine (www.nymag.com) A weekly magazine with feature stories and great listings about anything and everything in NYC, with an indispensable website.

New Yorker (www.newyorker.com) This highbrow weekly covers politics and culture through its famously lengthy works of reportage, and also publishes fiction and poetry.

Time Out New York (http://newyork.timeout.com) A weekly magazine, its focus is on mass coverage, plus articles and interviews on arts and entertainment.

Radio

NYC has some excellent radio options beyond commercial pop-music stations. An excellent programming guide can be found in the *New York Times* entertainment section on Sunday. Our top pick is **WNYC93.9FM and 820AM** (820-AM & 93.9-FM; www.wnyc.org). NYC's public radio station is the local NPR affiliate, offering a blend of national and local talk and interview shows, with a switch to classical music in the day on the FM station.

Smoking

Smoking is strictly forbidden in any location that's considered a public place; this includes subway stations, restaurants, bars, taxis, and parks.

and Los Angeles, California). Almost all of the USA observes daylight-saving time: clocks go forward one hour from the second Sunday in March to the first Sunday in November, when the clocks are turned back one hour. (It's easy to remember by the phrase 'spring ahead, fall back.')

Toilets

Considering the number of pedestrians, there's a noticeable lack of public restrooms around the city. You'll find spots to relieve yourself in Grand Central Terminal, Penn Station and Port Authority Bus Terminal, and in parks, including Madison Square Park, Battery Park, Tompkins Square Park, Washington Square Park and Columbus Park in Chinatown, plus several places scattered around Central Park.

The NY Restroom website (www.nyrestroom.com) is a handy resource to scout out a loo.

Tourist Information

In this wonderful web-based world you'll find infinite online sources to get up-to-the-minute information about New York.

In person, try own of the five official bureaus (the Midtown office is the shining star) of **NYC & Company** (☎212-484-1200; www.nycgo.com):

Midtown (☎484-1222; 810 Seventh Ave btwn 52nd & 53rd Sts; 🕗8:30am-6pm Mon-Fri, 9am-5pm Sat & Sun; [S]B/D, E to 7th Ave)

Lower Manhattan (City Hall Park at Broadway; [S]R/W to to City Hall)

Harlem (163 W 125th at Adam Clayton Powell Jr Blvd; [S]1 to 125th St)

Chinatown (cnr Canal, Walker & Baxter Sts; [S]J/M/Z, N/Q/R/W, 6 to Canal St)

The **Brooklyn Tourism & Visitors Center** (☎718-802-3846; www.visitbrooklyn.org; 209 Joralemon St btwn Court St & Brooklyn Bridge Blvd; ⏰10am-6pm Mon-Fri; [S]2/3, 4/5 to Borough Hall) has all sorts of info on the other favorite borough.

Borough Tourism Portals

Each borough has a special tourism website:

Bronx (www.ilovethebronx.com)

Brooklyn (www.visitbrooklyn.org)

Manhattan (www.mbpo.org)

Queens (www.discoverqueens.info)

Staten Island (www.statenislandusa.com)

Neighborhood Tourism Portals

In addition to each borough, many of the city's most popular neighborhoods have their own websites (either official or 'unofficial') dedicated to exploring the area. Some of our favorites include the following:

Lower East Side (www.lowereastsideny.com)

Chinatown (www.explorechinatown.com)

Upper East Side (www.uppereast.com)

Soho (www.sohonyc.com)

Williamsburg www.freewilliamsburg.com

Travelers with Disabilities

Federal laws guarantee that all government offices and facilities are accessible to the disabled. For information on specific places, you can contact the mayor's **Office for People with Disabilities** (☎212-788-2830; ⏰9am-5pm Mon-Fri), which will send you a free copy of its *Access New York* guide if you call and request it.

Another excellent resource is the **Society for Accessible Travel & Hospitality** (SATH; ☎212-447-7284; www.sath.org; 347 Fifth Ave at 34th St; ⏰9am-5pm; [S]6 to 33rd St,, 🚌M34 to 5th Ave, M1 to 34th St), which gives advice on how to travel with a wheelchair, kidney disease, sight impairment or deafness.

For detailed information on subway and bus wheelchair accessibility, call the **Accessible Line** (☎718-596-8585) or visit www.mta.info/mta/ada for a list of subway stations with elevators or escalators. Also visit **NYC & Company** (☎484-1222; 810 Seventh Ave btwn 52nd & 53rd Sts; ⏰8:30am-6pm Mon-Fri, 9am-5pm Sat & Sun; [S]B/D, E to 7th Ave); search for 'accessibility.'

Visas

Visa Waiver Program

The USA Visa Waiver Program (VWP) allows nationals from 36 countries to enter the US without a visa, provided they are carrying a machine-readable passport. For the updated list of countries included in the program and current requirements, see the **US Department of State** (http://travel.state.gov/visa) website.

Citizens of VWP countries need to register with the **US Department of Homeland Security** (http://esta.cbp.dhs.gov) three days before their visit. There is a $14 fee for registration application; when approved, the registration is valid for two years.

Visas Required

You must obtain a visa from a US embassy or consulate in your home country if you:

- Do not currently hold a passport from a VWP country
- Are from a VWP country, but don't have a machine-readable passport
- Are from a VWP country, but currently hold a passport issued between October 26, 2005, and October 25, 2006, that does not have a digital photo on the information page or an integrated chip from the data page. (After October 25, 2006, the integrated chip is required on all machine-readable passports.)
- Are planning to stay longer than 90 days.
- Are planning to work or study in the US.

Women Travelers

In general, New York City is a pretty safe place for women travelers, as long as common sense is used. If you are unsure which areas are considered dicey, ask at your hotel or phone **NYC & Company** (☎212-484-1200; www.nycgo.com) for advice; of course, other women are always a great source for the inside scoop. Depending on the neighborhood you're in, you are likely to encounter somewhat obnoxious behavior on the street, where men may greet you with whistles and muttered 'compliments.' Any engagement amounts to encouragement – simply walk on. Finally, if you're out late clubbing or at a venue further afield, it's a good idea to save some money for a cab fare home.

Behind the Scenes

SEND US YOUR FEEDBACK

We love to hear from travelers – your comments keep us on our toes and help make our books better. Our well-traveled team reads every word on what you loved or loathed about this book. Although we cannot reply individually to postal submissions, we always guarantee that your feedback goes straight to the appropriate authors, in time for the next edition. Each person who sends us information is thanked in the next edition – the most useful submissions are rewarded with a selection of digital PDF chapters.

Visit **lonelyplanet.com/contact** to submit your updates and suggestions or to ask for help. Our award-winning website also features inspirational travel stories, news and discussions.

Note: We may edit, reproduce and incorporate your comments in Lonely Planet products such as guidebooks, websites and digital products, so let us know if you don't want your comments reproduced or your name acknowledged. For a copy of our privacy policy visit lonelyplanet.com/privacy.

OUR READERS

Many thanks to the travelers who used the last edition and wrote to us with helpful hints, useful advice and interesting anecdotes:

Adam Adams, Lieuwe van Albada, Lella Baker, Gisela Corvetto, Alyx Cullen, Nick Dillen, Eveline van Drielen, Qiu Leyu, Alan Manning, Daphne Papadopoulou, Wilmar van de Sande, Dianne Schallmeiner, Annette Skupien, Eileen Stevens, Robert Strauch, Renee Teernstra

AUTHOR THANKS

Brandon Presser

Wow. What an undertaking. The success of this new-look NYC guide would not have been possible without the help and support of a ton of people. First and foremost, an infinity huge thank you to Jennye for being the guiding light at the end of a seemingly endless tunnel, and to Joanne for being the dearest friend one could ever hope to have. A special nod goes to my wonderfully talented and dedicated coauthors Cristian and Carolina, and at Lonely Planet big thanks to Gabby, Brice and Heather. Additional thank yous to New York know-it-alls Mollie, Allidah, Greg, Nikki, Benjamin and Robert.

Cristian Bonetto

First and foremost, an epic thank you to my beautiful friend and mobile encyclopedia Kathy Stromsland. Many thanks also to Anthony Leung, Zora O'Neill, Patti Golden, Sean Muldoon, Jacque Burke, Andrew Carmellini, Jason Zinoman, Adam Craig, Jeff Orlick, Helena Tubis, Julian Lesser, Katie Trainor, Craig Hopson, Jan Lee, Alesha Oak, Allen Banick, Stephanie Choi and Les Hayden. Extra grazie to my diligent co-writers, Brandon Presser and Carolina Miranda, and to Jenny Garibaldi for the commission.

Carolina A Miranda

Thanks to the countless friends (Sam, Robin, Bobby, Suzan, Robby D, Franck the Tank, Suzan, Marissa and countless others) for the free advice, the food tips and the hangovers. To Cristian and Brandon: no matter how well I think I know this town, it always takes an outsider to show me something new. And to my husband, Ed, who I drove insane during the writing of this book: I owe you infinite faux-vintage-cocktails-served-by-bespoke-shirted-hipsters-with-pointy-mustaches. ♥ U ALL, C.

ACKNOWLEDGMENTS
Illustrations p230-1 by Javier Zarracina.
Cover photograph: Midtown, btrenkel/
Gettyimages

Many of the images in this guide are available for licensing from Lonely Planet Images:
www.lonelyplanetimages.com.

THIS BOOK

This 8th edition of Lonely Planet's New York City guidebook was researched and written by Brandon Presser, Carolina Miranda and Cristian Bonetto. Previous editions were written by Ginger Adams Otis, Beth Greenfield and Regis St Louis. This guidebook was commissioned in Lonely Planet's Oakland office, and produced by the following:

Commissioning Editor Jennye Garibaldi

Coordinating Editor Gabrielle Innes

Coordinating Cartographer Mark Griffiths, Brendan Streager

Coordinating Layout Designer Carlos Solarte

Managing Editors Anna Metcalfe, Martine Power, Angela Tinson

Managing Cartographers Alison Lyall, Amanda Sierp

Managing Layout Designer Chris Girdler

Assisting Editors Elin Berglund, Briohny Hooper, Justin Flynn, Andi Jones, Evan Jones, Bella Li, Kate Mathews, Joanne Newell, Karyn Noble, Sonya Mithen, Mardi O'Connor, Simon Williamson

Assisting Cartographers Rachel Imeson

Assisting Layout Designers Frank Deim, Sandra Helou, Paul Iacono, Wibowo Rusli, Kerrianne Southway, Wendy Wright

Cover Research Naomi Parker

Internal Image Research Nicholas Colicchia

Thanks to Imogen Bannister, Daniel Corbett, Laura Crawford, Janine Eberle, Ryan Evans, Larissa Frost, Liz Heynes, Laura Jane, David Kemp, Kate McDonell, Erin McManus, Wayne Murphy, Darren O'Connell, Trent Paton, Piers Pickard, Lachlan Ross, Michael Ruff, Julie Sheridan, Laura Stansfeld, John Taufa, Gerard Walker, Clifton Wilkinson, Amanda Williamson

Index

See also separate subindexes for:

✕ **EATING P406**

🍷 **DRINKING & NIGHTLIFE P407**

☆ **ENTERTAINMENT P408**

🔒 **SHOPPING P409**

🏃 **SPORTS & ACTIVITIES P410**

🛏 **SLEEPING P411**

🔲 SHOPPING

Sights 000
Map Pages **000**
Photo Pages **000**

New York City Maps

Map Legend

Sights

- 🏖 Beach
- 🔵 Buddhist
- 🏰 Castle
- ✝ Christian
- 🕉 Hindu
- ☪ Islamic
- ✡ Jewish
- ❗ Monument
- 🏛 Museum/Gallery
- 🔵 Ruin
- 🍷 Winery/Vineyard
- 🐾 Zoo
- 👁 Other Sight

Eating
- 🔵 Eating

Drinking & Nightlife
- 🔵 Drinking & Nightlife
- 🔵 Cafe

Entertainment
- 🔵 Entertainment

Shopping
- 🔵 Shopping

Sleeping
- 🔵 Sleeping
- 🔵 Camping

Sports & Activities
- 🔵 Diving/Snorkelling
- 🔵 Canoeing/Kayaking
- 🔵 Skiing
- 🔵 Surfing
- 🔵 Swimming/Pool
- 🔵 Walking
- 🔵 Windsurfing
- 🔵 Other Sports & Activities

Information
- 🔵 Post Office
- 🔵 Tourist Information

Transport
- 🔵 Airport
- 🔵 Border Crossing
- 🔵 Bus
- 🔵 Cable Car/Funicular
- 🔵 Cycling
- 🔵 Ferry
- 🔵 Monorail
- 🔵 Parking
- 🔵 Subway
- 🔵 Taxi
- 🔵 Train/Railway
- 🔵 Tram
- 🔵 Other Transport

Routes
- Tollway
- Freeway
- Primary
- Secondary
- Tertiary
- Lane
- Unsealed Road
- Plaza/Mall
- Steps
- Tunnel
- Pedestrian Overpass
- Walking Tour
- Walking Tour Detour
- Path

Boundaries
- International
- State/Province
- Disputed
- Regional/Suburb
- Marine Park
- Cliff
- Wall

Geographic
- 🔵 Hut/Shelter
- 🔵 Lighthouse
- 🔵 Lookout
- 🔺 Mountain/Volcano
- 🔵 Oasis
- 🔵 Park
-)(Pass
- 🔵 Picnic Area
- 🔵 Waterfall

Hydrography
- River/Creek
- Intermittent River
- Swamp/Mangrove
- Reef
- Canal
- Water
- Dry/Salt/Intermittent Lake
- Glacier

Areas
- Beach/Desert
- Cemetery (Christian)
- Cemetery (Other)
- Park/Forest
- Sportsground
- Sight (Building)
- Top Sight (Building)

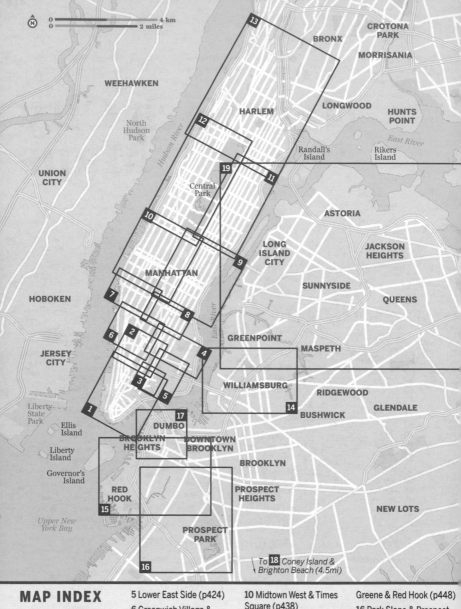

MAP INDEX

LOWER MANHATTAN & TRIBECA

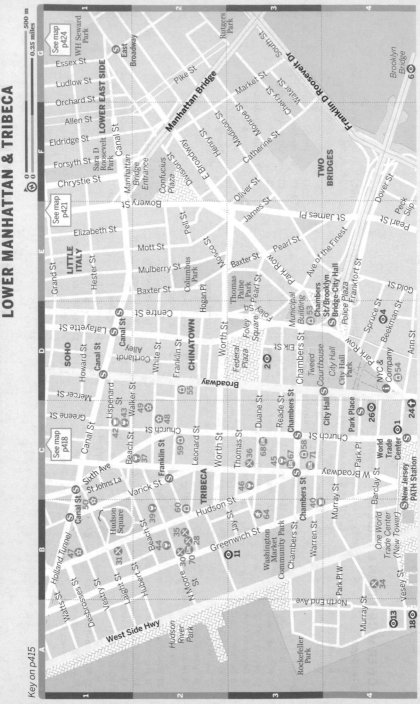

See map p424

See map p421

See map p418

Key on p415

500 m
0.25 miles

WH Seward Park

Essex St

Ludlow St

Orchard St

Allen St

Eldridge St

Forsyth St

Chrystie St

LOWER EAST SIDE

Sara D Roosevelt Park

Canal St

East Broadway

Pike St

Rutgers Park

Market St

Water St

Cherry St

Monroe St

Madison St

Henry St

E Broadway

Division St

Confucius Plaza

Manhattan Bridge Entrance

Bowery St

Manhattan Bridge

Franklin D Roosevelt Dr

Brooklyn Bridge

Catherine St

Oliver St

James St

St James Pl

Dover St

Peck Slip

Pearl St

TWO BRIDGES

Elizabeth St

Grand St

Hester St

LITTLE ITALY

Mott St

Mulberry St

Baxter St

Columbus Park

Hogan Pl

Mosco St

Pell St

Baxter St

Pearl St

Ave of the Finest

Park Row

Gold St

Beekman St

Spruce St

Ann St

Thomas Paine Park

Pearl St

Chambers St/Brooklyn Bridge-City Hall

Frankfort St

Police Plaza

Municipal Building

Centre St

Lafayette St

Canal St

Howard St

Mercer St

Greene St

SOHO

Canal St

Cortlandt Alley

White St

Franklin St

CHINATOWN

Worth St

Broadway

Federal Plaza

Foley Square

Elk St

Tweed Courthouse

City Hall

City Hall Park

Park Row

NYC & Company

Sixth Ave

Canal St

St Johns La

Varick St

Lispenard St

Walker St

Beach St

Church St

Leonard St

Worth St

Thomas St

Duane St

Reade St

Chambers St

Park Place

Franklin St

TRIBECA

Hudson St

Jay St

Greenwich St

Washington Market Community Park

Chambers St

Murray St

W Broadway

Church St

City Hall

World Trade Center

New Jersey PATH Station

One World Trade Center (New Tower)

Barclay St

Park Pl

Vesey St

Murray St

Warren St

North End Ave

Park PIW

Holland Tunnel

Watts St

Desbrosses St

Vestry St

Laight St

Hubert St

Beach St

N Moore St

West Side Hwy

Hudson River Park

Rockefeller Park

Hudson Square

Sixth Ave

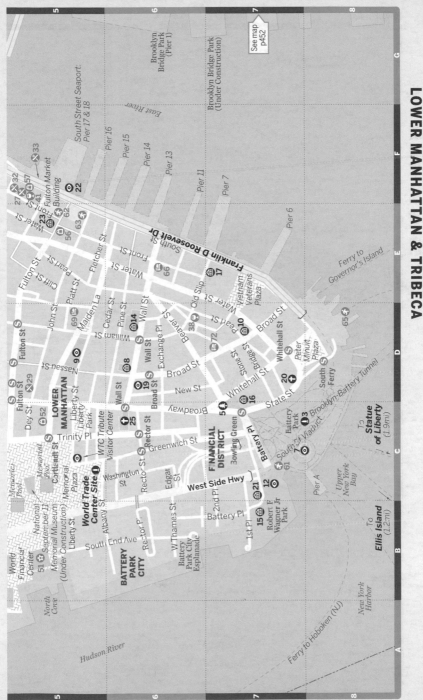

LOWER MANHATTAN & TRIBECA

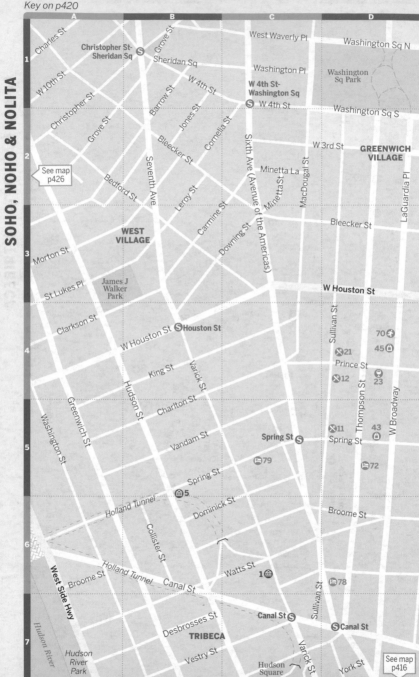

SOHO, NOHO & NOLITA

A · B · C · D

1
Charles St
Christopher St-Sheridan Sq Ⓢ
Grove St
West Waverly Pl
Washington Sq N
W 10th St
Sheridan Sq
Christopher St
W 4th St
W 4th St-Washington Sq Ⓢ W 4th St
Washington Pl
Washington Sq Park
Washington Sq S

2
See map p426
Grove St
Bedford St
Seventh Ave
Barrow St
Bleecker St
Jones St
Cornelia St
Leroy St
Sixth Ave (Avenue of the Americas)
Minetta St La
Minetta La
MacDougal St
W 3rd St
GREENWICH VILLAGE
LaGuardia Pl

3
Morton St
WEST VILLAGE
Carmine St
Downing St
Bleecker St
St Lukes Pl
James J Walker Park
W Houston St

4
Clarkson St
W Houston St Ⓢ Houston St
King St
Hudson St
Varick St
Charlton St
Sullivan St
Ⓧ21
Prince St
Ⓧ12
Thompson St
70 👟
45 🔒
23 🍴
W Broadway

5
Washington St
Greenwich St
Vandam St
Spring St
Spring St Ⓢ
Ⓧ11
Spring St
43 🔒
📷79
Ⓧ
📷72

Holland Tunnel
🏛5
Dominick St
Broome St

6
West Side Hwy
Broome St
Holland Tunnel
Collister St
Canal St
Watts St
1 🏛
Sullivan St
📷78

7
Hudson River
Hudson River Park
Desbrosses St
TRIBECA
Vestry St
Canal St Ⓢ
Hudson Square
Varick St
Ⓢ Canal St
York St
See map p416

A · B · C · D

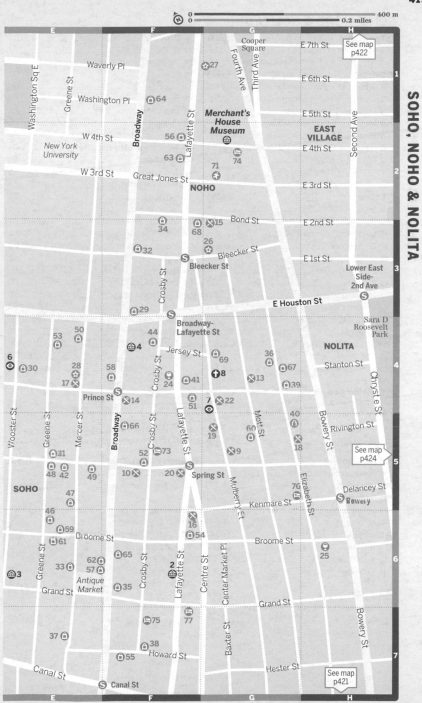

0 — 400 m
0 — 0.2 miles

E 7th St
See map p422

Waverly Pl

Washington Sq E

Greene St

Washington Pl

Cooper Square

Fourth Ave

Third Ave

E 6th St

★ 27

E 5th St

🔒 64

Broadway

Lafayette St

Merchant's House Museum
🏛

EAST VILLAGE

Second Ave

New York University

W 4th St

56

🔒 63

🏛 74

E 4th St

W 3rd St

Great Jones St

71
✚

E 3rd St

NOHO

E 2nd St

🔒 34

68 ✕ 15

Bond St

E 1st St

🔒 32

26

Bleecker St

E Houston St

Lower East Side-2nd Ave

🔒 29

Bleecker St

Crosby St

Broadway-Lafayette St

Sara D Roosevelt Park

53

50

44

Jersey St

🔒 69

36

NOLITA

6 ⊙

🔒 30

28

58

17 ✕

24

🔒 41

✚ 8

✕ 13

🔒 67

Stanton St

Chrystie St

Wooster St

Greene St

Mercer St

Prince St

✕ 14

Broadway

🔒 66

Crosby St

🔒 51

7 ⊙ ✕ 22

Lafayette St

Mott St

40

18

Bowery St

See map p424

52

🖥 73

✕ 19

60

Rivington St

10 ✕

20 ✕

Spring St

✕ 9

48 42

49

Mulberry St

Kenmare St

Elizabeth St

70

Delancey St
Bowery

SOHO

47

46

Greene St

59

61

Broome St

Broome St

🔒 25

🏛 3

33

62

57

🔒 65

2

Antique Market

🔒 35

Center Market Pl

Grand St

Grand St

Baxter St

Bowery St

37

🖥 75

77

38

55

Howard St

Hester St

Canal St

Canal St

See map p421

SOHO, NOHO & NOLITA *Map on p418*

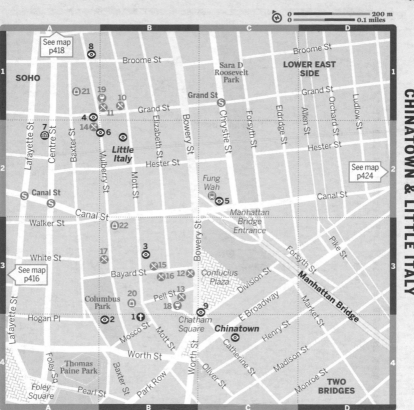

EAST VILLAGE

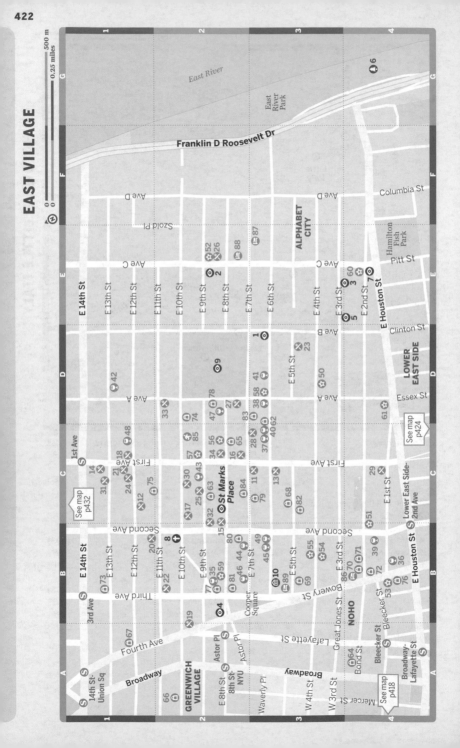

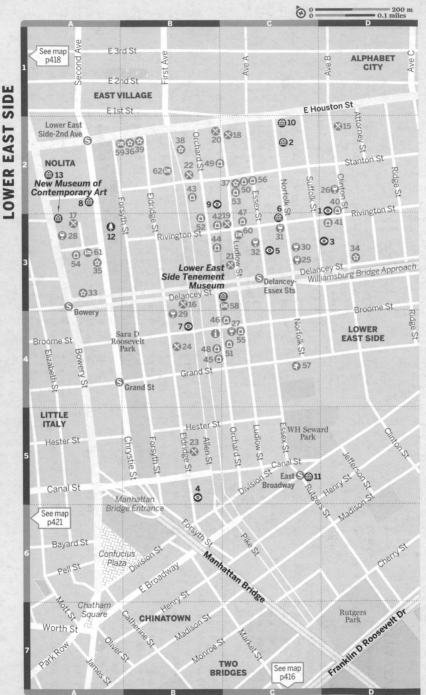

LOWER EAST SIDE

LOWER EAST SIDE

GREENWICH VILLAGE & THE MEATPACKING DISTRICT

CHELSEA

See map
p430

WEST
VILLAGE

MEATPACKING
DISTRICT

The High Line

Abingdon Sq

Christopher St-
Sheridan Sq

James
J Walker
Park

Hudson River
Park

Pier 40

Hudson River

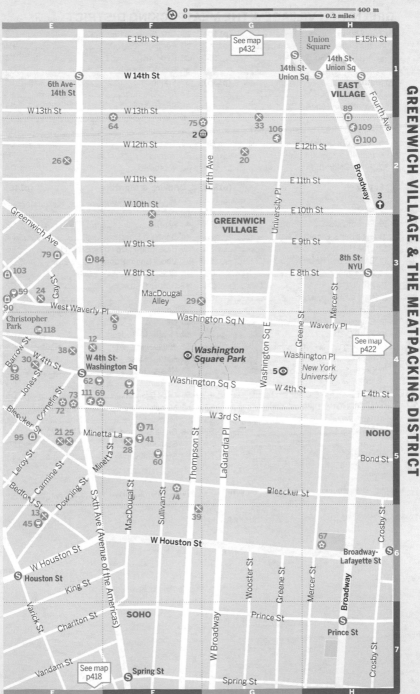

GREENWICH VILLAGE & THE MEATPACKING DISTRICT

GREENWICH VILLAGE & THE MEATPACKING DISTRICT

CHELSEA

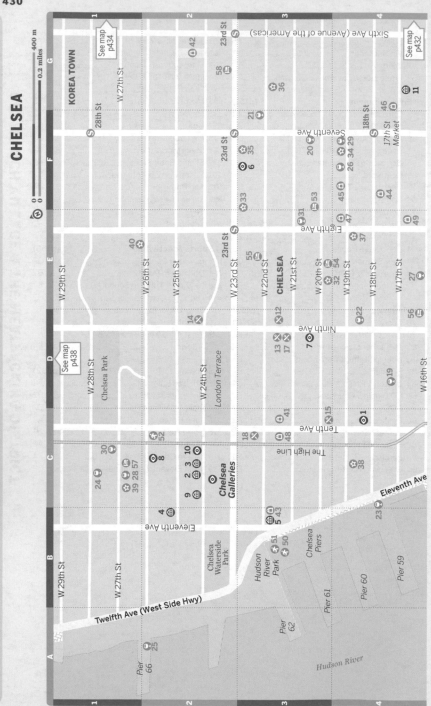

KOREA TOWN

CHELSEA

Chelsea Galleries

See map p434

See map p438

See map p432

Sixth Ave (Avenue of the Americas)

Seventh Ave

Eighth Ave

Ninth Ave

Tenth Ave

The High Line

Eleventh Ave

Eleventh Ave

Twelfth Ave (West Side Hwy)

Chelsea Park

London Terrace

Chelsea Waterside Park

Hudson River Park

Chelsea Piers

Hudson River

W 29th St
W 28th St
W 27th St
W 27th St
W 26th St
W 25th St
W 24th St
W 23rd St
W 22nd St
W 21st St
W 20th St
W 19th St
W 18th St
W 17th St
W 16th St
28th St
23rd St
23rd St
23rd St
18th St
17th St Market
W 29th St

Pier 66
Pier 62
Pier 61
Pier 60
Pier 59

400 m
0.2 miles

CHELSEA

◎ Top Sights (p132)
Chelsea Galleries................C2
Chelsea Market...................D5

◎ Sights (p137)
1 Alexander & Bonin.............C4
2 Andrea Rosen Gallery.........C2
3 Barbara Gladstone Gallery...C2
4 Cheim & Read....................B3
5 Chelsea Art Museum...........B3
6 Chelsea Hotel....................F3
7 General Theological
    Seminary.......................D3
8 Greene Naftali...................C2
9 Mary Boone Gallery............C2
10 Matthew Marks Gallery......C2
11 Rubin Museum of Art........G4

◎ Eating (p146)
Amy's Bread.................(see 16)
12 Billy's Bakery.................D3
13 Blossom........................D3
14 Co.................................D2
15 Cookshop.......................C3
16 Eeni's............................D5
    l'Arte Del Gelato............(see 16)
17 Le Grainne......................D3
    Sarabeth's....................(see 16)
18 Tia Pol...........................C3

◎ Drinking & Nightlife (p149)
19 1Oak............................D4
20 Bar Veloce......................F3
21 Barracuda.......................F3
22 Bathtub Gin.....................D4
23 Chelsea Brewing Company...C4
24 Eagle NYC.......................C1
25 Frying Pan.......................A2
26 G Lounge........................F4
27 Hiro...............................E4
28 Home.............................C1
29 Peter McManus Tavern......F4
30 Park Elephant..................C1
31 Rawhide.........................E3

◎ Entertainment (p151)
32 Atlantic Theater
    Company........................C3
33 Clearview's Chelsea...........F3
34 Dance Theater
    Workshop......................F4
35 Gotham Comedy Club........F3
36 Irish Repertory Theater......G3
37 Joyce Theater..................E4
38 Kitchen..........................C4
39 Sleep No More.................C1
40 Upright Citizens
    Brigade Theatre..............E1

◎ Shopping (p157)
41 192 Books.......................C3
42 Antiques Garage Flea
    Market...........................G2
43 Balenciaga......................F4
44 Barneys Co-op.................C1
45 Behaviour.......................E3
46 Housing Works Thrift Shop...G4
47 Nasty Pig........................E4
    Posman Books...............(see 16)
48 Printed Matter..................C3
49 Universal Gear.................E4

◎ Sports & Activities (p158)
    300 New York................(see 50)
50 Chelsea Piers Complex......B3
51 Little Athletes Exploration
    Center...........................B3
52 New York Gallery Tours......C2

◎ Sleeping (p332)
53 Chelsea Hostel.................F3
    Chelsea Hotel................(see 6)
54 Chelsea Lodge.................E3
55 Colonial House Inn...........E3
56 Dream Downtown.............D4
57 Hôtel Americano...............C1
58 Inn on 23rd St.................G2
    Maritime Hotel..............(see 27)

UNION SQUARE, FLATIRON DISTRICT & GRAMERCY

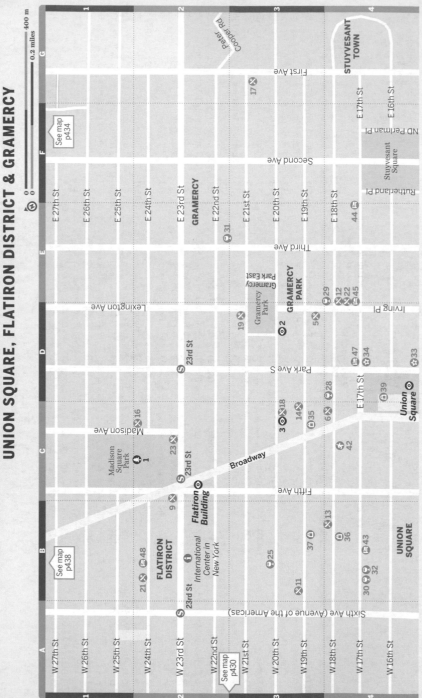

UNION SQUARE, FLATIRON DISTRICT & GRAMERCY

MIDTOWN EAST & FIFTH AVENUE

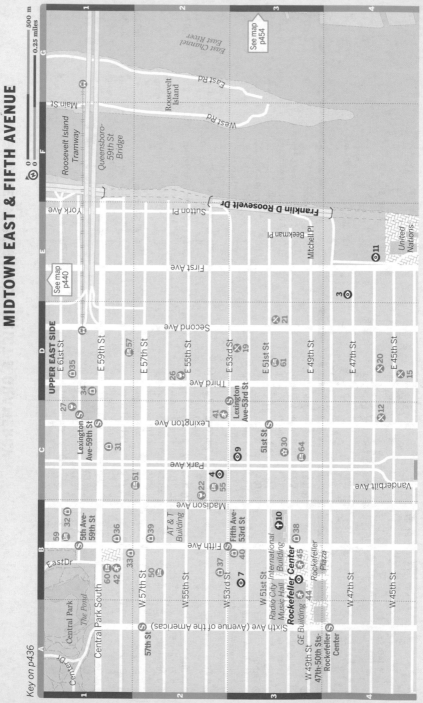

Key on p436

See map p440

See map p454

UPPER EAST SIDE

Central Park

Central Park: The Pond

East Dr

Central Park South

East Channel East River

Roosevelt Island

Roosevelt Island Tramway

Queensboro-59th St Bridge

Main St

Roosevelt Island

East Rd

West Rd

East Rd

Franklin D Roosevelt Dr

York Ave

Sutton Pl

Beekman Pl

Mitchell Pl

United Nations

First Ave

Second Ave

Third Ave

Lexington Ave

Park Ave

Madison Ave

Fifth Ave

Sixth Ave (Avenue of the Americas)

Vanderbilt Ave

E 61st St

E 59th St

E 57th St

E 55th St

E 53rd St

E 51st St

E 49th St

E 47th St

E 45th St

W 57th St

W 55th St

W 53rd St

W 51st St

W 49th St

W 47th St

W 45th St

Lexington Ave-59th St

Lexington Ave-53rd St

51st St

5th Ave-59th St

5th Ave-53rd St

57th St

47th-50th Sts-Rockefeller Center

AT&T Building

Radio City Music Hall

GE Building

Rockefeller Center

Rockefeller Plaza

International Building

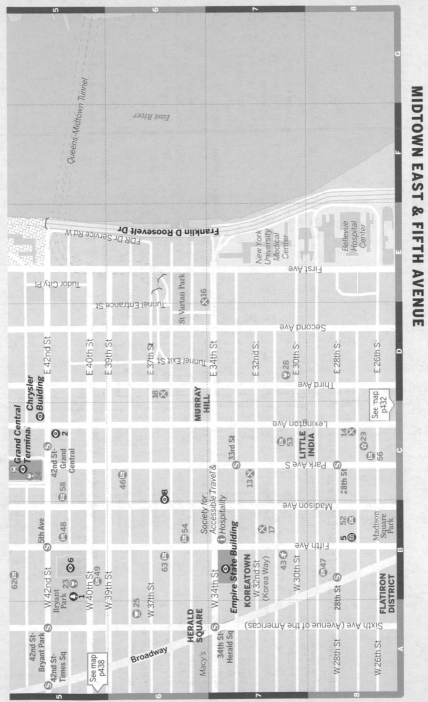

MIDTOWN WEST & TIMES SQUARE

Key on p437

500 m
0.25 miles

See map p442

See map p434

Hudson River

Hudson River Park

Twelfth Ave (West Side Hwy)

Eleventh Ave

Tenth Ave

Ninth Ave

Eighth Ave

Broadway

Seventh Ave

Sixth Ave
(Avenue of the Americas)

Fifth Ave

Central Park South

Central Park

The Pond

West Dr

East Dr

Columbus Circle

Time Warner Center

Fordham University

Dewitt Clinton Park

HELL'S KITCHEN

THEATER DISTRICT

TIMES SQUARE

THE DIAMOND DISTRICT

Times Square Visitor Center

NYC & Company

Worldwide Plaza

Museum of Modern Art

AT & T Building

St Patrick's Cathedral

International Building

Rockefeller Center

GE Building

Radio City Music Hall

W 60th St
W 58th St
W 57th St
W 55th St
W 53rd St
W 51st St
W 49th St
W 47th St
W 45th St

E 59th St
E 57th St
E 55th St
E 53rd St
E 51st St
E 49th St
E 47th St
E 45th St

5th Ave-59th St
59th St-Columbus Circle
57th St
57th St-7th Ave
50th St
49th St
47th-50th Sts-Rockefeller Center

5th Ave-53rd St
Fifth Ave-53rd St

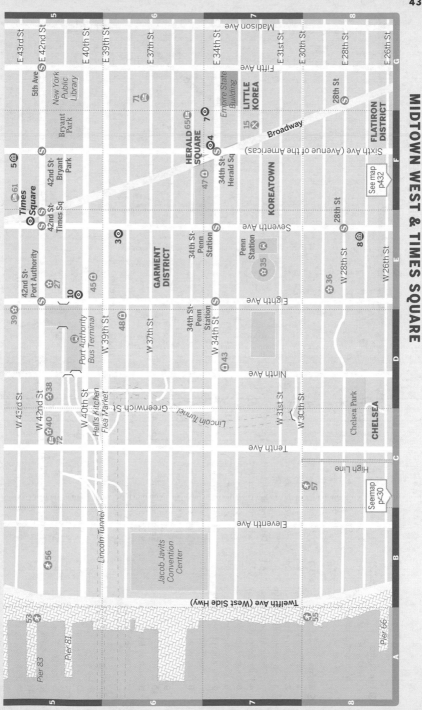

UPPER EAST SIDE

See map p454

John Jay Park

East End Ave

Franklin D Roosevelt Dr

East River

Rockefeller University

York Ave

Second Ave

First Ave

Third Ave

Lexington Ave

Park Ave

5th Ave

Metropolitan Museum of Art

Conservatory Water

Central Park

The Pond

Hunter College

68th St-Hunter College

Roosevelt Island Tramway

Queensboro-59th St Bridge

See map p434

See map p442

E 82nd St
E 80th St
E 78th St
E 76th St
E 74th St
E 77th St
E 72nd St
E 70th St
E 68th St
E 65th St
E 63rd St
E 61st St
Lexington Ave-63rd St
Lexington Ave-59th St
5th Ave-59th St

UPPER WEST SIDE

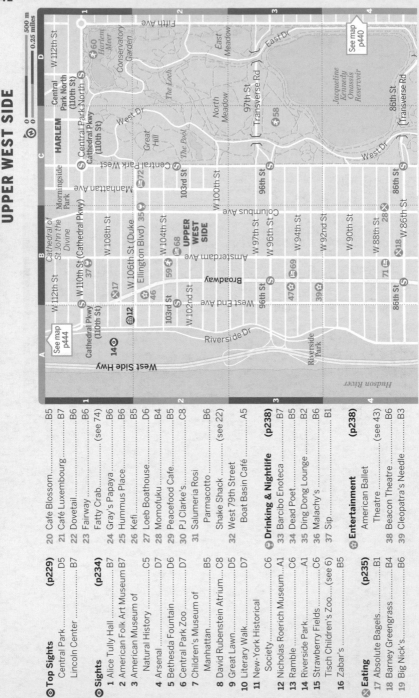

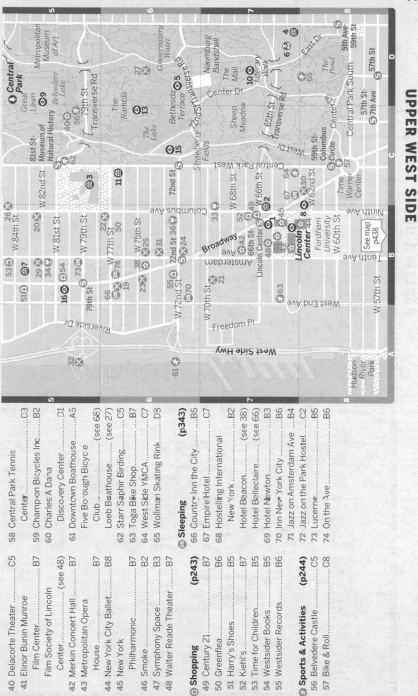

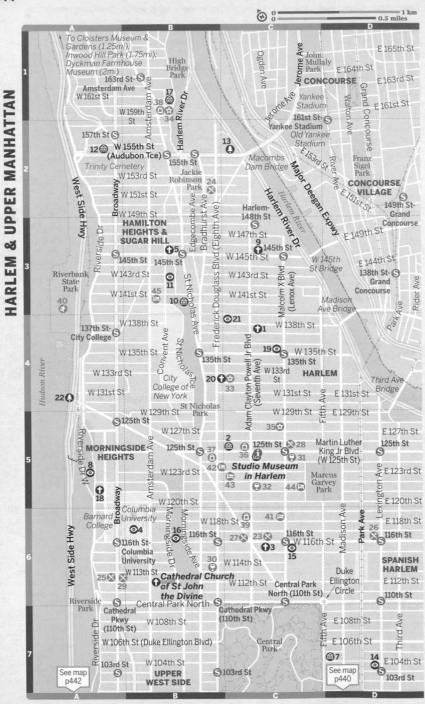

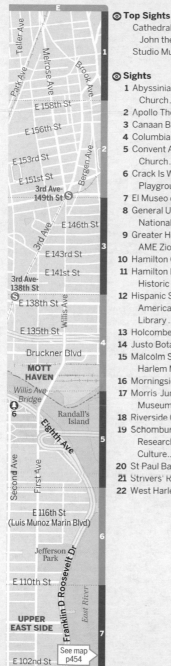

WILLIAMSBURG

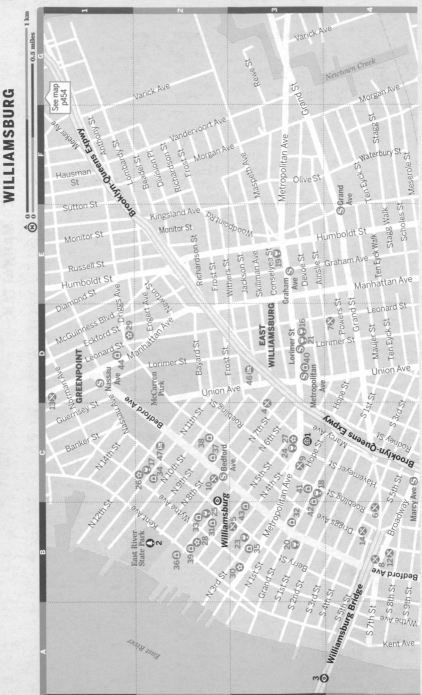

WILLIAMSBURG

BOERUM HILL, CARROLL GARDENS, COBBLE HILL, FORT GREENE & RED HOOK

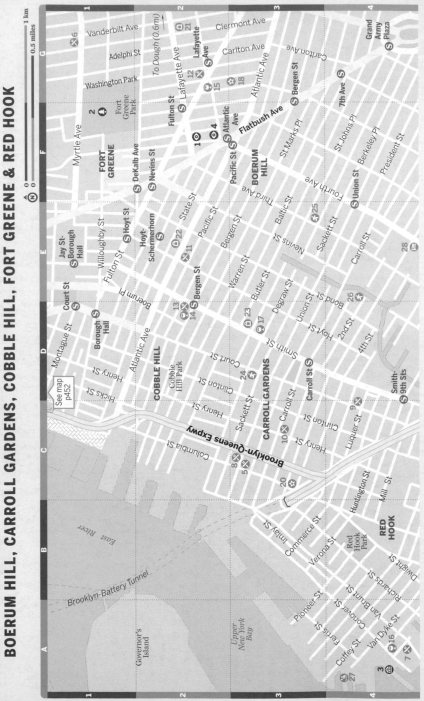

0.5 miles
1 km

Vanderbilt Ave
Adelphi St
Washington Park
Myrtle Ave

To Dough (0.6mi)

Clermont Ave
Carlton Ave
Atlantic Ave
Carlton Ave

Grand Army Plaza

Lafayette Ave
Clermont Ave

Fort Greene Park

FORT GREENE

Fulton St
Lafayette Ave

Bergen St

7th Ave

DeKalb Ave
Nevins St

Atlantic Ave
Flatbush Ave

St Johns Pl

Berkeley Pl

President St

Pacific St

BOERUM HILL

St Marks Pl

Union St

Jay St–Borough Hall
Willoughby St
Fulton St

Hoyt St

Hoyt St

Hoyt–Schermerhorn

State St

Pacific St

Third Ave

Fourth Ave

Court St

Boerum Pl

Bergen St

Warren St

Baltic St

Nevins St

Sackett St

Carroll St

Montague St
Borough Hall
Borough Hall

Atlantic Ave

COBBLE HILL

Cobble Hill Park

Court St

Clinton St

Butler St

Degraw St

Union St

Bond St

2nd St

4th St

Hicks St
Henry St
Henry St

CARROLL GARDENS

Smith St

Carroll St

Smith–9th Sts

Columbia St

Brooklyn-Queens Expwy

Henry St

Clinton St

Luquer St

Huntington St

Mill St

RED HOOK

East River

Brooklyn-Battery Tunnel

Governor's Island

Upper New York Bay

Imlay St

Commerce St

Verona St

Red Hook Park

Dwight St

Richards St

Van Brunt St

Pioneer St

Conover St

Ferris St

Coffey St

Van Dyke St

See map p452

Sights (p272)
1 Brooklyn Academy of Music........F2
2 Fort Greene Park.......................F1
3 Waterfront Museum....................A4
4 Williamsburgh Savings Bank Tower.......F2

Eating (p280)
5 Calexico Redhook......................C3
6 Chez Lola................................G1
7 Fairway.................................A4
8 Ferdinando's Focacceria..............C3
9 Frankies Spuntino....................C4
10 Lucali.................................C3
11 Mile End..............................E2
12 No 7..................................G2
Prime Meats...........................(see 9)

13 Seul...................................C3

Drinking & Nightlife (p285)
14 61 Local..............................D2
15 Der Schwarze Köelner.................G2
16 Sunny's...............................A4
17 Zombie Hut...........................D3

Entertainment (p288)
18 American Opera Projects..............A4
BAM Howard Gilman Opera
House.................................C4
BAM Rose Cinemas....................(see 1)
BAMcafé...............................(see 1)
19 Ball House............................D5
Brooklyn Academy of Music...........(see 9)

20 Jalopy.................................C3

Shopping (p292)
Black Gold..........................(see 9)
21 Brooklyn Flea Market (Fort Greene)...G2
22 Eva Gentry...........................E2
23 Smith + Butler.......................D3

Sports & Activities (p294)
24 Area Yoga Center.....................G3
25 Brooklyn Boulders....................E3
26 Gowanus Dredgers Canoe Club........E4
27 Red Hook Boaters....................A4

Sleeping (p346)
28 Hotel Le Bleu.......................E4

PARK SLOPE & PROSPECT PARK

See map p448

BOERUM HILL

CLINTON HILL

Pacific St

Atlantic Ave

33

Pacific St

St Marks Pl

Bergen St

14

29

30

Flatbush Ave

18

7th Ave

CARROLL GARDENS

Union St

Lincoln Pl

Union St

20

12

Carroll St

President St

15

1st St

7

3rd St

PARK SLOPE

6

Garfield Pl

4th Ave-9th St

24

5th St

26

Sixth Ave

Seventh Ave

27

7th St

9th St

Eighth Ave

28

7th Ave

36

Prospect Park West

Prospect Ave

13

23

15th St

Picnic House

9

Prospect Park Ballfields

19th St

25

21

16th St

19

15th St-Prospect Park

West Dr

18th St

25th St

25th St

27th St

5

Fifth Ave

29th St

WINDSOR TERRACE

Terrace Pl

Vanderbilt St

Green-Wood Cemetery

36th St

McDonald Ave

E 2nd St

E 4th St

Fort Hamilton Pkwy

Clinton St

Court St

Smith St

Hoyt St

Bond St

Nevins St

Warren St

Butler St

Degraw St

Carroll Park

Carroll St

2nd Pl

Union St

Carroll St

4th Pl

2nd St

Nelson St

4th St

Gowanus Canal

Smith-9th Sts

GOWANUS

Second Ave

2nd St

Third Ave

Fourth Ave

Fifth Ave

11th St

13th St

Prospect Ave

17th St

19th St

21st St

23rd St

25th St

Prospect Pkwy

Prospect Ave

Gowanus Expwy

Gowanus Expwy

Tenth Ave

Sherman St

11th Ave

Prospect Park Southwest

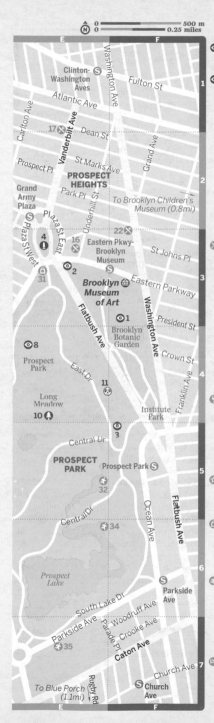

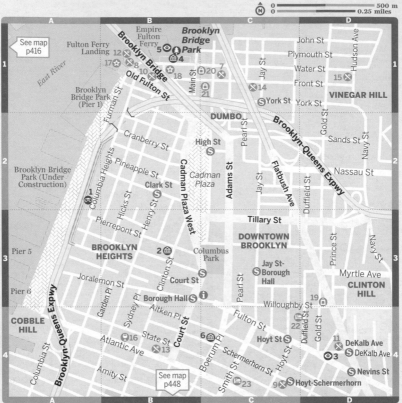

CONEY ISLAND & BRIGHTON BEACH

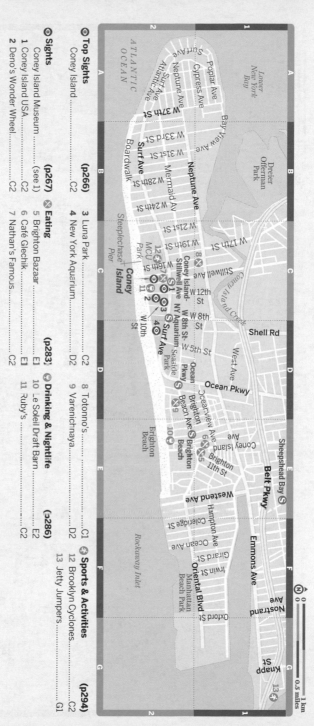

QUEENS

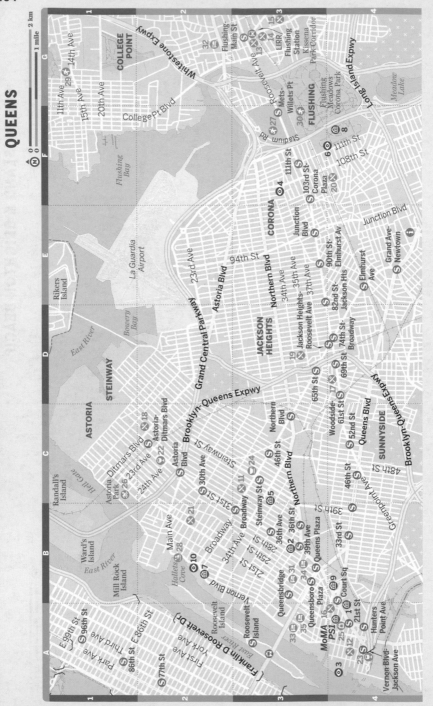

N

0 _____ 2 km
0 _____ 1 mile

COLLEGE POINT

14th Ave
11th Ave
15th Ave
20th Ave

College Pt Blvd

Whitestone Expwy

32

Flushing-
Main St
15
14
13
LIRR
Flushing
Station
Roosevelt Ave

Kissena
Park Corridor

Long Island Expwy

Meadow
Lake

27
Mets-
Willets Pt
30

FLUSHING

Flushing
Meadows
Corona Park

8

6
111th St
108th St

Flushing Bay

**La Guardia
Airport**

**Rikers
Island**

East River

Bowery
Bay

111th St
4
103rd St-
Corona
Plaza
20

Stadium Rd

CORONA

Junction
Blvd

Junction Blvd

STEINWAY

Grand Central Parkway

23rd Ave

Astoria Blvd

94th St

Northern Blvd
34th Ave
35th Ave
37th Ave

90th St-
Elmhurst Av
82nd St-
Jackson Hts
Elmhurst
Ave

Grand Ave-
Newtown

i

ASTORIA

**Randall's
Island**

Hell Gate

**Ward's
Island**

East River

**Mill Rock
Island**

Astoria
Ditmars Blvd
18
23rd Ave
Astoria-
Ditmars Blvd
24th Ave
22
26
Astoria
Blvd
30th Ave
31st St
21
24
11
Steinway St
5

Brooklyn-Queens Expwy

Northern
Blvd
46th St

**JACKSON
HEIGHTS**

19
Jackson Heights-
Roosevelt Ave
74th St-
Broadway
69th St
65th St

Woodside
61st St
52nd St
17
Queens Blvd

SUNNYSIDE

Brooklyn-Queens Expwy

46th St
48th St
Greenpoint Ave
39th St
33rd St

E 99th St
96th St
Third Ave
Park Ave
86th St
77th St

Franklin D Roosevelt Dr
First Ave
York Ave

**Roosevelt
Island**

Main Ave
28
Halletts
Cove
10
7
Broadway
34th Ave
25th St
21st St
31st St
28th St
36th St
38th St
2
Steinway St
36th Ave
39th Ave
Queens Plaza

Vernon Blvd

Queensbridge
31
34

Queensboro
Plaza
9
Court Sq
1
21st St

MoMA
PS1
16
25
12
3
23
Vernon Blvd-
Jackson Ave

Hunters
Point Ave

29

QUEENS

Van Wyck Expwy
Grand Central Pkwy
Willow Lake
Forest Hills
71st Ave
67th Ave
FOREST HILLS
63rd Dr-Rego Park
Woodhaven Blvd
QUEENS
Eliot Ave
Juniper Valley Park
Grand Ave
69th St
Long Island Expwy
MASPETH
See map p446
Humboldt St
Greenpoint Ave
Nassau Ave

Our Story

A beat-up old car, a few dollars in the pocket and a sense of adventure. In 1972 that's all Tony and Maureen Wheeler needed for the trip of a lifetime – across Europe and Asia overland to Australia. It took several months, and at the end – broke but inspired – they sat at their kitchen table writing and stapling together their first travel guide, *Across Asia on the Cheap*. Within a week they'd sold 1500 copies. Lonely Planet was born.

Today, Lonely Planet has offices in Melbourne, London and Oakland, with more than 600 staff and writers. We share Tony's belief that 'a great guidebook should do three things: inform, educate and amuse'.

Our Writers

Brandon Presser

Coordinating Author; SoHo & Chinatown, East Village & Lower East Side, Greenwich Village, Chelsea & the Meatpacking District and Union Square, Flatiron District & Gramercy After earning an art history degree from Harvard University and working at the Musée du Louvre, Brandon swapped landscape canvases for the real deal and joined the glamorous ranks of eternal nomadism. Today, Brandon works as a fulltime freelance writer and photographer. He's penned over 40 guidebooks to far-flung destinations across the globe, from Iceland to Thailand and many 'lands' in between. When he's not on the road he calls New York City home – he lives a block from Union Square. Brandon also wrote the Planning, Sleeping, Day Trips from New York City, New York City Today, History and Survival Guide chapters.

Read more about Brandon at:
lonelyplanet.com/members/brandonpresser

Cristian Bonetto

Lower Manhattan & the Financial District, Midtown and Queens Raised on a diet of Sesame Street, Cristian's fondness for stoops and subways began in his diaper days. Since then, the one-time TV and theater scribe has played both tourist and local in New York City, writing about the city's food, architecture and art for numerous international publications. When he's not downing dirty martinis in Manhattan, you'll find him on assignment in Italy, Scandinavia or Southeast Asia. Cristian also wrote the NYC Table, Painting the Town Pink and NYC on Screen chapters.

Carolina A Miranda

Upper East Side, Upper West Side & Central Park, Harlem & Upper Manhattan and Brooklyn Carolina has lived in New York for almost two decades (Coney Island, Park Slope, Manhattan and Bushwick). During her time in the city, she's attended the roller derby, canoed through industrial canals, watched basement performance art, seen operas at Lincoln Center and gotten engaged on the roof of the Metropolitan Museum. Her stories have appeared in Time, ARTnews, Budget Travel and on National Public Radio. She is a regular contributor at WNYC. Find her on Twitter at @cmonstah. Carolina also wrote the With Kids and Arts and Architecture chapters.

Published by Lonely Planet Publications Pty Ltd
ABN 36 005 607 983
8th edition – Aug 2012
ISBN 978 1 74220 020 0
© Lonely Planet 2012   Photographs © as indicated 2012
10 9 8 7 6 5 4 3 2 1
Printed in China

Although the authors and Lonely Planet have taken all reasonable care in preparing this book, we make no warranty about the accuracy or completeness of its content and, to the maximum extent permitted, disclaim all liability arising from its use.

All rights reserved. No part of this publication may be copied, stored in a retrieval system, or transmitted in any form by any means, electronic, mechanical, recording or otherwise, except brief extracts for the purpose of review, and no part of this publication may be sold or hired, without the written permission of the publisher. Lonely Planet and the Lonely Planet logo are trademarks of Lonely Planet and are registered in the US Patent and Trademark Office and in other countries. Lonely Planet does not allow its name or logo to be appropriated by commercial establishments, such as retailers, restaurants or hotels. Please let us know of any misuses: lonelyplanet.com/ip.